Computer Programs for Qualitative Data Analysis

A Software Sourcebook

Computer Programs for Qualitative Data Analysis

Eben A. Weitzman
Matthew B. Miles

SAGE Publications
International Educational and Professional Publisher
Thousand Oaks London New Delhi

For information address:

SAGE Publications, Inc.
2455 Teller Road
Thousand Oaks, California 91320

SAGE Publications Ltd.
6 Bonhill Street
London EC2A 4PU
United Kingdom

SAGE Publications India Pvt. Ltd.
M-32 Market
Greater Kailash I
New Delhi 110 048 India

Printed in the United States of America

Library of Congress Cataloging-in-Publication Data

Weitzman, Eben A.
Computer programs for qualitative data analysis: A software sourcebook. / Eben A. Weitzman. Matthew B. Miles.
p. cm.
Includes bibliographical references and index.
ISBN 0-8039-5536-7 (cl.).—ISBN 0-8039-5537-5 (pb)
1. Social sciences—Data processing. 2. Social sciences—Computer programs. I. Miles, Matthew B. II. Title.
H61.3.W45 1995
300'.285'536—dc20 94-40467

95 96 97 98 99 10 9 8 7 6 5 4 3 2 1

Sage Production Editor: Astrid Virding
Sage Typesetter: Danielle Dillahunt

Contents

Acknowledgments

We would like to thank the developers of each of the 24 programs reviewed here for their cooperation with this project. In almost every case, they provided us with free copies of their programs, and often spent significant amounts of time talking with us and checking our reviews for accuracy and fairness. We would like to extend special thanks to Thomas Muhr (developer of ATLAS/ti) and Tom Richards (developer of NUD•IST), who had thoughtful advice and reactions beyond their programs.

This book benefited greatly from the thoughtful efforts of our reviewers. We recruited Markku Lonkila, Vernay Mitchell, Susan V. Opotow, Renata Tesch, H. Stephen Turley, Sally Uhl, Diana Rivera-Viera, and Bruce Wilson. Mitch Allen at Sage Publications recruited Dale Berg, Julie Caplow, Nigel Fielding, Kathleen Gilbert, Mark Horney, Ray Lee, and Stephen Wolfel. Each of the reviewers gave the manuscript a careful reading and made significant contributions to its improvement—as well as to our understanding of broader issues in the development and use of qualitative analysis software.

Julie Flynn, Lenny Levitsky, Libby Schmaltz, and Sadi Seferoglu did wonderful graphic work, and Michael Moon and Judy Woolcock helped manage the Herculean task of getting all the right copies out to all the right people.

Mitch Allen, our editor at Sage, has our heartfelt thanks for his patience and support throughout the extended process of writing this book. Astrid Virding, our production editor, went above and beyond the call of duty, devoting great amounts of helpful, creative energy to the project.

We would not have been able to devote ourselves so fully to this project without financial assistance from several sources. We are grateful to the Regional Educational Laboratory for Educational Improvement of the Northeast and Islands and to Peter Gerber at the John D. and Catherine T. MacArthur Foundation for funding the project, and to Sara Miller McCune and David McCune at Sage Publications for support during preparation of the manuscript.

Our special thanks go to each other for teaching/sharing our respective areas of expertise and for hard work, good times, and friendship. Learning this developing field together was a great adventure—we often felt like explorers on a new continent, discovering spectacular new landscapes. The adventure will continue.

* * *

We owe a special debt of gratitude to the late Renata Tesch, who played a crucial role from the mid-1980s onward in the development of software for qualitative data analysis. Always at the leading edge, she strongly supported the building of an international community of developers, disseminators, and users concerned with improving programs and practice. She not only wrote prolifically but facilitated others' work as well in journals and edited collections. In our case, she provided steady encouragement, clarification, new ideas (the matrix of features in Chapter 9 was stimulated by her work along similar lines), update information on programs and developers, and critical readings of early drafts. We—and her many colleagues worldwide—have lost an able, thoughtful friend. This book carries on the dialogue that Renata did so much to support.

PART I

The Basics

Part I is intended to introduce the reader to the world of computer programs for qualitative data analysis. Chapter 1, "Introduction," has four parts. The first provides a brief history of developments in computer-assisted qualitative data analysis. The next describes the book's audiences and purposes. Then we explain how we produced the book, with comments on our biases and our procedures. The last section gives some specific advice on how to use the book in an active, personalized way to get what you need from it.

Chapter 2 presents the four key questions you need to ask yourself when you're choosing software for qualitative data analysis, as well as two broad, cut-across issues. It also provides an adaptable worksheet for you to use, to organize, filter, and keep track of what you learn as you work your way through the various parts of the book.

Finally, Chapter 3 sets up the rest of the book by explaining the five basic types, or "families," of software reviewed here and their basic functions.

1

Introduction

"Which computer program should I use to analyze my qualitative data?"

This book was written to help answer that question. To begin with, we should comment on the question itself. First and foremost, there is no computer program that will "analyze" your data. We could borrow a bromide here: "Computers don't analyze data; people do." Like its parent statement about guns, this is a half-truth. Guns do make it very easy for people to kill people. And computers make it much easier for people to think about the meaning of their data. They are not a substitute for thought, but they are a strong aid to thought.

A second comment: The phrase "my qualitative data" masks some important issues. Choosing a program depends very crucially not only on what your data are like—the extended text and images you gathered through interviews, observations, and documents—but on how you like to approach them, intellectually speaking, and just what you want to accomplish in the way of analysis.

A third comment is that the word "analyze" covers a wide range of activities, from editing and annotating field notes to data storage and retrieval, coding, writing memos, drawing conclusions, graphic mapping, and report writing. Programs differ widely in how good they are at these specific tasks of analysis.

A final comment on the original question: the phrase "which computer program" implies choosing one that's "best." In fact, it's often the case that, depending on your analysis plans, it may make sense to use two or more programs that can work on different tasks.

We'll return to these issues as we go. In this introductory chapter, we review the current situation regarding computer-assisted qualitative data analysis, then discuss the book itself: its purposes and audiences, how we came to write it and how we proceeded, how the book is set up, and how to use it most effectively for your purposes.

Computer-Assisted Analysis: A Minihistory

Ten years ago, most qualitative researchers were typing up their handwritten field notes, making photocopies, marking them with pencil or colored pens, cutting them up, sorting them, pasting them on file cards, shuffling cards, and typing their analyses. A few were beginning to use word processors for their written-up field notes, and a few were starting to explore database programs as a way to store and access their voluminous text.

Most textbooks on qualitative studies at that time (e.g., Bogdan & Biklen, 1982; Goetz & LeCompte, 1984; Lofland & Lofland, 1984; Miles & Huberman, 1984) had either no discussion at all or, at most, a page or two on the use of computers in qualitative research. The only programs most people had heard of were those that carried out quantitative content analysis of text. (There were in fact a few other programs just emerging: Drass, 1980; Seidel & Clark, 1984; Shelly & Sibert, 1985.) Journal issues devoted exclusively to the topic (Conrad & Reinharz, 1984) were just beginning to appear.

But in less than 10 years, there has been a phenomenal development in this domain. There's been an outpouring of journal articles, a series of international conferences on computers and qualitative methodology, thoughtful books on the topic (Fielding & Lee, 1991; Tesch, 1990), and new journal issues (Tesch, 1991). Software is frequently discussed on electronic bulletin boards—both generic ones and those devoted to specific programs. In a 1991 survey of qualitative researchers by Miles and Huberman (1994), three quarters of respondents reported using computer software for data entry, coding, search and retrieval, display, and concept building—with a mixture of satisfaction and dissatisfaction.

As Miles and Huberman (1994) emphasize:

> By now it's largely taken for granted that you need a good word processor to do qualitative research. Handwritten or dictated field notes, along with tape recordings, must be converted into analyzable text, which then needs to be reduced, displayed and used to draw and verify conclusions. Ordinary typing and retyping is far too slow and costly.
>
> But it's also fair to say that the researcher who does not use software beyond a word processor will be hampered in comparison to those who do. As Tesch (1989) points out, computer-aided analysis can reduce analysis time,[1] cut out much drudgery, make procedures more systematic and explicit, insure completeness and refinement, and permit flexibility and revision in analysis procedures. Ragin and Becker (1989) add that the microcomputer is especially useful for "case-oriented" researchers, those interested in "interconnected arguments about interrelated events" rather than in sheer statistical "variation." Computing, they suggest, can move studies beyond the "handicraft production" that has characterized much qualitative research. (pp. 43-44)

Things have happened so fast that many qualitative researchers feel bewildered and uncertain. A few are still relying on typewriter and scissors. Others are working mainly with a familiar word processor, while beginning to realize its limitations. And although quite a few have begun using qualitative analysis software, they're uncomfortably aware of their program's limitations and are seeking more powerful help. Until now, there was no organized assembly of current information on relevant programs.

About This Book

Audiences

This book is written for qualitative researchers who want to initiate, extend, or update their use of computer software for qualitative data analysis.

The phrase "qualitative researchers" is meant to serve as a big tent. Readers may have had years of prior experience in qualitative studies or may only have launched a fledgling study or two, perhaps as part of a course on qualitative methods. (If you have had no experience at all with qualitative work, the book will be very hard to make sense of.)

The big tent also includes qualitative researchers of many different varieties and persuasions. There is really no systematic, agreed-on way to sort out types of qualitative research,[2] but we believe that researchers doing grounded theory, narrative studies, ethnography, interpretivist and hermeneutic work, critical theory, and collaborative or action research may all find useful ideas in the book (see Chapter 10). The book doesn't presume a "correct" or official style of qualitative analysis.

Finally, the tent includes people who may not quite think of themselves as qualitative researchers at all, but who are faced with making sense of qualitative data. These might include, for example, the quantitatively trained researcher who needs to process results on open-ended questions, the consultant who's making a summary of several dozen diagnostic interviews, the evaluation expert who's examining the results of focus group discussions, the cognitive researcher who wants to represent students' mental maps, the content analyst who wants to understand the meaning

1. It's sometimes argued (e.g., Horney, 1994) that computers don't save time because of (a) the learning time needed and (b) their "encouragement" of new, more complex tasks that might not have been attempted otherwise. Our countercomments are (a) that learning time is rarely more than a few days and (b) the new, more complex tasks are in fact being done more efficiently and accurately, particularly in large databases, so that there is, at the very least, higher quality for the "same" time investment.

2. We don't presume to sort out qualitative researchers and their analytical approaches according to a coherent scheme. Many efforts of this sort have been made (e.g., Crabtree & Miller, 1992; Jacob, 1987; Miles & Huberman, 1994; Tesch, 1990; Wolcott, 1992); all are illuminating, and all are unsuccessful to some degree. See also the very useful chapters on "strategies of inquiry" in Part 3 of Denzin and Lincoln (1994).

of words and phrases used frequently in a political campaign, or the literary scholar exploring Shakespeare's uses of metaphor.

Purposes

The book has two purposes: (a) supporting choice of programs and (b) helping with early program familiarization and adaptation. It's *not* designed to teach methods of qualitative data analysis. Let's review these aims in detail.

Supporting intelligent choice. The primary purpose of the book is to aid in the choice of programs that can assist qualitative data analysis. The aim is to provide clear, critical information for researcher decision making about which programs to adopt. We take an independent, user-oriented approach like that of *Consumer Reports*. We do not distribute or support any of the programs reviewed here, and we have taken a dispassionate view of developers' claims about the "obvious" merits of their programs.

There are now several dozen programs that qualitative researchers can use to support their work. Yet, as with the scattered and burgeoning literature of the field, there hasn't been a single up-to-date place the researcher can go to find out which programs are useful for what purpose and how they work. The late Renata Tesch's (1990) groundbreaking book focused on six programs in depth and discussed many others briefly. But since 1990 development has moved rapidly; four of the six she examined have been substantially updated and expanded, one (TAP) has gone off the market, and one (Textbase Alpha) is unchanged from the version Tesch carefully reviewed.

Even a current, in-depth review like that of Richards and Richards (1994), though it deals with key issues and different types of software, mentions under a dozen programs and doesn't provide the at-the-elbow help that researchers need as they consider the basic questions of "Shall I?" and "Which?"

Even after you've answered the question "Shall I?" in the affirmative, the "Which?" question is particularly hard to answer. The potential uses of software in qualitative studies are very diverse, as outlined in Table 1.1.

How can you handle these tasks in any particular study? Let's say you are already using a word processor. It may easily cover items like 1, 2, 3, 8, and 14. If you know how to write "macros" (automated procedures) to perform repetitive tasks, you may also be able to accomplish items 4, 6, and 9.

But most of the other, more complex tasks listed in Table 1.1 are well beyond your word processor's capabilities. In most studies, it's more helpful to find and use additional analysis software to deal with such tasks.

TABLE 1.1. Uses of Computer Software in Qualitative Studies

1. Making notes in the field
2. Writing up or transcribing field notes
3. Editing: correcting, extending, or revising field notes
4. Coding: attaching keywords or tags to segments of text to permit later retrieval
5. Storage: keeping text in an organized database
6. Search and retrieval: locating relevant segments of text and making them available for inspection
7. Data "linking": connecting relevant data segments to each other, forming categories, clusters, or networks of information
8. Memoing: writing reflective commentaries on some aspect of the data as a basis for deeper analysis
9. Content analysis: counting frequencies, sequence, or locations of words and phrases
10. Data display: placing selected or reduced data in a condensed, organized format, such as a matrix or network, for inspection
11. Conclusion-drawing and verification: aiding the analyst to interpret displayed data and to test or confirm findings
12. Theory-building: developing systematic, conceptually coherent explanations of findings; testing hypotheses
13. Graphic mapping: creating diagrams that depict findings or theories
14. Preparing interim and final reports

SOURCE: Miles and Huberman (1994, p. 44).

This book reviews 24 programs that we've roughly clustered into five major "families." *Text retrievers* are good at hunting for words or phrases in your database and collecting them for your scrutiny. *Textbase managers* can also retrieve and in addition help you manage and sort your data in a systematic, organized fashion. *Code-and-retrieve programs* let you apply keywords, or codes, to meaningful chunks of your data, such as lines, sentences, or paragraphs, and then retrieve those chunks, by codes or combinations of codes. *Code-based theory-builders* have code-and-retrieve features and also include functions like building a conceptual structure, annotation and memo writing, and formulating and testing hypotheses. Finally, *conceptual network-builders help you formulate and represent conceptual schemes through a network of "nodes" and "links."*

The clustering is rough because program features overlap and because each program has a different configuration of features. For any given category, we cross-reference to other programs that can perform the same functions nearly as well. This book is designed to help you make informed choices among the welter of options.

Familiarization and adaptation. A second purpose of the book emerged as we wrote it. If you have purchased a program, or have access to it through a computer lab, the reviews can also be used as a sort of mini-manual, helping you learn your way around the program and start using it effectively. (For example, after getting a sense of the program's structure and functioning, you can look at the "screen shots" reproduced in our figures and learn what you do to get the program to act that way.) We also suggest "workarounds," ways to adapt the program for your purposes.

The format of each review normally includes the following topics, which can be read either as you're choosing possible programs or during early use:[3]

Title box: The program's name; operating system(s); the developer's name, address, and phone/fax/e-mail numbers; the price; the hardware requirements

Overview: A quick thumbnail sketch: how the program is set up, what it looks and feels like, what it can do, and its outstanding features

Database structure: How the program is set up to organize your data

Data entry: How you bring your data into the program and set it up for analysis

Working on the data: How you set up and carry out coding and sorting of your data; how you annotate your text, write memos about it; how different parts of your database are linked

Searching: How you hunt for and retrieve items in your data (such as coded segments, words, or phrases) that you need for your analysis

Output: How the program gives you results, and through what methods (on screen, printer, copying to disk)

Theory building: How the program helps you think about your data systematically, develop propositions or hypotheses, test them, and generate a coherent explanation of what you are finding

Graphics editing: The program's abilities to work with data or results in a diagrammatic, network-like form

User friendliness: The program's ease of learning, its supports for learning, and its ease of use once learned

Miscellaneous: Anything of interest that doesn't fit logically elsewhere, including automation or customization and network use

Update: Recent information on the developer's plans to revise or extend the program; notes on new versions received after the review was completed

Comparative remarks: Comparisons with other programs that can do similar things

Summary

References: Items specific to this program (the manual, key articles, and so on)

3. For some programs, we do not follow this review outline precisely but adapt it to fit a program's special characteristics. We usually omit a heading when a program completely lacks some feature (such as theory building or graphics editing) or has no update information.

A nonpurpose. Books need to be defined by what they are *not* trying to do. This book is not aimed at teaching methods of qualitative data analysis. The reader who wants to extend competence in analysis methods should consult recent texts, such as Silverman (1993), Denzin and Lincoln (1994, esp. Pts. 4 and 5), Miles and Huberman (1994), and Wolcott (1994).

How We Produced the Book

The reader deserves an account of how we went about our work, to help in assessing the credibility and usefulness of the results.

Background

In 1991 this book's topic had been considered an integral part of the second edition of Miles and Huberman (1984). Weitzman and Miles began the process of critical review of software and did a prototype report (Weitzman & Miles, 1991). As the second edition revision continued, it became increasingly apparent that software reviews could not be included within the space limitations of an already large book. Ideas about choosing appropriate software were included in an appendix (Miles & Weitzman, 1994) along with general ratings of 22 programs.

We then decided to produce a book of full-scale reviews; it can be easily used as a companion text to the second edition, though it need not be linked that way.

The Authors and Their Biases

Weitzman's background is in political science and social psychology. He has interests in computer usage, conflict resolution, cross-cultural conflict, alienation and commitment, and organizational development.

Miles is a social psychologist who has focused his work on planned change in education, doing qualitative studies since the mid-1970s. His current research interests are advances in qualitative data analysis, school restructuring, and educational reform in developing countries.

Our collaboration has been especially fruitful, because Weitzman brought to it strong technical skill in computing, and Miles a strong background in qualitative research. We learned a lot from each other and the experience of review writing as we went. Miles, for example, began the book with Level 2 computer skills and moved up to Level 3 (see definitions in Chapter 2). Weitzman, who already had Level 3+ computer skills, learned more about alternative approaches to qualitative studies.

How would we describe our biases? Here are some we're aware of:

1. Qualitative research goes better when it's systematically planned and designed.
2. Arguments about epistemological purity don't get research done.
3. Qualitative research is a craft, not a rule-driven enterprise. Still, there can be better and poorer qualitative studies.
4. Computer software can support qualitative data analysis in intellectually meaningful ways.
5. There's no "best" program; the best choice for anyone depends on prior computer and research experience, on the time horizon, on the project at hand, and on the analyses planned.
6. "Better" programs as we see them tend to be easy to learn and to use, flexible, and powerful (in the sense of permitting precise, coherent, extensive analyses). They keep us close to our data rather than distracting us with their routines. They permit us to understand complexity without oversimplifying it. See also our discussion in Chapter 10 of what a "good program" should include at the minimum.

Our Procedures

Program selection criteria. Clearly, we could not cover the full universe of programs conceivably useful for qualitative data analysis. We aimed to include

- a reasonable sampling of programs across our five program types
- good coverage of programs often cited as used in qualitative studies, particularly those developed specifically for that purpose
- commercial packages that seemed especially promising to us for qualitative analysis
- programs for DOS, Mac, and Windows

We deliberately excluded

- programs no longer available to the public, without support from developers or distributors
- programs reviewed in Tesch (1990) but *not* updated or revised since then
- programs we heard about later than May 1994

Our review methods. We asked developers for review copies, explaining our plans for the book. We received current versions and sometimes "beta-test" (prerelease) versions, along with program documentation.

The review procedure varied; in many cases, we started by doing the tutorial or tour that came with the program; for others, we read through the manual or other documentation carefully, then worked with the program. In a few cases, it seemed easiest to load the program and start exploring it, referring to documentation when help screens were not illuminating enough.

We often used the data files that came with most programs as demonstration material; in a few cases, we used data of our own. We did not use a standard set of data across programs and did not have a standard "testing" routine that we applied to all, because the programs differed so widely.

The first draft by one of us was reviewed in detail by the other, and revised, often with a second round of critique and advice. The resulting draft was reviewed by (a) the program's developer, who was invited to provide corrections and suggestions, and did so in nearly all cases; (b) eight reviewers we recruited representing a wide range of sophistication in terms of software and qualitative research; and (c) seven reviewers recruited by our publisher.

Corrected/revised drafts based on this feedback were prepared by the original writer, then revised after final feedback from the other. We consider each review a joint product.

Program ratings in the matrix of features (Chapter 9) were produced by the original author and revised after discussion with the other, with feedback from the program developer and in a few cases from reviewers.

Using the Book

This brief review of the parts of the book and the chapter structure is sequentially presented, but we want to emphasize at the start that the best way to use the book is to jump around in it from topic to topic, not to read it sequentially from start to finish. That is, we recommend a *hypertext style of reading* (if that term is not familiar to you, jump to the Glossary).

Part I, "The Basics," is essentially background and framing of the issues.

After Chapter 1, which you're reading, Chapter 2 starts with the question of how to choose software. That question cannot really be posed: "Which program is best?" Rather, we suggest that you first need to ask yourself four basic questions:

1. What kind of a computer user am I?
2. Am I choosing for one project or the next few years?
3. What kind of project(s) and database(s) will I be working on?
4. What kind of analyses am I planning to do?

Chapter 3 provides an orientation to the territory. It covers the types and functions of software, which, as noted above, we have sorted into major families: text retrievers, textbase managers, code-and-retrieve programs, code-based theory-builders, and conceptual network-builders. These families are not "pure types" but overlap considerably.

Part II, "Software Reviews," looks at specific programs. Chapters 4 through 8 examine 24 programs, roughly sorted into the five major families we've just described: text retrievers, textbase managers, code-and-retrieve programs, code-based theory-builders, and conceptual network-builders. The review format has been described above. In Chapter 9, we provide a matrix cast in a *Consumer Reports*-like format; it shows detailed program features and ratings for each of the 24 programs, which are clustered as in Chapters 4 through 8.

Part III, "Reflections and Resources," begins (in Chapter 10) with an overview of the current state of the art, then outlines some hopes for future development. Resources include an appendix with contact information for all the programs' developers, a glossary of key terms, a brief list of annotated cross-cutting references, a master reference list, and the index.

How to Jump Around in the Book

There are many routes through the book. Here are some possibilities.

1. Beginning with Part I will give you a good grounding. Review the questions and start the worksheet (Table 2.1) in Chapter 2. Browse in Chapter 3 to get a feeling for program types. Then browse in the reviews of a few programs that might make sense in terms of your own situation. Then check Chapter 9 for some further scanning and cross-program comparison. Using the matrix can help you clarify your needs further, sort out a pool of useful candidates, and winnow these down by reading through their reviews.

2. Go directly to a program you're interested in. Look through the program carefully; try it if you have access to a copy. Check it back against your worksheet ideas from Chapter 2. Don't close up too quickly. Jump to other programs mentioned in the "Comparative Remarks" section for that review to see how they are similar and different. After that, try a program in a different "family" and repeat.

3. Remember as you jump that you may well be looking for two or three programs, not just one.

4. Always jump to the Glossary whenever you run into a term you're not sure you understand. The Glossary is intended to be comprehensive; it demystifies arcane terms and specifies how they're being used in this book.

5. Go to the overview table at the start of Part II that summarizes the main characteristics of the 24 programs, then start browsing in ones that look interesting.

6. Go immediately to Chapter 10 to get a sense of where the field is and what sorts of analytical needs may be most relevant for your own approach to qualitative research. Then come back to options 1 or 2 above.

7. If you think you need a certain type of program (such as a textbase manager), work through all the reviews in that specific chapter, then jump to the other related programs that are mentioned at the start of the chapter.

The book is designed to provide a reasonable amount of detailed information about the characteristics, strengths, and weaknesses of the 24 programs we reviewed. Using it should get you to the point of (a) narrowing the field to a few candidates; (b) asking colleagues or friends who may be using those programs for more information; (c) asking a developer for specific information, a brochure, a demo version; (d) trying out the program if you have access through a computer lab; or (e) making a purchase. Remember too that the program reviews can be used as "mini-manuals" to help with early familiarization as well as with workarounds and adaptations.

You should keep in mind that nearly all the software reviewed in this book will be upgraded and improved in the next few years (see "Update" sections in most reviews). So our reviews provide a kind of "floor" that may well be exceeded by later versions of the programs. We expect to upgrade the book itself periodically as well.

A last remark: Using the book is a learning process. Writing it was one for us. We often felt stupid and uncomprehending as we worked our way through programs. Not being initially clear about terms and meanings is par for the course for anyone. It's easy to get puzzled because you don't understand a program's basic assumptions and analytical approach—or perhaps even hate them. But things get clearer when you ask, explore, make things explicit.

Using the Glossary liberally will help, but it's not the same as coming to understand the ins and out of a particular program. We encourage you to talk with interested colleagues (as discussed in Chapter 2) when you don't understand something.

2

How to Choose Software

KEY QUESTIONS[1]

"What's the best program?" There's no answer in the abstract. Choosing the right software, for you, depends on your own level of work with computers, on your time perspective, on the particular project you have in mind, and on the type of analysis you are expecting to do. We want to avoid the trap of saying that there's a best program, even for a particular combination of these factors, because researchers come up with creative adaptations of software all the time, getting programs to work quite well for tasks for which they were never intended. It's important for the researcher to look at each program freely, avoiding the constraints imposed by thinking that "this program is for this type of analysis only." We talk about some of the functions and features that are needed for different styles of analysis in Chapter 10.

A careful look at the issues below will help you know what to look for in more detail, in relation to specific programs. Specifically, there are four key questions for you to ask and answer that will go a long way toward helping you choose a software package:

1. What kind of computer user am I?
2. Am I choosing for one project or the next few years?
3. What kind of project(s) and database(s) will I be working on?
4. What kind of analyses am I planning to do?

In addition to these four key questions, there are a couple of cut-across issues to bear in mind:

How important is it to you to maintain a sense of "closeness" to your data?

What are your financial constraints when buying software, and the hardware it needs to run on?

With these basic issues clear in your mind, you will be able to look at the specific programs in a more active,

1. This material, as well as portions of Chapter 3, is adapted, with extensions, from Miles and Weitzman (1994, pp. 311-315).

deliberate way, seeing what does or does not meet your needs. You can then turn to Part II, where we provide in-depth reviews of 24 programs, in Chapters 4 through 8. In Chapter 9, you will find a matrix of features and ratings that lets you easily compare programs according to the specific functions and features you've decided are relevant to your needs.

To help with the process of answering these four key questions and putting them to use in your choice of software, we've provided a worksheet in Table 2.1. We suggest you work in pencil, on a photocopy, so that it's easy to revise or start over when your needs change. The left column lists the four issues we discuss here, with their subissues indented below. Next is space for you to jot your brief answer to the question, followed by a space you can use to note the implications of the answer for program choice or to make any other notes. Finally, there's a column for candidate programs, where you can jot down the names of programs that appear to satisfy a particular need or programs that are ruled out by that need (you might want to write these in red or with a minus sign next to their names).

Obviously, you don't yet have all the information you need to fill out the worksheet or you wouldn't be reading this book. You may want to start by filling in the "Answer" column as you read through the rest of this chapter. You may also be able to make a few entries under "Implications/Notes." As you work your way through other parts of the book (see our suggestions for hypertext-style reading in Chapter 1), you'll be able to fill out more of the worksheet. We invite you to adapt this worksheet to your own needs and work style: Change the meanings of the columns, come up with different systems for filling it out using colors or symbols, or, if this sheet doesn't work for you at all, make your own. Maybe you'll want to make a copy for each candidate program you're considering and take more extensive notes about how each candidate addresses each of the issues (you'll probably want to rename the columns). See whether you find it most helpful when working with the text of the reviews, with the ratings matrix in Chapter 9, or, more likely, with some combination of the two. We turn now to the four key questions. Afterward, we'll discuss the cut-across issues.

Question 1: What Kind of a Computer User Are You?

Your present level of computer use is an important factor in your choice of a program. If you are new to computers, your best bet is probably to choose a word processing program with advice from friends and begin using it, learning to use your computer's operating system (e.g., MS-DOS, Windows, or Mac) and getting comfortable with the idea of creating text, moving around in it, and revising it. That would bring you to what we'll call Level 1.

Or you may have gotten acquainted with several different programs, use your operating system easily, and feel comfortable with the idea of exploring and learning new programs (Level 2).

Or you may be a person with active interest in the ins and outs of how programs work (Level 3) and feel easy with customization, writing macros, and so on. (We won't deal here with the "hacker," a Level 4 person who lives and breathes computing.)

If you are Level 1, give a lot of attention to the "user friendliness" of the programs you are considering. Check the Glossary frequently for any unfamiliar terms—we've tried to be careful to define everything that might seem arcane. Find a friend or colleague (see below on why this is important) who's at Level 2 or 3, preferably one who's also a qualitative researcher (if your friend is not, he or she may easily misinterpret what the program is trying to do for you—so be careful), to help you interpret unclear features of the programs you're considering. Always connect the functions and specific features of the programs to your project and analysis plans. Your friend can also support your choice of a program and your initial tryout of it.

If your computer use is at Level 2, you should have little difficulty in using the detailed information in Part II to make some preliminary choices. Again, use the Glossary! Be sure a choice fits your project and its analysis needs—especially if you choose an ambitious or demanding program. Naturally, try to find friends who are already using the program you are interested in. Clarify any questions you have with a Level 2 or 3 friend—one who's also a qualitative researcher. You may want to consult a Level 3 friend for assistance during installation and early use.

If you are a Level 3 computer user, you'll have no difficulty in assessing detailed program features. (You may still need to refer to the Glossary for terms that are specific to this class of software.) Most Level 3 people get a real kick out of the surprising, powerful, enjoyable things computers and software can do (that's why you wound up learning as much as you did, right?). But don't let particularly interesting features seduce you away from the questions: What is my project like? What's my time perspective? What kind of data will I collect? And what sort of analysis am I planning? Stay with those questions.

In general, both during your choice of programs and as you're looking forward to early use of programs, we strongly emphasize the importance of friends: You don't have to struggle through nobly alone. If "friends" sounds squishy, think of this as "professional networking." You may not have friends who are computer whizzes, or who are qualitative researchers, but chances are you have, or can find, helpful colleagues. If you're a student, your professor(s)

TABLE 2.1. Worksheet

Issue	Answer	Implications/Notes	Candidate Program(s)
What kind of a computer user are you? (Level 1-4)			
Are you choosing for one project or the next few years?			
What kind of database and project is it?			
Data Sources: Single vs. Multiple			
Single vs. Multiple Cases			
Fixed Records vs. Revised			
Structured vs. Open			
Uniform vs. Diverse Entries			
Size of Database			
What kind of analysis is anticipated?			
Exploratory vs. Confirmatory			
Coding Scheme Firm at Start vs. Evolving			
Multiple vs. Single Coding			
Iterative vs. One Pass			
Fineness of Analysis			
Interest in Context of Data			
Intentions for Displays			
Qualitative Only, or Numbers Included			
Closeness to the data important?			
Cost constraints			

may be able to help you, at least with the research end of things; so may your fellow students. If you're a professor, independent researcher, consultant, data analyst, or the like, you may have colleagues or students who can help, or you may be able to find new ones through professional associations. No matter what occupational hat you wear, you can find colleagues through a growing number of electronic resource groups. The latter, some of which are listed in Chapter 10, consist of a number of e-mail discussion groups, or "lists," which are much like electronic bulletin boards. You can post messages, and other "list members" will reply. Questions about software use in qualitative research are almost always answered within a day or two by knowledgeable people who are happy to share what they know. All these people are who we mean by "friends."

They help you with sorting out the pros and cons when you're choosing programs. And, when you start with program use, trying to do it all alone, or from the manual and tutorial alone, often proves difficult. Learning anything new is an interactive process. Friends supply support, tips, new ideas, and tricks of the trade quickly and easily. Friends don't make you feel stupid. Friends learn from each other.

Finally, a non-minor question is whether you are an MS-DOS or Mac user.[2] Though more than a few programs are available for either, it's often one or the other. People used to the intuitive, point-and-click, icon-grabbing Mac style get impatient with typing out commands. MS-DOS users like being able to issue a typed, precise command from anywhere in the program. Microsoft Windows, which runs on MS-DOS based computers, gives a feel much like a Mac. There are two ways you can go with this: You can let your choice of computer drive your choice of software, or you can let your choice of software drive your choice of computer. Which way you go is an entirely personal choice and depends on such factors as these: which type(s) of computer you already know how to use; how willing you are to learn another one; whether you have access to, or resources to acquire, either or both types of computer; what the costs would be if you switched; and if you're collaborating, what kind of computer your colleagues use.

A question that parallels the computer-use-level question is this: How experienced a qualitative researcher are you? If you're a very experienced qualitative researcher, the implications of the capabilities of the programs may often be obvious. You may have strong preferences about the way you like to work and be able to easily see which features and which programs will support that style. At the other extreme, if you're a novice to qualitative research, some of what we say may be unclear to you, not because you're new to computers, but because you're a novice qualitative researcher. If you don't know what data reduction, coding, or data display are, it may be hard to make a choice. In this case, we again urge you to find support from others who can help you figure out what you're likely to need to do once you get started. Support may also be essential in answering the questions in this chapter. Again, supportive others don't have to be friends who happen to be experts: They can be professors, colleagues, or researchers you contact on the e-mail lists. The books on qualitative analysis mentioned in Chapter 1 are also an important source of support.

Question 2: Are You Choosing for One Project or the Next Few Years?

A second significant issue is whether you're choosing software just for this project or for the next few years. Your word processor doesn't care what you're writing about, so most people pick one and stick with it until something better comes along and they feel motivated to learn it. But particular qualitative analysis programs tend to be good for certain types of analyses. Switching will cost you learning time and money. Think about whether you should choose the best program for this project, or the program that best covers the kinds of projects you're considering over the next few years. For example, one of the code-and-retrieve programs[3] might look adequate for the current project and be cheaper or look easier to learn. However, if you're likely to need a more full-blown code-based theory-builder down the road, it might make more sense to get started with one of those now (assuming you choose one that includes good code-and-retrieve capabilities).

Question 3: What Kind of Database and Project Is It?

The third general question is about your project and its contemplated database. As you look at detailed software features, you need to play them against these issues.

Data Sources: Single Versus Multiple

You may be collecting data on a case from many different sources (say your case is defined as a student, and you talk with several teachers, the parents, friends, and the student herself). Some programs are specifically designed to handle data organized like this; others aren't designed this

2. If you use Unix, you're not out of luck: Several of the programs reviewed here are available for Unix-based computers as well.

3. We describe the broad program families, such as code-and-retrieve programs and code-based theory-builders, briefly in Chapter 1 and in more depth in Chapter 3.

way but can handle multiple sources pretty well; and some really don't have the flexibility you'll need. Also, look for programs that are good at making links, such as those with hypertext capability, and that attach "source tags" telling you where information is coming from.

Single Versus Multiple Cases

If you have multiple cases, you usually will want to be able to sort them out according to different patterns or configurations, or work with only some of the cases, or do cross-case comparisons. Multi-case designs can get complicated, as in nested designs. For example, your cases might be students (and you might have data from multiple sources for each student). Your students might all be "nested" in (grouped by) classrooms, which might be nested within schools, which in turn might be nested in districts. Look for software that will easily select different portions of the database, and/or do configurational analysis across your cases; software that can help you create multiple-case matrix displays (see below) is also useful.

Fixed Records Versus Revised

Will you be working with data that are fixed (such as official documents, the plays of Shakespeare, or survey responses) or data that will be revised (with corrections, added codes, annotations, memos, and so on)? Some programs make database revision easy, and others are quite rigid; revising can use up a lot of time and energy. Some won't let you revise data at all without starting over.

Structured Versus Open

Are your data strictly organized (for example, responses to a standard questionnaire or interview) or free-form (running field notes, participant observation, and the like)? Highly organized data can usually be more easily, quickly, and powerfully managed in programs set up to accommodate them—for example, those with well-defined "records" for each case and "fields" with data for each record. Free-form text demands a more flexible program. There are programs that specialize in one or the other type of data and some that work fairly well with either type of data.

Uniform Versus Diverse Entries

Your data may all come from interviews. Or you may have information of many sorts on the same person or case study site: documents, observations, questionnaires, pictures, audiotapes, videotapes (this issue overlaps with single versus multiple sources, above). Some programs handle diverse data types easily, and others are narrow and stern in their requirements. If you will have diverse entries, look for software designed to handle multiple sources and types of data, with good source tags and good linking features in a hypertext mode. The ability to handle "off-line" data—referring you to material not actually loaded into your program—is a plus.

Size of Database

A program's database capacity may be expressed in terms of numbers of cases, numbers of data documents (files), size of individual files, and/or total database size, often expressed in kilobytes (K) or megabytes (MB). (Roughly, consider that a *single*-spaced page of printed text is about 2 to 3K.) Estimate your total size in whatever terms the program's limits are expressed, and at least double it. Most programs are more than ample, but you should check.

Question 4: What Kind of Analysis Is Anticipated?

Your choice of software also depends on how you expect to go about analysis. This does not mean a detailed analysis plan but a general sense of the style and approach you are expecting.

Exploratory Versus Confirmatory

Are you mainly planning to poke around in your data to see what they are like, evolving your ideas inductively? Or do you have some specific hypotheses in mind linked to an existing theory that you'd like to check out deductively? If the former, it's especially important to have features of fast and powerful search and retrieval, easy coding and revision, along with good text and/or graphic display.

If, on the other hand, you have a beginning theory and want to test some specific hypotheses, programs with strong theory-building and testing features are better bets. In either case, you may want to look for programs that test propositions or those that help you develop and extend conceptual networks.

Coding Scheme Firm at Start Versus Evolving

Does your study have a fairly well-defined a priori scheme for codes (categories, keywords), perhaps theory-derived, that you will apply to your data? Or will such a scheme evolve as you go, in a grounded theory style, using the "constant comparative" method (Strauss & Corbin, 1990). If the latter, it's especially important to have on-screen coding (rather than being required to code on hard copy) and to have features supporting easy or automated revision of codes. Hypertext link-making capabilities are helpful here too. "Automated" coding (in which the program applies a code according to a rule you set up, such as when a certain phrase, or a combination of other codes, exists) can be helpful in either case.

Multiple Versus Single Coding

Some programs let you assign several different codes to the same segment of text, including higher-order codes, and may let you overlap or nest coded chunks (see the discussion of chunking and coding in Chapter 3). Others are stern: one chunk, one code. Still other programs will let you apply more than one code to a chunk but won't "know" that there are multiple codes on the chunk; they'll treat it like two chunks, one for each code.

Iterative Versus One Pass

Do you want—and do you have the time—to keep walking through your data several times, taking different and revised cuts? Or will you limit yourself to one pass, for intellectual or resource reasons? An iterative intent should point you toward programs that are flexible, invite repeated runs, make coding revision easy, and can make a log of your work as you go. (This is related to the question of whether your records are fixed or revisable during analysis.)

Fineness of Analysis

Will your analysis focus on specific words? Or lines of text? Or sentences? Paragraphs? Pages? Whole files? Look to see what the program permits (or requires, or forbids) you to do. How flexible is it? Can you look at *varying* sizes of chunks in your data? Can you define free-form segments with ease?

Interest in Context of Data

When the program pulls out chunks of text in response to your search requests, how much surrounding information do you want to have? Do you need only the word, phrase, or line itself? Do you want the preceding and following lines/sentences/paragraphs? Do you want to be able to see the entire file? Do you need to be able to jump right to that place in the file and do some work on it (e.g., code, edit, annotate)? Do you want the information to be marked with a "source tag" that tells you where it came from (e.g., Interview 3 with Janice Chang, page 22, line 6)? Programs vary widely on this. This question has strong implications for the "closeness to the data" issue.

Intentions for Displays

Analysis goes much better when you can see organized, compressed information in one place rather than in page after page of unreduced text. Some programs produce output in list form (lists of text segments, hits, codes, and so on). Some can help you produce matrix displays. They may list text segments or codes for each cell of a matrix, though you will have to actually arrange them in a matrix for display. Look for programs that let you edit, reduce, or summarize hits before you put them into a text-filled matrix with your word processor. Some programs can give you quantitative data (generally frequencies) in a matrix. Others can give you networks or hierarchical diagrams, the other major form of data display; these features are currently better developed than those for matrices.

Qualitative Only, or Numbers Included

If your data, and/or your analyses, include the possibility of number crunching, look to see whether the program will count things and/or whether it can send information to other programs specifically designed for quantitative analysis such as SPSS, Systat, or BMDP. Think carefully about what kind of quantitative analysis you'll be doing, and make sure the program you're thinking about can arrange the data appropriately. Consider too whether programs can link qualitative and quantitative data in a meaningful way (in terms of the analytical approach you're taking).

Cut-Across Issues

The two main cut-across issues, again, are closeness to the data, and financial resources. Let's dispense quickly with the latter question first. Software varies dramatically in price. The range of prices for the programs we review here is $0 to $1,644 per user. In addition, programs vary a lot in the hardware they require for running efficiently. You obviously can't use a program if it's too expensive for you or if it requires a machine you can't afford. You can find the information you need on both these issues in the title box for each review, as well as in the ratings matrix in Chapter 9.

The remaining issue, closeness to the data, is a little harder to get a handle on. Working with qualitative data on a computer can have the effect of "distancing" you from your data. That is, you may wind up looking at only small chunks of text at a time, or maybe even just line-number references to where the text is. This is a far cry from the feeling of deep immersion in the data that comes from reading and flipping through piles of paper, which so many experienced qualitative researchers value so highly.

Other programs are set up so that this effect is minimized. They typically keep your data files on screen in front of you at all times; show you search results by scrolling to the hit, so that you see it in its full context; and allow you to execute most, or all, actions from the same screen where you're viewing your data files. Programs that allow you to build in hypertext links between different points in your data, and provide good facilities for keeping track of where you are in the database, can in some ways help you get even closer to the data than you can with paper transcripts.

Having said all this, we should also make the point that having software that enhances the sense of closeness to the data may not be a crucial issue for everyone. Some researchers don't mind relying heavily on printed transcripts to get a feeling of closeness while working with the computer, while others think such heavy reliance defeats the purpose of qualitative analysis software. Furthermore, some research projects simply don't require intense closeness to the data on the part of the researcher. You may be doing more abstract work and in fact *want* to move away from the raw data. We won't deal with the pros and cons of these differing approaches here.

Moving On

Having worked through these questions, you now have some sense of your needs in two general areas: YOU—what kind of computer user and qualitative researcher you are (right now) and whether you're choosing for now or for a few years—and YOUR WORK—what kind of project and database you're choosing a package for, and what kind of analyses you will be doing once you get started. Having your thoughts on these issues at least tentatively in order should enable you to take an active, deliberate approach to the reviews and ratings in the next chapters: You know what your needs are and you'll be able to recognize things that will or won't meet them.

3

Software Types and Functions

General Types

We begin with some gross distinctions. Most programs are actually a blend or combination of these general types, so it doesn't pay to be purist here. From the point of view of making a final choice, you have to look at the specific functions of a program and see if it does what you need it to do. But from the point of view of understanding the basic types and functions of software, it's worthwhile to try to sort them out a little. As a starter, we can name the following general types: word processors, text retrievers, textbase managers, code-and-retrieve programs, code-based theory-builders, and conceptual network-builders. (Richards & Richards, 1994, have provided a roughly similar typology with more detail, though our definitions vary somewhat.)

While it may be that a program we characterize as, say, a textbase manager is a better text retriever than most of those we characterize as text retrievers, we've tried to characterize them in terms of where their "heart and soul" is. This isn't perfect, but it makes it possible for us to organize the book a bit and for *you* to organize your approach to learning about the programs. Then, once you decide that what you need is, for example, good text retrieval capabilities, you'll be able to decide whether you're better off with a text retriever-type approach to text retrieval or a textbase manager-type approach to text retrieval. This overlap works to your advantage. It means that you'll often have several workable options, and can focus on subtle differences that will really optimize your choice. To help with the first cut, we've provided a table at the beginning of Part II that gives a general sense of each program's capabilities.

We'll begin with three types of "generic" programs—word processors, text retrievers, and textbase managers—which weren't necessarily developed with the needs of qualitative researchers in mind. Then we'll move on to the specialty types.

Word Processors

These are basically designed for the production and revision of text and are thus helpful for taking, transcribing, writing up, or editing field notes, for transcribing interviews, for memoing, for preparing files for coding and analysis, and for writing report text. Most word processors have decent facilities for searching for character strings (any sequence of characters, including spaces—maybe part of a word, a whole word, a phrase, a social security number, and so on) in the text. Some of the more cutting-edge word processors around these days, like Microsoft Word for Windows, will even let you create hypertext links (which connect two points in the text so you can jump back and forth between them), pop-up memos, and annotations.

There are ways to use a word processor to get a *very* pale imitation of some qualitative research program-like functions. For example, you can type your codes into the text and set them off with { }. Then you can search for the string "{happy}" to find text with the *code* "happy" and not just the word "happy." You can even write macros that will collect, say, all paragraphs coded "happy" and copy them to another place.[1] (But you usually can't search for paragraphs that are coded "happy" but NOT coded "birthday," or paragraphs that are coded "happy" AND coded "classroom.")

But this kind of workaround approach is probably not worth the trouble, especially because the results can't compare with those possible with the dedicated packages reviewed here. Because of this, and also because they change so fast, we don't list or rate specific word processors here. The computer trade magazines, like *PC Magazine* or *PC Computing* for DOS computers, or *Macworld* or *MacUser* for Macintosh computers, review the leading word processors regularly and can be very helpful in making a choice. Those magazines, however, rarely deal with the other types of software we deal with here. They also provide much briefer summaries of program capabilities, as necessitated by the differences between magazine article and book formats.

Text Retrievers

Software packages such as Metamorph, Orbis, Sonar Professional, The Text Collector, WordCruncher, or ZyINDEX are dedicated, sophisticated text search programs. They specialize in finding all the instances of words, phrases (or other character strings), and combinations of these you are interested in locating, in one or several files. To varying degrees, they can find things that are misspelled, sound alike, mean the same thing, or have certain patterns (like any three numbers, a hyphen, two numbers, a hyphen, and four more numbers: that is, any social security number). They can often do interesting operations with what they find, like marking or sorting the found text into new files, or linking annotations and memos to the original data, or launching new processes or other software packages to work on the data. Some have content-analytic capabilities as well: counting, displaying words in their context, and creating word lists and concordances (organized lists of all words and phrases in their contexts).

As we'll see, this category overlaps a lot (in terms of where actual programs fit) with the next one, which we've called "textbase managers." Some of the more sophisticated programs in each category have many of the essential features of both categories. In addition, many of the programs listed as code-and-retrieve or code-based theory-builders incorporate a lot of text retrieval functions. We'll still aim for the "heart and soul" sorting, for clarity.

Textbase Managers

As compared with text retrievers, programs of this type provide more in the way of *organizing,* sorting, and making subsets of your text systematically, and then provide for search and retrieval. Examples are askSam, Folio VIEWS, Tabletop, and MAX. Some deal with highly structured text organized into "records" (that is, specific cases) and "fields" (numerical or text information appearing for each case) and some easily manage "free-form" text. Some can include quantitative information.

Textbase managers differ as a group from text retrievers in their specialized capabilities for managing and organizing your data, and particularly for creating different subsets of your data for further analysis. In addition, they search for and retrieve various combinations of words, phrases, coded segments, memos, or other material (you can generally store and search for references to externally stored documents, pictures, or audio- or videotapes). Their search operations may be close to, just as good as, or sometimes better than those in the text retriever category. Some of them have advanced hypertext (see discussion under "Data Linking/Hypertext," below), annotation, memoing (see discussion under "Memoing/Annotation," below), multimedia, and even coding functions.

We now turn to three types of software packages specifically intended for qualitative data analysis: code-and-retrieve programs, code-based theory-builders, and conceptual network-builders.

Code-and-Retrieve Programs

Code-and-retrieve programs—often developed by qualitative researchers, as opposed to commercial software houses—specialize in helping you divide text into segments or chunks, attach codes to the chunks, and find and display all the chunks with a given code (or combination of codes). They take over the kinds of marking up, cutting, sorting, reorganizing, and collecting tasks qualitative researchers used to do with scissors and paper and note cards. Examples are HyperQual2, Kwalitan, QUALPRO, Martin, and The Ethnograph. They should (although they don't

1. For example, the late Renata Tesch of Qualitative Research Management, Inc., has shown in detail how this can be accomplished, as has Morse (1991), who focuses on using Macintosh word processors with macros.

always) provide the capability of searching for character strings as well as codes.

These programs often provide support for some sort of memo writing, although they don't always link the memos directly to the text or code(s) they're about (more on what we mean by "linking" below). They may provide some hypertext capability, although usually not of an extensive sort.

Code-and-retrieve programs—even the weakest of them—are a quantum leap forward from the old scissors-and-paper approach: They're more systematic, more thorough, less likely to miss things, more flexible, and much, much faster. Their basic code-and-retrieve functions, and memo-writing features when they have them, are a useful aid for theory-building efforts. In this sense, most code-and-retrieve programs can be considered theory-building tools. The programs in the next section are (with one exception) code-and-retrieve programs too, but they also have specialized functions of various types that go a step further in specifically aiding theory development.

Code-Based Theory-Builders

Like the code-and-retrieve programs, these are also often researcher developed. They usually include the same types of capabilities as the code-and-retrieve programs. So, if code-and-retrieve programs can be good theory-building tools, why do we make this distinction? Because the programs we've grouped here have special features and/or routines that go even further in supporting your theory-building efforts than do the programs grouped under code-and-retrievers. For example, they might help you to make connections between codes (i.e., categories of information) to develop higher-order classifications and categories, to formulate propositions or assertions that imply a conceptual structure that fits the data, and/or to test such propositions to see if they apply (we describe briefly how some of these approaches work in the section "Conceptual/Theory Development," below). It's these sorts of capabilities we look for when we try to distinguish between code-and-retrievers and code-based theory-builders. They're often organized around a system of rules or based on formal logic. Examples are AQUAD, ATLAS/ti, HyperRESEARCH, NUD•IST, and QCA. It's important to remember through all of this that no program will actually build theory for you, nor would you want one to. Computers don't think, and they can't *understand* the meaning of your qualitative data. But programs differ in the amount and kind of support they offer to *your* theory-building efforts.

Some of these packages also outdo the code-and-retrieve programs in basic code-and-retrieve functions. For example, they often have more sophisticated search routines. In addition, some are adding the ability to code and retrieve data other than text, like pictures, audio, even video: They'll keep track of where on a videotape (that's hooked up to your computer with the appropriate hardware) a coded segment is, and play it for you when you search for the relevant code. Several of the programs reviewed here will let you incorporate graphics into your database. We couldn't include specialty video-coding software packages usable for annotating, storing, and retrieving video data, such as Videologger (Krauss, Morrel-Samuels, & Hochberg, 1988), VideoNoter—revised to CVideo—(Roschelle & Goldman, 1991), Learning Constellations (Goldman-Segall, 1990, 1993), and VTLOGANL (Hecht, Roberts, & Schoon, 1993); but one of these, CVideo, can be used as an add-on to the code-based theory-builder NUD•IST (see review in Chapter 7). Two of the textbase managers, Folio VIEWS and askSam, and one of the text retrievers, Sonar Professional, can work with video segments linked into documents if your computer has multimedia capabilities. As discussed in Chapter 10, we expect this to be a growing area in the next few years, especially if there's heavy user demand.

Conceptual Network-Builders

Software of this sort also helps you build and test theory, but you work with systematically built graphic networks. You can see your variables shown as nodes (typically rectangles or ellipses), linked to other nodes by lines or arrows representing specified relationships (such as "belongs to," "leads to," "is a kind of"). The networks are not just casually hand drawn, but are real "semantic networks" that develop from your data and your concepts (usually higher level codes), and the relationships you see among them. Examples are ATLAS/ti (note that this one is also listed as a code-based theory-builder—it can represent anything you're doing with your text, codes, memos, and so on as a network), MECA, and SemNet. Programs with strong network-drawing capabilities, like Inspiration and MetaDesign, while not developed specifically for qualitative data analysis, have all sorts of features like extended text in nodes, pop-up memos, outlining, and/or hypertexting that make them more than just diagrammers; they're also real *conceptual* network-builders, just of a different sort.

Functions and Features: What to Look For

Let's turn in more detail to what these types of software packages can do for you. Any given program incorporates a particular set of functions for doing qualitative analysis work and may overlap several of the categories above. We'll sketch these here briefly. We'll also discuss two critical cut-across issues: *program flexibility* and *user friendliness.* Chapter 9 lists general functions, and specific features that let you carry out those functions, for each program in a matrix. It also explains all of the functions and features in the matrix.

Data Entry/Database Structure

Programs vary a lot in how they, first, let you enter your data and, second, organize and store it. Some programs are set up so that the work of data entry is done in the program itself: You start up the program and type your text in directly. Other programs require that you type up your data in another program, usually your word processor (some programs will let you do it either way). Programs that have you type up your data elsewhere also vary in how much they constrain the *way* you type up your data; sometimes you can format it any way you want (which is good if you already typed it up before you chose your analysis package, or if you're using a scanner to load text onto your computer), and sometimes you must follow very strict formatting rules, like limiting lines to 59 characters, single spacing text with an extra line between paragraphs, using hanging indents, or inserting special characters (like @ or ~) to delimit blocks of text or pages. Meeting strict data preparation requirements can be labor intensive. Researchers who have chosen such programs sometimes find that they shy away from using them for smaller, shorter-term projects where there will be less chance for the time investment to be recovered. These issues are discussed in the "Data Entry" sections of the reviews.

Once the data have been entered, it's important to know how they will be organized and stored: What is the structure of the program's database? In some programs, the data, having been typed in directly or imported, are stored in an "internal" database. That is, all of the relevant text is kept in one file on your disk, in a special "proprietary" format that your program alone can read, though it still looks normal to you (this is the way most software works—your word processor, database program, spreadsheet, scheduler, and so on all generally store data in proprietary format). We'll call this an "internal-files" approach. When you import data into an internal-files program, what actually happens is that the program makes a copy of your data and converts the *copy* into proprietary format for you to work with while leaving the original *untouched.*

Other programs leave your text in their original files on the disk. This typically means the program works with plain ASCII files. Sometimes it can also mean that the program works with files in the proprietary format of your word processor rather than converting them into the program's *own* proprietary format. This we'll call an "external-files" approach. Some of these programs set up a special index to those files so that they know just where all the text resides. For example, a code-and-retrieve program that works this way, rather than "importing" your text and directly placing your code references in it, will create a separate file with an index of the locations in your text file that you have coded. Then, if you tell it you want segments coded "happy," it will refer to the index, look up line and column numbers (and filenames) where "happy" was applied, and *then* go to the right text file and retrieve the appropriate range of text.[2] Programs that take an external-files approach typically leave your data files untouched, keeping track of any work you do in separate files, which are indexed to line and column numbers in your data files. Usually this means that, if you edit or alter the data files, the program will no longer have accurate indexes and so will do things like retrieve the wrong text in response to search requests or lose the correct location of hypertext links and annotations.

Another database structure issue is how data are organized. If the program takes an external-files approach, your data will be organized to some extent by how you divide your data among the different files you write up: such as a file for each interview or a file for all data on a given site. An internal-files program may take a more or less structured approach. Some programs follow a traditional database design in which data are arranged in a table of records (rows) and fields (columns). Records usually correspond to the unit of analysis or case (say, a person or a site), and fields to various variables. This allows you, for example, to sort the records so that you can see all cases in various orders or groupings and keep all the information for each case together. Other programs allow a more unstructured design in which your data may just be flowing text or a hybrid structure of flowing text with the option to place records and fields within it at any point. These sorts of structural issues are discussed in the "Database Structure" sections of the reviews.

Chunking and Coding

In this domain, programs can help you segment or "chunk" your data, such as into separate words, phrases, lines, sentences, paragraphs, or free-form segments, and then attach codes or keywords to the chunks. Some programs force you to establish your chunks before you even import your data, say, by dividing them into pages or paragraphs. Then you can apply codes only to these fixed chunks as wholes. Other programs allow completely free-form chunking. In these, your data all appear on screen and you can drag the mouse over the precise chunk of text you want to code, determining the start and end points of the chunk to the letter. In these setups, you can virtually always create chunks that overlap and nest within one another so that you can, say, apply one code to a sentence, then apply another code

2. Actually, some internal-files programs use indexes also, usually as a strategy to increase search speeds.

to the whole paragraph it came from. Or you can make the entire response to a question a large chunk, and apply various codes that apply to the response as a whole. Then you can go through and do a finer coding of smaller parts of the response. Often, even when you can do free-form coding, there are still easy ways to automatically select a whole line, sentence, paragraph, page, or file. We think this is a key issue: Virtually any style of research will benefit from a more flexible, versatile chunking setup. A rigid setup can cripple some research projects, even though others may fare all right.

Some programs have one-step (on-screen) coding; others require you to work with a hard copy printout (two-step). Codes are attached in several ways: one or several to a chunk or on overlapping or nested (one completely within another) chunks. A given program may support one or more of these schemes. Sometimes you define a chunk as you code it; sometimes you set up all your chunks ahead of time and apply codes later. Many programs let you do hierarchical or multilevel coding (e.g., "rain" has successively higher level codes of "precipitation," "weather," and "climate"). Some programs don't support this. You need to use a "workaround"—a way of getting the program to do something it wasn't designed to do. A common "workaround" that researchers use for this problem is to incorporate any higher-level codes into a code's name (e.g., instead of "rain," you'd have "climate\weather\precipitation\rain"). Of course, this doesn't work so well if you have a lot of levels or if "rain" is a subcode of more than one higher-level code. Also, if a program only allows you 10 or 15 characters per code, you'll have a hard time doing this.

Some programs have features that make reorganizing codes easy (e.g., if you add "snow," you can tell the program to include it under the higher level codes, and if you decide that lower level codes of "powder snow" and "corn snow" need to be connected to a new code, "skiing conditions," you can easily revise and update your originally assigned coding scheme). Programs also vary in how easy they make it to rename codes, or to replace one or several with another, or to correct or revise specific applications of codes to chunks.

Many programs also attach "source tags" so you can see later where a retrieved chunk came from (which interview, when, with whom, and so on). Some programs will show you your complete coding scheme in list, hierarchical tree, or other network form. Coding is discussed in the "Working on the Data" sections of the reviews.

Memoing/Annotation

Qualitative analysis is aided when you can reflect on your data, mark it up, write memos about it, and so on. It has become increasingly clear to us that any good code-and-retrieve or code-based theory-building program should include a memoing facility of some sort. Some programs let you make marginal or side notes, or annotations. Some let you write extended memos about the meaning of data or codes (though they vary in the extent to which they actually link the memos to the things they are about). Several let you apply codes to these "second-level" inputs. By implication: Some programs do not have any of these functions. These issues are also addressed in the "Working on the Data" sections of the reviews.

Data Linking/Hypertext

As you work on data, you are constantly seeing connections between different parts of the qualitative database. Some programs are good for making and recording links *within* parts such as fieldnote text, codes, annotations, memos, and "off-line" data (such as audiotapes or documents that are not actually in your database but that can be referred to when you need them). They may also let you make links *across* these parts of the database (e.g., linking codes to memos). Programs with strong linking functions, perhaps in a "hypertext" mode, let you "browse" or "navigate" easily through the database.

There's an important distinction to be made here between merely recording a *reference* and actually creating a *link.* Let's illustrate the distinction by considering different ways programs handle memos.

Some programs store memos in a separate file and give you a place to type in a reference to the text or code the memo is about. You can then search to see if there are memos about a text passage or code you're interested in. For example, you might have a memo containing reflections about an aspect of a school's change process, that were prompted by a particular passage in an interview. When reading the interview subsequently, you would not see that there was a memo attached to this passage. You'd have to exit the view of the interview, pull up the module with your memos in it, and search for any memos associated with the line numbers of the passage you were interested in. You can also see, when you're reading through your memos, references to the text or code each one is about, so that you could switch to the text-viewing module and go look at that segment. While the memo and the thing it's about are *conceptually* linked, they're not *operationally* linked in the program; you have to travel back and forth on your own.

In contrast, some programs create an actual, working link between your memos and the things they are about, so that, whenever you look at a text passage or code, the memo is right there for you to see (usually in a smaller window on screen), and vice versa. Alternatively, instead of immediately seeing the linked memo (or text or code), you may see a little icon that you can select, or have some other way to request that you be jumped directly to the memo (or text or code).

It's the ability to make these jumps, and navigate around your data by moving among associated ideas rather than moving linearly through the text, that really qualifies something as hypertext. There are different approaches to hypertext, each with its own unique advantages. The first is hypertext using fixed, explicit, or "hard" links. In this approach, you set up a link, designating its start (or source) and end (or destination) points. Any time you activate a link like this, typically by mouse-clicking on the source point, you will be instantly jumped to the destination point (in some programs, you can jump in either direction). The hard link approach has the advantage of allowing you to set up permanent links between related parts of your database.

The other approach to hypertext is implicit, dynamic, or intelligent hypertext (McAleese, 1993). In this approach, there aren't fixed links; instead, the computer carries out various actions. For example, while you're reading your text, some programs will let you highlight some text, and instantly execute a search for other places where that same text occurs, so that you jump around among the places in the text where the same topic is discussed. Some programs send your search hits to a new window on the screen. When you click on a hit, the program automatically searches for the place it came from and will jump you there so you see the hit in context. This approach sometimes uses hard links that initiate actions (rather than jumping to a specific spot) such as sorting your database or carrying out a search. The intelligent hypertext approach can be more flexible, and can create links between related material for you, so that you can browse along new paths.

Note that what code-and-retrieve programs do is create links between codes and text passages (except for a couple of really disappointing ones that just create references). This is so intrinsic to code-and-retrieve software, however, that we don't mention it when we talk about linking in those programs, except in the rare cases when it's missing. Along with coding and memoing, data linking is discussed in the "Working on the Data" sections of the reviews.

Search and Retrieval

Most programs can look for material you want, and show it to you, either alone or together with other instances of what you asked for. One issue is how fast this can happen. Another is whether the program will find segments by code and/or can search for "strings" of characters (usually words or phrases occurring naturally in the text). Some programs will find not only the word or phrase you asked for but all synonyms for it. Some have "wildcard" searching (e.g., "decisi*" will get you "decisive," "decision," "decision-making," and so on).

An important issue is how search requests are made—what sort of logic is used. Software developers have taken a variety of approaches to allowing you to ask sensible questions of the data. For example, many programs support "Boolean" requests (power AND conflict, power OR conflict, power NOT conflict, and so on). In more sophisticated implementations, these can be strung together using algebraic parentheses to formulate very precise search requests, as in (power AND conflict) NOT teacher. A few of the code-and-retrieve programs can look specifically for overlapping or nested chunks (find a place where a chunk coded "power" OVERLAPS a chunk coded "conflict," find a chunk coded "power" NESTED in a chunk coded "conflict"). Another alternative is "set logic," which is similar to Boolean logic but also allows such requests as "find me all chunks with at least 3 of the following five terms." Some programs can look for items that are near each other in the text or that precede or follow each other. Some programs, regardless of the type of search logic, can look just within a certain portion of the database (for example, only female respondents, or only in second-grade classrooms, or classrooms taught by women)—an important and useful feature.

Another very significant issue is how the program shows you the results of a search. When the program finds a chunk that matches your search request (sometimes called a search "hit"), it may show it to you by displaying the whole document it came from with the hit highlighted so you can scroll up and down and see as much context as you want, or it may give you a little of the surrounding context. Or it may just show you the hit completely out of context. If it doesn't show you complete context, you may or may not be able to jump right to where the hit came from. Some programs give you good information about where the hit came from—who it's about, what part of the database it's from, and so on—and some do not. If you're doing multiple searches, some programs will let you keep the results of each on the screen in separate windows.

A nice function to look for here is whether the program makes a log or record of searches and retrievals as you go. That enables you to build up a database of search requests that includes the ones that did something useful for you, along with annotations and memos made along the way. Some programs let you repeat a search simply by selecting it from the log; you may have the option to update or expand the old search as well. Search-and-retrieval functions and features are discussed in the "Searching" sections of the reviews.

Conceptual/Theory Development

As noted above, some programs have special functions that directly support your theory-building efforts. They may do this via rule-based or logical approaches, and some through building semantic networks. Some programs permit you to develop, and test, "if . . . then" propositions or hypotheses: You specify a rule (or set of rules) that you think is true, and the program will tell you whether and for which and how many cases it holds. Others allow you to do "configurational" analysis across several cases to find case-specific patterns of predictors associated with an outcome, as described by Ragin (1993b). In this approach, working with true/false variables (such as presence or absence of a code), you specify the outcome variable you're interested in, and the program goes through the cases in your database and generates a list of all the combinations of predictors associated with this outcome, removing redundancies. It then uses Boolean logic to reduce these patterns, finding the common, necessary elements of the patterns.

A fairly different approach to theory building uses the construction of visual networks, in which relationships are depicted graphically, to help you clarify and test ideas. Some of these operate on very strict, often hierarchical logic, where relationships must be represented in fixed ways, and others allow you to work in a more free-form way, arranging diagrams as you like. For network-building programs, look for whether nodes (the boxes or symbols that represent the entities in a network—typically concepts or text passages) must be simply labeled or can have text attached—and whether links (which are represented graphically by lines or arrows) are of a single, unspecified type, or of multiple types (such as "is part of," "leads to," "follows," "is a kind of," "belongs to")—or types you yourself specify. Theory-building features and functions are discussed in the "Theory Building" sections of the reviews.

Data Display

Most programs show you results on screen or will send them to a printer or another file. Some work on alternate or split screens, or in windows. Some programs can output text or numerical data to help you enter them in a matrix display; others will display networks. If the program does frequency counts, it may be able to send results directly to a statistical program. Programs that produce graphics vary in the aesthetic quality of their output. These issues are summarized in the "Output" sections of the reviews.

Graphics Editing

As we have said, some programs let you create and edit networks composed of "nodes," depicted with symbols such as rectangles and ellipses, connected by "links," which are depicted by lines or arrows. Nodes can be variables, or codes, or memos, or even have large amounts of text attached to them. The links can be one or two way (single- or double-headed arrows) and may also be labeled with titles. Look for editing flexibility (for example, when you move nodes, the links should move along with them—these are called "intelligent links") and a range of graphic styles. In the reviews of those programs with graphic capabilities, a "Graphics Editing" section is provided discussing the program's features in this domain.

Network and Team Use

Not all programs will run properly on a network or LAN (for local area network). Those that do, vary. Some programs can simply be loaded onto one of the network's common hard drives and then used by different users in a completely separate way. But other programs will allow multiple users at multiple workstations to work on the same documents at the same time, collaborating in rich ways that wouldn't be possible without the computer.

In addition, some programs are particularly good at supporting team use, with features that control the level of access different users have to the data, record what gets done by whom, and when, and have techniques for managing and merging work products of team members. Such features are available not only for simultaneous, or "real-time," collaboration over a network, but for work done separately on separate computers, and for simple "turn taking" at the same computer, as well. These features are discussed, for programs that have them, under the "Miscellaneous" sections of the reviews.

Other Considerations

We've summarized the main functions programs can carry out. As you're considering a particular program, there are also some considerations that cut across all these functions.

One is *flexibility.* Does the program do only what it's built for, or can you "work around" its features, doing other things you want to do without too much hassle? Must the program be used as is, off the shelf, or can you customize, adapt it, write "macros," create new routines within it? Workarounds are addressed in various places in the reviews, and issues like customization and macro facilities are discussed in the "Miscellaneous" sections.

The second consideration—a very fundamental one—is *user friendliness.* How hard is the program to learn? And once you've learned the program, how easy is it to use? (The answers to these two questions are often different!) Will the time and effort required to learn and use the program be justified in terms of what you're getting? And how good are the supports for learning: the manual or other documentation (you may be using these a lot at first); the tutorials; the help screens; and the technical support on the other end of the phone line? For both these issues, ask other users and see the "User Friendliness" sections of the reviews in Chapters 4 through 8.

PART II

Software Reviews

Part II consists of five chapters of in-depth software reviews, one chapter for each of the five "families" of software discussed in Chapter 3: text retrievers, textbase managers, code-and-retrieve programs, code-based theory-builders, and conceptual network-builders. Within each chapter, we have presented the reviews in alphabetical order—there is no hidden meaning to the sequencing. Once again, no program is a "pure" type, and there are plenty of overlaps across the families. Our counsel is to keep the needs you've identified in mind and look at each program for itself, in terms of what it can do for you.

Before delving into the reviews, you may want to read Chapter 9. In explaining the ratings matrix presented there, it discusses program functions and features more specifically than we have so far. It will help you put what you read in the reviews into context. The headings in Chapter 9 differ slightly from those in the reviews, but we provide pointers to the review headings to look for.

For convenience, we repeat the format for the reviews here.

Title box: The program's name; operating system(s); the developer's name, address, and phone/fax/e-mail numbers; the price; the hardware requirements

Overview: A quick thumbnail sketch: how the program is set up, what it looks and feels like, what it can do, and its outstanding features

Database structure: How the program is set up to organize your data

Data entry: How you bring your data into the program and set it up for analysis

Working on the data: How you set up and carry out coding and sorting of your data; how you annotate your text, write memos about it; how different parts of your database are linked

Searching: How you hunt for and retrieve items in your data (such as coded segments, words, or phrases) that you need for your analysis

Output: How the program gives you results, and through what methods (on screen, printer, copying to disk)

Theory building: How the program helps you think about your data systematically, develop propositions or hypotheses, test them, and generate a coherent explanation of what you are finding

Graphics editing: The program's abilities to work with data or results in a diagrammatic, network-like form

User friendliness: The program's ease of learning, its supports for learning, and its ease of use once learned

Miscellaneous: Anything of interest that doesn't fit logically elsewhere, including automation or customization features and network use

Update: Recent information on the developer's plans to revise or extend the program; notes on new versions received after the review was completed

Comparative remarks: Comparisons with other programs that can do similar things

Summary

References: Items specific to this program (the manual, key articles, and so on)

Occasionally, one of these sections will be missing from a review. This is not an oversight (we double-checked!), but because that topic was not relevant for the program being reviewed.

Comparing programs is a big part of what you'll be doing here, and we've provided two main sets of comparisons. The ratings matrix in Chapter 9 gives a big comparison across all the programs, giving detailed ratings of functions and features. The "Comparative Remarks" section of each review, on the other hand, looks holistically at a particular program, and compares it with various other programs that have similar functionalities.

Whenever we could, we've provided toll-free telephone numbers for contacting developers and/or distributors of the programs. Readers outside the United States should know two things about these numbers. First, they always begin with the three-digit area code "800," and so these phone numbers are often referred to as "800 numbers." Second, it's up to the owner of an 800 line whether or not to have the line accept calls from outside the United States. We don't know which do and which don't; try and you'll find out.

Finally, we provide in Table II.1 a one-page summary of program functions, without getting into specific features. This table will also tell you what type of computer(s) or operating system(s) (Macintosh, DOS, Windows, Unix, or mainframe) the program is available for. There are two types of ratings in this table. The square symbols for Coding, Database Management, Memoing, and Theory Building tell you simply whether the program is designed for this function, isn't designed for it but can do it at least in a limited way with workarounds, or whether it simply can't do this thing at all. Note that there's no judgment made or implied about how well the program carries out this function—we felt this would be too reductionistic for such functions in a general table. The round symbols for Search & Retrieval, Matrix Building, Network Display, and User Friendliness, on the other hand, are strength ratings, using the same set of symbols as in the big ratings matrix in Chapter 9. These were categories that lent themselves more readily to these judgments in this format.

Table II.1. Summary of Program Fucntions

	Program	Version	Operating System	Coding	Search & Retrieval	Database Management	Memoing	Data Linking	Matrix Building	Network Display	Theory Building	User Friendliness
TEXT RETRIEVERS	Metamorph	3.5	Mc D U M	□	●[a]	□	□	■	—	—	—	⊙
		4.0	Mc W U	—	●[a]	□	■	■	—	—	—	●
	Orbis[b]	1.0	D W	□	●	■	□	—	●	—	—	⊙
	Sonar Professional	8.5	Mc W	—	●	□	■	■	—	—	□	●
	The Text Collector	1.7	D	—	●	□	—	—	—	—	—	●
	WordCruncher	4.5	D	—	⊙	□	—	■	—	—	—	○
		Beta	W	—	●	□	■	■	—	—	—	⊙
	ZyINDEX	4.0/5.1	D/W	—	●	□	■	■	—	—	—	○
TEXTBASE MANAGERS	askSam	5.1/1.0	D/W	—	●	■	□	■	—	—	—	⊙/●
	Folio VIEWS	3.1	D W	■	●	■	■	■	○	—	—	●
	Tabletop	1.x	Mc W	—	⊙	■	■	—	⊙	—	■	●
	MAX	3.5	D	■	○	■	—	■	—	—	—	⊙
CODE-AND-RETRIEVE PROGRAMS	HyperQual2	1.0	Mc	■	○	■	■	■	○	—	□	⊙
	Kwalitan	4.0	D	■	⊙	□	■	■	—	—	□	●
	Martin	2.0	W	■	○	□	■	□	—	—	—	●
	QUALPRO	4.0	D	■	○	□	□	—	—	—	—	⊙
	The Ethnograph	4.0	D	■	⊙	□	■	—	—	—	—	⊙
CODE-BASED THEORY-BUILDERS	AQUAD	4.0	D	■	○	□	■	□	⊙	—	■	⊙
	ATLAS/ti	1.1E	D	■	⊙	□	■	■	⊙	●[c]	■	●
	HyperRESEARCH	1.55	Mc W	■	⊙	□	—	—	○	—	■	●
	NUD·IST	3.0	Mc W	■	●	■	■	□	●	⊙	■	●
	QCA	3.0	D	—	○	—	□	—	○	—	■	○
CONCEPTUAL NETWORK BUILDERS	Inspiration	4.0	Mc W	—	⊙	—	■	■	—	●	—	●
	MECA	1.0	Mc D U	—	—	—	—	■	—	⊙	■	○
	MetaDesign	3.0/4.0	Mc/W	—	○	—	□	■	—	●	—	●
	SemNet	1.1Beta	Mc	—	⊙	—	■	■	—	●	■	●

■ *Designed for this purpose, as we see it (may be more or less effective)*

□ *Not really designed for this purpose, but can do at least in a limited way*

— *Can't do this*

● *strong*

⊙ *OK*

○ *weak*

— *absent*

NOTE: Operating system: Mc = Macintosh; D = DOS; U = Unix; M = mainframe; W = Windows.

a. For raw text retreival, in a class by itself.

b. Available as add-on module for XyWrite 4.0 or NotaBene 4.0 word processors; ratings include word processor features.

c. Weaker than Inspiration and MetaDesign on graphics, but can create networks from data.

4

Text Retrievers

The programs in this chapter are basically good at hunting for words, phrases, or other "strings" of characters in your database, and then bringing them to you for your scrutiny, either one at a time and/or collected in a batch. They may range considerably in the details of how you give them a search request and how your search "hits" look when you get them. Some can do frequency distributions or crosstabs of your hits as well.

Other programs that overlap significantly with this category, and the chapters they are reviewed in, include the following:

□ □ □

Metamorph, Version 3.5/4.0[1]

Available for DOS, Windows, Unix, Macintosh, and MVS, and will be customized for other operating systems on request

Thunderstone
Expansion Programs International, Inc.
11115 Edgewater Drive
Cleveland, OH 44102

Phone: (216) 631-8544
Fax: (216) 281-0828

Price: $1,644
Faculty: $400

Hardware Requirements:
For DOS and Windows
- 286 or better CPU
- Hard disk with at least 4MB free space
- 450K of free DOS RAM (that's *free,* not total)
- An LPT1 parallel port

Overview

Metamorph is an extremely powerful search-and-retrieval program that uses artificial intelligence techniques to find not only the word(s) you ask for, but any form of that word, or any other word that means the same thing; if you're looking for a quantity, it will find any expression of that quantity. We know of no other program that can replicate those features, and they are the primary reason for a qualitative researcher to use Metamorph: It has the potential for serious advances in qualitative data analysis—especially the searching aspects.

For this review, we looked at both the DOS and the Windows versions of the program; they are sold together as one package for the single version price. The program is also available for Unix, MVS, and Macintosh and will be custom "ported" to other operating systems by request; all resemble the DOS version. There were substantial differences between the DOS and Windows versions. In gen-

1. The current version numbers are 3.5 for the DOS version and 4.0 for the Windows version.

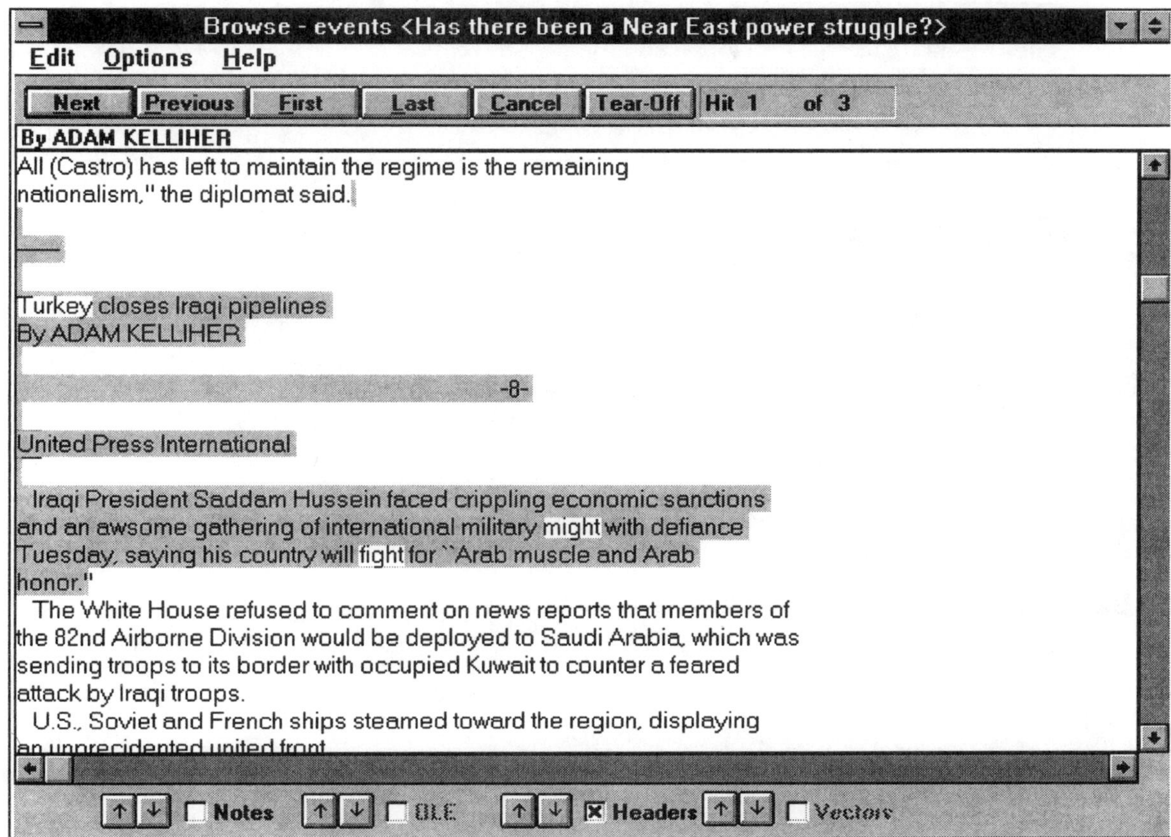

Metamorph Figure 1. You view your search results in the browser. The whole hit is highlighted in gray. The three words that matched the query are "Turkey," "might," and "fight." Just above the text window is a narrow window that shows the header (source tag) "By ADAM KELLIHER." The actual query that was entered shows in the title bar at the top of the screen.

eral, the Windows version, which is newer, is much more user friendly and has a couple of significant improvements, while the more difficult, and blindingly fast, DOS version gets you several important and powerful additional functions and features (though you also get a stripped-down, easy-to-use version of the DOS program called EZMM, which still has essentially the same search power). As we understand things from the developers, the versions for other platforms most closely resemble the DOS version. Because the Windows version is, deliberately, more accessible to a wider range of users, we'll focus on it here, making occasional references to the DOS version as we go. In a special section later in the review, we'll talk about the differences between the two versions in some detail.

The program has a mode that allows you to ask questions of the data in English (e.g., "Has there been a Near East power struggle?"). Found chunks ("hits") can be reviewed on-the-fly, in context, and sent to any output file you want. The program has a nice "browser" in which you review search results (see Figure 1). In the DOS version, hits can be automatically sent to an output file, and you can easily edit the original data files in midsearch. And you can establish up to 10 types of indexing tags (source tags) to appear with your search results (how this works differs between versions—see below).

In addition, the program allows you to link pop-up notes and OLE objects (such as spreadsheets or graphics) to your text. It also has a powerful linking facility that launches actions based on strings of characters found in the text. So you might set it up to load your spreadsheet program whenever it sees a spreadsheet filename in the text and open the specified file. Or you might have it start a secondary Metamorph search, say, for your memos whenever it saw the words "Memo here" in the text. The DOS version has even more sophisticated linking capabilities.

Database Structure

Metamorph, like The Text Collector, has no internal database; it searches through text files you have on your

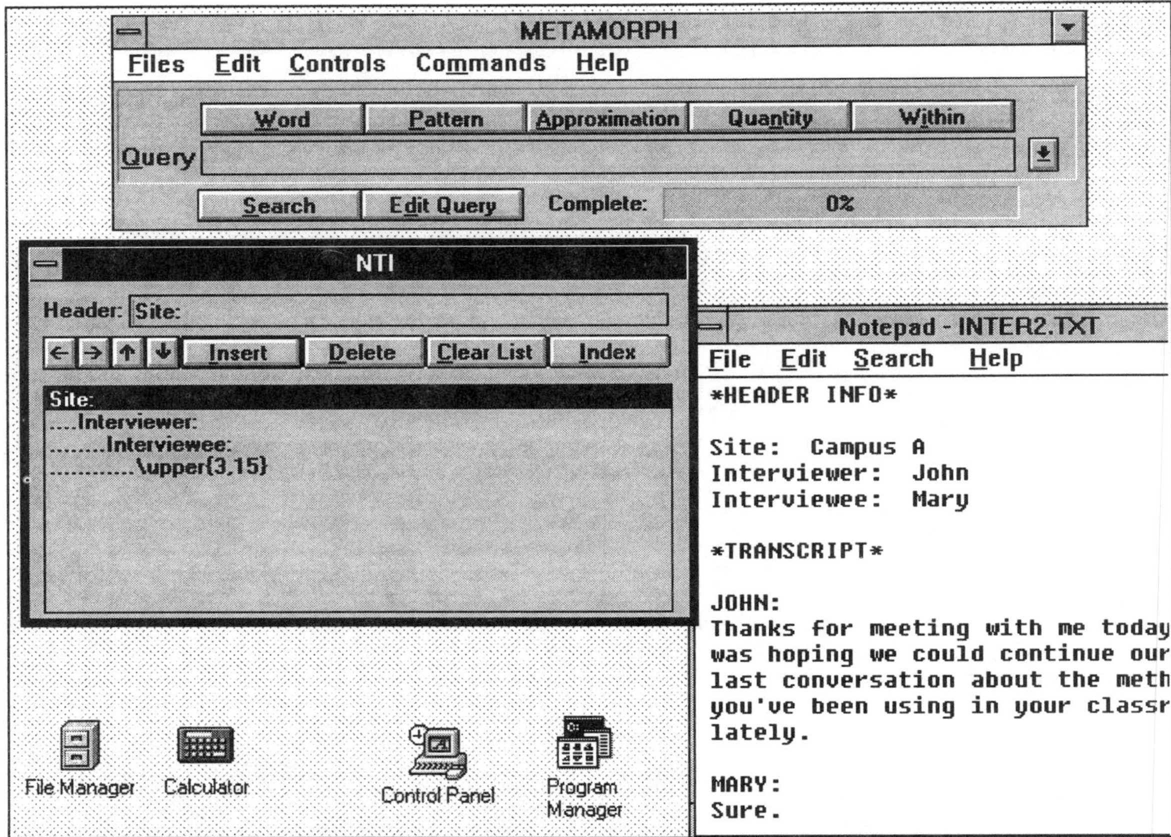

Metamorph Figure 2. Setting up to apply NTI headers to the file Inter2.txt. The first three header levels are just simple strings (in this case a word followed by a colon) that appear at the beginning of a header line in the text (at right). The fourth one (\upper{3,15}) is a little more complicated. By using REX syntax, I've set up a header that will capture any series of 3 to 15 uppercase letters at the beginning of a line. Because the name of a speaker in my transcript always appears in uppercase letters on a line by itself (e.g., JOHN:, MARY:), these will always appear as the fourth-level headers with any hits extracted from the following text.

hard or floppy disk. Generally, you search through ASCII files. If you search a document in another format, say, a document from your word processor that you have not converted to ASCII, the text just won't show any of its formatting (indents, double spacing, centering, underlining, and so on)—no big deal. But if you try to search something like a dBASE file, you won't get readable results.

You select the set of files to be searched through the File Select dialog box. The list of files to be searched *at any one time* is limited to 1,024. However, you can save a list of files to a special list file. Later, you can use the name of such a list file as a single entry in the file list, and all the files listed in it will be included in the search. Because you can even include the name of one list file in another list file, there is, in effect, no limit. List files serve as what other programs call file catalogues: collections of files you can easily call all at once.

Data Entry

As noted above, you generate your data with your word processor or text editor and usually create an ASCII file. There is no need to import or index files before you search them.

Hierarchical Outline/Source Tags

Using a function called NTI, you can assign source tags in the form of hierarchical outline headers to show up with search results. The headers are created from strings of characters that exist in your text and are identifiable in some way. For example, if every page of your document has a page number enclosed in hyphens at the bottom (e.g., -1-), you could instruct the program to find all such strings of characters and assign them to the text on that page as a header, or source tag. If all of the section headers you used when typing your document are surrounded by double asterisks, you could have the program find all strings surrounded by double asterisks and assign them as headers (tags) to following chunks. You can define up to 10 different types of headers for a file. Thus any retrieved chunk can have headers showing (for example) the interviewee, page, and section where the chunk came from.

If the strings you're looking for appear flush against the left margin, each on a line by itself, this process is easily accomplished. For example, if you have a line that starts with "Interviewer:" and then the interviewer's name before each interview, you just tell the program to define an "Interviewer:" header, using everything on that line as the header. Then you'll get headers like "Interviewer: Rebecca" or "Interviewer: John." Figure 2 shows a setup in NTI for three types of headers and a sample text file it would work with.

You can also use strings for source tags that aren't flush left and on lines by themselves (see Figure 2). However, this procedure is not easily accomplished. You have to be able to identify the regularly occurring strings (which can include nonprinting characters like carriage returns, tabs, and other formatting codes) and then be able to create the routine to locate them. This involves learning a rather complex command syntax called REX, which we will discuss further below. If you are able and willing to take this on, Metamorph comes packaged with a number of separate programs for finding and identifying such recurrent strings. (If you're not, the next paragraph will sound like nonsense, so just skip ahead.)

One such program, ISTXT, reports on whether a file is in English and whether or not it is an ASCII file. It can be used in batch processes to screen files to be passed to a Metamorph search. Another, RECON, performs reconnaissance on a file, reporting the frequencies of all patterns of nonalphanumeric characters—such as carriage returns (paragraph markers) or tabs—in the file. Still another, HEX, gives hexadecimal translations of all characters in the file, visible or not, because you can include hexadecimal numbers in REX commands.

These programs, taken together, provide fairly powerful tools for identifying strings to feed to NTI. If you're the sort who likes to get into the technical nitty-gritty, or if your organization has someone who does, you can do some powerful stuff with NTI. The one major limitation with it is that a tag applies to everything up until the next tag. This means you can't just stick a tag on a chunk unless you have a new tag to take over *immediately* afterward. Therefore one might not want to use this for coding. Another implication of this is that if you wanted some of these headers to appear as source tags for any text retrieved from the file, you would set them all up as a first-level header at the beginning of the file and have all subsequent headers at lower levels of the hierarchy.

Working on the Data

By way of introduction to this section, we must point out that you do not have to work on the data at all. You can simply search and make reports, as will be discussed under "Searching" and "Output," below.

You can't edit your text files in Metamorph. If you want to modify a text file, you'll have to quit your search, delete the file from the list of files to be searched, start a new search on some other file(s) to make Metamorph forget about the file and let another program use it, and then edit it with an editor like Notepad (which comes with Windows but will open only relatively small files) or your word processor. Then you'll have to go back and add the file back into the list to be searched.

This section will describe the facilities Metamorph offers for annotating your text (in midsearch if you like) and for linking things to it. Some of this is easy and some of it is quite difficult, so remember that you don't have to get into any of this to use the incredibly powerful search routines.

Metamorph 4.0 for Windows allows you to create four types of "attachments" to your text files, and it does this through its own indexes, never actually altering the text files themselves. The types of attachments are (a) NTI headers, which were discussed above; (b) notes, which are little pop-ups you can use for annotations and memos; (c) OLE attachments, which let you attach any OLE object; and (d) vectors, which let you insert icons to launch other programs as you are browsing search results. Except for headers, all attachments are "attached" to a range of text, which is highlighted in yellow when it comes up in a search. You can right-click with the mouse (click the right-hand button) on this range to activate the attachment.

Notes

Notes show up in a little window, which shows five lines at a time (about 30 characters per line) when you're initially composing a note and only two lines when it pops up later (see Figure 3 for both). For some reason, these windows are *not* resizable. You can have up to 30K of text (a little over 10 single-spaced pages) in a note, though, and there's a scroll bar so you can read through it. Obviously, you won't see much text at a time in such a small window. For longer notes, you'll probably want to copy to an output file or the clipboard and then print them out for easier reading. When you add a note, Metamorph automatically stamps it with the date and time.

You can't search for text in notes, as you can in, say, Folio VIEWS, but once you pop up a notes window you can scroll back and forth through all the notes attached to the current file. There's no automatic way to print out notes, so you have to copy to another file. As we'll discuss under "Output," below, this procedure is annoying but not horribly

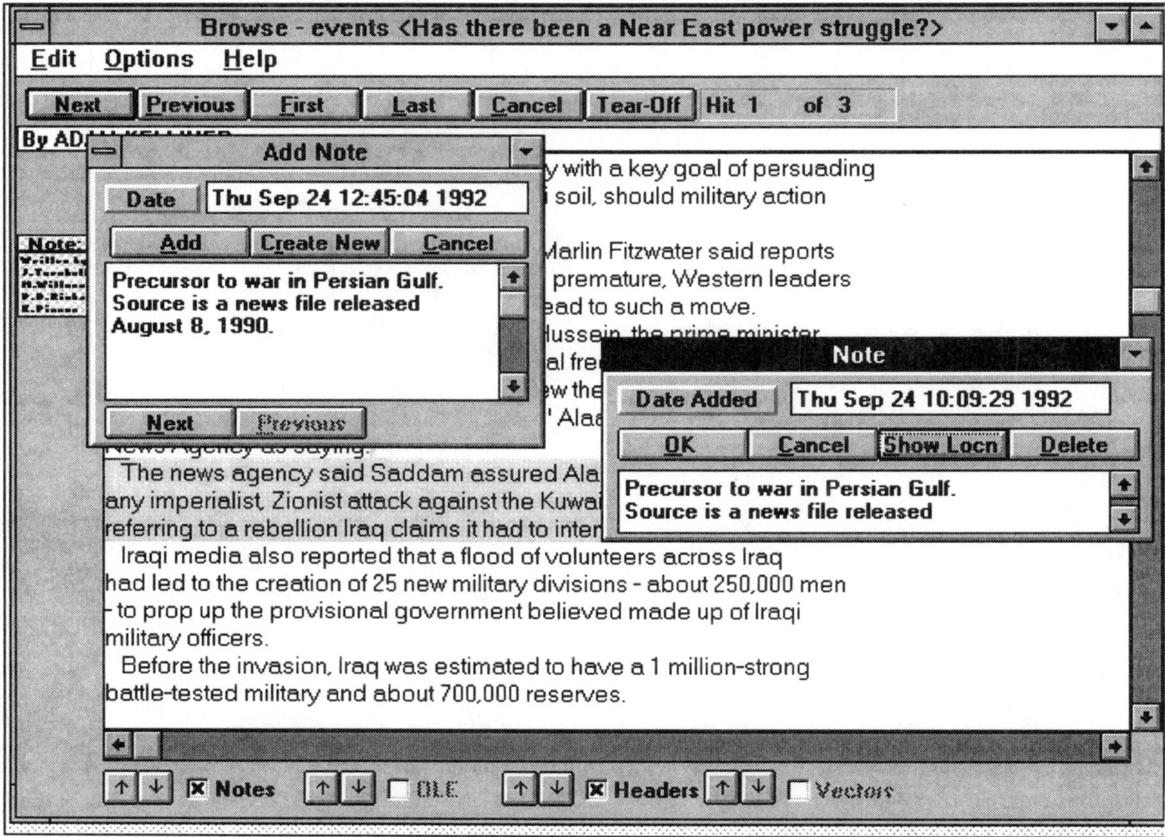

Metamorph Figure 3. Two different ways to look at the same note. When you first write a note, in the Add Note box, you see more lines, but they're a little shorter. When you call it up later, you only see two lines at a time! If you want, you can call up the Add Note box and then scroll through all the notes until you get to the one you want, but is it worth it?

restrictive. Outputting the text that a note is attached to does *not* send the note along as well; you must output it separately. Unfortunately, the little Note icon in the left margin of the browser always says, "Written by:" and the names of the programmers who created Metamorph, not the author of the note.

OLE

Another type of attachment you can make is an OLE (for "object linking and embedding") link. This means that when you create an OLE attachment in Metamorph you have the option of calling up another OLE-supporting Windows program that you have (like a spreadsheet program or graphics program) and creating the "object" (e.g., a spreadsheet, chart, or drawing) that will be attached to your text file. Again, the text the attachment is made to will be highlighted in yellow and an icon will appear on the left. By clicking with the mouse, you can make the object pop up in a window. You can also edit or print the object by having it load up in the program you used to create it (just use a different combination of mouse clicks). All of this worked fine with the OLE attachments that had been made to the sample files. When we tried to make our own, we were able to make the attachments but got repeated (misspelled) error messages, like "Looking betond [sic] file" when we came back and tried to pop them up. The developer reports that this is a bug that's been fixed.

Vectors

Vectors are a little more complicated than notes and OLE links. A vector attachment does two things: First, it recognizes a character string in the text; then, based on what's in the string, it performs some action—usually launching another program. You have to set it up ahead of time with strings to recognize and actions to perform when it does. The easiest and most obvious application is to set

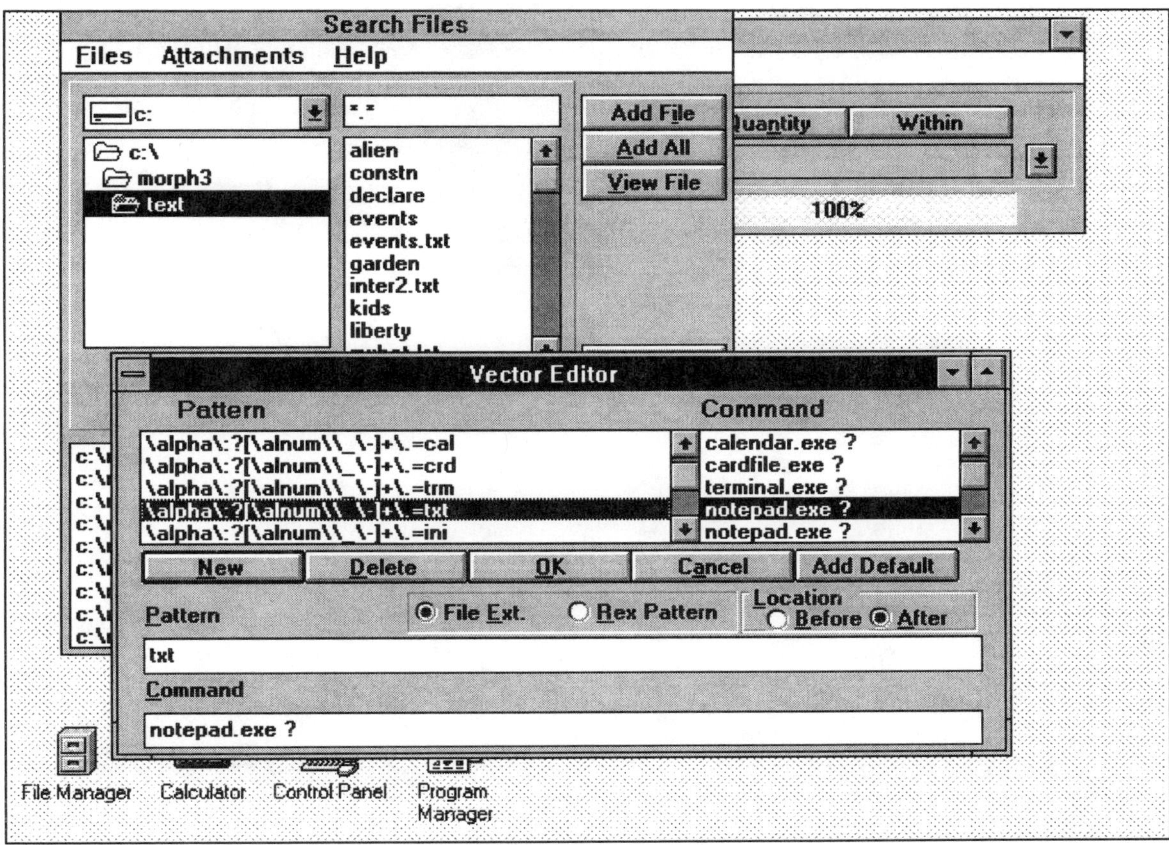

Metamorph Figure 4. The Vector Editor. The selected vector will, for any file name that ends in .TXT (usually an ASCII file), load up Notepad with that file in it ready for editing. All you have to do is type "txt" in the Pattern box and "notepad.exe ?" in the Command box (the ? stands for the file name) and Metamorph adds in the rest of the complicated syntax automatically.

it up to recognize file names in the text and then load up the file in its associated program. For example, if the name of a graphics file with a diagram in it appears in the text, you could just right-click on the file name and the graphics program would appear with the file already loaded.

To cause this to happen, you will have gone into the vector editor (see Figure 4) and created an entry that says, for example, for every filename that ends in ".PCX" load up Paintbrush with that file in it. Metamorph will set up the syntax for routines based on file names and their extensions, so it's really pretty easy. When you click "OK," Metamorph will attach "vectors" to all the matching strings it finds in the text files currently selected. These will be highlighted in yellow in the text and can be activated just like notes and OLE objects.

You can also do fancier stuff with vectors, but it gets more complicated. (Don't worry if you don't follow this paragraph; in *this* case, what you don't know won't hurt you.) Essentially, you can find almost any string of characters or pattern of characters (e.g., the pattern for a social security number is any three digits, a dash, any two digits, a dash, any four digits: ###-##-####) using REX, and set up a vector for it to issue any command. In addition, you can have the string that was found become part of the command.[2] So, if you had a file containing data on your subjects, you might attach a vector to all their ID numbers, in the text files, that would open up that file in some other program, like a flat-file database (or the DOS version of Metamorph). If that other program accepted search terms as command line parameters (as does the DOS version of Metamorph), then you could have it start up with a search for the ID number that was found in the first place. This would be accomplished by passing the ID number found in the text to the other program as a command line parameter.

2. That's how in the examples above the correct graphics file got loaded into Paintbrush. Some programs accept "command line parameters," information like filenames and program options as part of the command—on the "command line"—that starts them up. So you might type "word mytext.doc" to start Microsoft Word with the file "mytext.doc" loaded up and ready to edit.

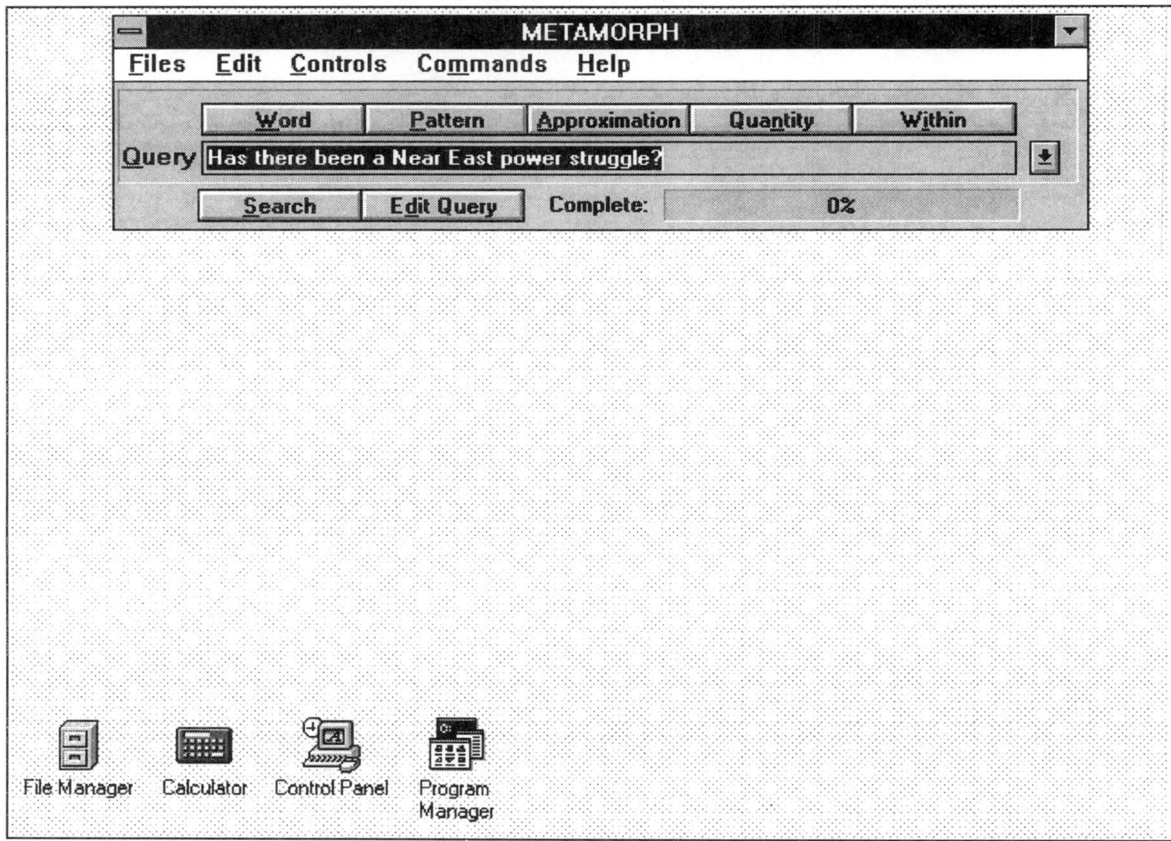

Metamorph Figure 5. The Query box, with an Ask mode query typed in and ready to go. Note the cluster of buttons around the Query line for getting help with creating different types of queries, which can all be mixed and matched. These are all described in the various subsections of the "Searching" section.

The DOS and other versions of the program actually have a more powerful version of vectoring via a program called MMVEC. We'll describe this in the section on the DOS version, below.

Searching

This is what Metamorph is primarily for, and it handles search requests in a way we have not seen anywhere else. It expands your search request to find virtually anything that means the same thing, whether you have asked for words or quantities or alphanumeric patterns (such as dates, phone numbers, serial numbers, and so on). In addition, you can combine the many different kinds of searches (concepts, numbers, patterns, and approximations) all in one query. Metamorph is able to use all its search routines together in finding a single hit. Before discussing how Metamorph expands search requests, let's lay a little groundwork.

Search Modes

Metamorph offers two approaches to typing in your queries: Ask and Search (in the DOS and other versions, these are explicitly different commands, whereas in the Windows version, they're just different ways of typing in the query—see below). In *Ask* mode, you simply type a question, such as "Has there been a Near East power struggle?" (the example in the tutorial). Metamorph, using lists of "noise words," such as "a, but, then, of" and question words, such as "Has there been," strips the query down to the important words: "Near East power struggle." If there are quantities expressed, either in words (e.g., "more than five hundred") or numerals, it automatically calls its Numeric Pattern Matcher to handle the quantity (more on this, too, later). Items in queries in Ask mode are treated as linked by AND logic; all must be present for a hit to be found.

In *Search* mode, you type in just the search words. You have access to OR logic (actually, Metamorph's search

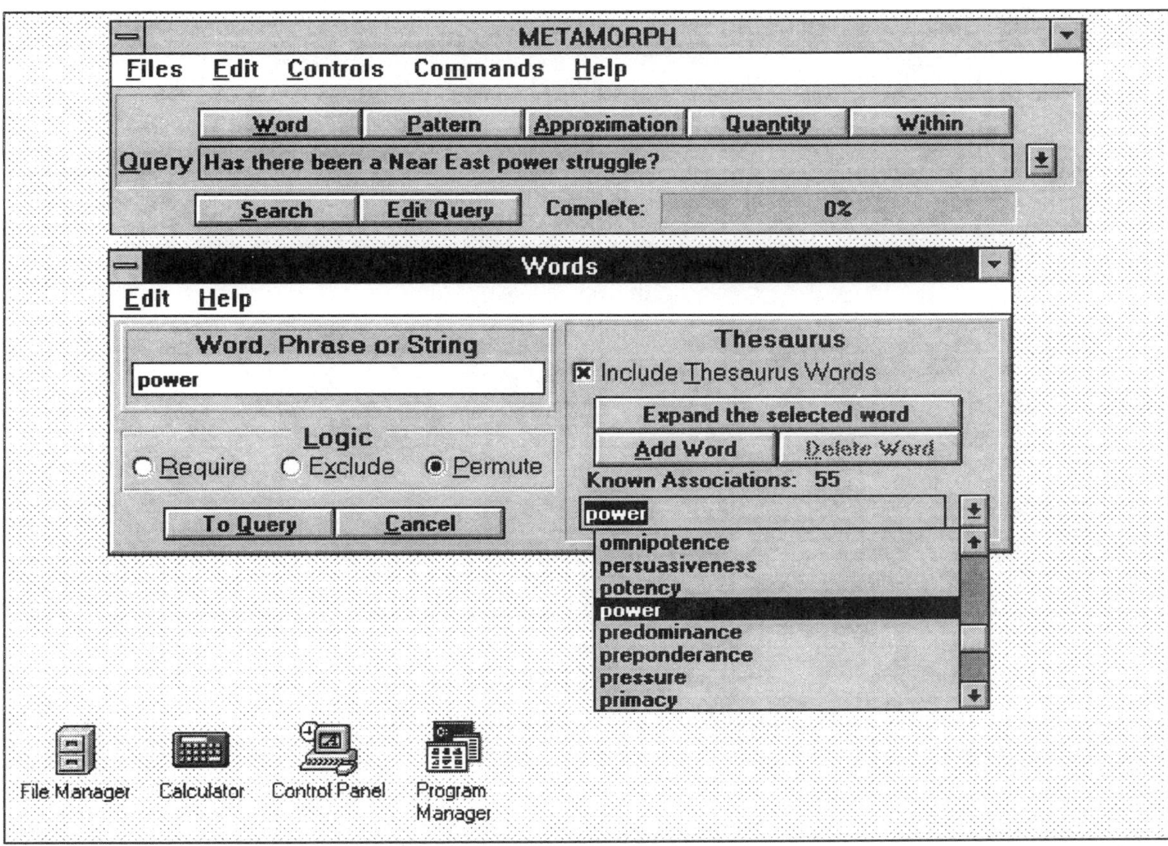

Metamorph Figure 6. The Word box lets you edit equiv sets. The To Query button will paste the current word into the Query line. ("Permute" refers to @ or OR logic: see section on "Search Logic," below.)

logic is more complex than the Boolean logic you'll find in most programs, but more on this later) and can call the Numeric Pattern Matcher, the Approximate Pattern Matcher, and others explicitly. This mode more closely resembles the search modes in other search packages. The new "Query Box" in the Windows version (see Figure 5) makes using all these different types of pattern matchers easy to understand and do.

Text Unit Delimiters

Any program that searches for co-occurrences of words (including codes) has to be told how close together those words have to be in order to be considered to co-occur. In The Text Collector, for example, words have to co-occur within a "context block." In Metamorph, such chunks are simply referred to as delimited text units. Text units can be automatically defined as lines, sentences, paragraphs, pages, or numbers of characters, or can be manually defined to be delimited by any user-specified string of characters (visible or not). You can either pick such delimiters off a list, as you would in The Text Collector, or include the text unit definition you want in the search request, requesting sentences, for example, by ending the query with "w/sent." If you do not include such instructions, Metamorph will automatically use whatever definition was used last (sentences are the default).

Concept Searching

As we indicated above, one of Metamorph's most powerful features is its ability to expand a search request to capture alternate ways of saying the same thing. For English words, it does this with two procedures (either of which can be turned off at will). One is called morpheme processing. Metamorph has lists of all English suffixes and prefixes (which you can add to or remove from) and it removes any of these from the search words to derive the root, or morpheme, of the word. By searching for morphemes, the program should find all cognates of a word, finding, for example, "cooperate" and "cooperative" when you ask for "cooperation."

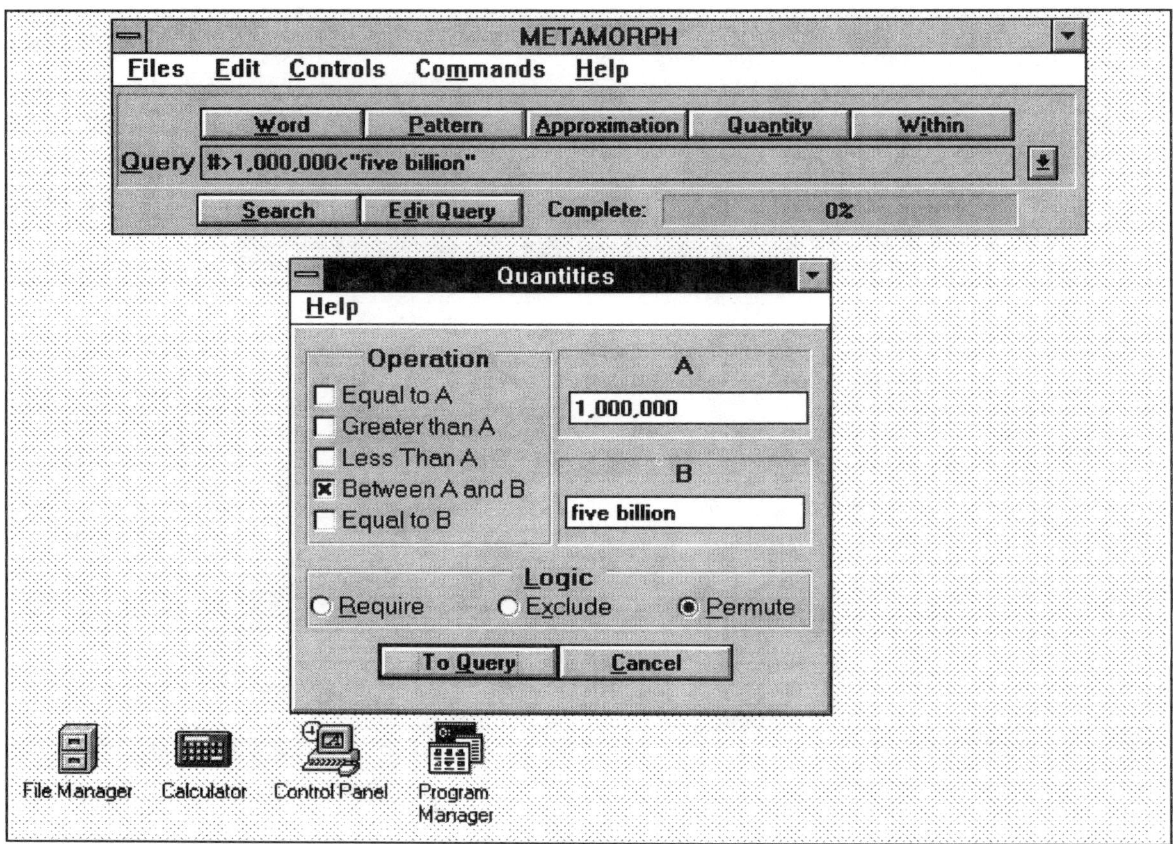

Metamorph Figure 7. The Quantity dialog box helps you set up Numeric Pattern Matcher requests. You just type in the quantities, in words or numbers, and specify a relationship on the left. Metamorph will then find any combination of words or numbers that expresses the quantity you're looking for.

The other technique Metamorph uses is to expand each English word in the search request into a list of equivalents (or "equivs") maintained in a file of over 250,000 associations. The example used in much of the Metamorph materials is the query: "Near East power struggle." Metamorph recognizes the phrase "Near East" and expands it to a list of all countries in the Near East. Then it takes the word "power" and expands it to a list of almost 60 equivs, such as "might," "force," "strength." Finally, it expands the word "struggle" to a list of almost 30 equivs, such as "fight," "battle," "conflict." The search will then locate any sentence (or other desired unit) that contains any cognate of any word in the Near East list, AND any cognate of any word in the power list, AND any cognate of any word in the struggle list. The idea is to get you any sentence that refers to a Near East power struggle whether those particular words appear or not!

Can you get stuff that's completely irrelevant to what you're interested in? You bet. But the folks at Thunderstone don't see this as a problem, and they may be right. First of all, their stance is that the important thing is to make sure you get everything you need, because you can always ignore or throw out the garbage. (Let's just hope you don't wind up buried under a pile of garbage!) In addition, you can always turn off morpheme processing and/or equiv processing. You can even specify which words in the search get morpheme processing, equiv processing, both, or neither. Perhaps most important, using the Words dialog box, you can customize any of the equiv sets (see Figure 6). You can add words to or subtract them from the set of equivs for any word or acronym (whether it already exists in the equiv file or you're adding it for the first time). You can also select any word on the list of equivs for a given root word and have all of the equiv word's equivs added to the current list.

Finding Quantities

The Numeric Pattern Matcher (NPM) is called by preceding the quantity with the # symbol (the quantity can appear in the same query with nonquantity expressions).

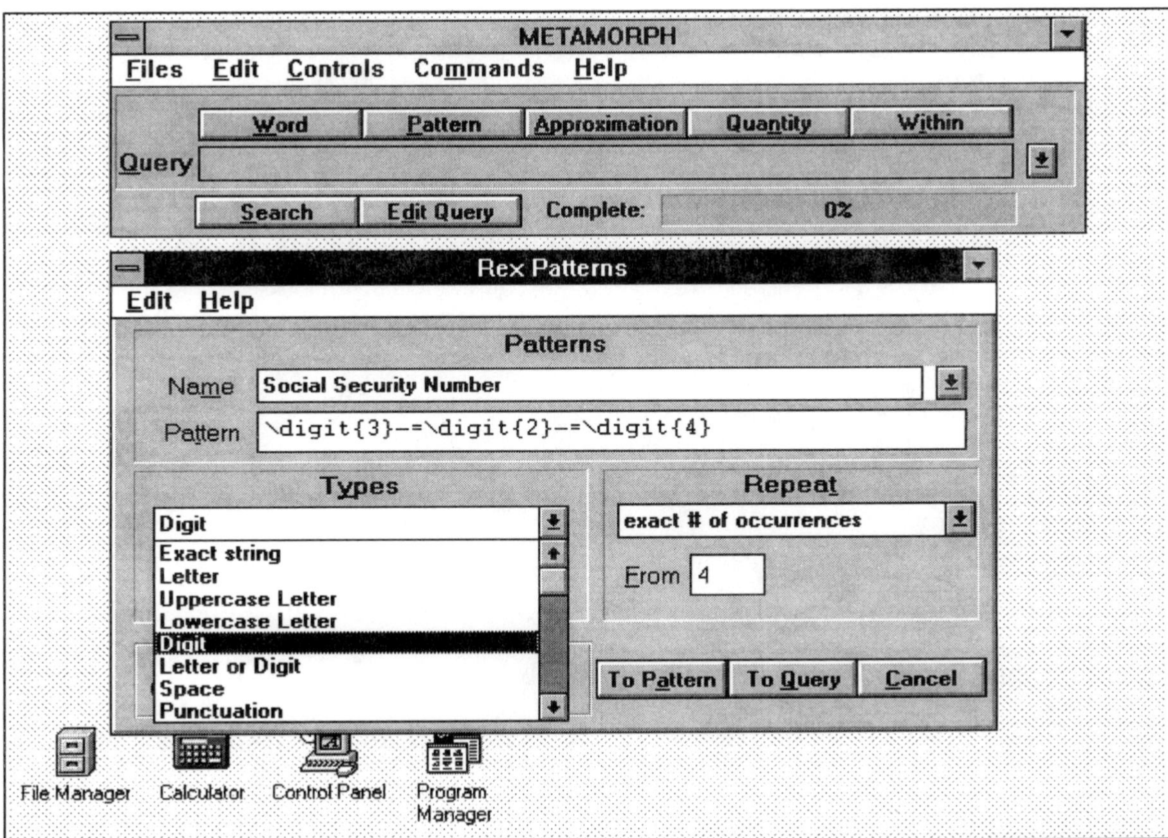

Metamorph Figure 8. The Patterns box does the translation to REX syntax for you. You just select the type of character you want to look for from the list on the left (if you choose Exact string, you get a box to type it into) and specify how many of them in a row you're looking for. Showing here are the options I selected to paste in the last part of a social security number pattern. four digits in a row. Metamorph has automatically made the translation to "\digit{4}" for me. In the Name box, above, I've assigned a name for this pattern, so I can call it up again without having to reconstruct it.

The options you can select from the Repeat box are One occurrence, At least one occurrence, Zero or more occurrences, Zero or 1 occurrence, exact # of occurrences (shown), Range of occurrences, No occurrences, and No operator (meaning you're not making any specification about repetition).

NPM can recognize a quantity expressed in words, numerals, or a combination of the two, though it's best if you type your query in numerals. It also recognizes greater-than, less-than type logic. Having read the quantity you enter on the query line, NPM is then able to find that quantity in the text expressed in any form. Specifying a quantity to be searched for is made very easy in the Windows version through the Quantity dialog box (see Figure 7).

Matching Regular Expressions with REX

Another of Metamorph's powerful search tools is its Regular Expression pattern matcher (REX). REX provides what is essentially a very sophisticated wildcard syntax, allowing you to create patterns of digits, characters, spaces as well as particular characters, and the Patterns dialog box in the Windows version makes it easy to use (see Figure 8). You could easily describe, for example, what a social security number looks like, so that any such pattern of digits would be found. You could also describe what your headers look like, say, an extra blank line, and then some text offset by asterisks, ending with another blank line. REX is very powerful and is used not only for searches but for defining text unit delimiters, NTI header strings, and so on.

As mentioned above, the Patterns dialog box in the Windows version of the program means you don't really have to learn the syntax (when a REX string was needed for use in NTI, it proved easier to first figure it out with the Patterns dialogue and then copy it). This is important because it is a difficult syntax to master, and the documentation is inadequate: While the Windows version manual gives a coherent explanation, it's complicated and has lots of rules and exceptions to those rules; different aspects of it are described in different parts of the DOS and Unix manual, and some not at all, and you probably would not find all the information there without reading through the manual from cover to cover. So if you're using any of the other, non-Windows versions of the program (DOS, Unix, and so on), you may need a Level 3 or 4 friend to help you use REX.

Fuzzy Searches: The Approximate Pattern Matcher

Another brilliant feature of Metamorph is its Approximate Pattern Matcher. As its name suggests, this feature allows you to specify the percentage of approximation of the search string you want allowed for something to qualify as a hit. For example, if you want to find someone's last name, but aren't sure how it's spelled, you might ask for a 75% approximation of their name. Thus, if you think one of our names is spelled "Weissman" and ask for a 75% approximation (by typing "%75Weissman"), you would find the correct spelling, "Weitzman," if it exists in your text. (You would also find anything else that was at least a 75% match to Weissman, like Whiteman or Waltzman.) There's also a dialog box for approximations, but the syntax is so simple it doesn't seem necessary.

Search Logic

In Search mode, you can specify complex search logic. Again, it's a little tricky. Fortunately, the Windows version allows you to pop up an Edit Query box, which maps out just how your query is being treated (see Figure 9). Look at it for a moment, then we'll explain further.

Perhaps because of the fact that, when you ask to find a word, generally you're finding the set of all equivalent words, Metamorph uses "set logic" rather than Boolean logic. If you just type in a few words, they're treated as an AND list; a sentence must have each of the search terms (if you're using equiv processing, then it's actually one word from each set of equivs) to be a hit. You can say you want sentences that do NOT have a word by preceding that word with a hyphen (minus sign).

OR statements happen in one of two ways. First, the set of equivs for a word, say the 59 equivs for "power," are basically treated as a big OR list; any one OR another of the words in the list will suffice. The second way to get OR logic is with the @ sign, followed by a digit, which actually represents the number of intersections of sets required for a hit. What? you ask.

OK, suppose we give the query: "@0 power struggle Near East." 0 intersections are required, so this is a simple OR statement: We want sentences that have power OR struggle OR Near East. But if we ask for "@1 power struggle Near East" then we want sentences that represent at least one intersection among the sets power, struggle, and Near East. Is set logic beginning to swim to the surface from high school memory? The idea is that if there are terms from each of two sets in a sentence, that's one intersection of the two sets. If there are terms from each of three sets, that would be considered to be two intersections, and so on. Zero intersections, again, requires a term from one set with no required intersections with other sets. Note: Sentences with more intersections than specified on the query line will also be retrieved.

You can combine mandatorily *included* words (marked with a +), mandatorily *excluded* words (marked with a –), and words affected by @ logic in one complex logical request (any words not marked with + or – will be affected by the @ specification). You cannot, however, use parentheses to nest parts of the logic as you do in a Boolean search. We're not sure yet, but this may not be too big a problem given the flexibility of the available logic.

Given the complexity of the search logic, the Edit Query box (Figure 9) is an important addition and is available only in the Windows version. It lets you see just what the query you've written will really do and lets you fix it if it's not correct.

The Search Process

Once you have selected the files you want to search, you type in your query or construct it with the various dialog boxes discussed above, all of which are opened with the buttons arrayed around the query line. If you want, you can edit the equiv lists for any of the words as well.

The Windows version of the program offers *only* an interactive search mode. (This is somewhat disappointing because the other versions of the program allow you to have all output sent automatically to a file, which you can then review—a nice option. Still, if you can only work one way or the other, interactive is usually better. We'll discuss output in this version in a moment.) When you click on "Search," Metamorph begins the search, opens up the "browser," and starts showing you hits, in context, as the search continues in the background (see Figure 1). In the browser, you can scroll through the entire source file the hit is located in. There are menu items to jump from hit to hit, forward or backward, or to the first or last hit in the search. NTI headers can be displayed in a window at the top of the browser, and icons appear on the left for notes, OLEs, and vectors. As you review your search results in the browser, you not only can review existing notes and OLE attachments, you can apply new ones as well. You can also launch any vectors you've set up.

Another important option that's unique to the Windows version is that you can modify your query in midsearch!

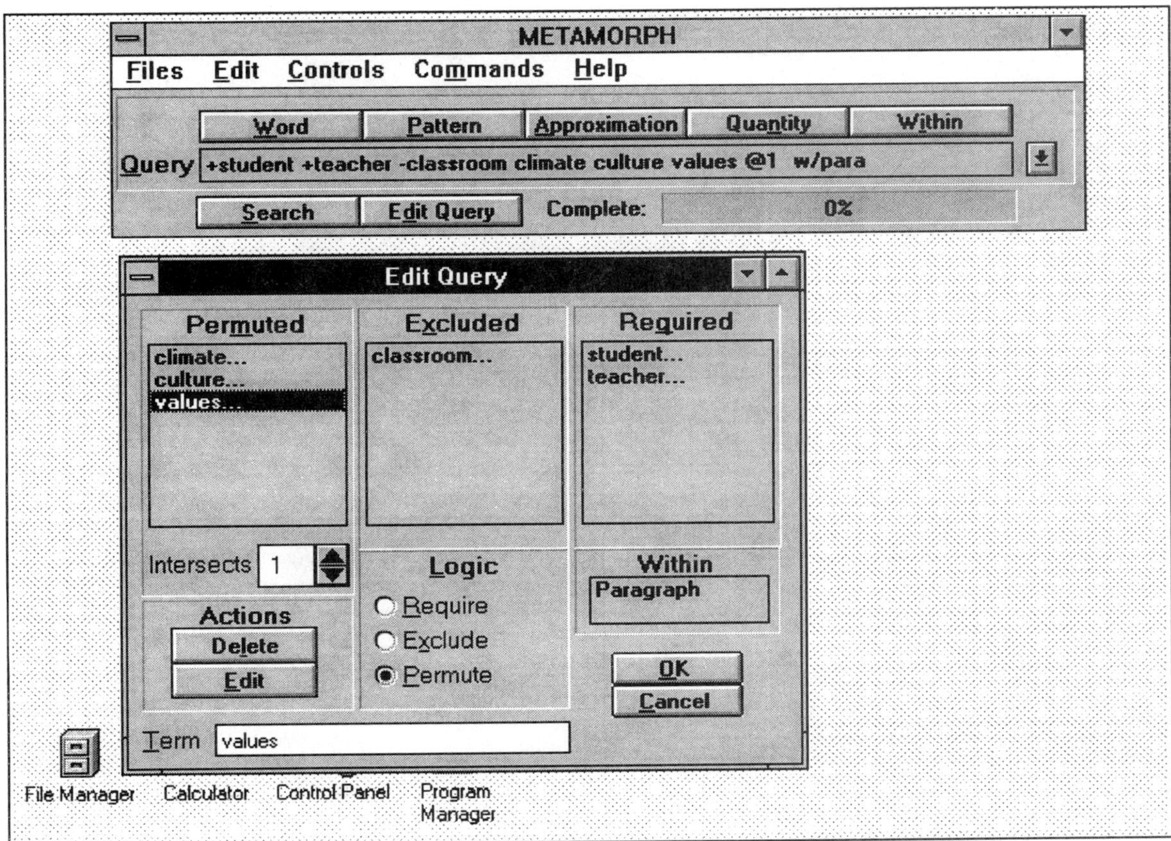

Metamorph Figure 9. The query on the Query line at the top may look like gibberish, but the Edit Query box breaks things down so you can see what it all means: We're looking for paragraphs, specifically those that involve both teachers and students, have some bearing on culture, climate, and/or values, and take place outside the classroom. The Permuted box shows terms that are affected by @ (OR) logic, and the Intersects box below it shows that we are requiring at least one intersection among the terms "culture," "climate," and "values"—at least two of them must be found (if any one would do, we would specify 0 intersects). The Excluded box shows that paragraphs with a mention of classrooms should NOT be retrieved, and the Required box shows that both students and teachers MUST be mentioned.

If any term is in the wrong place, you just drag it to the correct box with the mouse and the syntax in the Query line gets fixed automatically!

While you're in the browser, you just double-click on any word on the screen, and up pops the Words dialog box. You can edit your equiv lists if you're getting garbage or missing important stuff. You can also add/delete words to/from the query and change the permute/exclude/require logic conditions for any of the words, either to get rid of garbage or to make sure you get important information you've been missing.

You can have multiple browsers with the results of different searches in each of them. There's a "Tear-Off" button that creates a freestanding copy of the browser with all the information currently in it and places it as an icon at the bottom of the screen. That way, you can tear off the results of a search, leave that browser at the bottom of the screen, conduct a new search, and go back to the results of the first search whenever you want. Unfortunately, you can't save a torn-off browser; you can only keep it until you quit from Windows.

There is a query log that is retained from session to session. If you want to go back to an old search without having to type the query again, you can click on a button next to the Query line, and a list drops down showing all the queries you've made before (there's a feature that lets you edit this query history, so you can delete queries you don't care about saving). But if you've changed the list of files you want included in the search, you'll have to go back to the File Select dialogue and select them all over again.

Output

Metamorph provides no printer support, and the Windows version doesn't even provide a way to automatically send all the results of a search to an output file. You create all output by copying individual chunks of text to the clipboard. You can either use a utility called the Clipboard Saver that sends everything sent to the clipboard to a text file, or else paste your "clippings" individually to another file. The Saver is probably the way to go. You can easily change the name of the file it's sending text to, so you can alternate among different output files for text from the same search.

If you press <Ctrl-Insert>, the combination for copying to the clipboard in Windows, the current hit gets sent to the clipboard, along with the source file name and any NTI headers (index tags) that apply. (One very annoying glitch: If the cursor isn't in the highlighted hit, even though the correct text will go to the clipboard, the headers that go with it will be those that apply to the cursor position! If you're not careful, you can easily wind up with the wrong headers on your text.) If you want to change the range of text that gets clipped (say your hit is a sentence and you'd actually like the whole paragraph it's in to be output as one chunk), you just select the text you want with the mouse and then press <Ctrl-Insert>. You can then edit and print from your text files with any text editor (like Windows' Notepad) or your word processor.

User Friendliness

The Windows version represents an enormous stride forward for Metamorph in user friendliness, and it really will be fairly easy for almost any user: Remember, you don't have to use things like NTI headers and vectors—they're just available if you want them. Metamorph for Windows is designed for what the programmers at Thunderstone refer to as the "casual user." By this they mean anyone up through a Level 3½ computer user. For example, they provide the various dialog boxes for constructing queries so you won't have to learn a lot of difficult search syntax. They've also eliminated some very useful functions in the name of simplicity, but we'll talk about this more below when we compare versions.

Essentially, the program is easy to learn and easy to use. One drawback is documentation (though this is much less of a problem with the Windows version). The on-line help for the Windows version seems to be a stripped-down version of the manual, running in a special version of Metamorph called MetaBook, which facilitates looking for needed information very nicely. But, quite a few things aren't adequately explained. On-line help in the DOS version is discussed below, in the special section on that version, and is excellent. The manual for the DOS version, which explains all the ins and outs of the program, is really tough. It is written for programmers, by the admission of the company, but it is also, in our opinion, poorly written and organized. For example, parts of REX syntax are explained in two completely different parts of the manual, and the user interface itself isn't described until Chapter 9. On the other hand, the manual for the Windows version, like the program itself, is aimed at the "casual user" and is much more user friendly. The discussion is pitched to introduce a Level 1 or 2 user to the advanced concepts in Metamorph. The discussion of REX (probably the trickiest thing about the whole program to grasp), for example, could probably be followed by most Level 2 or eager and willing Level 1 users.

Tech support on the phone is very good, and they're very patient with dumb questions (believe us, we know). They are committed to staying on the phone with you and holding your hand through any process. If you still can't get it, they'll send you a modem on loan, with some software that lets them take over your machine over the phone line, and set things up for you. Now that's support!

DOS, Unix, MVS, etc. Versus Windows

As mentioned at the outset of this review, the Windows version represents a significant change from the other versions of Metamorph, largely in the direction of becoming more directly accessible to the end user. For example, all the dialog boxes available from the query box that help you build a query without remembering syntax are new additions: If you want a REX pattern in the DOS or Unix and other versions (for simplicity, collectively referred to hereafter as the "DOS version"), you'll have to figure out how to write it from the manual. The DOS version is also easy to use for its basic functions. But it is intended for and sold largely to developers and consultants or large installations with professional systems programmers. These professionals then do a lot of the work of setting up headers and vectors and so forth and provide a custom-tailored, ready-to-go package to the researcher who just wants to ask a question and get an answer. Though it can be extremely powerful, even for a novice user, it is not for anyone who doesn't have the assistance of, or isn't her/himself, a Level 3 or above computer user. To put it another way, the program provides an extremely powerful set of tools to build the applications you want—it does not necessarily provide all those applications right out of the box, although you can begin searching almost immediately.

Unfortunately, the Windows version, in the name of accessibility, gives up some important features that the programmers at Thunderstone believe are nonessential for the "casual user." In this section, we'll mirror the overall struc-

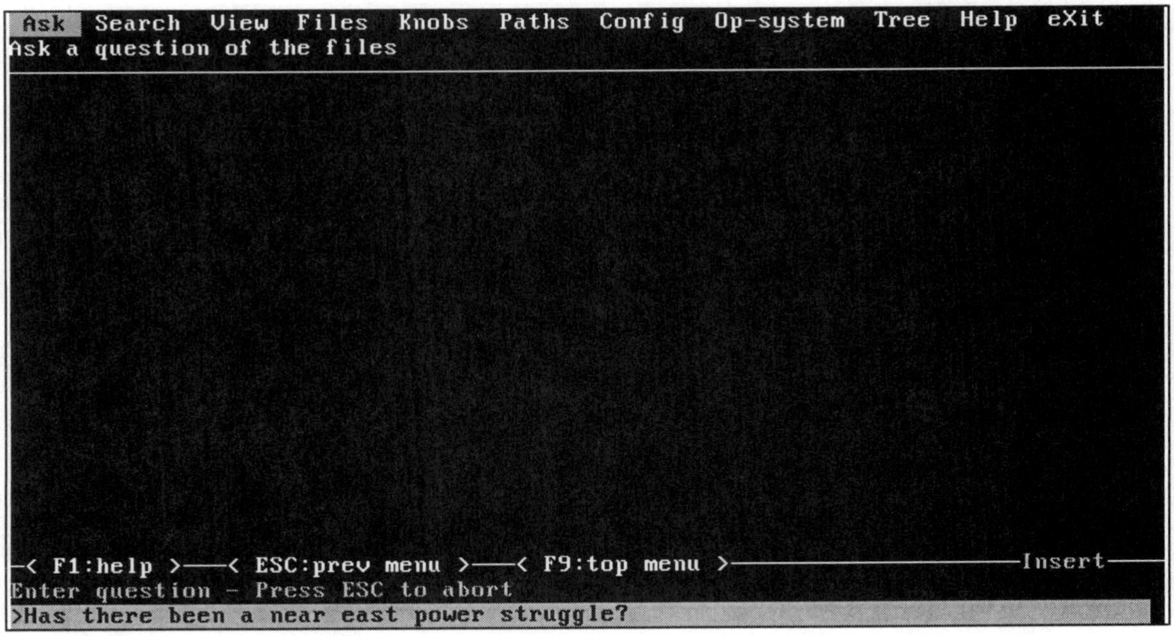

```
Ask  Search  View  Files  Knobs  Paths  Config  Op-system  Tree  Help  eXit
Ask a question of the files

-< F1:help >--< ESC:prev menu >--< F9:top menu >-----------------Insert--
Enter question - Press ESC to abort
>Has there been a near east power struggle?
```

Metamorph Figure 10. DOS version: Asking a question in "Ask" mode by typing it in as a normal English question.

ture of the review, just hitting on the areas where there are clear differences. Remember, though, that the DOS and Windows versions come as a two-for-the-price-of-one package, so you won't be irrevocably committing to one or the other when you buy. (If you buy for Unix, MVS, Macintosh, or other systems, what you get will be like the DOS version only.) Figures 10 and 11 give you a look at the initial search screen and the file browser, so that you can begin to get a sense of the differences in feel.

Data Entry

Again, you generate your data with your word processor or text editor and usually create an ASCII file.

Hierarchical outline/source tags. In the DOS version, you use a function called Mindex, instead of the Windows version's more highly evolved NTI. Mindex tags (headers) apply to all chunks between one header in the text and the next. As with NTI, you can define up to 10 different types of tags for a file (so you could have headers that are flush left and all caps, headers that are surrounded by double asterisks, headers that are surrounded by hyphens, and so on).

One big weakness of Mindex compared with NTI is that it doesn't have the facility for easily recognizing headers that are on lines by themselves and taking the whole line as a header. You'll *have* to deal with REX (this is one big place that your system manager-type person comes in handy).

The other major problem with Mindex occurs if you have more than one level of header in your file and want the levels treated hierarchically: You can't do it. For example, suppose you had these headers as an outline for a file of semistructured interviews:

I. Your role
II. History of the school
III. The new program
    A. Description
    B. How adopted
IV. Implementation problems

You would set up two types of tags, one to find the Roman numeral first-level headings and one to find the capital letter second-level headings. Everything would go along just fine until you hit section IV. At that point, "Implementation problems" would replace the previous first-level header, "The new program," but because there was no new second-level header, "How adopted" would still apply. The approach taken in the Windows version, via NTI, does not suffer from this problem.

Working on the Data

Once again we remind you: You do not have to work on the data at all. You can simply search and make reports. This section will describe the facilities the DOS version of Metamorph offers for editing your text (in midsearch if you

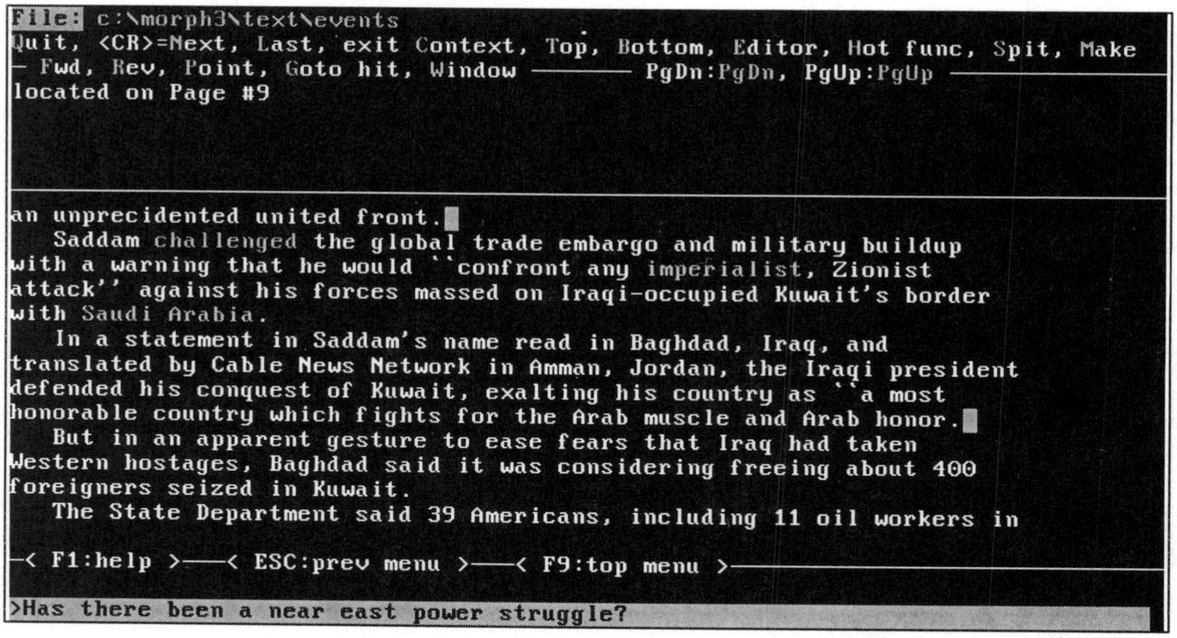

```
File: c:\morph3\text\events
Quit, <CR>=Next, Last, exit Context, Top, Bottom, Editor, Hot func, Spit, Make
- Fwd, Rev, Point, Goto hit, Window ———— PgDn:PgDn, PgUp:PgUp ————
located on Page #9

an unprecidented united front.
   Saddam challenged the global trade embargo and military buildup
with a warning that he would ``confront any imperialist, Zionist
attack'' against his forces massed on Iraqi-occupied Kuwait's border
with Saudi Arabia.
   In a statement in Saddam's name read in Baghdad, Iraq, and
translated by Cable News Network in Amman, Jordan, the Iraqi president
defended his conquest of Kuwait, exalting his country as ``a most
honorable country which fights for the Arab muscle and Arab honor.
   But in an apparent gesture to ease fears that Iraq had taken
Western hostages, Baghdad said it was considering freeing about 400
foreigners seized in Kuwait.
   The State Department said 39 Americans, including 11 oil workers in

-< F1:help >——< ESC:prev menu >——< F9:top menu >————————
>Has there been a near east power struggle?
```

Metamorph Figure 11. DOS version: Viewing a hit in "Browse" mode. The words that matched the query terms "near east" (Saudi Arabia), "power" (imperialist), and "struggle" (challenged) are highlighted (they appear a darker gray in this figure). The gray rectangles mark off the hit (I was searching within sentences). Note that, due to the way Metamorph looks for sentences, you'll sometimes wind up with a two-sentence hit when you want just single sentences.

like) and for hypertexting. Some of this is easy and some of it is quite difficult, so remember: You don't have to get into any of this to use the incredibly powerful search routines.

Editing. Remember that in the Windows version there is no provision for editing your text. When in "browse mode" in the DOS version—that is, you're viewing a file being searched or an output file ("messagefile")—you can hit the "e" key and be popped into a text editor at the point in the file you were viewing, and can make any edits you want. This is very nice for inserting codes or annotations into the text.

The one drawback is that, because the program keeps track of text by "byte offset" (the number of characters from the start of the file), which is recorded in the messagefile, when you pop back to browse mode the markers enclosing your hit chunk will then be out of position. This is fairly easy to overcome by re-executing the same search, but doing it a lot could get tedious.

The editor itself is "not bad," with some nifty features. It will remember up to three blocks of cut, or deleted, text for you to paste, or insert, elsewhere. It also provides a couple of different ways to undo edits, and it supports macros. On the other hand, it's a plain text editor: no formatting, underlining, and so on. It's fairly simple, though the control-key and alt-key combinations are confusing. But with the on-line help screens, you'll be using it fairly comfortably before long.

Linking/hypertexting. The linking functions in the DOS version are less user-friendly than those in Windows (notes, OLE, vectors) but also more powerful. Specifically, the program has a good facility for linking chunks of text to other things, which can then be invoked with a keystroke when browsing such a chunk. These linked things can include other chunks of text, graphics, actions in other software, or additional Metamorph searches. Imagine that you do a search, a chunk of text matching the search pops up on your screen, you hit the hot-key, "h," and something happens: maybe an annotation pops up, maybe you're shown a graphic, or maybe a new search is initiated to pull up other things that you want to see whenever you see the current chunk. (If you want to accomplish the kind of hypertexting where you have fixed links between one point and another, you are going to have to master some mighty fancy footwork, but first let's talk about some simple things you can do.)

How do you link these objects and actions to chunks of your data? When you are browsing a file and hit the hot-key, "h," Metamorph carries out some action based on the hit chunk you were browsing. In the simplest setup, it looks in a hot-list file for instructions you have set up for that chunk. These instructions can be anything from displaying a short message on the screen (a code or footnote) to editing another file (e.g., of memos or annotations) to starting another Metamorph search—say, to find a particular annotation in a large annotation file—after which you would return to browsing/searching the file you were in when you hit the hot-key.

If you want to get fancy about hypertexting (*Level 1 and 2 users may want to skim or skip the following paragraph*), you can use Metamorph's "vector" program, MMVEC, which is significantly more powerful than the vector facility in the Windows version. It is not, however, a simple "point to this and point to that" routine: You're going to have to program it to do what you want.

MMVEC is able to search for strings in the chunk being browsed when you hit the hot-key, and pass substrings of them as arguments to a command. How would that be useful? You might, for example, create an "overview file," listing headings, or maybe abstracts, and embed in the entries file names and byte offsets for the full text (tools are provided for automating such procedures). You could then do searches in the overview file, perhaps looking for certain terms in your abstracts. Then, when a hit occurred, MMVEC could locate the file name and offset information that you had embedded in the hit, and pass that information to another Metamorph search as the text to be searched, or it could pass that information to the Metamorph editor, MMEDIT, so that the editor would go straight to the portion of text in the full text file. Thus you could search (for example) an abstract file (or heading file) and automatically be passed to the full text the abstract is associated with. You can also execute any other command or program and pass it any string of text in the current hit.

Searching

Search modes. In the DOS and other non-Windows versions of Metamorph, you must explicitly choose between the two search modes: Ask and Search. In Ask mode, you type a question (e.g., "Has there been a Near East power struggle?") (Figure 10). Metamorph strips the query down to the important words: "Near East power struggle." If there are quantities expressed, either in words or numerals, it automatically calls its Numeric Pattern Matcher to handle the quantity. Items in queries in this mode are treated as linked by AND logic; all must be present for a hit to be found.

If you choose Search mode, you type in just the search words; no noise or question words will be filtered. You have access to OR (actually, set logic) and NOT logic as well as the default AND and must call the Numeric Pattern Matcher, the Approximate Pattern Matcher, and others explicitly. For example, in Search mode, you call the Numeric Pattern Matcher by preceding the quantity with the # symbol (the quantity can appear in the same query with non-quantity expressions).

Equiv editing. In the DOS version, you can edit equivs either on-the-fly, or ahead of time by editing a list of user modifications with a text editor. As compared with the Word dialog box in the Windows version (see Figure 6), working on the equivs ahead of time with a text editor is very clunky.

On the other hand, the on-the-fly option is very nice. Turning on the "edit" feature will cause the program to show you lists of equivs for all your search terms, one at a time, before executing a search (see Figure 12). You can review each list and edit it if you want, either permanently or just for this search, using options to add or delete words. In addition, each equivalent word is marked by its "class," or part of speech (noun, verb, pronoun, preposition, conjunction, interjection, modifier, and unknown), and you see each list sorted by class. You can change the class of a particular word or delete an entire class. This might be useful, for example, to get rid of all the verb equivalents to your search term when you're looking for "things" and just want nouns.

Various pattern matchers. Calling the various pattern matchers in the DOS version must be done explicitly,[3] and there are no dialog boxes to help you. So, in Search mode, you precede a quantity you want matched by NPM with a "#," a term you want matched with, say, 75% accuracy by the Approximate Pattern Matcher with "%75," and a REX pattern with a "/." Furthermore, in the last case, you'll have to remember or figure out REX syntax yourself (with the help of the manual); there's no handy dialog box to translate for you.

The search process. The DOS version offers you two ways to have your results handled: You can see them in a browse mode, which is somewhat similar to that in Windows, or have them all sent to an output file (see "Output," below). First we'll discuss the browse mode.

Once you have typed in your query, Metamorph begins the search and starts showing you hits, in context, as the search continues in the background. In this "browse mode" (Figure 11), you can scroll through the entire source file the hit is located in. As mentioned above, you can hit "e" to edit the file or "h" to invoke a hot-function (described under "Linking/Hypertexting," above). There are menu items to jump to the top or bottom of the file or back to the current hit. You can perform REX (Regular Expression) searches within the source file (remember that a REX "pattern" can

3. The exception to this is that, in Ask mode, NPM will automatically be called to match quantities.

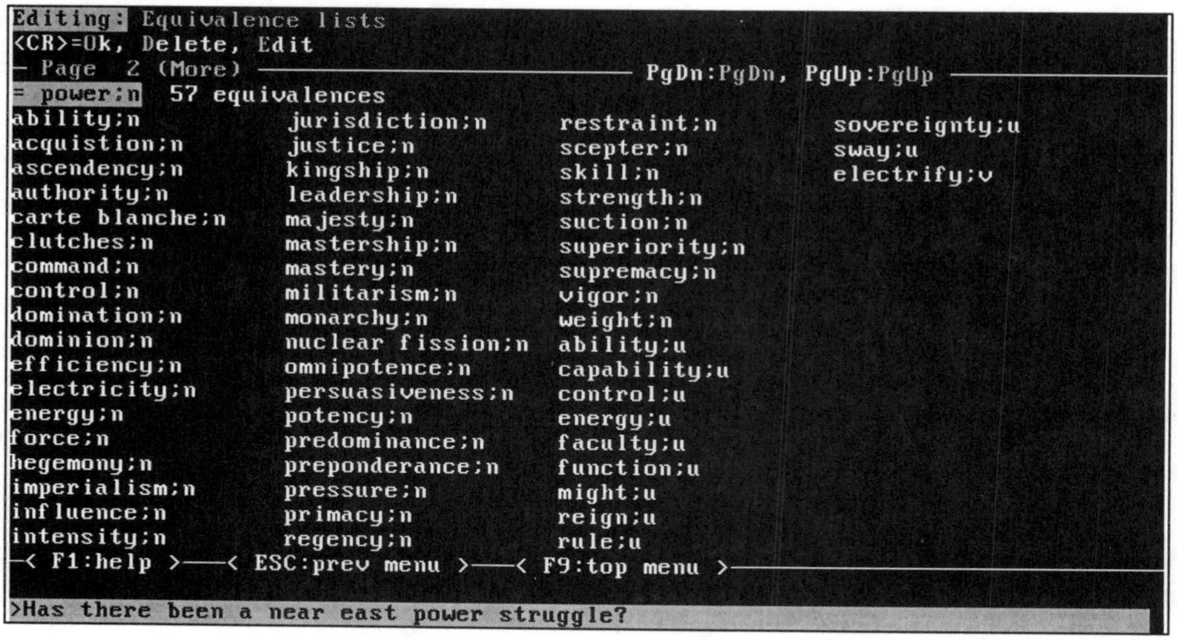

```
Editing: Equivalence lists
<CR>=Ok, Delete, Edit
- Page  2 (More) ─────────────────────── PgDn:PgDn, PgUp:PgUp ──────
= power;n  57 equivalences
ability;n              jurisdiction;n       restraint;n         sovereignty;u
acquistion;n           justice;n            scepter;n           sway;u
ascendency;n           kingship;n           skill;n             electrify;v
authority;n            leadership;n         strength;n
carte blanche;n        majesty;n            suction;n
clutches;n             mastership;n         superiority;n
command;n              mastery;n            supremacy;n
control;n              militarism;n         vigor;n
domination;n           monarchy;n           weight;n
dominion;n             nuclear fission;n    ability;u
efficiency;n           omnipotence;n        capability;u
electricity;n          persuasiveness;n     control;u
energy;n               potency;n            energy;u
force;n                predominance;n       faculty;u
hegemony;n             preponderance;n      function;u
imperialism;n          pressure;n           might;u
influence;n            primacy;n            reign;u
intensity;n            regency;n            rule;u
─< F1:help >──< ESC:prev menu >──< F9:top menu >──────────────────
>Has there been a near east power struggle?
```

Metamorph Figure 12. DOS version: Editing the equiv list for the word "power." At the end of each word is a semicolon and a letter indicating the part of speech the word belongs to. n = noun, u = unknown, v = verb. Others available are P = Pronoun, p = preposition, c = conjunction, i = interjection, and m = modifier.

just be a word or phrase that you want matched exactly, it doesn't have to be a complex pattern). There are also options to Point to a block of text (by default, the hit) and Spit it, along with source file name and Mindex headers (source tags), to any output file. Hit the Enter key, and you pop to the next hit. Hit L (for Last), and you pop back to the last hit.

Output. The basic output of the search is the messagefile (see Figure 13), a feature completely removed from, and sorely missed by us in, the Windows version. You can see this before, during, or after the full hit context browse if you wish. (In browse mode, the messagefile is created in the background, and you can get to it with a keystroke at any time.) The messagefile consists of messages like "search engine started," "opening file News.txt," and so on: basic process information. It also includes the query, and for each hit the words that actually satisfied the query, which is nice because you can often tell at a glance whether or not the hit was appropriate. The messagefile shows Mindex headers associated with each hit as well as the text of the hit itself. If you cursor over to the hit, and hit "c" for Context, you will immediately be back in the full text browse mode. This happens *even if you have called up an old messagefile*. In other words, you can review the results of a search either as it happens or at *any time in the future,* with full access to context (assuming the source file is still on your disk). Finally, the messagefile gives you the number of hits found in the search.

The messagefile represents a significantly better log of your work than the simple query log in the Windows version. In fact, because the messagefile is itself a searchable text file, you can submit the results of earlier searches as data for new searches, a capability that makes system closure possible.

Another nice feature is that each of the types of messages described above, including the hits themselves, can be included in or excluded from the display of the messagefile. So you could review, say, just the Mindex headers and the words that satisfied the search term as a quick way to scan through and see which hits are actually worth reading. Or you might just want to see the actual text of the hits, maybe with Mindex headers or the query that produced them. In addition, there is a fairly easy-to-use utility program that lets you strip out the types of messages you are interested in and send them to a report file, with some limited formatting control. You could, for example, pull out Mindex headers, the messages identifying the words that matched the query, and the hit text.

User Friendliness

User friendliness is *not* what this program is about. If you want to be able to do incredibly rich searches, and

```
File: c:\tmp\mmmsg.003
Quit, <CR>=Next, Last, Context, Top, Bottom, Editor, Hot func, Spit, Make
                                        PgDn:PgDn, PgUp:PgUp
502 power struggle
201 search engine started
203 opening the file "c:\morph3\text\alien"
203 closing "c:\morph3\text\alien", hits: 0, bytes: 10826
203 opening the file "c:\morph3\text\constn"
203 closing "c:\morph3\text\constn", hits: 0, bytes: 45312
203 opening the file "c:\morph3\text\declare"
501 attempts jurisdiction
403 018 located on Page #3
300 c:\morph3\text\declare 6754 122 42 8 100 12
We have warned
them from time to time of attempts by their legislature to extend an
unwarrantable jurisdiction over us.
301 End of Metamorph hit
203 closing "c:\morph3\text\declare", hits: 1, bytes: 8539
203 opening the file "c:\morph3\text\events"
501 opposition leaders
403 018 located on Page #1

-< F1:help >--< ESC:prev menu >--< F9:top menu >-

>power struggle
```

Metamorph Figure 13. DOS version: Viewing a messagefile. Each type of message has a unique number identifying it. The first line, "502 power struggle," gives the query that started the search (502 messages always do). "501 attempts jurisdiction" gives the words that satisfied the query to produce the following hit (501 messages always do). The highlighted (in this figure, darker) 300 message gives the hit location followed by the text of the hit. The 403 message immediately above the 300 message contains Mindex header information for the hit. This messagefile can be called up *at any time in the future*, and by selecting the 300 message and choosing "Context," you can see the hit in its source file in the browse mode.

don't mind a manual that's written for heavy-duty systems-type people, you can get going fairly easily and do some great work. Furthermore, if you use EZMM (described under "Miscellaneous," below), you can do powerful searches with almost no learning at all.

Remember, though, that the manual really is tough (see the main "User Friendliness" section). *On the other hand,* there is an on-line version of the full manual (not a stripped down one as in the Windows version) that you can search with Metamorph. Given the power of the Metamorph search engine, this is great to use: You don't even have to worry about coming up with the right word as you do when you're looking through an index—Metamorph's equiv processing will find what you're looking for. This overcomes some of the difficulties with the organization of the manual; in fact, in evaluating the Windows version, we found ourselves resorting to the on-line DOS manual to find information, and then trying to extrapolate to the Windows version. However, these search capabilities do *not* help with the way it's written.

If you want to get into Mindexing, or defining custom delimiters, you're going to have to stretch more than a bit if you're a Level 2-type person. If you want to get into hot functions of any complexity, it's serious roll-up-your-sleeves time.

But, no matter what version you're using, you still get the same good tech support.

Miscellaneous

Both DOS and Windows versions of Metamorph will run on a network. Multiple users can maintain their own configurations of options, and search the same files concurrently, as long as the network has been set up to allow such file sharing.

In addition, there are some significant features of both versions we haven't discussed. The DOS versions (remember, these include all versions *except* Windows) of these features get really technical, while the Windows versions are pretty easy but may be more limited. For those so inclined, here's an overview. We'll specify whether these are DOS or Windows version features as we go.

EZMM (DOS Version)

There is a special, simplified version of the DOS version called EZMM, for "Easy Metamorph," that is just that; it's a simple query line version without all the options (see

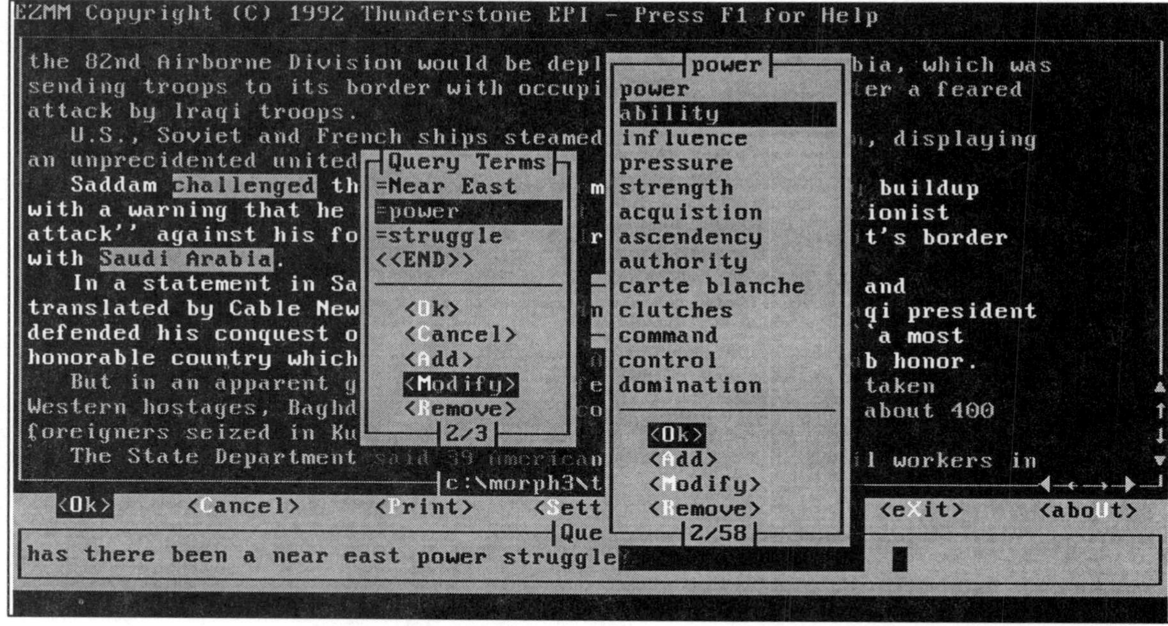

Metamorph Figure 14. The simplified DOS version, EZMM. In the background, a hit is displayed in bright white, and the words that matched the search term are shown in reverse video. Although this is a much simplified version of the program, it retains all of the full version's search power, including the ability to edit equiv lists using the pop-up lists in the foreground.

Figure 14). By default, it takes the default "profile" for the DOS version, including all options settings and the list of files to be searched. If you want to search a different set of files, you can just include them as part of the command (as a command line parameter) when you start up the program. So, if you want to search your interview files, which are named "inter01.txt," "inter02.txt," and so on, you'd type, at the DOS prompt:

ezmm inter*.txt <Enter>[4]

You'd then get a simple query line, without all the options and other headaches to worry about, all set up to search your interview files. All you do is enter your queries, look at your results, and send them to an output file. *If and only if* your profile is set up for on-the-fly equiv editing, you get a supersimplified equiv editing screen so you can review and make changes before the search goes on.

4. Remember that * is a wildcard, meaning it stands for any other characters that might be there. So "inter*.txt" means any filename that starts with "inter" then has anything else and ends in ".txt"—in other words, "inter01.txt," "inter02.txt," and so on.

Macros (All Versions)

You can give search requests short names and then execute the search by simply entering the macro name on the query line. An example in the manual suggests replacing the REX expression /19\digit\digit, which will match any year in the twentieth century (actually the digits 1 and 9 followed by any other two digits) with the macro name "Year." If you then enter $Year on the query line, it will automatically be expanded to the full REX expression. The Windows version comes with a number of such patterns predefined, so macros are easy to use without actually learning REX.

Profiles (DOS Only)

You can save the full set of options you like to use with Metamorph in a "user profile," and you can save as many profiles as you want. Then, instead of resetting all the options, you can just call up a profile. Profiles can even include the list of files to be searched and the search terms.

Batch Mode (All Versions)

You can string together multiple searches in one batch file. In the DOS version, there are extensive options for starting searches from the command line. You can set up an entire profile file with all options, files, and search terms in it and have it executed in the batch search. If you are working in a multitasking environment, you can run concurrent searches. You can review results as they happen in browse mode or just review the messagefiles later.

In the Windows version, all the batch mode does is start up a search or list of searches. You cannot choose a particular profile (there are none); you just get the most recently used set of options. There are no special start-up options, and you have to review results as they happen in the browser.

Other Features

Pipe mode: Live TTY data (DOS and Unix only). If you subscribe to live data services, such as a news wire, you can set up Metamorph to profile the data *as it comes in* and send the results of different searches to different places or people. You can even send the results of one search to a finer search. This apparently works much better in Unix.

Application program interface and ITS Writer (DOS only). These options, available at additional cost, allow you to build Metamorph into other applications. The ITS Writer (Interactive Text Systems Writer) allows you, with fairly simple commands, to build a menuing front end for the program, allowing you to develop search systems for a particular textbase for yourself or other users. The API provides you with the machine instructions you would need if you were writing your own software and wanted it to be able to call up Metamorph.

Comparative Remarks

The program Metamorph most closely resembles, at first glance, is The Text Collector. Metamorph is much harder to use and it costs a *lot* more. But it does a tremendous amount that The Text Collector never dreamed of. Compare the two carefully before making a decision.

Other programs to compare are Folio VIEWS, ZyINDEX, and Sonar Professional, all of which require you either to import and/or to index your data before you can search it. *This is a major difference:* Do you need to be able to really work with and manipulate your data with a textbase manager like Folio VIEWS? Do you need to have your text files free on your hard disk and search them whenever you want with Metamorph? Or can they be kept on your hard disk but left untouched for use with an indexing program like ZyINDEX or Sonar?

Folio VIEWS, in particular, and ZyINDEX, to a lesser extent, incorporate some synonym expansion and word-root stripping features, but they aren't nearly as powerful as Metamorph's morpheme and equiv processing. On the other hand, VIEWS is *very* easy and intuitive to use and has lots of powerful features of its own.

Summary

Metamorph is a super-high-powered text searching program, and then some. While it has some drawbacks, mainly a trade-off between ease of use in the Windows version and power in the DOS and other versions, it can do things no other program can. If you can afford it, and either you or someone in your organization has the skills and wherewithal to make the thing work right (less of a problem with the Windows version, or EZMM), you will get a tremendous amount out of this program, especially if you have a large, rich database you want to do quick, sophisticated searches in, and are not expecting to do any coding.

Reference

Thunderstone Software. (1991). *Metamorph Version 3.4 for DOS & Unix: Operations manual.* Cleveland, OH: Author.

Orbis 1.0 for XyWrite 4.0

Available for DOS

The Technology Group
36 South Charles Street, Suite 2200
Baltimore, MD 21201

Phone: (410) 576-2040
Fax: (410) 576-1968

Price: $149
(Plus price for XyWrite 4.0, $495,
or educational price, $125)

Hardware Requirements
- IBM PC, PS/2, or 100% compatible
- 286 or higher processor recommended
- 384K free RAM
- Hard disk with minimum of 2MB free (up to 7 MB for all options)
- DOS 3.3 or higher
- For WYSIWYG display, EGA, VGA, CGA, or Hercules monitor

Overview

Orbis is a sturdy, fast, text-retrieval program designed to be used with two different word-processing packages, XyWrite 4.0 and Nota Bene 4.0, both of which are powerful and sophisticated. It cannot be used as a stand-alone program. But it's a very practical choice if you already use one of these programs, or want to, and would like a fast, straightforward text search-and-retrieval facility to accompany it. Its great advantage is its integrated character: You can move back and forth easily between the word processor and your database, doing searches as needed and incorporating the results in what you are writing—whether that is preliminary analysis, later analysis, or final report writing.

Essentially, Orbis "indexes" your data files, creating a separate set of "management" (indexing) files, then searches *those* files. Your basic data files remain unchanged. It's thus best for data sets that you don't expect to change or revise very much (although reindexing is quick). It doesn't let you do coding (although you can insert codes in your text and retrieve them like any other words). This review is based on the XyWrite 4.0 version of Orbis, but the features are largely the same for Nota Bene 4.0. However, Orbis for XyWrite will only run with XyWrite; you need the Nota Bene version to run with Nota Bene.[1]

Database Structure

Orbis works with free-form text files that are not organized by records and fields, and creates, as just noted, separate indexing files. The indexing files must be on your hard disk. Orbis can handle up to a million files, with 2 million "entries" each (which you can define as paragraphs, pages, and so on), and there can be up to 8 million characters per *entry*, so you need not worry about capacity.

To make your chunks, you define a standard entry size by a hard carriage return (i.e., paragraph), a blank line (which could define one or several paragraphs, thus providing some flexibility), a page-end marker, or a file as a whole.

1. Nota Bene is distributed by Nota Bene, 285 West Broadway, Suite 460, New York, NY 10013. Phone: (212) 334-0445. Fax: (212) 334-0845. Prices: Orbis, $129; Nota Bene, $459 (academic, $179). Orbis, Nota Bene, and Ibid (a bibliographic program) are sold as a package for $339; other combination discounts are available.

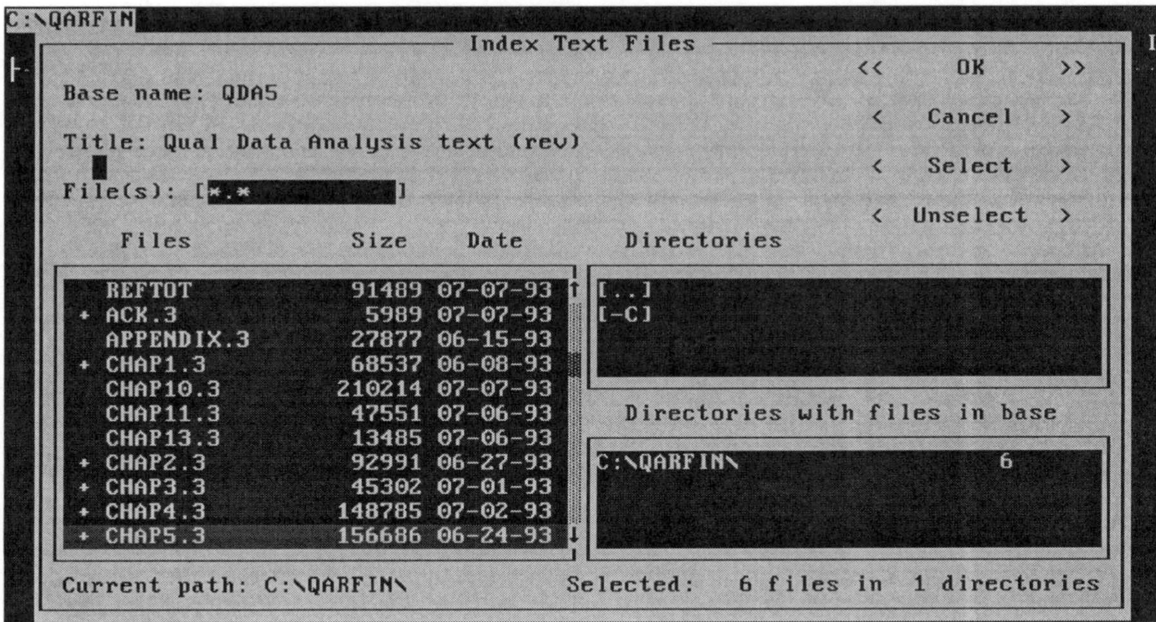

Orbis Figure 1. Setting up a textbase. A name (QDA5) and longer title have been assigned. The box at left shows that six files have been selected from the subdirectory C:\QARFIN by clicking on them twice, for inclusion in the textbase. The box at the lower right shows that only QARFIN is involved; other subdirectories could be drawn on if wished. Following this selection, Orbis will index the files in the textbase.

Data Entry

Your text is created in XyWrite or in ASCII text.[2] You may also convert text to XyWrite from a wide range of other word processors, including WordPerfect, Word, Ami Professional, Framework, Multimate Advantage, WordStar, and others. It's easiest to have all the text files in one subdirectory on your hard disk, though you can draw from different subdirectories (or even a diskette) if your data are organized that way. However, your Orbis management files, where the data are indexed, *must* be on your hard disk. As the manual says, for practical purposes, they are your textbase.

You enter Orbis from XyWrite and choose "Text-base" from a XyWrite menu. After you specify the name and title of your textbase, the screen may look like Figure 1.

A mouse is optional, but convenient. To include files in the database, you look at the subdirectory where your files are (lower left box), and click on a filename twice if you want to select it for the database. Figure 1 shows that six files have been selected; each has a plus sign beside it. When all the files you want are included, you're asked to set "parameters": whether to include an "omit list" of words such as "a," "and," or "the," which will not be included in searches (it's actually quite a big list, and you might want to review and edit it), whether you want case (uppercase, lowercase) to be respected during searches or not, and what the "end marker" of a chunk is: carriage return, blank space, page end, or file. Note: These parameters cannot be changed and they apply to the entire textbase you're setting up. However, if it turns out you don't like them, it's easy to set up another textbase with different parameters.

2. XyWrite documents are actually in ASCII but have extra ASCII command characters inserted. Orbis will accept "pure" ASCII as well.

Working on the Data

Orbis is not a coding program but just retrieves words in their context. The simplest way to work around this is to open the file in XyWrite and assign codes in capital letters (CAPS) to your text files, either embedded in the text or at the beginning or end of chunks. Then create the textbase and set the parameters to be case sensitive. (Alternatively, Orbis also lets you mark words during file preparation by attaching an @ or # to them; it will find "@code" or "#code" as well as "code" without any marker. For multiple-level coding, you could thus use @ or # for first and second levels and CAPS for the third level. As we'll see later, Orbis will search for a block of text as well as for individual words, so you could ask for "@code1 #code2 CODE" if you had coded a chunk that way). Multiple

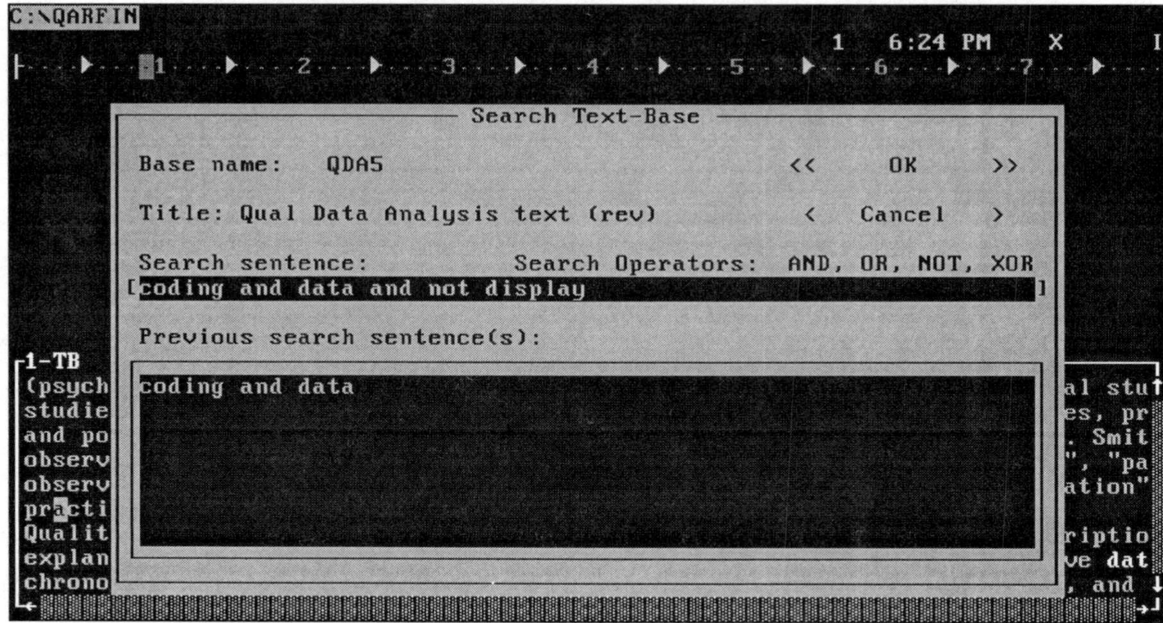

Orbis Figure 2. Specifying search sentences. In the search sentence area above are entered the words being looked for, linked by Boolean operators. In the lower box is a previous search sentence ("coding and data"); these cumulate as you proceed. In the background is the "text retrieval window" from the preceding search request (see also Figure 3); the "search textbase" window has popped up to permit entering a new search sentence ("coding and data and not display").

codes per chunk are no problem. But while all this is easily done on screen, it still is a workaround and has nothing like the ease of programs that are specifically designed for coding. Choosing Orbis only makes sense if (a) you want the integrated text retrieval and word processing capabilities and (b) the coding workaround doesn't bother you.

There is no line numbering facility, and line-by-line coding would have to leave enough space on the line for codes; so Orbis is awkward at that level. Nesting and overlapping codes are thus difficult to apply.

XyWrite's normal search-and-replace function can be used to rename or combine codes. A code list is not automatically generated, but you can use the XyWrite facility for creating indexes (mark each code and ask for an index—this has the extra value of showing you pages that codes appear on). However, neither XyWrite nor Orbis will make a list of all the words in your text, as some other programs will.

Your text can be marked up or annotated with XyWrite's "redlining" facility; additions will be shown on screen in green, deletions in red. (When printed, additions appear within brackets, [like this], and deletions are crossed out.) The program will also insert tags showing who wrote the annotation and when, a useful feature when multiple researchers are using the same database.

There is no real memoing facility as such, in the sense of memos' being attached to specific codes or files. The workaround here is simply to open another file in an alternate window (XyWrite lets you run nine at a time), give it a name that will help you remember that it applies to a certain text file, and write the memo—perhaps inserting a reminder in the text file (such as MEMO4 or MEMO16).

Remember, again, that Orbis must index your text files (and reindex them after any change whatsoever). The program lets you know if this "refreshing" is required. Indexing and reindexing are fairly quick, however. For example, a database of 16 files, about 620 double-spaced pages (1.2 megabytes), took about 2 minutes to index when created on a 386 33MHz machine. After a one-word change in one file, the reindexing took only a couple of seconds. Adding a complete new file was almost as quick.

Searching

When you choose Search from the Orbis menu, you get a screen like Figure 2. In the "search sentence" area, you enter search requests, using Boolean operators AND, OR, XOR, NOT. In this case, the search will be for instances of "coding" and "data," excluding chunks that include the word "display." These operators apply within the chunk size you have chosen (line, paragraph, several paragraphs, file).

```
C:\QARFIN
Item 4 of 26                         1 TB  C:\QARFIN\CHAP3.3  6:30 PM    X     I

 ORBIS  Match: <   -   ><   +   >  Entry: < ^PgUp >< ^PgDn >  Info: < ^F10  >
Computer Use
     The First Edition of this book had less than half a page on computers as
data storage and retrieval. In under ten years, there has been a phenomenal de
new software; there are now on the order of two dozen programs well suited to
qualitative researchers. In our survey, three quarters of our respondents repo
computer software for purposes of entering data, coding, search and retrieval,
displays or building concepts.    [9]
     By now it's largely taken for granted that you need a good word processor
qualitative research. Handwritten or dictated field notes, along with tape rec
```

Orbis Figure 3. Search hits displayed. At the upper left, we see that this is the fourth of 26 hits. Below, in the text retrieval window, is the chunk, with the hits highlighted. It extends beyond the screen, but you can scroll left or right. The file from which the chunk came (CHAP3.3) is shown at the upper right, with the name of the source directory (C:\QARFIN) given as well. You go to the next hit with <+>, or the previous one with <->. <Control-PgUp> and <Control-PgDn> take you to previous or following "entries" (in this case, paragraphs). The top half of the screen is open, and XyWrite can open a window there in which you can paste, edit, or summarize text from the text retrieval window. There can be up to eight such working windows in addition to the text retrieval window.

You can also define categories or synonyms for a "NEXIS" search (an approach drawn from the commercial database of that name). To do this, you first make a special file. For example, a NEXIS file might read:

weather rain hail sleet snow

Entering "+weather" as a search sentence will get you hits not only for "weather" but for all the other terms as well, which in this case you consider as subcategories of weather. NEXIS searches can also be used to set up synonym searches; adding to the NEXIS file, we might have

weather rain hail sleet snow
argument dispute conflict disagreement

Asking for "+argument" will get you all the chunks that contain the synonyms you've defined. You can still use "+weather" too.

In Figure 2, a previous search sentence for this session with the textbase is shown below. These can be reactivated or revised to a new search sentence if you wish. Wildcard searching is possible. You can mix Boolean, wildcard, and NEXIS search requests in one search sentence. You can also define a block of text—either in the document you're working with in XyWrite (see below) or in the text retrieval window itself, which appears once you start the search (Figure 3). Orbis will then find all instances of the text block in the textbase.

Searching is fast. You see hits almost instantaneously, even when there are a large number of hits. (Orbis starts showing you hits with the message "1 of ???" even if it isn't all the way through the textbase, and keeps searching in the background while you view hits. But it all happens quickly (in a 600-page database, the "1 of ???" message lasted only a second or two).

At the upper left (Figure 3), you see the hit number (4 of 26); at the upper right, the file from which the hit comes (CHAP3.3). (There are no more precise source tags than this: You can't know what page of the file the hit came from. If the filename identifies the source—person, date, and so on—then you'll know where the hit came from, otherwise not.)

Below you see the chunk, with the hit(s) highlighted. It's possible to page up to preceding chunks or down to following chunks, whether or not they have hits in them, and to jump immediately to the next hit. At any point, you can move to an "information" screen, which summarizes the number of hits in each file (thus if you were searching for something you'd defined as a code, you'd have code frequencies, which you could print with PrintScreen). You can also go straight to a specific *file* for hits if you wish. The information screen also shows you words in the search sentence that were not found.

Note in Figure 3 that the text retrieval window appears in the bottom half of a split screen. XyWrite is still functioning as you search. You can open a new working file in the top half of the screen (or in any of the seven other remaining windows) and copy hits into it, editing/summarizing them as you wish.

You can also use XyWrite's tabling facility to enter hits, edited/summarized or not, into a matrix display to aid your analysis. You can create matrices with up to 12 columns and an indefinite number of rows. To find the raw text for a particular matrix cell, you'd do an AND search using the two relevant terms or codes that stood for that particular row-column intersection. Usually you will need to reduce or edit the raw text, which you can do in the alternate window, then import that into the appropriate matrix cell. (These features illustrate the strong value of the word processor-text retriever linkage.)

There is no automatic facility for assembling all hits and moving them to a file, which is an important limitation. However, with XyWrite (or with Nota Bene), you could write a macro to do that.

When you finish a search, you can jump back and start a new one; all your search sentences are retained and are visible, as we saw in Figure 2. As noted, you can also highlight a word in a chunk shown in the text retrieval window—or in your alternate window—and do a search for it in the textbase.

Remember that Orbis only finds text strings in the form of words or blocks of words. If you've defined codes as above, it will find those as well. There are no real limits on how many strings/codes you can define.

Though Orbis records your search sentences used with your textbase, keeping up to 10 of them, and thus gives you a short-term running log, it does not keep a record of hits or provide a full audit trail. And if you revise or update the textbase, the old search sentences disappear, so you have no log at all!

Output

Search results can, as we've noted, be seen on screen, or pasted into another file chunk by chunk, or pasted into the cells of a matrix (chunk by chunk). Any of these products can be printed using XyWrite. Not having the automatic possibility to export all your hits at once to a disk is a weakness.

Any annotations you've done via XyWrite's redlining facility are back in the original text files; their text, and/or the associated tags showing author and date, can be searched for using XyWrite's regular search facility in "expanded view." Orbis itself can only search for the text of annotations, because it does not function in "expanded view." Memos, as noted above, reside in other files and can be retrieved and printed if you've named them to make that easy. There's no graphics output (but graphics can be pasted into your analytical text if you've drawn them and stored them somewhere). There's no numerical output other than word frequency counts.

Theory Building

As a text retriever attached to a word processor, Orbis/XyWrite is not especially strong in the theory-building domain; its only theory-relevant features are XyWrite's outlining facility and the NEXIS search option. It's a straightforward tool for finding things quickly and managing text. You're on your own for making theoretical sense of what you find.

User Friendliness

Orbis is easy to learn and use. For a Level 2 person who already knew XyWrite, the tutorial took under 3 hours. It took another couple of hours to create a new textbase and search it easily. Both the tutorial and the manual have symbols in the right and left margins showing the precise keystrokes or mouse moves you use to get what you want. The manual (The Technology Group, 1993a) is clear and well written. The help screens are also clear.

Both Orbis and XyWrite are forgiving, give you clear messages when you've done something wrong, and have good help screens.

XyWrite 4.0 is a full-featured, sophisticated word processor. If you have not been using it (in earlier or present versions) already, the learning time may be a good-sized investment—a few days to feel modestly fluent. But it's basically straightforward, with easy-to-remember mnemonic commands, plenty of pull-down menus, mouse capability, and a very thorough, carefully written manual (The Technology Group, 1993b). And it's *very* fast.

The same general comments apply to the other word processing program with which Orbis can be used: Nota Bene, which is also distributed by The Technology Group. Nota Bene's strength lies in its features designed for the scholarly community: a strong bibliographic database facility; different academic style manuals; usability in a wide range of foreign languages and printer alphabets including Greek, Hebrew, and Cyrillic characters; table of contents and index production; and so on. Like XyWrite, Nota Bene manages footnotes well and produces indexes and tables of contents. Both programs are easy to use once learned.

We might remark that we don't review other word processors in this book (many of them have features that are equal to or better than XyWrite's). But we haven't seen others that have a text retriever attached.[3]

The technical support line is not toll free, and you encounter a voice-mail set of instructions. If tech support personnel are occupied, you are asked to leave a message with details. A call back within an hour or so, with a clear answer, seems typical.

Miscellaneous

Orbis is modestly customizable: You can create a "hot-key" to start it up quickly, move its position in XyWrite's menus, and edit the omit list. The latter is important; the list contains not only words like "the," "to," and "is" but words like "above," "among," "forgot," "himself," "neatness," "ongoing," "soon," "take," "vary," and "when." You might well want to look for such words, depending on your project. If so, you must delete them from the omit list. The alternative of bypassing the omit list completely is another way, but that uses a lot more memory and slows down searches. Note: You can add words to the omit list if you want to.

XyWrite itself is very customizable: It's easy to change defaults, keyboard files, menu and help files, and printer files; there is a customization manual (The Technology Group, 1993c). You can do the usual keystroke macros as well as use XPL, the XyWrite programming language, to produce more complex macros.

XyWrite (and thus Orbis) can be installed on a network. As noted earlier, XyWrite's redlining facility permits logging the date, time, and individual ID when annotations or revisions are made, a useful feature for research teams.

3. We have heard mention of WPIndex, an add-on for WordPerfect; another add-on program is being developed for DataPerfect.

Update

XyWrite now has a Windows version. A new version of Orbis compatible with it was expected in 1995.

Comparative Remarks

Orbis with XyWrite is a less sophisticated searcher than, say, Folio Views, askSam, Metamorph, Sonar Professional, The Text Collector, or ZyINDEX and has very modest database management capability. But the linked programs are very effective in doing what they promise: finding text strings in a large textbase that you're interested in, and editing and managing both your basic text and retrievals from it.

Summary

Orbis, used either with XyWrite or Nota Bene, brings together a strong word processor with a reasonably good text retriever. For many researchers, especially those who already use either of the word processors, it will be a very practical choice with minimal front-end learning investment.

You have to work around the lack of coding support, the limited search options, and the limited facilities for collecting search hits. You don't get explicit theory-building support. What you see is what you get: a good package integrating word processing and text retrieval.

References

The Technology Group. (1993a). *Orbis for XyWrite*. Baltimore, MD: Author.

The Technology Group. (1993b). *XyWrite 4.0: Command reference guide*. Baltimore, MD: Author.

The Technology Group. (1993c). *XyWrite 4.0: Customization guide*. Baltimore, MD: Author.

Sonar Professional, Version 8.5/2.5[1]

Available for Macintosh and Windows

Virginia Systems Software Services, Inc.
5509 West Bay Court
Midlothian, VA 23112

Phone: (804) 739-3200
Fax: (804) 739-8376

Price: $795
$295 for nonprofessional version
Educational discounts only for university bookstores

Hardware Requirements:
For Macintosh
- 4MB PAM
- System 7 or higher

For Windows
- 386 or better
- Windows 3.1
- 4MB RAM minimum, 8MB recommended

Overview

Sonar Professional is a text search program, with some important additional capabilities, that works by building indexes of your documents; your documents can be created by a tremendously wide array of other programs and left in their native format. It has a few important drawbacks, but its pleasant, easy interface is fun to use, and there are a bunch of different fast and powerful ways of getting around in your data.

Sonar gives you access to complex, nested Boolean searches, proximity searches, synonym searches, and phonetic searches, and all of these can be combined as you wish. There are seven data fields—filename, date, keywords, and four user-definable fields—for every document in the "document information database," which can be used as search criteria as well. You can attach memos to pages of your documents (but not to specific chunks of text), and you can search the memos. Sonar will produce frequency lists of words that occur near a word of interest and will let you use this frequency list to view the new words in context. Printed reports are good, with source tags, search terms marked, and memos printed with text.

Sonar will also try to find indirect associations between two words by doing what it calls "Relational" searching: looking for co-occurrences of both words with the same intermediary "link" words. This might be a useful theory-building feature if you keep in mind that proximal words may *or may not* be related in reality.

There are versions of Sonar for both the Macintosh and Windows. The two versions are virtually identical. For this review, most work was done on the Macintosh version, and we will generally speak in terms of the Macintosh (e.g., we'll say "folders" rather than "directories").

Database Structure

Your data are documents on your hard disk, created with other programs. As of this writing, the Macintosh version supported documents created by Design Studio 2.0, Frame-

1. The current Sonar Professional version numbers are 8.5 for Macintosh and 2.5 (upcoming revision) for Windows.

Maker 2.1 and 3.0, FullWrite Professional 1.0, MacWrite 4.5, MacWrite Pro, MacWrite II, Microsoft Word 1.05, 3, 4, and 5, Microsoft Word 1.xx and 2.0, More and More II, PageMaker 3.0, 4.2, and later, QuarkXPress 3.0 and later, RagTime 3.0, Ready Set Go! 4, 4.5, Trapeze, WordPerfect 1.0.3, 2, and 3, and WriteNow (various aspects of Sonar's performance change significantly from package to package—check to make sure the support for your package is adequate to your needs). QuickTime movies embedded in documents can reportedly be played by Sonar, and images are displayed in a separate window, but we were unable to test these features. The Sonar Image version of the program will also facilitate scanning and editing of images. The Windows version supported Word for Windows 1.0 and 2.0, WordPerfect 5.1 for DOS and Windows, and Microsoft Works 1.0 and 2.0.

Sonar indexes all the files in a folder (directory) at once, so you have to set up folders just for your documents, and you have to organize your folders keeping in mind that each folder will constitute a separate, selectable index. When you're searching, you can create and save named groups of indexes, which act, in essence, as a larger index. File size is limited by RAM: If you want to index a 5MB file, you probably need about 5-6MB of RAM. The manual advises placing no more than 400-500 files in a folder for reasons of search speed, although it says you can in practice place "several thousand" files in a folder. You are further advised that searching 100 folders with 10 documents each is slower than searching 10 folders with 100 documents each. While it's clear that optimum performance will be achieved somewhere between folders with too many files each and having the same files spread out over too many folders, there's no clear advice about where this point is.

There are two ways you can tell Sonar to subdivide a file (for Sonar's purposes only—your files are never changed by Sonar). First, you can define "blocks" of text, which can be used in searching as the search context (distance within which two terms must co-occur to satisfy an AND request). To do this, you give Sonar any nonalphanumeric character to use as the block delimiter or choose to use carriage returns. The default character is "_" and you could insert this (or another of your choosing) in your files everywhere you want a new block to begin. Or you might have a file that has a particular character between blocks. For example, if, when you download a bunch of e-mail messages in one file, they're separated with some character, then you'd be all set up to have each message treated as a separate block. The manual also suggests using blocks for defining fields. The example given is of a resume: You put a "_" after education, after experience, and so on. Each section then becomes a "field." If you use "." as your block separator, then you'll get sentences as blocks, but you'll also have a new block starting everywhere there's a "." in an abbreviation and so on. If you use carriage returns, then every paragraph will be a block.

The second way to subdivide a file is to create subdocuments within it. You insert a line at the top of each subdocument that has a string of three of the block separator characters, a name for the subdocument, and three more of the block separator characters. So if the separator were "*" you might have "*** docname ***." Now when you search, each subdocument will be treated just like a regular document in all summaries and results, and the subdocument names you provide will be reported as the file names. This can be a useful feature if you have lots of small documents, like memos or notes, in one file but want them considered separate documents when searching. This could apparently also enhance search speed. It can also be useful for big files because the file size limitation above applies to documents rather than files. So, with 5-6MB RAM, you could index a file containing multiple 5MB subdocuments.

Data Entry

As already indicated, you prepare your data with a word processor or desktop publishing package. Whether or not character formatting (bold, underline, and so on) shows up in your Sonar searches depends on which program you used. If you want to use blocks (other than paragraphs) or subdocuments, you'll need to put in the necessary separators. No other text preparation is necessary.

The indexing process itself is fairly easy to learn and do, with just a few options to set (it looks like a lot here, but it's only seven menu items, most of which you'll set once and ignore). The one big obstacle here (and it's an important one) is that many of these settings affect your searches, and to change them you have to reindex each affected folder.

There are basically seven options you can set before you index. (a) If you're indexing text-only documents, or documents from a word processor that Sonar doesn't directly or fully support, you tell Sonar the number of lines of text you want per page, and the number of the first page, and Sonar will use this information to report page numbers for retrieved text. (b) There's an option to force Sonar to index all files, even if they're not from supported programs, and the program will do its best to index the text in the documents while ignoring the control characters (formatting and so on) in the file. (c) You can tell Sonar whether or not to use a supplied, editable noise word list to keep common words like "a," "the," "be," and so on out of the index. Think about this one carefully, because to change the setting you'll have to reindex the folder. (d) You can have hyphens removed from words, so that they are treated as whole words, or hyphens can be treated as spaces. Again, to change, you have to reindex. (e) You tell Sonar whether you have subdocuments in your files. (f) You define your

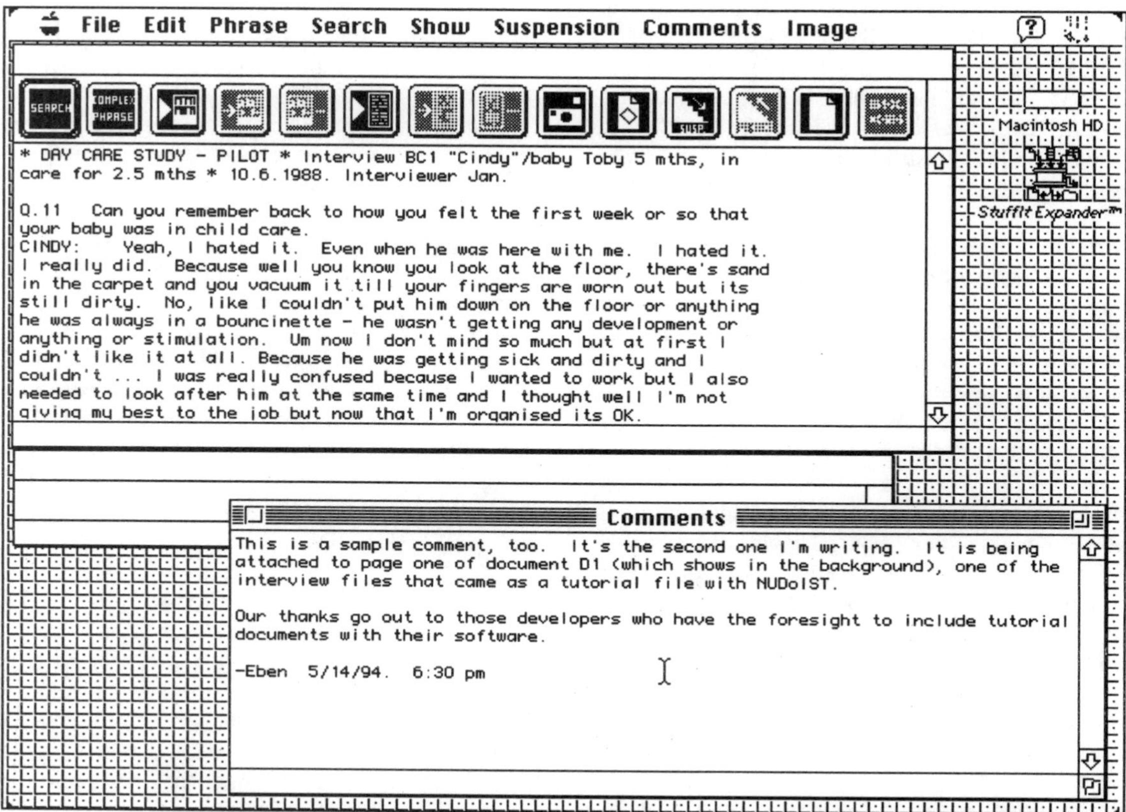

Sonar Figure 1. Viewing the comment (lower window) associated with the current page, above. The main window shows the first page of the first document in the index, until you do a search.

end of block character. (g) Finally, you can choose to create an "archive" of files on removable media, such as a floppy disk or (more likely) CD-ROM. When you search an archived index, the removable drive (with the actual files on it) does not have to be available. Sonar will tell you the name of the disk, folder, and file a hit is in, and after you supply the disk, it will show you the data.

One other issue has to be decided by you: You must decide before you index your data whether or not you want searches to be case sensitive (i.e., respect capitalization). But this is not available as a menu choice; to change this option, you have to move one of Sonar's program files from one folder to another and rename it. If you later change your mind, you'll have to move the file back and reindex your data.

Index times seemed to vary considerably (as usual, these are imprecise stopwatch tests). Several batches of documents were indexed on a Macintosh IIci with 5MB of RAM. The times varied so much that it is difficult to project index times with bigger data sets. Some of the results were as follows:

Number and Type of Documents	*Total Size*	*Time to Index (Min:Sec)*
9 Text Only	48KB	1:15
7 Text Only	52KB	0:25
7 Microsoft Word	236KB	0:30

Working on the Data

If you want to edit your data, you do it with your word processor. There's an option to have Sonar warn you if it starts searching a file you've modified but not reindexed. If you tell it to continue, it will do its best to search and display the file, though the results may not be quite right. This is a helpful feature you won't find in most document-indexing search programs.

There are two ways you can work on your data from within Sonar. You can write memos, one per page, and you can add data to the document information database to use in searching.

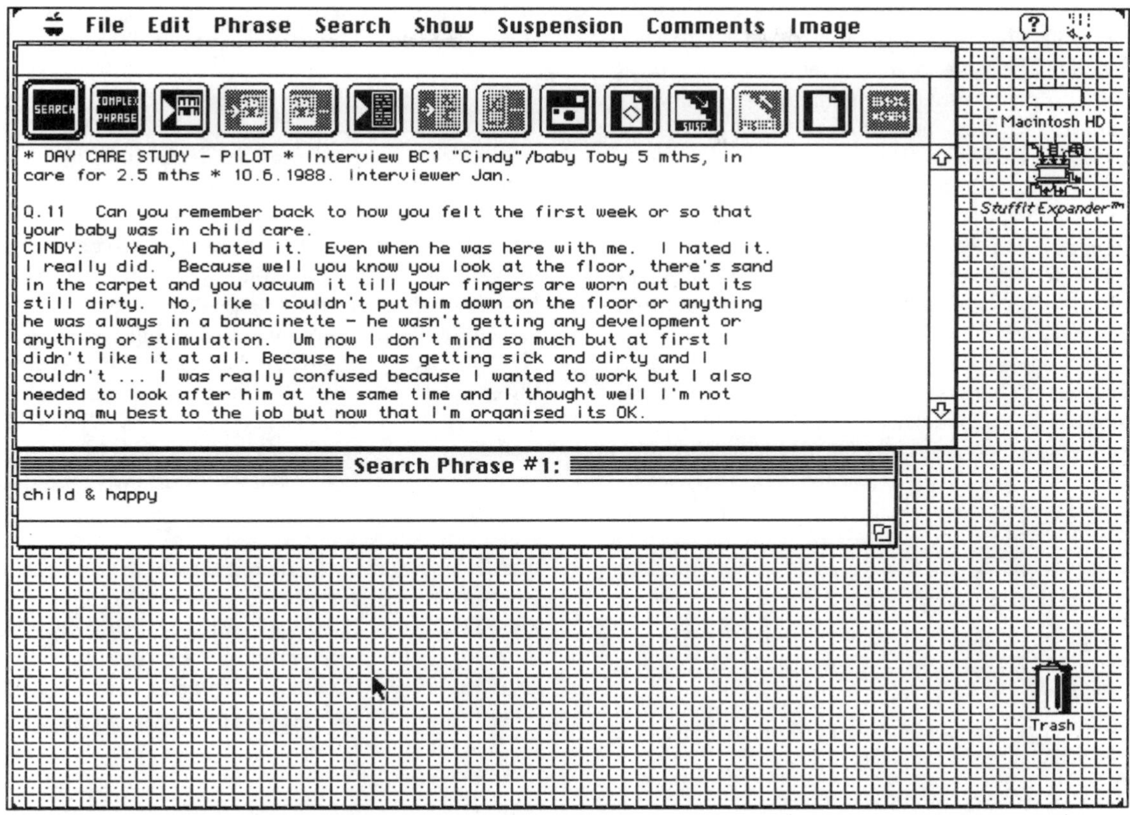

Sonar Figure 2. The search request "child & happy" has been typed into the query box at the bottom. This will find documents that have both words, regardless of how close together they are. (If you've specified blocks of text in advance, the request will find co-occurrence within blocks.)

Memoing with Comments

Memos are called comments, and you can attach one to each page of your documents. Comments can hold 32K worth of text, or about 10 single-spaced pages. If you open the comment window, it will change as you move around, always showing the comment for the page you're viewing (see Figure 1). Comments can be searched but only for a simple character string (word or phrase)—no Boolean or other sophisticated searching here—and the results can be output, together with the attached page of text, as well as being viewed on screen.

Document Information

The document information database has a record for each indexed document (or subdocument!), and has seven data fields that can be used singly, in combination, or in combination with any other kind of search, for searching for documents. The first two fields, for filename and date, are filled automatically (though you can edit the date if you want to use something other than the file creation date). The third field is for keywords for the file and can hold up to 70 characters. The other four fields are called User Field 1 to User Field 4. You can rename these fields and put up to 220 characters of text in each. However, you only get one set of names for these fields, which applies to *all* your indexes—a serious limitation.

Searching

Searching is easy to learn and do. There's a query box at the bottom of the screen at all times (see Figure 2). You can simply type a word or phrase and it will be inserted into the query box—you don't have to do anything to select the query box first—hit <Enter> and the search is executed. Or you can select a word or phrase in the text with the mouse, then click on the Search button, and that word or phrase will be searched for. You can type anything from a one-word search to Sonar's most sophisticated searches directly into the query box. If you press ⌘-N, the string you've typed is stored momentarily, and you can type another one. You can do this repeatedly, and when you're ready, you press <Enter> and all the strings you've typed are searched for, as though all were connected by OR.

By default, search context is the entire file, unless you have defined blocks and turned on the block searching option in the search preferences dialog box. If you want to look for strings within closer proximity, you must specify the proximity in terms of numbers of words; there are no options for line, sentence, paragraph, or page contexts.

There's just one wildcard, *, which matches any number of any characters. There is no support for matching regular expressions (or patterns such as social security numbers or phone numbers), a curious omission in a dedicated search package.

The search syntax is simple. AND is represented by &, OR by |, and NOT by ~. Parentheses are supported and you can use them to make queries as complex as you want. There are also five search modifiers:

:x means to find the terms within x words of each other (proximity).

= forces the terms to appear in the same order in the text as in the search request (sequence).

! specifies that terms can occur in any order.

^ disables block searching for a particular pair of terms, so that when block searching is on, you can still search for documents that have two words, even if they're not in the same block.

means "itself." This is a little hard to get a grasp on logically, but it lets you make searches like "convers* ~:1# conversation"—which means "every word that starts with 'convers' *except* 'conversation.' "

There are three operators and five modifiers: a very simple set to learn and yet it gives you great search power. If you prefer, though, there's a complex phrase dialog box that lets you create a Boolean query, using proximity, for up to three phrases (see Figure 3).

Again, the search commands are very simple, but you can do very complex things with them. The proximity operator applies to specific *parts* of a Boolean expression, so part of an expression can be asking for words to co-occur within one proximity and part of it asking for other words to co-occur within another. For example, take the query "A &:10 (B & C)." What does this actually mean? Because there's no proximity operator between B and C, they only have to co-occur within a file. But the proximity operator connecting A to (B & C) means that you're looking for places where A co-occurs with B OR with C, given that B AND C are both in the same file. Each time A co-occurs with B or with C is treated as a single "occurrence," or hit.

Document Information Searching

In the document information dialog box, there's a search button for searching for documents based on data in the document information database. This button brings up another dialog box with three boxes: one to select a field, one to select an operator, and one to type in a string or date to look for. The operators available here are Containing (meaning the field contains this string somewhere in it), Not Containing, Equal To (the field's contents are exactly this—more restrictive than just containing it), Not Equal To, Less Than, Less/Equal To, Greater Than, Greater/Equal To.

In addition to being available this way, the document information searching dialog box is available from the complex phrase dialog box (Figure 3). Choosing it from there will paste the document information search you define into one of the phrase slots in the complex phrase dialog box, so that you can combine document information with text strings in searching. Further, the syntax for searching on these fields is fairly easy and can be used by hand in the query box once you feel comfortable enough to try it on your own.

Synonym and Concept Searching

Sonar comes with a built-in thesaurus, which you unfortunately cannot view or edit, though you can define your own synonyms in addition with "concept" files (you can create as many as you want but only one can be open at a time). If you enclose a word *or phrase* in { }, it will be automatically expanded during the search to all synonyms either in Sonar's thesaurus or in your open concept file, any of which will satisfy the search request. There's a great shortcut here: If you strike the [key, Sonar will place { } in the query box, with the cursor in the middle so you can type in your word or phrase.

If you choose to create a concept file, you do it from within Sonar. Sonar opens up an editor window for you, and you begin typing in groups, or families, of synonymous words and phrases. You type one word or phrase per line and leave a blank line between families.

Phonetic Searching

Sonar also allows you to define phonetic searches. To do this, you place / characters between the phonemes of a word, like this: he/ro/ic/. Sonar has a file containing groups of similar sounding phonemes, which you can edit. When Sonar searches for "heroic," it will also search for spellings that substitute phonemes from the same groups as "he,"

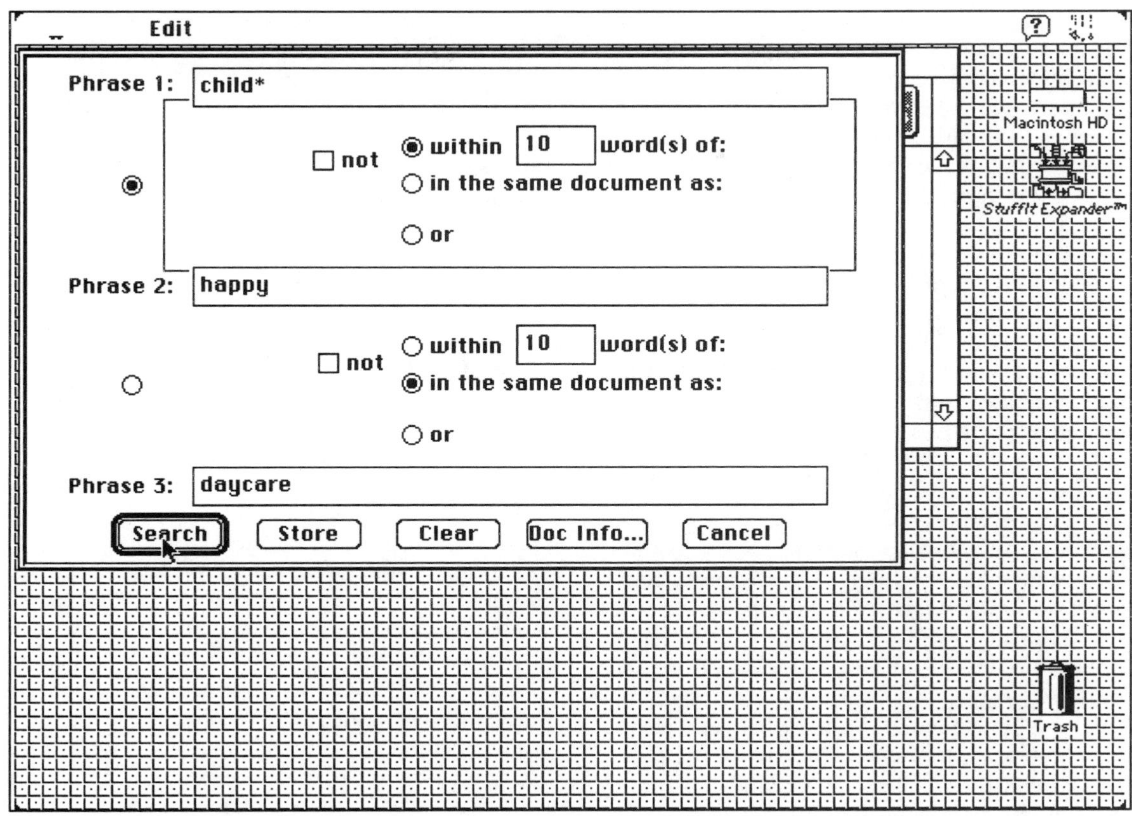

Sonar Figure 3. The Complex Phrase dialog box. There are boxes for each of three phrases. "Radio buttons" and check boxes let you specify AND ("within x words," and "in the same document" are AND searches as well as proximity operators), OR, and NOT for each pair of phrases. The bracket on the left from Phrase 1 to Phrase 2 (and the darkened radio button next to it) indicates that the combination of Phrases 1 and 2 should be looked for first, as though you had put parentheses around this part of the search. To give this request from the query box, you'd type: "(child* &:10 happy) & daycare." The Doc Info . . . button lets you add a search statement from the Document Information database as one of the three phrases.

"ro," and "ic." So it will find misspellings like "hairoik," "hurrohic," and so on.

Associated Word Searches

After executing a search for a simple word or phrase, you can click the Assoc. Words button. This will produce a frequency list of all words that occur within a specified number of words of the search string. You specify in a dialog box the distance you want—how many words (default is 10) and in which direction (before, after, either side). The resulting list can be ordered either alphabetically or by frequency. If you click on a word in the list, a search is initiated for all the places where it and the initial string co-occur. If you hold down the <Shift> key when you click, you'll get a whole new associated words list for the word you click on. There's a way to hop back and forth among the various nested searches you're generating here, and we'll talk about it under "Viewing Search Results," below.

Link File Searching

Sonar will let you create "link" files where you store a list of search terms. You can then search for all of the strings in a link file, as though they were connected with ORs.

Relational Searching

There's a more interesting use for link files, though. Sonar will use the terms in a link file to look for indirect relationships between two other strings you supply in a relational search. What, you ask?

First, Sonar does a proximity search (default is 10 words, either side) for the two strings you supply. If it finds any hits, it tells you there's a "direct" relationship and shows you the hits. Next, it looks to see whether any of the strings in the open link file co-occur within 10 words of *both* of the strings. If so, your search strings are said to be "indirectly" related through their common neighbor in the link file.

For example, say you do a relational search for A and B. If C is in your link file, and co-occurs with *both* A and B (not necessarily in the same place), then Sonar will tell you that "A » C » B" meaning that A is related to C, which is related to B. This is called a second generation relationship. Clicking on a » will initiate a search for all co-occurrences of the adjacent terms. This allows you to examine the co-occurrences on which this proposed relationship is based and determine whether or not they're meaningful. A little brief experimentation says sometimes they are and sometimes they aren't, as you might guess. For example, a relational search for "happ*" (to see what things were associated with being happy or with happiness) proposed that "happ* » CHILD » CAREER » FAMILY." This might suggest that there were relationships between happiness and having children, between having children and having a career, and between having a career and things having to do with a family (certainly, one could place many equally banal interpretations on this). Looking at the actual data, though, showed that it didn't all support a consistent interpretation. For example, sometimes "happ*" and "child" co-occurred where a person was talking about his or her own happiness about having children, but sometimes it was a person talking about his or her *child's* happiness. Some of the other "co-occurrences"—for example, some of those between "child" and "career" and some of those between "career" and "family"—where actually in separate, unrelated sentences or even paragraphs. On the other hand, some of the retrieved data would support meaningful interpretations of the proposed relationships. Moral of the story: *Be careful.* An epistemological note here too: Remember that this is all based on a list of potential link words that *you* put in the link file and is thus subject to all the strengths and weaknesses of *your* theoretical assumptions.

After looking for second generation relationships, Sonar looks for third generation relationships (two link words, C and D, both from the link file, so that A » C » D » B), fourth generation, and so on. Default is to go to fifth generation (four link words), but you can set this to whatever you want. Actually, you don't see any of these results until the whole thing has been processed. You are then presented with a list of all the relationships, from second generation up. Each item in this list is called a "genealogy" (another use of genealogies is discussed below), and the whole list can be saved, then recalled and navigated later on.

There's another twist on this. If you want, you can just type in one phrase instead of two. Sonar will then do its relational search routine, building out from this phrase through the ones in the link file, without the restriction of having to wind up at a second term.

Viewing Search Results

When you first enter Sonar, you select a group of indexes (which you can name as a group), and right away you see the first document in the main window (when you reopen Sonar subsequently, your last group of indexes is remembered and appears automatically). This viewing window is fully scrollable and remains so at all times, and can be resized, up to the full screen, to show more or less text at once. If you want to get at the file in its native application, you can launch the application, with the document in it. When you execute a search, the window scrolls to the first hit, and the search term(s) are marked with a box (see Figure 4). Which hit is first is determined by "relevancy." The file with the most hits is considered the most relevant to the search, and its hits are presented from top to bottom. If you don't like this, you can have files presented in alphabetical order instead.

Sonar uses the term "occurrence" rather than "hit." There are buttons to hop to the next or previous occurrence, or the next or previous document. As you jump from occurrence to occurrence, you'll see various search terms being boxed and unboxed, as different combinations of them—different occurrences—are displayed. This can be both confusing and disconcerting, but it may be a worthwhile price to pay for the extra flexibility in defining searches. Unfortunately, it doesn't work consistently: When exactly the same paragraph appeared in two different files, different sets of "occurrences" were found. You can also scroll the window to see the rest of the file in either direction. Three other buttons give you different summaries of your search, and two of them can be used to navigate the results, as described below.

Instant index. The instant index button produces an index showing, for each phrase in a search, the documents it is found in and the page numbers for each document where it is found. This list can be printed or saved.

Go to document. Another button produces a list of all the documents that contain a given search phrase (if you've searched for multiple phrases, you have to do this one at a time) and the number of times the phrase (string) occurs in that document. Click on a document name, and the main

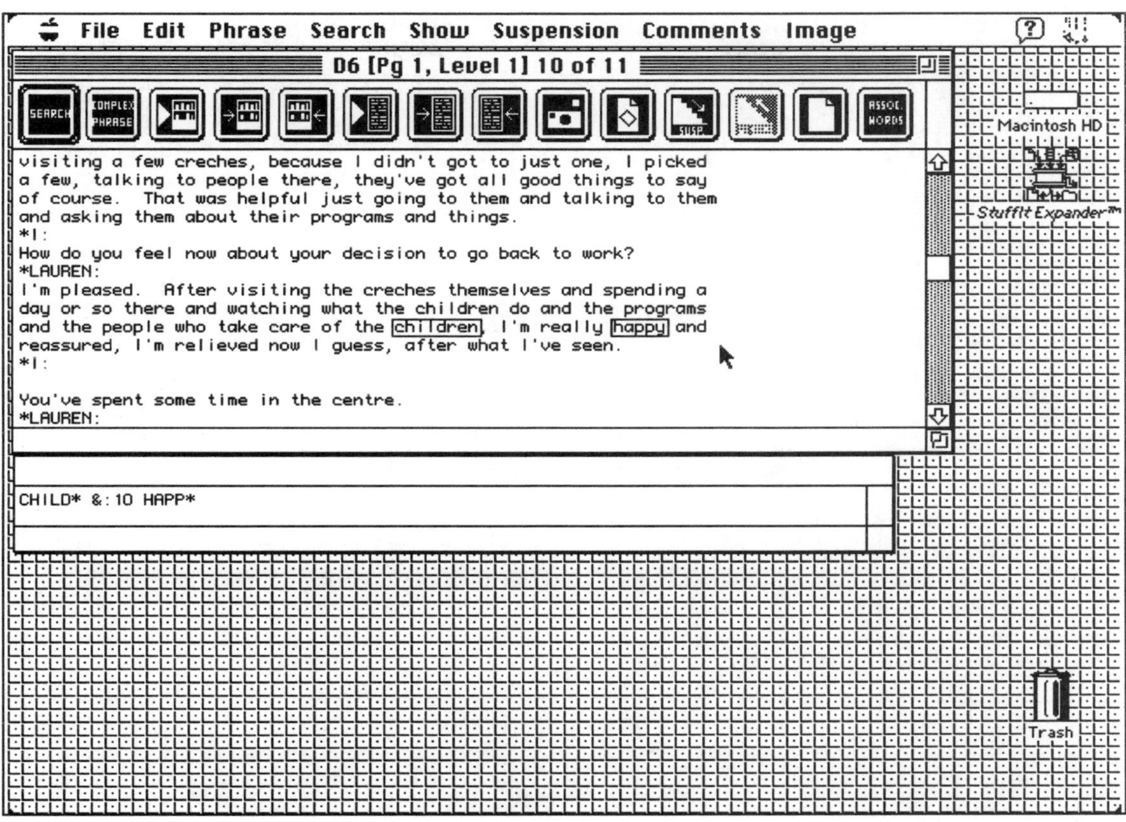

Sonar Figure 4. Viewing the results of a search for words that start with "child" (child*) within 10 words of (&:10) words that start with "happ" (happ*), as defined in the query box. The words "children" and "happy," which matched the search request, are boxed in the main window.

search window jumps to the first hit in that document. This gives a hypertext functionality.

Go to occurrence. There's also a button that produces a list of all the "occurrences," in a line of context each, like a KWIC concordance (see Figure 5). Click on a line and the main window jumps to that occurrence. Again, this is a sort of hypertext directory of your hits. This list can get very long, because a hit from a search for multiple phrases can be broken down into several occurrences.

Suspend and Resume. The Suspend button lets you interrupt the current search, of whatever type, and do other things, such as run other searches. The Resume button takes you back to the suspended activity. Suspends can be nested, that is, you can suspend an operation, even when something else is already suspended, and so on, as far down as you want (Sonar always shows you what level of suspension you're up to). The Resume button then steps you back through your suspended sessions.

This is a very important and useful feature, and relates back to a number of the processes we've already discussed. In several instances, such as from an associated word list, a relational search, a go to occurrence list, or a go to document list, we clicked on an item in a list or a » link symbol and launched a search. Each time, we suspended an earlier search—the one that produced the list. So after perusing all associations between two terms in a relational search, or the associated words for a word in an associated word list, we could get back to where we started by clicking the Resume button, repeatedly if necessary, and then go on to explore the next item.

If you're going to change your selection of search folders after you suspend a session, you'll have to remember to Save Context before you suspend. Then when you resume, you can get back the set of folders you were searching originally.

Genealogy. The list of suspended sessions is called a "genealogy" and can be called up at any time (see Figure 6).

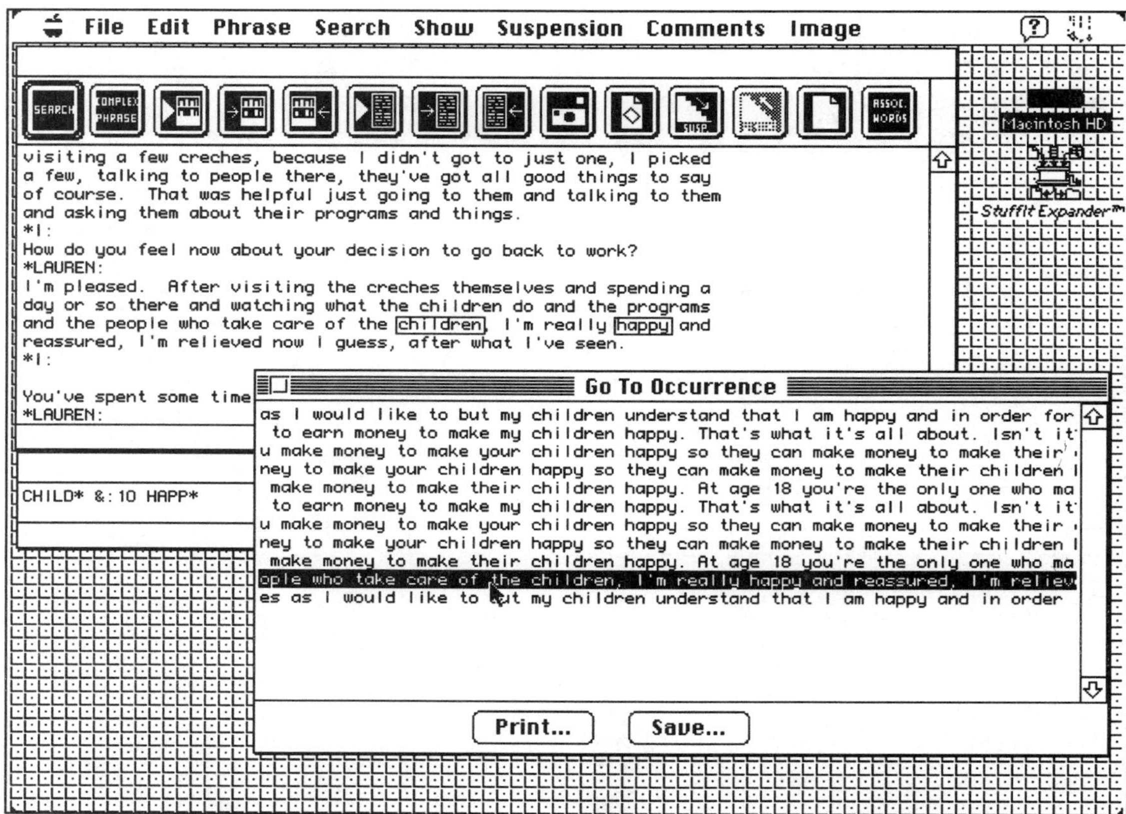

Sonar Figure 5. The Go To Occurrence list for the search defined in Figure 4. Clicking on an occurrence line (in this case, the second from the last) highlights it in the list and causes the main window in the background to display the hit in context, with boxes around the search terms.

(Remember that the output of relational searches were also called genealogies.) The different suspended processes are listed, connected with »s. Clicking on a » will jump you straight to that process. This is true whether you suspended sessions by explicitly clicking the Suspend button or simply by clicking on items in an associated word list, relational search, occurrence list, and so on.

Genealogies can be saved and reloaded later, so that they can function as a savable, executable audit trail of your work. There are a couple of limitations here, though. First, genealogies are only created when you suspend processes (or do a relational search), not whenever you do a search. So if you're just doing one search after another from the query box, never doing anything to cause a suspend, you don't get a genealogy. Second, each time you resume a process, it disappears from the genealogy. So if you want to save a genealogy for later reuse, make sure you save it while all the processes you want in it are suspended.

Output

Output is another strong point of Sonar. Every one of the lists we've discussed has a Print button, allowing you to print out that list. If you want to send text selectively from your results to the printer, there's a Print Selection menu item that will print text that's been selected with the mouse.

Append

To send text selectively to an output file, you can select with the mouse and copy to the clipboard. Usually, copying something to the clipboard erases whatever was there before. However, Sonar gives you an Append option so that you can collect multiple chunks of text on the clipboard. Each chunk is identified with the name of the document and page number it came from. You can send your own notes—annotations or memos, in effect—to the clipboard to accompany these data by typing them into the query box and giving the Append command, ⌘-S. This is

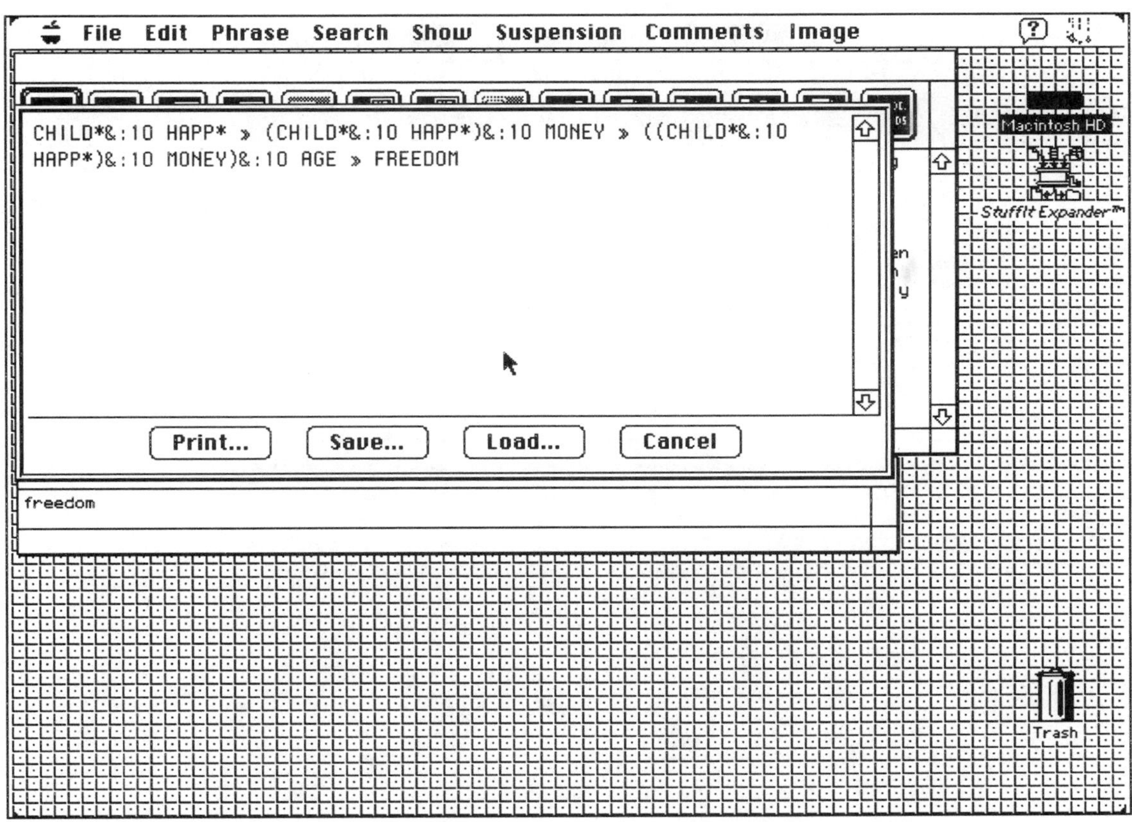

Sonar Figure 6. A "genealogy" showing a list of suspended searches, each being represented by the actual search request. Here's what it's showing. (a) I searched for "child*" within 10 words of "happ*"; (b) from an associated word list for the previous statement, I selected "money" so it searched for that statement within 10 words of "money"; (c) from an associated word list for the search in (b), I selected "age" and searched for those co-occurrences; and (d) I did a new search for "freedom."

an unusual, and very useful, feature. Identifying information and your notes appear flush left, and the copied text is indented.

From the clipboard, the accumulated text can be pasted into a word processor. Sonar also has a special clipboard viewer that has buttons allowing you to print the clipboard's contents directly, save them to a text-only file, or add them to an existing text-only file.

Search Reports

Sonar also creates nice, simple reports from your searches and sends them either to a file or to the printer. Nothing fancy here, but basically what you need, and it's all well laid out and easy to read. At the top of the report, you get the total number of occurrences in the report. Then you get each occurrence in context, with source tags for document name, page number, and search request as well as the comment for the page it's on, each occurrence being separated by a dashed line. You can specify how many words of context you want and can choose before, after, or on both sides of the search phrase itself. Or you can get the whole document.

There's an option to minimize duplication, and this is very useful. If more than one occurrence exists within an overlapping range of context, it'll all be put together as one chunk. Another option lets you have search terms shown in uppercase letters for easy identification in the printouts. Unfortunately, this option doesn't work for words or phrases that have been found using wildcards or synonym/concept searches. There are also options to turn on and off the inclusion of the total occurrence count and the comment.

Topic Reports from Comments

You can also produce a report based on a search through your comments. This works just like the search reports,

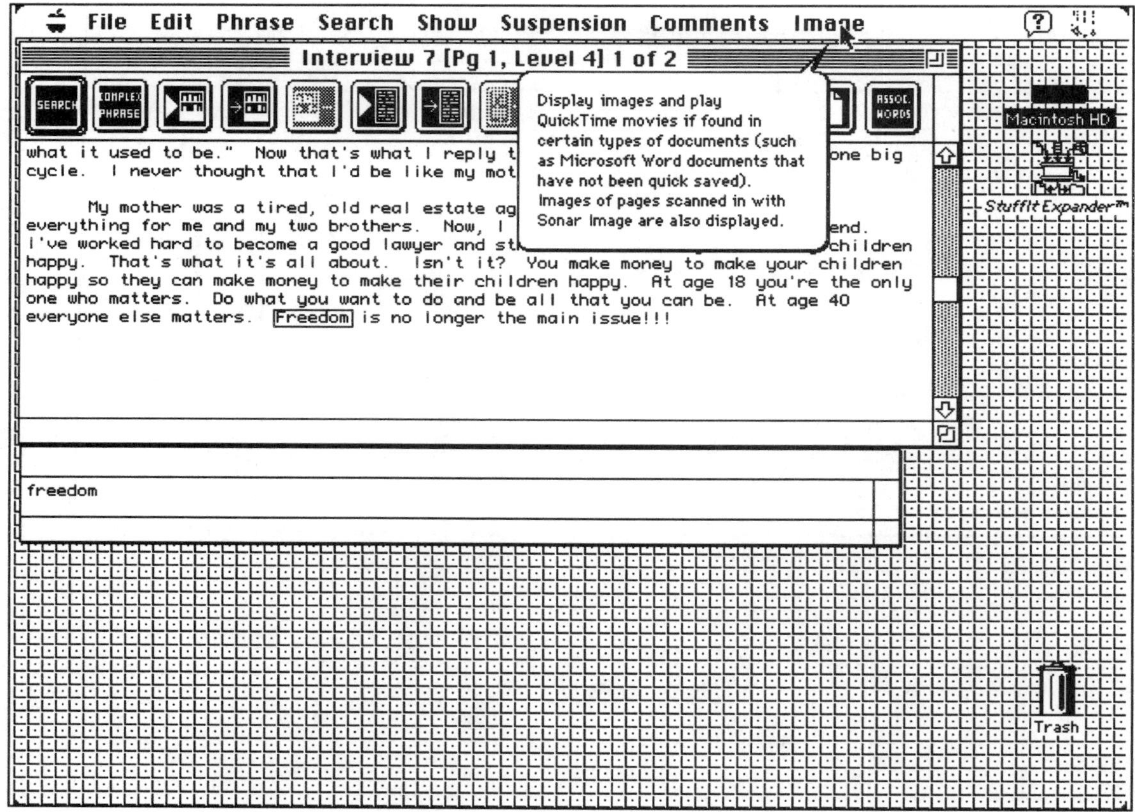

Sonar Figure 7. Balloon help, a feature of Macintosh System 7 that is only supported by some programs, such as Sonar, causes a little cartoon speech-style balloon to appear, giving a help message to whatever the mouse cursor points to. You can leave this on while you work. It is currently showing the help message for the Image menu. If you pull down a menu, or open a dialog box, you can get balloons for every menu item and most dialog box items. There are *no* balloons for the buttons.

except that comments print first, with their associated page of text below.

Theory Building

Aside from its memoing capabilities, the closest Sonar comes to theory building is with its associated words and relational searches. Whether or not you consider these useful (or legitimate) theory-building approaches will depend on your theoretical and methodological orientation. We suspect some folks will find them very useful. As we mentioned earlier, in playing around with the relational search function, we found plenty of examples of legitimate connections, and plenty of bogus ones too. Obviously, it would be a mistake to accept such results without rigorous and close examination of the text on which the proposed relationships were based. It would also be a mistake to lose track of the fact that Sonar is only working with the list of terms you give it in the link file as potential link words.

Graphics Editing

You cannot edit graphics in Sonar, although you can resize the image window in which they are displayed. Graphics are not displayed or printed in the text where they are embedded but are displayed in a pop-up image window and can be printed separately from there. The Sonar Image version of the program, however, allows you to both scan and edit images. We did not have a copy of this version (we don't have a scanner) for testing.

User Friendliness

All in all, this is an outstandingly user-friendly program. It is both enjoyable (research *is* fun, after all, but some other programs tend to obscure that) and easy to learn and use. If there's one big problem here it's that there's no tutorial whatsoever—no sample files, no section of the manual that walks you through the basics with your data, nothing. On the other hand, the manual is relatively small, so it's not too much to get through; it's clear and well written, with lots of illustrations, and has an excellent, thorough index. In contrast to many of the other manuals we've had to slog through, we were able to find everything we needed through the index. On-screen help is available through System 7's balloon help feature, which Sonar supports. With this feature turned on, a little help balloon pops up for anything you point the mouse at, such as menu and dialog box items (see Figure 7). Unfortunately, there are no help balloons for the buttons on the main window.

Technical support is available 9 to 5 eastern time, Monday through Friday. You pay for the call to Virginia, though having to leave a voice-mail message resulted in their paying for the callback. The support people were patient, knowledgeable, and helpful.

Miscellaneous

The indexing process can be somewhat automated via macros. Sonar's index module supports Apple's AppleScript, a macro language. Using the Script Editor, you can record the steps you take in indexing a folder or folders. The Script Editor will also allow you to edit a script, say, to use it with new folders or multiple folders. Scripts can then be replayed as a shortcut to actually carrying out the actions step by step in Sonar.

Sonar can be run on a network. It will support multiple, simultaneous users.

There's a stripped-down version, called Sonar (as opposed to Sonar Professional), which costs $500 less, but it doesn't seem worth it. You lose *all* of the following: phonetic searching, synonym/concept searching, comments, report generation, suspend/resume, context saving, AppleEvents (which gives you the ability to launch other applications), image/movie support, associated words, link file searching, relational searching, and genealogies. At $295 and so little left in the way of features, why bother?

At least one bug turned up during testing: The document information search dialog box didn't work properly, so that if you tried to change the operator the computer crashed. Tech support said they'd heard of, but not been able to duplicate, this error, but they thought it was a problem with running on System 7.0.x, rather than 7.1.x, where the problem doesn't occur, and said they'd check it out.

Update

The Macintosh version of the program has now been upgraded to run on the new PowerPC-based Macintosh computers. The version has been changed from 8.5 to 8.5PPC. This version will run on either a regular Mac or a Power Mac.

Comparative Remarks

The most similar program to Sonar reviewed here is ZyINDEX, another document-indexing search program, which is available only for the PC. Sonar outshines ZyINDEX in virtually every way. It is much more user friendly, gives you much more useful and flexible ways to navigate around your data, and has better, more flexible output options. ZyINDEX does come out better in its support for some regular expression pattern matching.

Sonar is far more user friendly than WordCruncher, much simpler on the text-preparation count, and has a few more search options. WordCruncher may be better for working with very large archived files for which you want to establish an outline-type structure, especially if you want traditional content-analytic functions.

Orbis/XyWrite is just as user friendly but is less sophisticated as a searcher and report maker; its main plus is the close integration with a full-featured word processor. That lets you alternate easily among search, analysis, and writing.

Another possible comparison is with Folio VIEWS (which on the Macintosh is currently available in a read-only version, though the full version is due out soon), to which all your data must be imported. Importing gives you a lot more flexibility than indexing, and Folio VIEWS has a lot more powerful features than Sonar, but by the same token an indexing program like Sonar lets you leave your files free on the hard disk, where you can continue to edit them in their native programs (which in this case are available in a wide assortment).

Compared with Metamorph, a text searcher that doesn't need to index your data, how Sonar stacks up depends on your needs. For raw search power (and speed), Metamorph is miles ahead of Sonar. However, Sonar's other search features (associated words, various indexes and hypertext-like lists, relational searches), comments, and output options will be significant advantages over Metamorph for some users.

Summary

Though this program has some serious problems and oversights—such as the lack of options for searching by line, sentence, paragraph, or page; the quirky way hits are highlighted; and so on—we liked it a lot. It's a very user-friendly text retriever that really adds something on top of that: special search and navigation features, good memoing, and good reporting. It also supports an uncommonly broad range of file formats for your data. If you want a text retriever, especially with these extra features, and don't mind working with a program that has to index your files, Sonar Professional deserves your serious consideration.

Reference

Virginia Systems Software Services, Inc. (1994). *Sonar: Macintosh combined user's guide, Sonar and Sonar Professional, Version 8.5.* Midlothian, VA: Author.

The Text Collector, Version 1.7

Available for DOS

O'Neill Software
P.O. Box 26111
San Francisco, CA 94126

Phone: (415) 398-2255

Price: $69

Hardware Requirements:
- IBM PC series (or compatible)
- 128K RAM
- PC-DOS or MS-DOS 2.0 or later

Overview

A first impression, as well as a final one: This is a sweet little program. You feel it from the moment you pick up the stark, utilitarian little manual (which looks as if it were produced on a desktop printer). The Text Collector is a no-frills, easy-to-learn, fast, flexible program for doing just what the name implies: collecting chunks of text from one or many files and storing them in an output file or files. It runs in just 128K of RAM, from floppies or a hard disk, and (according to the publisher) on any monitor and with any dot matrix, daisy wheel, or laser printer.

Let's get a little more specific. The program retrieves and sorts chunks of text from input files to output files (leaving the input files intact). You can simply browse through files, marking chunks of text to be saved to output files. Or the program can search through a file or group of files, looking for matches to the search term(s) you specify. You can work interactively, reviewing each find and deciding whether to move the matching chunk to the output file, or you can have the program create an output file with all matches, which you can then comb through and refine. There are lots of options for controlling the process, the more important of which we'll discuss below.

Database Structure

The Text Collector has no internal database. It simply searches through files on your hard or floppy disk(s). It can search files in many formats, including word processing files, database files (such as dBASE), and computer source code files. You can set up free-form databases by organizing your data files in directories or having The Text Collector save lists of files to search.

There is *no limit* to the length or number of files you can search at once except for disk capacity. You do not have to import files or even index them. For faster operation, you can load The Text Collector onto a RAM disk[1] and have it store its temporary files there.

Data Entry

You do not enter or import any data into The Text Collector. Your data consist of the information you have created with other software, such as your word processor or database manager. The Text Collector simply allows you to search, sort, and output that data.

Working on the Data

The program itself does not support coding, editing, graphics, making tables, or theory building. This is not to say it is not useful for qualitative analysis—on the contrary. The

1. A RAM disk is like an imaginary temporary floppy disk set up in the computer's fast RAM memory. Its advantage is speed. RAM disks require special software.

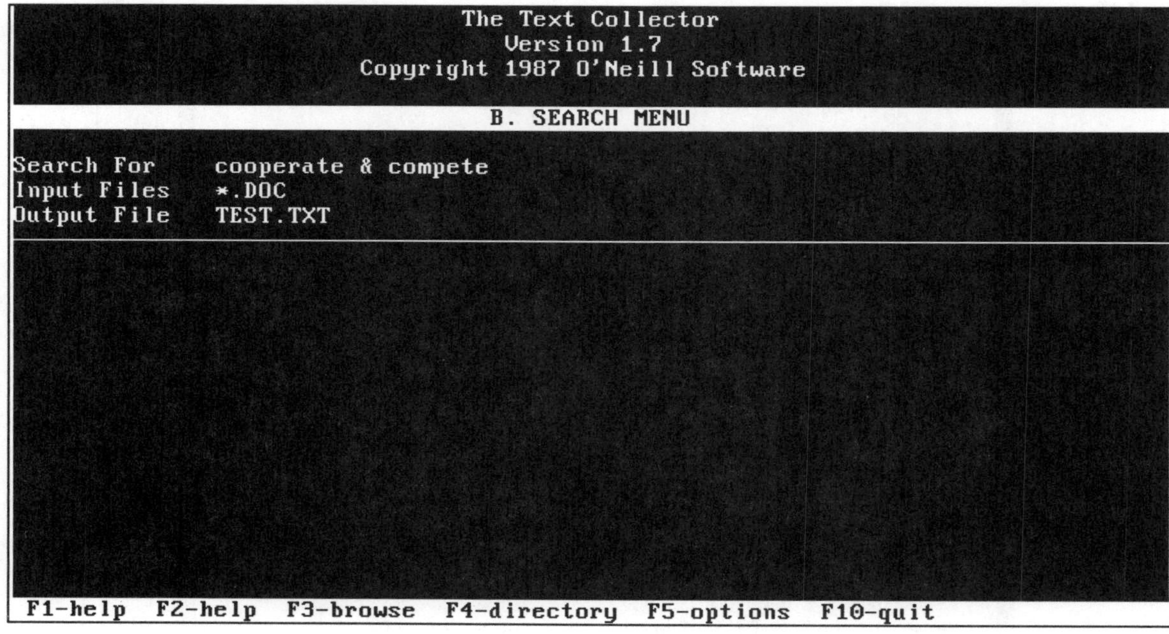

Text Collector Figure 1. A search has been defined for all context blocks with both the words "cooperate" and "compete" in all files with .DOC extensions. Output will be sent to the file TEST.TXT.

program works quite well for saving all chunks on a topic to a new file. You can always put codes in your data with your word processor, then search for and retrieve chunks based on those codes. For example, you could insert the code "change" in your text with your word processor, setting it off with, say, curly braces: {change}. Then if you searched for the string "{change}" you would only find the code "change" and not simply the word "change." Alternatively, you could type your codes in all uppercase letters: CHANGE. Then you could do a case-sensitive search (meaning only match if the case—upper or lower—is the same) for the string "CHANGE."

Searching

The Text Collector has excellent support for Boolean operators: You can use AND, OR, and NOT, and you can abbreviate them to symbols. Parentheses can be used for complex statements and can be nested as many times as you like. (See Chapter 2 for a more detailed discussion of these issues.)

Context Blocks

One of the most important concepts for searching with The Text Collector is that of context blocks. Basically, this is the chunk that the program retrieves when it finds a match to your search term, and which you can have written to the output file. You can define this as a word, sentence, line, paragraph, parentheses, quote, database record, or even a whole file. Depending on the mode you're working in (see below), you may be able to change the context on-the-fly. In addition, you can create custom contexts by providing start and end delimiters. For example, we defined the word "References" as a start delimiter and a forced page break as an end delimiter, and the program collected the reference lists from every document on the hard disk into one new file.

Context blocks have another meaning in The Text Collector. If you define a complex search, say, for *both* the words "cooperate" and "compete," the program finds all instances in which both words are within the same context block. The size of the context block therefore affects whether or not a match is found: If you've set it to paragraphs, the words must co-occur in a paragraph; if you've set it to sentences, they must co-occur in a sentence; and so on.

Search Modes

As mentioned above, there are several ways to carry out a search in The Text Collector; you have a choice of browse mode, automatic search mode, and command mode. Each mode has a number of options.

```
                                   OUT.DOC
\AA\DOC\TEXTCOLL.DOC The Text Collector has no internal database.  It
simply searches through files on your hard or floppy disk(s).  It can
search files in many formats, including word processing files, database
files (such as dBase), and computer source code files.  You can set up
free-form databases by organizing your data files in directories, or
having The Text Collector save lists of files to search.
\AA\DOC\TEXTCOLL.DOC There is NO LIMIT to the length or number of files
you can search at once except for disk capacity.  You do not have to
import files or even index them.  You can load The Text Collector onto a
RAM disk, and have it store its temporary files there for faster
operation.
\AA\DOC\TEXTCOLL.DOC You do not enter or import any data into The Text
Collector.  Your data are the information you have created with other
software, such as your word processor or database manager.  The Text
Collector simply allows you to search, sort and output that data.
\AA\DOC\TEXTCOLL.DOC The program itself does not support coding, editing,
graphics, making tables, or theory building.  This is not to say it is
not useful for qualitative analysis:  on the contrary.  The program works
quite well for sorting all chunks on a topic to a new file.  You can
always put codes in your data with your word processor, then search for,
and make chunks based on, those codes.

F1-help F2-tag F3-search F4-sort F5-save F6-print F7-format F8-next F9-prev
```

Text Collector Figure 2. Browsing the output file "OUT.DOC," which contains the results of a search for the word "search" in an earlier version of the file containing this review. Each context block begins with the full pathname of the file (\AA\DOC\TEXTCOLL.DOC). The search term, "search," is highlighted in each block. Line numbers have been added to the output file.

Browse mode. This is the most basic search method. It allows you to find scattered blocks of text and save them in another file or send them directly to the printer. The file being browsed appears on screen, and you can scroll around in it at will. If you ask to browse more than one, you see them one at a time and can switch among them with a keystroke. You can sort the file as you browse (see below). You can redefine the size of your context blocks on-the-fly, so that you can, for example, find a paragraph with the words "cooperate" and "compete," then select out text from the paragraph by the word or sentence. You can search for all occurrences of a search term, in which case they are all highlighted and "tagged" for output (more on tagging later), or you can search for one occurrence at a time, manually tagging if you want. You can also ask to see only the chunks that match the search in a list on screen.

Automatic search mode. In automatic search mode, you set your options, then go to the search screen (see Figure 1) and supply a search expression, input file(s), and output file. The program then finds all matching chunks and copies them to the output file. When it's finished, you can browse the output file (see Figure 2) and use any of the procedures mentioned above under browsing to zero in on what you want.

Alternatively, you can have the program simply create a list of the names of files in which the search expression is found (the context block, for search purposes, is thus the whole file). Then you can conduct further automatic searches or browse operations on this list of files.

Finally, you can conduct an *interactive automatic search.* Using this method, each time the program finds a match, it puts you into browse mode and loads up the file in which the search expression was found. You then use the browse procedures to output the text you want (there are some very nice options for automating the process). When you're done with a file, The Text Collector continues to search for other files that contain material matching the search expression.

Command mode. This mode allows you to enter the search expression, specify input and output files, and a couple of options, at the DOS prompt. The real advantage of this is that you can define a series of such searches in a regular DOS batch file and execute the searches sequentially, rerunning them whenever you want.

Tagging

When you search a file in browse mode, matching chunks can be automatically "tagged" for output. As indicated above,

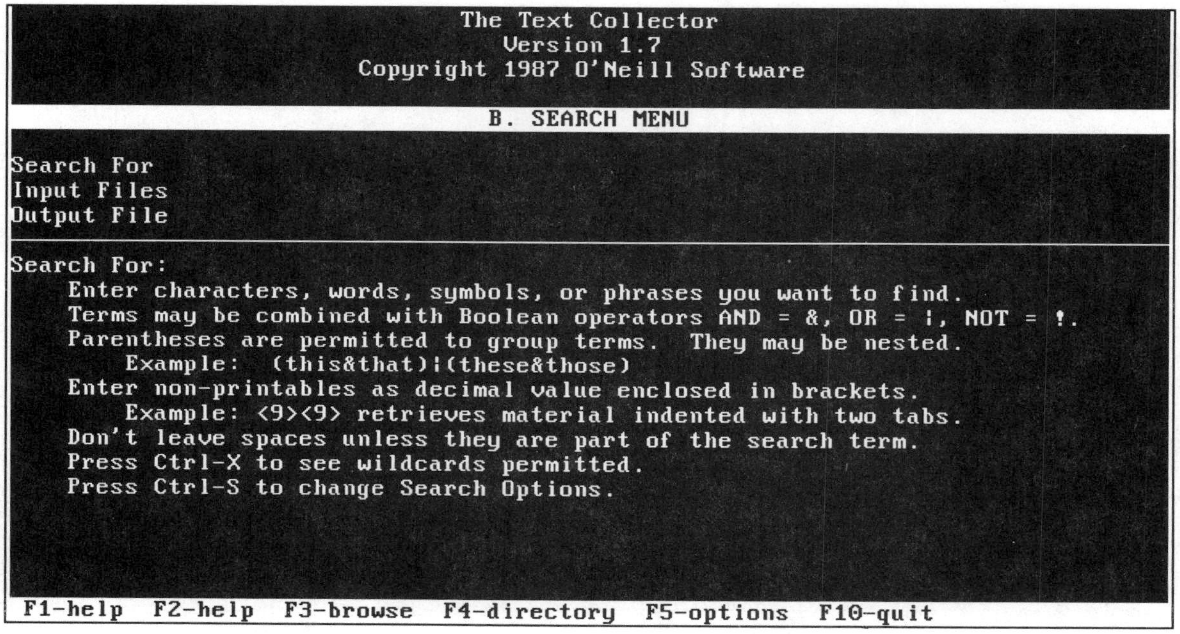

```
                        The Text Collector
                           Version 1.7
                  Copyright 1987 O'Neill Software

                          B. SEARCH MENU

Search For
Input Files
Output File

Search For:
    Enter characters, words, symbols, or phrases you want to find.
    Terms may be combined with Boolean operators AND = &, OR = |, NOT = !.
    Parentheses are permitted to group terms.  They may be nested.
        Example:  (this&that)|(these&those)
    Enter non-printables as decimal value enclosed in brackets.
        Example: <9><9> retrieves material indented with two tabs.
    Don't leave spaces unless they are part of the search term.
    Press Ctrl-X to see wildcards permitted.
    Press Ctrl-S to change Search Options.

 F1-help  F2-help  F3-browse  F4-directory  F5-options  F10-quit
```

Text Collector Figure 3. The Search Menu, with the cursor (not shown) in the "Search For" field, and corresponding help below.

you can also manually control what text goes to the output file, by "tagging" blocks of text with a keystroke. You can do this either as you review search results or simply as you read through the file. Because what gets tagged is a whole context block (chunk) at a time, if your current context block is paragraphs, you will need to change the context options if you want to tag just a sentence. This is easily done.

One key implication of this system is that if you are sorting text as part of a qualitative analysis, you have the ability to define overlapping segments. For example, you could tag the second and third sentences of a paragraph and send them to one output file, clear the tags, then tag the first through fourth sentences of the paragraph and send them to another file.

Directory Control

The Text Collector gives you a number of options for controlling the files that are taken as input for a search. You have the simple option of specifying a list of files and/or paths, including wildcards. However, The Text Collector gives you some more interesting options as well. You can examine directories and visually select the files and subdirectories you want included in your search. You can have a list of files sorted by date or name, and you can limit them by date as well. Once you have gone through a list selecting files, you can have the resulting list of files saved and used for future searches.

Other Search Options

The Text Collector has a number of nice search options. For example, you can conduct an "alpha search" in which everything other than alphanumeric characters are ignored. So, if you search for "de-emphasize," the program will also find "deemphasize" and "de emphasize" because it ignores things like spaces and hyphens. This is nice for finding words or phrases that are hyphenated, punctuated, or split between lines.

The program also supports phonetic searches (see the Glossary), but not too reliably. The program finds a lot of garbage because it ignores spaces and vowels—a problem acknowledged in the manual.

One other search option that deserves mention is the unusually flexible wildcard scheme. In addition to the DOS wildcards "*" and "?" there are separate wildcards for alphanumeric characters, lowercase letters, uppercase letters, numbers, spaces, non-ASCII characters, and ASCII characters. You can also differentiate between a single instance (with DOS wildcards, you'd use a "?") and multiple instances (with DOS wildcards, you'd use a "*") by using the lower- or uppercase of the wildcard. The wildcard scheme is laid out in The Text Collector's help screen as follows:

<a> or <A> alphanumeric character (letter, number, or under score)

<l> or <L> lowercase letter (a to z)

<u> or <U> uppercase letter (A to Z)

```
                         The Text Collector
                            Version 1.7
                   Copyright 1987 O'Neill Software

                           B. SEARCH MENU

Search For
Input Files
Output File

Input Files:
    Enter names of files you want to search through.
    Separate multiple entries with a space.
    Wildcards '*' and '?', disk drives, and path names are permitted.
        Example:  *.DOC  *.TXT  *.ASC
        Example:  A:*.*
        Example:  A: B: C: *.BAT
        Example:  C:\PATH\*.DOC
    Leave entry blank to search files from last directory reviewed.
    To search across directories:
        Set "Expand Directories" to YES (Press Ctrl-D twice).
        Include a backslash (or path) in your response:  C:\*.BAT

 F1-help  F2-help  F3-browse  F4-directory  F5-options  F10-quit
```

Text Collector Figure 4. The Search Menu with the cursor (not shown) in the "Input Files" field, and corresponding help below.

<n> or <N> number (0 to 9)

<s> or <S> space (tab, space, carriage return, linefeed)

<o> or <O> non-ASCII character < 33 or > 126 (end of word)

<x> or <X> ASCII character > 32 and < 127 (start of word)

Lowercase = single; uppercase = multiple

Can combine within brackets: <uLs>

The example at the bottom of the help listing above, <uLs>, is asking for a single uppercase letter <u> followed by any number of lowercase letters <L> followed by a space <s>. The result is any word starting with a single capitalized letter and followed with a space—in most cases, the first word of each sentence. Obviously, combinations of these wildcards allow extraordinary flexibility in defining wildcard searches.

Output

Output from searches is sent either to the screen and then to an output file or else directly to an output file, depending on the search mode you're working in. The output file can then be brought into your word processor for further work (like making tables). You can also print a file you're browsing or an output file, as we'll discuss under "Printing," below.

The program gives you some control over the format of your output. For example, you can have every chunk identified with a source tag (the name of the file it came from—more options when you print) either at the beginning or at the end of the chunk. You can specify whether and how you want the chunks in the output file sorted and whether or not you want line numbers in the output file. Finally, you can ask to have chunks separated and specify how they are separated, for example, by a blank line or a row of asterisks.

Sorting

Sorting of output can be done either automatically as part of the search or interactively while you're in browse mode. The sort options are not terribly complex. You can sort in ascending or descending alphabetical order, have case ignored or used as a sort criterion, and specify a "start byte." This last option lets you tell the program to start, say, at the tenth character in the chunks for sorting. This is useful, for example, if you are using data from a database manager, which might have control codes or field names at the beginning of the chunks, and you want to sort based on the contents of the fields, not the names.

Printing

Printing from the Text Collector is exceptionally simple and quite reliable. There is one menu for setting margins and another for options like headers, which can include a title, file name, date, and page number. There is no need to mess with drivers or printer installation. There are simple menu options to define formfeed symbols or special line-

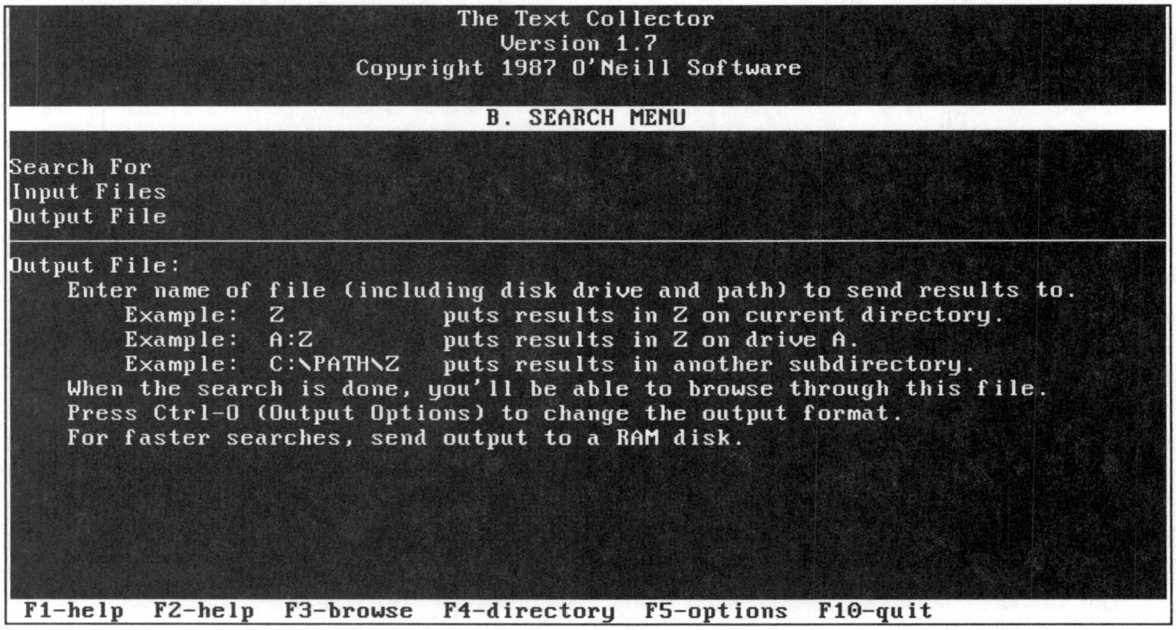

```
                        The Text Collector
                           Version 1.7
                  Copyright 1987 O'Neill Software

                          B. SEARCH MENU

Search For
Input Files
Output File

Output File:
    Enter name of file (including disk drive and path) to send results to.
        Example:  Z          puts results in Z on current directory.
        Example:  A:Z        puts results in Z on drive A.
        Example:  C:\PATH\Z  puts results in another subdirectory.
    When the search is done, you'll be able to browse through this file.
    Press Ctrl-O (Output Options) to change the output format.
    For faster searches, send output to a RAM disk.

 F1-help  F2-help  F3-browse  F4-directory  F5-options  F10-quit
```

Text Collector Figure 5. The Search Menu with the cursor (not shown) in the "Output File" field, and corresponding help below.

feed symbols for old or quirky printers. Don't let the brevity of this paragraph fool you into thinking the printing options here are lacking; they're just so simple and efficient there's not much else to say.

User Friendliness

One of the nicest things about The Text Collector is that it is easy and fun to use. The program is completely menu driven, with excellent help screens (described below) explaining almost every menu item and option on-the-fly. Most menu items can be accessed instantly with control-key shortcuts. The manual is easy to understand, and most of the options in the program are fairly simple.

If there is one weakness in terms of user friendliness, it's that the logic of the program can sometimes be hard to follow. To define a complex search (such as the example of collecting all text between the word "References" and a forced page break everywhere on the hard disk), you may need to set a number of options correctly in order to get desired results. It can sometimes be difficult to figure out what you need to do or what you did last time. Fortunately, the program allows you to store entire search requests and options configurations for reuse.

Good tech support is available from the developer, Dennis O'Neill, though you pay for the call to San Francisco. It was hard to come up with a question to ask him because everything's easy to figure out, and nothing went wrong. So we called with a question we had already answered, and a couple of queries about how to do things we pretty much knew the program couldn't do. After some phone-machine tag, he suggested that we leave questions on his machine if we missed him a second time. We did and found detailed, helpful, patient answers to all questions on the answering machine the next morning. He seems to make his calls each morning, so the whole process took a day and a half; if you leave your questions the first time, you will probably have the answers the next morning.

Help Screens

One of the particularly friendly features of the program is the option of ever-present, easily understandable help screens. Most available screens in the program are divided by a horizontal line. If you do not specify otherwise, the bottom portion of the screen always contains instructions for filling in whatever item you have placed the cursor in. For example, consider Figures 3 to 5. These show three views of the Search Menu. In Figure 3, the cursor is in the "Search For" field, and instructions for filling out that field appear below.

In Figure 4, the cursor is on "Input Files," with corresponding help, and in Figure 5, "Output File" is selected. The instructions in these help screens are almost always adequate to explain what you need to do.

Miscellaneous

It's worth mentioning that The Text Collector is probably not a program you'll use all by itself; most folks will use it in tandem with a word processor: writing, searching, collecting, summarizing, making tables, and so on. Types of projects for which it may be particularly useful include those with big databases and those with a not-too-micro emphasis in coding.

Automation

The closest thing The Text Collector has to a macro is a default file. You can save as many of these as you want. Each default file contains all the settings for the program. Once you have all the options and search criteria set the way you want, you save that setup (with a keystroke or two) into a file with the extension .DEF. Then whenever you want that setup, you retrieve that .DEF file. You can also change the start-up default file if you want.

There's also a batch mode (see "batch programs" in the Glossary) that lets you run The Text Collector either from the DOS prompt or from a DOS batch file. You can specify search terms, input and output files, or simply a .DEF file that defines all of these parameters. When you run The Text Collector in batch mode, you never see the program on the screen; it just does its work and gives you back the DOS prompt. Thus you can set up batch files to run frequently needed searches. You can also set up batch files to accomplish "recursive" sequences of searches. To use the manual's example, you could conduct a search (e.g., to select cases matching some criterion), then conduct a second search using just the files found in the first search as input, and then conduct yet another search on the output file from the second search.

Comparative Remarks

We first looked at The Text Collector in the summer of 1991. At the time, we hadn't seen the more powerful search packages and were very impressed. Coming back to it now to update the review, having explored the likes of Metamorph and Folio VIEWS, we're every bit as impressed, and maybe a little bit more so. The Text Collector does not quite have the power of a program like Metamorph, but it's much easier to use, and much more affordable, *and* it can read files in their native formats (e.g., word processing files) with no problem—something most of the big commercial packages can't do without your seeing a whole lot of garbage on the screen. While it doesn't have features like synonym searching, hypertext, or a replayable record of all your searches, it does have good support for Boolean logic, nice features like alpha searching, and—especially—on-the-fly context switching. The combination of browse mode and automatic and interactive searches makes this program, at $69, a standout.

Summary

The Text Collector is not the most powerful qualitative data analysis package on the market, but its ease of use, flexibility, and speed will make it a good choice for many users, especially those with big databases and a relatively macro approach to coding. You can be up and running in practically no time: Give yourself an hour to learn your way around and expect to be a little slow until you get the hang of it. You can use it easily in tandem with your word processor. The program will not code; it will not extract meaning for you or build outlines or paths. It will not create hypertext links. What it does is search and sort text, and it does so fast and easily.

Reference

O'Neill Software. (1987). *The Text Collector: User's manual.* San Francisco: Author.

WordCruncher, Version 4.5 for DOS

Available for DOS

Johnston & Co.
P.O. Box 6627
Bloomington, IN 47407

Phone: (812) 339-9996
Fax: (812) 339-9997

Price: $395
Faculty: $299

Hardware Requirements:
- IBM PC: AT or better recommended
- DOS 2.1 or better, preferably 3.2.
- Hard disk: 1.2MB free or 2 floppy drives
- 512K RAM, 640K recommended

Overview

WordCruncher is a complex text retrieval program, with two major parts. The first part, WCView, retrieves words, substrings, and phrases, using a wide range of search requests, and does so quickly from documents (or a collection of linked documents) as large as 4 billion characters. It will collect search hits (which it calls "references"), count frequencies and do z-scores, and prepare keyword-in-context concordances and conventional indexes.

The second part, WCIndex, works with ASCII documents you've prepared in your word processor. You insert "marker codes" that organize the text at three levels that you specify—for example: Book, Chapter, and Page; Work, Section, and Line; Interviewee, Question, and Paragraph; or even, for example, Study, Individual, and Data Fields. (WCIndex will insert these for you automatically as well, if your text is set up right—see below.) WordCruncher's metaphor for your text files is that they're "books"; a batch of books is kept on a "bookshelf." Up to 1,000 files can be put into a single "book" if you wish.

It's designed to be used together with WordPerfect (via WordPerfect Library), so you can export search hits and process them, and run macros. But it is not set up to work with other word processors as such, so you have to save your files to ASCII format. (According to the 4.5 update manual, the DOS version was to have been designed to include a special switching facility that would let you pop back and forth between WCView and whatever other task you are doing, but this feature has been abandoned.)

WordCruncher is best when you're looking for *words* and their location in large-scale, semistructured, archived documents that you're not going to code, change, or edit, such as historical documents, medical records, legal opinions, or the plays of Shakespeare. Such documents are not fully free-form, but they don't have records and fields in the usual sense. Rather, they usually have an outline structure (book, chapter and verse, and so on).

It's much more complex and harder to learn than many programs, but it's fast, and its search and output options are fuller than those in Orbis (though they're more limited than those of Metamorph). So it's a good tool if you are not especially interested in coding and want to take a content-analytic approach to a substantial amount of fixed text—counting words, seeing keywords in context, producing concordances.

WordCruncher also has some hyperlinking functions, and you can insert "bookmarks" at particular points in the text whenever you want and pop back to them by hitting a letter key you've defined; bookmarks can also be used to set the boundaries of a search within a file.

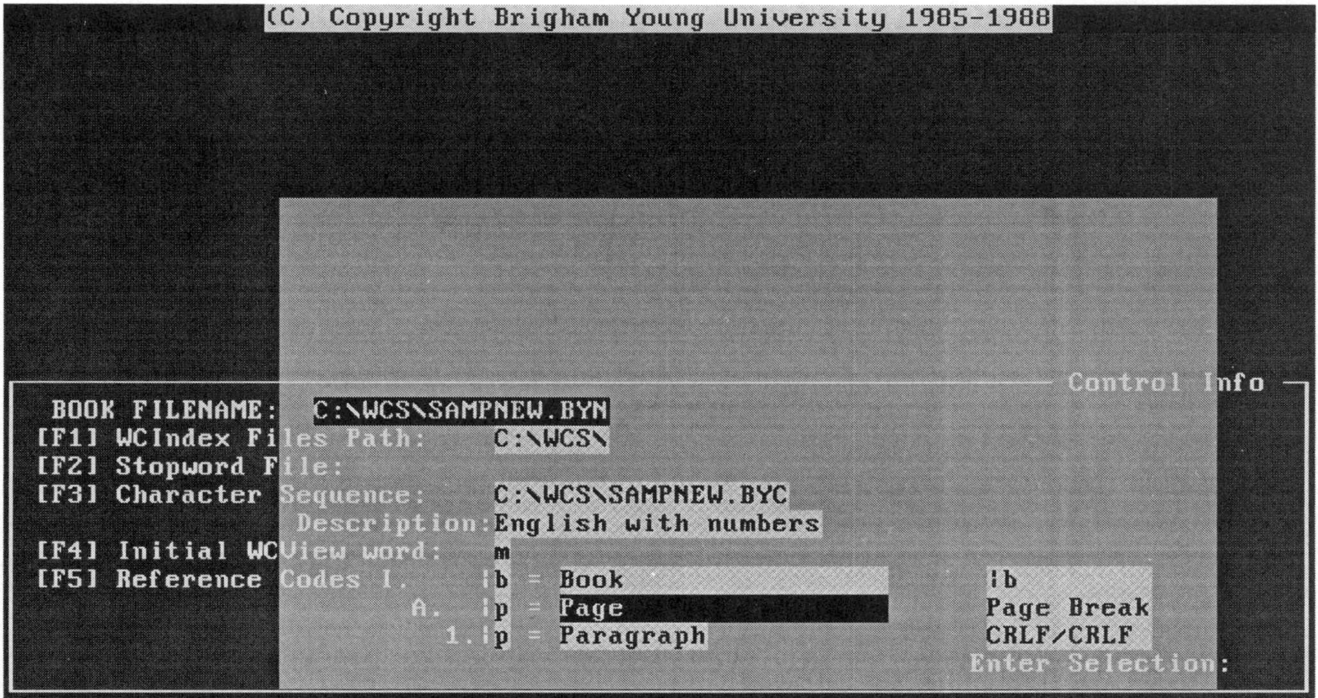

WordCruncher Figure 1. Specifying automatic marker application. In this instance, the user has indicated that the three levels to be marked are Book, Page, and Paragraph, and is about to correct the small "p" signaling "page" to a capital "P." At the right, the "¦ b" indicates the marker code for "book." The second-level marker (at the right) has been set to occur at page breaks (it could also have been one or two carriage returns). The third-level marker has been set to two carriage returns (it could also have been set at one return or at the end of each sentence).

This review is based on the DOS Version 4.5, with some brief added commentary on a beta-test copy of the Windows 5.0 version, with preliminary documentation. (As of this writing, the Windows version is only available to institutions, vendors, and resellers, who may tailor it and develop documentation for their versions. A public Windows version was expected in early 1995—see "Update," below.)

We should say in general that the program is complex and sometimes quite hard to follow and understand—more so for WCIndex than for WCView. The documentation is sometimes confusing and is written for technically oriented users (Level 3 plus). Stay with us; we'll try to be as clear as possible.

Database Structure

WordCruncher works with ASCII text files that have to be precisely formatted to indicate the three-level structure of the file (the "book"), as described in the "Overview," above. This structure can, however, be enlarged to five levels with some effort by typing in extra marker codes for levels 2 and 3.[1] It makes a separate index of all the words in each file, except for the "stopwords" you specify (a list of "nuisance words" you want to omit from searches), and then searches that index. As noted, separately indexed files can be linked into a single "book" for searching.

WordCruncher actually creates a whole range of files named with special extensions (all starting with BY for Brigham Young University, the birthplace of the program): .BYB has your basic text files; .BYX is an index of them; .BYA has abbreviations for book names; .BYC has special characters used in French, German, and Spanish; .BYD is for dictionaries, and .BYT for thesauruses, each indexed by .WCI; .BYF is frequency counts; .BYM is error messages; .BYL links files together; .BYN is for new files that need to be automatically indexed; .BYS is stopwords. In some cases, it's important for you to know and remember these file extensions, a feature that doesn't feel user friendly at all.

For small files, the disk space required for the index files is up to three times the text file size; the manual says that for a large text file (7MB) the index files might be only 3MB or so.

1. The Windows version allows for 10 different marker codes, which need not be hierarchically organized.

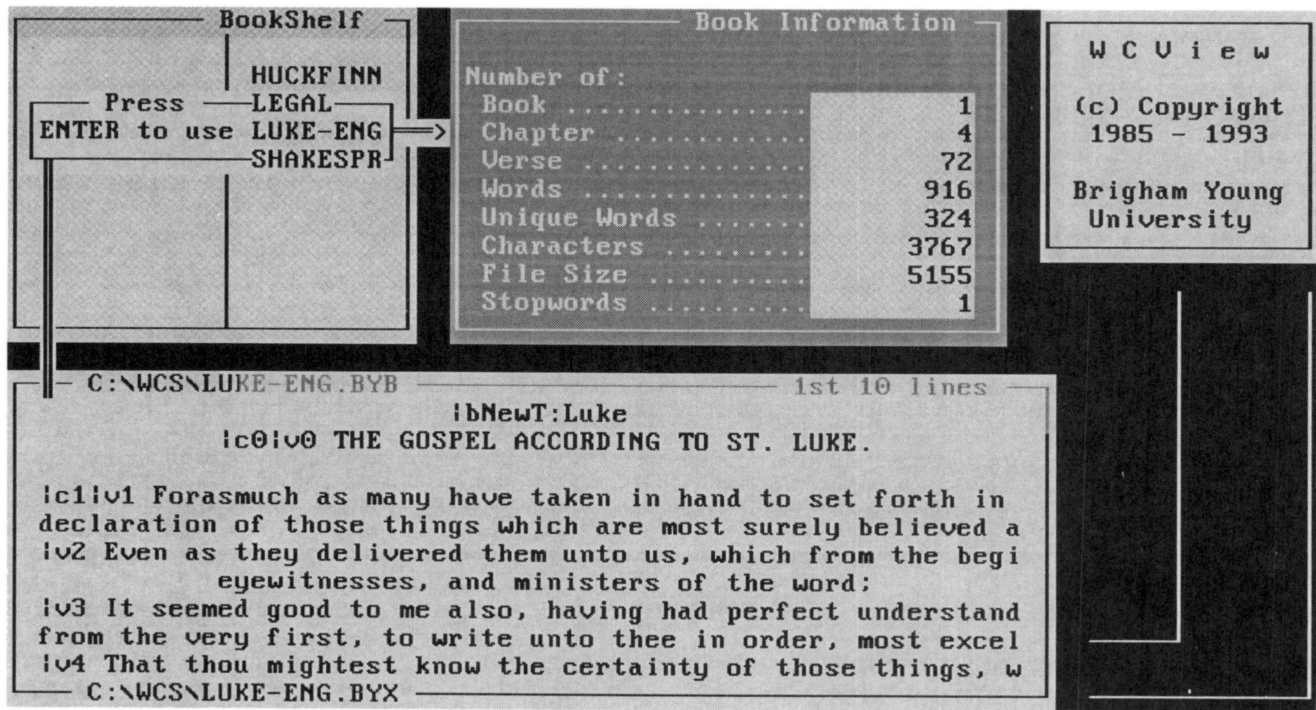

WordCruncher Figure 2. The "bookshelf." The user is preparing (top left) to select the book "Luke-Eng" from among three other titles on the shelf. The information box (top center) shows that the book has 4 chapters, 72 verses, and 916 words, of which 324 are unique. The headings in the information book change automatically if you choose another book (e.g., one with headings called "work," "section," and "line"). The number of text characters and the total file size are also given. Only one "stopword" is in force (these are words excluded from searches and can be specified as wished).

Below are displayed the first ten lines of the indexed "book." The marker "¦ b" indicates the book (abbreviated as "NewT: Luke"); the markers "¦ c0" and "¦ v0" are attached to the title (this can be used for other prefatory material). From then on, we see the markers "¦ c1¦ v1" for chapter 1, verse 1, and for subsequent verses in that chapter.

The capacity of the program is very large; there can be 1,000 "books" in a single file, each with 2,000 second-level marker codes, and each of those with 8,000 third-level marker codes. That multiplies out to 16 million third-level markers, which might be attached to paragraphs, sentences, or lines.

Data Entry

You begin with ASCII files, which are typically created in your word processor and converted to generic ASCII. Files can also be created via an optical scanner. In either case, cleaning of the text, formatting, and so on needs to be done before you proceed with indexing. Remember, these files should be ones you *don't* expect to change or revise (if you do, they will have to be reindexed).

If you want to use already marked documents, they may be commercially available, according to the developer. An example is the "Constitution Papers" (Electronic Text Corporation, 1987), which includes everything from the Magna Carta and the Mayflower Compact to the original constitutions of many states, Paine's *Common Sense,* and the Articles of Confederation. The developer will also prepare your text for a $35/hour charge.

Working on the Data

You make decisions about what you want each level of the file structure to be. Only the first level has any substance attached to it (the title of your "book"). The second and third levels are simply numbered; the second level might be a section, chapter, or page. The third level is in effect the smallest unit of your book; it might be a line, sentence, verse, or paragraph, for example. You give appropriate titles for each level.

Note that WordCruncher has no real coding facility in the usual sense. Rather, you can (tediously) enter markers using your word processor (which WordCruncher calls "ref-

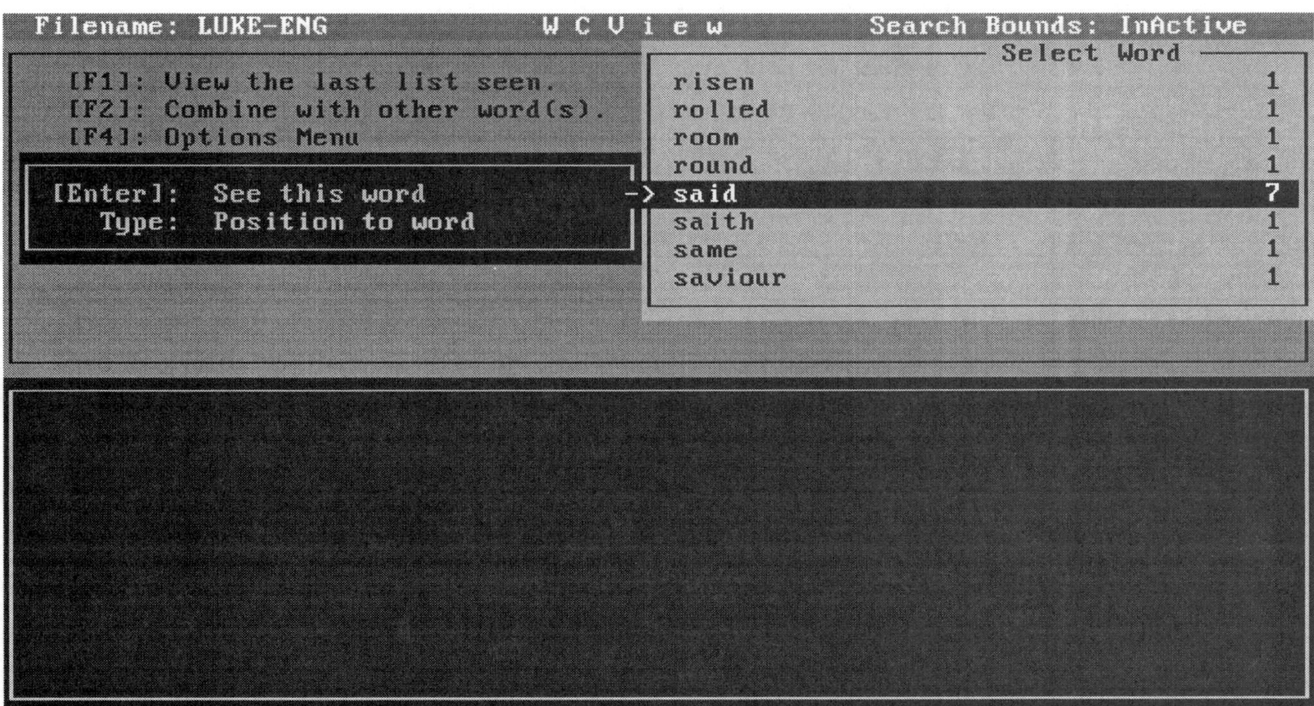

WordCruncher Figure 3. Search request for a word. The complete word list for the "book" appears at the right. It can be scrolled through, but it's quicker to simply start typing the word you want; the program jumps to it immediately (if the word has been indexed in the text). Here the word "said" has been selected. You see at the right that there are seven hits.

erence codes"), showing where each level begins. Doing this by hand, you could begin, for example, with "¦ bTwain: HuckFinn," to indicate the abbreviated name of the book you want WordCruncher to index, then insert "¦ P1" (or any relevant number) to indicate the page number, then "¦ p1," "¦ p2," and so on to indicate the beginning of each paragraph on the page. Remember that you define the meaning and labels for the levels, so they could just as well be "book," "chapter," and "verse" or "interviewee," question," and "line." If you are a Level 3 computer user, the easiest way is to write a macro to accomplish all this. The developer acknowledges that indexing has "a learning curve" but claims it to be simple "once you get the hang of it."

When you ask WCIndex to index the file you've prepared, it will spot errors (missing, erroneous, or out-of-sequence markers); you then have to exit, start your word processor, correct the .BYB file, and then start indexing again.

Fortunately, WCIndex contains a routine that will insert the second- and third-level marker codes for you automatically, working with a .BYN file that doesn't yet have the markers—assuming that your ASCII text is properly formatted. Figure 1 shows the choices you have: naming the three levels; choosing whether second-level markers will be omitted, created after every carriage return, after two carriage returns, or after a page break; and choosing whether third-level markers will be omitted, created after sentences, or after one or two carriage returns. WCIndex then indexes the .BYN file, creating a .BYB file.

But even this isn't too easy; as you find out in the tutorial, the .BYN routine will number your first paragraphs on each page "p0" unless you place a double carriage return after each page break, and if the program has indexed something you didn't want it to, you then have to edit the basic text file (.BYB file), *not* the .BYN file, and reindex it. (WordCruncher can automatically reindex files if you have edited them or added new material.)

A first-level marker code can have a label of up to 20 characters to show your book's title. The second level can have up to an 8-character label (such as Three, Sixteen, or Ques4). If you choose the "enhanced citations" option, you can extend the length of first- and second-level codes up to 78 characters, the full screen width. The program can accept up to 2,000 second-level units per "book" (i.e., per any particular first-level marker). Third-level marker codes are simply numbered consecutively from 0 up to a maximum of 65535; there can be 8,000 of them for each second-level marker. Recall that the program can accommodate up to 1,000 "books" in a single .BYB file, so you can in principle have 2 million second-level markers (e.g., "pages") and 16 million third-level markers (e.g., "paragraphs").

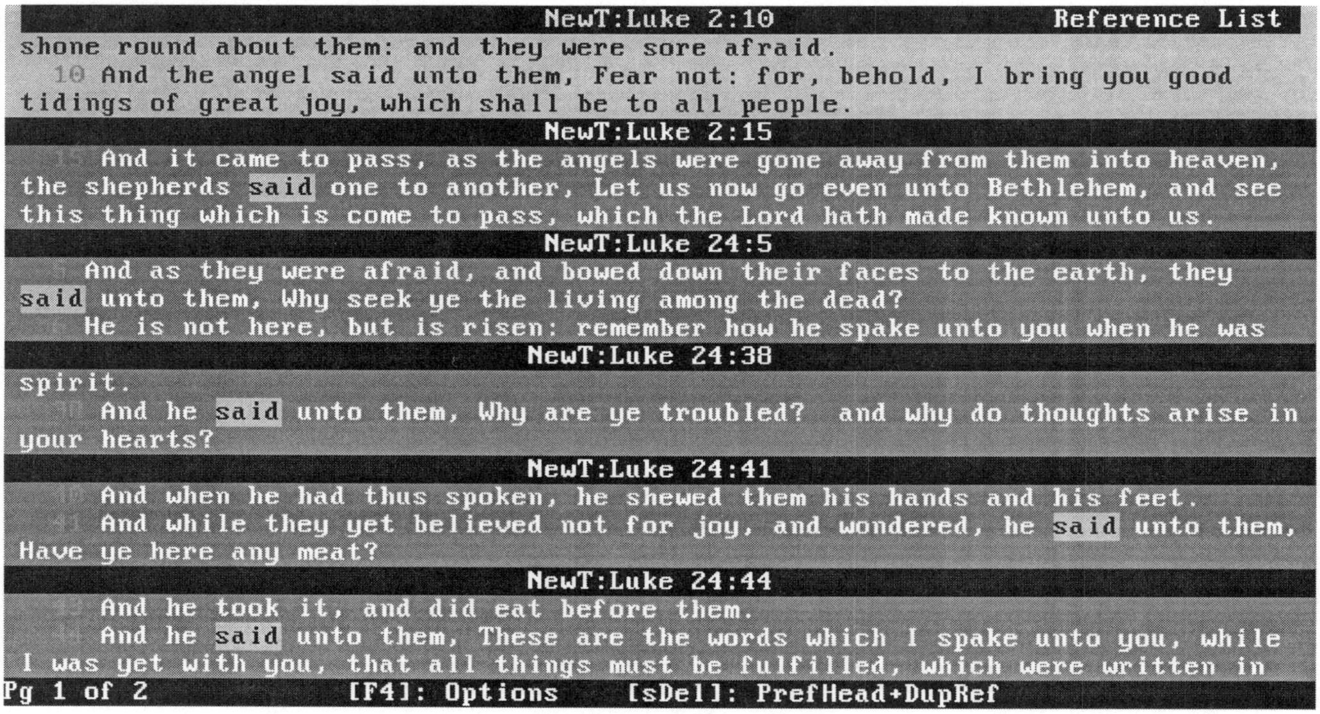

```
                        NewT:Luke 2:10                   Reference List
shone round about them: and they were sore afraid.
  10 And the angel said unto them, Fear not: for, behold, I bring you good
tidings of great joy, which shall be to all people.
                        NewT:Luke 2:15
     And it came to pass, as the angels were gone away from them into heaven,
the shepherds said one to another, Let us now go even unto Bethlehem, and see
this thing which is come to pass, which the Lord hath made known unto us.
                        NewT:Luke 24:5
    And as they were afraid, and bowed down their faces to the earth, they
said unto them, Why seek ye the living among the dead?
    He is not here, but is risen: remember how he spake unto you when he was
                       NewT:Luke 24:38
spirit.
     And he said unto them, Why are ye troubled?  and why do thoughts arise in
your hearts?
                       NewT:Luke 24:41
     And when he had thus spoken, he shewed them his hands and his feet.
     And while they yet believed not for joy, and wondered, he said unto them,
Have ye here any meat?
                       NewT:Luke 24:44
     And he took it, and did eat before them.
     And he said unto them, These are the words which I spake unto you, while
I was yet with you, that all things must be fulfilled, which were written in
Pg 1 of 2          [F4]: Options     [sDel]: PrefHead+DupRef
```

WordCruncher Figure 4. A "reference list" (collection of hits). Six of the seven hits are displayed. The search word, "said," is highlighted, and the three-line context of the first hit is highlighted in a window (any of the other hit contexts that you wish to see in the Expanded Window can be highlighted). Verse numbers are shown at the left.

Here the default context of three lines is in force. You can immediately enlarge the context size to up to 22 lines if you wish—all the hits will immediately appear in a larger context, which can be scrolled within.

Searching

Once your data are indexed, they're put on the "bookshelf" along with other "books," and you can pick one of them to search (see Figure 2). Remember that you can actually link a number of files into one larger searchable "book" if you wish. You do this by creating a list of file names to be linked, making sure the reference codes are the same across files (e.g., third-level codes are always lines) and by indexing that file. This was easily accomplished in the tutorial.

Reference Searches

Because WordCruncher files have a three-level structure, you can search for a specific reference—you see a table of contents, in effect, and you cursor to the level 1, 2, and 3 markers you want (e.g., Macbeth, act 5, scene 8). That reference will appear in the Expanded Window, where you can scroll up and down in it to preceding and following material.

Word Search and Display

Single word. First, the simplest: To find all instances of a specific word, you just begin typing it; as soon as it's recognized in the midst of an alphabetical word list or "Word Wheel" (Figure 3), you see the number of hits. If you hit Enter, you'll see what WordCruncher calls a "reference list"—namely, all the hits, each highlighted in its context.

Figure 4 shows a reference list with a very small context size of three lines for each hit (this is in effect a series of adjacent windows). You can scroll up or down from window to window (in effect, from hit to hit). The context size within each window can be immediately enlarged to up to 22 lines if you wish. You cannot scroll within the hit context, but if you go to what's called the Expanded Window by hitting Enter again, you will see the full text with the hit highlighted, and you can then scroll up and down in the text (Figure 5).

You can highlight blocks of text in the Expanded Window to be sent to a printer or file. You can also choose to print just the references (context size can be varied), or the complete third-level segment (e.g., "verses") they appear in, or the complete second-level segment (e.g., "chapter") they appear in.

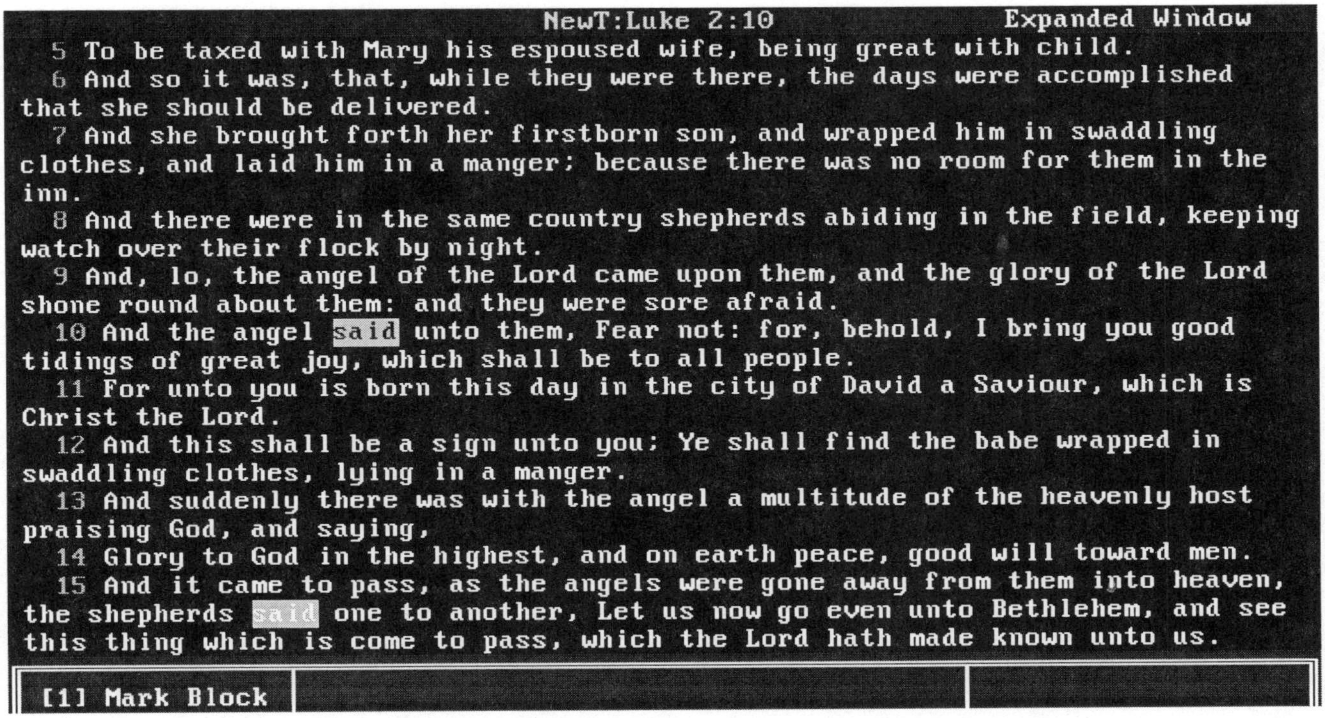

```
                              NewT:Luke 2:10              Expanded Window
  5 To be taxed with Mary his espoused wife, being great with child.
  6 And so it was, that, while they were there, the days were accomplished
that she should be delivered.
  7 And she brought forth her firstborn son, and wrapped him in swaddling
clothes, and laid him in a manger; because there was no room for them in the
inn.
  8 And there were in the same country shepherds abiding in the field, keeping
watch over their flock by night.
  9 And, lo, the angel of the Lord came upon them, and the glory of the Lord
shone round about them: and they were sore afraid.
  10 And the angel said unto them, Fear not: for, behold, I bring you good
tidings of great joy, which shall be to all people.
  11 For unto you is born this day in the city of David a Saviour, which is
Christ the Lord.
  12 And this shall be a sign unto you; Ye shall find the babe wrapped in
swaddling clothes, lying in a manger.
  13 And suddenly there was with the angel a multitude of the heavenly host
praising God, and saying,
  14 Glory to God in the highest, and on earth peace, good will toward men.
  15 And it came to pass, as the angels were gone away from them into heaven,
the shepherds said one to another, Let us now go even unto Bethlehem, and see
this thing which is come to pass, which the Lord hath made known unto us.
 [1] Mark Block
```

WordCruncher Figure 5. Expanded Window, showing a hit in full context. Here the user highlighted the first hit (verse 10 in Figure 4), hit Enter, and got this display: All the text in the book is accessible. Note that a second hit (in verse 15) is also highlighted, but in a different color, showing that it's not part of the originally requested hit. You can jump to each succeeding (or preceding) hit if you choose. In this display, you can also mark any block of text you like for immediate printing or filing.

WordCruncher will delete duplicate references (which might appear if the search words occur twice in the same segment), along with prefatory material not marked by reference codes, if you hit <Shift Del>. There's also a useful facility: You create a "selected" reference list as you look at the reference display. You can delete highlighted references, add highlighted references to the selected list, or simply ask for a specified number of references after a highlighted reference. You can step out of the list-making, do a search for new words, and add references from that search to the list, which can be printed with the options noted above.

Anything you retrieve comes with "citations"—source tags, in effect, which are the three levels of marker codes—say, book, chapter, and verse in the Gospel of Luke example.

Other word search modes. You use a wildcard * to ask for prefixes (thus "over*" will get you "overbearing," "overloaded," "oversight," and so on) or suffixes (thus "*ing" gets you participles) or for other substrings. You can also request an exact phrase, such as "in my opinion." You can also specify a list of all the words you want and find all their occurrences (inclusive OR); such lists can be saved. These could be related words (e.g., synonyms, if you wish).

More thoroughly, you can use a "thesaurus" of synonyms to do searches for words—all or some of the synonyms will be found, as you wish. A sample thesaurus is enclosed with the program to show you how it works—but you have to create your thesaurus yourself, in relation to a particular book or bookshelf.

Combined word lists. The "combined list" facility lets you specify *two* lists, each with one or more words/phrases. You select Boolean operators AND, OR, or NOT to show how you want to relate the word(s) in list 1 to those in list 2. You also can choose or ignore the sequence of the words if you wish, as well as specifying their proximity (within the same window, same segment—such as chapter or verse—or within any number of characters you specify). Figure 6 gives an example of the search specification. This lets you find, for example, what WordCruncher calls "partial phrases": two or more words occurring in sequence near each other.

Figure 7 shows the immediate counts of the hits resulting from the search in Figure 6, and Figure 8 shows the "reference list" display of hits.

When you get such a reference list, as noted earlier, if you ask for "options," a box pops up (Figure 8) that lets

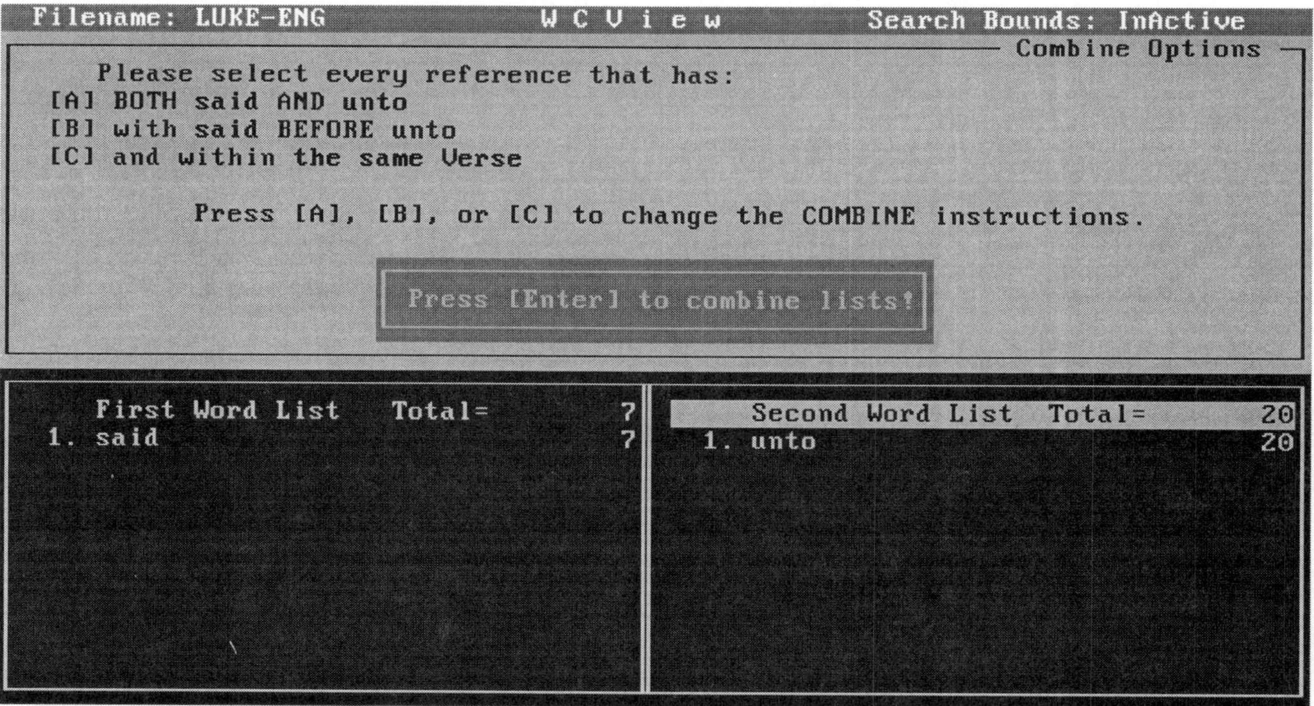

WordCruncher Figure 6. A "combined" search request for the LUKE-ENG book. The user has selected the word "said" for one list and the word "unto" in a second list. (More words could have been included in each list.) The A, B, and C keys have been used to specify a search request, as indicated.

(The A key cycles between AND, NOT, and OR; the B key cycles between "before," "after," and "either"; the C key cycles between "verse," "chapter," and any number of characters you like.) The C key choices will naturally vary according to how you have named levels 2 and 3 when you set up the data file.

you delete duplicate references (these seem to be inevitable), or a range of other undesired references, before you send results to file or printer. The basic .BYB file and its associated indexed .BYX file do not change.

You can also ask for frequency distributions (as in Figure 9). WordCruncher will also compute standardized z-scores for word frequencies, will compute "expected" word frequencies based on their appearance in the entire file, and will tell you how far the obtained frequency in a particular chapter or other search range differs from that.

A serious weakness is that WordCruncher does not make a log of your search requests, to which you could return to repeat or refine a search. Each search is simply produced; you have to note or remember what you were looking for. (You can get back to the immediately preceding screen if you want.) Of course, you can save any search result to disk, or print it, but there still is no log.

WordCruncher's searches are very fast. Using a large book, the "Constitution Papers" (Electronic Text Corporation, 1987), size 2MB, containing 44 historical documents on a 386 (33MHz) machine, single-word searches, multiple-word OR searches, and complex Boolean requests were all accomplished in under a half second, even when the number of hits was over 1,500. A concordance in index form for 1,392 references to "liberty" or "constitution" was created in about 20 seconds; it occupied 45 pages (58K).

Other Search Features

Bookmarks. A bookmark lets you jump directly to it from anywhere in the text file. To place a bookmark from the Expanded Window, you pop to the bookmarks display. You can then set bookmarks either at a particular marker (such as Chapter 6, section 2) or at a particular word; you assign the bookmark to a letter key, then return to that point in the text at any time you want. You see a list of bookmarks—across all books in the current bookshelf—with citations (chapter, verse, and so on) but *you* have to remember the significance of the bookmark—why you put it there and gave it that particular letter. (You do not see an icon where the bookmark was placed.) Bookmarks can be added, de-

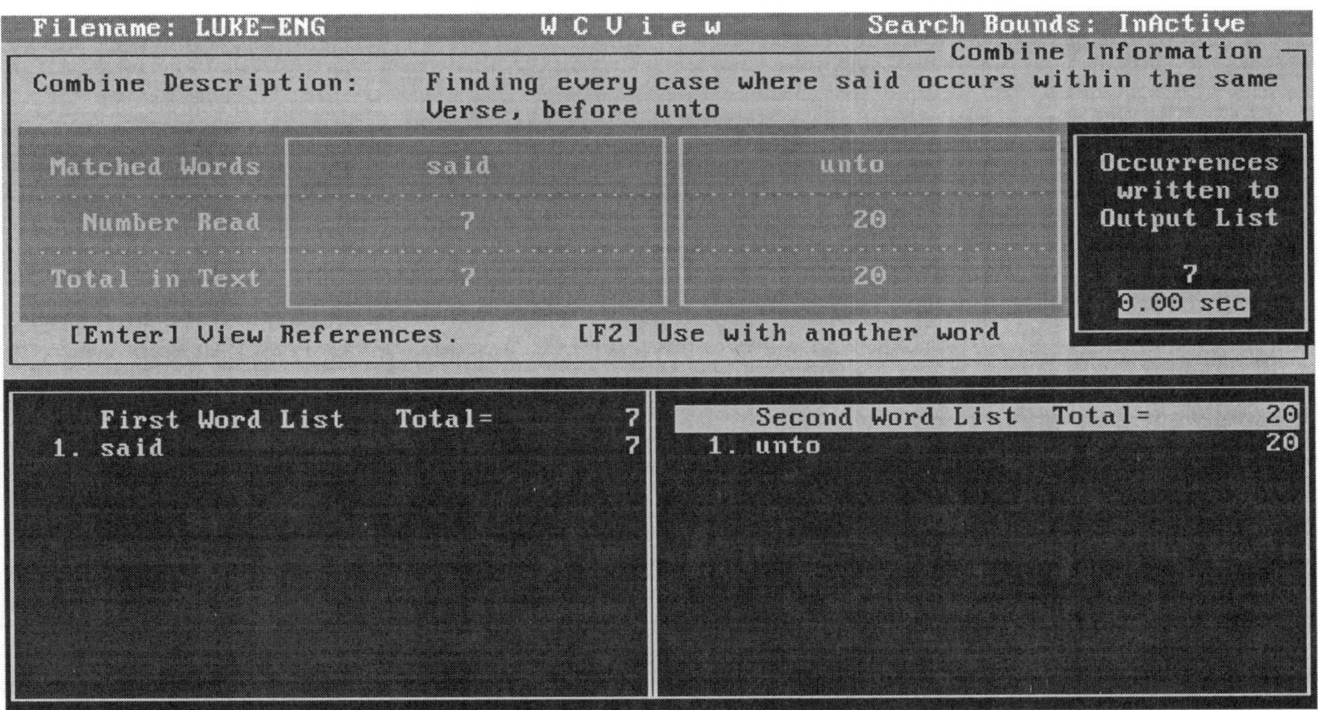

WordCruncher Figure 7. Output for a "combined" request—the quantitative results of the search specified in Figure 6. Word frequencies for each search word, and for the "combined" search, are shown.

leted, or moved to different keys at any time. Each book, given our alphabet, can accommodate 26 bookmarks.

You can also use bookmarks to set "search bounds"—the beginning and end of a search range (e.g., the complete document, which you set by pressing <Home> and <End>) or only Chapters 6 and 7, or only part of a chapter (which you set by typing the letters of a beginning and ending bookmark). Then when you do a search, it will be restricted to the text within that range. The documentation isn't clear, but it appears that only one such set of bounds can be applied at a time in a book (i.e., there can't be multiple search ranges). Search bounds are a simple way to segment your data; they are saved to disk but can be turned on or off during a search. Search bounds remain even if you delete bookmarks, but they can be deleted or revised.

Hyperlinking. There is also a hyperlinking feature, but it's difficult to figure out how to do it from the upgrade summary (Johnston & Co., 1991-1992). You must first define several control characters as delimiters that define the "start" or "stop" of indexing operations, so the hyperlink icon itself can be excluded from indexing. (The "character sequence" screen in WCIndex had no help on how to do this.) Then you manually insert the control characters in the .BYB file *before* indexing (or reindexing, presumably); the documentation shows some examples of how it would look. There is apparently no facility that lets you use a hot-key or other device for inserting hyperlinks.[2] Such links can be made from any point in your text—but only to *marker codes,* not to specific words. After the file is indexed, the control characters show up as icons; you can jump to the linked marker with <Alt-F1>. The upgrade summary says that hyperlinks can also be made to a graphic or made to an external task, but doesn't explain the latter. All in all, this is decidedly user unfriendly, in sharp contrast to the simplicity of hyperlinking in most other programs—and indeed in the Windows version of WordCruncher, as we'll see.

The upgrade summary describes features it calls "word-based hyperlinking" within the Expanded Window display, where you are viewing the whole text; you can position on a word, then with <Control-left arrow> you jump to the Word Wheel (the name for the list of all words) or with <Control-right arrow> directly to a reference list for that word. You can also "jump" from hit to hit with <Control-PgDn> or <Control-PgUp>. These features are very convenient but hardly "hyperlinking" in the usual sense; you're just starting a new search and then scrolling through hits.

2. The Windows version naturally has an easier, more usable hyperlinking facility.

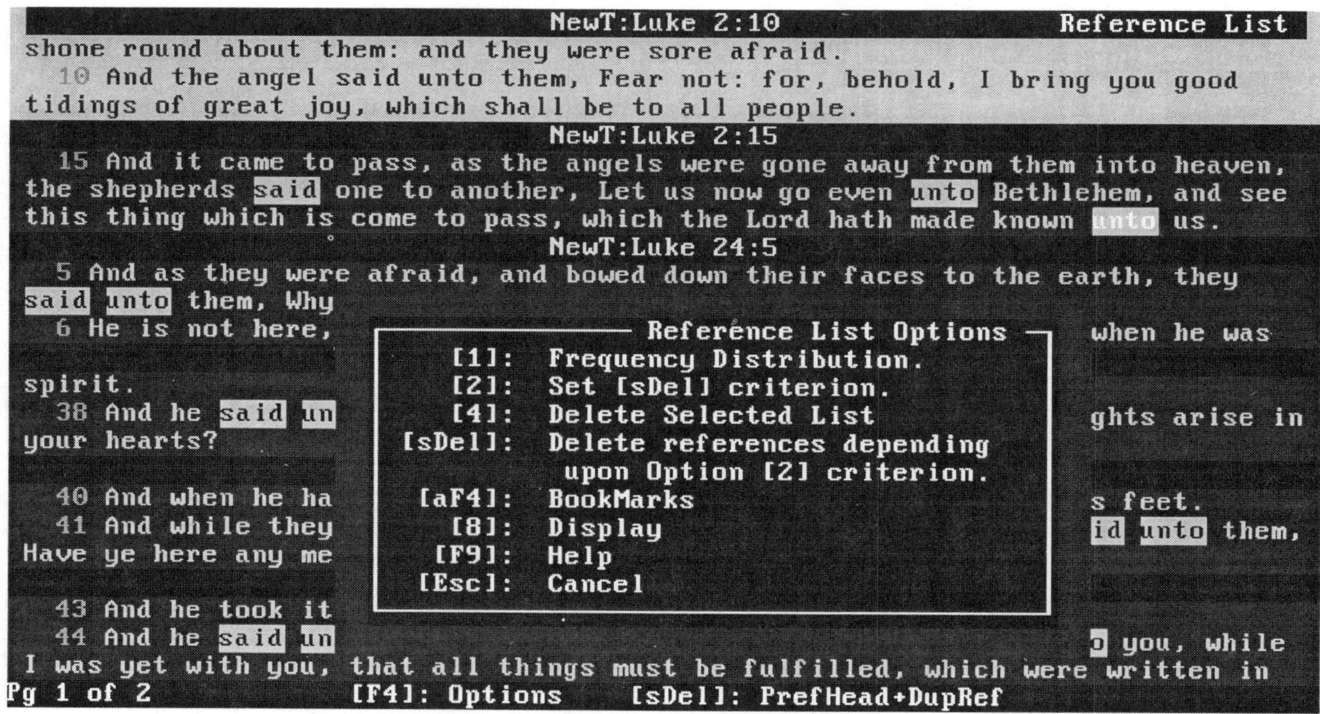

WordCruncher Figure 8. Display of search hits, with options window. The text results of the combined request from Figure 6 appear in the background, with the words "said" and "unto" highlighted when they appear in the proper sequence and within the specified distance. An "options" window has been popped up; the user can now request frequencies or delete some of the hits ("references")—for example, those that are repetitive or meet some other criterion (such as only those from, say, Chapter 2). "Bookmarks" can also be set to specify a range for another search within the text, or simply to enable you to return to a specified point in the text later.

Concordances. Finally, WordCruncher will produce KWIC (keyword in context) concordances. That is, it will collect and show you each occurrence of a word you're searching for, in the line where it occurs (or in up to a 100-character context); you also see the citation (page, paragraph, and so on). In the display, the word can be abbreviated to a first initial if you wish; if you then restrict the character context to, say, three characters, you'll just get a list of citations, each with the initial. You can also just get the word and a list of citations. You can also get a conventional index of words in the text and their line or page numbers. But if you select a list of words shorter than the list of all words, it does not alphabetize them for you—you have to do that.

Your search request for a concordance or index can be a list of some or all words in the text or in a specified block of text. Within the concordance facility, you can only make an OR list of words. But for fancier list-making, you can use all the operators regularly used for searching to create your word list (wildcards, substrings, phrases, location within same paragraph, and so on) and save it in an ASCII file. Then you call up that file and use it to create the concordance or index.

In short, WordCruncher lets you find specific material from a large database organized in its three-level format and will do a moderate amount of content-analytic counting for you. It was originally built to support textual and literary analysis but could be used as well for any database that you aren't coding or revising, but just need to find and count things in. (As with Orbis, you could, of course, insert codes, marking them with some special character such as @ or #, but that workaround seems even more difficult here because of the lack of easy, integrated connection to your word processor—unless you use Word Perfect. The Windows version does make linkage to your word processor easy.) However, remember that if you do a code-insertion workaround, you'll have to reindex the database each time you insert new codes—a serious limitation.

Output

It's fairly easy to look at output on screen, then send it to printer or file. A useful feature is that you can type in a comment to serve as a header for the output. However, the DOS Version 4.5 is set up to work with only three printers

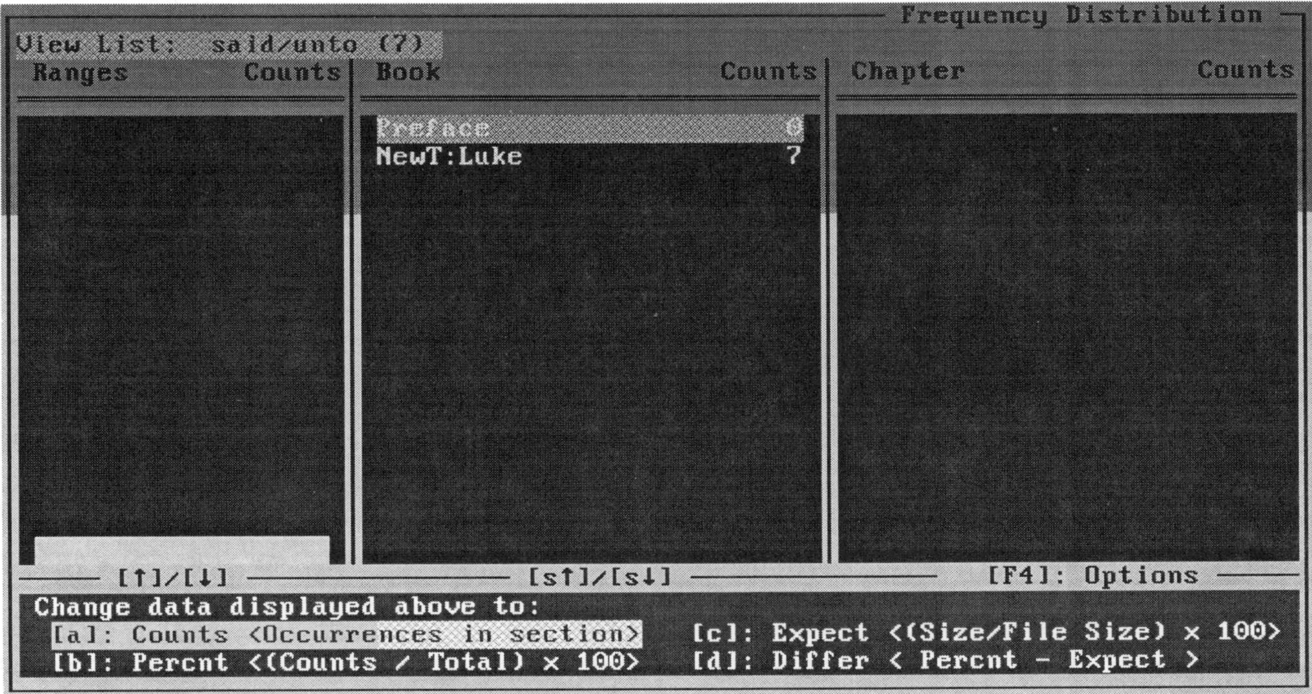

WordCruncher Figure 9. Frequency output. The frequency count of the "said"-"unto" combined request, is here shown as 7. At the bottom, the display can be immediately changed to show the results as percentages, or to compute "expected" percentages based on the hit's occurrence across the entire file, or to compare expected versus actual percentages in the section of the file being searched. No boundaries for "search ranges" have been set, so that column is blank; no chapter counts have been requested either.

(NEC 2200 Pinwriter, HP Laser Jet Plus, and Epson Graphics); if you have any other printer and want highlighting to show up as bold or italicized, you have to enter specific commands for your printer, a task that's daunting even with your printer manual in hand.

User Friendliness

The manuals (Electronic Text Corporation, 1989a, 1989b) are quite thorough but quite complex and not too friendly. They also have errors; their indexes are incomplete and faulty. (For example, a number of features—thesaurus, tunes, concordance—have no entry, and the "overview of features" at the beginning of the WCView manual—Electronic Text Corporation, 1989b—has many misnumbered page references. The 4.5 upgrade summary, 1991-1992, alludes to a nonexistent facility for switching between WCView and other applications.)

The newer tutorial (Johnston & Co., 1993) is pretty straightforward; it took a Level 3 person about 4 hours to go through an introduction to the two major parts of the program, WCView and WCIndex. The process was hampered by missing pages. We suspect, however, that real fluency with the program would not come easily or quickly; the older tutorial in the manuals (Electronic Text Corporation, 1989a, 1989b) looks more difficult. The developer is optimistic and cited an instance of a Level 2 person's learning the program in a week, with a half dozen support calls.

Help screens are reasonably clear but are not always available in the midst of routines. Most error messages are carefully explained in the manual, but some errors ask you to call customer support.

Tech support is provided via phone, with practical, specific help each time a call was placed, though the developer was concentrating on finalizing the Windows version and didn't always get back promptly. Happily, the rather stern pay-for-technical-support setup described in the manuals is no longer in place.

Miscellaneous

You can customize colors for the different specific portions of the screen display. A basic keyboard template for use of the function keys is provided, but you can reassign function keys and combinations as you wish. The expanded view can also be customized (e.g., each sentence or each phrase can begin on a new line if you wish, and marker codes can be shown or suppressed).

WordCruncher also contains "tunes" that you can assign to specific displays or to error messages; these might help a visually impaired user.

There is a provision for creating "dictionaries," which are simply lists of words in your text, with accompanying definitions, which you yourself create and then index with WCIndex (a sample is included). If a dictionary has been set up, you can pop to it from words highlighted in a search, from the last word in a search list, or from the word under your cursor in the Expanded Window display. A dictionary might be useful, for example, when the multiple users in a research team include some members less experienced with the content. It could also be used for code definitions in the usual sense (but remember that doing coding at all with WordCruncher means a difficult workaround). (See also the provision for "thesauruses" described earlier.)

Appendix E of the WCView manual provides actual examples of how WordCruncher can be customized for purposes ranging from a standard records-and-fields database (a workaround that isn't too useful) to a study of amino acid sequences in proteins and the sections of a policy handbook. They were produced by the developer, who naturally understands how to tune WordCruncher to the needs of a specific project, but for most users the effort may be too great.

Note that if you try to run the DOS version as a DOS application under Windows, you'll have problems; some of the commands (e.g., Alt-spacebar) immediately kick you out into Windows. You'll have to correct this by setting up a .PIF file (see your Windows manual) and disabling the Windows key combinations that WordCruncher uses.

WordCruncher can also be customized to read special characters in German, Spanish, and French. The Windows version is said to change the language of menus to any of these if you wish, and also includes Hebrew.

Differences Between Versions

The Windows version—soon available to the general public—looks superior to the DOS 4.5 version in most (but not all) respects, judging from the beta-test copy we saw.

The basic structure (the indexing program and the viewing program) is the same, but the user interface is much more friendly, using familiar Windows features. The help screens are better (they are actually set up on-line as a book, with hyperlink icons, so you can reference them easily). The Windows version also makes it easy for you to shift back and forth between WordCruncher and your word processor, whether or not it's WordPerfect—though you'd better have plenty of memory (with 4MB; and running a word processor, XyWrite 4.0, memory ran out several times). Note: You also need a fast machine (386 or 486) and 10-15MB free on your hard disk (beyond Windows).

Unfortunately, there is no provision for automatically doing the tedious job of entering index markers in a file (which the DOS version does have); you still have to put all your markers in your ASCII file by hand and include hyperlinks you want to make (see below). Then you call up a "template" file that you've prepared. You can use an existing template from another file, or you create one using a dialog box; it lets you specify the meaning of your various reference codes and how citations will be shown. This template shows WCIndex how to index the file. With the ASCII file and the template ready, you use a dialog box to "convert" the file to the .ETB format required by the program, then WCIndex indexes the file for you, producing an .ETX file that has the index, book names, and a character list. (The documentation says that automatic marker entry from some word processor files may be implemented in the future.)

In the Windows version, you can use ten levels of indexing rather than the DOS version's three, and they do not need to be hierarchically related (e.g., you could index a chapter in a multiauthored book by a specific author's name).

Searching is easy: You can click directly on words in the text to get all the references. There is a dialog box, the Search Manager, for creating Boolean expressions more easily than in the DOS version. It comes on screen at the same time as the Word Wheel (the quickly accessible list of all words in the text)—see Figure 10. You can also search in a "Table of Contents" mode to find, for example, the text in Chapter 2, page 19. However, the Windows version does not include KWIC (keyword in context) searches and won't produce concordances.

As you do successive searches, each appears in a new window (which is itself a set of smaller windows, as in the DOS version), and the windows cumulate on screen; you can rearrange them in a number of convenient ways (Figure 11), bring one you want up to the top, and so on.

The Windows version, happily, also makes a log, showing the names of all the screens you have looked at (e.g., main menu, a specific book, a section of a book, or the help screen). Clicking on any of these general headings brings you back to where you were. However, the log gives no date or other precise information about what you were doing at that point.

The frequency distribution options are about the same as in the DOS version, though the Windows version does not do z-scores.

Hyperlinking is done through an editing window; when you put the cursor on a reference marker and choose "Add Glyph," WordCruncher starts up a second copy of the book you are working in, in another window. In that window, you position the cursor on the *destination* of the link, then click

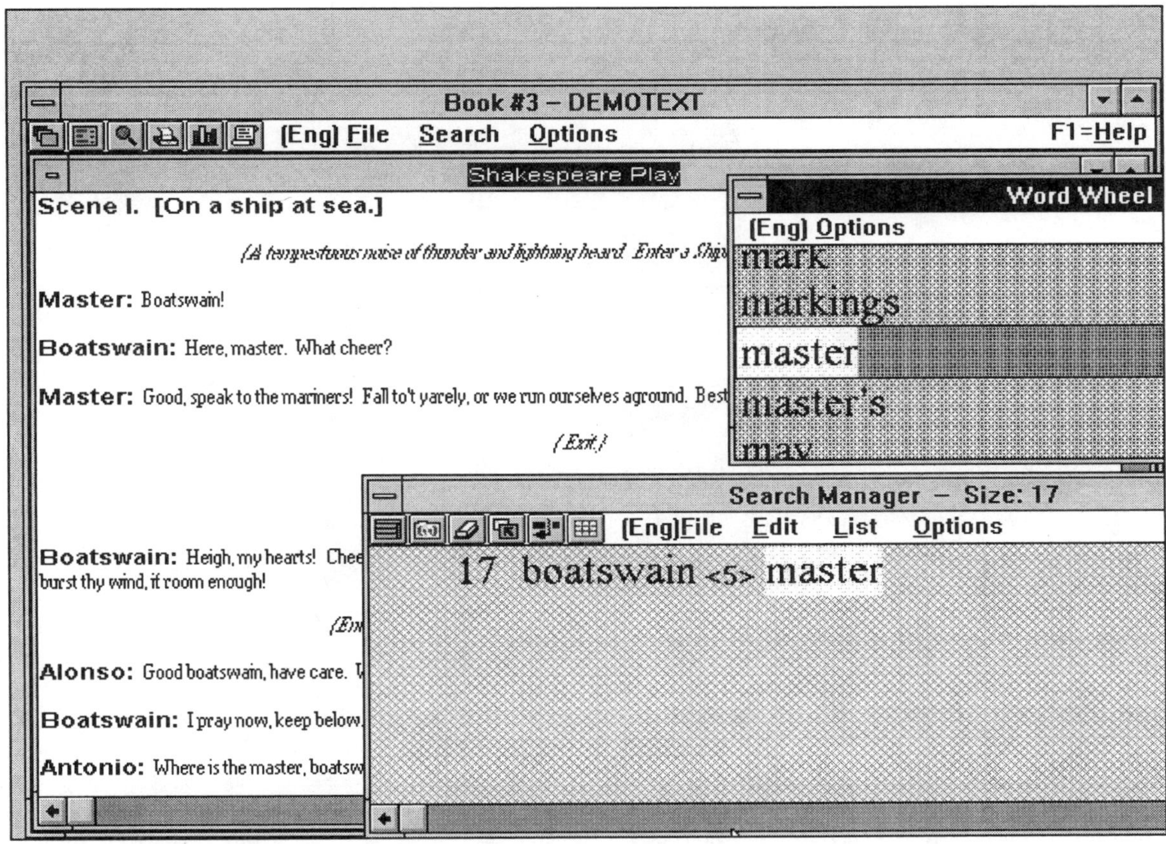

WordCruncher Figure 10. How the Windows version does searches. The Word Wheel pops up along with the Search Manager; the latter shows that there are 17 instances of the words "boatswain" and "master," within five words of each other, without regard to sequence of the words (shown by the < > symbol). The full expanded text appears in the background; the search terms are highlighted (not visible in this display).

while Control is held down. That inserts a glyph (a character or symbol used as an icon), which appears immediately in the original text. (This process is not described clearly and required technical help from the developer.)

Adding or deleting hyperlink glyphs does not change the text indexing. You can also make hyperlinks to external texts or to other Windows programs. Glyphs can also be used to insert bookmarks, or "user notes" (in effect, annotations). In the future, linking to off-line audio or video material is contemplated. Hyperlinks can be made between text and graphics files; just as a text link goes to a specific place in text, you can define a specific "hot spot" in the graphic image, to which you'll pop when you click on the hyperlink glyph. There's also a graphics editor for working on images, but it lacks a facility for creating .ETG files, the indexed file including graphic images. (See "Update," below.)

The editing window also lets you edit your text if you wish. However, the beta-test version we saw did not have an associated reindexing feature implemented (a fairly crucial feature if you want to be able to edit your files).

There is an interesting facility for linking two files synchronously (e.g., an English and a Spanish version of the same text); they will scroll in parallel.

The Windows version documentation (Brigham Young University, 1993a, 1993b) is often technical and unfriendly, because it's aimed at vendors and resellers, some of whom are in turn preparing the final manual. At several points it doesn't correspond with what you see on screen (e.g., how you request frequency distributions), and the indexes are poor.

On balance, if you use Windows or expect to, when the automatic indexing and reindexing features in the Windows version are implemented, it will be a better bet than the DOS 4.5 version. However, features such as automated file preparation, KWIC searches, and z-scores are missing in the Windows version.

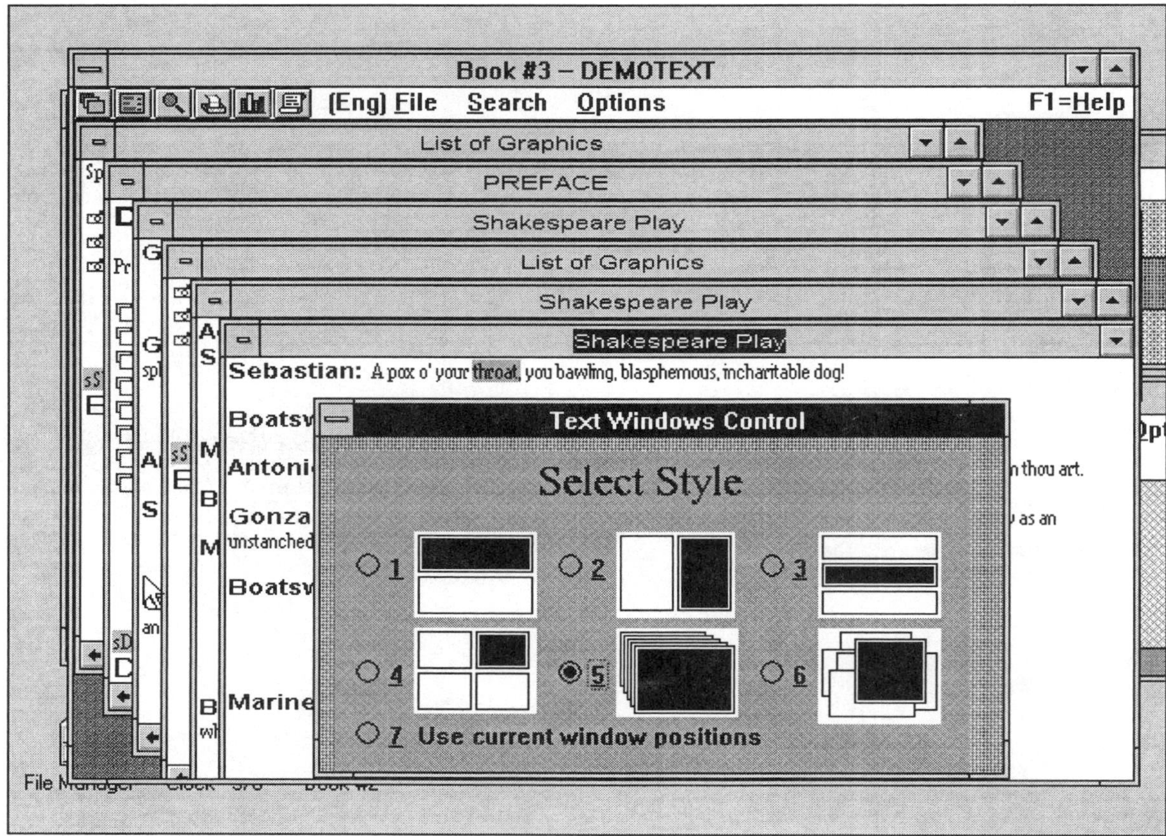

WordCruncher Figure 11. A cascade (sequence) of searches (Windows version) showing the stack of prior windows in the background, and the choices offered for rearranging the windows in the Text Windows Control box.

Update

If you are interested in WordCruncher for Windows, you'll have to wait until a firm, well-documented Windows Version 5.0 is publicly available. It was expected in January of 1995—but then it has been under development since 1990, so expect it when you see it. According to the developer, it will have the ability to search within specific document sections (such as Question 8 of an interview) and a "co-location" feature that will count words appearing within a set distance of a search term (said to be useful in finding related words and concepts). A new graphics editor with .ETG facility was ready in the fall of 1994.

Comparative Remarks

WordCruncher's elaborate text preparation and reindexing features make it harder to use than text retrievers like Orbis or Sonar Professional. Folio VIEWS is much more flexible and friendly and has stronger searching and hyperlinking facilities. WordCruncher's search capabilities are more limited than those of Metamorph, ZyINDEX, or Sonar Professional.

On the other hand, if you want to do content-analytic work with big, archived semistructured databases and—even better—can find already prepared ones, WordCruncher's content-analytic strengths may make it a reasonable choice for you.

Summary

WordCruncher is a rather complex program for retrieving text from a large, relatively permanent database, organized in a three-level outline format and performing content-analytic functions (frequency counts, z-scores, KWIC concordances, book indexes). It won't help you with coding, and it has no real theory-building capabilities, but if you are essentially working in archived data, its retrieval speed is good. The DOS version is considerably harder to learn and use than the Windows version, which, however, lacks some useful features (automatic indexing, z-scores, KWIC searches). The forthcoming Windows version was expected to be publicly available in early 1995.

References

Brigham Young University. (1993a, October 9). *System documentation, WordCruncher for Windows (evaluation copy): WCView for Windows*. Provo, UT: Author.

Brigham Young University. (1993b, August 19). *System documentation for WordCruncher for Windows: WCIndex for Windows*. Provo, UT: Author.

Electronic Text Corporation. (1987). *The Constitution Papers* (WordCruncher Bookshelf Series, Bicentennial Edition 1787-1987, 10 disks). Provo, UT: Author.

Electronic Text Corporation. (1989a). *WordCruncher: WCIndex Retrieval Software* (version 4.30). Provo, UT: Author.

Electronic Text Corporation. (1989b). *WordCruncher: WCView Text Retrieval Software* (version 4.30). Provo, UT: Author.

Johnston & Co. (1991-1992). *WordCruncher 4.5: Upgrade summary and reference guide*. American Fork, UT: Author.

Johnston & Co. (1993). *WordCruncher: Getting started*. American Fork, UT: Author.

ZyINDEX for Windows 5.14

Available for Windows

ZyLAB Division
ZyCO International, Inc.
19650 Club House Road, Suite 106
Gaithersburg, MD 20879

Phone: (301) 590-2760
(800) 544-6339
Fax: (301) 590-0903

Price: $395

Hardware Requirements:
- IBM PC, PS/2, or compatible
- High density diskette drive (3.5 in. or 5.25 in.)
- Hard drive or network drive
- DOS 3.1 or higher
- Windows 3.0 or higher

Overview

This is a text search program (and a strong one) that works by building indexes of your documents, and it has a few useful bells and whistles attached. ZyINDEX actually consists of two programs, ZyBUILD and ZyFIND. You use ZyBUILD to prepare an index of the files you want to be able to search, and ZyFIND to search them and view your hits in full or restricted context. You can search using Boolean and/or set logic, synonyms, filenames and dates, numeric operators (<, >, =, and so on), fields (which you define), proximity, and sequence. You can combine any of these operations in a single search. You can also create hypertext links and add pop-up annotations (4K) for your text. One unusual advantage is that you can index and search files not only from a wide variety of word processors but from the database programs dBASE III, IV, and FoxPro, the spreadsheets Microsoft Excel and Lotus 1-2-3, and PKZIP compressed files. You can also add graphics files to your indexes; they can be searched by filenames and dates or by the text in any notes you attach. Another unusual feature is that you can "archive" older versions of your files, so that if a document has been revised five times, a search will be able to turn up text even if it only existed in, say, the third revision. Finally, whenever you are viewing a retrieved document, you can click a button to "launch" the document, opening it up in its native program—whether that is a word processor, spreadsheet, database manager, or graphics package—to permit you to edit, print, or query it.

Despite its search power, the program is somewhat disappointing. The interface is unpleasant, the documentation is *very* hard to pull information from, some operations are quite slow, and while it's supposed to be a file "viewer," which usually means you see things the way they would appear in their native programs, everything appears in the same ugly system font and with formatting lost. User friendliness is generally low; the program can be difficult to learn your way around, and the various supports (manual, online help) are weak. Also, output options are somewhat restricted and clumsy (e.g., it takes a lot of steps every time you want to send a chunk of text to an output file). If one of the program's unique features—like searching database and spreadsheet files in native format, keeping an archive of earlier versions of a document, or launching applications—is essential for your work, this may well be the program for you. Otherwise, if you want a powerful text searching program, you're probably better off with The Text Collector,

Folio VIEWS, or Metamorph. We'll draw specific comparisons in the "Comparative Remarks" section, below.

Database Structure

Your data are in files on your hard disk. Using the ZyBUILD program, you build indexes of the files you want to be able to search. You can leave the actual data files in any directory(ies) you want. The multiple files that are created for each index are kept in subdirectories of the ZyINDEX program directory, with each index in its own directory.

You can build indexes of very large collections of documents: up to 20 gigabytes (that is, 20,000 megabytes) of ASCII text per index. Individual files can be as large as you want, up to the DOS limit of 4 gigabytes. Each index can index 50 million files.

During the build process, ZyBUILD needs a lot of disk space, and it's very complicated to figure out how much. You need to have about 1.25 times as much "free space" as the largest file you're going to index, *plus* space for the dictionary file (which holds a list of all the unique words for the index you're building), which could get big and is constantly changing as the index is built. It becomes extremely difficult to make a meaningful estimate. Make sure you have plenty of space. One tech support representative recommended having at least 10MB of "elbow room."

And, once the index is built, it takes up about 40% as much space as the indexed files for small (10-50MB) indexes, going down to about 25% as much space as the indexed files for large (more than 300MB) indexes.

Indexes can be used as a way of grouping files. Multiple indexes (up to eight) can be searched at once, and adding and removing indexes from the current list is easy and quick.

You can define fields for the files in a particular index (or fields can be shared across indexes). To define a field, you specify a character string (usually a word or phrase) to signal the beginning of the field, and one to signal the end of it. If you were searching a database file (or any file with field names marking the beginning of each field of data), you could use field names as the start and end markers (fieldname1 starts field1, and fieldname2 ends it). But you could also define larger ranges of text as fields. So, for example, in searching the file containing this review, you might use the string "Database Structure" to start a field and the string "Data Entry" to end it. The resulting field would then be the entire text of the current Database Structure section. You could then search for occurrences of a word within this field.

If your data are arranged in columns, for example, in a text matrix, you can use column positions as another way to specify fields. You can actually define three (and only three) columns of data. When building an index, you specify where your data columns begin and end using column position on the page. For example, the first character (letter, number, or space) on a line is in column 1, the second in column 2, and so on. You give ZyBUILD column positions for the start (CL1) and end (CL2) of one column of data. This actually defines three columns: from the beginning of the line to CL1, from CL1 to CL2, and from CL2 to the end of the line. The space on each line in each of these three columns can be treated as a field.

You do not "chunk" your data in ZyINDEX. Search context (the range within which two terms must coexist to be found with an AND statement) is specified by you as part of your search request, as described under "Searching," below. Your choices include the file (the default), page, paragraph, sentence, line, field, and columns.

Data Entry

You neither input data directly nor import it into ZyINDEX. As explained above, your data are in files you've created with your word processor, spreadsheet, database manager, or graphics package. To make these files available for ZyINDEX, you create indexes for them using ZyBUILD (see Figure 1). If you edit a data file, you will have to rebuild any indexes it is referenced in—a time-consuming process (see below).

File Comments

When you index a file, the first 60 characters of text in the file are captured as a "comment" for the file, which can be included in various displays along with the file. If you don't want the first 60 characters of the file, you can specify a character string that marks the place where you would like the comment taken from. So, for example, when we indexed a batch of software reviews from this book's manuscript, we wanted the comment to come from the beginning of the "Overview" section rather than the top of the information box that begins each review. In ZyBUILD we were able to specify the search string "Overview," and the file comments were then created as the first 60 characters immediately *after* the word "Overview."

Section Headers

If you have section headers (one level only) marked in the text in some unique way, say on a line by themselves beginning with "##," you can have ZyBUILD find these headers and use them in the index. (You can actually use a simple, moderate-strength pattern-matching syntax to find patterns of characters rather than literal strings.) Then, whenever ZyFIND displays text from that file, it will show you the section header (the whole line) for the section it came from. The manual and help screens give almost no information about how to specify your headers for ZyBUILD, so it's difficult to say just how powerful or flex-

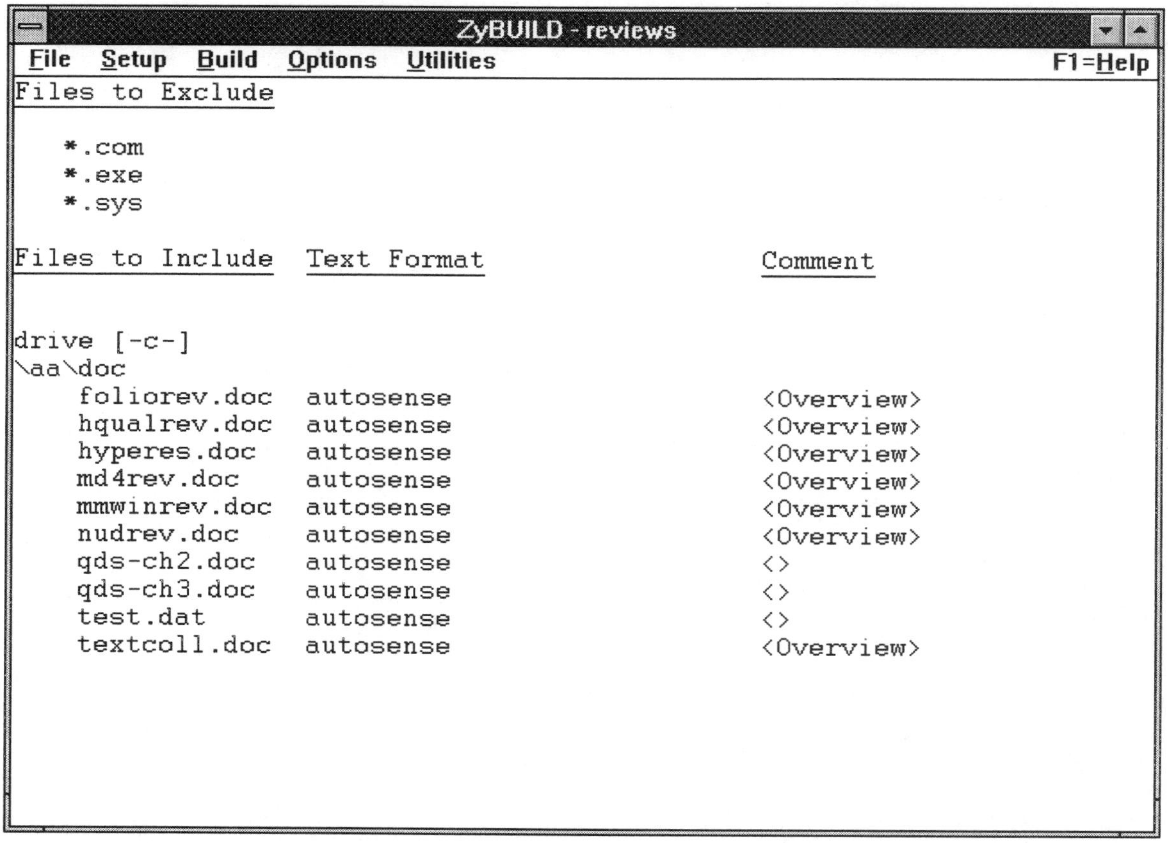

```
ZyBUILD - reviews
File  Setup  Build  Options  Utilities                                   F1=Help
Files to Exclude

   *.com
   *.exe
   *.sys

Files to Include   Text Format                        Comment


drive [-c-]
\aa\doc
    foliorev.doc   autosense                          <Overview>
    hqualrev.doc   autosense                          <Overview>
    hyperes.doc    autosense                          <Overview>
    md4rev.doc     autosense                          <Overview>
    mmwinrev.doc   autosense                          <Overview>
    nudrev.doc     autosense                          <Overview>
    qds-ch2.doc    autosense                          <>
    qds-ch3.doc    autosense                          <>
    test.dat       autosense                          <>
    textcoll.doc   autosense                          <Overview>
```

ZyINDEX Figure 1. ZyBUILD. Double-clicking anywhere in the lower portion of the window pops up a dialog box allowing you to change the list of Files to Include. The Files to Exclude list lets you specify file types to exclude, so that you can, for example, select all the files in a directory without accidentally indexing program files.

ible this facility is. The impression is that it's a simple, useful tool for marking headers, as long as you only have one level of header and they can all be distinguished by a common character string.

Archiving Files

As mentioned earlier, you can "archive" earlier versions of a file. If you set the archive option when you build an index, then when you rebuild to update for edited files, ZyINDEX will remember what the old version(s) looked like. You will then have the option of searching not only the current version of the file but all or specified earlier versions as well. This is described in more detail under "Searching," below.

Generating Hypertext Links

You can embed codes in your text files that cause ZyBUILD to set up hypertext links when it indexes the files (you can also create links one at a time while viewing text in ZyFIND, as discussed below under "Working on the Data"). There are two ways to do this: You can embed codes that specify a link from one spot in the text to another spot in the text of the same or another file, or you can embed codes that specify a link from one spot in the text to another file as a whole, so that activating the link simply retrieves the "destination" file. In either case, the codes you embed mark the beginning and end of the range of text you want to serve as the "source" of the link. This range will appear highlighted in blue when the text is retrieved in ZyFIND, and double-clicking anywhere in it will jump you to the "destination" end of the link. If the destination is a specific range of text, you'll have to mark that with codes also. This procedure is much more cumbersome than the procedures described below for creating links in ZyFIND, and it's not clear why one would choose to work this way.

Index Building Speeds

Building an index of nine files containing 4,103K (about 4 megabytes) took 1 minute and 48 seconds on a 33MHz

486 with 8MB of RAM. However, on slower systems or with larger collections of files, it could get much slower and quite tedious. The manual says that, with a 33MHz 386, build speeds for 10MB of documents will be about 4MB per hour with < 2MB free space, going up to 12MB per hour with > 10MB free space (note that speed goes *down* as the size of your document collection goes up). Even the faster rate on a 386 would imply 20 minutes to build the sample index described here. One tech support representative said the fastest build rates she had seen were about 20-25MB per hour. This is still much slower than the rate we got, which may be somewhat anomalous.

The implication seems to be that one should expect build operations to be time consuming, especially with slower computers or bigger collections of documents. Remember also that, any time you edit any of your files, you're going to have to rebuild your index.

Working on the Data

Within ZyFIND, there are a couple of ways you can work on your data, other than searching it. You can annotate the text or write memos by adding notes to specific points in the text or editing a file's comment, and you can create hypertext links.

Memoing/Annotation

The program supports annotation in two ways. You can attach pop-up "note" windows to words or phrases in the text. Or you can access the file comment, which can hold 60 characters.

Notes can hold up to 4K and can be used for memos as well as annotations. You select some text, hit <Ctrl-N> or make a menu selection, and a window pops up for you to write the note in. When you're done writing the note, you can choose to save it as "Public" or "Personal." In a multiuser setup (see "Network and Team Use" under "Miscellaneous," below), the latter are available only to you. Notes can be searched, but first they must be added to the index. When you save the note, there's an option to flag it for indexing. But it is not actually added to the index until the next time you build the index. The text to which the note is attached appears highlighted in gray. A double-click with the mouse anywhere in this region will pop the note back up.

The file comment is created at the time of indexing, as described earlier. However, you can edit the comment at any time while viewing a file in ZyFIND. The comment can be made to appear in a number of places, including at the top or bottom of the ZyFIND file viewer, as part of the file listing in the search results list (described under "Searching," below) and in the header or footer of printouts of text files.

Hypertext Links

You can create hyperlinks to jump from place to place, within a file or between files, and either or both files can be text or graphics, as long as they are in the index. Earlier, we described the process of specifying links before indexing, which can be awkward. However, creating links from within ZyFIND is easy. You select some text to act as the destination of the link, then copy this text to the clipboard. Next, you go to the place in the text where you want the jumping off point, or source of the link, to be, select some text there, and choose Paste Link from the Edit menu. The source text now appears highlighted in blue; double-clicking it with the mouse will cause you to be jumped to the destination text.

Later, when you "activate" a link, ZyFIND opens up a new file viewer window, positioned at the destination text, which appears in reverse video (white text on black background). This slows down jumps, and can be annoying, but it has one advantage: You can use the Window menu as a kind of log of your jumps. Dropping down the Window menu gives you a list of all open windows, in the order in which they were opened. Selecting the most recent window, for example, hops you back one step in your "hypertrail."

Bookmarks

You can insert "bookmarks" anywhere you want in the text. Just highlight some text, select Bookmark from the Edit menu, and give the bookmark a name. Subsequently, anytime you've got the index with the bookmark loaded, you can jump straight to a bookmark by hitting <F4> or making a menu selection and then choosing the bookmark you want.

Searching

When you load up ZyFIND, you are presented with the "Enter a Search" window (see Figure 2). Whatever indexes were in use during your last ZyFIND session are still selected, but you can add to or delete from this set easily. At the bottom of the window is the Search Request box, where you can enter your query. You can type in simple or complex queries directly.

The Boolean operators AND, OR, and NOT are supported, and parentheses can be used to create more complex, nested expressions. Set logic is also supported in the form of a "quorum" operator, which lets you search for co-occurrences of a specified number of the terms you list (e.g., if any two of the five terms listed occur, retrieve the text). You can search for number ranges with operators for less than (<), less than or equal to (≤), equal to (=), not equal to (< >), greater than (>), or greater than or equal to (≥). The two DOS wildcard operators are supported: * for

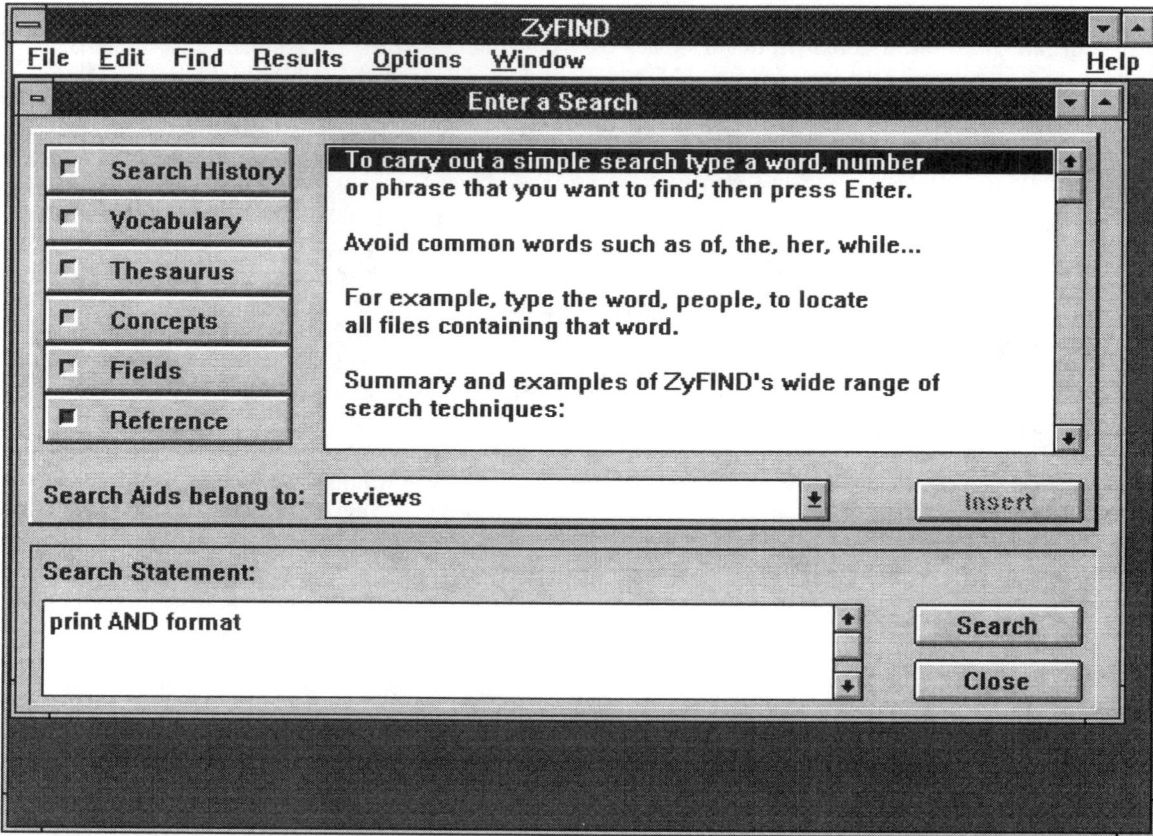

ZyINDEX Figure 2. The ZyFIND Enter a Search window. Your search statement can be entered in the box at the bottom. The top half of the window is for search aids; the buttons on the left select them, and the box on the right shows the search aids themselves. In this case, Reference has been selected, and some simple help information appears. The other options are explained in the text. The "Search Aids belong to" box lets you select which index the program will look in if you select one of the other search aids.

any number of occurrences of any characters, and ? for one occurrence of any character. In addition, you can define "classes" of characters. If you put a list of characters between square brackets, such as [abc], you are asking for any *one* of these characters—it's like a special, restricted wildcard. You can also specify a range of characters, like [c-f] or [6-9]. You can search for files by filename and file modification date. These are the ways you can search for graphics files in addition to searching for text in notes attached to the files.

When viewing search results, you can use the mouse to select a string in the text and launch a new search for other occurrences of the selected text. You can conduct this search in all the currently selected indexes, all the files that were retrieved by the current search, or only the current file.

The "progressive search" option—useful in large databases or when one string is very frequent—allows you to progressively narrow in on information of interest. After you conduct a first search, you can search again, restricting the new search to those files retrieved in the current one. You can continue to search in narrower and narrower sets of files.

When you search in archived files, you can restrict the versions of a file that you want included in the search by number. When you view the text, you can request markers that indicate where editing has taken place. A "+" in the left margin indicates that the marked line (or text in it) was added in the version being viewed, while a "–" indicates that the line (or text in it) was subsequently deleted.

Search Aids

You can choose among a number of "Search Aids" at the top of the window (see Figure 2; the choice buttons are on the left, the aids themselves appear in the box on the right). Clicking on *Search History* displays in the box to the right a log of all the search requests you've made in the

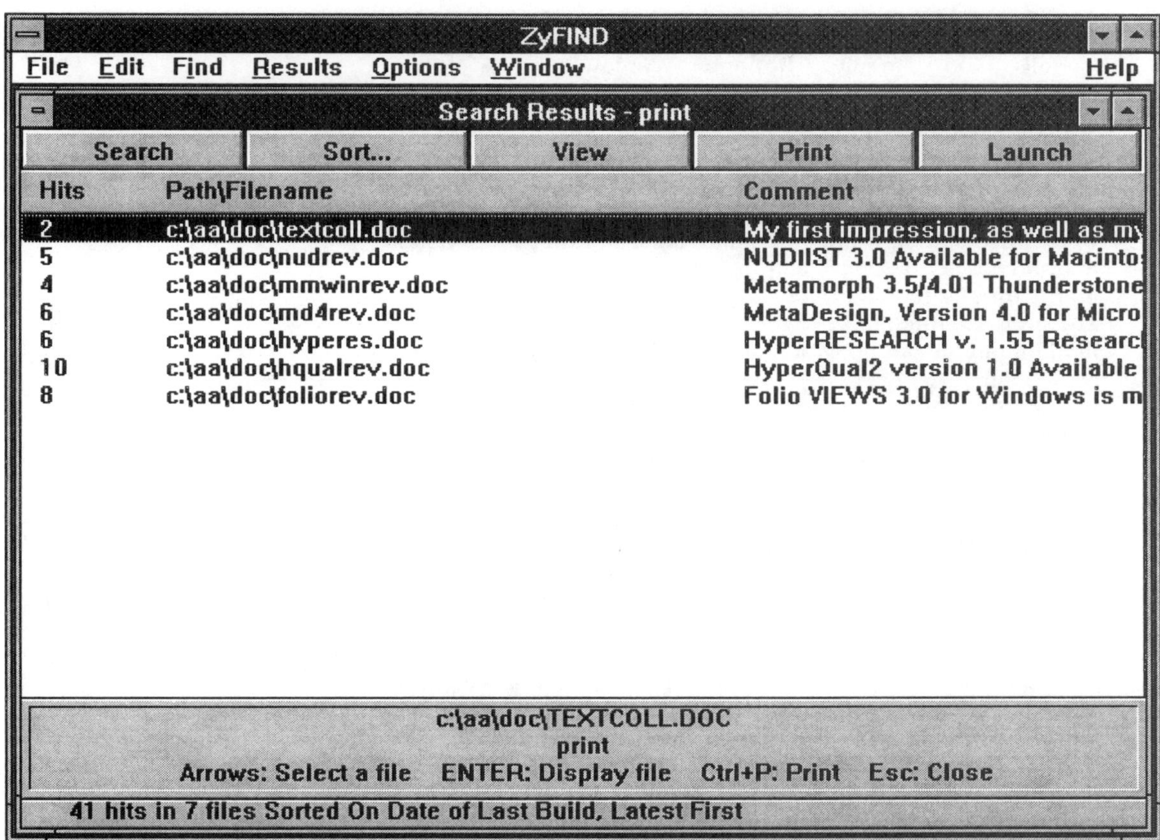

ZyINDEX Figure 3. Standard display of search results. Number of hits, path and file name, and comments are listed in columns. The footer has been customized to show the path and filename of the currently selected file, the search string ("print"), and some keystroke information.

current session, so that you can reuse them or paste them into more complex searches.

Vocabulary gives you an alphabetical list of all the words (and nonword strings) in the index, and the number of times each word occurs in the index. The list offers intelligent search: As you start typing a word, the list tries to match letter by letter. So if you start typing the word "word," when you type the "w," the list immediately scrolls to the first word beginning with "w." When you type the "o," the list scrolls to the first word beginning with "wo," and so on. As soon as the correct word is found, you can hit <Enter> to paste it into the Search Request.

Thesaurus gives you a list of synonyms of the selected word in the Search Request as well as the number of times each synonym occurs in the index. You can add any of these, one at a time, to the query, where they are added as OR terms. You can add synonyms for a particular index, but you cannot modify the global thesaurus.

Concepts are essentially search macros: queries that you name and save for future use. These can be typed in directly by typing @conceptname, or they can be selected from a list. Concepts can contain any search query, including references to other concepts.

Fields are defined by a starting and ending word, as described earlier under "Database Structure," and can be defined at any time. Click on a fieldname in the list (which will be displayed at top right), and "IN fieldname { }" appears in the Search Request box, with the cursor between the curly braces. You then type in the expression (any term or combination of terms) you want to appear within the field in order for a hit to be retrieved. Note that you can also type in a field search directly.

Field searches can be done even if the field is not defined, by doing what is called an "on-the-fly" field search. To do this, you specify the start and end strings for the field as part of the search. So, to use the earlier example for searching the "Overview" sections of these reviews, you could type "overview TO database structure {user friendliness}" to look for the phrase "user friendliness" in the "Overview" section, even if you hadn't already defined this as a field.

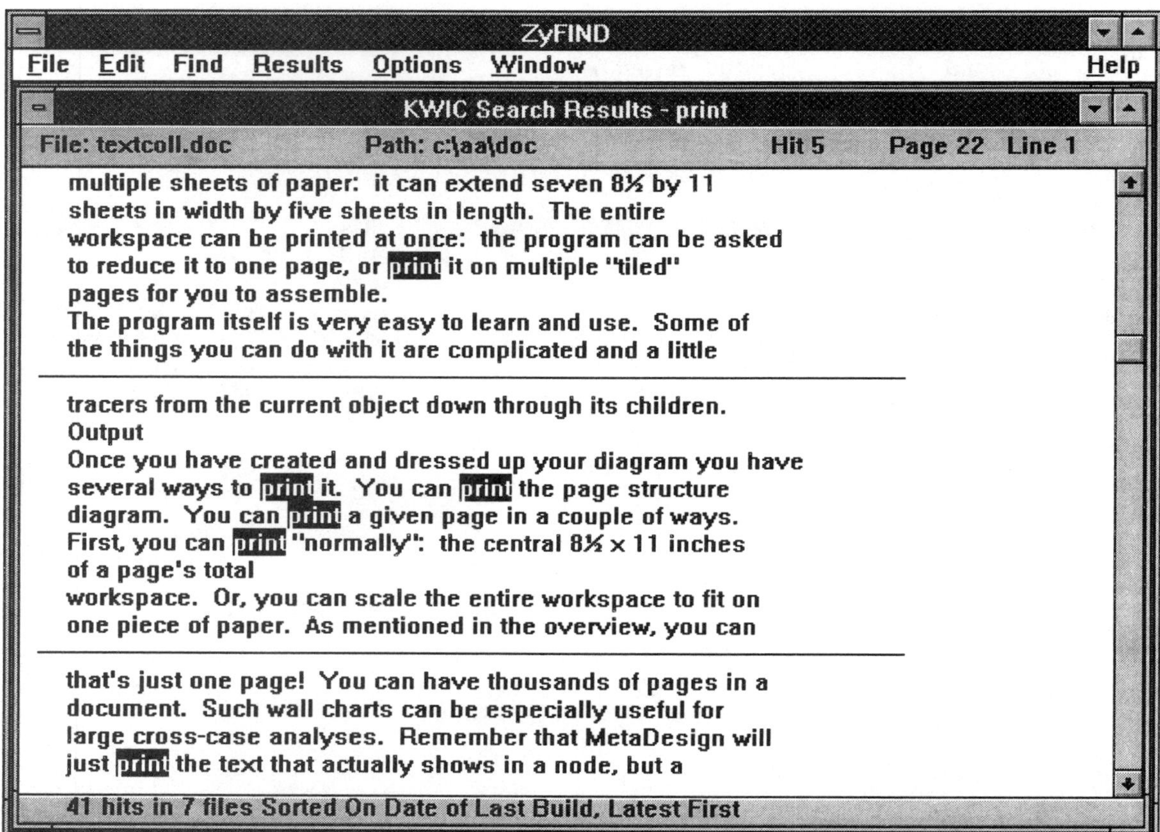

ZyINDEX Figure 4. KWIC view of the search for "print." Context has been set to three lines above and below the hit. The "context" in the middle has the hit term on more than one line and shows the overlapping contexts as one batch.

Search Context

Search context (the distance within which terms must co-occur to satisfy, for example, an AND request) by default is the entire file. You can control context with a high degree of flexibility and specificity, but you must do so explicitly for each search.

There are a variety of "separators," or delimiters, that you can use to specify context. You have access to EOD (end of document), EOS (end of sentence), EOL (end of line), EOP (end of paragraph), EOG (end of page), and CL1 and CL2 (column markers defined when indexing). If you wanted to search for co-occurrence by sentence, for example, you would have to type "EOS to EOS {search term}." It probably makes sense to define fields for sentences, paragraphs, lines, or whatever other units you may want to use for search context, so that you can paste these expressions right in.

There are also a variety of ways to conduct proximity searches. The Within operator allows you to specify proximity by number of words (e.g., classroom w/5 violence finds the word "classroom" within five words of the word "violence"). Or you can use it with one of the separators so that, for example, Minnesota w/3/EOP Maine finds Minnesota within three paragraphs of Maine.

The Precedes operator is like the Within operator, except that it specifies which term must come first. The Range operator allows you to specify different proximity distances before and after a word, so that you can find a term within one distance before or another distance after another term.

Finally, the To operator allows you to find one term between two others. This allows you to create on-the-fly fields, as discussed above.

Viewing Search Results

When you execute a search, you are presented first with a results list. You can see this in two customizable formats.

Standard results list. The first is a list of the files in which hits were found (see Figure 3). By default, you'll see the

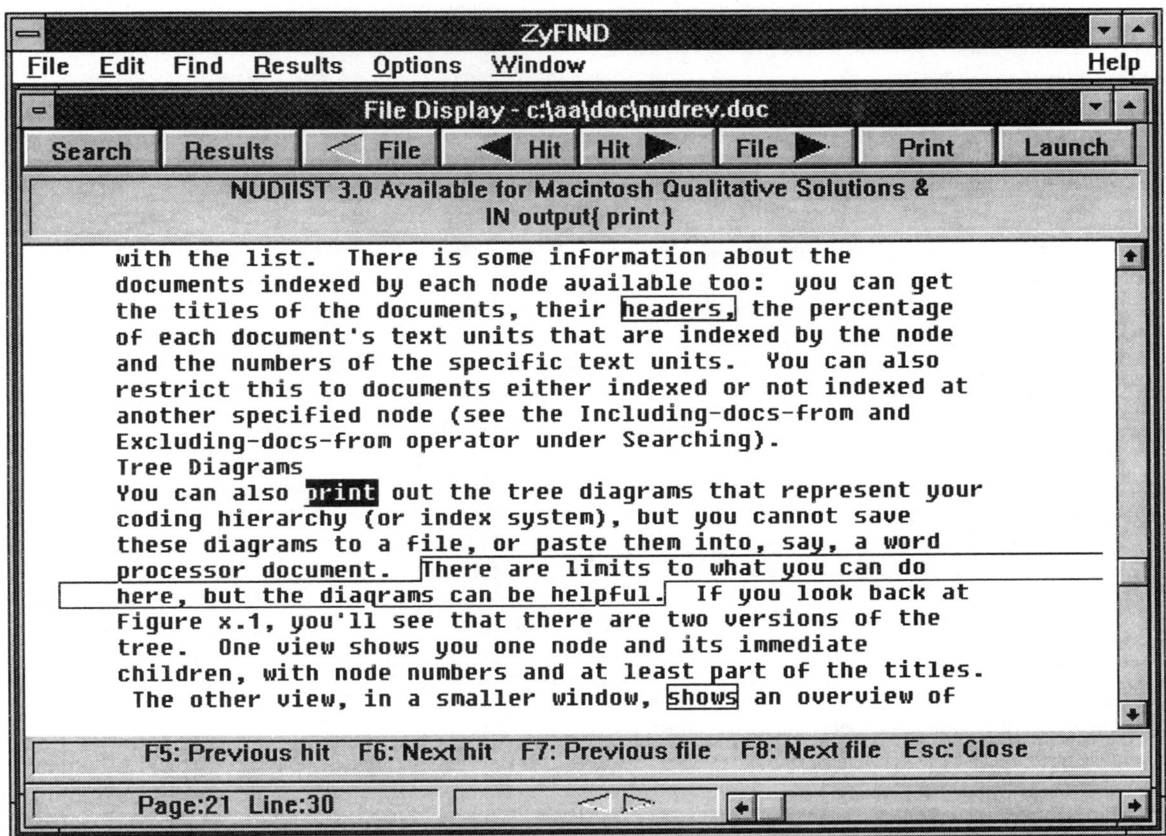

ZyINDEX Figure 5. Viewing a file in the File Display. The name of the file being viewed appears in the title bar. The comment, and below that the search request (for the word "print" in the Output field), appear in the header, just above the text. In the footer, just below the text, is an optional list of keystroke actions you can take. In the status line at the bottom are the page and line number from the original file. The highlighted word "print" near the middle of the screen is the search term that was found (on screen, this can be highlighted in yellow). The boxed word "headers," near the top, and the boxed sentence near the middle both have notes attached (on screen, these can be highlighted in gray, instead of boxed). The boxed word "shows," near the bottom, is the source end of a hyperlink (on screen, this can be highlighted in blue, instead of boxed).

number of hits, path and filename, and part of the comment for each file (as shown in Figure 3). In the title bar above, you see the search request that generated these results. This display is highly customizable. Your choices of information to be displayed include hits, hit density (the manual says this is a function of the number of hits and the size of the file but doesn't tell you what the function is—not very helpful), file modification date, file modification time, filename (with or without path), and comment. You can have the list sorted in ascending or descending order based on filename, path and filename, comment, number of hits, hit density, file modification date/time, or the date and time the file was added to the index (the default setting). At the bottom of the window, you can add a "footer" with the comment, path, search statement, and/or a list of keystrokes for various standard actions.

KWIC results list. The second option is a keyword in context (KWIC) mode in which you specify from one to ten lines of context for each hit (see Figure 4). You get one "context" for each hit. If the context for one hit overlaps with that of another hit, the whole range is displayed together. There is a header for the window that displays the filename and path, hit number, page number, and line number, all of which change as you scroll around. Moving around in the KWIC mode, unfortunately, is annoyingly slow. You can move the cursor around what shows on the screen just fine, but whenever you try to scroll beyond what's showing on the screen, you have to wait while ZyFIND retrieves the next batch of text. Again, on a 33MHz 486 with 8MB of RAM, it repeatedly took intervals of 5 seconds or more before the list would scroll, even though the search had produced just six hits in two files, with only three lines of context around each hit. This happened even after trying to scroll back up through material that had already been displayed.

Viewing hits in context. To see your hits in full context, you double-click on an entry in the results list or click on the View button at the top of the window (see Figure 3). This opens up the file display window (see Figure 5). Here you can view hits in full context, but all formatting is lost. In word processor documents, this is usually just ugly, and maybe it's difficult to find headers and such (which you might usually spot by centering, underlining, and so on). In spreadsheets, it makes the results useless: The contents of each cell are listed one under another, in a single column. We couldn't make heads or tails of the tables ZyFIND retrieved. Database files fare somewhat better. You get one field per line for each record, with the field name, a colon, and the field contents neatly arranged. After all the fields for one record are listed, those for the next begin. This setup makes it easy to set up ZyINDEX's fields to correspond to those in your database.

Using the file display, you can also attach and read notes, and make and travel along hyperlinks. The actual hit terms are highlighted in yellow, text to which notes are attached are highlighted in gray, and source points of links are highlighted in blue. There are buttons at the top of the screen to jump to the next or the previous hit in the current file and to go to the next or previous file in the results list. There are also buttons to print (the whole current file, a selection of text, or a range of pages) or to "launch" the file in its native program (so if you're viewing, for example, a document you wrote with WordPerfect, WordPerfect will start up with the document opened up in it). You can customize the header and footer areas of the window to display (for the header) the various buttons, file comment, section headers, and/or the search query and (for the footer) the comment, section headers, search query, and/or a list of keystrokes for different actions.

Output

There are options to print out the results list (in either standard or KWIC mode) or the files that are retrieved by searches, and you can output selections of text to ASCII files. You can also use the Windows clipboard to copy and paste, for example, to your word processor.

When printing from the file display, you can print by file, page, or selection. You can define headers and footers with the search term, file comment, and/or path and filename of the file. You can also choose fonts. You won't see any of the highlighting in your output.

You can also choose the Save As selection from the File menu, supply a filename, and have the entire file, a selection of text you've highlighted with the mouse, or a range of pages in the current file saved to an output file. If the file already exists, you can choose to have the new text either overwrite or be appended to the existing text. The latter option would allow you to send multiple chunks of text to the same output file. You can include the same header and footer information as when printing, and this information will appear above and below each chunk you send to the file.

If you want to print the text in a note, you have to open that note, select all the text you want to print, and then print the selection. Although the program claims you can get header and footer information here, none appeared. Although notes can hold 4,000 characters, the notes box only allows 34 characters per line, and this is the way notes print out. So what would normally be a little more than a single-spaced page winds up being one very narrow column on a few pages.

Either form of results list, standard or KWIC, can be printed. The only information you can put in a header or footer is the search statement. In the KWIC view, each context block begins with a listing of the filename (but not the path), the page number, line number, and hit number (if there is more than one hit in the context block, this information refers to the first one). The search terms are well marked with brackets and underscores, like so: [_word_]. Context blocks are separated with dashed lines.

Theory Building

The 4K notes are on the small side for writing deep reflective or theoretical memos, and they don't print out with the text they're linked to. The hyperlinks can be helpful for establishing connections among different parts of the data, which can be a useful theory-building feature. A researcher interested in changes in data could make good use of the archive feature for theory building. For example, if you take a hermeneutic approach to steadily rewriting or annotating your text, you could see in retrievals what revision number, and date, a given retrieval was from.

Graphics Editing

ZyINDEX can index, retrieve, and display graphics files from several formats: TIFF (CCITT 3 & 4), PCX, BMP, and EPS. It can also display graphics that are embedded in Word for Windows and WordPerfect for Windows documents. However, you cannot edit graphics from within ZyINDEX, except by using the launch feature to open up the graphics file in its native program.

User Friendliness

This is not a user-friendly program. Even though it has a graphics interface, and the basic functions are relatively easy to use, they often take a while to learn. Many operations, as discussed throughout, are slow and awkward.

As mentioned in the "Overview," the documentation is very difficult to pull information from, working either from the table of contents or the index. ZyLAB would do well to follow the lead of the producers of other big search packages like Metamorph and Folio VIEWS and provide an on-line manual making use of the program's search capabilities. The standard Windows-style help system is no more helpful than the manual. In either case, even if you can find the information you're looking for, you're likely to find it incomplete or difficult to understand. We certainly did.

The technical support people are available from 7:30 a.m. to 6:00 p.m. central time on weekdays, and they are helpful. But they try to get you to make a toll call to Buffalo Grove, Illinois, even though you can get through on the 800 number. The manual only lists the toll number, but there's an 800 sales number as well. If you call and ask for technical support, you'll probably be told that they're all busy and will call you back. They usually call back the same day. If you're out, they leave a message asking you to call them back on the toll line. We always ignored this, called back on the 800 number, and waited for another call back; you should too.

Miscellaneous

Program Stability

An item related to user friendliness is that the program is not completely stable. All too often—actually, even once would have been too often—the program caused general protection faults, an error that basically means the program has crashed, although the rest of the Windows environment, and any other applications you have running, are *usually* still OK. There were other little oddities as well. For example, when the upgrade from version 5.1 to 5.14 arrived, there were no longer icons when a window was minimized, just a title. ZyLAB seems to be moving fairly quickly with upgrades, so perhaps they'll eventually get this all worked out.

Network and Team Use

ZyINDEX can be used on a network. The person who creates an index is defined as the owner and has "full rights," meaning he or she can work with the index in all the normal ways. Other users can either be granted full rights as well or "read-only rights." These users can search the index, read public notes and traverse public hypertext links, and output the text they find. They cannot, however, modify the index in any way (e.g., by adding notes, updating the index).

Regardless of a user's level of access rights, he or she can only read or traverse public notes or links or the personal notes or links he or she has created. This is true even for the index's owner.

Comparative Remarks

ZyINDEX does not stack up well against the competition in many respects, although it does have a few unique features. It requires you to index your files, like Sonar, but it doesn't give you nearly as useful indexes and summaries of your search results as Sonar does, and it doesn't have some of Sonar's really interesting features, like associated word and relational searches. The Text Collector and Metamorph don't require indexing. ZyINDEX doesn't seem to be any faster than these nonindexing programs—in fact, it's slower than all but Metamorph for Windows, with which it's about on a par—so the advantages of indexing are unclear, at best.[1] Furthermore, it doesn't give you access to the kind of powerful manipulation and editing of your data that Folio VIEWS manages by actually importing the data.

The Text Collector is easier to use, and a lot cheaper, though less powerful. It has much better output options and flexibility. But ZyINDEX has more sophisticated search options, hyperlinking, and notes.

ZyINDEX's field definition function is easier than Folio VIEWS's, and VIEWS doesn't have an archive function. Other than that, though, VIEWS strikes us a better choice on almost any criterion. It is a much faster searcher, has more and better linking and memoing features, doesn't lose formatting, has multiple hierarchical levels, and has fields and highlighters. Above all, it's much more pleasant to use.

Summary

While ZyINDEX is generally much less desirable than an internal textbase program such as Folio VIEWS 3.0, or an indexless searcher like Metamorph or The Text Collector, it might be the right option if you need one of its few unique features. For example, you might really want the archive feature. Or you might prefer it over Folio VIEWS if you don't want to import your files, and over Metamorph if your files include database, spreadsheet, or graphics files.

Reference

ZyLAB Division, Information Dimensions, Inc. (1993). *ZyINDEX for Windows user's guide.* Buffalo Grove, IL: Author.

1. Remember, though, that our speed evaluations are based on subjective evaluations or, at best, a rough stopwatch test.

5

Textbase Managers

The programs in this chapter are related to the "text retriever" family, but with some important added functions. They keep your data in a systematic, ordered fashion—whether that involves "records" and "fields," free-form text, or even quantitative information linked to text. They help you manage complex databases, and can sort or segment them into meaningful subsets to help you make comparisons and contrasts. They're also good at search and retrieval.

Other programs that overlap significantly with this category, and the chapters they are reviewed in, include the following:

☐ ☐ ☐

askSam, Version 5.1/1.0b[1]

Available for Windows and DOS

askSam Systems
P.O. Box 1428
Perry, FL 32347

Phone: (800) 800-1997
(904) 584-6590 (Support)
Fax: (904) 584-7481

Price: $395
$99.95 Educational
$1,095 Network 5-station pack, $547.50 Educational

Hardware Requirements:
For Windows
- IBM or 100% compatible 386 or better
- 4MB RAM
- Hard disk with at least 5MB free space
- High density diskette drive (3.5 in. or 5.25 in.)
- DOS 3.1 or higher; Windows 3.1

For DOS
- IBM PC, XT, AT, PS/2, or compatible
- 384K RAM
- Diskette drive (3.5 in. or 5.25 in.)
- Monochrome, CGA, EGA, or VGA monitor
- PC-DOS or MS-DOS 2.0 or higher

Overview

askSam is a fast and flexible database management system (DBMS) that integrates database, word processor, and text retriever capabilities. Its particular strength, when compared with other programs reviewed here, is its ability to handle any combination of structured and unstructured data, placing both types on the same screen and giving you full DBMS-style, field-based control of your data. It is flexible enough to be useful for more than managing and analyzing your data: It can also be a good choice for storing references and abstracts (or, for that matter, the actual text) of the literature you're using; for use as a personal information manager (PIM), a program that acts as an electronic

1. The current askSam version numbers are 5.1 for DOS and 1.0b for Windows. Version 2.0 was in beta-testing at the time of this review, and its new features are described in the "Update" section.

datebook, to-do list, phone book, and note taker; and for managing databases of notes, memos, faxes, and so on. While it can't do all these things as well as various specialty packages, it does incorporate them all into one bundle.

askSam provides some hypertext capabilities. It can do fairly complex Boolean searches, proximity searches, searches by field, numeric searches, date searches, and searches combining all of the above elements, and complex searches are pretty easy to define. It has a powerful and flexible report-generating mechanism that allows you to sort and select records based on complex criteria and gives you strong control in designing your output, including grouping records and totaling fields. It does not support coding, although fields can be used to store codelike information about records. askSam can give you a KWIC-like listing of keywords in context, but it won't give you source tags (e.g., page and line numbers) as a true KWIC listing does.

There are both DOS and Windows versions of askSam. The Windows version is quite user friendly, in terms of both learning and ultimate ease of use (although it does tend to crash every so often), has better word processing features, and can hold graphics and other OLE objects (such as video and audio). The DOS version is more difficult to learn and use (though it is still "moderately" user friendly) but, as is often the case, is faster, requires less RAM (and less powerful hardware, generally), and has a number of powerful features that haven't yet made it into the Windows version. For example, the DOS version has a full database programming language suitable for application development, which allows you, among other things, to create relational databases. It will let you index fields, which can increase search speed in large files. The DOS version also lets you define up to 10 "templates" per file, which allow you to easily insert different field structures (and boilerplate text) into different records or different parts of the same record. By contrast, the Windows version allows just one of the equivalent "Entry Forms" per file. Finally, the Windows version keeps your records separate from each other, though they can be up to about 300 pages long, while the DOS version restricts records to 20 lines but lets you link them together into one continuous document.

Based largely on the user-friendliness issue, we decided to focus this review on the Windows version. (Readers who have been frustrated with the DOS version should read on!) Under "Miscellaneous," below, we'll further discuss comparisons between the two versions.

Database Structure

As mentioned just above, askSam for Windows divides your data into records, which it calls "documents." (Don't let this confuse you; most of us are used to thinking of *documents* as *files,* but in askSam they're not—documents are *records.* A file can have many documents.) You might organize interview data so that you had one interview per document, survey data so that you had one case (or respondent) per document, or observational data so that you had one observation period per document.

Each document can hold up to about 16,000 lines of text, which comes to about 300 pages, and can hold any combination of free-form unstructured text as well as formal, structured fields. askSam uses an "internal files" strategy: Your data are either typed directly or imported into special askSam format files. A file can contain as many documents as the size of your hard disk will allow.

Fields can be placed anywhere you wish in a record. To define a field, you simply type its name (one word only, though you can use a - or a _ to link multiple words), in the position you want, followed by a [(see Figure 1). (You can redefine the field character from [to : or anything else you like.) By default, a field will continue to the end of a line. If you want more than one field on a line, you just specify where a field ends with a] (as was done with the City[field in Figure 1). If you want a field to be more than one line long, again you just place the] wherever you want the field to end. The same field can occur more than once in a record and can be as long as you want, but fields cannot overlap.

For askSam to recognize your fields, you must define them in the Entry Form. To do this, you go to the Entry Form with a menu command and then type in your field-names (but without actual data in the fields), just as you would in a record. This does two things at once; it defines your fields, and it sets up a template you can use for creating new documents. The layout of the fields in your documents, though, does not have to be kept the same as in the Entry Form. As long as the fields are listed in the Entry Form, askSam will be able to use them for searching and manipulating your database.

Data Entry

Data can be entered directly, imported, or pasted into askSam using the Windows clipboard.

Direct Data Entry

Direct data entry is one of the very pleasant things about askSam. If you've got unstructured data, you can simply type in text, and askSam acts as a basic Windows word processor. If you want to enter more structured data, the data Entry Form can make the process very easy.

Entry Forms can be used as a template for creating new documents (although you can also create documents without them) and can contain not only fields but any kind of

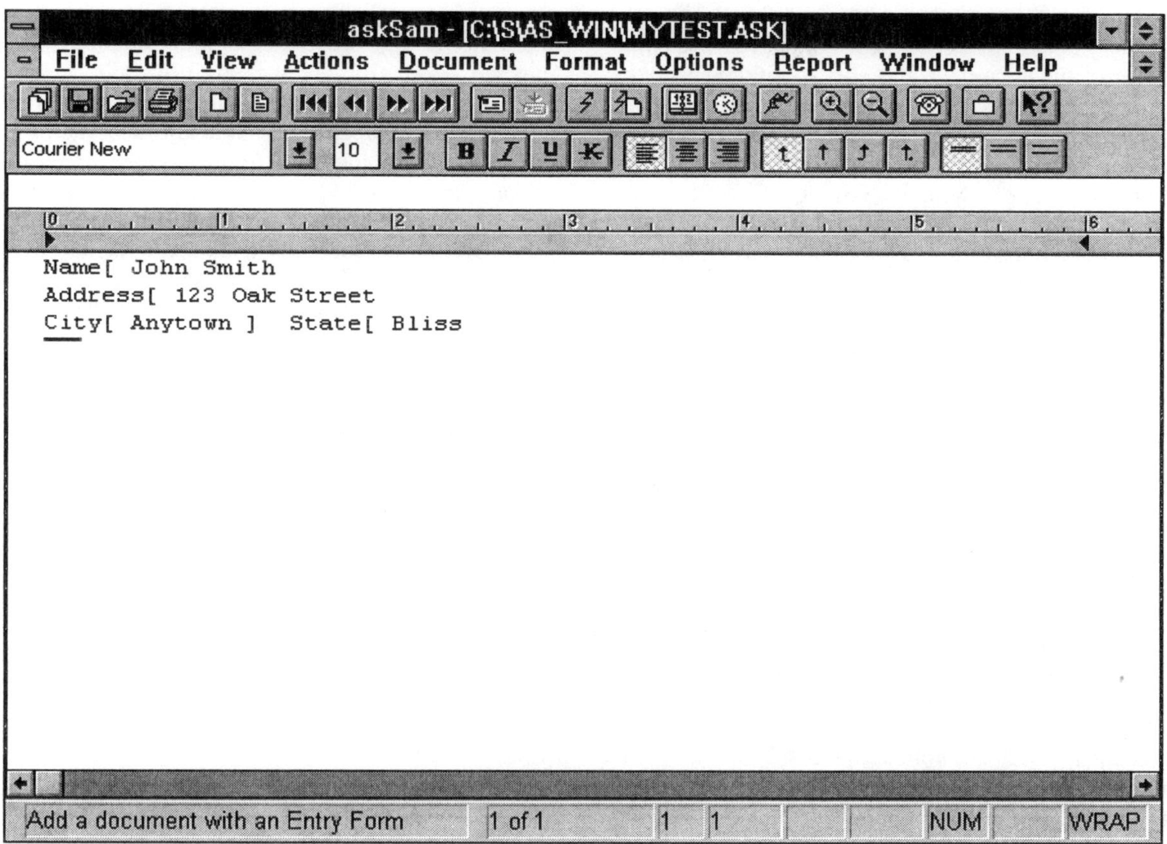

askSam Figure 1. Viewing a document in askSam. The fields defined are Name[, Address[, City[, and State[. The City[field is explicitly ended with a] because there is another field (State[) on the same line. Many of the program's commands are available via the first row of buttons, at top. Just below are a row of buttons for formatting text. The white band between this formatting bar and the ruler is a command line, where you can issue any askSam command directly. At the lower left corner of the screen, in the status bar, is an explanation of a button the mouse cursor (which doesn't show here) was pointing to (sixth button, first row).

boilerplate text (like headers, labels, or interview questions) or graphics (such as a logo) that you want to appear in every document you create from the Entry Form.

When you call up the Entry Form, it looks just like any other record—a blank screen—and you can edit it just like any other record. You can put boilerplate text and graphics, as well as fieldnames (remember that simply typing a fieldname[is enough to define the field), anywhere you want in the Entry Form. After you've saved it, when you create new documents (records), they can either be empty or look just like the Entry Form. If you choose the latter (just hit <F5> to create a new document with the Entry Form), all of the text in your Entry Form, including the fieldnames, appears in the new document. You can now type in the data for this document as you would in any word processor.

Or you can hit <Alt-E> to turn on Data Entry mode. In this mode, data entry behaves the way it would in a traditional database: The cursor begins in the data area (one space past the [) of the first field in the document, you type in the data for that field, hit <Tab> or <Enter>, and the cursor pops to the next field's data area. <Shift-Tab> will take you back to the previous field.

If you want to type more data into a field than you left room for, you simply switch off Data Entry mode and continue typing; because you've gone back into the word processor-like mode, your text is inserted at the cursor. If you know that you're going to need to do this a lot, you can still get Data Entry mode-type of navigation. To do this, insert the characters ^^ in the data area of any of your fields in the Entry Form. Then, when you're entering data in a document, hitting <F3> will always jump you to the next field.

There are other control codes (in addition to ^^) that you can use in an Entry Form. ^D will automatically stamp (insert) the current date when you create a new document with the Entry Form. ^T will stamp the time. ^N will stamp the number of the document. *But,* this is not the absolute record number of the document. Rather, it records the number of the document among those that were created from the Entry Form. So if you create three documents with the Entry Form, then one without, the next document you create with the Entry Form will be stamped as number 4, even though its record number is 5. This number stays the same even if you sort your database.

Importing Data

You can import data to an askSam database from ASCII text-only files, WordPerfect 5.x files (with formatting), Rich Text Format (RTF) files (a format used by a number of programs, including Microsoft Word, for transferring formatted text, including .BMP graphics, from one program to another), and dBASE III and IV (.DBF) type files. In all of the above cases, you have a variety of options for specifying where the file gets split into documents.

An attempt at importing an RTF file met with fair results. Fonts, underlining, italics, and centering were all correct. Borders around paragraphs were lost, and footnote text was inserted into the text where the footnote reference mark had been—all in all, not bad.

Importing dBASE files is terrific. askSam automatically puts each dBASE record in a separate document. In addition, it places the name of each field from the dBASE file in the document according to the askSam convention and creates an Entry Form, so the file is all ready to be used as an askSam database. It also imports memo fields from dBASE databases, which is important because dBASE stores these in separate files.

Templates

askSam for Windows comes with a variety of "templates" (not to be confused with Entry Forms), which you can use to create standard types of databases. Templates are basically empty databases (though they can have documents with data) containing an Entry Form and a batch of predefined Reports (discussed under "Output," below), and you can easily create your own templates, or modify the ones that come with the program. When you create a new file, you can create it from a template, which basically makes a copy of the template under the new filename. The templates that come with askSam all start with a document explaining the use of the template, and some have sample data as well.

There are templates for interview data, "clippings" (information from documents), notes, address/phone books, calendars, to-do lists, tracking phone messages, storing e-mail, and so on. Each of these templates comes with a number of useful Reports, tailored to the purposes of the template. As an example of a template, the *interview* template (actually, it's called "question.ask") is shown in Figure 2. It offers fields for name, age, sex, race, date, and time at the top of each document. Below, it has text for each of the interview *questions.* Below each question is a field for typing in the interviewee's response. This setup would facilitate sorting and searching and organizing output by any of the demographic-type fields as well as searching for particular text either across responses or within the answers to particular questions.

The *clippings* template has fields for publication, date, issue, title, author, page, keywords, and abstract. This could easily be modified to more exactly match academic journals, and reports could be set up to approximate styles such as APA, Chicago, and so on. The *notes* template has just four fields—for date, subject, note number, and the note itself. Reports that come with it let you create lists of the first three fields, sorted either by date or by subject. Such a list could be used with the hypertext feature (discussed under "Searching," below) to jump to the notes themselves.

Working on the Data

Sorting the Database

One of the things that databases are particularly useful for is sorting. For example, you might want to sort your records (documents in askSam) in chronological order, by age of subject, by research site, or in any number of other ways. An askSam database, like a more traditional database, can be sorted based on multiple fields. (When you sort on multiple fields, the file is first sorted on the first specified field. If there are "ties"—say two or more documents have the same value for a field—those documents are sorted on the second field, and so on.) The file can also be sorted on the first word in each document. You can specify whether or not case (upper or lower) matters in sorting and whether you want ascending or descending order. You can have articles ("a," "the," "in," and so on) ignored. You can have documents sorted on the last word in a field (which you might want if you have entered names as Firstname Lastname), on the first word in the field, or based on all the words in the field.

Coding

There's no real built-in way to code your text, but there are a couple of ways to work around this issue. One way is by using fields to represent codes for an entire document. For example you could define a field, Characteristics[, and

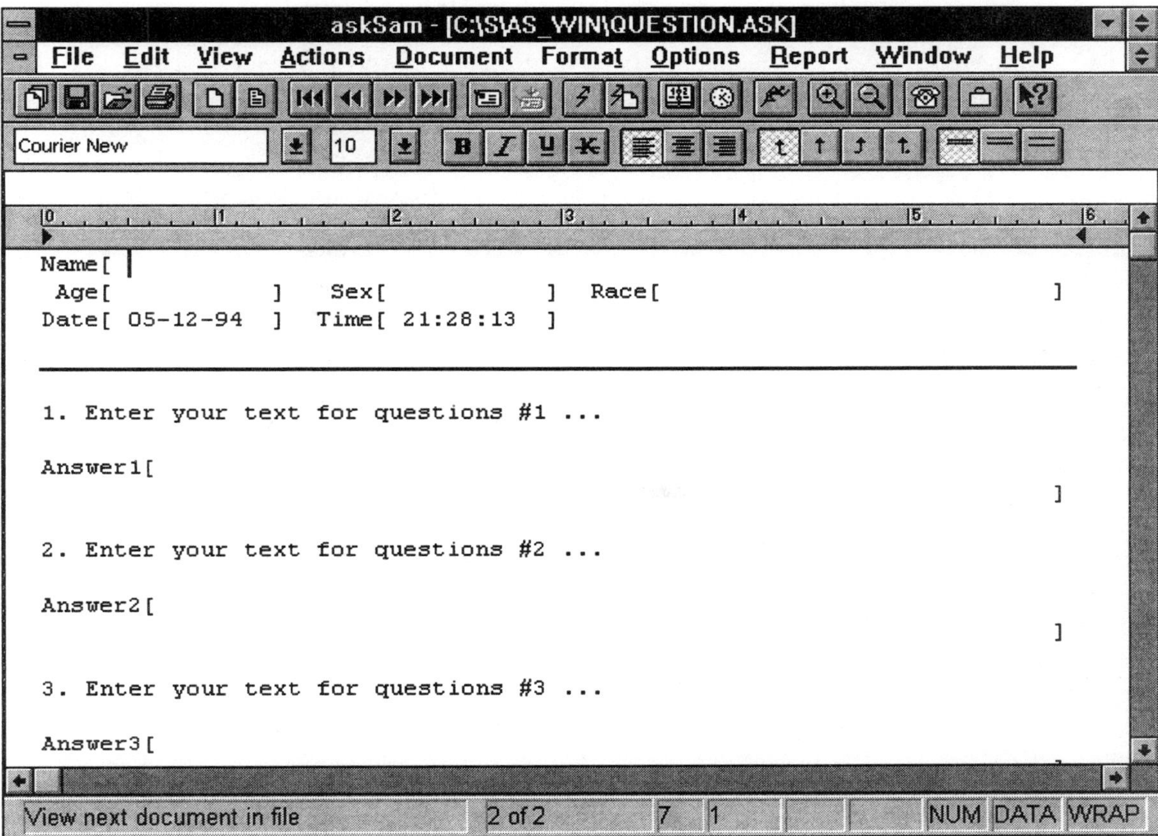

askSam Figure 2. This template sets up a database for holding interview data. The Entry Form automatically creates new documents like this one. There are basic demographic-type fields at the top, a separator line, and fields for answers to each question. In data entry mode, you just hit <Tab> to navigate from field to field, making data entry easy. You could easily edit the Entry Form in any way you wanted, such as to have different fields at the top, or to show the actual questions instead of "Enter your text for questions. . . ."

then fill it in with the characteristic code you wanted on each record (document), such as "Enthusiastic." You could even put multiple "characteristics" into this field. Another approach to the same basic strategy would be to create a field called Enthusiastic[and simply place a Y in it. Then you could search for records that had a Y in the Enthusiastic[field.

If you, like most people, want to code specific passages within your documents, you may be able to find an acceptable workaround as well. For example, if there's a particular chunk of text you want coded "Enthusiastic," you could add in a field definition for that chunk by typing Enthusiastic[at the start of the chunk and] at the end of it. This could be done quite flexibly, but it runs into the limitation that fields can't overlap. Yet another strategy would be to simply place a code word in the text, set off by some unique identifying string, and search for that code word.

Storing Facts Not in Text

This is a strong point of askSam. You can simply create fields to hold demographic or other information that doesn't actually exist in the text.

Marking Up the Text

askSam for Windows gives you access to a variety of character formatting attributes, including font styles and sizes (including TrueType), bold, italic, underline, strikeout, and color. The usefulness of these is, however, reduced by the fact that if you use a Report you lose all formatting.

Memoing/Annotation

There are a variety of strategies available for memoing and annotation. You could, for example, place a Notes[or

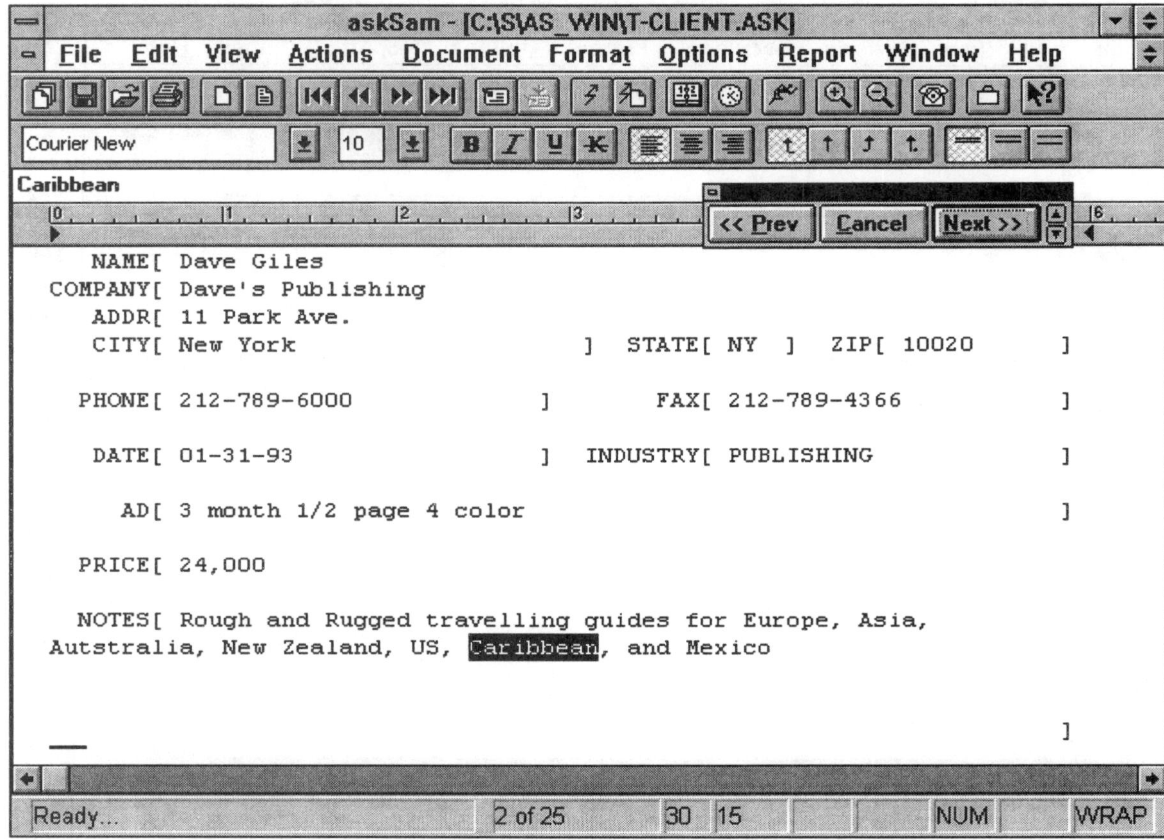

askSam Figure 3. Viewing the results of a search for the word "Caribbean," which appears on the command line (simply entering a term on the command line will start a search for it) and is highlighted where it appears in the text. The floating button bar at upper right has buttons to go to the Previous or Next document with a hit, or to cancel the search. The little up and down arrows on the right end of the bar will jump you to the next or previous hit in the current document. You can also edit and scroll around in the text any time you want, then continue to view the search results.

Memos[field in your documents. Annotations could be typed directly into the text. Memos could also be stored in a separate file, such as one created with the notes template described above. askSam's hypertext facilities would make it possible to link memos to specific documents and particular chunks of text within them.

Searching

The search options in askSam are many, varied, and strong. It was surprising to find, though, that a number of the things you'd want to do weren't possible—more on these as we go. Despite the complaints we'll have from time to time here, the overall picture is that askSam is a good, strong searcher.

Every type of search you can do in askSam for Windows can be constructed with a helpful, easy-to-use dialog box. Whenever you enter a search term or fieldname in a dialog box, there's a drop down list of either the last 20 or so search terms, or of the fieldnames for the current file.

Searching from the Command Line

There's also a command line at the top of the screen (see Figure 1) where you can type any kind of search request if you know the command syntax. Working from a command line can be much faster if you're comfortable with it—compare typing "dir *.bak<Enter>" in DOS with what you have to do in Windows: open up the File Manager, navigate to the directory of interest, pull down the View menu, select By File Type, and type in "*.bak"—but you have to know the commands. A very helpful feature for learning the command syntax, if you like working from a command line, makes askSam show you the equivalent command(s) for any action you take from a menu or dialog box before it actually executes the action. This shows in a pop-up message box that you can study (or copy down) before allowing the action to proceed.

To get to the command line, you can just hit <Esc>. So once you find out that you can just put Boolean operators in curly brackets, it can be easy to just type "<Esc>conflict {OR} cooperation" instead of going through a dialog box. More complex searches may still be easier to define with the dialog boxes.

Viewing Search Results

Once you launch a search, askSam begins showing you the documents that match the search, one at a time, moving you through your database (see Figure 3). Search terms are highlighted in the text, and you have the option of having every occurrence of a term highlighted or only the first in each document. A small, movable control bar (see the upper right portion of Figure 3) lets you jump from hit to hit within a document and forward and back among the documents that matched the search request. You can also scroll around in and edit the text whenever you like. Unfortunately, you're not given any information about how many hits you have.

Local Find, Replace, Global Replace

Let's start with the simplest kinds of searches. If you want to find a simple character string, *within the current document,* there's a Find option on the edit menu that works just like those in most word processors: Type in a string in the resulting dialog box, and you go to the first (or next) occurrence of the string. Also like a word processor, there's a Replace option, which will replace one string with another. Finally, there's a Global Replace option that will replace a string throughout all the documents in a file. Replace lets you check each hit before it's replaced (like any decent word processor will) but Global Replace does not. Search-and-replace operations could be useful, in addition to editing, for revising codes, changing fieldnames, or cleaning up a file you've just imported so that it will work well with askSam (e.g., replacing long, multiword fieldnames with short, single-word ones).

Boolean Searches

Boolean searches are constructed in a dialog box (Figure 4) or, as we've noted, on the command line if you know the syntax. The search context (the distance within which terms must co-occur to satisfy an AND search) for a Boolean search is always the document, so you're looking through your database for the documents where some terms co-occur. You type in search terms at the top of the dialog box and paste them into the "list" at the bottom. If you want to search for a single character string, you just type in that one string. You cannot use parentheses, so you have to control the logic with the order in which you enter things. This can be confusing (and the manual is no help), but we'll try to explain it here.

Take, for example, the Boolean expression "happy AND smiling OR sad AND crying." This could mean many different things. Using parentheses, the search "(happy AND smiling) OR (sad AND crying)," which means find me text that either has both "happy" AND "smiling," OR has both "sad" AND "crying," is very different than the search "happy-AND (smiling OR sad) AND crying," which means find me text that has at least three terms: "happy," "crying," AND either (or both) "smiling" OR "sad." In fact, the second one doesn't make much sense.

In askSam you get some control over this by ordering the terms in the search list and by how you specify your ANDs, but you don't get as good control as with parentheses. If you don't specify an operator between two terms, then you are using an "implied AND," while if you do explicitly select AND, you're using a "specified AND." There's a big difference. Implied ANDs are evaluated *before* ORs, and specified ANDs are evaluated *after* ORs. So, in our examples above, if you used implied ANDs—"happy (implied and) smiling OR sad (implied and) crying"—you'd get the first search (the ANDs get looked at first, then the OR) while if you used specified ANDs—"happy AND smiling OR sad AND crying"—you'd get the second search (the OR gets looked at first, and then the implied ANDs come into play). All in all, not as friendly as search query-making should be.

Searching in Fields

You can search for strings of text within specific fields. The Search in Field dialog box simply lets you type in a search term and a fieldname. This will find all documents that have the search term in the specified field, and both the search term and the fieldname will be highlighted in the text. To find a Boolean combination of terms within a field, you have to use the Multiple Search Request dialog box described below.[2]

Numeric Searches

The numeric search function also works with fields, so you can find records where a particular field has a specified

2. You can also do this from the command line, but you need the reference manual from the *DOS* version (Seaside Software, 1991a) to get the syntax. You don't get this manual if you buy the Windows version.

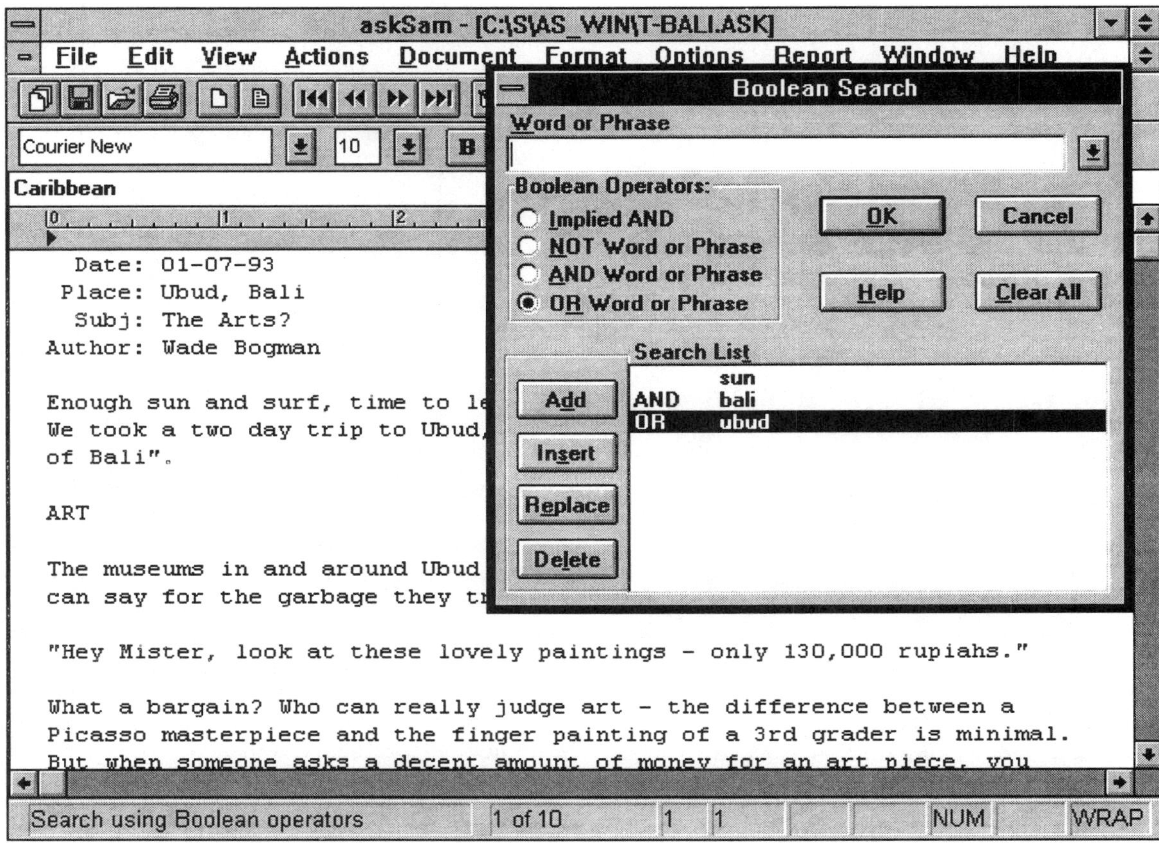

askSam Figure 4. Defining a Boolean search with the Boolean Search dialog box. Search terms are first typed into the Word or Phrase box at the top and then pasted into the Search List box, below. You choose the Boolean operator with the radio buttons between the two boxes. The search defined here is equivalent to "(sun AND bali) OR ubud." If we used an implied AND in front of "bali" (no operator would appear), then the search would be equivalent to "sun AND (bali OR ubud)." Note that the document in the background has both fields, at the top, and free-form text, below.

numeric value or range of values. It lets you choose a field, a numeric operator—less than (<), less than or equal to (≤), equal to (=), not equal to (< >), greater than (>), or greater than or equal to (≥)—and a numeric value. When you view the results of a numeric search, you don't see the matching value highlighted. The idea seems to be that you simply want to select these documents, rather than look at the particular value, although you could easily do the latter with a report (see below under "Output"). Reports also let you generate totals and subtotals on numeric fields within and across groupings of records.

Proximity Searches

Proximity searches let you do an AND search where two terms have to co-occur within a smaller distance than the whole document. Each of the two terms can be a simple word or phrase, but not logical expressions (e.g., no OR lists). You can specify the number of words, lines, sentences, or paragraphs (these are called proximity units) within which the two terms must co-occur. You can specify that the first term occur before, after, on either side of, or in the same proximity unit (line, sentence, or paragraph—you can't have two words co-occur in the same word) as the second. You can limit the search to the first proximity unit of each document. To review the results, you can either view them in the normal way or have the found units sent to a new file, where you'll see them listed all in one document, separated by dashed lines—*but* with no source information: a serious weakness.

Date Searches

If you have fields with dates in them, there are three types of searches you can do on them, all of which can be particularly useful in longitudinal studies. A simple date

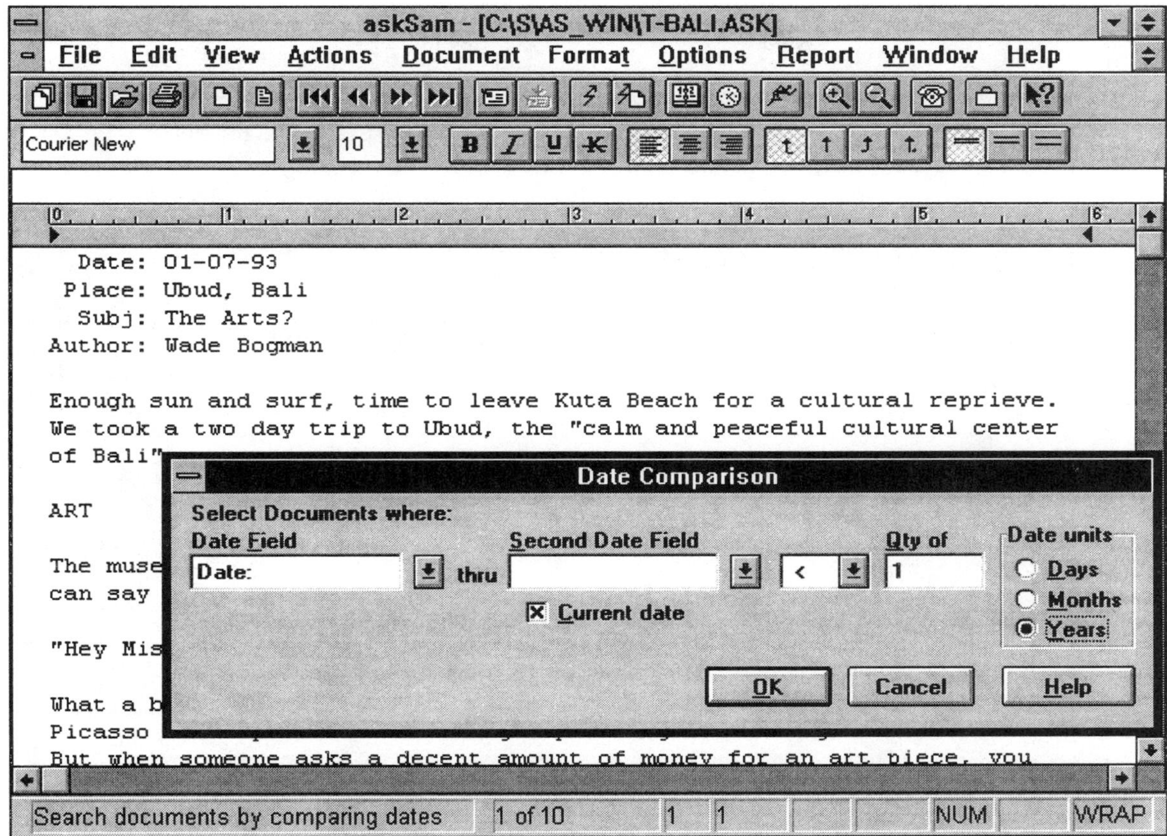

askSam Figure 5. Defining a Date Comparison search for documents where the date in the Date. field is less than 1 year different than the current date. Note that the second date could be another date field (e.g., if you were interested in the interval between enrollment and graduation) or a specific date other than today's. The dates can be compared in terms of days, months, or years.

search lets you compare the date in a date field, using the numeric operators, with today's date, a date you type in, or another date field. So, for example, you can find all documents where the date is no later than (≤) 1/1/84.

A date range search lets you compare a date field with two other dates that you type in. So you can look for documents where the date is no later than 1/1/84 but is after (>) 4/15/80.

The date comparison search dialog box (see Figure 5) has boxes for you to select the names of two different fields, a numeric operator, and in which you can type a number of days, months, or years. One date is subtracted from the other, and the result is compared, according to the operator you select, with the number you type in. So you could ask for documents where the two date fields (say, Enrollment[and Graduation[) are more than 4 years apart. A further option lets you put in an actual date instead of the second date field and compare that with the first date field.

Multiple Search Requests

The Multiple Search Request dialog box (see Figure 6) lets you combine character string, field, date, numeric, and proximity searches into one search request using the Boolean operators AND, OR, and NOT. So, you could find documents where the word "male" was in the Gender[field AND the word "enthusiastic" occurred in the same sentence as the word "teaching." The buttons on the left side of the dialog box let you pop up the various search request dialog boxes to define the different elements of the search. The buttons on the right let you assign Boolean operators to each element.

If you want to find documents where "enthusiastic" and "teaching" both occur in the field for answers to question 1 (call it answer1[), you can define two different field searches (one to find the word "enthusiastic" in answer1[and the other to find "teaching" in answer1[) and connect them with an AND, so that both must be true for a docu-

askSam Figure 6. Defining a Multiple Search Request. In this case, we're looking for the documents that have the word "Bali" anywhere, AND have the word "Arts" in the Subj. field, AND have the word "good" within three words on either side of the word "surf." (After you choose a software package for your project, you have our permission to go.)

ment to be retrieved. Note though, that, if you've got two occurrences of the same field in a document, and one term is in one occurrence of the field, and the other term is in the other occurrence, the document *will* be retrieved. This may or may not be what you want. It may also be a further limitation on the workaround strategy suggested under "Working on the Data," above, for coding with fields.

Also note that you cannot embed search elements within one another. So you cannot combine a field and a proximity search to find all documents where the words "enthusiastic" and "teaching" occurred in the same paragraph *within* answer1[. This is another real weakness.

Show (KWICs)

The Show command is similar to a KWIC. It lets you output all occurrences of a text string, with a specified amount of context around it, to a new file that you immediately see. You can choose the number of words, lines, sentences, or paragraphs before, after, or on either side of the string. You can also output just the line, sentence, or paragraph that contains the string. The way this differs from a standard KWIC is that you get no source information, whereas you normally would expect to get the filename, some document identifier (though this could be tricky because document numbers can change), page number, and perhaps line numbers—again, a serious weakness.

Wildcards

Wildcards are limited to the DOS * and ? (* matches any number of any nonspace characters, and ? matches any single character). You can use wildcards in Boolean, field, and proximity searches.

Hypertext Searching

Hypertext is implemented via hypertext searching. You can highlight some text and execute a search for that text in either the current file or another file (just click on a button or press a <Ctrl-key> combination). At first glance, this may seem like a kind of progressive searching and not much like real hypertext linking at all. However, when combined with the Report functions described further under "Output," below, you can get some very useful hypertexting going. This approach to hypertext has been referred to as intelligent, or implicit, hypertext, as contrasted to the explicit type of hypertext we see more often, in which there are fixed link points in the text (Kibby & Mayes, 1993). (Explicit hypertext is coming with Version 2.0. See the "Update" section, below.)

For example, say you want to search a notes database. You can create a report that lists the Date[, Subject[, and Number[fields for each document, one per line. This is sent to a new file, which you immediately see. You can scan through this list, select the line for a document you'd like to see, and click the hypertext search button (see Figure 8). Because the line you selected had enough information to uniquely identify the document you're looking for (its date, subject, and document number), your hypertext search jumps you right to that note. Thus the report becomes a sort of hypertext directory listing of the database.

But wait, it gets better. Reports can select only those documents that match a search, and all kinds of askSam searches are available. To continue the above example, you could have the reported list narrowed down only to references to those notes that contained a particular topic.

Search Macros

Again, search macros rely on the use of reports. As mentioned above, reports can include search requests. Any time you want to execute a search stored in a report, you simply run that report (there's a button to click to jump to the list of reports to run). If you haven't designed an output format for the report, you view all the search hits in context, just as you would if you had executed the search from a search dialog box.

Counting

There are a number of ways you can count things in askSam. First of all, there's a Count command, which lets you count either the number of occurrences of a text string in your database or the number of documents in your database that contain that text string. Second, when you define a search in the Multiple Search Request box, you can ask to be shown the number of documents that match the request, but you must do this *instead of*, and not in conjunction with, the actual search. Third, you can have counts done as part of a report. You can group records according to common values in specified fields and get counts of the records that fall into various groups and subgroups.

Output

You can print data directly by file, document, or range of pages, but not by a selection of text. You can define headers and footers for your printouts, with page numbers, number of pages in the batch being printed, date, time, filename, and path. Formatting is retained when you print directly, though it is lost when you generate a report. A .BMP (bitmap) graphic that was pasted in (one of those supplied as a screen background with a Gateway 2000 computer) showed significantly diminished print quality as compared with printing the same graphic from Paintbrush or a word processor; all gray scales were lost, and the whole image was in stark black and white. However, the askSam logo that's embedded in the "readme" database retained its gray-scale shading.

Reports

One of askSam's best, most powerful features is its report writer. Reports search for, sort, and output selected information from documents in a database to a new file, which can be viewed, hypertext searched from, or printed. You have a great deal of flexibility in defining the appearance and contents of a report, although *all character formatting is lost when data get sent to a report.*

When you create a report, there are three areas you work on. First, you "select" the records to be included in the report through the Multiple Search Request dialog box (which gives access to all types of searches). Next, you specify any sorting you want done on the output. This is done through the same dialog box you use for sorting the database, described earlier, with all the same options.

Finally, you go to the layout screen (see Figure 7), where you define the layout of the report for each document (data from each retrieved document will appear one below the other in a list, separated by a line, or on separate pages, as you wish). This layout screen looks a lot like a regular document, and you can type and edit boilerplate text in it freely, though you cannot apply character formatting. Any text will appear with every retrieved document (so we're talking just about boilerplate, not actual data). In the lower left corner of the screen is a floating toolbar, a movable group of icons that gives you access to all the layout tools. You can place fields anywhere on the screen, either by typing the fieldnames (as you did when you defined your Entry Form) or by clicking on the Place Field button, picking from a list, and then clicking with the mouse on the spot you want the field to appear. As you do this, the status bar at the bottom shows the line and column numbers of the location of the mouse cursor, which can be very helpful in aligning things carefully. Wherever a fieldname is placed, the actual contents of the field will appear when the report is run (see Figure 8). If you want the fieldname itself in-

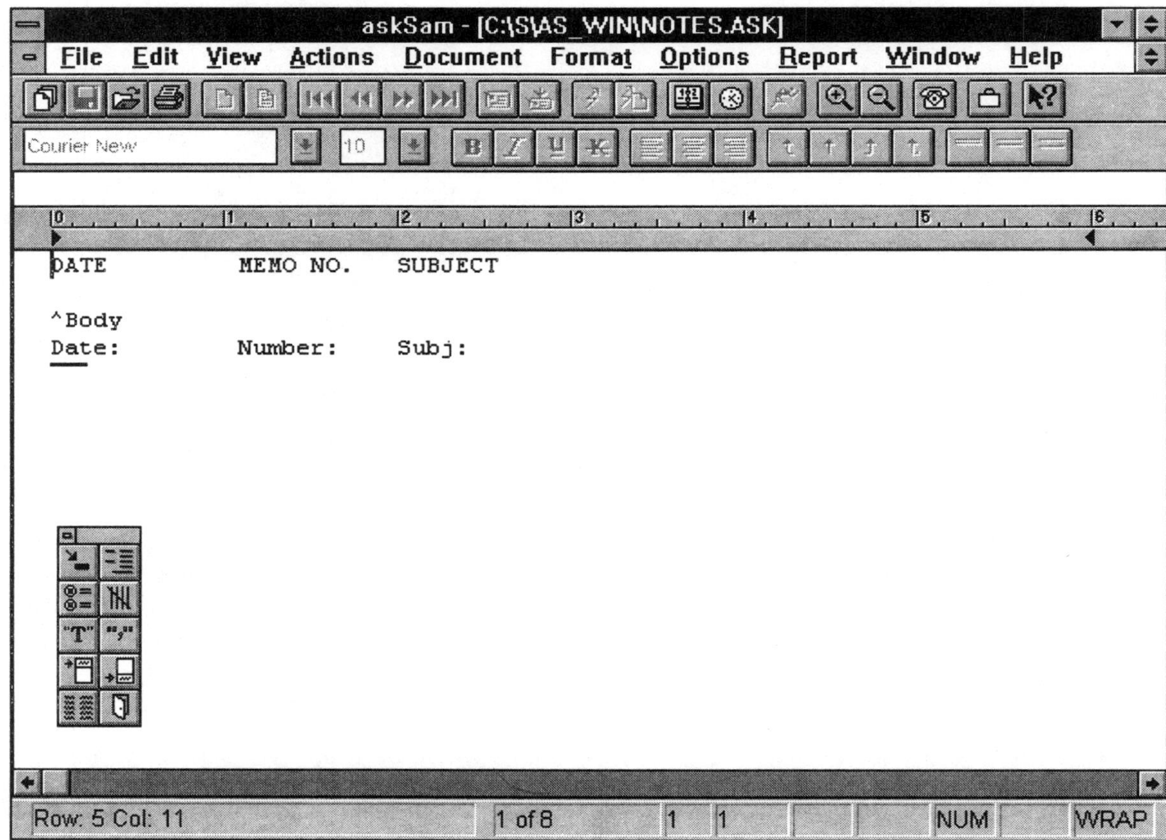

askSam Figure 7. Designing a report layout. The floating button bar at lower left gives you access to most report-design functions. The first row of text is boilerplate—headers that will appear at the top of every page, though a header could also be made to appear with every record. Below this will be a series of rows (records) showing date, number, and subject for every retrieved document (see Figure 8). The line that reads "^Body" separates the header from the part that appears for every record. Without this, the line of text would simply appear above every row.

cluded in your report, you type it in as text without the field character (e.g., [).

There are options that let you tailor data output. For example, if you are creating a report of addresses, you'll want a comma after the City[field. But some cities have longer names than others. Relative field length options let you put the comma right after the city name or leave exactly two spaces between the state and the zip code. You can also force the data from a field to print in a column of a specified width; if the data are longer, they will wrap to the next line, staying within the boundaries of the column you've defined.

Documents can be grouped in reports based on fields. So you could, for example, have all the data from each research site grouped together. If you define groups, you can have totals for numeric fields across each group. As mentioned earlier, you can also get counts of the number of documents that fall into each group. askSam is quite sophisticated in its ability to handle groupings and subgroupings on multiple fields, and subtotals and totals on a given group or across groups.

Theory Building

askSam is not what we'd classify as a theory-building program, but it does have some useful features for building theory. Hypertexting in askSam does not let you create permanent links between one spot in your data and another, although you could, for example, insert unique strings that only appear at two hyperlinked spots—for your first hyperlink, you could insert {1} at both ends; for your second link, {2}; and so on. Further, some very sophisticated hypertexting can be accomplished with the creative use of reports or with the use of fields specifically

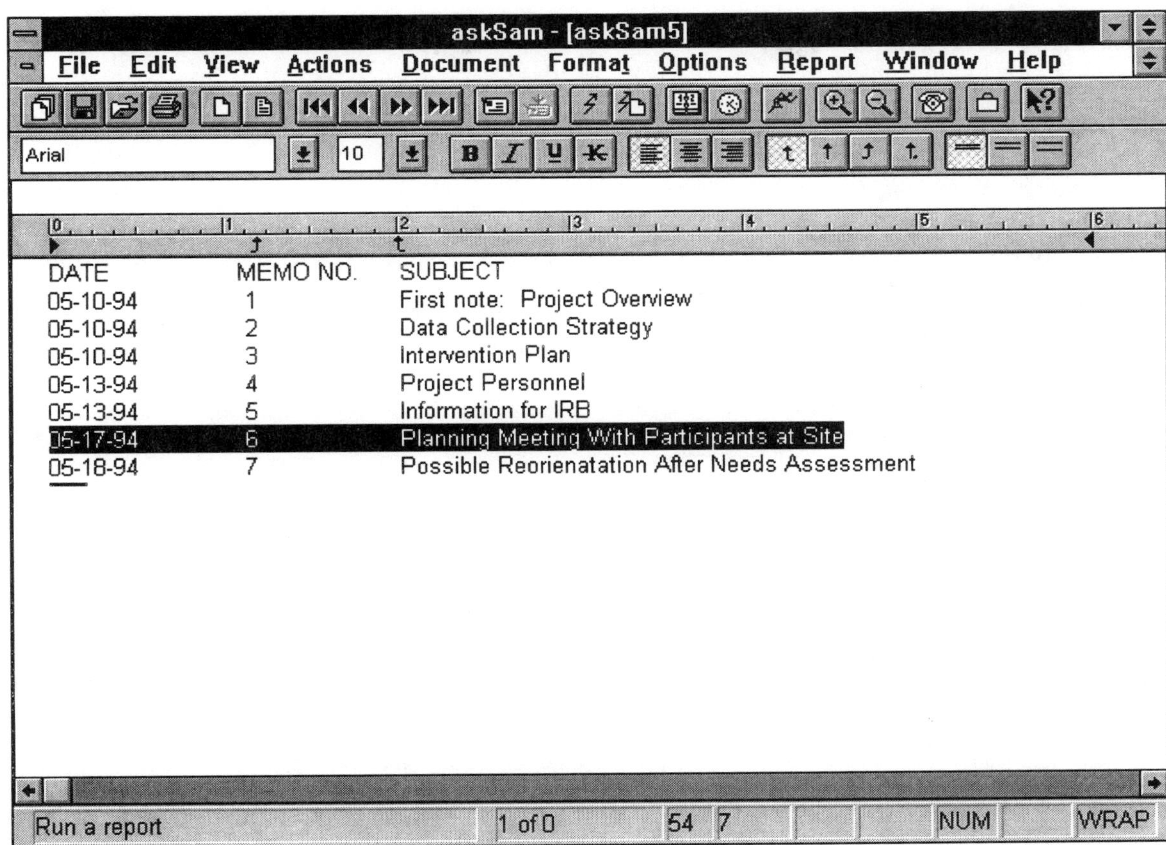

askSam Figure 8. The report generated by the layout defined in Figure 7. The line for memo number 6 has been selected. Doing a hypertext search for this text in the notes database will jump us straight to the right memo, because there's enough unique information here that only that memo will be found.

designed to facilitate hypertext searching (see the discussion under "Hypertext Searching," above).

Graphics Editing

askSam lets you paste bitmap graphics (or anything else that can be placed on the Windows clipboard), or other OLE graphic objects, into documents, Entry Forms, or report layouts. Once they are pasted in, they can be resized but not edited. Remember that OLE objects, whether linked or embedded, can still be edited in their native applications (just double-click and up pops, say, Harvard Graphics, with the graphic loaded and ready to edit).

User Friendliness

User friendliness is a strong point of the Windows version of askSam. The program itself is pleasant and relatively easy to use, although a few things could be made easier (you shouldn't have to pull down a menu and select from it every time you want a search dialog box—they should all be available with your choice of keystroke or toolbar button). The program also suffers from some serious bugs, as described under "Miscellaneous," below.

The tutorials are very helpful and easy to follow and took much less than the 3½ hours (2:15 for the lessons on structured data and another 1:20 for unstructured data) suggested by the manual. They really show you all around the program, give you lots of interesting ideas, and leave you ready to start working. The manual isn't bad but at times gives inadequate or confusing information (e.g., the rule behind the business about implied and specified ANDs isn't explained, it's just illustrated with an example that doesn't tell you anything about how another search would work). It doesn't tell you anything about the commands that are available from the command line; as mentioned earlier, it was necessary to go to the reference manual from the *DOS* version (Seaside Software, 1991a) to get information about commands. You don't get this manual if you buy the Windows version. Too many things can't be found in the index (like "Technical Support"!).

On-screen help is available in two ways. First, at the lower left of the status bar, you usually see a brief explanation of whatever button or menu item the mouse cursor is pointing to. Second, there's the standard Windows-style help system. This wasn't bad, though—as is usually the case—it was a bit less informative than the manual. The version we had (1.0b) also had a tendency to bring up the wrong help screen when help was requested from a dialog box (we're told this has since been fixed).

Technical support is available from 9 to 6 eastern time. You're supposed to make the toll call to Florida, even though there's an 800 number for sales, PR people, and so on. We called the 800 number once and asked for tech support. After we argued for several minutes that our office phone system wouldn't let us call Florida (the truth), we were patched through. It seems unlikely that you could do this on a regular basis though. The tech support people are friendly and helpful, although they didn't know what the rule behind the implied and specified AND was either (we were able to figure it out together).

Miscellaneous

Bugs

Unfortunately, the Windows version of the program, as of Version 1.0b, is not yet very stable. It frequently crashed. (Most often, this happened when we tried to do a search it didn't like. For example, we entered "p*"—meaning any word that starts with "p"—as a term in a proximity search, and *crashhh*! Another time we mistakenly tried to search an empty, new file. When we were asked if we wanted to save the file, we realized there was nothing to save and so said "no," and instantly: *crashhh*!) Windows 3.1 has been designed so that, when a program crashes, Windows can usually protect itself and any other applications you've got running, so that only the bad application goes down. However, askSam managed to lock up the whole machine a couple of times, and at one point the first three pages of this review were lost (we were not happy). Lesson: SESO (save early and save often). askSam helps with this by making you save your work every time you try to leave anything you've changed. There were also problems with an askSam database created from a Psychlit download, which somehow corrupted itself, crashed, and lost the data.

askSam on Networks

askSam is available for use on networks, but the documentation we received did not contain information about how this works. If you're interested in network capabilities like having multiple users simultaneously working on a database, contact the developer for more information.

DOS Versus Windows

The DOS version of the program is an altogether more powerful database management system than the Windows version, and as a result is more difficult to learn and use. (Actually, the Windows version is intended as a more user-friendly, more widely accessible implementation of the program.) It's still enjoyable, and mostly easy to use once you get started. We were able to get in and get started searching in no time with the demo, but it took quite a while longer to figure out what else the program could do and how to do it. There is no tutorial, and the manuals are more dense and technical than the ones for the Windows version. On-screen help is provided via an on-line version of the manual, which works fairly well. There is no character formatting and no graphics or OLE support.

The DOS version has a full database programming language, only about 20 of the commands from which are available in the Windows version. With this language, you can reportedly (we didn't take the time to learn it) create your own applications, build new databases out of old ones, set up relational databases out of multiple files, and so on. You can also index fields, a technique used by traditional databases to significantly enhance the speed of searches in large files.

Rather than creating a single Entry Form for each file, as in the Windows version, you can define up to 10 "key templates" per file, which let you insert 10 different predefined field structures into your documents. As with Entry Forms, these can contain both text and fields. This gives you a lot more flexibility and could be particularly useful for databases where you had different types of records.

The DOS version also has a somewhat different database structure than the Windows version. Records are limited to a single 80-character by 20-line screen, and in Record mode you see them one at a time. You can switch to Document mode, in which the records appear linked together, and scroll by as though they were one, with visible breaks between them. You can also switch to Free mode, in which the lines between documents disappear. Further, there are such things as implied and contextual fields, which allow you to identify fields without typing in fieldnames and field characters.

"Hypertext" is much more sophisticated. You can still do hypertext searches as in the Windows version, though less flexibly. Also, you can set up hypertext menus, which list not only particular phrases you want to search from but also commands or programs you want to be able to execute. This is not what we usually think of as hypertext, but you can use these commands and programs to do things like find particular pieces of information, so that it is more similar than you might think. Hypertext facilities intended for use by developers often look like this (Metamorph is similar).

Finally, the DOS version is faster and less resource intensive (as DOS versions of most things are). You can run it on a floppy-only PC with 384K RAM and DOS 2.0 if you want to (but do you really?).

Update

With Version 2.0 of askSam for Windows, which was in beta-testing at the time of this writing, the program should receive a batch of significant new features. We mention here some of the more significant ones that appeared to be in good working order in the beta version.

Version 2.0 supports the attachment of named "bookmarks" to ranges of text (typically words or short phrases) so that you can jump to them from anywhere in a file. It also allows you to set fixed, or explicit, hypertext links. You attach the start point of a link to some text and then specify one of several different types of destinations. The destinations can be bookmarked text in the current document, current file, or another file. They can also be reports in the current file, or reports in other files, so that when you double-click on such a link a report is automatically run. Or the "destination" can be a menu command, so that when a link is double-clicked on some action is performed. Further, askSam's implicit style of hypertext has been extended. Double-clicking on a line in a report will now cause you to be automatically jumped to the document that line came from, whereas with Version 1.0 this could be accomplished only by a hypertext search for all documents that contained the same text as on the report line.

There is now a command that lets you select a group of files for searching. There are also two new options in the Search in Field dialog box that let you search for all occurrences of a field that have no data or for all occurrences of a field that are nonempty. In addition, the Global Replace command now allows you to set up multiple search criteria to specify the documents in which you want a replace operation carried out.

The options for getting data into askSam, and manipulating them once they're there, have also been improved. The import options now include Word 6.0, WordPerfect 6.0, comma and tab delimited ASCII, NEXIS files, and CompuServe Information Manager files. For about $30, you will be able to buy an add-on set of 10 additional import filters, including AmiPro and Wordstar. Even more interestingly, a new *Automatic Field Recognition* option allows you to simply tell askSam what field character is in your data, and it will automatically recognize your fields. Thus, in the Psychlit download example, all that would have been necessary would have been to tell askSam that the field character was a ":" and the rest would have been done automatically. The Data Entry mode has also been enhanced: You no longer have to switch out of Data Entry mode in order to expand long fields; as long as the field is already more than one line long, it will automatically expand as you type. There's also now an add-on you can get that lets you scan data directly into an askSam database.

Formatting and reporting options have also been enhanced. Formatting can now include "hanging indents," background colors, and sub- and superscripted text. Reports now can include formatting as defined in the report layout, but formatting from the original document is still lost. Report layout is made easier by the presence on screen of a list of fieldnames, which you can drag and drop into position on the layout.

Comparative Remarks

The closest competitor to askSam reviewed here is Folio VIEWS. In short, the choice should be easy: If you really want to use structured data, either by itself or together with unstructured data, and you want to be able to manipulate it by fields, as with a traditional database, choose askSam. Otherwise, choose Folio VIEWS.

Folio VIEWS is much better at formatting and printing, explicit hypertexting, memoing, and annotating. It offers hierarchical outlining of your data, nonhierarchical grouping of it, "highlighters" that can be used for coding, and free-form, overlappable fields. Its searches are more flexible and faster, allowing nesting of all the different aspects of a search request. It also appears to be a more stable, robust program.

On the other hand, askSam acts more like a traditional database. It makes better use of field structure, allowing you to easily create standardized field layouts or to tell it where to find the fields in data you import. For example, to use the Psychlit download we mentioned earlier in Folio VIEWS, we would have had to do a lot of elaborate work on the file, inserting codes to mark the fields before we imported it. In askSam, all we had to do was import the data, tell askSam that the field character was : instead of [, then go to the Entry Form and type in the fieldnames, and we were ready to go. Furthermore, askSam's use of fields in reports gives you powerful data manipulation possibilities, like sorting and rearranging your fields and creating hypertext directories, that you couldn't touch in Folio VIEWS.

Like askSam, MAX can also manage free-form text, structured text, and numbers—but it keeps different kinds of data (text, numeric, demographic) in separate, linked databases. MAX can in addition do coding, send numeric data to statistical programs, and handle general data management. But it has no word processing facilities and is less flexible than askSam in assigning fields, searching, and making reports.

Summary

askSam brings together the power and functionality of a traditional database manager with a truly free-form textbase manager. The Windows version gives up some of the raw horsepower of the DOS version but is much easier to use. It's still quite powerful and goes well beyond competitors like Folio VIEWS in field-based database management, though it falls short of Folio VIEWS in most other respects. It also has the potential to help you with a wide variety of project management chores, including PIM (personal information management) functions like scheduling, address list management, and to-do lists; archiving of memos, faxes, and e-mail; and literature abstracting and indexing. The DOS version is an even more heavy-duty database management system, specifically designed to handle mixtures of free-form text and structured data.

References

Kibby, M. R., & Mayes, T. (1993). Towards intelligent hypertext. In R. McAleese (Ed.), *Hypertext: Theory into practice* (pp. 138-144). Oxford: Intellect.

Seaside Software, Inc. (1991a). *askSam reference.* Perry, FL: Author.

Seaside Software, Inc. (1991b). *askSam user's guide.* Perry, FL: Author.

Seaside Software, Inc. (1991c). *Getting started with askSam.* Perry, FL: Author.

Tyk, S., & Mohler, K. D. (1993a). *askSam for Windows getting started guide.* Perry, FL: Seaside Software, Inc.

Tyk, S., & Mohler, K. D. (1993b). *askSam for Windows user's guide.* Perry, FL: Seaside Software, Inc.

Folio VIEWS, Version 3.0

Available for Windows, DOS, and Macintosh[1]

Folio Corporation
5072 North 300 West
Provo, UT 84604

Phone: (801) 229-6700
(800) 543-6546 (Sales)
(801) 229-6650 (Support)
Fax: (801) 229-6790

Price: $495
$150 Educational (Students and Faculty)

Hardware Requirements:
For Windows and DOS

- 286 or better IBM compatible PC
- Windows 3.0 or later
- DOS 3.0 or later
- 2MB RAM (4MB recommended)
- One high density (3.5 in. or 5.25 in.) floppy drive
- Hard drive with 17MB free space for full installation (can be done in as little as 2MB for *very* bare-bones installation)
- Graphics adapter and monitor (EGA or VGA recommended)

For Macintosh

- 68030 or better Macintosh
- System 7 or better
- 2MB RAM (4MB recommended)

Overview

Folio VIEWS 3.0 for Windows is much, much more than a textbase manager; it's a package that will serve extremely well for textbase management, search and retrieval, coding, hypertexting, memoing and annotation, and even multimedia applications. About the only things it lacks are theory-building, network editing, or dedicated matrix-building functions.

Although it's a database, you look at your data in a WYSIWYG Windows word processor. Records generally correspond to paragraphs (unless you don't want them to). VIEWS is a "free-form" database in that fields can occur anywhere within records and can vary in size. (See Figure 1.) You can edit your data anytime you want and all changes are dynamically (instantly and automatically) added to the full index kept for the search engine.

You can apply "highlighters" to the text, just as you'd use a highlighter pen, and you can have different named highlighters for different types of information. Because

1. This review focuses on Version 3.0 for Windows. Version 3.1 was just being released as this book was being completed, and its important new features are discussed in the "Update" section of this review. There is also a DOS version that we haven't reviewed here. VIEWS is currently available for the Macintosh only in a "Lite" edition, but a full version is expected around the time this book is published.

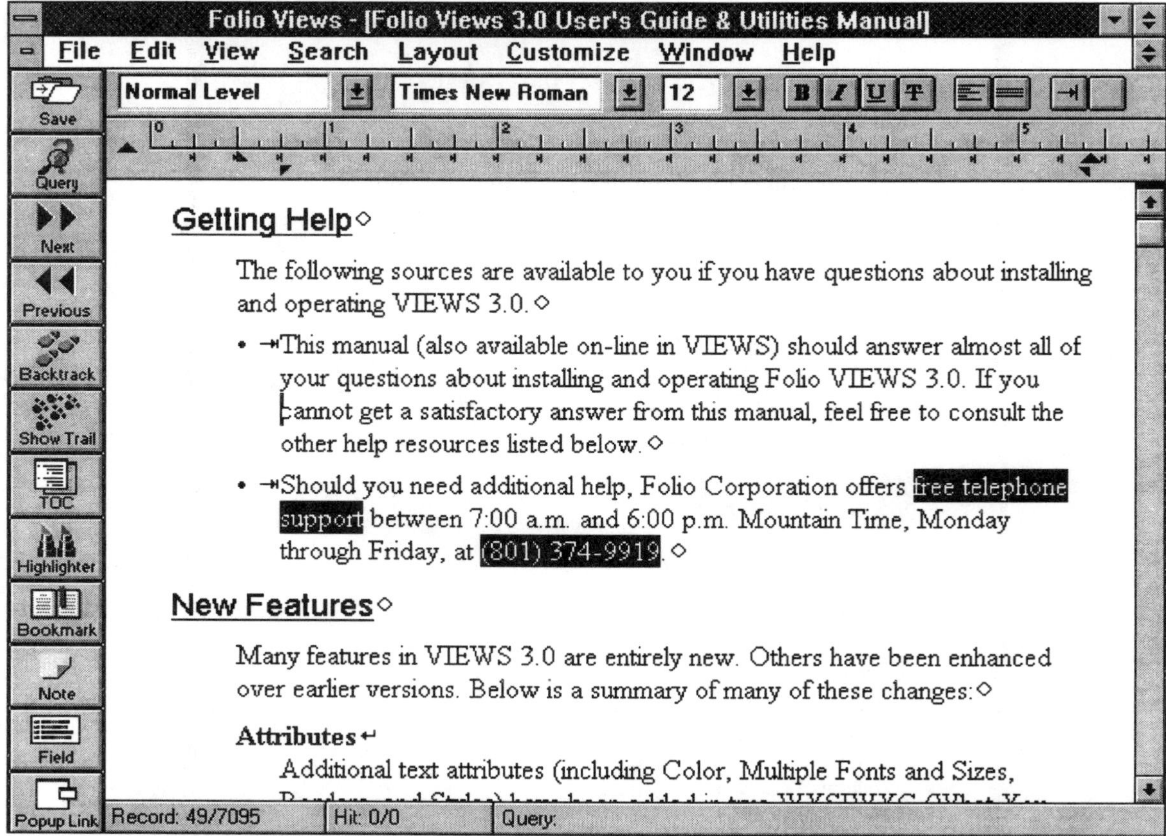

Folio VIEWS Figure 1. Looking at an infobase—in this case, the on-line manual that ships with the program. The end of each record is marked with a ◊. Text in the field "phone numbers" appears in reverse video (white text on black background). Note that this field only shows up in one record of those on the screen and is not continuous within this record. There is a "toolbelt" on the left that gives quick access to many functions, and the ribbon across the top facilitates easy formatting.

you can retrieve text based on highlighters, you can use these for coding in a code-and-retrieve style.

There is a table of contents (TOC) view, with expandable/collapsible level headings, which you can use to organize or navigate your document. In addition to hierarchical levels, you can also collect and define "groups" of text that aren't sequential.

There are two built-in ways to attach memos to text. Both methods give you pop-up windows in which to write: "Notes" being attached to paragraphs and "Popups" being attached to a word or phrase in the text. (You can also simply type annotations into the text, setting them off with any display attributes—such as color or italics—available in Windows.)

Above all, the program is *easy* and fun to use. Many functions can be executed with a click of the mouse, and the whole thing has a nice intuitive feel. The fact that VIEWS combines textbase managing, text search, and code-and-retrieval features makes it a particularly good choice for big cross-case analytic projects where you need good cross-case comparability that respects the richness and complexity of each case, or projects where you have lots of different types of data.

Database Structure

Folio VIEWS calls a database an "infobase," presumably to indicate that you can have many different kinds of information stored there. Data are either entered directly into an infobase or created in another program, like your word processor, and then imported. An infobase can be up to 16 terabytes (or 16 *million* megabytes) in size. A separate index of all words in your infobase is maintained, so that search results are practically instantaneous. The index is automatically updated as you type or edit, with no noticeable penalty in speed.

A Folio VIEWS "infobase" can have a wide range of structures, from virtually no structure at all, like straight text, to a highly structured database with records and fields, hierarchical levels organizing the records, and nonhierarchical groupings of nonsequential records. Note, though, that the traditional notion of records and fields as the rows and columns of a matrix becomes just a metaphor in Folio VIEWS. As we're about to see, though records can be single lines, they're more likely to be paragraphs or larger chunks of information, and fields do not have to be arranged in strict columns. Nonetheless, you can still *think* of it as a matrix, and doing so is helpful.

At the most basic level, an infobase can just consist of a bunch of text. Typically, your paragraphs will be treated as records for search purposes, though, if you like, you can adjust the boundaries of records. Whether you're working with just plain text, or setting up something that looks more like a traditional records-and-fields database, you may want to make such adjustments.

To put more than one paragraph in a record, you can insert a line break by hitting <Shift-enter> or a paragraph break with <Ctrl-shift-enter>. (The difference is that in the former case the two blocks of text will look like separate paragraphs but be treated as one by things like paragraph formatting commands.) If you want units smaller than paragraphs, like sentences, to be records, you'll have to break them into separate paragraphs.

If you are working with running text, you might want to define a record for each case, which might be, for example, individuals. You would then have many retrieval options for finding cases that met particular criteria. Or you might have many different types of source documents—like interviews, observations, reflective memos, transcribed documents, and so on—and want to put each of these in a separate record, so that you could, for example, limit searches to documents of a given type. Of course, there may be many situations where you'll want to stick with the standard one paragraph to a record format (which still leaves you lots of ways to group by case or source document, as discussed under "Levels" and "Groups," below). It all depends on your strategy.

Fields

Fields in Folio VIEWS are far more flexible than in a traditional database. You can apply them flexibly to any range of text. You can define fields of several types: numeric (either for whole numbers or numbers with floating decimal points), text, date, and time, and you can define as many named fields of each type as you want. For example, you could set up text fields for subject's name, observer, and site, an integer field for subject's ID number, and a date field for the observation date.

Very interestingly, fields can overlap, be nested, and appear more than once in a record. You can also define different display attributes for fields. Thus another way you could easily use fields is to code: Define a text field for each code, then code your text by applying fields.

You can search for all records that have a given field—which you might want to do if you used fields for coding—or records with particular combinations of words in that field—say, to find records with the name Deborah Crane in the "subject" field, not just anywhere in the text. (There's lots more you can do with fields when searching; see "Searching," below.) It's important to note that this means you aren't stuck with records as your chunk size for search purposes; you can search for co-occurrence by record or by field (and lots of other ways as well—see "Searching" again).

If you want fields, you simply select the text that you want to place in a field (using the mouse or keyboard) and "apply" the field by clicking on the field button on the toolbelt or issuing a command from a menu (see Figure 1). (You're then asked to choose an existing field definition or create a new one for this text.) You can also set up the field in the text ahead of time: Just apply it to a couple of blank spaces in the text (it's a good idea to type the field name in or next to this blank field, so you know it's there). Then you can place the cursor in the field and enter text anytime you want—you can enter as much text as you want and the field will expand to fit it. If you want standardized records, you could set up a blank master record, like a template, with the fields as you want them, then make copies of the master whenever you want to start a new record.

You can associate character attributes (font, size, underline, bold, foreground and background color, and so on) with a field, and they will automatically apply to all text in that field. This way you can easily see what text is in the field. (Using a background color is great, then you can see a solid rectangle of color under all the text in the field, which makes it *look* more like a field does in a traditional database. See Figure 1.)

Automatically applying fields. One of the few drawbacks to this setup is that you can't tell VIEWS to automatically apply fields to all similar text in all records. For example, we wanted to import a file full of e-mail, one message per record, and place the "From:," "To:," "Subject:," and "Date:" information in fields. (More typically, you might have typed up your fieldnotes in your word processor, with the subject name, ID, observer, site, and date all on the first few lines of the file and want those things automatically put in fields when you import into VIEWS.) In a traditional database program, it would have been a relatively simple matter to specify where the data for each field were located in the ASCII being imported and have them automatically placed in the correct fields.

In VIEWS, however, you have to do a bit of a workaround, which is hard to learn but fairly easy to do once you know how. This process is discussed at more length in the section on "Folio Flat File Format," under "Data Entry," below.

Levels

If you want to get even more structured, you can impose a hierarchy on your infobase by creating an outline, or table of contents, that organizes the whole thing. If fields are the substructure of your records, then table of contents "levels" are the superstructure. You can have as many as 255 levels of outline headers (though you probably wouldn't want more than 5 or so). You can have as many specific headers of a given level as you want. For example, the header "Levels," just before this paragraph, is a specific header, and is at level 2 in the outline of this review, as is the header "Fields," above. Both fall under the level 1 header, "Database Structure." The structure looks like this:

Database Structure	(level 1)
Fields	(level 2)
Automatically applying fields	(level 3)
Levels	(level 2)

You can toggle to the table of contents (TOC) view to see just the level headers, formatted like an outline. The TOC view has expandable/collapsible level headings, which you can use to navigate your document. (If you collapse a heading, you won't see its subs, but if you expand it, you will. See Figure 2.) It can also display search hits in user-specifiable context (say, 3 words either side or as many as 50 words on either side) listed under the headings: Double-click on the hit line and you pop to the hit in full text view or scroll to it if you have both the table of contents and full text view windows open. This is a very nice way to see a quick, initial summary of search results before you delve into the text.

Perhaps most important, you can use levels for searching, restricting searches to levels or specific headers. You can also ask for co-occurrence of search terms by level rather than by record. Thus you might organize data for a multicase, multisource type project using levels.

Let's say your cases are individuals, they are located at multiple sites, and you have observations, interviews, and archival data on each subject. You might set up first-level headers for sites and then second-level headers for individuals. Second-level headers are now your cases, and first-level headers group them by site. Then, you could set up third-level headers for each case for observations, interviews, and archival data. If you have multiple observations for each case, you could go to fourth-level headers and so on. The whole thing might look like this:

Header	*Level*
Site 1	(1)
Deborah Crane	(2)
Interviews	(3)
9/1/93	(4)
9/15/93	(4)
10/1/93	(4)
Observations	(3)
9/12/93	(4)
9/13/93	(4)
Archival Data	(3)
Performance review	(4)
Educational records	(4)
John Roberts	(2)
Interviews	(3)
9/5/93	(4)
10/20/93	(4)
Observations	(3)
9/18/93	(4)
9/19/93	(4)
Archival Data	(3)
Performance review	(4)
Educational records	(4)
Site 2	(1)
and so on	

The table of contents view in Figure 2 shows what this might look like in VIEWS.

You could now view, or limit any searches to, John Roberts, all interviews, September 12 observations, the September 1 interview with Deborah Crane, and so on. You could also look for any case (level two section) that has a certain combination of fields (which could be codes). But we're wandering into searching here. We'll return to these issues under "Searching," below.

Groups

Groups work similarly to levels: they define sets of records. Unlike levels, however, groups are not hierarchical. Text in a group does not have to be sequential. So, if you didn't have the structure described above, you could create a group for all text about Joe Hailey, a group for all interview text, and so on. Then even if your text about Joe is scattered, you can see it all at once or limit a search to it. This could be very useful, for example, if there's text about Joe in your interviews with lots of other people.

Data Entry

You can enter text directly into Folio VIEWS, or you can create it in your word processor first. VIEWS itself

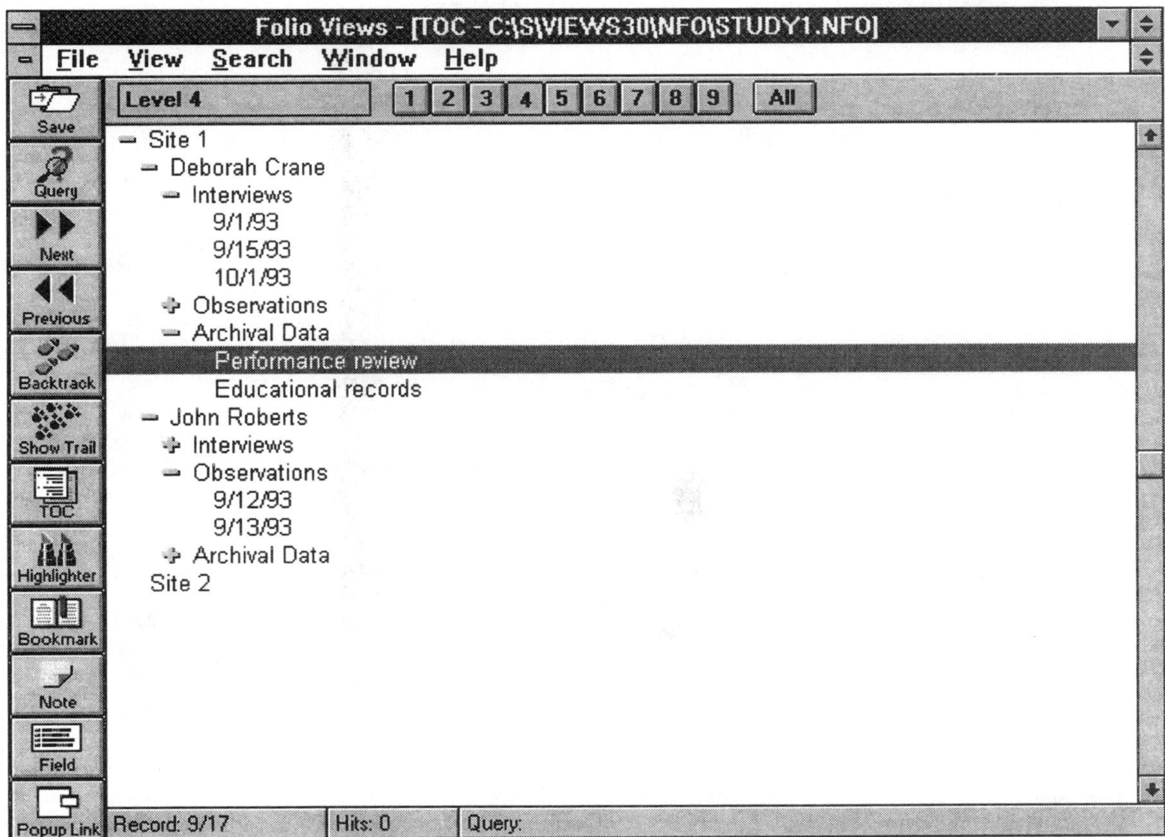

Folio VIEWS Figure 2. Table of Contents view for a hypothetical study. The "+" signs next to some headings can be double-clicked with the mouse to expand those headings (reveal hidden lower level headings) and the "–" signs next to others can be double-clicked to collapse subheadings.

functions as a good, easily learned Windows word processor, so entering data directly is a breeze; you have lots of standard editing and formatting options. VIEWS even has a style sheet with styles for each level, highlighter, field, and hypertext link type as well as paragraph and character styles.[2] The index is automatically updated in "real time" (as you work), so that it always reflects exactly what's in your infobase.

VIEWS can directly import from Microsoft Word (DOS and Windows, but not versions 6.0) or WordPerfect (DOS and Windows, *including* versions 6.0), retaining all your formatting, embedded objects (like graphics and spreadsheets), and even translating your outline (Word) or table of contents (WordPerfect) levels into VIEWS levels. VIEWS will, in fact, retain much of what you can do with these word processors, including redlining, borders, summary info (Word) or document summary (WordPerfect), tables (Word only), styles (Word only), hypertext links (goto buttons in Word, cross-references in WordPerfect), and bookmarks (Word only). Footnotes, annotations, and endnotes are placed in pop-up notes. One of the few things VIEWS won't import correctly is text in columns.

For other word processors, you must convert your text to ASCII or one of the supported word processors before importing. VIEWS can also import data from the LEXIS and NEXIS services—no surprise since Folio's parent company, MEAD Data Central, produces them also.

Just about any other object that can be pasted in the Windows environment (through OLE or the clipboard) can be pasted into an infobase. You can paste in graphics, charts, equations, animation, video, sound—you name it. VIEWS

2. A style is a predefined format that you can apply to a batch of text, and a style sheet is the collection of styles for a document. The better word processors have style sheets that let you set up styles for different kinds of paragraphs or types of text. Styles make text formatting easy and consistent. To apply formatting with a style, you just select the text and choose the style, and all paragraph and character formatting for the style is automatically applied.

has a very nice "Object Manager" that keeps track of all the different kinds of objects you have on your hard disk (or have the software to create) and allows you to name, rename, preview, edit, and place them in your infobase. Thanks to OLE, if you double-click on, say, a Microsoft Excel spreadsheet in your infobase, Excel will start up to let you edit the spreadsheet. OLE also lets you make live links, so that if you ever change the data in Excel, the portion of spreadsheet in your infobase will change too.

Folio Flat File Format

You can, if you want, do a lot of work on a file before you import it, to set up aspects of your infobase uniformly and automatically. This involves working on your infobase in Folio Flat File format (FFF). FFF format files are ASCII files with codes inserted to mark all of the different kinds of things you can have in an infobase. For example, <FD:From> would mark the beginning of text in a "From" field, and </FD:From> would mark the end of it. You can export an infobase to FFF format, or you can start working on an ASCII file, inserting codes, and thus turning it into an FFF file. You can use a separate search-and-replace utility (Folio Search and Replace—FSR) to automatically insert such things as records, fields, and levels in FFF format, and then import the file [back] into an infobase. While hard to learn how to do, for large infobases this could be a big work saver and create consistency you might otherwise be hard pressed to get.

To illustrate, let's return to the e-mail example. It seemed it should be possible to have VIEWS automatically put all text in a line that started with, for example, "From:" in a "From" field, but it wasn't that easy. Instead, it was necessary to export the infobase to FFF format, use FSR to insert the field codes, and then import it back into a new infobase.

FSR is a very sophisticated search-and-replace utility that comes with VIEWS. We had to use it to find each instance of text for the "From" field (which always began with "From:" and ended with a carriage return) and insert field-beginning and field-ending codes (<FD:From> and </FD:From>). FSR lets you specify all sorts of special conditions, combinations, and patterns of characters to look for so that you can do operations like this. But the syntax is *hard* to learn, and the manual for it is poorly organized. We eventually gave up trying to figure out how to do the example and invested in a 20-minute toll call to Utah for tech support.

Thanks to the kind folks at tech support, we now understand how to write the basic query to do the kind of operation described and could probably figure out how to do a similar operation (depending on *how* similar it was) on a new project without help. Once they explain it to you, you could too, whether you're a Level 2, 3, or 4 computer user. If you're an eager Level 1 user, you could probably do it too, but it'll be a lot less painful with the help of a Level 2 or 3 friend.

Working on the Data

You can edit your data freely whenever you want, and all changes are added instantly to the index. Remember, it's a good Windows word processor. VIEWS supports the full range of Windows 3.1's scalable fonts, colors, and so on that you can apply to your text, manually or using styles. You can define headers and footers to print with each page. There's even a spell-checker.

But there are an awful lot of other things you can do to your data before you even think about searching. A brief overview: As mentioned above, you can code with fields, and you can also code with something called highlighters, which we'll discuss in a moment. You can insert bookmarks that you can jump to from anywhere and five different kinds of hypertext links. There are two different kinds of pop-up notes you can use to annotate or memo your data (confusingly, one kind is called Notes, and the other Popups). There's also a facility that lets you "tag" records of interest. Then you can restrict your view to tagged records and just work on those. Finally, you can set up a "shadow file" in which you can do virtually any operation without affecting the original file.

Highlighters

Highlighters are based on the metaphor of using a highlighter pen on hard copy. You can define as many different named highlighters, with different colors or other display attributes, as you want.[3] They can be applied to overlapping or nested segments: Just highlight text with the mouse, click on a button, and up pops a list from which you can choose the highlighter you want or define a new one. Highlighters are actually very much like fields except that you do *not* define different data types (like text, numeric, and so on). Like fields, highlighters would also be very well suited for coding. You can use highlighters just like fields for search requests; you can just get records (or levels) with a particular combination of highlighters or find particular combinations of words in highlighters. We'll explain how to do this and more in "Searching," below.

3. Many qualitative researchers have experimented with using colors for different categories of codes, and this can be an extremely helpful approach. It is helpful to see the colors on screen, but it would be nice to have a color printer so you could see them on your hard copy. You don't need a fancy color printer either; a decent color ink jet printer can currently be had for $200 to $400.

Hypertext: Links and Bookmarks

Again, the program is a standout when compared with any other program we've looked at. You can define five types of hypertext links: jump links, pop-up links, program links, object links, and query links (all described in the next paragraph). To create a link, you select the text you want it attached to, pull down a menu, and choose the type of link you want. You'll get a dialog box that lets you name your links. Link points can be attached to a range of text, like a word, or a sentence, and they are identified with text attributes you choose, like color and underlining. To activate the link, you double-click on that text. You can backtrack through your link jumps or call up a "trail" of all jumps you've made and choose the place you want to return to (here's where naming your links comes in handy).

Jump links are traditional hypertext links. They allow you to jump from point to point in the text (you define both points). Your start and end points do *not* have to be in the same infobase, so you can define a link that will jump you from a point in one infobase to a point in another. *Popup links* cause a Popup note to appear, and are discussed further under "Memoing," the next section. *Program links* launch another application: You double-click on the link and another program (your word processor, statistical package, animation program, and so on) starts up. *Object links* bring up any OLE object, like a graphic in a box, or some other multimedia object. *Query links* perform a predefined query (search) whenever you double-click them. So, for example, you could link some text that talks about Johnny's feelings about the lunchroom to a query that retrieves every record marked with the lunchroom highlighter that has Johnny's name in it.

You can actually use query links to create what amount to other kinds of links. The tutorial uses query links to make a particularly useful additional kind of link: a *group link*, which changes the current view of the database so that you just see and work with the text in a particular group. This is accomplished by defining a query link that searches for all records in a given group. This has the effect of collecting and displaying only the data in that group.

If there's a place you want to be able to jump to from anywhere, you can insert a bookmark. Bookmarks are also nameable and can be placed throughout the text. Anytime you want to get to a bookmarked place, you just click on a button and up pops a list from which you choose the bookmark you want to get to.

Memoing: Notes and Popups

We've already hinted that you can memo in a couple of different ways. Notes are little pop-up windows in which you can type 4,000 characters of text, which is long enough for most memos. Each paragraph can have a Note, and a little icon like a Post-It appears in the margin, next to the paragraph. Double-click on the icon, and up pops the Note.

Popups also hold up to 4,000 characters. Unlike notes, they're not limited to one per paragraph and don't have icons. Instead, you apply a Popup link to a range of text, like a person's name (remember that a link can have any text attributes you choose, like color or underlining, to identify it, so the loss of icons isn't a problem). Then, whenever you double-click on the person's name, up pops the Popup. But like any other link, the range of text you apply it to can be as short or as long as you want.

Additionally, the extensive support of hypertexting would make it quite practical, and pretty easy, to keep longer memos elsewhere in the same infobase or another one, with jump links to pop you back and forth.

Tagging

Anytime you're looking at a record, you can "tag" it. Tagged records are marked with a thick red bar in the left margin. You can tag as many records as you want, in different parts of the infobase. There's a menu option to "keep tags," which lets you see only tagged records on the screen. Thus you can quickly scan through and tag a bunch of records on a topic and then look at them all together. You can also then easily select them all at once to, say, make them into a group or apply a highlighter to them. You can also choose to print all tagged records.

Shadow Files

Shadow files are intended to allow different users to do all their annotating, editing, highlighting, and so on without touching the actual (master) infobase. You could also do this for your own work to leave the original data in original form. When you call up a shadow file, it looks just like the master infobase (it just works a bit slower). As you edit and make other changes, everything seems to be going normally. But the master infobase is not affected at all. If the master is edited, you have the option of incorporating the changes into your shadow file or not.

Searching

The search engine is a powerful one, and it is *fast* because every word is indexed. You construct your queries (search requests) in an ingenious dialog box called the "query box" (see Figure 3).

As you construct a query, you can do all your search scope selections from a list (they get automatically pasted into the query box) or type them in yourself. (Scope lets you specify whether you want to search the whole infobase or limit your search by level, field, and so on—more on

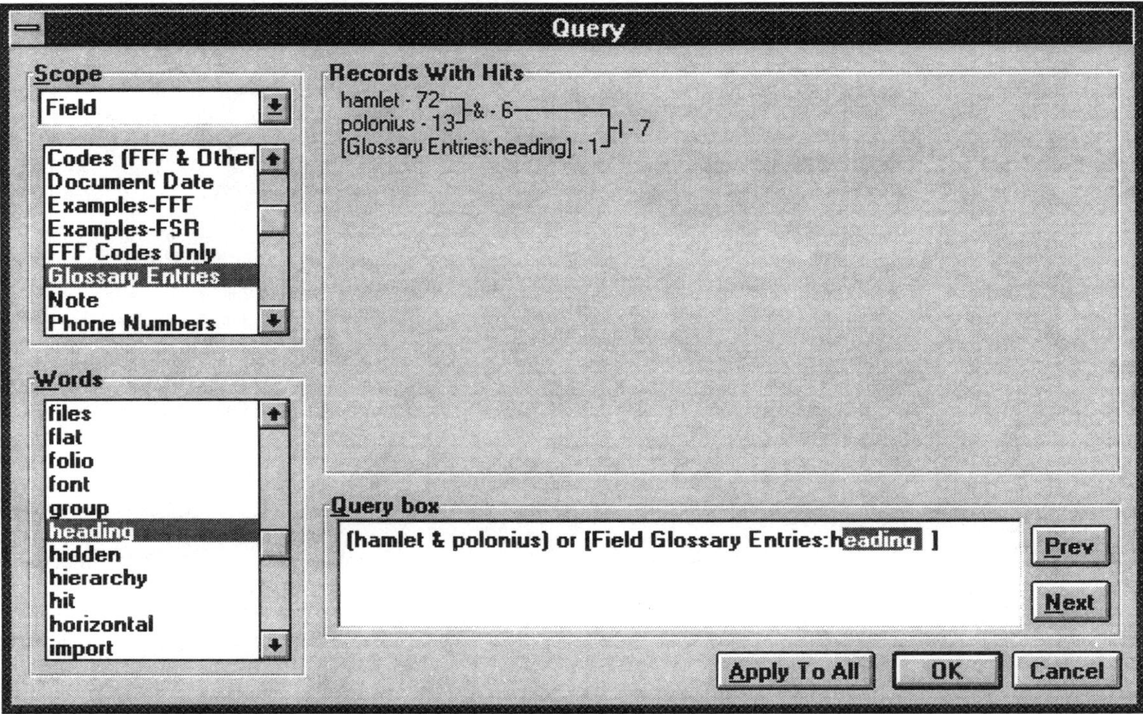

Folio VIEWS Figure 3. The Query dialog box. The query is typed in the "Query box" at lower right, and specifies a search for records with either the combination of the words "hamlet" and "polonius" or the word "heading" in the field "Glossary Entries" (only the first letter of "heading" has been typed—VIEWS fills in the rest of the word). The "Records With Hits" box shows a graphical map of the query, showing how many hits there are for each segment of it. The "Scope" list was used to specify the second part of the query. It has been set to "Field" and the "Glossary Entries" field has been selected from it (and this selection was pasted into the query box). The "Words" list shows all words that exist in the current scope (the Glossary Entries field), and the word "heading" is highlighted.

this in a moment.) There is always a list of all words in the current scope showing, and you can select from it. VIEWS has "intelligent searching": If you just start typing a word in the query box, VIEWS tries to match the rest of the word from the list—you just type as many letters as you need to get the right word and hit <Enter>. In the results box, you see a map of the query you're building *as you go,* which shows which terms are combined, in what order, with what operators connecting them, and the number of hits for each segment of the query. This turns out to be a very useful feature; each time you add a term to your query, you instantly know how many instances of it there are in the text and how it will affect the total query results when combined with the other terms. Thus you can do a lot of fine tuning of your query before you ever run it. The query box is scrollable, so you can call up any query you made earlier in the session. About the only limitation is that queries are limited to 1,000 characters—not much of a problem.

AND, OR, XOR, NOT (&, |, ~, ^) and parentheses (logic nesting) are supported, as are numeric operators (=, <, >, ≤, ≥, < >) for date, time, integer, and real number fields. The standard DOS wildcards, * and ?, are supported. There are options for thesaurus (synonym) searching and stem (word-root) searching as well. Thesaurus searches let you find synonyms of a word, and stem word searches let you find words with the same root. A stem search for "run" will find "run," "running," and even "ran" —in other words, any cognate of the word "run."

When you run your search, you can look at the results in a couple of ways. First, you can see hits in full context in the infobase. You just click on the "Next" (or "Previous") button in the toolbelt, and you get jumped from one hit to the next. The actual terms that defined your query are highlighted. If you want, you can ask to see *only* records with hits; the screen looks the same, but all records except those with hits disappear. You can also view your hits in the table of contents view, as described earlier under "Levels" in "Database Structure." Under each level header, you see the actual hit word(s) optionally embedded in up to 50 words of context on either side. You can double-click on any of these entries and pop to the full text view at the hit record.

Understanding Search Context and Scope

The search scope option in the query box lets you use levels, groups, highlighters, fields, notes, and pop-ups as a basis for expanding or restricting the scope of your search. This can have two different types of effects, which we'll call search context and search scope to clarify the matter. While Folio VIEWS doesn't explicitly make this distinction, the different effects are available, so we recommend thinking about it this way.

Search context is the range (record, field, level, and so on) within which both terms of an AND request must occur—or both terms of a NOT request must not occur—to be found. Search scope specifies the parts of the infobase (all of it or a particular level, group, or field) that will be included in the search (this essentially segments or subsets the data). Again, VIEWS does not explicitly make this distinction, and you adjust both context and scope with the scope list of the query box.

Search context. By default, the *search context* (the range within which both terms of an AND request must occur to be found) is the record. (When you view your results, you can see either the hit in its surrounding text or only the records with hits.) You can, however, expand or restrict the search context.

You can expand the context to sections as defined by header levels or groups. So, going back to our hypothetical level structure, you could find, say, any interview with both the highlighter for school climate in it anywhere and the word "principal" in it anywhere. You can mix a request like this with a request for some other terms co-occurring within a record.

Inversely, you can *restrict* the search context to fields or highlighters. Thus, if you want to find some combination of words or phrases if it occurs within a section coded with a field or highlighter, you can.

There are also two types of proximity searches where you specify a number of words within which terms must co-occur; in ordered proximity searches, the terms must appear in the order you specify; in unordered proximity searches, they can be in any order. (Note: these are only AND searches.) This may have the effect of creating contexts either larger or smaller than a record (records may vary in size).

Search scope. You can leave the *search scope* as the entire infobase, or you can restrict it to specific sections as defined by levels. You can also say which levels or particular headers you want included. Another alternative is to set the search scope as a particular group. Further, you can use fields or highlighters as scopes, thus restricting the rest of a search to text found in the field or highlighter. The search scope can be expanded to include, or restricted to only include, Notes and/or Popups (they're not included in the scope of a search unless you specify they should be).

Using Search Context and Scope

When you start manipulating context and scope, including levels, groups, fields, highlighters, Notes, and Popups, you can do some fantastically sophisticated searches, and you can do them easily. There are two ways to go about this (this is another distinction we're creating). Say you just want to retrieve by a code, like "School Climate." You might have named a highlighter (or a field) "School Climate" and applied it to relevant text. You just select that highlighter from the scope list or enter it yourself in the query box like this: "[highlighter school climate:]." When you execute the query, you get all text to which this highlighter has been applied. You can use all the logical operators to combine highlighters. Remember that the default context is record, so if you ask for [highlighter school climate:] AND [highlighter principal:], you'll get all records where both highlighters have been applied. This is like a normal Boolean combination of codes.

The second way treats highlighters (and fields, levels, groups, Notes, and Popups) either as search scopes or contexts as described above (though VIEWS always refers to them as scopes). You can add a search term that you want to find within that, for example, highlighter. So, you might enter [highlighter school climate:victim] to find occurrences of the word "victim" within passages highlighted (coded) school climate.

But you're not limited to text strings as terms to search for within the scope (in this case, the school climate highlighter). You can use the logical operators. Then you can ask for passages highlighted *school climate* that have both the words "victim" and "violence." Better yet, you can use the names of other scopes, thus nesting them in your search request: [highlighter school climate:[highlighter principal:]]. This way, you could find all instances where the two highlighters actually overlap rather than just co-occurring in a record (and you can search for anything you want in the intersection). Even better yet, you can nest scopes of different types: fields, levels, groups, highlighters, Notes, and Popups.

Theory Building

Though Folio VIEWS wasn't designed specifically as a qualitative analysis tool, and so has no *deliberately* included theory-building support, it does have a number of features that are quite helpful for theory-building efforts. It has excellent memoing and annotating features; extensive, flexible, and easy hypertexting capabilities; and, perhaps most important, it supports system closure.

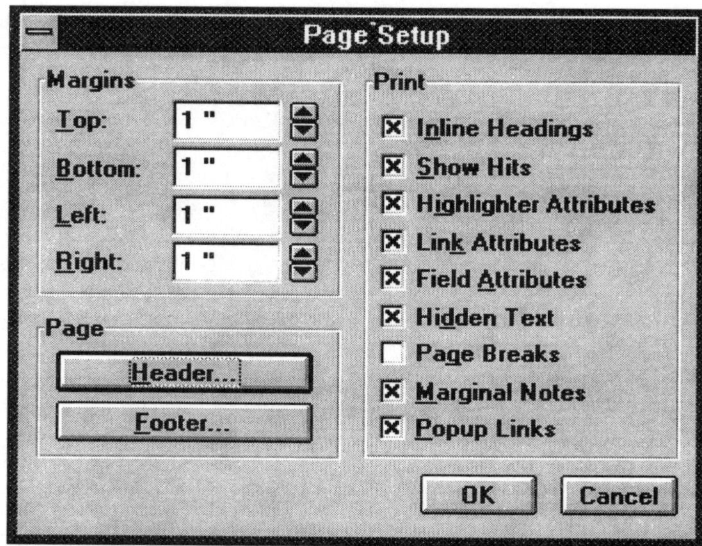

Folio VIEWS Figure 4. The page setup dialog box offers a wealth of options for information and attributes to include in printouts.

We've spotted at least two ways to accomplish the latter by making search results available for later analysis. After executing a query, you'd choose to view only records with hits. Then you'd have two choices. One method would be to select all the text left in the view (all records with hits) and copy them all to one place in the infobase (or in a new infobase). Then you'd have a contiguous set of all text that matches a given query. The second method would also involve selecting all text left in the view (all records with hits) but this time, instead of copying it all to one place, defining it all as one group. Then a search for the group would allow you to gather together all data from that search in one view. Alternatively, you could specify that group as a search scope as a shorthand way to nest the original query in a more complex one.

Either of these methods (and you could probably come up with more on your own) would allow you to use the results of your analyses as data for further analyses. Thus you have an essential element of system closure.

Output

Output is first rate.[4] For text, you get the full range of Windows fonts, including the scalable TrueType fonts, and the full complement of text attributes, including bold, underlining, italics, and colors. You can also print any type of graphic that you can link or embed. With the upgrade to Version 3.01, Folio says you can now import from or export to 27 different graphics formats (including .PCX, .BMP, .GIF, TIFF, .WMF, and so on).

"Inline headers" can be made to print above each record, showing you exactly where in the table of contents the record is from. You get all the level headers applying to a record, in hierarchical order, separated with backslashes (\). A header for a record from the example we used in describing hierarchy might look like this:

Site 1 \ Deborah Crane \ Interviews \ 9/1/93

Thus we would know that the record came from the 9/1/93 (level 4) interview (level 3) with Deborah Crane (level 2) at Site 1 (level 1).

There are in fact a wealth of options for printing, including having search terms marked with bold text or showing visual attributes (colors, underlining, and so on) of fields and highlighters (so you can see your coding!) as well as of links. You can also control the printing of notes and pop-ups (see Figure 4). In addition, you can limit printing to records by number, all tagged records, selected text, or the current "view." The last option refers not to the current screenful of information but to the *way* you're currently viewing the infobase on screen: Are you seeing the whole thing, or have you limited your "view" to records with hits, or only tagged records?

You can also define sophisticated running heads or footers to print on each page, into which you can paste any object, as well as page numbers, print dates, and various bits of information about the infobase (see Figure 5). Perhaps most interestingly, you can insert a code that will print

4. This discussion assumes you have a Windows 3.1 compatible printer.

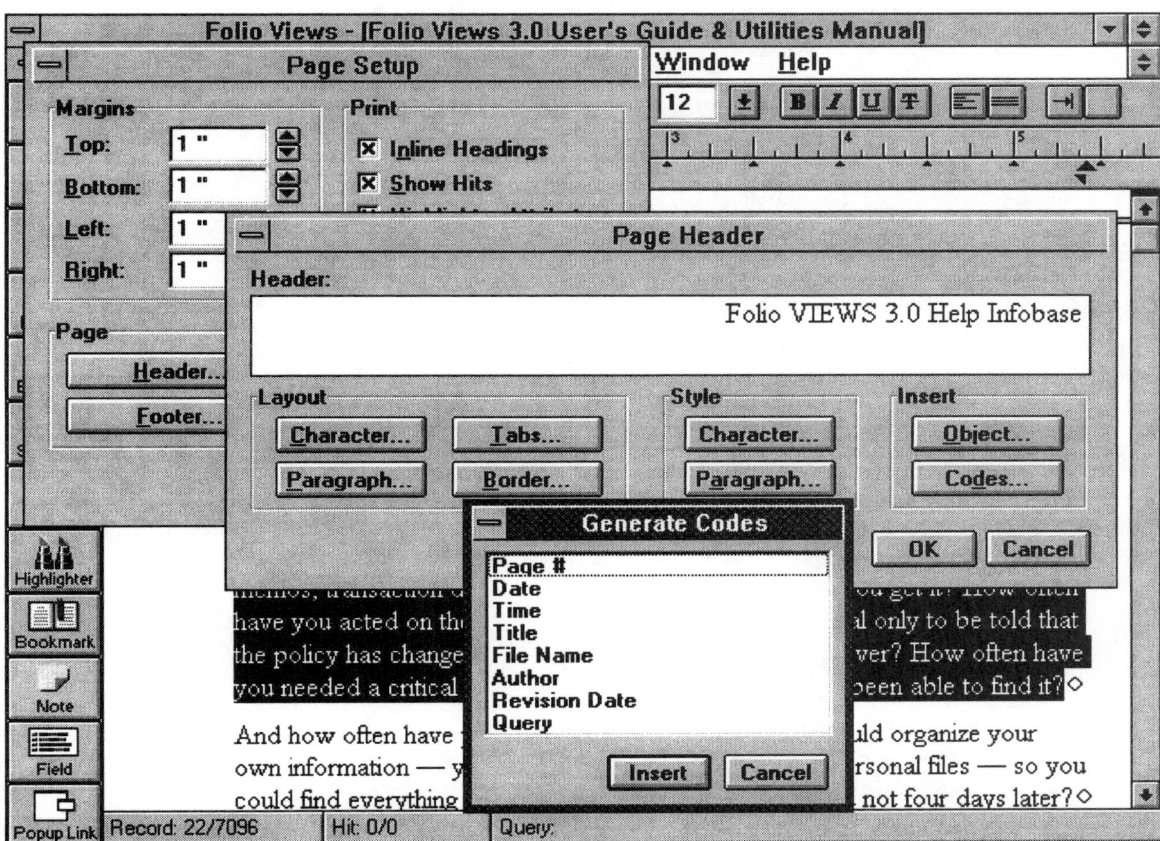

Folio VIEWS Figure 5. There are numerous options for page headers (running heads) and footers. The Insert Codes button is *not* for your analytical codes! It pops up this dialog box, which lets you insert codes in your running header (or footer) that tell the program to print page numbers, the current date and time, the infobase's title, filename, author, and latest revision date, and the query whose results are being printed.

the current query, so that all of your output will be labeled with the query that produced it.

The importance of these features should not be overlooked: it is all too easy when doing qualitative analysis with a computer to wind up with endless pages of printout and have no idea what analysis a given printout came from or where the text came from. The information VIEWS lets you put in running heads, together with inline headers and the other information and attributes you can control allow you to keep very good track of what everything is about and where it came from.

User Friendliness

Despite its complexity, Folio VIEWS 3.0 is a very user-friendly program. Almost all of its features are easy to learn and use. The manual is generally clearly written, and the whole thing itself comes in an infobase, so you can use the program's remarkable search features to get help. If there's one complaint we had with the manual it's that it is a little too focused on lengthy tutorials; some things are very hard to just look up without at least reading through the tutorial. (We realize this is an odd complaint, because the usual problem is lack of good tutorials. It's just that Folio relies a little too heavily on them.) This is a particular problem in the case of the FSR (Folio Search and Replace) utility that you need to use to automatically apply fields and such to consistent occurrences in the text. As a result, we gave up and called tech support and let them work out the syntax we needed.

There is often a fairly long wait on the phone queue for tech support, and depending on where you're calling Utah from, this can get expensive (you pay for the call). On the other hand, the people at tech support that we talked with were patient, friendly, knowledgeable, and helpful. You can also get help via CompuServe or Folio's own BBS.

Miscellaneous

Multiple Users

For each infobase, you can control access levels (various types of privileges) for specific users, who must log in and give a password (otherwise they are automatically logged in as "Guest," a user whose access rights you can also set). There can be 125 simultaneous users with read-write privileges on a network and an unlimited number of simultaneous read-only users. They can all be using the same infobase or different ones. You can define groups of users and specify access rights for them as a group, and still make changes for an individual in a group.

At the most restricted level, a user can only read and search the infobase (read only). As shown in Figure 6, you can define many different aspects of what a given user can do, including whether they can edit the text, headers, or footers; add and modify levels, fields, highlighters, and groups; and so on.

Another approach to managing multiple users is through the use of shadow files. Each user can have her/his own shadow file and "customize it" so that it presents the data in a way that suits her/his needs. Customizing a shadow file can include just about any operation you could do to a real infobase, including editing, highlighting, changing levels, applying fields, and so on. In other words, to each user it seems just as though s/he has her/his own personal version of the infobase, but the original, "master" infobase is never affected by her/his work. If *you* make changes to the master copy (like adding or correcting data), shadow file users can incorporate these changes through a "reconcile" facility.

Customization

There are quite a number of options you can set to customize the program. For example, there are 90 different tools that you can place on the toolbelt (see Figure 1), and you can have it placed vertically or horizontally, with words, icons, or both (as in Figure 1) for each tool. You can save many of the different viewing option settings as defaults, depending on how you like to work, and you can have a graphical title page appear momentarily when you load an infobase.

Other Platforms

Folio VIEWS 3.0 for DOS has recently been released, but we haven't had a chance to review it, and a Macintosh version is due out relatively soon (so far there's just a read-only Mac version called Folio Lite). Folio claims that any of the three versions of the program (Windows, DOS, and Mac) can read infobases created on other platforms seamlessly. We haven't been able to verify these claims but suspect that they are largely, but not completely, true. Limits are likely to arise around platform-specific issues like TrueType fonts, OLE 2.0, and so on.

Update

At least two major developments are in the works. Version 3.1 was just being released as final edits were being done on this book, and a fully functional Macintosh Version 3.1 (as opposed to the current read-only implementation of Version 3.0) is planned for the end of 1994 (such dates almost always slip; figure early 1995). The same date is predicted for Version 3.1 for DOS.

Version 3.1 includes a number of significant improvements. For example, Query Templates let you design your own dialog box to simplify issuing special queries. If, for example, you often want to select records according to the data in a "Gender" field, and then search for phrases appearing within a chunk coded with a highlighter, you could set up a Query Template with labeled boxes for you to type in the gender, search phrase, and highlighter name you needed whenever you wanted to do such a search.

There are also new features for working with shadow files, including intelligent ways to add new information from the master infobase to the shadow file as well as to add new information from shadow files to the master.

Another new feature that will be of interest to many qualitative researchers is integration with OCR software so that documents can be scanned directly into infobases. With this feature, if you have a scanner, hard copy items such as archival documents collected in the field can be easily added to an infobase for storage and analysis. You could also use this feature to put articles, book chapters, or even books (if you've got a lot of disk space) into a "lit search" database, where you could use all of the search, markup, linking, and annotating features of VIEWS as you read and prepare to write.

One other item worth mentioning is a new "Filter Add-On Pack," which gives you the capability to import data from an additional 50 programs, including FrameMaker, InterLeaf, Lotus 1-2-3, Lotus Ami-Pro, and dBASE.

Comparative Remarks

VIEWS stacks up well against other textbase managers, text retrievers, code-and-retrieve programs, and code-based theory-builders. We'll compare it with each group separately.

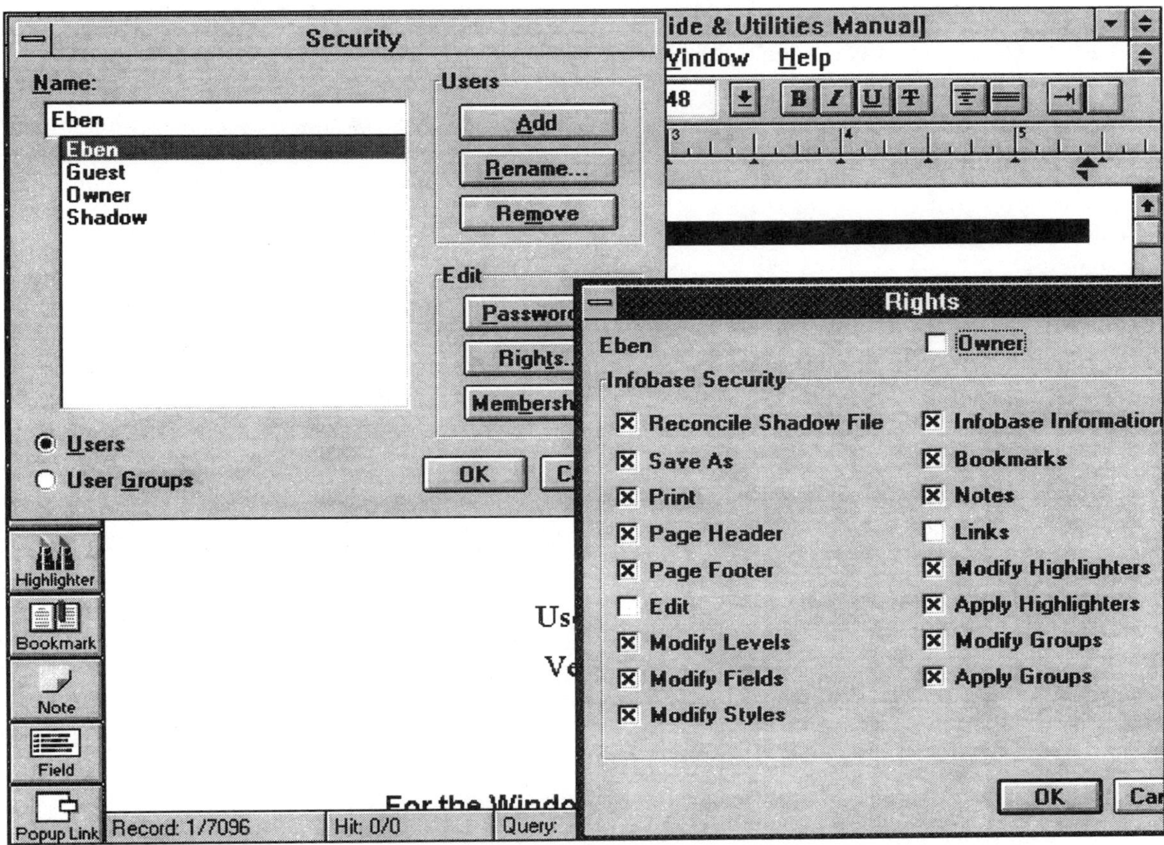

Folio VIEWS Figure 6. The "Security" dialog box allows you to add, remove, rename, and group users and set passwords for them. If you invoke the "Rights" dialog box, you can individually allow or disallow 17 different kinds of actions for each user or give the user full access by selecting "Owner" at the top.

Textbase Managers

Folio VIEWS 3.0 is the strongest of the textbase managers we've reviewed, being much easier to use, and incorporating a wider and more powerful array of features, than either MAX or askSam. Its only potential weakness relative to these programs is the difficulties involved in setting up structured records if you want them.

Text Retrievers

VIEWS is also about as good a text retriever as you're going to find, but it doesn't work on external files: You must build an infobase and import the data you want to be able to search. This nontrivial distinction aside, VIEWS's search features are the equal of any of the text retrievers, with the possible exception of Metamorph. The latter has a bit more in the way of raw retrieval power, but the range of options for searching with scopes in VIEWS makes the choice less than clear cut.

Code-and-Retrieve Programs and Code-Based Theory-Builders

Furthermore, VIEWS can also be used as a very good code-and-retrieve program by using highlighters and fields for coding. Its on-screen, mouse-based application of these is as easy as the coding routines in any of the code-based theory-builders (like HyperRESEARCH, ATLAS/ti, or NUD•IST) and better than those in most of the code-and-retrieve programs (like Kwalitan, The Ethnograph, or QUALPRO). However, you need a workaround to do some things, like getting a code list printed out, that a lot of these programs can do easily. In addition, its potential for organization of the data with levels, groups, and records exceeds those of any of the programs listed here—with the possible exception of the special-purpose casewise organization of data in HyperRESEARCH—and its search capabilities are absolutely unmatched by any of the programs in these two categories—with the possible exception of the special kinds of co-occurrence of code operators in NUD•IST. Furthermore, its annotation and memoing features are at least the equal of most of the programs in either of these categories.

What it does not have are any of the theory-building features found in the code-based theory-builders, including any kind of graphic-mapping features (though you can import or link in graphics created in another program). However, its hypertexting and other data-linking features are unequaled among the programs reviewed here in terms of ease of use, elegance, variety, and power.

Summary

This easy-to-learn, easy-to-use textbase manager is clearly the best in its class and is also an excellent text retriever and code-and-retrieve program. For heavy-duty theoretical work, you may prefer a program like ATLAS/ti or NUD•IST, though VIEWS does have excellent memoing, outlining, and system closure facilities. But the integration of sophisticated textbase management with powerful text search, sophisticated coding and retrieval, and extensive hypertexting capabilities make this program well worth considering for many qualitative researchers. It's especially good for "disorderly" projects where you're (for example) interviewing *and* observing *and* documenting with many individuals per site, writing memos, doing successive analyses on the results of earlier analyses, and so on, and where you may not need or want a tight coding scheme. Many evaluation and applied studies run like this.

Reference

Folio Corporation. (1993). *Folio VIEWS personal electronic publishing software: User's guide, Version 3.0, for the Windows graphical environment.* Provo, UT: Author.

MAX, International Version 3.5

Available for DOS

Udo Kuckartz
Free University of Berlin
Institute for Social and Adult Education
Arnimallee 12
D-14195 Berlin, Germany[1]

Phone: 49-30-838 5539
Fax: 49-30-838-5889
Distributor's phone/fax: 49-30-813 7201
("Hotline" Thursday 9 a.m. to 1 p.m. Berlin time)

Price: $220

Hardware Requirements:
- IBM PC 286 or better
- MS-DOS 2.0 or better
- hard disk
- 640K RAM (540K if you do not load a small (100K) text processor at the same time)

Overview

MAX is a database program designed to code and work with narrative text (which can be more or less structured) *and* numerical data on a number of cases. It works most easily when the cases are persons, though it could be used when you have comparable data across a number of cases defined as complex groups or organizations. The numerical data can include both "profile" (demographic, background) information about the cases and ratings, scales, or other measures of variables appearing in the cases. MAX's strength is its ability to manage and link both sorts of data. Its abilities to work with qualitative data are more limited than those of most code-and-retrieve programs.

MAX was deliberately designed to be run in alternation with your word processor, to save bulk and cost. You use your word processor for entering, storing, formatting, and printing data. You cannot run MAX and a full-size word processor at the same time, but you can exit from MAX to use your word processor, and when you return to MAX, get right back to where you left off. Or you can run MAX under Windows as a non-Windows application, and switch back and forth easily between MAX and your word processor. The manual says that, if you're running MAX under DOS, you can use a modest-size (up to 100K RAM) text editor (such as DOS EDIT, IBM PE2, or NORTON EDITOR) for looking at or revising files that you've loaded along with MAX; you go to the external editor, then return to MAX when you wish. (Version 3.5 does have a modest editor built in, which lets you enter text directly.) There's no way to print within MAX, though you can use the DOS "print" command.

MAX also outputs numerical data to statistics programs, such as SYSTAT and SPSS, and to other programs accepting dBASE format.

1. U.S. distribution and minor technical support are from Qualitative Research Management, 73425 Hilltop Road, Desert Hot Springs, CA 92240. Phone. (619) 329-7026.

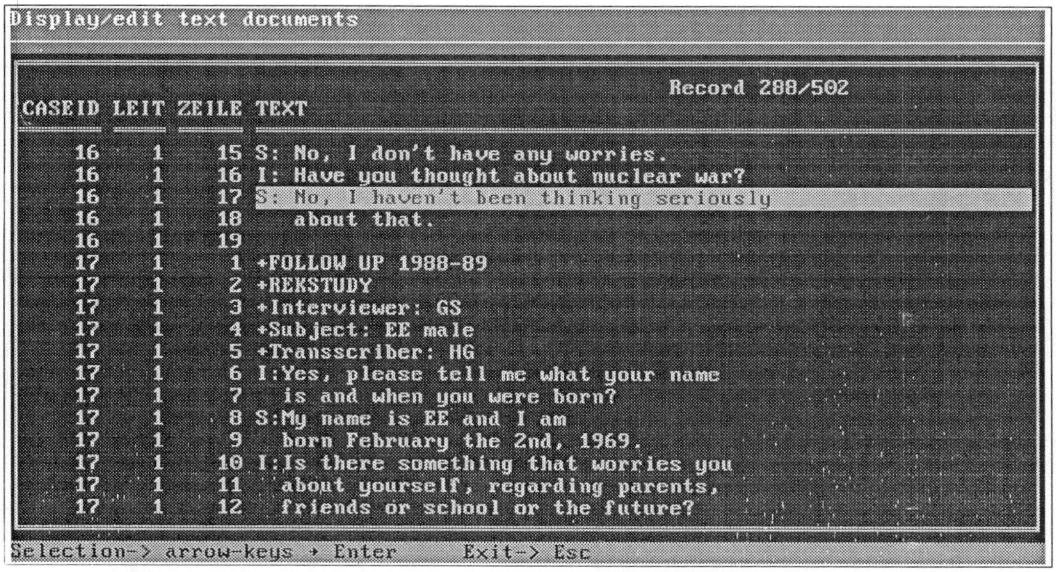

```
Display/edit text documents

                                            Record 288/502
CASEID LEIT ZEILE TEXT
  16     1    15 S: No, I don't have any worries.
  16     1    16 I: Have you thought about nuclear war?
  16     1    17 S: No, I haven't been thinking seriously
  16     1    18    about that.
  16     1    19
  17     1     1 +FOLLOW UP 1988-89
  17     1     2 +REKSTUDY
  17     1     3 +Interviewer: GS
  17     1     4 +Subject: EE male
  17     1     5 +Transscriber: HG
  17     1     6 I:Yes, please tell me what your name
  17     1     7   is and when you were born?
  17     1     8 S:My name is EE and I am
  17     1     9   born February the 2nd, 1969.
  17     1    10 I:Is there something that worries you
  17     1    11   about yourself, regarding parents,
  17     1    12   friends or school or the future?
Selection-> arrow-keys + Enter      Exit-> Esc
```

MAX Figure 1. Displaying and editing a line-numbered text file that includes multiple cases. The data have been organized by block. Here we see the end of block (Leit) 1 (which includes the first questions in the interview—name, birth date, and worries) for case ID 16, and the beginning of block 1 data for case ID 17. Lines 1-5 have standard fields for header information for each case (the study phase, the study name, interviewer, subject, and transcriber). At the top right, we see that the cursor is on Record (line) 288 of 502 in the document. The columns at the left show that this is case ID 16, block 1, line (Zeile) 17.

You can edit any of the columns, moving across them with the arrow keys, and can scroll up and down. You cannot add text beyond the right margin (MAX just stops you and will not word wrap).

This review is based on an early draft of the manual (Kuckartz, 1993), which, while clear, was not wholly updated from Version 3.4 to explain Version 3.5. It also included a good deal of German text in the examples.

Database Structure

MAX works with six connected databases: text documents; numerical data, which the program calls "multiple-choice"; profile data on characteristics of your cases; your code list; "coding indicators" (showing segments of the text to which codes are attached); and labels (names for different types of data—multiple-choice, profile, and structured text blocks (such as the responses to Question 6 or Item 24). All these are discussed more fully below under "Data Entry."

MAX can accept up to 999 text documents. Each can refer to a unique case if you wish (usually, as noted, an individual) or can contain multiple cases. A document can be very large—98,000 lines, or up to 5.9 megabytes. However, there can only be 99 text blocks (chunks of text you define—see below) per document. MAX will accommodate 999 codes, and the number of codes per block, or per segment of 1 or more lines, is unlimited. The program can accommodate 24 profile variables and 60 multiple-choice items (supposedly expandable to 1,024 items).

Data Entry

Text Data

First the text (or "narrative") data: You create text data (either outside MAX or using its text editor) as ASCII files, each headed with a unique ID number, using 60-character lines or less. If your text data are structured, like questionnaire open-ended responses or structured interview text, you organize them in "blocks"—say, the answer to Question 6. You add in a block number (such as /2 or /5) at the beginning of the block, and end the block using two hard returns <Enter, Enter>. Thus you'll have structurally comparable blocks of text across all your cases—even though the text within each block will be unique to that case. You also use a menu option to assign labels to text blocks, which can be up to five lines in length. Thus a complete interview question could be entered. (These labels are printed when blocks are retrieved.)

```
 F2 -> MARK BEGINNING       F3 -> MARK END            ESC-> QUIT
Li.    Text                                                   Blck    Doc

  5  | * Translator: IC                                      | 1    |  11
  6  | I: Will you now tell me your name ?                   | 1    |  11
  7  | S: ABH                                                | 1    |  11
  8  | I: And when where you born ?                          | 1    |  11
  9  | S: 30 May 1969                                        | 1    |  11
 10  | I: Is there something in the future                   | 1    |  11
 11  |    causing  you concern in regard to                  | 1    |  11
 12  | S: Yes, my parents. They'll surely                    | 1    |  11
 13  |    die from stress or selling                         | 1    |  11
 14  |    the house no one wants to buy.                     | 1    |  11
 15  |    Something of the business                          | 1    |  11
 16  |    has to be sold, rescured. There's                  | 1    |  11
 17  |    a little stress around this                        | 1    |  11
 18  | I: Do they thus cause you a little                    | 1    |  11
 19  |    concern?                                           | 1    |  11
 20  | S: Yes - mainly my father -  he's                     | 1    |  11
 21  |    an evening drinker and all that.                   | 1    |  11
 22  |    One's always                                       | 1    |  11

Text segment line 12 To  17              stress
Accept this coding into database?                              YES   NO
```

MAX Figure 2. Coding the text. The text is line-numbered at the left. At the right, the block and document numbers are given. The code "stress," shown at lower center, has just been applied to lines 12 to 17 and will be confirmed as part of the database. To do this, you cursor to the start line, hit <F2>, then to the end line, and hit <F3>. Hitting <Enter> will pop up the code list, and you choose the one you want to apply. To do multiple codes for the same set of lines, you repeat the process and choose another code.

If your text data are free-form (and thus not structurally comparable across cases), you are advised by the manual to leave the entire text as a block. If your text exceeds 999 lines, MAX will automatically start block 2 at line 1,000 and keep assigning new block numbers every 999 lines thereafter.

As noted, you can have multiple persons in the same file if you wish, but the data must always begin with an asterisk and an ID number. When you import your ASCII files, MAX copies them (the raw files are untouched, as in any program that works with external files), attaches line numbers to text, and sets up a file for profile data.

After this you can do very minor line editing (correcting errors or adding text within a line). To protect the line numbering, MAX will not allow you to add text beyond the end of a line—so it may be wise to keep your line length short during data entry, as in Figure 1, to give yourself a little slack for editing. You can delete a line if you wish (it just leaves the line numbered but blank).

Figure 1 shows the edit/display screen. Editing within MAX is very limited (to line editing, essentially, without copy, cut, or paste functions); if you want to seriously revise, annotate, or update your text, you have to use your word processor *before* you import files to MAX. Essentially, MAX works with largely "finished" texts, not ones you want to edit, revise, and ruminate about.

Numerical Data

Now the numerical ("nonnarrative") data: First, the "profile" data for respondents has up to 24 slots for items like age, gender, occupation, and so on. There are also five standard fields MAX creates when you import a file, which can optionally be used as document headers (researcher, respondent, date, time, and duration).

The so-called multiple-choice data feature allows for up to 60 items per respondent. This version of the manual (Kuckartz, 1993) doesn't explain how to expand the quantitative database to the purported 1,024 items. The items can be any numerical data, such as questionnaire responses, or categories or ratings generated by the researcher from analysis of open-ended responses.

Data can be entered in either of two ways: by *all items* for a respondent or by an item for *all respondents*. (Imagine a matrix with respondents as rows, and items as columns: You can enter data either horizontally by respondent or vertically by item.) You set the labels for variables and type in their values. However, MAX does not ask you to specify the range of values, as in statistical packages, so it can't check out-of-range values. You are on your own with whatever (numerical) codebook you have prepared in hard copy, covering your variables and their values.

```
Modify/delete coding

Schlagwort Nr.    6
Schlagwort    subject

 10   1   54 I:So you are optimistic about
 10   1   55    life after you managed to get
 10   1   56    out of this?
 10   1   57 S:Yes.

          10 |   1 |   47 |   48 |   2
          10 |   1 |   22 |   22 |   6
          10 |   1 |   22 |   22 |   6
          10 |   1 |   24 |   26 |   6
          10 |   1 |   54 |   57 |   6
          11 |   1 |   12 |   17 |   8
          12 |   1 |   11 |   15 |   1
          12 |   1 |   19 |   25 |   1

ALT+T -> list text segment                  ESC-> EXIT
```

MAX Figure 3. Checking code applications with an eye to revision. The user chose "Modify/delete coding" and asked for code applications in document 10 (document 12 follows). In the list of applications below, the user moved the cursor to the application of code 6 beginning at line 54 and ending at 57. <Alt-T> brings up the coded segment above (without context) so the appropriateness of the code can be judged. A new code number can be substituted, or the code application can be deleted by entering zero in the right column.

Both profile and multiple-choice data can be revised and added to at any time. However, the on-screen values of profile and multiple-choice data are expressed as *numbers,* so you are back to your hard copy "codebook" again to know what you are doing; the program doesn't store the meaning of those numbers (e.g., 1 for male, 2 for female) for you.

Working on the Data

Coding requires you to start with a catalog of numbered codes (specified at only one level), which is always updatable. A code can be up to 40 characters. In the code list, shown alphabetized or by code number, the code name can be edited to any other form. *But* the code *number* that MAX assigned stays the same—and code numbers are what get attached to text. So if you changed the meaning of the code when you changed the label, you would still get the same chunk when you retrieve using that numbered code. The new meaning might or might not fit the chunk, so you'd have to review to be sure. (You can revise your coding of a chunk if you want to.)

Assuming that you have a code list, you enter the "Code functions" module and choose "Assign code to text segment." You specify the document. The text you're coding appears (Figure 2), you set starting and ending line numbers for the code application, and then hit <Enter>. The alphabetized code list pops up and you highlight the one you want applied. You can't just attach new codes spontaneously—you must first think of a new code, leave the coding module, add the new code to the catalog, *then* return to coding and attach it to specified lines.

Codes can overlap or nest but cannot go across blocks. Each code, as noted, is assigned a number. You have a choice of working on screen or via hard copy.

Coding can jump around in the text and need not be done in sequence. To check your coding, you can ask for a list of "coding indicators," which displays the line numbers to which a particular code has been attached (or the line numbers for all the code applications in a document). If you want to change an application, you choose "Modify/delete codes" and cursor to that application. To see the actual text of those lines, you hit <Alt-T>, and they pop up (Figure 3). These coding indicators can be deleted or revised, so you can reconsider or correct the coding you've done. You can also get a frequency listing of codes.

You can delete a code from your coding list with all its applications, and you can rename a code, which does a global replace of all its applications. (Remember: The code *number* stays the same.) There is a facility for joining two codes (you create a new code for the joint name, then spec-

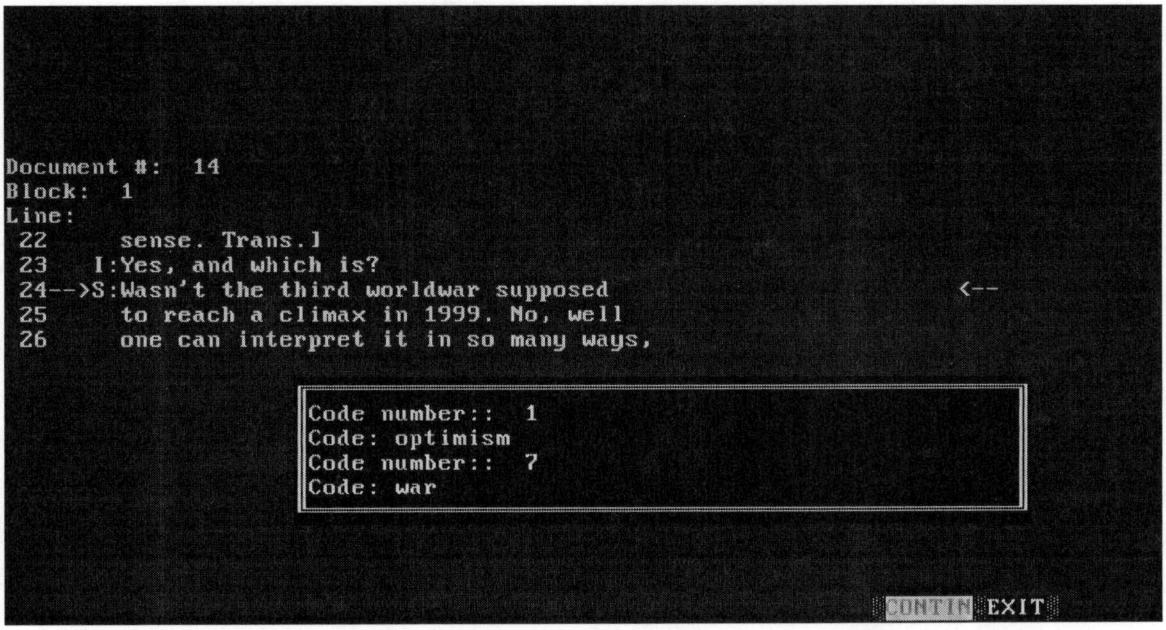

```
Document #:  14
Block:  1
Line:
 22      sense. Trans.]
 23    I:Yes, and which is?
 24-->S:Wasn't the third worldwar supposed                    <--
 25      to reach a climax in 1999. No, well
 26      one can interpret it in so many ways,

                    Code number::  1
                    Code: optimism
                    Code number::  7
                    Code: war

                                                   CONTIN  EXIT
```

MAX Figure 4. Result of a string search. The user asked for the string "wor." The hit line is marked by arrows left and right. Pressing <Alt-S> has popped up the lower box, showing that the codes "optimism" and "war" have both been applied to this line. Hitting <Enter> when "Continue" is highlighted will bring up the next hit.

ify the other two). But there is a bug: When MAX was asked to join "family" and "stress" into a new code called "family stress," it just put all the chunks coded "family" into "stress" and emptied the categories "family" and "family stress." The developer is working on the bug, but says it can be avoided by leaving the code functions module before doing "join" or by only joining already existing codes. In any case, there's no record of which codes the joint code joins. That's a real limitation if your working style is to combine codes to develop new higher-order codes as you go.

You can send any document to a file, with the numerical codes attached (they appear as numbers in the right margin of the line-numbered text, line by line). You can see it with a "View file" option (or look at it/revise it with your text editor or word processor). There's a limit of five codes per line in this mode.

Basically, MAX's coding approach is designed for structured text, where you usually have fairly clear conceptual ideas in advance and want to limit richness and maintain comparability across a number of cases. It's less easy to use in a more grounded-theory style with free-form text; for that you need programs like ATLAS/ti, Martin, Kwalitan, or NUD•IST.

MAX has database management functions, including lists of text documents, information on which documents have numerical data linked to them, lists of line numbers to which particular codes are attached, summaries of profile and multiple-choice data, and lists of labels. It does backups for you. Basically, it helps you keep track of what you have and provides fairly direct access for straightforward analyses. You can also run DOS commands from within the program. There is a facility for deleting and backing up whole documents.

Searching

You can search for strings of up to 20 characters (there's also an "exact match" option that only finds a string if it's a whole word rather than embedded in a word), along with AND for up to five strings, OR for up to five strings—but no NOT. (You cannot do expressions mixing AND and OR.) You see the string—the line it appears in is marked by arrows right and left—in a small context: two lines before and two after. If you hit <Alt-S>, you'll see which codes have been applied to the line with the hit (Figure 4).

But you can't scroll in the hit's larger context or go back through the text; you are carried forward, hit by hit, until the last hit, or you quit. The feeling is rigid and tedious.

Coded segments can be retrieved and collated. The simple version of this is only via OR (you can get as many different codes as you want). You can do better than this by selecting data subsets (see below).

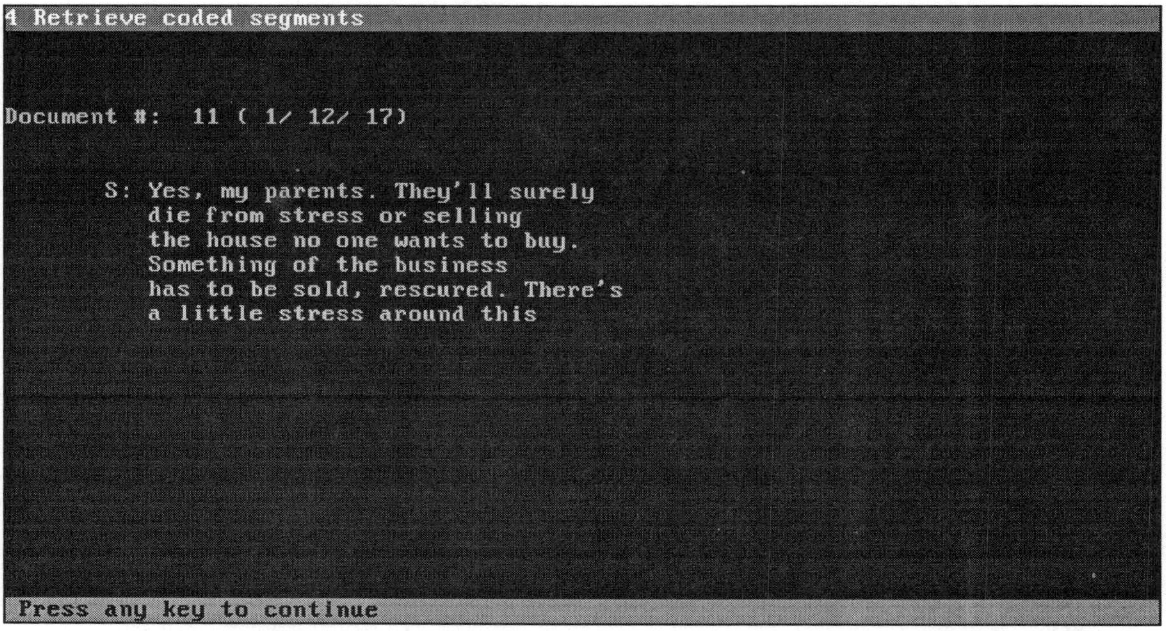

```
4 Retrieve coded segments

Document #:  11 ( 1/ 12/ 17)

        S: Yes, my parents. They'll surely
           die from stress or selling
           the house no one wants to buy.
           Something of the business
           has to be sold, rescured. There's
           a little stress around this

 Press any key to continue
```

MAX Figure 5. Retrieving a coded segment. The single code "stress," assigned in Figure 2, has been searched for, and appears briefly on the screen, then goes off. The hit appears as all the lines to which the code had been applied (12-17), without further context. The document number (11) and block number (1) are shown, along with the line numbers. The original code does not appear with the hit. Pressing any key takes you to the next hit.

Figure 5 shows how a hit looks during code retrieval. You see the document, block, and line numbers, but no other source information. As with string retrieval, you can't scroll around in the hit's context and can only proceed to the next hit, not the preceding one. In both string and code retrieval, you don't know how many hits you are dealing with—a serious limitation. You could be scrolling down through a hundred or only a handful.

MAX, with its data structure, does have advantages. When you're retrieving by code, you can look at specified subsets of data. You can retrieve by respondent, looking at all their text blocks, or by text blocks (say, by Question 6 responses), looking across all respondents (think of it as a big data matrix). You can also get a combination of blocks for each respondent (e.g., Question 6 and Question 11).

Most useful of all—this is perhaps the distinctive heart of the program—you can choose the "Quantitative and text data" option under Retrievals and Sortings to select documents with AND, OR, NOT, according to profile data (certain respondents, say, all women in their first 2 years of teaching) and/or multiple-choice data on those respondents (say, all those who scored below average on a morale measure). MAX will tell you along the way which documents (cases) you've selected, as you're gradually refining the search, expanding or contracting the pool (Figure 6). Then you can retrieve from your subset of respondents the code segments you're interested in; multiple retrievals are possible from the defined pool.

It appears that you can also work the other way: You'd find cases of interest using string or code retrieval, jot down the document and block numbers, then look at numerical data for those cases. This is another instance of how MAX is fairly bare-bones; it would be nice to be able to select cases using code retrieval and then automatically see numerical data for them, without having to write down and then key in numbers.

MAX does not log your searches and retrievals.

The "Retrievals and Sortings" menu also has options that let you sort data according to the numbered sequence of text blocks (useful when text blocks don't appear in their numbered order in all interviews), retrieve certain text blocks, list the values of data collected with multiple-choice instruments as well as the categories you've used in clustering open-ended data, and do word counts.

In general, on the data-linking front, MAX does a good job of connecting qualitative and quantitative data on a set of respondents. That's probably its main strength. But note that MAX traffics in numbered documents. You have to have good hard-copy lists of which documents are which,

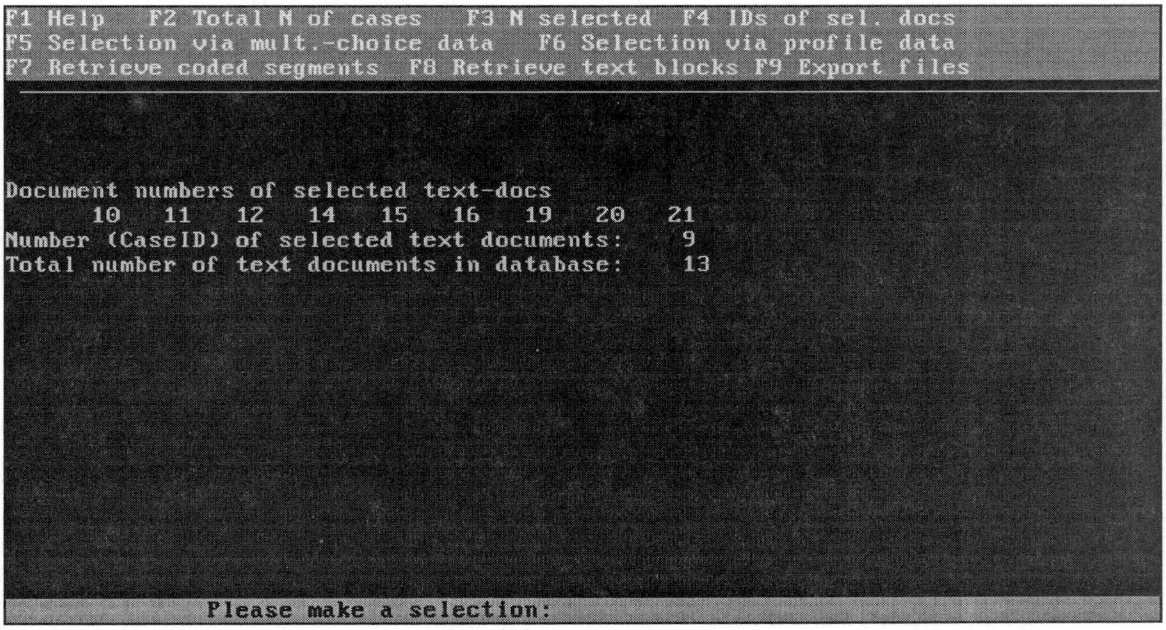

```
F1 Help   F2 Total N of cases   F3 N selected  F4 IDs of sel. docs
F5 Selection via mult.-choice data   F6 Selection via profile data
F7 Retrieve coded segments  F8 Retrieve text blocks F9 Export files

Document numbers of selected text-docs
     10   11   12   14   15   16   19   20   21
Number (CaseID) of selected text documents:    9
Total number of text documents in database:    13

           Please make a selection:
```

MAX Figure 6. Selecting documents (cases) for analysis. The various function key commands are all listed at the top. The user has hit <F6> and (on another screen) asked for cases where profile variable 1 (sex) has the value 1 (male). Hitting <F4> gives you the case IDs, <F3> gives the N of cases selected, and <F2> tells you the total number of cases involved. You can also do more complex selections using not only profile variables (<F6>) but (<F5>) multiple-choice data (e.g., those cases with a score of less than 10 on Scale 1). <F7> will enable you to retrieve coded segments from your selected set of cases, and <F8> will let you retrieve specific text blocks (such as the answers to interview Question 6). With <F9> you can export files with your results (though the procedure is not clear from the manual or help screen).

which blocks are which, and what the possible values are of your profile and multiple-choice data.

Output

The output of searches goes to screen or ASCII file, or both. Remember that there is *no* printer support (you'll have to use the DOS "print" command or print the ASCII file with your word processor). Any output file can be viewed (but not processed) within MAX.

MAX will prepare the profile and multiple-choice data *and* the coding-indicator data (line numbers and codes attached, also total lines per code) in dBASE format, which lets you export them to SYSTAT and SPSS as well as to many different spreadsheet and graphics programs. It also lets you produce numerical ASCII files, more slowly if your statistical package doesn't accept dBASE matrices. (You can also prepare text files to be exported to TEXTPACK PC, a traditional content analysis program that counts word frequencies, shows keywords in context, and so on.)

User Friendliness

MAX is fairly easy to learn, and easy to use for people who are accustomed to doing surveys including open-ended responses, or who have some quantitative background. It has the flavor of survey research, with an added-on code-and-retrieve feature. It's all menu driven, and the draft form of the manual is quite clear. The final version of the manual was expected in the fall of 1994. There is only one help screen (under "Quantitative and text data") in Version 3.5, but it is still in German.

Technical support in the United States is supplied by Qualitative Research Management, who also distribute the program. QRM deals with minor issues immediately; for more serious issues, QRM calls the developer, who will call you back and problem-solve.

MAX is not particularly flexible or customizable; you do things the way it says you have to. Not being able to back up or look at larger context during retrieval is a perfect example. However, it's fairly forgiving in that you can always <Esc> back out of what you're doing, and you can always revise codes and their application,and revise the values of profile and multiple-choice data.

Miscellaneous

The manual says not to run MAX with memory-resident programs, which will interfere with the function keys.

There's a password facility to prevent unauthorized access, but MAX files are not secure as such.

Your data files must reside in the same directory as MAX; you cannot, for example, make subdirectories to keep files from two projects separate. That's an important limitation.

Update

A Windows version exists in German, but there is no fixed date for it in English. It uses a hierarchical coding system and is word-based rather than line-based, according to the developer. The screen can display case names, the code list, and interview text in simultaneous windows.

Comparative Remarks

Folio VIEWS and askSam are other programs that can manage quantitative data along with text. They're better at searching, handling text, and creating reports than MAX, while MAX is better at processing quantitative data (and can also export it to statistical programs). askSam does not support coding as such—you have to do workarounds using data fields; in Folio VIEWS, you can use "highlighters" and free-form "fields" effectively as a coding method. Folio VIEWS is a richer environment for working with, marking up, annotating, memoing, coding, and manipulating text. Both Folio VIEWS and askSam are stronger at sorting and reorganizing data. Tabletop Senior also manages both sorts of data but cannot handle extended text and is primarily useful for cross-case analysis. It has no coding facility either.

As we noted earlier, MAX is hard to use in a grounded-theory style; for that, ATLAS/ti, Kwalitan, Martin, HyperQual2, or NUD•IST are better.

Summary

On balance, MAX is especially useful for quantitative-qualitative linkage, when you have comparable open-ended or semistructured and numerical data from a good-sized batch of people, as in the case of a standardized survey interview or questionnaire. It's a good bet for that kind of application, where you just want to get a good quick summary of what you have and make sense of it. To put it another way, MAX is useful when your approach is *variable*-oriented and *deductive* rather than inductive in approach.

But the qualitative side is not strong on coding—single-level codes, whose meaning can get lost in the blur of code numbers and line numbers—and is very limited on search and retrieval (limited fixed context, no scrolling back). The package does what it says it will, but is *not* useful for someone interested in deep, multilevel, iterative, reflective analysis of qualitative text.

So use MAX for what it's good for, and don't try to use it for extended free-form data, single cases, or grounded-theory development. That will just frustrate you.

Reference

Kuckartz, U. (1993). *MAX user's manual.* German version—Berlin: Free University of Berlin, Author. English version—introduction, translation, and design by R. Tesch, Desert Hot Springs, CA: Qualitative Research Management.

Tabletop

Available for Windows and Macintosh

TERC (Technical Education Research Centers)
2067 Massachusetts Ave.
Cambridge, MA 02140
Phone: (617)547-0430
Distributor: Broderbund Software
P.O. Box 6125
Novato, CA 94948-6125

Phone: (800) 521-6263

Price: $100

Hardware Requirements:
For Windows
- Windows 3.1 or better
- IBM PC 386 or better
- 4MB RAM desirable
- Hard disk with 1.5MB free

For Macintosh
- Mac II or better
- System 6 or better
- 2.5MB of RAM
- Hard disk with at least 3MB free

Overview

Are you ready? Tabletop may be a bit demanding for you. It's designed for use with students from the fourth grade up. But if they can do it, so can you.

Tabletop is a straightforward records-and-fields database with graphic-exploratory analysis features that make it attractive when you want to do preliminary cross-case analysis. Each case in your database is represented by an icon, and you can have them arranged in histograms, two-way plots, crosstabs, and Venn diagrams.

As you set up these displays, the icons flow around the screen and settle into the appropriate place. It's a rapid, graphical way to see what you have; each icon can be labeled (and relabeled) with any fieldname you like (such as the name or ID of your case, a number such as age, or a string such as language spoken). Any display can be printed or sent to file, and Tabletop keeps a retrievable record of your various displays. You can annotate your analyses. Basically, Tabletop lets you poke around in your data to see patterns and look at interactions of variables across cases. If you haven't guessed it by now, it's also very user friendly. It's really a database, not a textbase program as such, and it lacks the elegance of the complex textbase programs we've reviewed, but its very directness and simplicity are a plus.

TERC, the developer organization, is disseminating the program widely in schools, considering it a means for "helping students engage with concepts of constructing, organizing, analyzing and interpreting data."

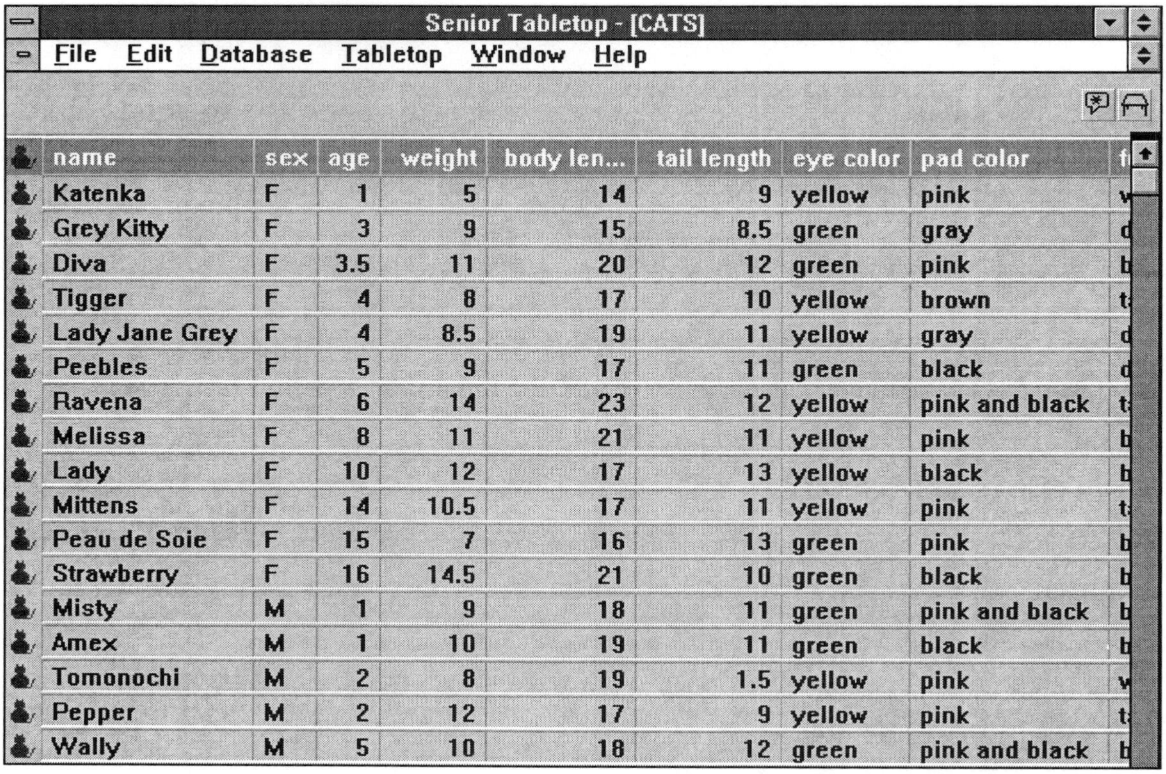

Senior Tabletop - [CATS]

File Edit Database Tabletop Window Help

name	sex	age	weight	body len...	tail length	eye color	pad color	f
Katenka	F	1	5	14	9	yellow	pink	v
Grey Kitty	F	3	9	15	8.5	green	gray	d
Diva	F	3.5	11	20	12	green	pink	b
Tigger	F	4	8	17	10	yellow	brown	t
Lady Jane Grey	F	4	8.5	19	11	yellow	gray	d
Peebles	F	5	9	17	11	green	black	d
Ravena	F	6	14	23	12	yellow	pink and black	t
Melissa	F	8	11	21	11	yellow	pink	b
Lady	F	10	12	17	13	yellow	black	b
Mittens	F	14	10.5	17	11	yellow	pink	t
Peau de Soie	F	15	7	16	13	green	pink	b
Strawberry	F	16	14.5	21	10	green	black	b
Misty	M	1	9	18	11	green	pink and black	b
Amex	M	1	10	19	11	green	black	b
Tomonochi	M	2	8	19	1.5	yellow	pink	v
Pepper	M	2	12	17	9	yellow	pink	t
Wally	M	5	10	18	12	green	pink and black	b

Tabletop Figure 1. A sample database supplied with the program (SOURCE. TERC, 1989). Icons for each record (in this case, cats) are at the left, and the fields are arranged in columns, beginning with the cat's name and proceeding through sex, age, and so on. The database has been sorted by sex, age, and weight. The remainder of the database is off screen to the right, and below, and can be scrolled to. Any item including fieldname can be edited. Columns can be moved or resized by clicking and dragging.

The icon at the far top right is for switching to the "tabletop" to create data displays; the one just to its left lets you write an annotation (memo) about the database.

This review is based on a pilot copy of the Windows version.

Database Structure

Tabletop organizes your data in traditional database form: a matrix of records (rows) by fields (columns). Each record is one of your cases, which might be an individual, a group, or a research site. The fields are the variables you have for your cases and can be of different types: numerical, string, or Boolean (true/false) form. You can also specify fields as in a spreadsheet, using a formula such as Bodymass= Kg/m^2, where you've already defined fields including Kg as weight in kilograms and m as height in meters. A field can, of course, include the name or ID of each case. There doesn't seem to be a limit on string size, but for practicality you'll want 10 or 12 characters or so, because the values will appear in full in your data displays (see below).

The developer, Chris Hancock, estimates that the program can manage about 200 cases, each with about 50 fields (Windows with a 386 or 486 machine, and Mac IIci) with perhaps 600 cases possible for a Mac with a PowerPC chip. Most qualitative studies don't go over a few dozen cases at most, so capacity isn't a problem.

Figure 1 shows a database, CATS, that comes with the Windows version of the program.

Data Entry

To enter data, you choose the File menu and click on "New database." You're presented with a screen that lets you enter the first fieldname, such as Site and, if you like, data for that field for one or more records (Figure 2). To add more records, you just hit <Control-Enter> and type in the record data. To add a new field, you hit <Control-F> and type in the new field name. Depending on how you

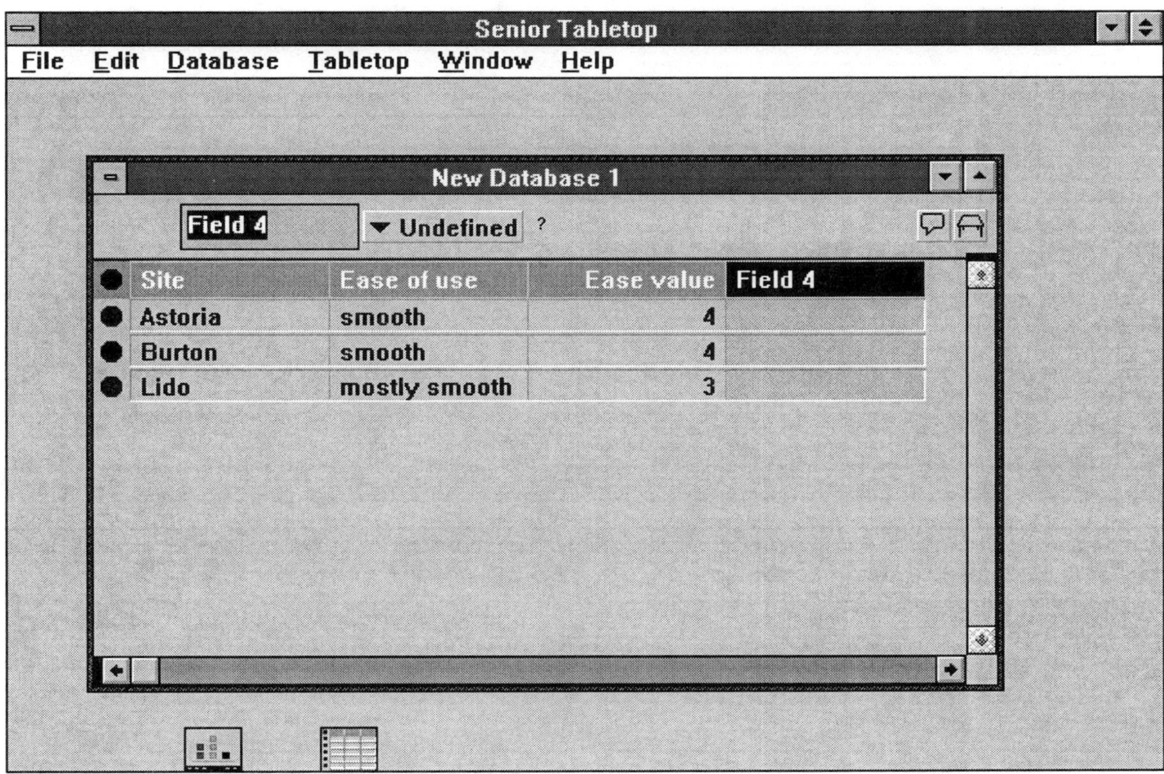

Tabletop Figure 2. Creating a new database. The user has created three fields and is about to define a fourth; typing in the new fieldname and <Enter> will do the trick. The field type is Undefined, but typing in text or a number will automatically convert the field to the right kind. Clicking on Undefined gives you the option to define the field as a string, Boolean true/false, number, or to base it on a formula (such as the ratio between the values in two other fields). The user has also entered a few records (Astoria, Burton, and Lido); more can be added at any time by hitting <Control-Return>. New fields can be made by pressing <Control-F>.

like to work, you can enter all the records for a field before going on to a new record, or just concentrate on getting all the fields in place first.

If you do the latter, you can then click on Questionnaire in the Database menu (Figure 3), which shows you all the fields. You can then enter all the data for one case.

Your data can be edited at any time. If you don't like the arrangement of rows and columns, you can move them by clicking on the row or column and dragging to the new position. When you do this, you have to watch carefully; a symbol appears at the edge of the matrix to show you precisely where the row or column can be deposited.

This work goes quickly: It was possible to create a database (from Table 8.6 in Miles & Huberman, 1994, p. 216) containing 12 cases and 10 variables in about 15 minutes. You save your database as a .DB file. Databases can be imported from the Microsoft Works database format or from ASCII text delimited by tabs or commas.

You can join one or more databases by clicking on Join in the Database menu. If the field structure is comparable, you can "Append" databases to each other, adding new cases. If the fields are not fully comparable, but have some overlapping fields for the same set of cases, you can use the Merge command. If not, the program will just leave some of the fields blank for which there are no data.

You can write annotations (really memos) for the database as a whole or for specific fields (for details, see "Theory Building," below).

Working on the Data

The records (cases) in your matrix can be sorted by up to three variables. For example, you might sort the "CATS" matrix first by sex, then age and weight, using the three boxes provided. That will show you right away by inspection that some younger cats, female and especially male, can be pretty heavy.

But the real strength of Tabletop lies in its other displays—Venn diagrams, scatterplots, and bar charts. You

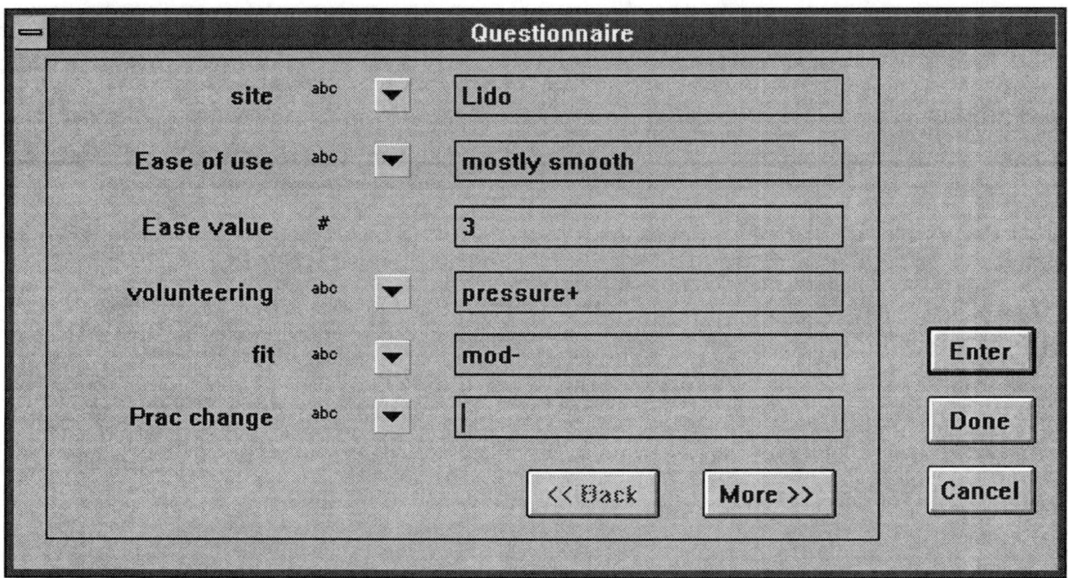

Tabletop Figure 3. Entering data via the Questionnaire. Once all the fields are set up, if you prefer to enter data case by case, you can call up Questionnaire from the Database menu. You're presented with the fields (abc means a string entry, # means numerical) and can type in your data, hitting <Tab > to move between fields. The Questionnaire will scroll down or up with the More and Back buttons to cover all the fields. The cases in the database are schools in the process of implementing innovations, and the variable "Ease of use" describes how "rough" or "smooth" the early implementation was. Other variables will be explained as we go along.

click on the "tabletop" icon to go to them, and you're first presented with a screen full of the icons for each of your cases, spread around in random order.

Venn Diagrams

For Venn diagrams, you click on the Venn icon. A loop appears on the screen, and you click on the fieldname you're interested in (a list of all fields appears). Then you click on the operator you want, also from a list (equal, not equal, equal or greater than, equal or less than), and a third term (this can be a fieldname or number). For example, a request might be, as in Figure 4, for the cases that have in the field called "Size value" a rating of 4 or more. When the request is complete, all the icons for records start moving around at once, carrying their labels with them (moving gently enough so that you can follow a particular one if you want) until the right ones are in the loop. In the databases used for this review (12-24 cases, 10-15 variables), this usually takes about 10-15 seconds on a 33 MHz 386 machine, faster than this on faster machines. If an icon is too crowded near another for readability, you can move it by clicking and dragging.

You can choose any label you want for the icons from the list of field names, and change the label any time you like. This is an extremely helpful feature, because you can check out alternate meanings of the arrangement you see. Furthermore, by clicking on the Operation and Compute buttons, you can immediately get counts of the icons in the loop, or a mean, median, mode, percentage, lowest or highest values, or the total. These operations can also be performed on numerical variables.

If you click on the Venn icon again, a second loop will appear, and you specify directions for it as well. The same features as above (alternate labeling, statistics) are available for the whole display. If you are interested in a specific region of the display, such as the intersection, you can highlight it by clicking with the mouse. You get a description in words of what the intersection means (e.g., Size value ≥ 4 AND Pracchg value ≥ 3 in Figure 5). You can compute statistics on it (Figure 6), mark those icons with boxes or special colors if you want, or print the selected region out graphically. You can also open a new screen with only your selected items—zooming in on them, so to speak. Marked icons will stay marked for subsequent analyses, so you can track them as you go along.

Tabletop will let you add a third loop as well if you wish.

For any type of display—Venn, scatterplots, or bar charts—you can click on a particular icon and you'll see all the data for that record in a little box (Figure 7).

And you can write an annotation (actually, a memo) at any point as you go; it can be revised, extended, or deleted (see below under "Theory Building").

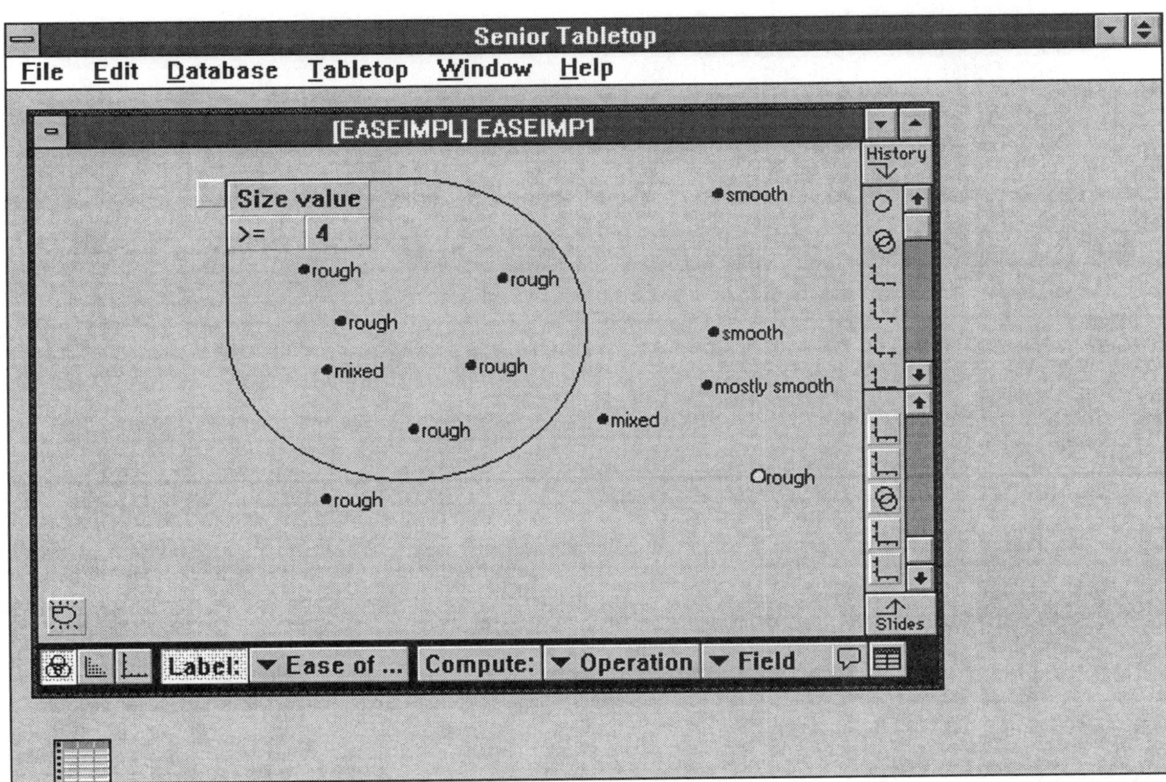

Tabletop Figure 4. Using the tabletop to create a Venn diagram. At the upper left, the user has chosen a fieldname (Size value), an operator (greater than or equal to), and a numerical value (4). Each icon with those characteristics has flowed into the Venn loop. The user has also chosen a label to apply to each icon, which in this case is Ease of use. Thus it's clear right away that five of the six cases whose Size value (the size of an innovation) was over 4 (the approximate median) also experienced "rough" use of the innovation. There are two "rough" cases with smaller-size innovations, however—to be pursued further in Figure 5.

Clicking on the Operation button lets you choose from a range of counting operations (such as median, mean, mode, total, smallest, largest) for any of the fields you choose from the Field list next to it; Compute gives you the results. You could also ask for a histogram.

The icon just to the right of the Field button will open a window for annotation/memoing about what you are finding from the display. The next icon will pop you back to the database display.

On the History bar at the top right you see a series of icons that represent each of the past 20 displays. The Slides bar at the lower right is for specific displays you want to save.

Scatterplots and Crosstabs

For scatterplots and crosstabs, you click on the "axis" icon (see, for example, Figure 7, third icon from left at bottom). You specify the Y and X axes by clicking on a list of field names for each. Then the category names and/or scales appear automatically, and the icons start flowing into place. If you want to refine the display, you click on "Show Axis Edit Bar" in the Tabletop menu; you can then adjust the size of intervals (which Tabletop calls "steps") for continuous variables. A Reset button will bring you back to the original step sizes. As with the basic database, if you don't like the order in which categorical data have been presented (Tabletop naturally doesn't know the "correct" order that exists in the researcher's mind), you can move the row or column by clicking and dragging. Tabletop will remember the revised order and use it from then on. If both fields are categorical, you'll get a matrix as in Figure 8. Note that you can also have plots that have both axes for continuous variables, or plots that have a continuous versus a categorical variable.

Crosstabs can be produced for either categorical or continuous data just by asking for the "Count" statistic; each cell then displays its frequencies. (Tabletop doesn't compute chi-squares or similar statistics but it will do mean, median, percent of total, and highest and lowest values).

As with Venn diagrams, the option for changing labels is illuminating. For example, in Figure 9, the problem was trying to understand why the Proville site was such an outlier. Changing the labels for all the icons from "Site

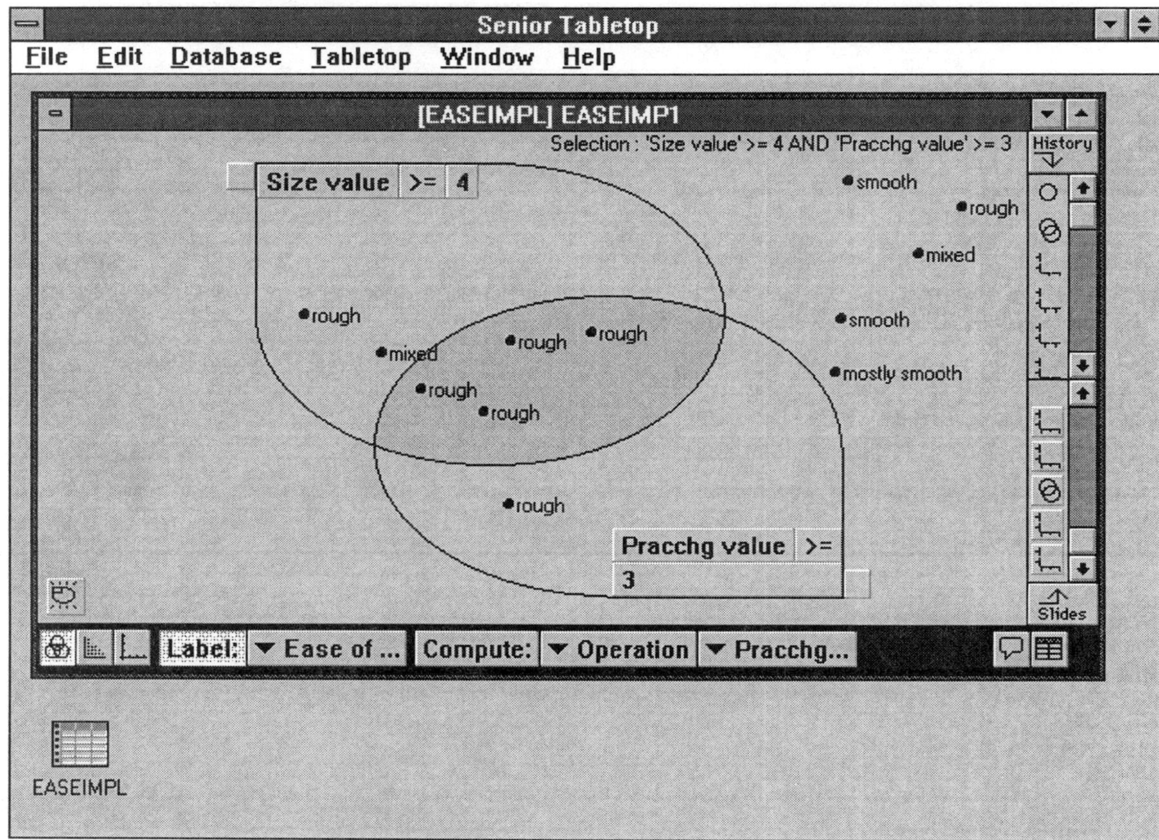

Tabletop Figure 5. Continuing the Venn diagram. The user has opened a second loop, defining it as values of Pracchg (amount of change in practice which the innovation requires) ≥ 3. The two variables together (OR) account for all but one of the cases of rough use (see Figure 6 for more).

The user has also defined the intersection of the two variables, and the meaning of the defined area is reported at the top right.

name" to "volunteering" (Figure 10) helped make it clear that the presence of negatively felt pressure was associated with "roughness" of implementation. In effect, you are looking at the relationship of two variables and speculating as to which third variables may be involved as mediating or intervening influences. Here too the option of marking a particular set of icons can be useful.

The Tabletop menu also lets you click on "Show Plot Recorder," a method for logging your work. As you proceed through different displays, revising the variables and labels, each display automatically generates a new icon in a bar at the right, up to a total of about 20 (Figures 4, 5, 6, 7). If you go over 20, the earlier ones are discarded. Clicking on any of those icons will bring you back to that display. You can deliberately save a few key displays by clicking on the "slides" icon; up to about 10 such "slides" (one display each) can be accommodated. The entire current "history" and the slides you've identified can be saved as a .TT file. If you open that file later, you can click on icons in the history, or a slide, and can go right on from there, specifying new variables, labels, displays, and so on.

Bar Charts

If you click on the "frequency" icon, and give a field-name for the X axis, you'll get a bar chart/histogram; the icons just stack up on each other. Tabletop will compute its usual statistics for each vertical stack if you wish.

Searching

Tabletop doesn't "search" in the usual sense of finding codes or strings. Rather, as just described, you ask for the data you want to see in Venn, bar chart, or scatterplot/cross-tab format, and you get them, displayed by cases. It's a kind of visually-assisted sorting and searching.

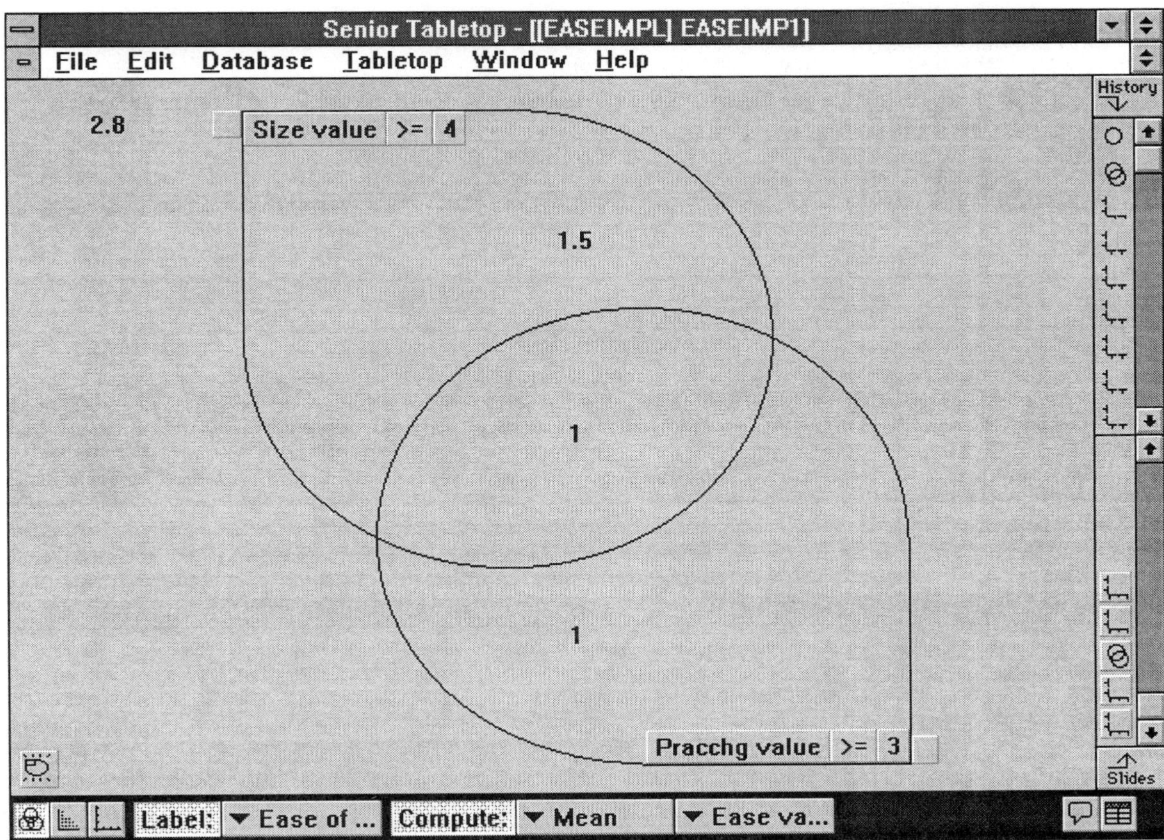

Tabletop Figure 6. Displaying statistics. The user, working from the display in Figure 5, has requested computation of the means of the cases on "Ease value" in different parts of the Venn diagram. The number 2.8 at the upper left refers to the mean of all the cases outside the two loops.

Output

Tabletop's strength is in its screen displays, but you can also send any display directly to a printer or to a file. The graphic quality is OK, but the typestyle came out for us as standard Courier or Dutch, not the way it looked on screen. Your database can also be printed.

Tabletop will not export the computed figures in a display, but according to the developer, you can export a field (and thus presumably several) from your database to your word processor.

Theory Building

Tabletop's strength is in exploratory data analysis, specifically across cases. You can sort out subsets of data with the Venn facility and examine relationships between a succession of two variables at a time, with a "shadow" third one via the use of labels, as noted above. You stay close to your data and begin to have a real feeling of why the icons "Joe," "Beverly," and "Susan" may be behaving as they are as they flow around in display after display, in contrast to those called "Chris," "Ginger," and "Fred." The developer of Tabletop calls this "data modeling," saying,

> Data [do] not come by the bale or by the pound, or even by the kilobyte; data [are] built in structures. These structures are in turn amenable to manipulations which yield results to which we may assign meaning . . . we can begin to make sense of data when we consider the data, the structures and the manipulations as a coherent whole—a *data model.* (Hancock & Kaput, 1990, pp. 1-2)

There is an "annotation" feature, which lets you record your musings in a work session as you go. That annotation text, unless you suppress it, simply stays on screen above each of the subsequent displays as you create them. You can revise and update the annotation as you go, and if you use the history feature and save your work, you can pull

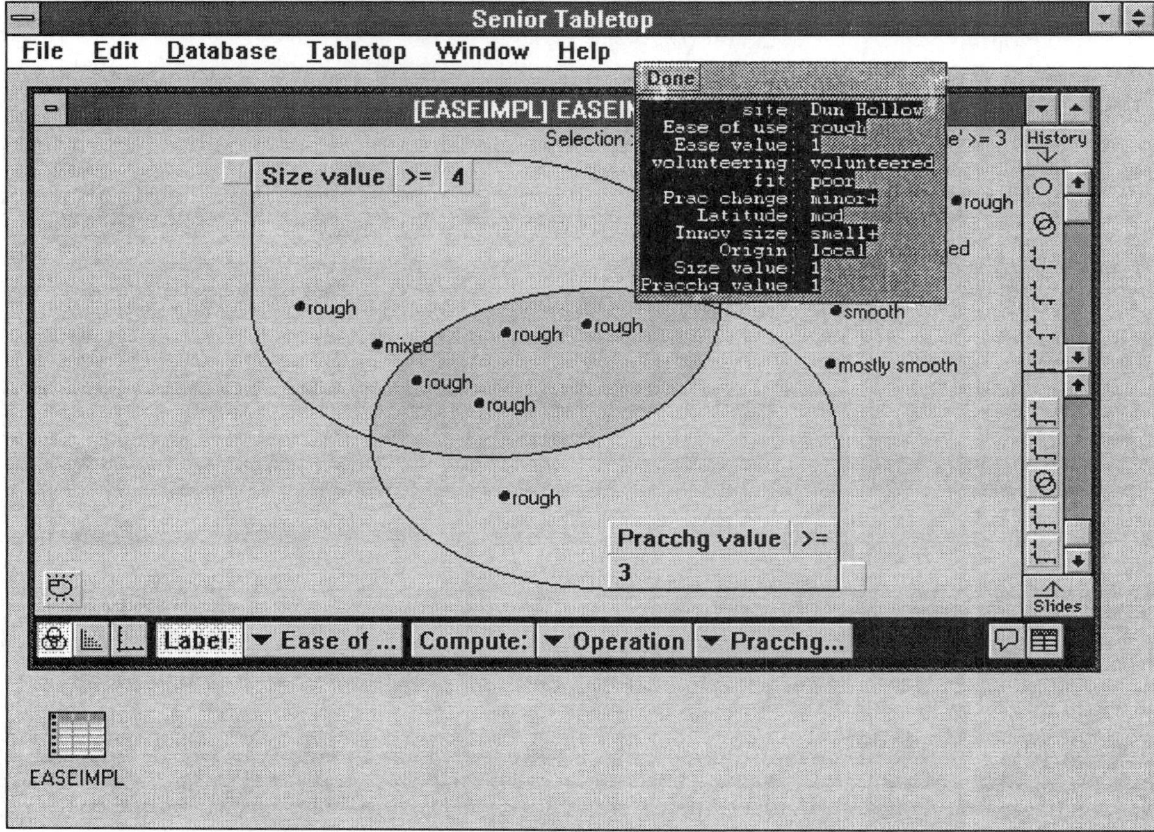

Tabletop Figure 7. Looking at the data for a single case. The user has double-clicked on the deviant "rough" case at the upper right, which pops up a box with all the information for that case. Though the innovation's size and the practice change it demanded were small at Dun Hollow, we can see that the innovation was a poor "fit" to the school, and users had little "latitude" to improve its fit. This led, we can speculate, to the "rough" use.

Such a finding could be summarized in the annotation for the display, appearing above it.

up and see the various versions of the annotation as it developed. Annotations can also be added to your basic data matrix as a whole or to specific fields. What the program calls annotations can be up to 64K (about 20 single-spaced pages). That length, and their linkage to displays, fields, and matrices, certainly qualify them as memos. You can't search their text, however.

Graphics Editing

Graphics editing in the usual sense is very limited. However, as noted above, you can change scale intervals and category placement, mark specific icons or classes of icons, and create new icons for one, some, or all records.

User Friendliness

Are you a fourth grader or older? If yes, Tabletop is user friendly for you. You do need a little familiarity with Windows or the Macintosh, of course.

TERC developed a Curriculum Writer's Guide to support classroom use, but it's not generally available. (See the "Update" section, below.) We worked from the "condensed quickie version" (TERC, 1994). The latter was quite clear (except on how to create a database), even though the screen shots were from the Mac version. There is no real tutorial, but a sort of minitour; its screen shots and annotated explanations were very useful. Program fluency was a matter of a couple of hours.

The help screens were hardly implemented at all in the test version.

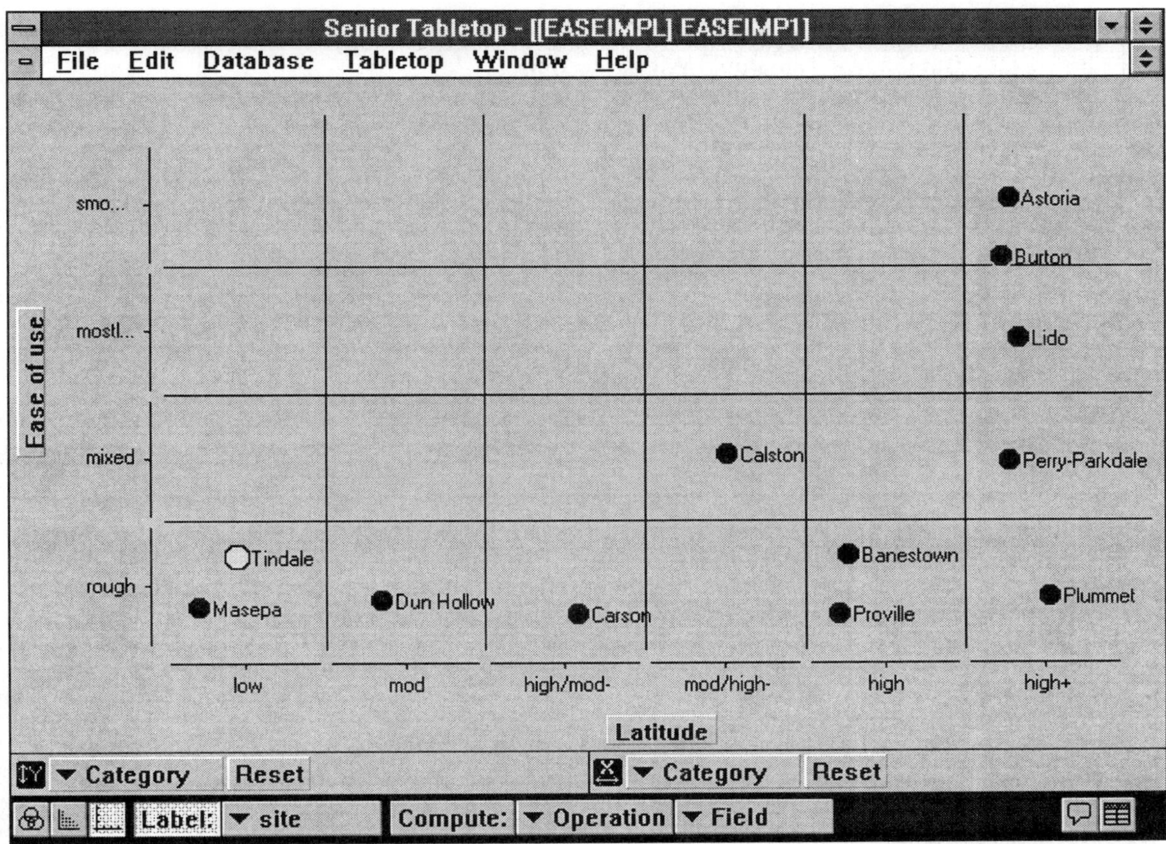

Tabletop Figure 8. A crosstab/scatterplot of two categorical variables. The user has clicked on the "axis" icon at the lower left, then clicked on the Y axis button at center left to choose a fieldname from the list. This is repeated for the X axis at center bottom. The index bar just below the display shows that both axes are for categorical variables. The icons then arrange themselves as shown; the user has chosen the site names as labels. It's easy to see that "smooth" or "mostly smooth" use is associated with high latitude for adapting the innovation, but that "rough" use occurs regardless of the level of latitude.

The Tindale icon (lower left) has been selected by a click. It can then either be moved within its cell or clicked on twice to show full information, as we saw in Figure 7.

For now, you can get technical support from the developer, Chris Hancock, who patiently and cheerfully answers questions, even though he says he isn't a Windows ace. First-level tech support was to be supplied by Broderbund beginning in the fall of 1994; more difficult questions will be dealt with by Hancock.

Miscellaneous

Tabletop has limited customization. You can choose from a series of preset icons for your cases or create one yourself. An icon can be unique to a case, or standard across all of them. Icons can be shown full or half size.

A minor annoyance is that when you click on an icon to move it, as you drag, the cursor disappears, so you have to fly blind to the new location. The icon stays fixed, then pops to the new location.

Update

A manual is expected, oriented to classroom use. Tabletop will also be marketed to schools by Jostens Learning, Inc., 9920 Pacific Heights Blvd., Suite 100, San Diego, CA 92121, in conjunction with other curriculum materials. Phone: (619) 587-0087 or (800) 422-4339.

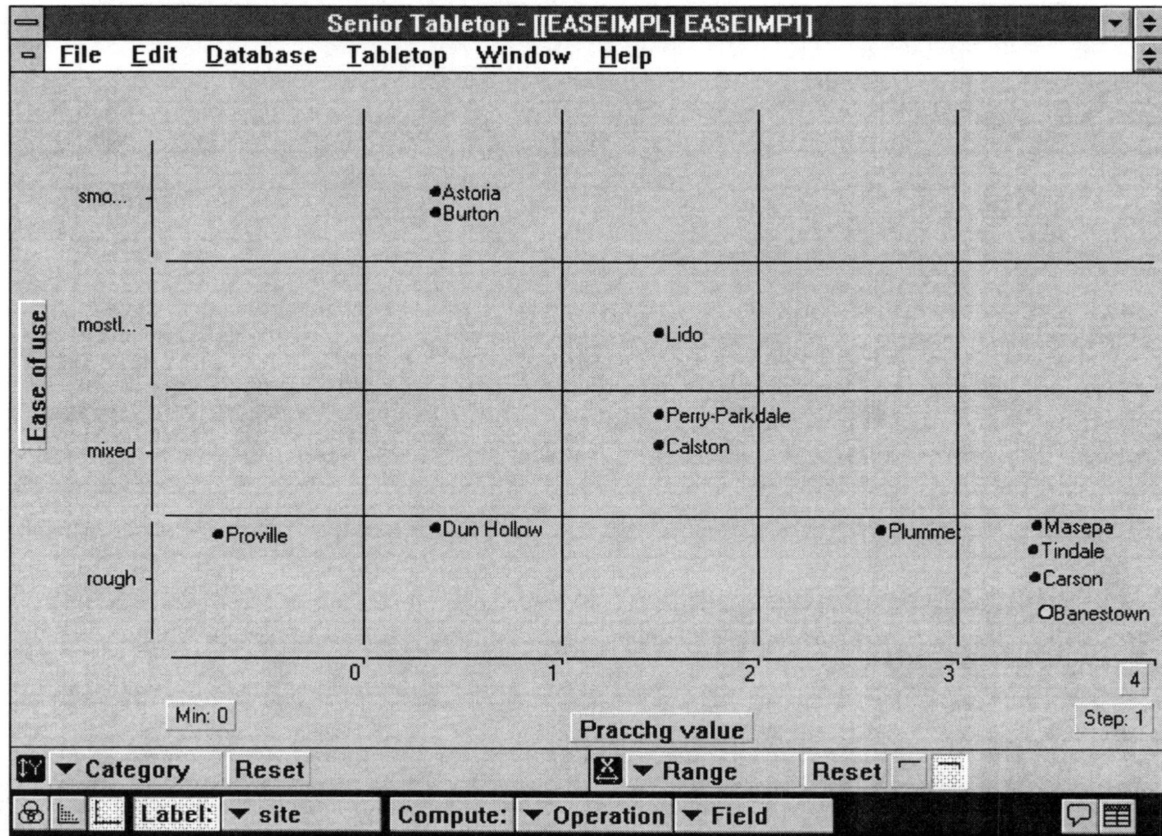

Tabletop Figure 9. Another display comparing a categorical with a continuous variable. "Ease of use," arranged as ordered categories, is compared with "Pracchg value," a rating of the amount of change in practice the innovation required. Clicking on "Range" permits you to change the step size on the X axis (now 1) to any other value. You can also opt for continuous values. The Reset button brings you back to the original setting. Note the general relationship (high practice change means rough use and vice versa), but Proville and Dun Hollow are deviant cases. We already know about Dun Hollow (Figure 7). For Proville, see Figure 10.

Comparative Remarks

Tabletop falls between traditional, more fully featured textbase managers and programs such as AQUAD and QCA that can do comparative cross-case analysis. It's much friendlier than AQUAD or QCA, and stronger in that it can use continuous rather than only Boolean true/false data, along with as many categories as you like for a field. Its Venn plus scatterplot facilities give you a much better idea of what's happening with your data; AQUAD and QCA give you no graphics at all. On the other hand, it can only deal with 3 or 4 variables at a time, while AQUAD and QCA can take up to 12 at once, accommodating much richer configurations.

All the textbase managers we reviewed can accommodate large amounts of text in fields, and most have much richer, faster, and more powerful searching facilities. So, if you have a big textbase, and are concerned not just with cross-case analysis but detailed within-case analysis, go for MAX, askSam, or Folio VIEWS for storing and exploring your data. Tabletop is really a small, relatively inexpensive, special-purpose program that lets you look across cases, once you have a good idea of what the key variables are and have good measures or statements of them. It's well worth buying as a supplement to almost any other program we've reviewed.

Summary

Tabletop is a simple database program with some thoughtful enhancements that let you examine cross-case relationships and patterns via Venn diagrams, bar charts, and scatterplots. You see case icons move into position in these displays; the flavor is direct. Tabletop keeps you honest and close to your data. Don't expect the usual textbase

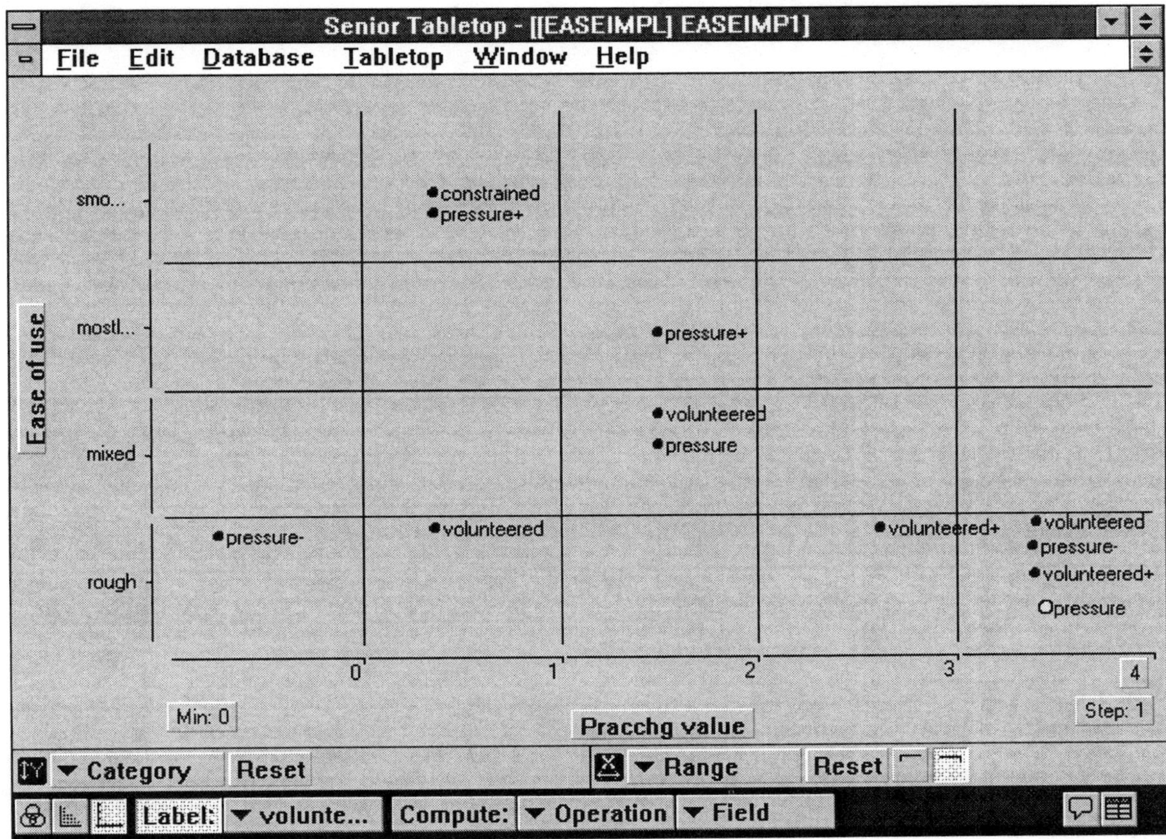

Tabletop Figure 10. Checking out a third variable. The user wondered if the variable "volunteering" might explain Proville's outlier status. Labeling the icons with that field shows that Proville (lower left corner) experienced pressure to adopt the innovation, and felt it as a barrier (pressure –). Note that the other case of "pressure –" at the far right also had rough use, but when pressure was seen as facilitative ("pressure +"), ease of use was smooth or mostly smooth.

searching and management features, but spend the small amount of money and time involved to enhance your abilities to do good cross-case analysis and interpretation.

References

Hancock, C., & Kaput, J. J. (1990, July). *Computerized tools and the process of data modeling.* Paper read at the 14th International Conference on the Psychology of Mathematics Education, Mexico.

Hancock, C., Kaput, J. J., & Goldsmith, L. (1992). Authentic inquiry with data: Critical barriers to classroom implementation. *Educational Psychologist, 27*(3), 337-364.

Miles, M. B., & Huberman, A. M. (1994). *Qualitative data analysis: An expanded sourcebook* (2nd ed.). Thousand Oaks, CA: Sage.

TERC (Technical Education Research Centers). (1989). *Use numbers.* Menlo Park, CA: Dale Seymour.

TERC (Technical Education Research Centers). (1994). *The Tabletop (Senior) user guide: The condensed quickie version.* Cambridge, MA: Author.

6

Code-and-Retrieve Programs

The programs we describe here assume that you want to "code" your data—that is, apply keywords to meaningful segments or "chunks," such as lines, sentences, or paragraphs of your text. They help you to set up the kind of "chunks" you want to use, to develop a list of codes, to attach the right codes to the right chunks—and then to search for and retrieve all the chunks to which one or several codes have been applied.

Other programs that overlap significantly with this category, and the chapters they are reviewed in, include the following:

□ □ □

HyperQual2 Version 1.0

Available for Macintosh

Raymond V. Padilla[1]
3327 N. Dakota
Chandler, AZ 85224

Phone: (602) 892-9173

Prices:
Stand-alone version: $180
"Stack" version (requires HyperCard 2.0): $360
Various multiple licenses and network deals available

Hardware Requirements:

- Macintosh computer (no minimums specified)
- 1MB RAM minimum (4MB recommended for System 7)
- HyperCard 2.0 *for Stack version only*
- Hard Disk

Overview

HyperQual2 (the new version of HyperQual) is a HyperCard-based Mac program for managing information and performing analyses in a qualitative study, and is almost a hybrid of a textbase manager and a code-and-retrieve program. Like the Windows program Martin, it is based on the metaphor of copying chunks of text to index cards, then coding, sorting, and writing memos about them. Being built on HyperCard, it incorporates some useful hypertext features. It will be appealing to those who like its unique structure and hyperlinking, and tedious for others who expect more in the way of analytical capabilities. The analytical strategy is one of locating "meaningful chunks," sorting them out, adding codes to your sorted "exemplars" (not to the original data), and annotating and memoing like crazy as you go. You don't explicitly do Boolean searches

1. Distributor: Developer or Qualitative Research Management, 73425 Hilltop Road, Desert Hot Springs, CA 92240. Phone: (619) 329-7026.

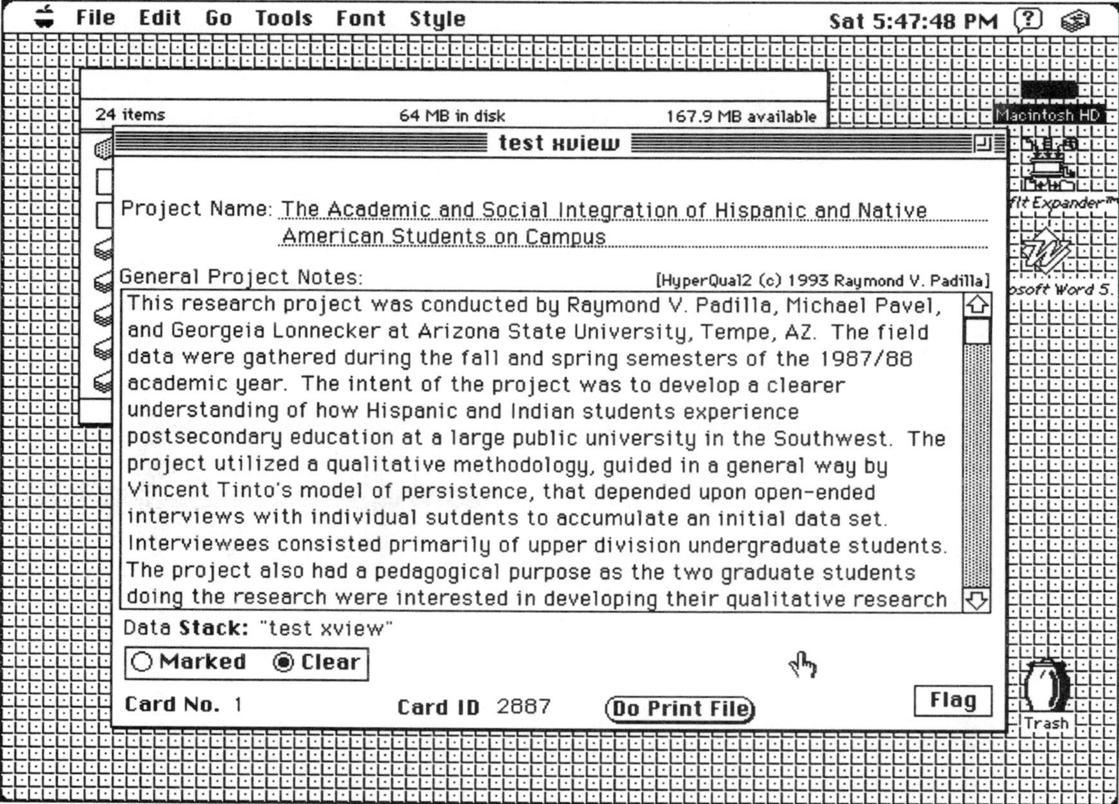

HyperQual2 Figure 1. A Structured Interview, or Xview, face card. The user fills out the Project Name and General Project Notes fields. The name of the stack, "test xview," appears at the lower left. Card No. 1 indicates this is currently the first card in the stack (this changes as cards are added/deleted). Card ID 2887 is a unique number assigned to this card by the program and can be used to hop to a card from anywhere else in the stack.

for codes. Rather, you sort out and merge your stacks of exemplars, creating new stacks based on different combinations of codes. This can be thought of—again, Martin is similar—as a flexible, close-to-the-data way to build your conceptual understanding of the categories and subcategories of meaning in your text.

HyperCard files are called "stacks"; the metaphor is a stack of index cards. HyperQual2 has five basic types of stacks, each designed for a different type of data, and then some additional ones that get created as a result of search and output operations. The five basic types are for (a) structured interview data; (b) observational data or unstructured interviews (or any other unstructured data); (c) documents (references, documents collected as data, research memos to be analyzed, and so on); (d) research memos; and (e) schemas: drawings, graphics, and so on.

In general, the program is very easy to learn and use, though a little cranky. For example, there are quite a few warnings in the manual about things you can do to crash the program.

There are two versions of the program available. The "stand-alone" version, at $180, runs by itself; you don't need HyperCard.[2] The "stack" version, at twice the price, requires HyperCard, which you must buy separately (unless it came with your Mac). Because of limitations of HyperCard Player (see footnote), there are certain things you can't do with the stand-alone version, like creating hypertext links between your text and your memos (a feature that was available in earlier versions of HyperQual). This review is based on the stand-alone version, though there will be occasional remarks about the stack version.

Database Structure

In HyperCard files ("stacks"), you are always looking at something that looks like an index card with various types of information on it. You can think of each card as a

2. This version incorporates HyperCard Player, a limited version of HyperCard sold to developers to build into their programs for this purpose.

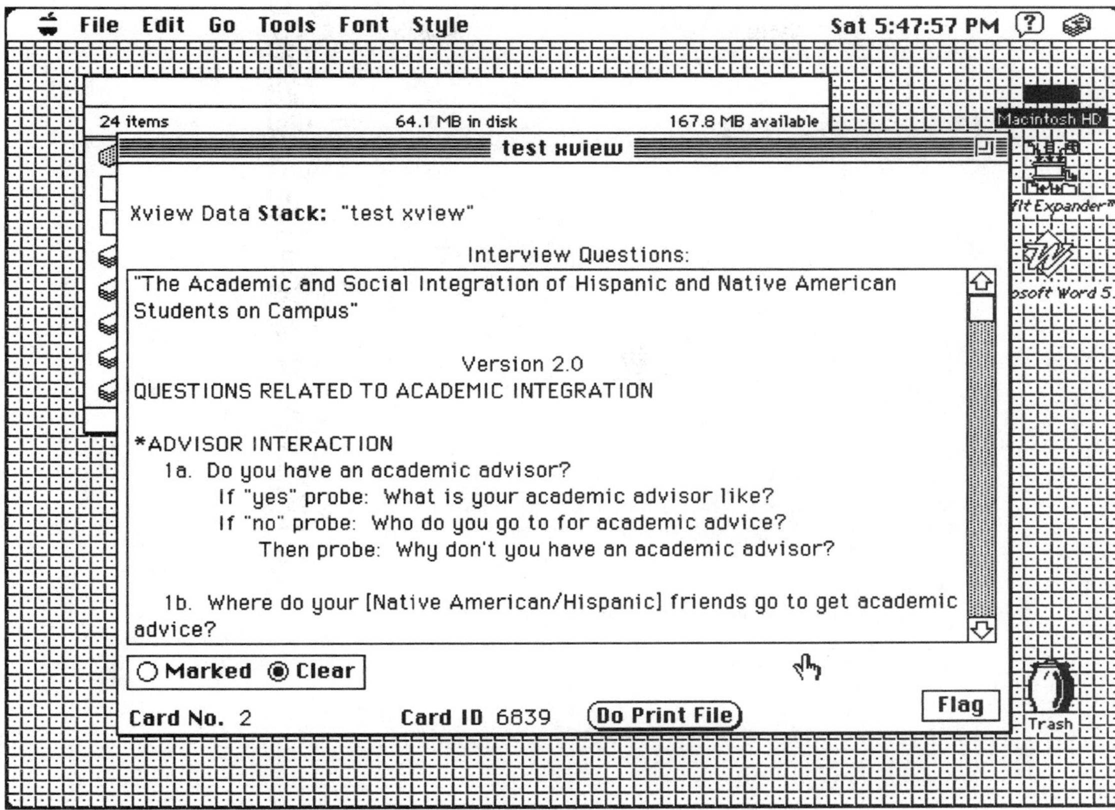

HyperQual2 Figure 2. An Xview interview schedule card. There's just one field to fill out here, with the complete text of your interview protocol. Question numbers can be used to retrieve questions when you're looking at the answers.

record in a traditional database—only they can be reshuffled, rearranged, and linked together in much more flexible ways. Like the records in a database, each card can have fields, and these can be arranged in different ways on the card. Any field can have as much as 30,000 characters of text (30K, or about 10 single-spaced pages—what it doesn't show you can scroll to). Different cards in the same stack can have different field structures, unlike a traditional database, where all the records in a file must have the same field structure. HyperQual2 has different types of stacks, some with as many as four different types of cards, each designed for distinct purposes and types of data.

This is not as confusing as it may sound. As we've noted, HyperQual2 has five basic types of stacks:

Xview: structured interview data

Site: observational data or unstructured interviews (or any other unstructured data)

Doc: documents (references, documents collected as data, research memos to be analyzed, and so on)

Memo: research memos

Sketch: drawings, graphics, and so on

The first three types are considered "data" stacks, intended to hold your initial data. Memo and Sketch stacks are meant for writing or representing things about your data and have different (fewer) capabilities and functions.

There are also "exemplar" stacks, one type corresponding to each of the three kinds of data stacks, to hold the specific chunks of data you select out from your data stacks and let you code and manipulate these chunks. You can have as many stacks of each type as you want.

Data Stacks

The data cards in data stacks all have roughly the same capabilities. From any of them, you can mark and select out "meaningful chunks" of text to new "exemplar" stacks.

Structured Interview (Xview) stacks. Xview stacks are specialized for handling transcripts of structured interviews. They have four types of cards: (a) a single face card (see Figure 1) with a field for the project name and a notes field,

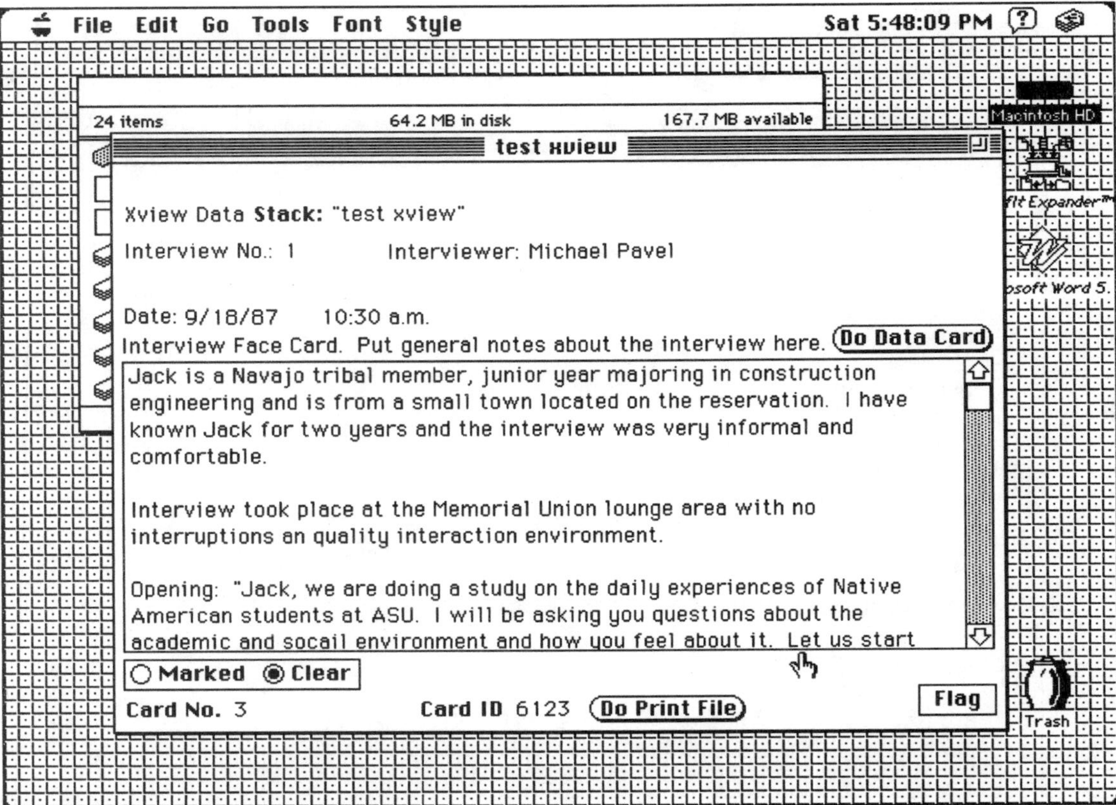

HyperQual2 Figure 3. An Xview interview face card. For each interview in the stack, you fill out one of these and follow it with the data cards for that interview. You fill in the information for Interview No., Interviewer, and Date and then type any general notes about the interview in the large box.

into which you might type the researcher's name, general information about the series of interviews or the project, important dates, and so on (remember, you can put up to 30K in any field); (b) a single card for the questionnaire or interview schedule (see Figure 2); (c) an interview face card for each interview (see Figure 3), with fields for interview number, name of interviewer, date, and general notes about the interview; (d) the interview data cards themselves (one *per question* for each interview; see Figure 4), with fields for interview number, question number, notes by researcher (again, up to 30,000 characters), and the actual response (30K). The presence of the interview schedule and the organization of data cards by question numbers allow you to jump from any data card to the question the interviewee was responding to on the interview schedule card, by just clicking on the Question No. field (see Figure 4).

Site/Unstructured Interview (Site) stacks. Site stacks are specialized for holding more free-form data, like notes from site observations or transcripts from unstructured interviews. They're very similar to Xview stacks, except that they don't have an interview schedule card, and the identifying information fields are slightly different to accommodate the difference in types of data. There are three kinds of site card: (a) a face card, which is the same as the Xview face card; (b) a site face card (see Figure 5)[3] for each site, with fields for site/interview number, observer/interviewer name, date, and general notes; (c) the site data cards (see Figure 6) with fields for observer's/interviewer's name, site/interview number, notes (30K), and data (30K).

Documents/Lit Reviews (Doc) stacks. Doc stacks can be used for storing information about, and (optionally) the actual text of, a wide variety of types of documents. For example, you could use them to store, annotate, and code your bibliographic references; documents you've collected as data; research memos you want to be able to code, chunk, sort, and analyze; and so on. Implied: You can do all the same

3. The data for Figures 5, 6, and 7 were provided by us. The data in all other figures are from the manual (Padilla, 1993).

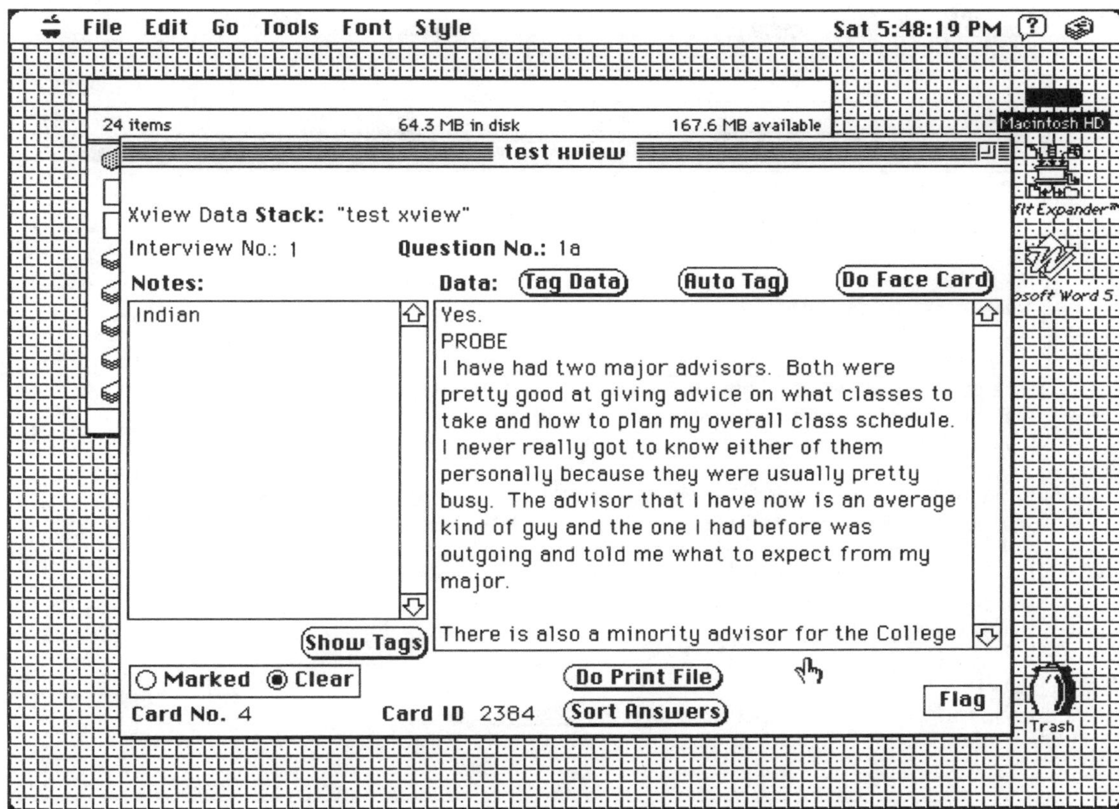

HyperQual2 Figure 4. Xview data card. The Interview No. is filled in automatically, and you fill in the Question No. Then you can type in the text of the answer to that question in the Data field, and any notes about it in the Notes field at the left. The functions of the various buttons, Tag Data, Auto Tag, and so on, are described as we go along.

things with data from a Doc stack that you can with data from Xview or Site stacks. Doc stacks have only one type of card with seven fields (see Figure 7). There are fields for reference information: author, title, publisher or journal, and year. There is a field for the actual text or excerpts from it (up to 30K) and a field for notes about the document (30K). There is also a field for keywords that can later be used to sort your Doc cards. This is a unique feature of Doc cards.

References can be output in a good approximation of APA style. You just have to create hanging indents and underline or italicize the appropriate part of the reference after importing to your word processor. (You'll also need to figure out a couple of workarounds, like putting volume and page number info in the "Publisher or Journal" field.)

Memo Pad and Sketch Pad Stacks

These last two of the five basic types of stacks are intended for holding memos and drawings about your analysis. They do not support many of the operations that the data stacks do.

Memo pad stacks. Memo stacks are designed explicitly for creating research memos. Unfortunately, the text you type into memo stacks *cannot* be chunked, sorted, and/or coded. (If you are interested in taking a system closure approach and doing these sorts of operations on your memos, you can set up a data stack for memos. Best suited for this would be the Doc stacks, which have fields for things like titles and keywords.) Memo stacks have one type of card (see Figure 8) with five fields for topic of memo, author, memo number, date, and the actual memo (30K).

In the stand-alone version, the ability to link these memo cards to data and exemplar stacks has been lost—a serious weakening of the program from the earlier HyperQual. In the stack version, as in previous versions, you can access HyperCard tools that let you place hyperlink buttons anywhere you want on a card, so that by clicking the button you can jump to another card. So you could create a "Memo"

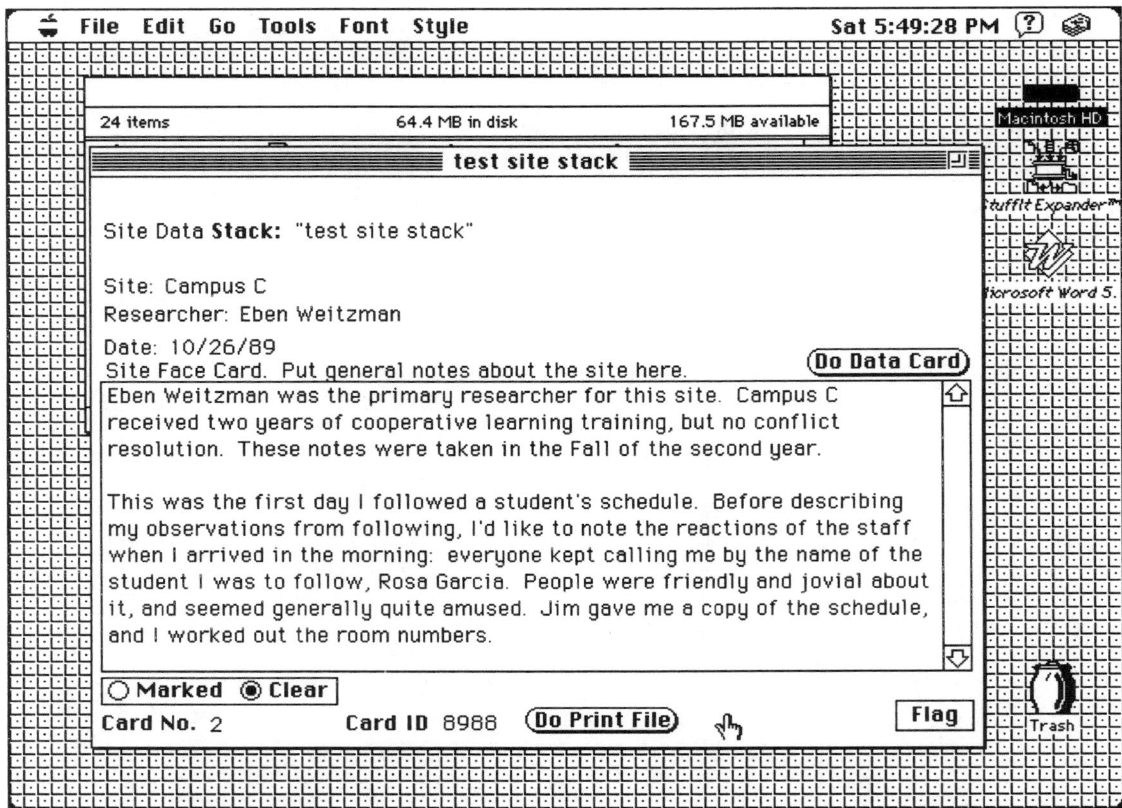

HyperQual2 Figure 5. The site face card from a site/unstructured interview stack. For each site, or each unstructured interview, you would set up such a face card, followed by the data cards for that site or unstructured interview. You type in the name of the site (or interviewee), researcher name, and date and then type in any general notes about the site or interview in the large box.

button on a data or exemplar card to jump you to a memo about the data on that card (see Figure 9).

Sketch pad stacks. Sketch stacks have totally blank cards on which you can draw with the HyperCard paint module. You could use this, for example, to store visual diagrams, such as networks, representing your emerging understanding of the relationships in your data. You can also paste in any drawings, photos, images, and so on, which can be imported with the HyperCard paint module, such as those from MacPaint or other graphics packages. Again, these cards are *not* linked to data or exemplar stacks in the stand-alone version, though in the stack version you could place hyperlink buttons in your sketches.

Capacity/Limits

You can have as many stacks and output files as will fit on your hard disk. Each stack can have up to 512 MB of data, or 16,777,216 cards. Again, you can have up to 30,000 characters of text in a field (technically, this is a little less than 30K, which would actually be 30,720 characters, but we'll call it 30K for simplicity's sake).

Data Entry

You can either type your text in directly or paste it in from the clipboard (from, say, your word processor). There are distinct advantages and disadvantages to each method. We'll suggest a compromise approach, which is workable only with System 7.

Direct Text Input

Typing your text directly into the cards makes some sense; you can fill in the various fields on the different types of cards in the stack at the same time as you type up your data. This can be important; it helps you see what information does and does not have to go into the text itself and encourages you to set things up in a way best suited to HyperQual2's structure.

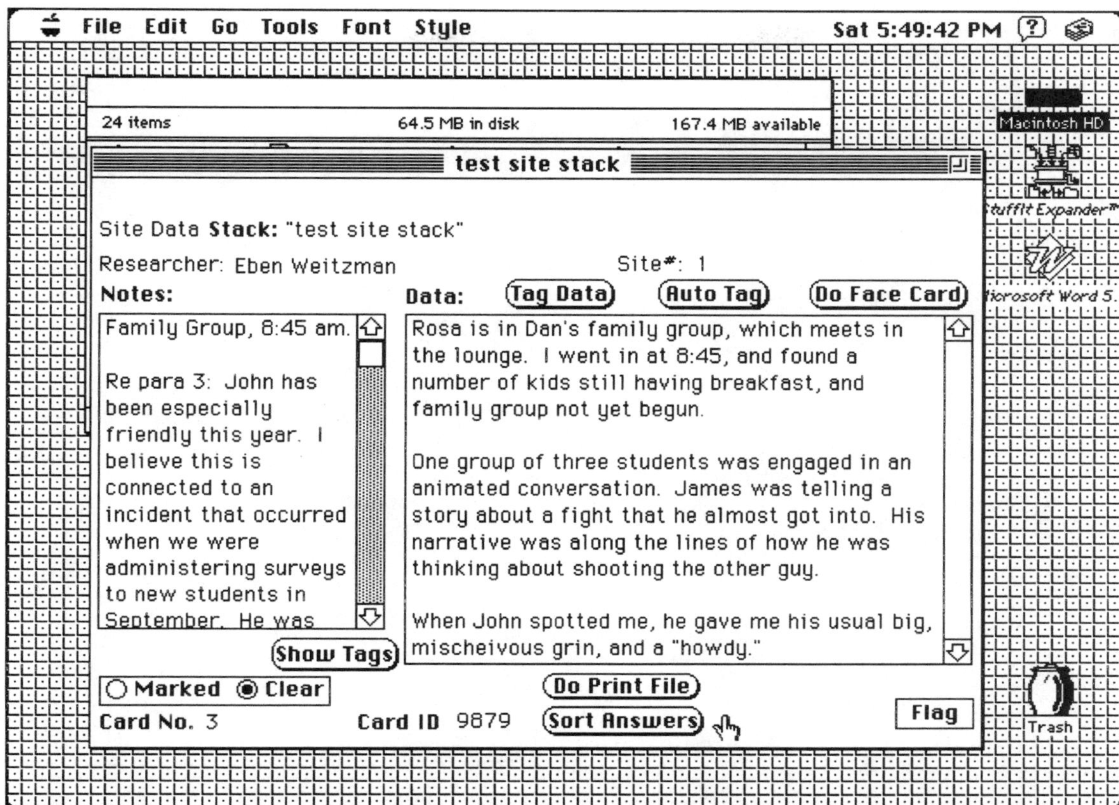

HyperQual2 Figure 6. A site data card. This is very much like the Xview data card. You type in the Researcher name, and the site visit (interview) gets numbered automatically. Enter the observation or interview data in the Data field and any notes about the data in the Notes field.

The down side is that the HyperCard editor is seriously limited. While it does support basic clipboard functions like cutting, copying, and pasting text, and also has a basic string search function, it is extremely uncomfortable for any extended typing. This is primarily because the cursor (arrow) keys are reserved for navigating among cards. So try to use the left-arrow key to back up a couple of spaces, and you wind up a couple of cards away, with the card you were on no longer visible on the screen and your place in the text lost. The Tab key is also reserved for navigating, so hitting Tab has similarly disruptive effects. The thinking is obviously that you can always use the mouse to move around, but for short distances especially, this is slow and cumbersome and completely counter-instinctual for a touch typist.

A virtually useless feature of the editor is that you can change fonts, styles (e.g., bold, underline, italic), and sizes, but these features disappear when you output your text. We'd advise against ever using this feature; you're going to get used to whatever emphasis you're trying to create—only to lose it when you really need it.

Indirect Text Input: Pasting and Importing Text

Your other option is to paste in text (or graphics for sketch pads) from the clipboard. (If you have the stack version, you can do some more sophisticated importing, described in the second paragraph below.) The advantage of this is that you can take advantage of the various editing features of your word processor when typing up longer passages of text. You can also paste in text from existing documents, like those you or someone else might have typed up earlier or scanned in from, say, archival site data. The disadvantage of the pasting method is that you separate the steps of filling out the face cards and various information fields from the process of typing up the data itself.

With the stack version you can, according to the developer, import data using HyperCard scripts (which are somewhere between a macro and a program in complexity). The advantage of this method is that you can put the data for all the fields of a card in one document, then have it broken up and put in the correct fields on import. The

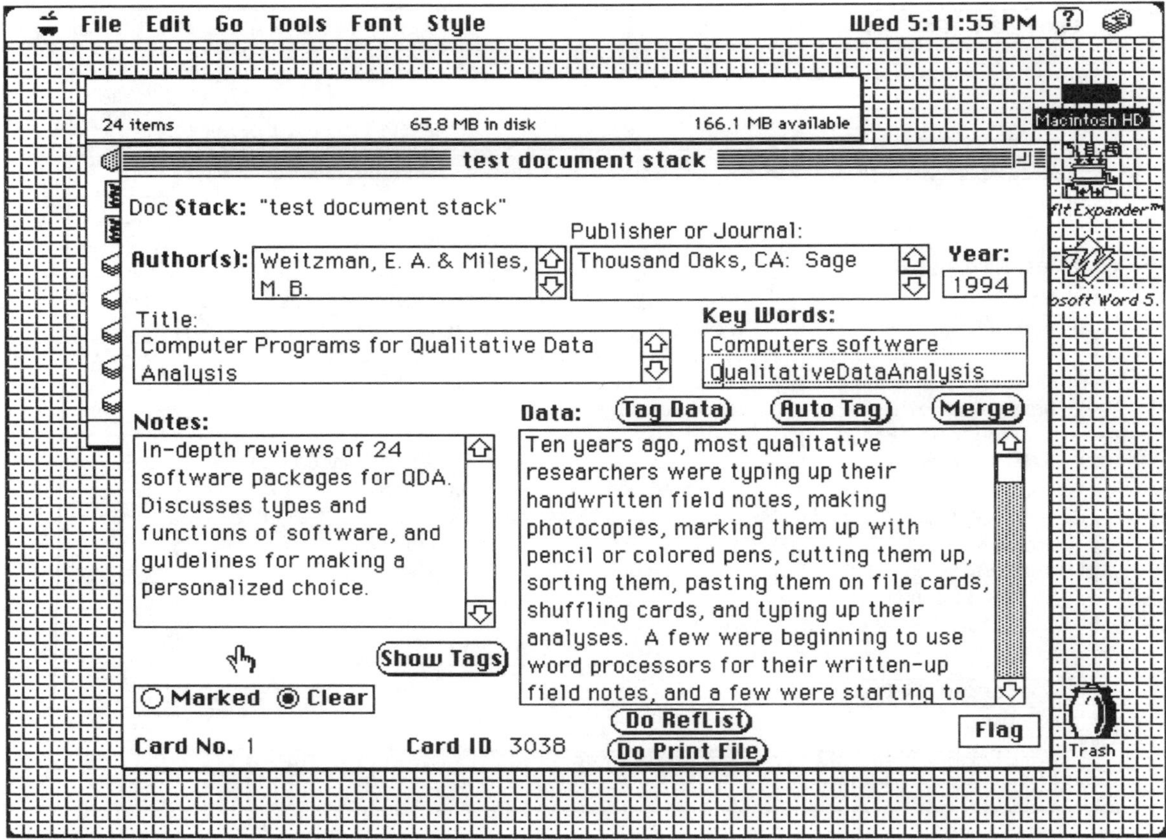

HyperQual2 Figure 7. A Document card. There are fields for Author, Publisher or Journal, Year, Title, and Key Words. You can type up to 30,000 characters of the text of the document in the Data field and notes about it in the Notes field. The keywords can be used for retrieving document cards.

developer says it's "pretty easy" to write the necessary scripts, but we weren't able to verify this.

A Compromise (System 7 Only)

If you have System 7, you can have more than one application open at once. In this case, your best bet may be to have both HyperQual2 and your word processor open at once, as in Figure 10. You could then type in the various information fields, move the cursor over to your word processor to type up the data, and paste it right into the card. This workaround comes about as close as you can get to what it would be like if HyperQual2's own editor were more useful.

Working on the Data

You go through your data by selecting out and coding chunks. You read the data, select meaningful chunks (which are called "exemplars," with the assumption that they are examples of categories of data) with the mouse, and proceed to send these chunks to a new or existing "exemplar" stack (see Figure 11). After selecting an exemplar, you click on the Tag Data button. First you're asked to name the exemplar stack to use. Then a box appears in which you can type the names of any tags (codes) you want applied to the whole exemplar in the exemplar stack (each exemplar in the exemplar stack gets its own card). *The data in the data card are never coded.* Thus you can create exemplars from overlapping or nested chunks of text in the data card, but when you apply codes, you apply them to these chunks as wholes, never overlapping or nesting code applications—just the chunks they apply to, as in Martin. Exemplar stacks have two editable fields, one for tags (30K, meaning you can have up to 30,000 characters worth of codes for each exemplar) and one for the exemplar (30K, meaning it can be as big as the data in the data card). There are also "locked" fields (which you can't edit) showing source stack, card, interview and question number, docu-

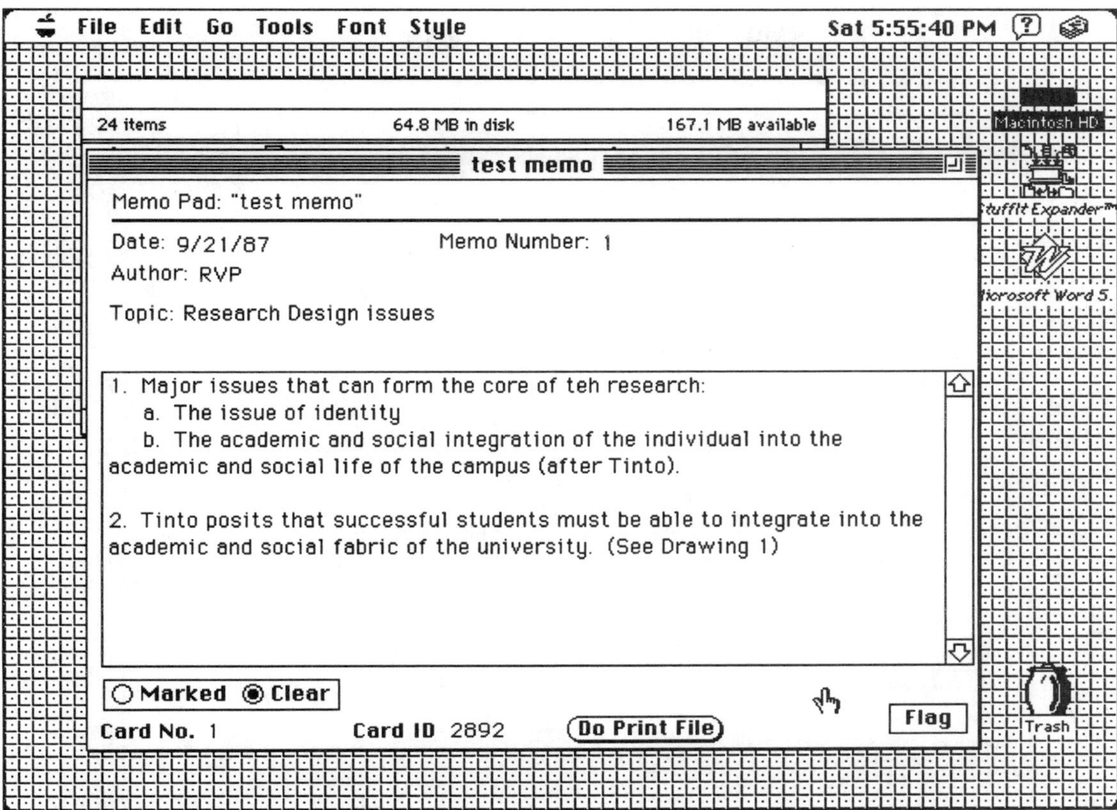

HyperQual2 Figure 8. Memo pad card. The name of the stack ("test memo") appears at the top. There are fields for Date, Author, and Topic, and the memo is numbered automatically. The text of the memo itself gets typed in the large field.

ment, and so on depending on the type of source data stack you're working from.

You can create multiple exemplar stacks in the process of sorting your exemplars, using different stacks to hold data belonging to different categories. However, because—as explained under "Searching"—you'll be creating a lot of new stacks as soon as you start searching and sorting through your data, you'll probably want to start out with just one, or perhaps a small number, of exemplar stacks (maybe one for each site or one for males and one for females).

Working with Tags (Codes)

HyperQual2 calls codes "tags." Tags can be virtually as long as you want but cannot contain spaces. If you want a multiword tag, you could just capitalize the first letter of each word, as in "SocialClimate," or use a character like the hyphen, as in "social-climate." When you select a chunk of text in a data card and click on the Tag Data button, a box pops up into which you can type the names of multiple tags (up to 30K worth) you want applied to the new exemplar.

Tags can be deleted from or added to an exemplar card or a whole exemplar stack (but adding may create duplicates, so you have to do a global delete first). You can also revise and replace tags throughout the stack.

Automated Coding

There's an Auto Tag button on all data cards that lets you automatically create and tag exemplars wherever a character string you're interested in appears in the text. You specify the character string (which must not exist in the name of the stack or the program will crash) which is typically a word or phrase, the name of the exemplar stack, and the tag(s) you want applied to the new exemplars. HyperQual2 then searches through the Data fields in the stack, and everywhere it finds the character string it marks off some text and copies it, with the new tag(s), to an exemplar card, making a stack of them.

The astute reader will be wondering how much surrounding text gets put in the new exemplar. The answer:

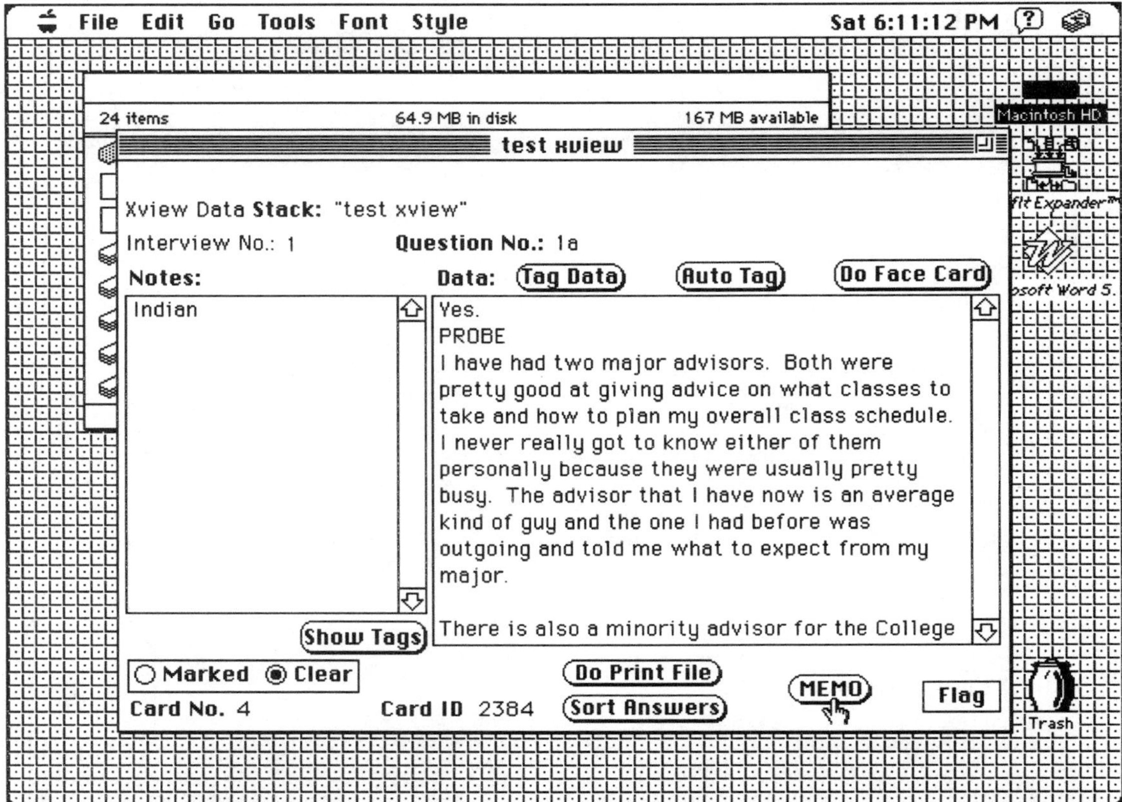

HyperQual2 Figure 9. An Xview card with a "MEMO" button—only possible in the more expensive stack version. Clicking on the MEMO button will jump you to the memo card you've attached to this data card. You can place as many such buttons as you want anywhere on the card. You can define them to jump you to any other card, such as a sketch or document or exemplar.

It's arbitrary, and you will almost certainly have truncated words at both ends. Here's how it works: If the data field has < 256 characters, the whole thing is dumped; if > 255, between 65 and 191 characters will be dumped if the hit is in the first or last 128 characters of the data field, otherwise 128 characters will be dumped. This is done *deliberately* by the developer, who feels that you shouldn't do something like this in an automated way but should have to review every found chunk and make sure it's what you want. To try to *force* you to do this, he makes the Auto Tag feature randomly truncate your exemplars, so you'll probably have to go back to the data card, mark the exemplars as you really want them by hand, one by one, and send them to a different exemplar stack. This can get a bit tedious.

Getting a Code List

There are a variety of ways to get a list of your codes, but they're not well tied together, and you may need to make several lists to get a complete one. If you click on the Show Tags button on a data card, the notes field changes to a list of all the tags that have been used in creating exemplars from data in *this* stack. You can print this list out. There is also a menu item that lets you show and print out the list of tags that are in use in a particular exemplar stack. However, any operations you do on tags in an exemplar stack will not change the list of tags that the data stack keeps. So, when you do Show Tags on the data stack, new codes you added while working in the exemplar stack will *not* show up, and tags you've eliminated from all of your exemplars still will. If there are tags you use in one exemplar stack but not in another, you'll have to generate lists from each of your exemplar stacks and probably also one from your data stack. You could merge these lists in your word processor, sort it, and delete duplicates, but this can be tedious work. One could wish for a more helpful way to get code lists.

Filtering and Merging Stacks

Exemplar stacks can be "filtered," or sorted, by tags. You type in the name of one tag you're interested in, and

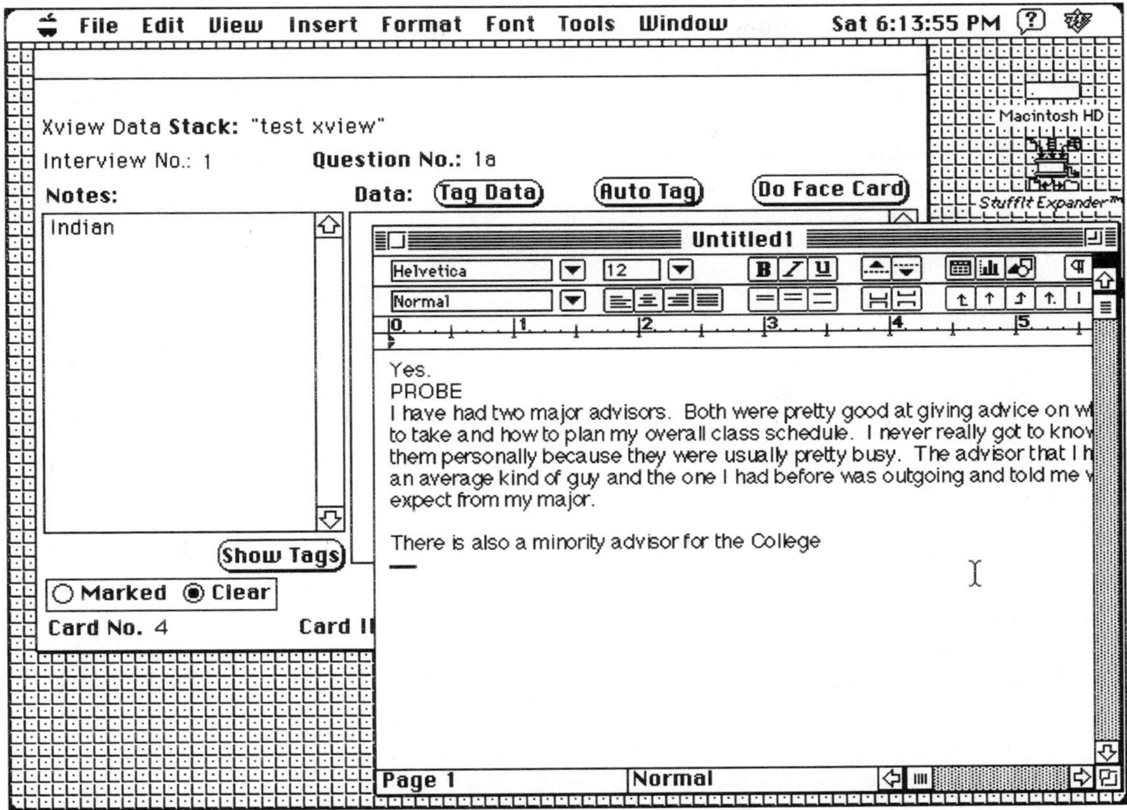

HyperQual2 Figure 10. Our suggested workaround for typing up longer data. Both the Xview card and a word processor (Microsoft Word) are showing on the screen at once (the Data field of the Xview card is hidden in this case, but it could be made visible if needed). When done typing the text, just cut from Word and paste into the Data field.

a new stack gets created that has only the exemplars from the current stack that have the filter tag (you can have the exemplars in the new stack keep all the tags they had in the previous exemplar stack, or only the filter tag).

You can also merge exemplar stacks. If you do this, the cards from one stack are added to another. But you must *never* try to merge exemplar stacks of the three different types (Xview, Site, and Doc), or the program will crash.

Doc stacks can be filtered by key words. This works just like filtering exemplar fields by tags, and Doc stacks also can be merged. Again, merge only with other Doc stacks.

It is important to keep in mind that, every time you filter, you create a new stack. When you merge, the current stack gets copies of all the cards in the stack you're merging in, which remains on the disk also. The implication is that you can eat up disk space in a hurry. How much and how fast depends on your analytical style, the size of the stacks being created, and how many of these stacks you can periodically get rid of.

Memoing and Annotation

As already described, there are basically two different ways you can store memos about your data. You can write them in a memo pad stack or you can write them in the Notes field of the data card. (Another alternative is to use a data stack for memos, instead of a memo pad stack, so that you can do more with them.) Exemplar cards have no note field. Information in a notes field is not linked to a particular spot in the data on the same card. It just goes with the entire entry. (In addition, remember that Xview and Site stacks have a face card with a field for general notes about the stack and interview or site face cards with a field for general notes about the interview or site.)

You can also annotate your text directly. There is no problem with typing directly into the text, either on the data card or on an exemplar card—perhaps marking off your annotation with ***s or some other character. *But* changes you make to text on one card will not be reflected in that text on another card, so if you annotate a data card, the

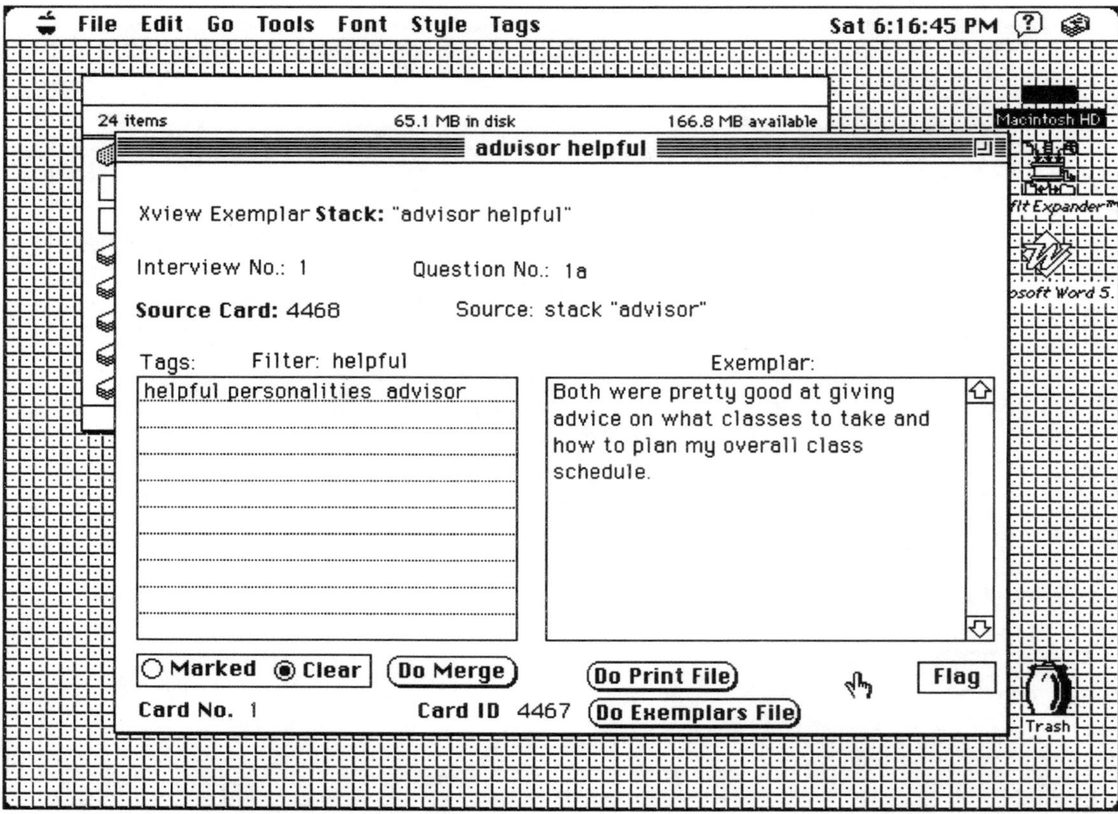

HyperQual2 Figure 11. An Xview exemplar card. All the data are placed here automatically, once you select a data chunk (exemplar) from the data card. You can edit the exemplar itself or the tags. "Filter. helpful" indicates that this exemplar stack was created by filtering an earlier stack on the tag "helpful." In other words, just those exemplars in the earlier stack that had this tag were copied to this stack. Different types of exemplar stacks differ only in the information at the top. Site exemplars show Researcher and Site # instead of Interview No. and Question No. Doc exemplars show the reference in APA format.

annotation will not appear on an exemplar created earlier from that text, or vice versa.

Searching

If you're looking for tags (codes), you can only simulate Boolean searches by filtering (remember, this means sorting exemplars into new stacks) and/or merging exemplar stacks. (This discussion applies also to searching Doc stacks using key words.) You can filter an exemplar stack on a tag, thus creating a new stack containing *only* exemplars with that tag. To simulate AND, you would then filter this new stack on the second tag. The resulting stack would only have exemplars that had both tags. Obviously, you're going to wind up with a lot of stacks in a hurry this way: Make sure you've got plenty of disk space, and delete unwanted stacks along the way.

To simulate OR, you can merge two exemplar stacks that have been filtered on different tags. The resulting merged stack would have any exemplar that had either the first tag OR the second. By doing repeated filter and merge operations, you can simulate complex Boolean searches. As in NUD•IST, the results of every search operation are thus retained in the new stacks and can be subjected to further analysis. However, the need for multiple operations to simulate the simplest AND or OR search, and the lack of any organizing structure to track or hold all these different stacks, can easily result in your becoming not only frustrated but what the developer calls HyperLost.

String searches are tedious. They are available only for data fields, for any card that has one (all but sketch pad). The HyperCard find function always goes to the first occurrence in a card. To see the next occurrence, you hit <Enter> while the hit is still highlighted. So if you stop to, say, send a chunk around the first hit to an exemplar, when

STACK: "test xview"   3/31/94

PROJECT: The Academic and Social Integration of Hispanic and Native American Students on Campus

PROJECT NOTES: This research project was conducted by Raymond V. Padilla, Michael Pavel, and Georgeia Lonnecker at Arizona State University, Tempe, AZ. The field data were gathered during the fall and spring semesters of the 1987/88 academic year. The intent of the project was to develop a clearer understanding of how Hispanic and Indian students
. . . .

INTERVIEW SCHEDULE:

"The Academic and Social Integration of Hispanic and Native American Students on Campus"

Version 2.0
QUESTIONS RELATED TO ACADEMIC INTEGRATION

*ADVISOR INTERACTION
1a. Do you have an academic advisor?
If "yes" probe: What is your academic advisor like?
. . . .

FACE CARD ID: 6123   Interview: 1   Interviewer: Michael Pavel   Date: 9/18/87   10:30 a.m.

Jack is a Navajo tribal member, junior year majoring in construction engineering and is from a small town located on the reservation. I have known Jack for two years and the interview was very informal and comfortable.
. . . .

INTERVIEW NO.: 1   Question No.: 1a   Card ID: 2384

Data:
Yes.
PROBE
I have had two major advisors. Both were pretty good at giving advice on what classes to take and how to plan my overall class schedule. I never really got to know either of them personally because they were usually pretty busy. The advisor that I have
. . . .

Notes:
Indian

HyperQual2 Figure 12. Sample output created by clicking on Do Print File from an Xview stack. The data from each card in the stack are listed in order. Note that I have abbreviated the text from each of the longer text fields, as shown with ellipses (. . .).

you repeat the search, you'll have to hit <Enter> again to get the second chunk. When you're up to the fifth hit, you'll hit <Enter> five times, and so on, assuming you don't lose count. HyperQual2 should be able to keep track of where you were, but it doesn't.

Output

You create your text output by sending text to an output file, which you can edit and print with your word processor. There are a number of ways to do this.

There is a Do Print File button on all cards (except sketch pads) that lets you create an output file of the data from either the whole stack or selected cards. If you select the whole stack, you get all the information from every card in the stack (including question or site numbers, notes, and tags). If you want just some of the cards in the stack, you go through and select them first individually with the Mark button (see any of Figures 1 to 11), then choose to print only marked cards. (Note that making an exemplar stack *is* creating a subset of data, which you could then print.)

For an Xview data stack, for example, you get the project card, the interview schedule, the first interview face card, all the data cards for that interview, the next interview face card, the data cards from that interview, and so on (assuming you have kept your cards properly ordered this way). The different types of data (from different fields and cards) are clearly identified, and the listings are well laid out (see Figure 12).

Some cards have special-purpose output buttons *in addition* to the Do Print File button. Doc cards have a Reflist button that lets you dump APA style references to a file, as described earlier. Exemplar cards have a Do Exemplars File button that makes a listing of exemplars without their tags (if you want tags, use Do Print File). The exemplars can be numbered if you want, and might be useful for making tables, e.g., of examples of quotes supporting an idea.

Xview and Site data or note fields can also be output by question or site number. You click on the Sort Answers button, specify the question or site number you're interested in, and choose to get information from either the data field or the notes field. An output file gets created with information from the specified field for cards relating to the question or site of interest.

Graphics output is created by printing sketch pad cards or stacks directly to your printer. There is a Print Cards button on each sketch card. You have the choice of printing the stack or just the marked cards, and you can print an image of the whole card, buttons and all, or just your graphic.

Theory Building

HyperQual2, like Martin, provides a useful approach to building theory about qualitative data through a process of selecting and sorting chunks of text into categories and subcategories, coding them as you go. However, it stops short of providing tools to explicitly support your thinking about the *relationships* among these categories.

While various exemplar stacks may represent subcategories of other exemplar stacks, the program provides you with no mechanism for storing or representing these relationships. The developer says that he typically uses a program like MacPaint or Inspiration to draw networks representing his emerging conceptual framework (you could also do this with the sketch stacks). This approach lacks the power of packages like ATLAS/ti and NUD•IST, which automatically link together the graphical representations of codes, text, and memos with the data themselves. Note, though, that, with the stack version, it would be possible to link parts of drawings to places in the text and memos through creating hyperlink buttons by hand.

Graphics Editing

Graphics editing in the sketch pads is carried out with HyperCard's built-in drawing capabilities, which are available in both the stand-alone and the stack versions of the program. There is a basic palette of drawing tools, including a freehand drawing "pencil" and tools for making rectangles, ellipses, lines, and irregular polygons. You can fill objects with various patterns and you can add text to your drawings. Using the clipboard, you can paste in a variety of different types of graphics images and then edit them with the HyperCard drawing tools. If you have the stack version, you can create hyperlink buttons to jump you from a data or exemplar card to a particular drawing, but with the stand-alone version you can't.

User Friendliness

User friendliness would probably be pretty good if it weren't for all the different ways you can cause the program to crash or mess up your data. On the one hand, the program is actually quite simple and easy to use. On the other, the manual is full of warnings about quirks caused by HyperCard (some of which are mentioned above). For example, if you misspell the name of the exemplar stack you want something sent to, you will crash the program, though you'll have a chance to catch the error: You'll be shown a list of filenames and asked to select the right one, *but don't do it*—the mismatch between the name you typed in wrong and the actual one you select will cause the program to generate a lot of error messages and place bad cards in your stacks! So you have no choice but to cancel the operation. When you do so, you will have to go back and reselect the chunk of text you wanted and retype the list of tags you wanted applied—this was very frustrating. Remember that you also can't specify a search string that exists in the stack name or the operation will fail. Further, the manual warns of several operations where you'll be told a stack is being replaced, when in fact it's being added to—why can't the on-screen messages be accurate? Although all these problems are supposed to be caused by limitations of HyperCard, the impression here is of a buggy program, even if the problems are predictable and avoidable once you learn them.

The manual is brief (56 pages) but gives a straightforward introduction to the program. There's no index, and there are some odd things about the manual's organization (you don't get told how to navigate around your stacks until the last chapter), but it is clearly written and its brevity makes it fairly easy to find what you're looking for. The manual does not explain the use of the drawing tools but refers the user to a HyperCard manual. As the user buying the stand-alone version may not have such a thing, this is not very helpful.

Tech support is available from the developer, Ray Padilla, and he is friendly, patient, and helpful. You can reach him from 6:30 p.m. to 9:00 p.m. mountain standard time, Monday through Friday, or on weekends. You pay for the call to Arizona (his introductory letter states that, at the price he's selling the program, he can't afford to return long-distance calls, but he will answer mail).

There is hardly any on-screen help: just a brief message for the opening screen reminding you what the different types of stacks are for. There's not really a tutorial, although the structure of the early part of the manual encourages you to follow along, using your data or what you see in the manual's figures. This works pretty well for getting oriented: Remember, the program's really pretty simple to learn.

Miscellaneous

The fact that HyperQual2 is built on top of HyperCard, which is essentially a hypertexting program, makes possible a number of useful possibilities. Many of the features of the cards actually provide hyperlink access to various navigation techniques and bits of information. Here's how they work.

Navigation

Simple navigation is accomplished with the cursor keys (right is next card, left is previous). HyperCard provides a Go menu, which has options to go to the next, previous, first, or last card in a stack. There's also a "recent" option, which displays a list of small images of cards. If you can tell from these shrunken images which card you want to go to, you just click on it and you're there.

HyperQual2 provides a host of more useful options. All of the field labels that appear in **boldface** on the cards are actually buttons, which are useful for navigation and for getting additional information. For example, clicking on the **Source Card** field in the exemplar stacks (see Figure 11) jumps you back to the source material (this is how you would see context and also how you would go back and chunk more carefully after an Auto Tag operation). The **Card ID** and **Card No.** fields on all cards (ID is fixed and unique; No. is number in the stack) are also buttons that let you type in the ID or No. you want to hop to. The Question No. field on Xview data cards is a button that will pop you to the interview schedule card and scroll you to the correct question.

Each card has a Flag button. One card at a time can be flagged. When a card is flagged, the flag button on the other cards changes to a "zip" button that zips you back to the flagged card. So if you're going to jump from an exemplar card to its source data card, you could flag the exemplar card first, so you could zip back. Likewise, if you were going to jump to an interview schedule from a data card, you'd flag the data card first so you could zip back.

If you have the stack version, you can insert hyperlink buttons anywhere you like (it's not too hard, but you have to find out how in the HyperCard manual—it's not in the HyperQual2 manual). Most significantly, you would probably put Memo buttons on your data cards to hop to associated memos. The Flag button would come in handy here too—before jumping to a memo, flag the data card so you can zip back.

Information Buttons

Every card has a **Stack** field, which is a button that will show you how many cards are in the stack. The labels for the **Data** and **Notes** fields are also buttons. They show you how many characters you've entered in the corresponding field so far, so you can tell if you're getting close to 30K.

Network Use

The stack version of HyperQual2 will run on a network. With this version, multiple users can work on the same stack simultaneously.

Comparative Remarks

In its approach to managing cards with (we hope) interesting excerpts of data, HyperQual2 is almost a Macintosh sibling of the Windows program Martin. However, it's a lot richer in its multiplicity of card types and navigation options. Where Martin lets you rearrange individual card icons on the desktop, and then put them in Martin's "folders" and higher-order "groups," HyperQual2 collects them in stacks. Though there's no mention of the Martin technique in the manual, you could do a workaround to take the same approach, by rearranging stacks on the desktop and putting groups of them in different directory folders (we tried this and, with System 7, which allows multiple stacks open at once, it worked quite nicely). To carry the Martin analogy a step further, if you wanted memos for a folder full of stacks, you could put a memo pad stack in the folder.

Although it's not apparent at first glance, HyperQual2 also has a bit in common, conceptually, with NUD•IST in that it encourages you to think in terms of hierarchical groupings of categories and subcategories, but it doesn't provide the overall, integrating network structure that NUD•IST does. It's also similar, conceptually, in that it provides for system closure by retaining the results of each search for further analysis and allowing you to treat memos as codeable data. However, NUD•IST's structure goes a lot further in supporting this kind of work.

In comparison with most other code-and-retrieve programs, HyperQual2 comes up quite short in terms of logical search requests. You can only select one tag at a time, or merge two stacks, in any one step. To carry out any kind of search for the intersection of multiple codes, or other more complex combinations of codes, takes multiple steps and generates multiple stacks.

On the other hand, its practical data management capabilities for multiple data types and structures are not found in other, comparable programs. These are not minor considerations, and they could be very helpful.

Summary

HyperQual2 is a good choice if the analysis style suits you, the structure isn't too rigid for your data, and the 30K limit on all fields isn't a problem. It is, again, absolutely unique in its structure of different types of cards and stacks for managing different types of data. This alone will make it attractive to many users. The other major aspect of its appeal is its hypertexting capabilities. Given this, it doesn't seem to make much sense to buy the stand-alone version: Most users will probably be better off paying twice as much for the stack version, and shelling out for HyperCard as well, although the developer says most folks buy the stand-alone. Be forewarned, however, about its drawbacks. The bugginess and the weakness of the editor should be taken into account in making a choice.

Reference

Padilla, R. V. (1993). *HyperQual2 for qualitative analysis and theory development.* Chandler, AZ: Author.

Kwalitan 4.0

Available for DOS

Vincent Peters
Postbus 9104
6500 HE Nijmegen, The Netherlands

Phone: 31-80-612038/615568
Fax: 31-80-612351
E-mail: U211384@vm.uci.kun.nl

Price: *f* 500 (about $250)

Hardware Requirements:
- IBM XT, AT, or compatible, IBM PS/2
- MS-DOS or PC-DOS 3.0 or better
- 350K RAM
- hard disk recommended (but can be run with 2 floppy drives)

Overview

Kwalitan is a thoughtfully designed program aimed at helping you think about your data in a grounded-theory style. It lets you code free-form text broken into segments, retrieve these, write "abstracts" or annotations of each segment if you wish, and write memos of several types. With these features, it's best for a database of moderate size (say, 30 or 40 interviews) that you want to examine, reexamine, revise, comment on, code easily, and think about—all in an iterative, developmental style. Everything is done on screen, with pull-down menus, and clearly stated help is available easily. It shows all the signs of a friendly program designed for qualitative researchers by a qualitative researcher and revised on the basis of user experience. It has no graphics capability, and its theory-building features are limited to a good memoing system and a hierarchical display of multilevel codes. Yet it's a very workable program to help you generate theory in your own terms, via close familiarity with your data.

This review is based on experience with version 3.1, the manual for 2.0 and the 3.1 supplement/update, and a test copy of the 4.0 version, which included some bugs. For example, if you're running Kwalitan under Windows, you can easily violate system integrity by pressing one or another key, and you have to exit and reboot. Less seriously, <Alt-H> doesn't get you help screens as promised; you have to use <Alt-F1> as in version 3.1. The developer says that these problems have been corrected for the release version of 4.0.

Database Structure

Your database is an integrated "work file," which contains as many specific free-form "documents" (files) as you like. This is useful: You might be working with all the interviews with Joe, or those with all principals, and so on. You can easily produce different or overlapping work files, a feature that's quite helpful in a complex or multicase study. Work files can be merged and documents added to or deleted from them. Your coding scheme for one work file can be sent to disk and used in a new work file. You work directly in the work file; there are no separate "indexing" files. You can revise your documents as much as you like, including changing segment boundaries.

Kwalitan can accommodate 65,000 files, with overall capacity depending on your disk storage capacity. Segments (chunks) can be any length you like; they're typically sentences, groups of sentences, or paragraphs. A

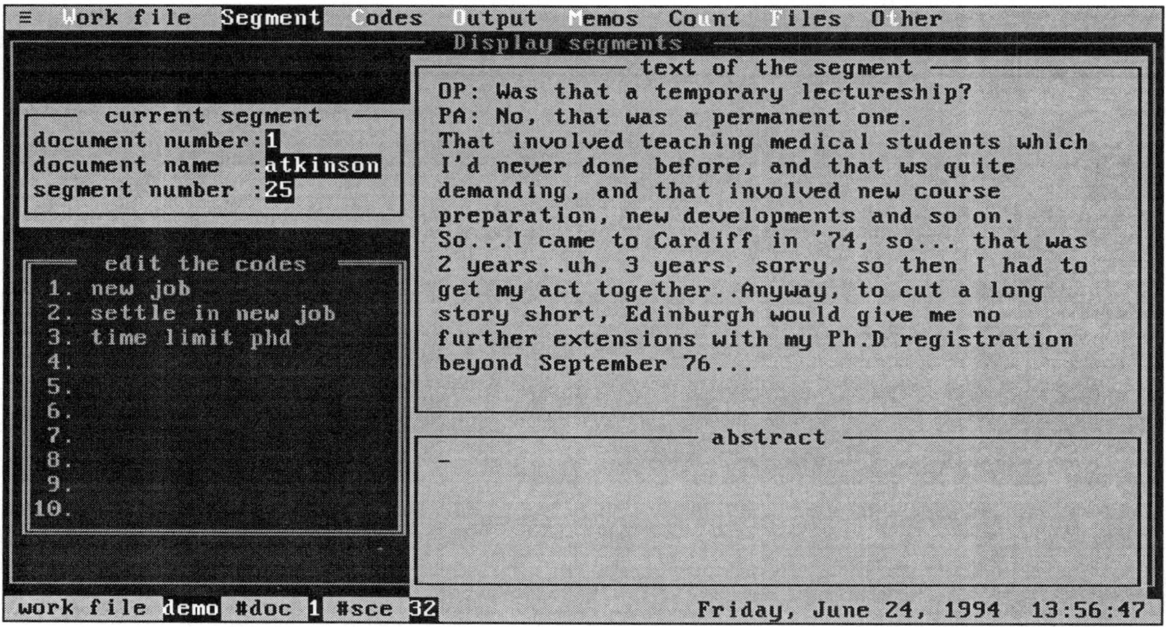

Kwalitan Figure 1. Adding codes. Looking at the text in the segment at the right, you type in new codes at the left, up to the maximum of 25 for this segment (identified at the top left).

chunk can be bigger than your screen display and can be scrolled through.

Data Entry

Kwalitan deals with text only. With your word processor, you create ASCII files, type in a filename and descriptive header information of your choosing, and then mark off "segments" or chunks with @ signs.[1] There is no way to segment files automatically, which is both a weakness and a blessing (it requires you to think about what a segment is, which may *not* at all be a paragraph or sentence). If you do want to segment automatically, you could get your word processor to insert @ signs whenever it sees a sentence (a period with a space after it) or paragraph (a carriage return). Segments can be any length you like. You have the option of adding a code at the beginning of each segment if you wish.

Each file becomes a "raw document," several of which can be called into what's called a "work file," where you apply codes, search, write memos, and so on. This is a very useful concept, as just noted. (It's a "virtual" work file, actually made up of nine linked files for documents, codes, memos, abstracts, and so on.) Once your "raw documents" have been called into the work file, the actual raw document files are no longer needed and can be stored elsewhere.

Each document in the work file is headed by a document number, a brief identifying code of your choice (8 characters), and some explanatory information of your choice (50 characters). This permits selection of documents during searches. At any time later on, segments can be further divided, merged, or extended to permit overlaps if need be. (This is a helpful corrective to the limitations of the "chunking first, coding next" mode.) You can edit your text at any time.

Working on the Data

When the document(s) are set up, you code each segment; the text is in a window at the right, and there is a box at the left for codes. (See Figure 1.)

You can scroll up and down through segments, thus seeing the context. You type in applicable codes (length, 20 characters, which can be a word or a phrase), which are steadily added to an alphabetical code list, which you can reference at any time. If you want to apply an existing code, you just scroll to it in the list and hit Enter. A code is applied to the whole segment; multiple codes are typical.

1. Version 3.1 called segments "scenes," reflecting the idea that a chunk should be of a meaningful length, and also called codes "keywords." Depending on the production of new documentation for 4.0, you may be working from the 2.0 manual and 3.1 supplement to it, and will have to make mental translations.

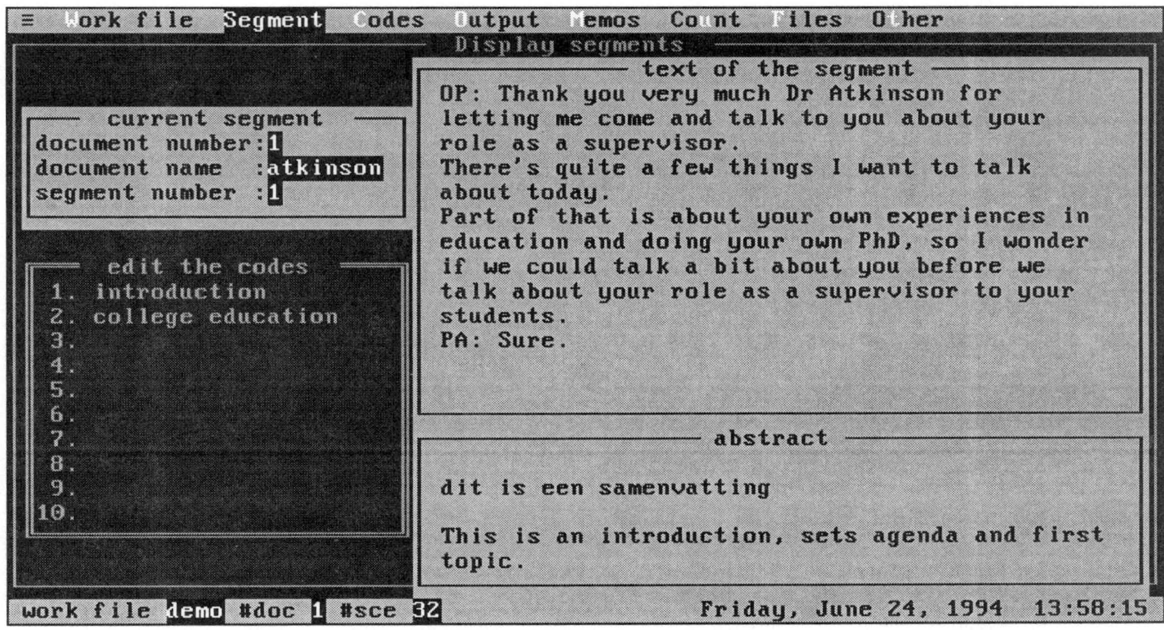

Kwalitan Figure 2. Writing an abstract of the segment. The original abstract, appearing at the lower right, was in Dutch ("samenvatting" means summary) and has been edited with added English text. The abstract can be hidden or displayed at any time.

There is an automatic feature: You can search for a naturally-occurring word or phrase in the text, and the program will apply it as a code to chunks where it finds it (you see the word capitalized in about two to three lines of context and can choose to accept or reject application of the code to that segment). You can edit and revise codes as you go; they are automatically added to the master list. Code capacity is 25 per segment—a reasonable limit for most people—but there does not seem to be any upper limit to the number of codes.

There is a sentence-numbering (not line-numbering) facility that you can turn on and off.

You can write brief (up to 250-word) abstracts of a segment, and either show these in a box at the bottom of the segment (see Figure 2) or hide the abstract (which is still available whenever you want it). You can also hide text and see just the abstract. This feature could be quite useful if you're building matrices with summarized text entered in the cells. Furthermore, what you write doesn't need to be an "abstract" necessarily—it could be a remark or annotation.

Memos can also be written; one type is a conceptual memo that's automatically attached to a code that you want to ruminate on or explain. Others are theoretical memos that cut across several segments or documents, method memos that explain how you did things, and "profile" memos that discuss aspects of a specific case. Any of these memo types can be attached to a work file or to several work files. You can also create separate memo files for each of several researchers or subtopics if you wish. You always have to tell Kwalitan the name of the file where a particular type of memo is stored. Memos can be edited at any time.

You get access to concept memos by the keyword to which the memo is attached. For the others, you open the memo file, get a list of memo titles, and pick from that. The memos can also be searched for any words they include; the result is a list of memo titles that you then select from to see the memo you're interested in. It's also possible to select a bunch of memos you're interested in, copy them to a file, create a document complete with @ markers, and then analyze it as you would any document in a work file.

Searching

You can search for *codes* using AND, OR, NOT; there's also a wildcard function. Furthermore, you can search for a major code, automatically including all its subcodes (see the discussion under "Theory Building," below). Co-occurrences are found within segments. You can also do searches for up to four *strings* in the text using AND or OR.

Kwalitan calls a search request "setting filters," because in addition to looking for coded chunks, or strings, you can also ask for particular documents, certain segments within the documents, certain cases defined by the "header" in-

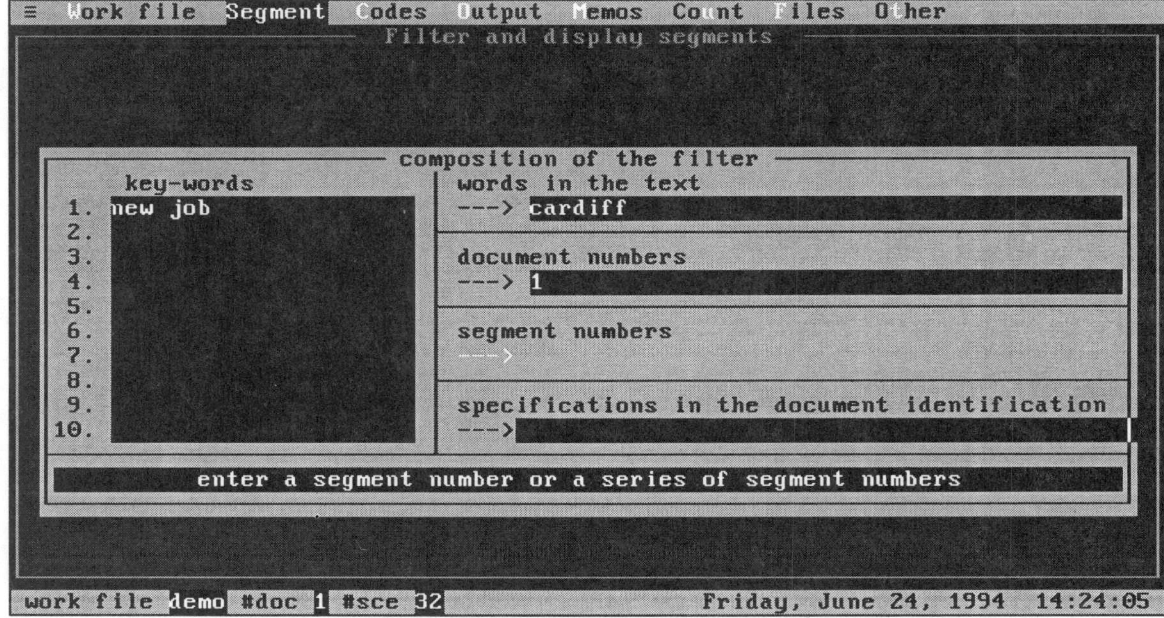

Kwalitan Figure 3. A search request. The researcher is looking for segments including the code "new job," indicated at the left, AND the word "Cardiff" (not a code), indicated at the right. Document No. 1 has also been selected. It's also possible to select specific segments, or documents with specific header information.

formation in the document description, and so on. Figure 3 shows the search request screen; in the example, filters have been set to look for segments only in document 1, with the code "new job" AND the word "Cardiff."

If you want to use OR with several keywords (up to 10), you just list the keywords; to use AND, you put + before the keyword; to use NOT, you put a caret (^) before the keyword. (It looks as if complex Boolean requests might not be too easy, especially without parentheses.)

Kwalitan searches quickly. A hit simply displays the whole segment in the right side of the screen (see Figure 1). In the release version of 4.0, the text you specified in the filter is highlighted; all codes for the segment are displayed as usual at the left. You can scroll through the hits forward or backward, but you do not see the context of preceding or following segments. (You can, however, note the segment numbers, exit search, go to general segment display, and find those segments. Or you can respecify your search to include the preceding and following segment numbers. This is quicker than it sounds, but it's still a workaround.) In the release version, the developer says you can choose the search function in Display Segments and specify search terms, and you'll get the first segment with a hit, from which you can scroll up or down to segments in the context.

You can send all the hits to a file or print them. If you want to edit or select material from hits before doing so, you can use the "abstract" facility and then print that.

Codes, which were only available in a list in version 3.1, are also available in version 4.0 in a tree (outline) structure with nine levels, so their linkage to each other is explicit (see "Theory Building," below). Codes and segments (scenes, chunks) are naturally linked. So are codes and conceptual memos. Abstracts (annotations) are linked to segments. Profile, theoretical, and method memos are linked to the work file as a whole.

You can see an alphabetical list of your codes, with their frequencies. The program also does a count of words in the whole work file, or in any document, or in a filtered set of segments, showing frequencies of each word, alphabetized.

Output

Output from searches can go to screen, a file, or your printer. Retrieved chunks are not editable "on-the-fly" (that is, one by one as you get them), but because they can be sent to a file, you can edit them later with your word processor. (And editing via abstracts, as just noted, is possible.)

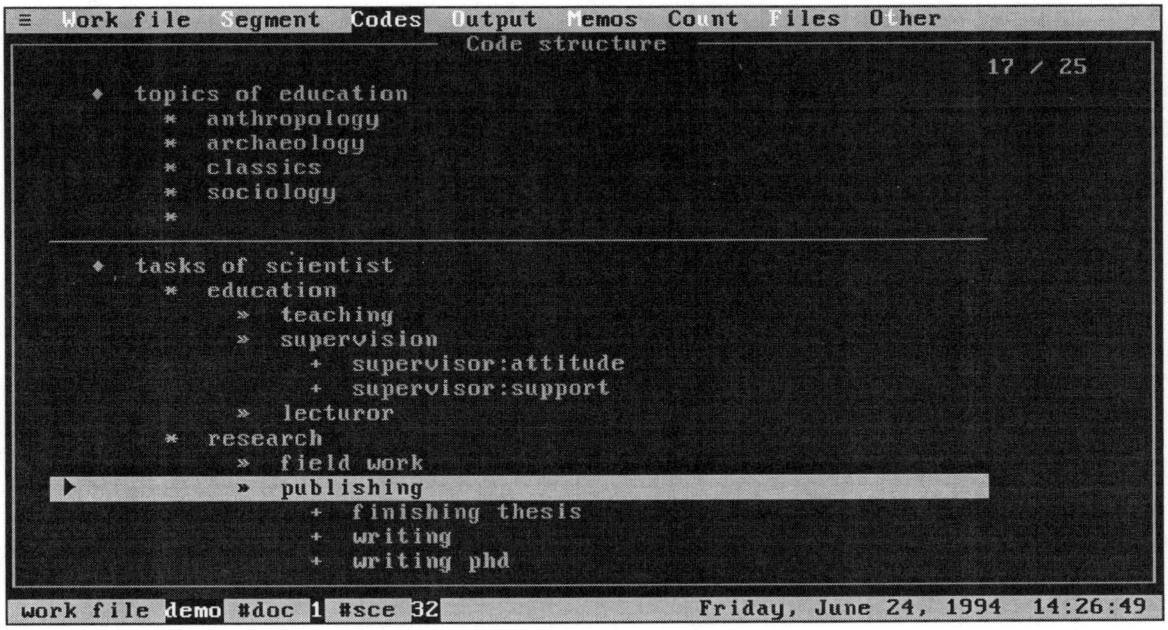

```
≡ Work file  Segment  Codes  Output  Memos  Count  Files  Other
                         Code structure
                                                          17 / 25
   ♦  topics of education
        *  anthropology
        *  archaeology
        *  classics
        *  sociology
        *
   ♦  tasks of scientist
        *  education
             »  teaching
             »  supervision
                  +  supervisor:attitude
                  +  supervisor:support
             »  lecturor
        *  research
             »  field work
 ▶           »  publishing
                  +  finishing thesis
                  +  writing
                  +  writing phd
 work file demo  #doc 1  #sce 32          Friday, June 24, 1994  14:26:49
```

Kwalitan Figure 4. The code structure. Each level of heading has a different symbol and is indented appropriately. You can delete codes or insert new ones, or change the level by using the right- or left-arrow keys. In this example, the left arrow would move "publishing" to the same level as "research." <Control-left arrow> would also carry along all the subcodes of "publishing"—"finishing thesis," "writing," and "writing phd." (See Figure 5 for the result.)

For printing, you set up a "print profile," which specifies whether the search criteria are reported, whether sentences are numbered, and whether abstracts should be printed. Memos of any type can be printed separately.

Version 4.0 can also create a quantitative data matrix that can be output to SPSS for quantitative analysis. The data file is accompanied by another "information" file listing the rows and column labels for the matrix so SPSS can read it directly. (The data matrix is in ASCII, in any case, so use by other programs may not be difficult.) You can draw on all or selected segments and/or from all or selected documents in your work file. The matrix columns are codes you're interested in, and the rows are segments or documents. You specify, for each cell of the matrix, a 1 or 0 (i.e., code occurs or does not within the segment or document), or frequencies, an option that's only useful when you've defined rows of the matrix as entire documents. Such matrices can be used for many purposes, including various quantitative clustering programs. Thus you could use the feature to cluster a number of cases, or a number of roles or individuals, assuming that you'd set it up so there was one document per case, role, or individual.

Kwalitan doesn't keep a log of your searches or what you went through with code revisions. It does not store search requests.

Theory Building

Kwalitan is designed to let you ruminate about your data in a grounded-theory style; see Wester and Peters (1989) for a good, carefully stepwise overview of that style. It's a thoughtful, flexible code-and-retrieve program that supports you in *thinking* about the meaning of your data.

The hierarchical coding display for 4.0 is a definite advance over 3.1. It shows you an outline ("tree") structure (see Figure 4). You can change the level of a code (i.e., a branch), optionally including all its subcodes, by using the left- or right-arrow keys. In Figure 4, for example, if you wanted "publishing" to be at the same level as "research," you'd tap the left-arrow key, and it would move left. Using <Control-arrow key> moves the entire topic left or right, with all its subheadings. See Figure 5, where this has been done.

You can also insert new "branches" equally easily, pulling codes as you wish from your larger code list (see the right side of Figure 5), and see the new outline. Note the flexibility: Kwalitan does not require you to have all your codes in hierarchical form, just the ones that make sense that way. You can print the entire structure. According to the developer, you can reuse it in another work file by simply opening the code scheme file (which has the suffix .CST) when you need it for a new work file.

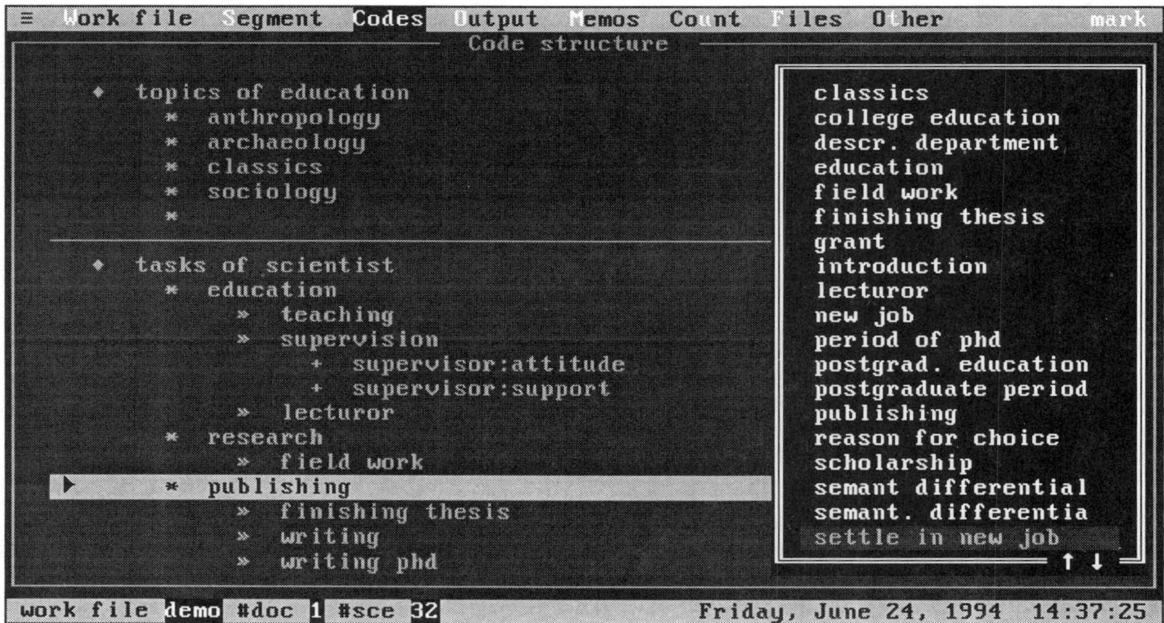

Kwalitan Figure 5. Working on the code structure. The code "publishing" and all its subcodes have been moved to the left one step. At the right, the researcher has popped up the alphabetical code list by hitting <F9> and found a code "settle in new job." Realizing that "settle in new job" should be a subcode for "new job," which appears above in the list, the researcher will next bring the "new job" code into the code structure at the left by highlighting it and hitting <Enter>. Then hitting <right arrow> will create a subcode space; highlighting "settle in new job" and hitting <Enter> will enter that subcode.

The coding tree is more than a display. You can use it to search for coded chunks; if you enter "%code," Kwalitan will retrieve hits not only for that code but for all its subcodes as well.

Though Kwalitan is very helpful for theory building in the grounded-theory tradition via memoing and multilevel coding, it doesn't have other theory-building functions like proposition-testing or showing networks of concepts. In that sense it's perhaps less elegant than, say, ATLAS/ti or NUD•IST—but it's strong on its own terms.

User Friendliness

It's fairly user friendly. The pull-down menus and the help screens are clear and straightforward. A nice feature is that <Control-F1> brings you an extra help menu defining all keystrokes for functions within the module you're working in; you can then choose them directly from the menu or use the function keys.

The program's feeling is a welcoming one, because you can see your text, codes, abstracts, and memos fairly easily, and you can navigate among them without too much difficulty.

The tour for familiarization took a Level 2 person a couple of hours, using the demo file provided. This involved working with a combination of manuals. The manual for 2.0 (Peters & Wester, 1990) is a bit stiff, though it does talk thoroughly about general strategies of analysis, as does the article by Wester and Peters (1989). The update supplement for 3.1 (Peters & Wester, 1993) is quite clear and useful. (The manual for 4.0 was not available during this review but was expected to be available in the summer of 1994.) The program is not hard to learn and is easy to use once you're on top of it.

The first version of Kwalitan, in Dutch, was produced in 1986. Since then the developer has worked regularly with a user group of about 150 in the Netherlands, making many improvements as a result. The developer will provide tech support by phone (roughly a dollar a minute to the Netherlands from the United States), fax (a bit cheaper per amount of information transferred), e-mail (much more reasonable), or by "snail mail." When 4.0 did not load, he got back immediately with help, which worked.

Miscellaneous

Kwalitan is quite good on practical utilities—you can copy, move, or erase files; move documents in or out of a work file; see a directory of everything at hand; rename, erase, or make subdirectories; and so on. Many software packages can be awkward on these counts.

The program seems fairly forgiving (you can always Esc back out of whatever you're doing). The facilities for customization are limited, it appears, to specifying alternate printing profiles and changing the screen display.

Update

Version 4.0 was scheduled for release in September 1994, with the English manual following soon afterward. A Dutch manual was to appear subsequently. We've discussed the new features of 4.0 during the course of the review. If there was a delay, you are quite well off with 3.1, which only lacks the coding tree and the quantitative matrix output.

Comparative Remarks

Kwalitan's searching capabilities are more limited than those of specialized textbase or text-retriever programs such as askSam, Folio VIEWS, or Metamorph. Better to use those when you have a very large or complicated database, or when you want features like synonym, sequence, or proximity searching.

Compared with other code-and-retrieve programs, however, Kwalitan stands up well. It's more user friendly than QUALPRO, HyperQual2, or The Ethnograph, has a stronger memoing facility than they do, and does coding more easily. HyperQual2 and Martin are built on such a different metaphor (notecards) that it's hard to compare Kwalitan with them directly. However, Kwalitan's data-linking capabilities are better than Martin's and not as full as HyperQual2's stack version, and Kwalitan lacks HyperQual2's graphics capabilities. Like Martin, it's better than HyperQual2 at building grounded theory.

Summary

Kwalitan, as a thoughtful code-and-retrieve program, is intelligently designed and practical. It shows the signs of a researcher-developed and user-refined product. If you want to take a reflective, grounded-theory-like approach to thinking about your data, revising and extending them as you go, it's a strong contender.

References

Peters, V., & Wester, F. (1989). *Kwalitan as a tool for qualitative data analysis*. Nijmegen, the Netherlands: University of Nijmegen, Social Science Faculty, Department of Research Methodology.

Peters, V., & Wester, F. (1990). *Qualitative analysis in practice: Including user's guide, Kwalitan version 2*. Nijmegen, the Netherlands: University of Nijmegen, Social Science Faculty, Department of Research Methodology.

Peters, V., & Wester, F. (1993). *Qualitative analysis in practice. Supplement: A short help to learn version 3.1*. Nijmegen, the Netherlands: University of Nijmegen, Social Science Faculty, Department of Research Methodology.

Wester, F., & Peters, V. (1989). *Qualitative analysis*. Nijmegen, the Netherlands: University of Nijmegen, Social Science Faculty, Department of Research Methodology.

Martin, Version 2.0

Available for Windows

Simonds Center for Instruction and Research in Nursing
School of Nursing
University of Wisconsin—Madison
600 Highland Ave.
Madison, WI 53792-2455

Phone: (608) 263-5336
Fax: (608) 263-5332
E-Mail: pwipperf@vms2.macc.wisc.edu

Price: $250

Hardware Requirements:
- IBM PC 286; 386 or 486 recommended
- 2MB RAM; 4MB recommended
- Hercules monochrome graphics; VGA recommended
- Windows 3.0
- Mouse
- 20-40MB hard disk recommended; needs .5MB free for program

Overview

Martin is a straightforward, very user-friendly program aimed at supporting users who have been accustomed to working with their data on file cards. You can annotate your text, copy chunks of data to a series of simulated "cards," attach one or more codes to each card, write an attached summary memo about each card, and group your cards into folders and then into a hierarchy of folders and folder groups. It resembles HyperQual2 in some respects, though it lacks HyperQual2's various types of data management cards and hyperlinking abilities. Think of it as a flexible, close-to-the-data way to build your conceptual understanding of your text.

Martin is essentially a "notecard" approach to qualitative analysis, originally developed to support "hermeneutic" researchers who like to read and reread their texts without necessarily "coding" them, and develop more and more overarching explanations of what they mean. In some respects, like HyperQual2, Martin lies on the boundary between "code-and-retrieve" and "code-based theory-builders."

Drass (1989) has pointed out some important potential limitations of "notecard" software (shared by some traditional textbase programs): difficulty in editing or changing the boundaries of chunks, which are seen as discrete and nonoverlapping "records," one to a card; inflexible approach to seeing the context surrounding a chunk, along with difficulty in seeing events or chunks in temporal order; and preset assumptions about the relations among chunks. In general, Martin is reasonably successful in avoiding these problems, as we'll see.

Database Structure

Martin starts with ASCII files, creating a set of working text files (with .PAR extensions) from them, and an overall "project" (.PJT) file, which can have multiple text files, along with all your cards, your codes, annotations and memos, the folders into which the cards are gradually sorted as you proceed, and the groups that contain several folders.

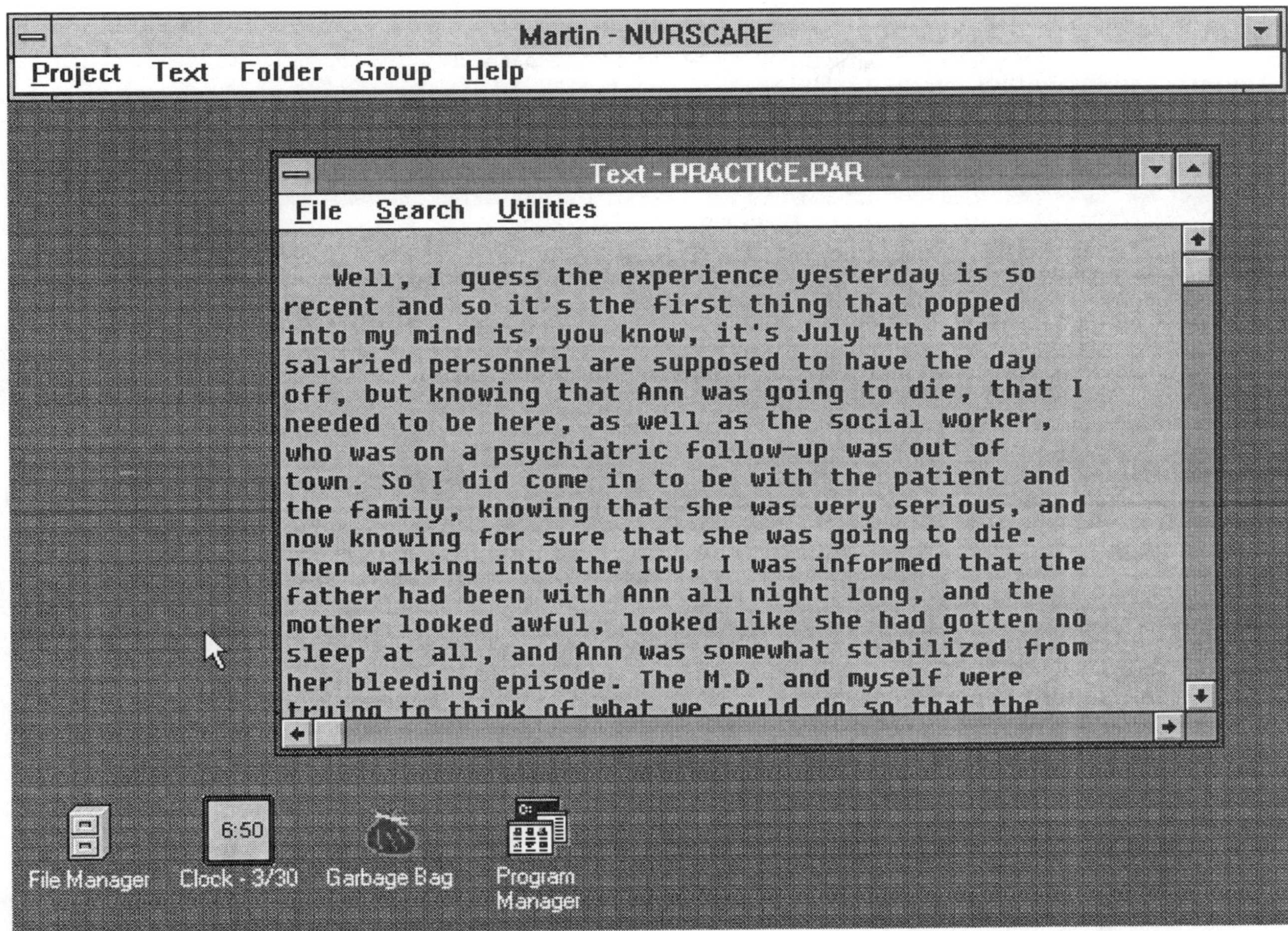

Martin Figure 1. A working text (.PAR) file, ready for the addition of notes and selection of passages for cards. The name of the project (NURSCARE) appears at the top. Martin's main menu options appear at the top left; they let you work at the project, text, folder, and group levels. The Garbage Bag icon lets you set aside items you don't want to keep; the program will ask you to confirm their deletion when you exit.

The manual suggests that any particular text file be kept under 50KB (practically, 18-20 single-spaced pages), so there'll be enough memory to include notes, cards, folders, and groups associated with it. There's no limit to the number of text files used in a project, other than your disk space. But this is not minor. A small one-page text file (like that in the manual), with a half dozen cards, a couple of folders, and associated brief memos, all the associated files, plus the backup .PJT file Martin creates, quickly added up to 10 times the length of the original text file. Martin creates some temporary files in this process; after you exit, the multiple is perhaps only 7X, according to the developer.

Data Entry

You prepare your text files in a word processor in ASCII format, with a .TXT extension; for later readability, it's best to keep line length at 80 characters or less (depending on how big you want your text window to be). Lines have to end with carriage returns because Martin doesn't word-wrap within the text window. (Your word processor should do this if you so specify when you save your text files as ASCII.)

A "project" consists of one or more text files. You either create a new project or recall an old one, then bring in your new .TXT file. Martin then creates what it calls a .PAR file, which is what you actually work with, making annotations, pulling out data chunks to go on cards, coding, adding summaries, making folders, and so on; all of this is stored in the .PJT file and its backup. The original .TXT file is untouched and can be moved off to a diskette if you like. The .PAR files are most conveniently kept in the Martin directory, though they need not be. The .PJT file and backup are automatically put in the Martin directory. Figure 1 shows a .PAR text file on screen.

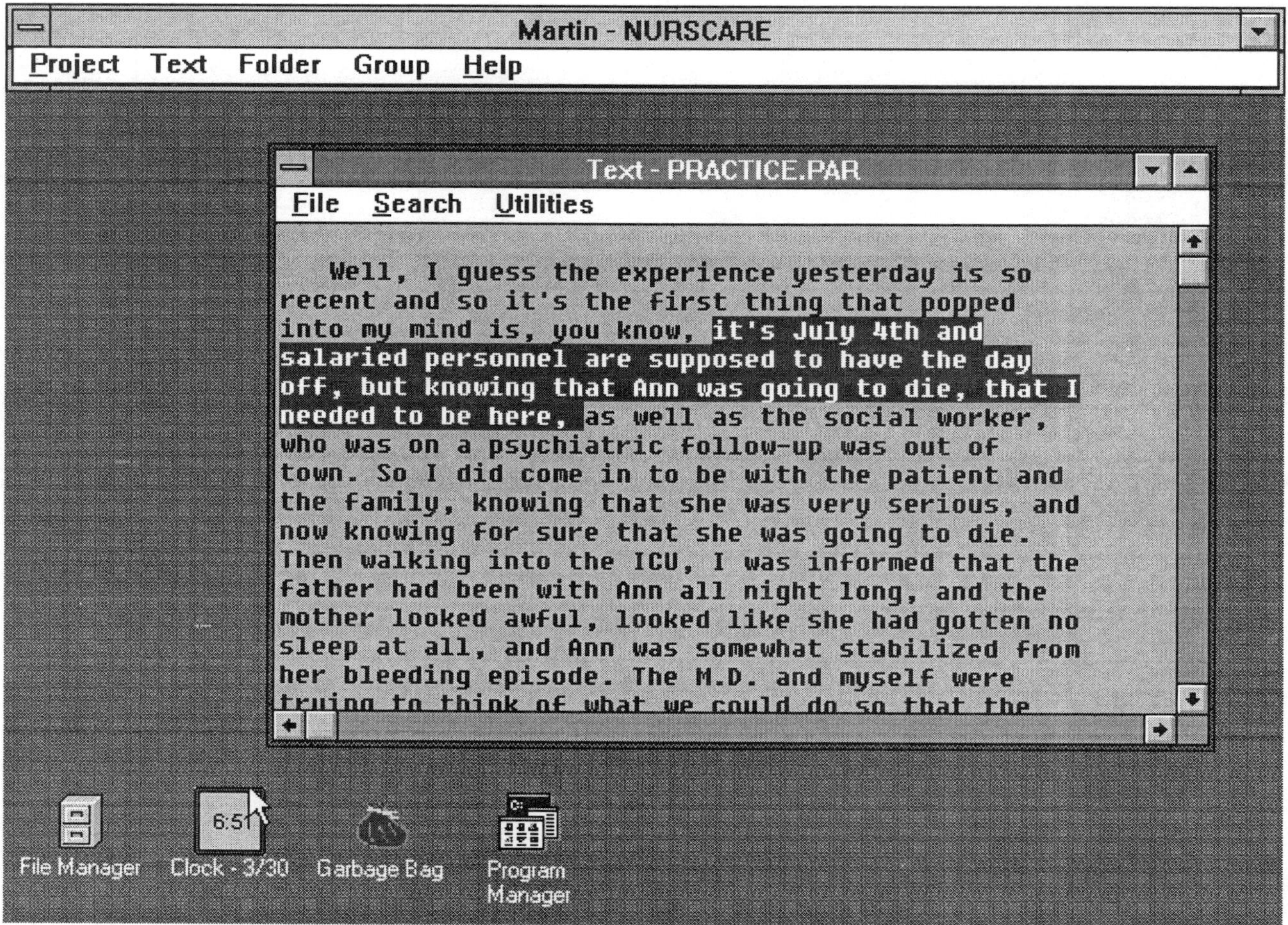

Martin Figure 2. Setting up a new card. The user has defined a chunk of text by dragging the mouse, and will then create a card by clicking on Utilities and selecting "Card."

Working on the Data

Martin has facilities for annotation of your basic text, making cards, giving cards titles, adding longer summaries (in effect, memos), coding, and sorting cards into more and more inclusive categories.

Notes

You can add annotations to the text by clicking on the Notes option under Utilities; the note word-wraps as you type, and can be up to 16KB (six single-spaced pages) long. When you "attach" the note to a particular point in the text, a numbered note marker appears there. To see the whole note whenever the text is open, you click on the number marker. Notes can be pulled up and edited at any time, removed from the text where you've attached them (the marker remains in the text, however), or moved to another location (e.g., into a detailed note for a folder or group, but not elsewhere in the text). Notes are not, however, searchable.

Cards

As you're viewing the text, you can define any block of it you like by dragging the mouse over it, as in Figure 2, then clicking on the "Card" choice in the Utilities menu. Cards can have text that overlaps with or nests within that on other cards. The text you've selected will appear on a new card. You type in a brief summary (up to a line) that identifies what's on the card and serves as a title. Martin then converts the card into an icon with the brief summary attached (Figure 3) and puts a numbered marker in the text.

You can continue on through the text making new cards, a strategy the manual encourages. But you can also pull up a particular card by clicking on its icon. When you do that,

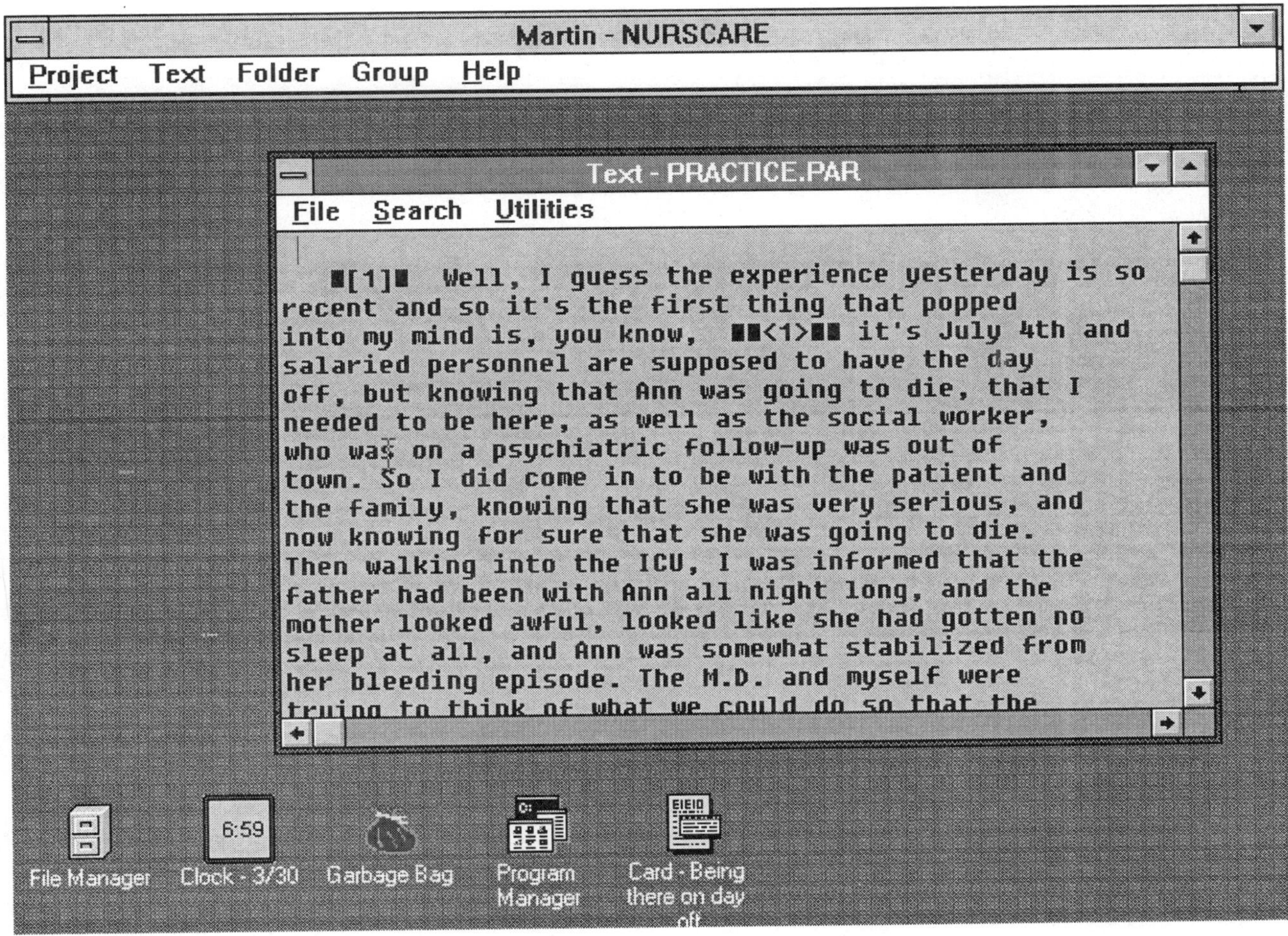

Martin Figure 3. The user has just finished creating a card with the brief summary title "Being there on day off." An icon showing the card's existence appears at bottom center. In the text, the number shows where the card's text begins. (The number 1 in square brackets signals the presence of a Note the user wrote earlier and attached to the text; the Note does not appear on this card—or any card—but can be pulled up by highlighting the number and clicking on "Notes" under Utilities.)

you can write a longer "detailed summary"—essentially, a memo—of up to 16KB (six single-spaced pages). Figure 4 shows this in action. (If you wish, you can copy, now or later, the content of specific cards into this memo as well, perhaps to serve as illustrations.)

You may also want to attach one or more "key codes" (up to 10 characters) that you might want to use to find cards later. Figure 5 shows the screen for adding new codes to the existing list and/or attaching codes to a card. There's no practical upper limit to the number of codes per card. Codes can be revised, and the revised versions will automatically appear on the cards they were assigned to (in the current project, that is). Codes can be deleted from a card. A code deleted from a *project* will be deleted from all the cards it was applied to.

If you close the text window, the cards you've created remain on screen; they can be viewed and edited. If you "iconize" the cards by clicking on the "minimize" arrow at the top right of each card (or if Martin has already iconized them as noted above), you then see a set of all your icons on the desktop, each identified by the "brief summary"; they can be moved around on screen into clusters to aid your thinking if you wish (Figure 6), as a preparation for putting them into folders. If you need to, you can pop specific cards back up on the screen to look at the text they include.

Folders

You can transfer cards into a larger category called a "folder," one at a time, by marking the icons for "transfer"

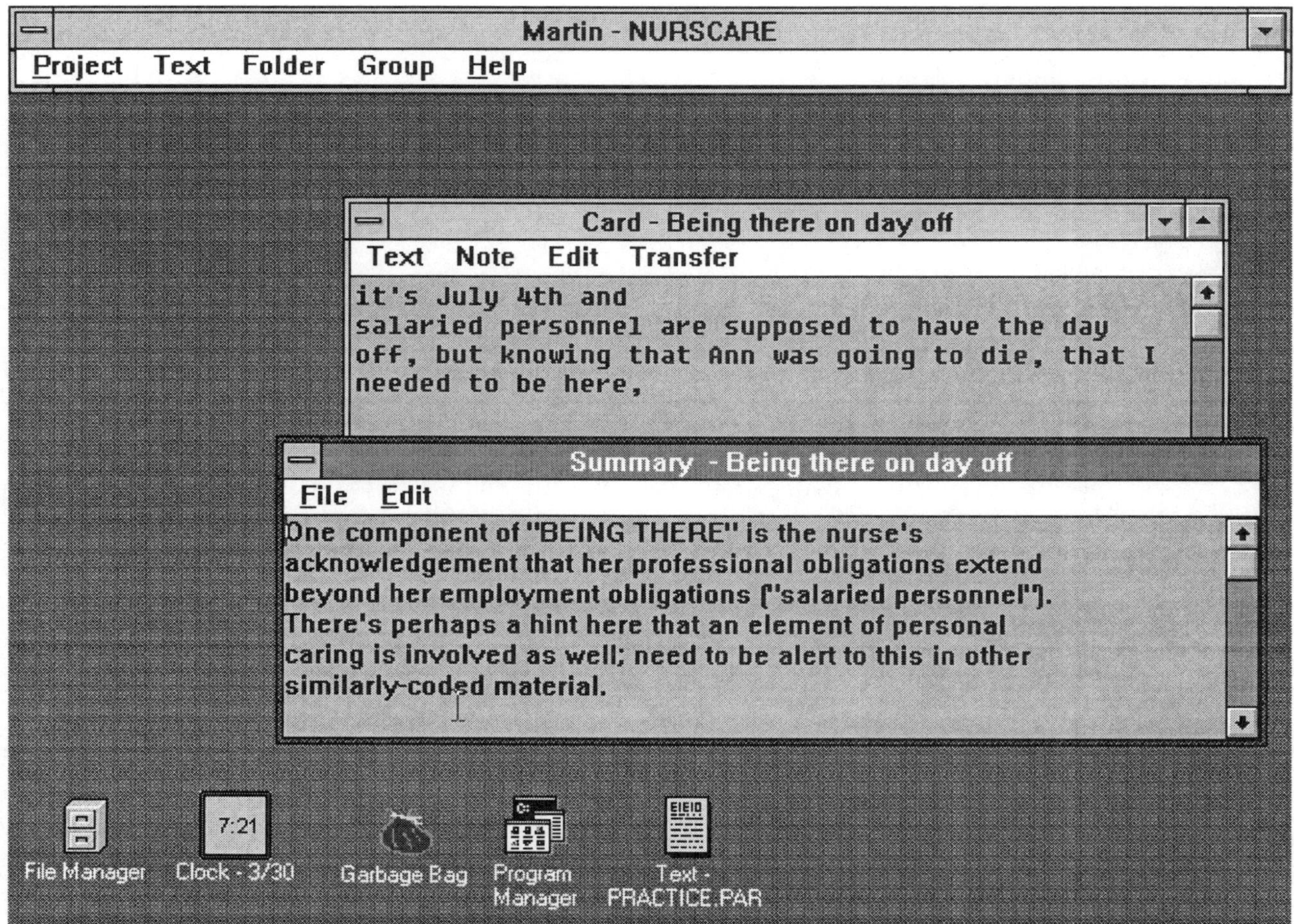

Martin Figure 4. Writing a detailed summary. The user has reduced the size of the card window so its text can be seen while the detailed summary (in effect, a memo) is being written in the lower window. In this case, the user is referring to a key code, BEING THERE, and clarifying its meaning. The so-called "brief summary" appears as the title of the card ("Being there on day off"), and this title is mentioned at the head of the "detailed summary" box as well. To see how the card looks when complete, see Figure 8.

by clicking on a "Transfer" box. Then you go to the Folder menu, create or open a folder (it will have a title, just as cards do), and click on "Get"; the card for each marked icon will then be transferred into the folder. You can then see all the card titles included, as in Figure 7.

If you wish, instead of marking cards one by one, you can enter the Key Code dialog box and specify the codes of the cards you want (they may be on the desktop as single cards or present in one or more other folders). You can simply ask for all the cards or select certain folders only. You can also confirm each card as it's presented for your OK. The manual warns that this process may be slow if extensive reorganizing of folders or groups is involved.

Note: Martin *moves* folder-resident cards you've chosen out of the old folder and into the new one. If you want to keep a card in both an old and a new folder, you have to make a duplicate card (click on "Duplicate") and mark only one of the cards for transfer. (The copied card will be identified as such in its folder.)

You can also write a detailed summary (memo) for a folder. There's no limit to the number of cards in a folder. A card can be removed at any time from a folder to the desktop if you wish. If you realize a card makes no sense, it can be discarded into the "Garbage Bag" (see below).

Once a card is in a folder, you can ask for "Information" about it (Figure 8). You see the name of the text file, the key codes, the brief summary, and the detailed summary and can also pull up the original text chunk. You can proceed to edit the card's features (though not the text chunk)

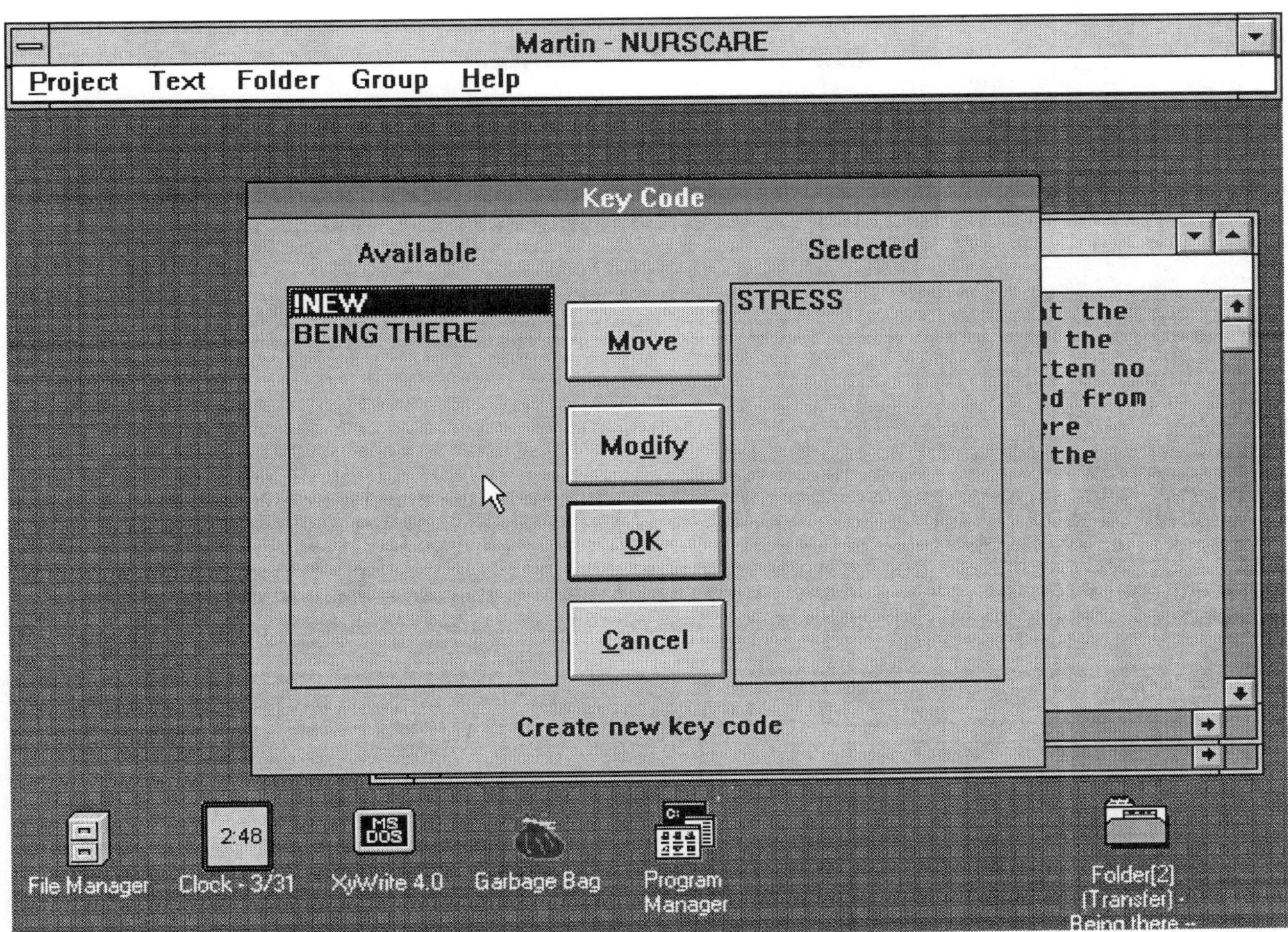

Martin Figure 5. Adding a new code to the list. The code BEING THERE already exists, as does the code STRESS, which had been "selected" for application to the just-previous card. The user has highlighted !NEW and will be presented with a screen asking for the code's name and a brief description (one line). The new code can be applied to the current card or simply held in the list. More than one code can be applied to a card, by moving the desired codes into the "Select" column. Codes added are automatically alphabetized.

as you wish. (You can also get this information before the card's in a folder, as you consider it for transfer.)

If you want to do something else with the card you're looking at (delete it, copy it, or transfer it), you click on "Call Up," which kicks the card out of the folder on to the desktop, and you do whatever you want with it, including moving it back in to the same folder after editing.

To people accustomed to sorting data by codes, Martin may seem strange at first: You are moving the *chunks* around, sorting them inductively into folders in a hands-on, flexible style. But note that, if you like, you can create a multilevel code list in a more a priori fashion, apply the codes to chunks, then sort cards by code into folders named for second-level codes, and then into groups with third-level code names.

Groups

Folders in turn can be iconized, moved around on the desktop, and collected into groups, which also can be iconized; new groups can be formed from several groups, so the process of generalizing is effectively unlimited. Any group can have a detailed summary memo included (you enter the Group menu and click on Note, then type the memo).

At the group level, you do not have the option of transferring folders by keywords, because they don't have any; you have to select folders one by one.

Analytical Strategies

The entire process is thus one of successive upward clustering, starting with chunks of first-level data. It's well

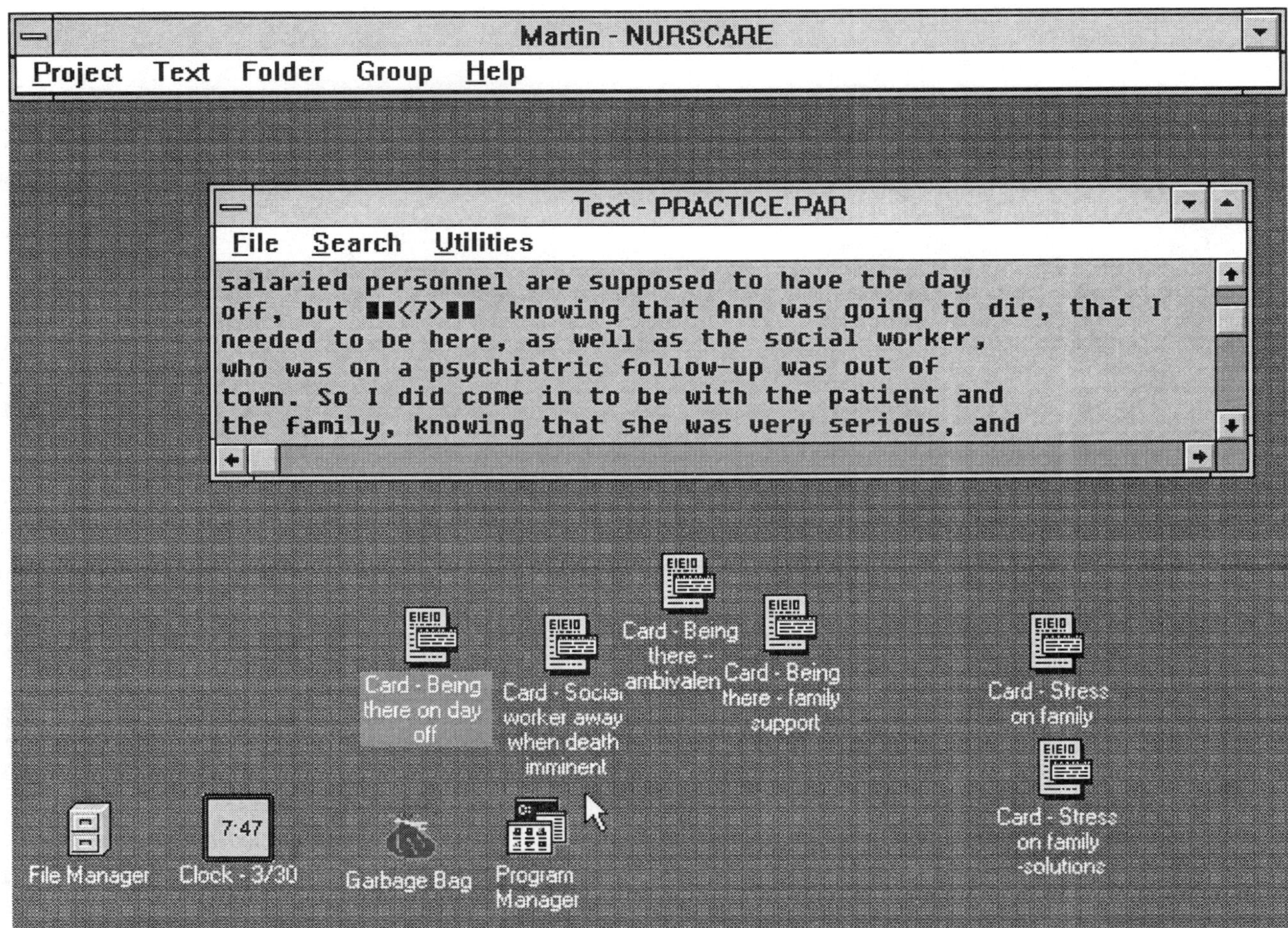

Martin Figure 6. Icons for cards (lower part of screen). The user has moved the icons into two clusters. The one at the right deals with stress on the family issues; the one at the left includes three different "Being there" items and one with the title "Social worker away when death imminent." The user is about to mark the four icons at the left for transfer into a folder.

suited to an inductive, grounded-theory approach as well as to a hermeneutic approach, where you are thinking about first-level data and considering what various chunks of it are instances of, seen at a more general level. The manual's section on "Using Martin" has a very thoughtful illustration of the entire process, using a study of nursing care.

As the manual points out, it's also possible for a knowledgeable analyst to create an a priori folder and group structure at the start, and move cards into it as the analysis proceeds. Folders and groups can be deleted, renamed, or transferred into other folders and groups.

Supportive Features

Martin has several very useful features that support your analysis. Whether you're proceeding inductively or deductively, the analytical process is usually disorderly, with a normal number of false starts, dead ends, and mistakes. Martin contains a "Garbage Bag" into which you drop unwanted material—cards, folders, or groups—as you go. When a session ends, this material will be discarded; you have the choice of keeping specific items if you want. You always get a warning prompt about the Garbage Bag's contents when you're exiting.

Everything else you've been working on (your cards, notes, folders, and so on) has been automatically saved—itself a great blessing—as you went along; any card, folder, or group will persist forever in your project unless you've discarded it in the Garbage Bag. Everything is also saved as you exit. When you start up again at a later session, you tell Martin the name of your project (.PJT file). Then your materials are restored to the screen *exactly* as they were when you left the project—a truly marvelous feature that

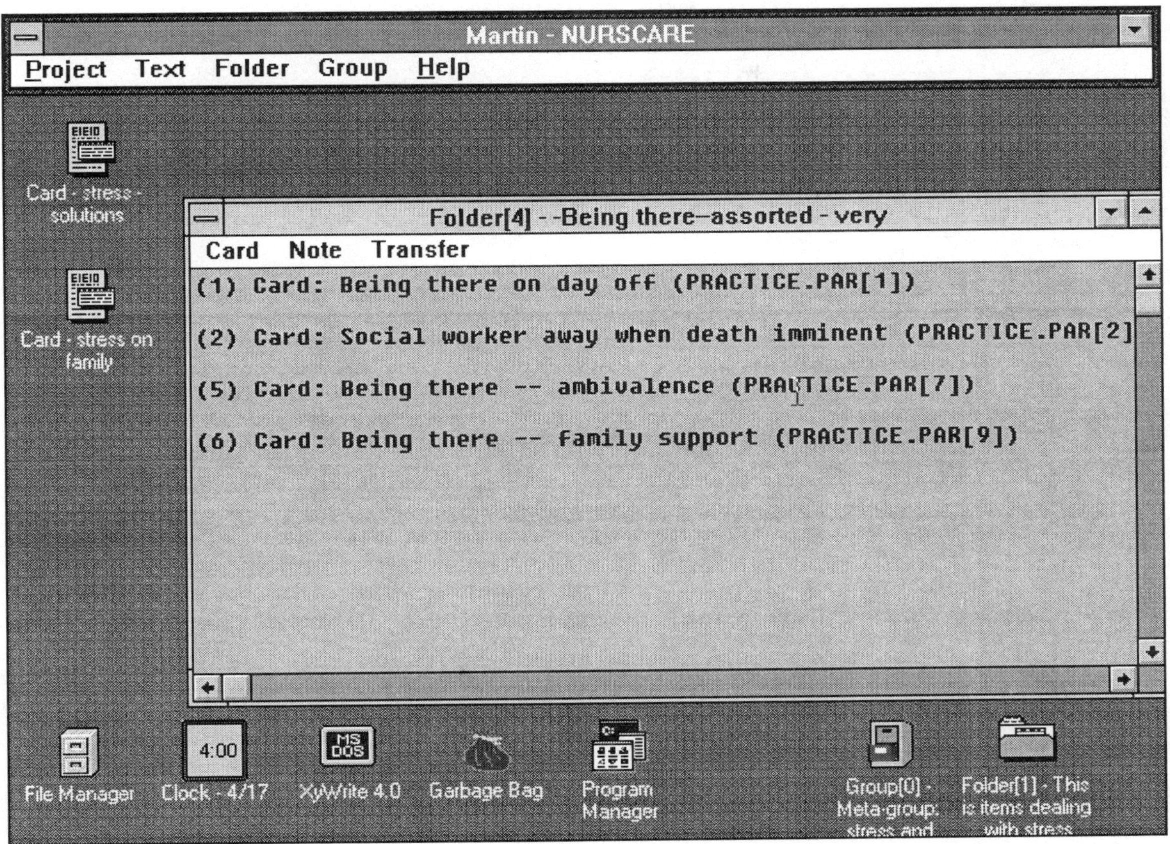

Martin Figure 7. Contents of a folder. All four cards marked for transfer have been moved into the folder. Each card's title is shown, along with its location in the original text file (PRACTICE.PAR); the numbers (1, 2, 5, 6) show the card numbers, which appear in the text file, as noted in Figure 3. The two icons for Stress on family (upper left) are still single cards, not yet put into a folder; though one has been created (Folder 1 icon, lower right) to receive them. The user has also created a group (called "Meta-group—stress and . .") that will eventually contain both the Stress on family folder and the "Being there-assorted-very" folder.

lets you pick up right where you left off. In effect, the .PJT file holds all of your analytical work together.

You cannot open two projects at once in Martin, but you can close one and open another, switching back and forth as you need to.

Searching

Martin's searching abilities are very limited. You open your text, click on "Search," then type in the string you're looking for. However, the search request is exact and case-specific (asking for "ann" will not get you "Ann"). There is no wildcard facility, but you can ask for a substring (typing in "pa" will get you "parent" and "patient"). You jump to the highlighted hit in the text, which is fully scrollable; <F2> will jump you to the next hit. This limited facility can be used to help you find something in the text you want to annotate and/or make a card for. You can also search the text for the numeral of a specific card or for a range of cards, such as all those with numerals less than 5.

In its card-oriented way, Martin can also do code-oriented searches. To do this, you can ask that cards with specific keywords (an OR list) be transferred into a folder. (The program maintains an updated, alphabetized list of your keywords for your project.) Martin will search through all or a specified subset of folders and groups to find the cards you want; you can accept or reject the transfer of each

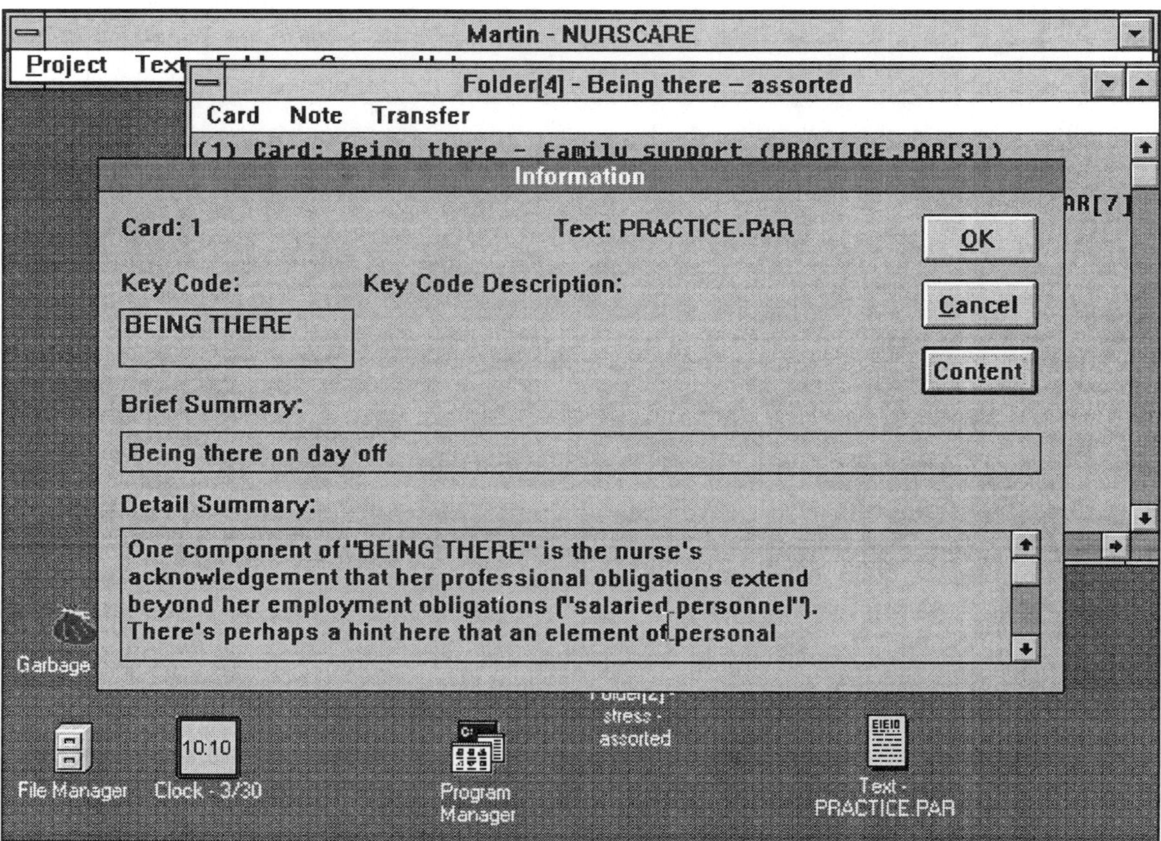

Martin Figure 8. Information about a specific card. The card titled "Being there on day off" (shown in Brief Summary box) has been selected from the list of four cards in the folder "Being there — assorted" (top of screen). Shown are the card's number (1) as it is marked in the original text, key codes (only one in this case, BEING THERE), and a Detail Summary—the memo the user wrote about this card—which can be scrolled through.

one as you go, or take all of them. *Remember:* Martin is moving cards out of folders to the new folder when you do this. Make duplicate cards if you don't want this to happen.

The developer suggests a workaround some users have tried: You do folder transfers, looking at the cards you get, but do not save your work. That gives you browsing information but does not disturb the folders' contents. (To do this, you'll have to set the automatic save feature for a long interval, like several hours.)

You can't search for specific folders or groups by keyword (they have none). When you open a group, you see all the folder titles, just as when you open a folder, you see all the card titles in it. So you scan the folder (or larger group) until you see what you want.

You cannot search for material in Notes attached to text or for material in detailed summaries (memos), or for card titles (brief summaries). It would certainly be nice to have such capabilities.

Output

Martin's strengths are in screen display. You can see your text, notes, cards, annotations, summary memos, folders, and groups on screen in multiple windows, either in full or in "iconized" form. *But*, depending on your system resources (RAM plus swap file), the developer says you may not be able to display more than 15 or so objects using Windows 3.0, or more than "the mid-30s" in Windows 3.1. As you work and icons are piling up, you need to go into the Windows Program Manager's Help screen from time to time to see the "resources remaining" figure. If you are running low, sorting objects into higher-order folders and groups frees up memory, and you can keep making cards and sorting them.

Martin steadily saves all your work to files.

If you ask Martin to "print" your work, it does not actually do so; it creates an ASCII .PRN file from the .PJT file.

```
***** Card on desktop *****
SUMMARY:
  stress on family
KEY CODE:
  Demanding features of patient/family situation (STRESS)
DETAIL SUMMARY:
  The family's presence is both physically and emotionally overloading.
  "hen walking into the ICU, I was informed that the father had been with Ann all night long, and the
mother looked awful, looked like she had gotten no sleep at all, and Ann was somewhat stabilized from her
bleeding episode. The M.D. and myself were trying to think of what we could do so that the family could
get some rest."
  (c:\martin\PRACTICE.PAR[3])

***** Folder on desktop *****
SUMMARY:
  Being there -- assorted
DETAIL SUMMARY:
  This folder pulls together stuff on the "being there" theme.
  SUMMARY:
    Being there on day off
  KEY CODE:
    Nurse's view of psycol./prof. availability for pt. (BEING THERE)
  DETAIL SUMMARY:
    This discusses the conflict between (or among) bureaucratic, professional, and probably personal
obligations.  See also card 2 on absence of social worker at the time.
    "you know, it's July 4th and salaried personnel are supposed to have the day off, but knowing that Ann
was going to die, that I needed to be here,"
    (c:\martin\PRACTICE.PAR[1])

  SUMMARY:
    being there - absent colleague
  KEY CODE:
    Nurse's view of psycol./prof. availability for pt. (BEING THERE)
  DETAIL SUMMARY:
    The idea of being there is also a function of whether colleagues are available or not.
    "but knowing that Ann was going to die, that I needed to be here, as well as the social worker, who was
on a psychiatric follow-up was out of town."
    (c:\martin\PRACTICE.PAR[2])
```

Martin Figure 9. Sample output. The user has asked for the "project" to be printed, giving its title. Martin created a .PRN file, which was then printed in the user's word processor. "All" printing options have been selected.

First comes a single card, with its descriptive title (SUMMARY), "stress on family"; then the description of the KEY CODE, plus its label (STRESS). This is followed by the DETAIL SUMMARY, which is a longer memo—only one sentence in this case. The text excerpt itself isn't labeled but appears in quotes. Then comes the source file information (drive, directory, text filename, and number of the card—3). (Any of these features except for the source information can be selectively suppressed if you wish.)

The display in Figure 9 then turns to folders; there's only one, "Being there—assorted"; in this excerpt we see the SUMMARY for it, and a DETAIL SUMMARY memo, then the two cards in the folder (see SUMMARY. "Being there on day off" and SUMMARY. "being there—absent colleague") indented; the same card-level information is provided as described above. If there were groups of folders, the cards in them would be shown as well.

Then you must print the file with your word processor, which you may want to have running under Windows as well, if you have enough memory. (You can also create print files in WordPerfect 5.0 or RTF formats.)

You can select a particular card, folder, group, or the project as a whole; Martin sends your request to a file, which you then print with your word processor (Figure 9). What you get for each card is the card title (brief summary), the description of the key code applied and the key code name, the detailed summary (memo), and then the actual text of the card. For each card's text passage, you get a source tag (just the drive/directory, filename, and card number).

Martin will also "export" your complete project if you wish; it creates an .EXP file in ASCII that can be read by any other computer showing the status, contents, and screen location of all project objects. (This file does have plenty of marker symbols—$, &, numbers, and the like—but gives you exactly the content displayed in each window.) You can also use this facility to "export" a project to another computer using Martin, which would then "import" it. Also, projects created with earlier versions of Martin are readable by Martin 2.0 using this facility. These features make using Martin in a research team very easy, a good deal simpler than copying all the files of a project by hand.

You can also "export" what you have done so far, then return to where you were and resume—so the "export" facility is a way of recording interim work. In all cases, the "exported" file is stored in the same directory you're using for Martin.

Theory Building

Martin's supports for theory building are sturdy and straightforward, essentially helping you form categories with more and more generality and conceptual power. It's a commonsense approach using the "notecard" metaphor, supplemented by annotation of your text and by memos written about specific cards, folders, and groups.

How well does it do at countering the worries expressed by Drass (1989) about notecard programs as analytical tools? Not badly. Chunks can easily overlap or be nested. Annotations ("notes") to your basic text can be edited, removed, or added at any time.

While the text passages on cards cannot be edited (appropriately so), you can easily discard a card you don't like and select text for another one. Card titles ("brief summaries") and memos ("detail summaries") can be edited at any time; codes can be changed. Multiple codes can be assigned to cards.

When you look at a card, you don't see context beyond the text you originally selected. But if you select the Call Up function, you'll see the card marker in its full text. Martin is not good at handling the temporal order of coded chunks in your text. There's some help if you marched through the text making cards from beginning to end, because the card numbers are assigned sequentially. But the numbers cannot be removed from the text file, so if you jumped back and forth in the text and didn't work in actual temporal sequence, you're out of luck.

Finally, Martin does make explicit assumptions about the relation of chunks; cards go in folders, and folders go into groups. But groups can also include other groups as well as folders. And there's no assumption that all cards and all folders will eventually belong to one Big Group up in the sky. Some folders and some groups may be completely disconnected from other folders and groups. It's not as tight or as limited a hierarchy as in some other programs (e.g., WordCruncher, The Ethnograph, AQUAD).

User Friendliness

Martin is basically easy to learn and use. The manual is a well-organized model of clarity and simplicity, working from general concepts to a quasi-tutorial to details of specific commands. There is, unfortunately, no demo file included, so you have to create a text of your own; a feature that (some would argue) requires you to get your hands on the program faster but (others would say) is annoying and slows you down. The manual includes a large number of well-described screen shots. It even offers an overview of Windows operations in case you're a new user.

When you call the listed phone number, you get an administrative person who will channel your request to the next available technical help person, who'll call you back. It was easy to reach Bob Schuster, the lead developer, with a request. Questions were answered clearly within an hour or so, sometimes immediately.

The help screens are quite complete and specific, using normal Windows conventions. You can move forward or backward through a help table of contents, click on needed information, or do a search for needed topics. There's a full glossary of Windows terms. A nice feature is that Martin keeps a history of the help topics you have looked at in a session, and you can get back to them quickly by clicking on the topic.

Martin is easy to use because its metaphor (annotated text plus a sorted collection of file cards) is a familiar one to many qualitative researchers who have worked that way B.C. (before computers). It is not complex, confusing, or hard to understand. The Windows interface is already familiar to many users.

You can get a free demo version (called the "working model") by requesting one. However, it does not allow you to save files, and thus will not bring you back to where you were in the previous session and will not auto-save. It also will not import files that have been processed by a copy of the full program that someone else might own. This has the effect of truncating the program as a new user experiences it; you have to take a good deal on faith. Fortunately, this review could be based on the full program.

There is no real tutorial, though Chapter 4 of the manual walks you through a sequence of analytical activities that you can experience vicariously. It's well done as these things go.

Miscellaneous

Martin backs up your work regularly, and you can set the period as you wish (default is 30 minutes). The manual notes that large projects may take several minutes to back up. A one-page practice text with a half-dozen cards, two folders, and one group took only a few seconds.

There are a few other customization features. You can suppress or permit a confirmation prompt when you are transferring objects (e.g., a card from one folder to another) or discarding objects into the Garbage Bag. You can set printing margins, so that when your word processor prints your files, lines won't be too long and wrap over to the next line.

And—very usefully—you can rename various levels of objects, giving them "aliases": Instead of "text," "card," "folder," and "group," you could, for example, call them "case," "excerpt," "pattern," and "theme."

Update

The developer is preparing Version 3.0 and considering whether to have it run under Windows 95.

Comparative Remarks

Martin's nearest neighbor is HyperQual2. Martin is simpler and easier to use than HyperQual2, but it lacks HyperQual2's ability to make hyperlinks and its useful range of data management cards. In effect, Martin just helps you work upward from data to more abstract levels; it doesn't let you make links laterally or diagonally *across* the categories you are developing.

It's hard to compare Martin with other code-and-retrieve programs that don't use the notecard/folder metaphor. Kwalitan is as good as Martin at supporting an inductive, grounded-theory approach, better at coding, and about as friendly. QUALPRO stacks up less well than Kwalitan on all these counts. The Ethnograph is strong at detailed, line-by-line, multiple-code applications, but more awkward to use than Martin. All three are better at searching than Martin.

As we suggested, Martin lies on the boundary between code-and-retrieve and code-based theory-builders. It's a lot easier to use than AQUAD, and stronger in inductive theory building. Generally, it's less powerful as a theory-builder—inductive or deductive—than NUD•IST, HyperRESEARCH, and ATLAS/ti.

Summary

Fundamentally, what you see in Martin is what you get: a simple, practical program for clustering key excerpts in your data and making gradual theoretical sense of them. It works on a "notecard" metaphor: You extract passages from your text, code them, sort them, write memos about them, and gradually build up a theoretical understanding of what your data mean. And it keeps you clear about where you are in your analytical flow.

If you want to reflect iteratively as you go, are not interested in developing a detailed coding scheme, and don't want to do close line-by-line analysis, Martin is a good contender. And it's a pleasure to use, especially if you are already comfortable with Windows.

You do need to consider the downside: Searching is *very* weak; cards are moved from folder to folder, not copied unless you deliberately set it up that way; you need a lot of disk space; and you may run out of memory (and desktop space) quicker than you'd like.[1]

References

Diekelmann, N. L., Lam, S., & Schuster, R. M. (1991). *Martin, v. 2.0 user manual.* Madison: University of Wisconsin—Madison, School of Nursing.

Drass, K. A. (1989). Text analysis and text-analysis software: A comparison of assumptions. In G. Blank et al. (Eds.), *New technology in sociology: Practical applications in research and work* (pp. 155-162). New Brunswick, NJ: Transaction.

1. The developer suggests that using virtual desktop software for Windows, or a higher resolution monitor, can help with the desktop space problem.

QUALPRO, Version 4.0

Available for DOS

Impulse Development Company[1]
3491-11 Thomasville Rd., Suite 202
Tallahassee, FL 32308
or
Dr. Bernard I. Blackman
2504 Debden Court
Tallahassee, FL 32308-3035

Phone: (904) 668-9865
Fax: (904) 668-9866

Price: Professional, $88
Student, $44

Hardware Requirements:
- IBM PC, XT, AT, 386, 486 and compatibles
- DOS 2.0 or better
- 128K of free RAM (actual use is 42K)
- Hard disk preferred; two floppies OK

Overview

QUALPRO 4.0 for DOS is a very simple code-and-retrieve program. It's modest in disk space requirements and is menu driven, fairly forgiving, and easy to learn. But it has some limitations: a narrow, constrained coding approach, little flexibility, and a search-and-retrieval style limited to collecting hits. For best results, as the developer emphasizes, you need to use it in parallel with your word processor.

QUALPRO presents you with menu choices when you start it up; you choose among (for example) "create a database," "use a database," or "help" by typing the choice's number or letter (there is no mouse capability). Then the program walks you through a series of questions, one by one (e.g., if you chose "use a database," it asks for the name of the database and the drive and path it's on; then it will display information about the database, such as its filenames or file groups). It has an old-fashioned mainframelike feeling: You are usually presented with questions one after another (rather than all together in a dialog box) with error messages if you don't do things right. You can always Esc back out of what you're doing, but you do have to follow the sequence of prompts and cannot scroll back up. The developer says this style was deliberately used to help novice users, and that experienced users can "bypass the structure" and work directly with the ASCII files via word processor. But most experienced users would prefer more flexibility within the program itself—and even novice users can usually learn faster from a dialog box style.

QUALPRO also has a series of "productivity tools" for working on your data (e.g., doing coding reliability checks, computing code frequencies, sorting data, viewing text, and finding uncoded files), which are accessed through the pro-

1. QUALPRO is also distributed by Qualitative Research Management, 73425 Hilltop Road, Desert Hot Springs, CA 92240. Phone: (619) 329-7026. QRM can answer minor queries but refers technical questions on the program to the developer.

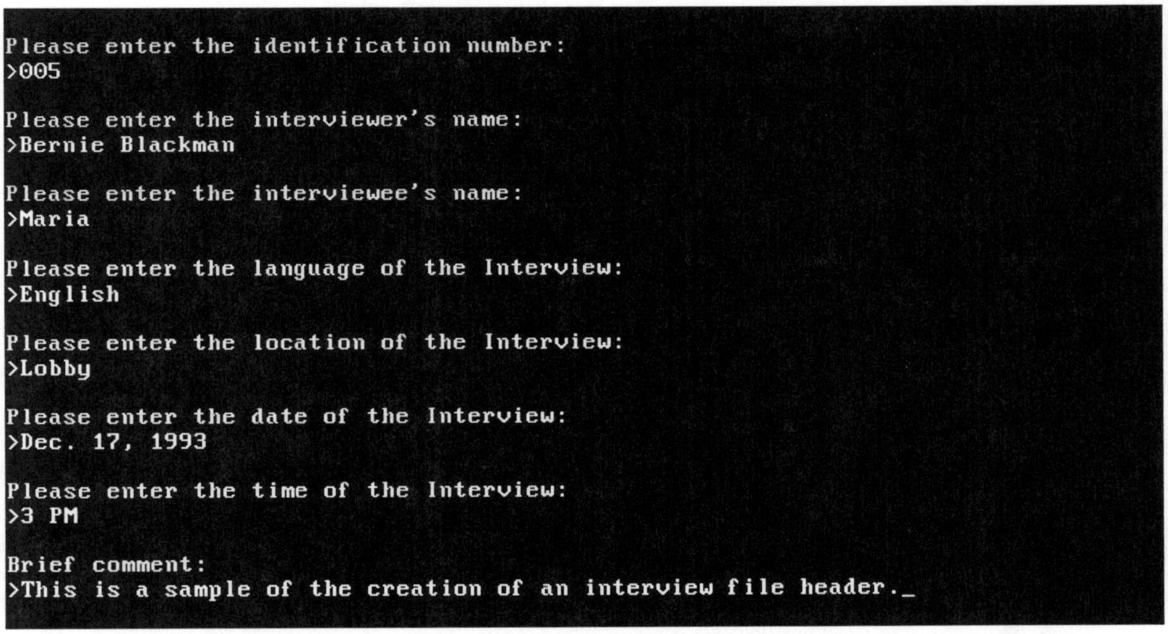

```
Please enter the identification number:
>005

Please enter the interviewer's name:
>Bernie Blackman

Please enter the interviewee's name:
>Maria

Please enter the language of the Interview:
>English

Please enter the location of the Interview:
>Lobby

Please enter the date of the Interview:
>Dec. 17, 1993

Please enter the time of the Interview:
>3 PM

Brief comment:
>This is a sample of the creation of an interview file header._
```

QUALPRO Figure 1. Filling in a file header. The items are filled in successively, but cannot be edited after the line is left. The file for which this is a header could be sorted by any of the provided information (ID number, English, Lobby, Maria, Dec. 17, 1993) or by codes, if they had been included in the Brief comment area. File headers for other types of documents (such as observations, documents, and memos) have a roughly similar structure.

gram shell. Those tools also work largely in a mainframe-like style, though the latter two do have a scrollable window.

Database Structure

QUALPRO works with your free-form ASCII text files. Each text file in the database is accompanied by two other files, one showing the lines to which you've applied specific codes (your files are not altered) and one with the header information for the file (face-sheet information on the respondent, date, researcher, and so on). All this is managed by a general "catalog" file for the database. The text files you want to include in a single database can be in different subdirectories or different floppies. The size of any particular file is only limited by disk space, but any given *textbase* is limited to 1,000 files. (If you're using floppies, you're limited to 36 data files per catalog.) Each code application is independent of all others; in principle, you could apply up to 1,000 codes to any piece of text. Each file is optionally organized into conceptually defined blocks, with size flexibly defined by you by inserting a blank line wherever you like (these could vary among sentences, paragraphs, several paragraphs, changes of speaker, interview questions, and so on). Text can also be looked at unblocked; all retrieved segments are then simply labeled "block 1." Codes are applied to any number of lines you like, and can overlap and nest, and extend across blocks. The value of blocks lies in reducing the amount of on-screen material and in providing some appropriate conceptual structure to your file.

Data Entry

You can type text in directly within QUALPRO (though editing is only line level—once you finish entering and editing a line, you cannot go back to it) or import ASCII files. Line length has to be under 69 characters (to allow for later printing of line numbers). Non-ASCII characters cause an error message, though the developer has thoughtfully provided a facility to strip them out; it also can be used to set the right length of line in imported text.

To specify blocks, you insert a blank line (two carriage returns) as noted above. QUALPRO automatically inserts a period within the blank line and two periods at the end of the file. If you are editing a file in your word processor, you need to know these conventions. To aid in later analysis, it's best to have a separate file for each interview, observation, and so on.

You can also specify file headers, which are useful in sorting subgroups of data. From the menu, you can choose

```
File name: EXAMPLE1                          Diary  Number: 001
Author: Bernie Blackman
Date: July 5, 1992          Time: 8:50 am
Brief Comment: Morning notes, breakfast and Maria


                                  * 1 *
 1    I awoke at 6:30 rested and thought immediately of breakfast. I washed 1
 2    in the basin Maria had provided, all the while thinking of breakfast. 2
 3    Would it be the same as yesterday? I shuddered from the cold air and  3
 4    the thought of breakfast.                                             4

                                  * 2 *
 6    Just then I met Maria face to face. She entered my room without      6
 7    knocking and began speaking rapidly about who I had to meet at lunch. 7
 8    Lunch meetings were very far from my mind since I still had to face   8
 9    Maria's breakfast. And would I be able to do it?                      9

                                  * 3 *
 11   I awoke at 6:30 rested and thought immediately of breakfast. I washed 11


Press the ◄┘ Enter key to continue or press the ESC key to cancel.
```

QUALPRO Figure 2. A file ready for coding. Line numbers have been attached, and data blocks separated. You can scroll down through the file, but not back up. You'll print hard copy, mark codes in the margins, then enter codes in the coding routine.

several different header types, including those for interviews, observations, documents, public records, contact summaries, diaries, and memos. There is also a "free-form" header with empty categories, and one with just the name of the file. You create headers in response to prompts: For example, if you choose an interview header, you'll be asked for items such as file ID number, interviewer, interviewee, language used, location, time, date, and a brief (one-line) comment, which could include codes if you wish. Figure 1 shows a sample header being filled in. Other header types are roughly similar.

When your data are complete, you can look at the prepared file, as in Figure 2, scrolling down (but not back up!) through it.

Working on the Data

QUALPRO adds line numbers and block numbers for you. Then you print hard copy and apply codes manually with a pencil (it's easiest to use brackets by a range of lines to mark off segments and write in code names beside the brackets). You then start up QUALPRO and type in codes (up to 15 characters) and segment-beginning and ending line numbers (the program is good in preventing logic and syntax errors, such as starting a code outside of the present block or doing line numbers in reverse order). Overlapping and nesting codes are OK. The manual recommends doing all the codes in a block before going on to the next block. However, codes can be applied across blocks if you wish.

The coding routine is simple. The data shown in Figure 2 were typed this way, as the manual suggested during the "tour":

WAKETIME,1,1 [applies code WAKETIME to line 1 only]

Other codes can be applied in the same way:

BREAKFAST,1,4

MORNING,1,9 [note that this overlaps into Block 2]

. [this period pops you into the next block]

BREAKFAST,8,9

.. [two periods signal end of coding]

If you make a mistake and type BREAK FAST and don't correct it, going on to the next line, QUALPRO will treat it as a new code, in addition to BREAKFAST. However, you can correct the code file later if that should happen (see below).

Practically speaking, coding cannot really be done with text on screen. The manual says you can, but in reality you would have to view the text on screen, jot down code names and line numbers, leave the text, enter the code Input

Last file no.: 2	1	2	3
QUALPRO Cross-TABS for XTAB.FRQ Last code no.: 4 Code Name	EXAMPLE1	EXAMPLE2	ROW SUM
1 BREAKFAST	2	1	3
2 MEETING	0	1	1
3 MORNING	1	1	2
4 WAKETIME	1	1	2
5 COL SUM	4	4	8

View Codes: ↑↓←→ PgUp PgDn Home End ESC=Exit

QUALPRO Figure 3. A crosstab display of codes across data files. The rows give code names, and the columns data file names. Frequencies are in cells.

option, apply the codes, then exit coding and go back to viewing the screen.

Codes are only defined at one level; the program does not help you develop second- or third-level codes. You could work around this by assigning main codes and subcodes, perhaps marking them off with colons (you can't use backslashes). But this sort of workaround is difficult because of the total 15-character limit to code size. QUALPRO will print you an alphabetized code list whenever you want it.

An important limitation is that coding is done in a line-editing mode—once you finish a line, that's it. Corrections are only possible later, after codes have been saved; you recall the file and can then append new codes or replace existing codes with new codes. You can also edit codes by exiting and reworking the code file via your word processor. The coding conventions are simple: The text CODENAME,1,6 applies CODENAME to lines 1 through 6 in the block you are working in. (You can also apply a code to line numbers across blocks.) The simplicity of the coding conventions means that you can easily create code files with your word processor—which might be a lot better than the locked-in, line-editing mode within QUALPRO. What you'd lose, of course, is the error-checking feature.

Coding does not alter your document. Text files are editable, but if you edit them after coding, *things get messed up,* because codes are line specified, and if your editing has shifted any lines, you will have to re-edit the codes, either within QUALPRO or with your word processor.

You can get frequencies of codes within each file, overall code frequencies, and a crosstab of code frequencies across files (as in Figure 3). All can be exported in ASCII. Another routine will give you a "code summary," showing code names and all the line numbers, in sequence, to which the codes have been applied. QUALPRO will also print you an alphabetized code list.

Two unique and useful features are a subroutine that lets you check the degree of agreement across coders, producing not only a reliability measure (Scott's Pi) and a "Table of Agreements" showing line-by-line comparisons between two coders, but a "Confusion Matrix" (a wonderful name). It shows coder A's line-by-line code frequencies in rows, code by code, and coder B's in columns, code by code. Thus you could see, for example, that coder A and coder B both gave BREAKFAST on 22 lines, but that, for 4 lines, A gave BREAKFAST and B gave WAKETIME, and that there were no lines where A gave BREAKFAST and B gave MORNING.

Another unique routine creates an output file that will show you every line of *uncoded* text (helpful as a recheck, especially if your coding scheme has evolved a good bit). But, as with code searches (see below), you see these lines without context (the material that has been coded preceding or following them). You do a summary table reporting

```
Code: BREAKFAST (1-4)     Block: 1 (1-4).     File: EXAMPLE1

 1   I awoke at 6:30 rested and thought immediately of breakfast. I washed 1
 2   in the basin Maria had provided, all the while thinking of breakfast. 2
 3   Would it be the same as yesterday? I shuddered from the cold air and  3
 4   the thought of breakfast.                                             4

Co-occurring codes:
WAKETIME (1-1)  MORNING (1-9)

Code: BREAKFAST (8-9)     Block: 2 (6-9)     File: EXAMPLE1

 8   Lunch meetings were very far from my mind since I still had to face   8
 9   Maria's breakfast. And would I be able to do it?                      9

Co-occurring codes:
MORNING (1-9)

Press the ◄┘ Enter key when you are ready to continue.
```

QUALPRO Figure 4. A retrieval output. All of the instances of code BREAKFAST have been collected. The actual lines (with block number and line numbers identified) are shown. You can scroll down but not back up. At the bottom, "co-occurring" code names are shown. other codes applicable to the lines involved but that had not been searched for.

the "catalog" that was searched, the number of files searched, the number of files with uncoded lines, the total uncoded lines, and number of uncoded groups of lines. This routine assigns "UNCODED" as a code to the lines involved, so that can be retrieved if you wish.

This combination of features gives QUALPRO unusual strength in checking, refining, and comparing the coding work of several coders (or of one coder on a test-retest basis).

Searching

This program *only finds codes,* not strings, and collects the coded segments for you (it does not work a hit at a time). You can retrieve code information using AND, OR, NOT operators in sequence (no parenthetical expressions); what you get, as in Figure 4, is simply the *actual lines* that were coded as specified by your request (no context is shown).

Line numbering on your collected hits can be shown or suppressed. In the collected hits, for each one, you also see the filename and block number, but no other source tags—you have to exit search and ask for file header information. You can scroll down but not back up through the collected hits—to do that, you'll have to save to a file and exit to your word processor or use the View option to look at the file you saved them to. If you mistype a code, or if there are no hits, you get no message, you're just flipped back to the original prompt—a bit disconcerting.

At the bottom of each hit, you see (unless you've suppressed it) the names of *other* codes attached to the hit (see Figure 4), even though they weren't part of your search request; their line numbers are included. This is a useful feature; the developer suggests it can help you see how codes may be linked. However, it's a bit cumbersome, because proximity of codes does not automatically mean conceptual linkage. To make conceptual sense, you still have to return to the main program and make a new retrieval request for the co-occurring codes, then page through *that* complete collected output to see in detail how they were applied.

A subroutine called SORT uses Boolean AND, OR, and NOT search terms, but not to find codes or strings. Rather, using header information, it sorts your files into subsets, so you can look for principals only, compare males and females, or see differences among early versus middle versus late interviews, and so on. It's a useful feature.

It actually creates new "catalog" files for, say, males and females; you can see the names of the files that have been included. Then you must still do a search in that "catalog" (textbase) by codes as above. Comparing males and females would mean doing two separate retrieval requests, one in each file—a somewhat tedious process. (However, a nice feature is that you can add keywords to the header information for your files at any time, and sort the data using them, without affecting the codes or text.)

The manual warns that (assuming use of an older, low-end machine) large files (size unspecified) may take a good while, like 5 minutes, to complete searches. With a faster machine, search is still not rapid (Morales, 1993, reports that a 486DX machine took "less than a minute" to find 20 code occurrences in a 2MB database).

Output

Output of all kinds is to screen, printer, or file, but choosing one precludes the others—if you look at a screen and then decide to save it on disk, you have to go back to the beginning of whatever retrieval you were doing, and this time tell it to save to disk (again, mainframelike rigidity). Text documents, search output, and uncoded lines can be printed with or without line numbers.

In a special utility, View, you can view your text files on screen, and scroll through them up and down, right and left, though you do *not* see line numbers.

You can customize page length and width for output, as well as the number of columns for the file-sorting SORT output, but nothing else in the program seems customizable.

Theory Building

QUALPRO has no theory-building capacity as such, in the sense of direct routines for data linking, proposition testing, multilevel coding, development of conceptual networks, or the like.

To do a memo, you make a separate file in QUALPRO format for each memo, or for several memos on the same topic. The memo files are automatically saved to the catalog you're using. QUALPRO usefully includes an "Append" feature, so memo files can be added to.

However, the memo files are *not* automatically linked to codes, or to any other file or text. You can, though, code them like any other file, and then sort them by the SORT routine, but you must have entered (or edited) appropriate header information for the memo file, naming the memo concepts or perhaps naming particular text files they're written about. For annotations, the developer suggests using some separate notepad utility, such as Sidekick or Windows 3.1 Notepad.

QUALPRO can be run as a non-Windows application under Windows 3.0 or 3.1, which enhances memoing, cut-and-paste operations, and use of your own word processor—which the manual emphasizes is a good idea.

User Friendliness

QUALPRO is quite user friendly on some counts, not on others. It's easy to learn, and simple to use, but it can be quite rigid and frustrating, as noted at several points above, if you're working within the regular program rather than your word processor.

The tutorial "tour" is well set up and took about an hour and a half for a Level 2 person. The manual is well organized and written clearly in a step-by-step style, with the beginning user in mind, including information on relevant DOS commands. The meaning of filenames is explained—a feature often missing in manuals; the appendix shows clear examples of file formats and outputs, which are not always easy to access in the program itself. Help screens, which are better implemented for the "productivity tools" than for the main program, can usually be accessed by hitting "?" whenever you're presented with a prompt you don't understand, and explanations are clear and relevant to where you are in the program. On-screen error messages are clear and straightforward.

The program is menu driven and pretty foolproof, but slow, because of the mainframe-like series of actions you have to perform to get what you want. It's forgiving, and you can usually escape out of what isn't working right. But you usually can't back up to the preceding line to correct something you did. You have to come back and edit the file later.

Tech support is supplied by the developer, Bernie Blackman, who answers his own phone.[2] The developer is also available for longer-term consulting and customized training on research applications by mail, e-mail (no address given) or telephone, at hourly or daily rates.

Miscellaneous

QUALPRO calls its routines beyond those of basic coding and sorting "productivity tools," which can be accessed through a shell (or directly from the DOS prompt), including those for code frequencies, coder reliability, sorting of subgroups, file stripping, code list production, crosstabs of codes by file, file viewing, and locating uncoded text. To access the routines directly from the DOS prompt, you have to know the right output filenames involved.

We did not encounter any bugs, and the developer is not aware of any.

Though Version 4.0 has added several features from the version (3.3) reviewed by Tesch (1990), her description is

2. QUALPRO is also distributed by Qualitative Research Management, 73425 Hilltop Road, Desert Hot Springs, CA 92240. Phone: (619) 329-7026. QRM can answer minor queries, but refers technical questions on the program to the developer.

worth your looking at if you are considering using QUALPRO.

Update

For Version 4.1, the developer intends to add utilities of a content-analytic sort such as string search, word frequency, and KWIC (keyword in context), along with multilevel coding. Both Version 4.1 and a new Windows version (labeled 5.0) are expected in 1995; as with all such promises, expect them when you see them.

Comparative Remarks

In comparison with other code-and-retrieve programs such as Kwalitan, HyperQual2, The Ethnograph, or Martin, QUALPRO is a more limited operation. Though it's simple to use, it's slow and fairly rigid in its main routines—even though the brochure and the documentation tout it as "flexible." It lacks the on-screen coding, memoing, and annotating features of Kwalitan and Martin, the data-linking capacities of HyperQual2, and the string search, speaker identification, codebook facility, and coded text output features of The Ethnograph. It's weaker on coding and on memoing/annotation than any of its code-and-retrieve partners.

On the other hand, QUALPRO's simplicity, its learning ease, the modest price, the unique, helpful facility for checking and comparing codes, and the output of uncoded text are clear pluses.

Summary

QUALPRO's simplicity could be useful if you have a small- to moderate-size database, a low budget, not much learning time available, and are happy with a line-by-line code-and-collect style. As the brochure says, it's designed for "almost anyone who cuts and pastes text manually," and it's pedagogically well set up. But you pay for QUALPRO'S simplicity with the limited options you have for coding, search, and analysis. If you're deciding on software to be used not just now but later on in more complex projects, it's probably not a good choice. However, if you use Windows, QUALPRO's limitations will be much less of a problem, because you can compensate with the features of your word processor, as the developer intended.

References

Blackman, B. I. (1993). *QUALPRO text database and productivity tools: User's manual, version 4 for IBM and PC compatibles.* Tallahassee, FL: *Impulse* Development Co.

Morales, A. (1993) Computer software review: QUALPRO v4.0. *NOTAS, 2*(1), 8.

Tesch, R. (1990). *Qualitative research: Analysis types and software tools.* New York: Falmer.

The Ethnograph, Version 4.0

Available for DOS

Qualis Research Associates[1]
P.O. Box 2070
Amherst, MA 01004

Phone: (413) 256-8835
Fax: (413) 256-8472
E-mail: qualis@mcimail.com

Price: $200

Hardware Requirements:
- IBM PC: any
- DOS: any
- Hard disk with 2MB free
- 460K RAM

Overview

The Ethnograph was one of the first code-and-retrieve programs on the scene, starting with Version 2.0 in 1985 (see Seidel & Clark, 1984). With an attractive name, it has achieved wide diffusion (over 4,000 copies have been shipped). In an informal survey of 126 qualitative researchers by Miles and Huberman in 1991 (Miles & Huberman, 1994), 43% of respondents said they were using some software for analysis. Of these users, 48% mentioned The Ethnograph. The program was basically designed for line-by-line coding of free-form data and retrieval of coded segments.

Earlier versions of the program, up through 3.0 (Seidel, Kjolseth, & Seymour, 1988), had mixed reviews; some users found it simple, useful, and easy to use, but others complained of its tedious, slow, cumbersome, limiting aspects. In many respects, a number of more recent programs (e.g., Kwalitan, ATLAS/ti, NUD•IST) have proved more lively, practical, and sophisticated while adding theory-building features, and The Ethnograph has been under active development to keep up with the pack.

Version 4.0, which we saw in two beta-test versions, does show substantial improvement and the influence of user needs. (The developer is a qualitative researcher and has written thoughtfully—Seidel, 1991—about the problems of software use in analysis.) It's set up in four basic modules for importing and managing data, coding, retrieval, and file management (see Figure 1 for the opening screen). The program includes on-screen coding, provision for memoing, a text editor, master lists of codes and speaker/section identifiers, and a codebook of definitions (a feature few other programs have). The Ethnograph also does better than most programs at displaying text with codes attached, and it's good at using face-sheet and speaker information both as source tags and as search criteria.

However, it's also fair to say that The Ethnograph still has some important limitations. The feeling is that its new features have not been well integrated into a friendly package. The user interface feels awkward (you work from a slow menu that requires you to move in and out of major modules to accomplish different tasks).[2] You have to respecify which files you want to work on each time you enter a new module, although the second beta version we saw provides you with a list of files you've been working

1. The Ethnograph is also distributed by Qualitative Research Management, 73425 Hilltop Road, Desert Hot Springs, CA 92240. Phone: (619) 329-7026.

2. The term "clunky," which we applied to The Ethnograph's interface in an earlier draft of this review, is probably too harsh. But The Ethnograph is not a well-integrated package like ATLAS/ti or Folio VIEWS, in which you can easily see and get to every function you need without having to jump in and out of modules.

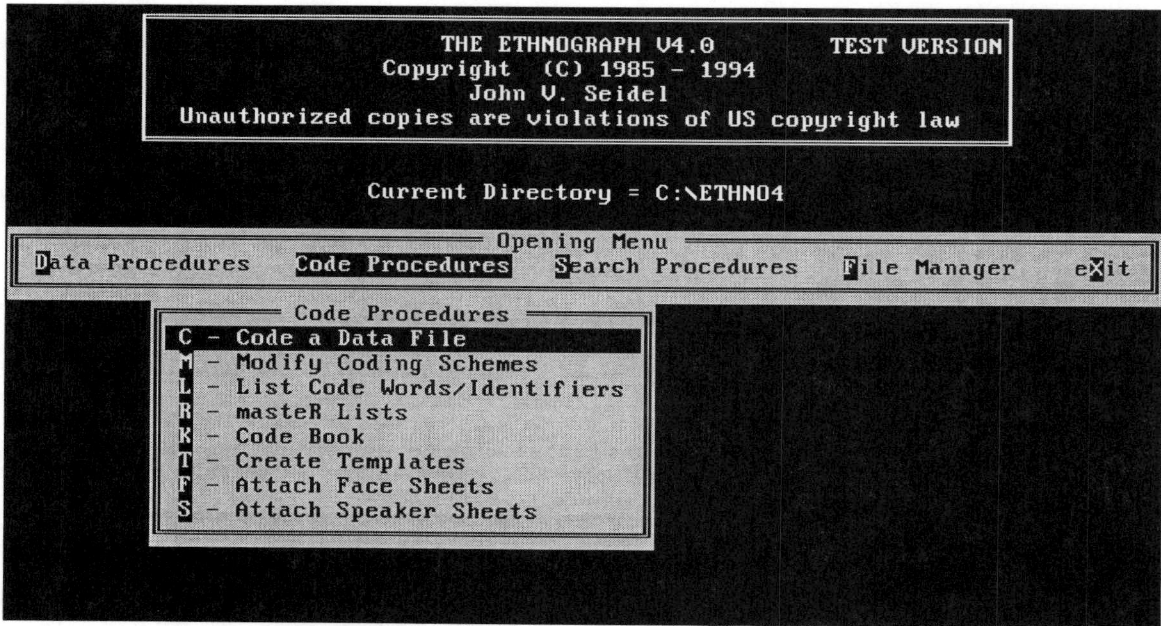

The Ethnograph Figure 1. The opening screen, showing the four modules. The menu for the second module (code procedures) has been pulled down, and the user is about to select "Code a Data File."

on to choose from. Other limitations include awkward search requests, the fact that search hits are normally presented without context (though you can expand the context for up to 10 lines, a hit at a time), absence of string search except during coding (though see the "Update" section), and little or no on-screen help. Though the intent of the program is to keep you close to your data as you code it and retrieve it line by line, the net effect (compared, say, with the intuitive, direct style of ATLAS/ti) is one of distance from your data—as long as you are working within the program itself. If you, like many users of the program, like to work actively with hard copy of your text and various printouts, marking them up and discussing them, then the "closeness" issue is moot.

In this preview (not yet a review), we depart from our usual rule of not describing "phantom" software that isn't yet available on the market, because of the prominence of the program. As a recent, eager electronic bulletin board user asked, "Does Version 4.0 of The Ethnograph exist?" Yes, it does, in a manner of speaking; it's been under development since 1989, but a number of promised features are still not implemented. Here we'll discuss what is in fact present in the beta-test versions we saw and will refer forward to the "Update" section on promised features as we go.

For a detailed description of Version 3.0, see Tesch (1990). We will not try to make comparisons between 3.0 and 4.0; the reader who knows 3.0 can make them, and other readers should be considering 4.0 in its own terms, keeping in mind that promises may or may not be kept, and that beta-test features sometimes disappear.

Database Structure

The Ethnograph produces a line-numbered file from your ASCII data file, then automatically produces up to 10 associated files that record code applications, your code master list, header information, speaker/section identifiers, memos, and others. These files are regularly updated as you add codes; your basic data files are untouched (and can even be deleted if you wish). A rough estimate is that you need floppy or hard disk space about double the size of your original data files.

A data file can be up to 9,999 lines (about 380K, 180 pages at 40 characters a line). However, if you are using the text editor, a given .ETH file (preformatted, with your basic data) can only be about 8,000 lines (300K, about 145 pages). The developer suggests staying at a 7,500-line maximum (136 pages).

Note: If you are converting ASCII files to the .ETH file format, the editor can only manage ASCII files of size 200K (that would be 5,000 lines, or 76 pages of 65 characters per line). A file larger than this can be divided with your word processor, then converted by the editor to sev-

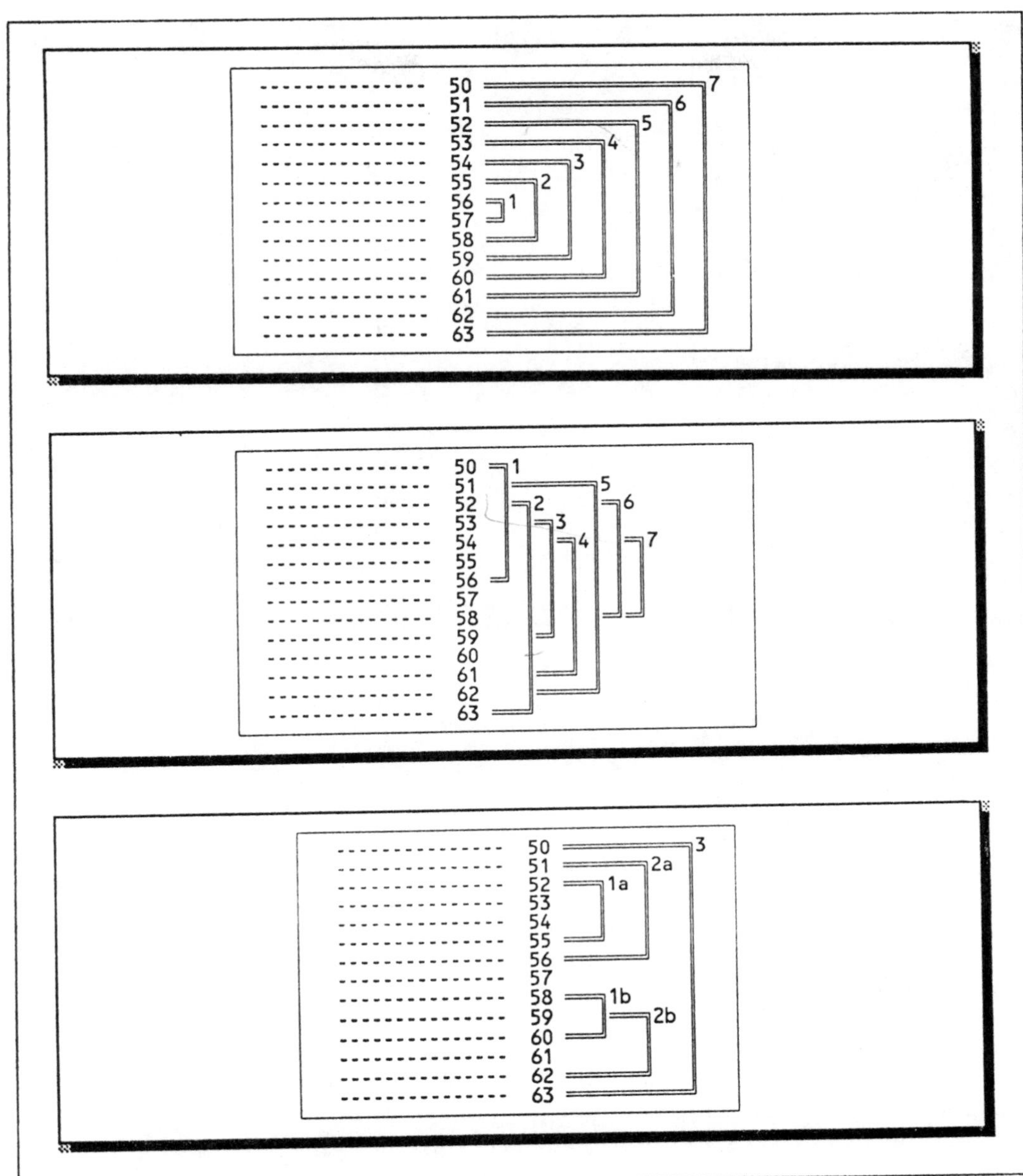

The Ethnograph Figure 2. Limits for overlaps and nesting (from documentation, pp. 8-4, 8-5). The first two boxes show how the limit of seven contiguous nests or overlaps applies. The third box shows five coded segments, but there are only three levels, because the 1a-2a and 1b-2b nesting/overlapping segments are noncontiguous.

eral .ETH files. Then you exit the editor and combine them using the program's Combine Files facility (up to The Ethnograph's limit of 9,999 lines).

The program can work with 200 data files at a time. This is the upper limit for the size of a "catalog," which is a collection of files you want to work on—for example, all the files from one project, or from one school, or for all females interviewed, and so on. Thus you can search in the catalog, call up and revise master code lists used in the catalog, print files, or carry out any other multifile task needed. (You can only code one file at a time, so the catalog function does not apply there.) Because the catalog is saved, you can call it up in later sessions without having to relist all the files again.

```
    CODING DATA FILE: CASE42                              METHOD: Code Sets
  he fell -- this guy fell off the back      25  |
  of his truck. The first thing that         26  |
$-SIGNS
  happened he had -- he had weakness or      27  |-$
  paralysis and numbness in both his         28  | |  Code Set Entry Window
  legs. Couldn't move for almost an          29  | |
  hour. And it began to come back. And       30  | |    Start Line:     27
  ever since that time he's had these --     31  | |    Code Word      Stop Line
  these weird sensations and pain --         32  | |  1 SIGNS            34
  pain has gone from his legs. Bladder       33  | |  2
  and bowel disturbance. Had a GU            34  |-$  3
  workup. They can't document that he        35  |    4
  has a (----------). I think he does.       36  |    5
  Impotence. And I think he contused the     37  |    6
  spinal cord is what he did.                38 -#    7
                                                      8
                                                      9
                                                     10
                                                     11
                                                     12
 F5=Scroll  F6=Master Code List  F7=Delete Code Set  F9=Abandon  F10=Accept
```

The Ethnograph Figure 3. Coding with the "code sets" method. The user has entered a start line (27), a code (SIGNS), and a stop line (34), then hit F10 to "accept" the coding. The code SIGNS with the identifying $ symbol appears in the text at the left, above the line where the code begins. At the right, vertical lines show the extent of the code application. The function keys named at the bottom allow you to scroll up and down in the text, to pop to a master code list, to delete the code set being worked on (which in this case included only one code), or to abandon coding.

Data Entry

The program will only accept files with the extension .ETH, formatted in a very precise way. They may have "contextual comments" that serve as header information for the whole file or major parts of it; they may have "speaker/section identifiers" that specify either who is talking or what the subsection of the data file is (such as "Question 16"). Each contextual comment and each speaker/section identifier applies to all the text up to the next comment or identifier, respectively, and must be followed by a colon. The importance of the comments and identifiers is that they appear as source tags for retrieved text.

(Later, if you wish, you can also create "face-sheet" variables, and "speaker-sheet" variables, which provide source information for a file as a whole and for speakers within it; they can also be used to select files for searching. See "Working on the Data" below.)

The body of the text is indented a recommended two spaces (the comments and identifiers are full flush left, a format sometimes called "hanging indent"). The text must be 40 characters wide or less, to allow for the display of code symbols at the right. Paragraphs are separated by a blank line.

Done completely by hand, this could get quite laborious. Using your own word processor, you'd have to write a macro to make life easier. Fortunately, The Ethnograph (a) includes directions for formatting .ETH files using WordPerfect and Word (both DOS and Windows versions) and AmiPro, and (b) has an internal text editor that can be used to create .ETH files directly or to convert an ASCII file into the .ETH format. (The latter works well if your ASCII file is impeccable; in using a messy file with a lot of blank spaces in it, it was necessary to work paragraph by paragraph rather than with the document as a whole.) You have to mark paragraphs, with a period in column 1, that do (or do not) start with a speaker/section identifier—which must be followed by a colon. If you omit the colon, the program will take the first 10 characters as an identifier, regardless, and you then have to edit the file, save it, and reimport it. You'll also have to edit the master list of identifiers, purging the old ones and adding the new ones—or rewrite the master list from scratch, which the developer suggests is easy.

And even though the editor will let you revise your data files, remember that The Ethnograph searches by line number, and any editing that changes the line numbering after codes have been attached will mess up retrieval.

```
      CODING DATA FILE: CASE42                           METHOD: Code Sets
+ EARL MICHAELS - PROGRESS STAFFING                1

#-PAT ID      $-PAT REVIEW
MD: Okay. Earl Michaels. Okay, oh, you             3 -#-$
  staffed him last week. Okay --                   4 -# |
                                                        |
#-PROBLEM
  Okay, he's got some musculoskeletal              6 -# |
  problems. What are you doing in                  7 -# |
  physical therapy?                                8    -$

!-TREAT
PT-1: Relaxation, muscle stretching --            10!

#-MOTIVE       #-EVAL        #-PAIN        #-PROGRESS    #-EVIDENCE
PT-3: He's well motivated and he's ready          12 -#
  to get better.  I think he's tired of           13  |
  the life style that he's been living.           14  |
  He's shown -- (------) pain slips               15  |
  steadily decreasing (-----).                    16 -#

MD: Are you all clear on what the final           18
  physical diagnosis was for him. You             19
 F1=Help  F2=Print  F3=Find  F4=Goto  F5=Memo  F6=View  F8=Code  F9(ESC)=Exit
```

The Ethnograph Figure 4. Scrolling in the text. This screen appears when you resume coding a previously coded text; you can also pop back to it by exiting the code set entry window in Figure 3. The options now available in the bottom row include printing this segment, searching for specific strings or codes in the text, going to a specific line, writing a memo, changing the view (keeping the text in view, seeing code sets only—see Figure 6—or "Nothing"—no text, just a coding box).

A copy of the editor can be detached from the Ethnograph and run independently (by, for example, a transcriber) to prepare data files—a useful feature.

We've noted that you can organize your files for a project into one or more "catalogs"; you can also select files from a "pick list" of all eligible data files and work with them in a session, without creating a catalog from them. If your filenames have been well set up (e.g., showing interviewees' role, gender, or "pre" or "post" timing), it will be easy to use the file selection and/or catalog feature to work with subsets of your data. (As we'll see, the face-sheet and speaker-sheet facility of The Ethnograph gives you even finer control of file selection when you are searching.)

You can also easily combine all or parts of several numbered or coded data files into a new single file; the program asks you for the line numbers to be included from each file (1 to 9999 gives you the complete file). The combined file is automatically renumbered; if you combined the coded versions, the codes remain but are attached to the new numbers. *However,* memos from the original files are not passed to the new combined file. Face-sheet and speaker-sheet values from the first file can be transferred to the combined file if you wish.

The Combine facility also permits you to divide files.

Working on the Data

As in previous versions, you can write codes on a hard copy of a line-numbered file if you wish, drawing brackets to show the lines at which each code application starts and stops, then in a second step type them in. However, Version 4.0 lets you code on screen. Code names can have only 10 characters. It would be nice to have longer, more meaningful codes—but the limitation does make it possible to show code words and chunk boundaries on screen—a trade-off.

You define text segments to which you're applying a code flexibly, by specifying a start line and a stop line. Any particular segment can have up to 12 codes applied to it, and code applications will often overlap or nest.

Any fully contiguous set of nested and overlapping code applications can have only seven levels of overlapping and nesting. Figure 2 shows some examples of this from the documentation.

If you choose the "code sets" option, you can apply a number of codes at once, provided that all the segments involved start on the same line (they do not have to end at the same line). Figure 3 shows how this works. If you choose the "quick code" method, you type in one code to a segment; it can then be immediately applied to later seg-

```
             Coded Version of CASE42    3/8/1994   18:18    Page 1
--------------------------------------------------------------------------
     + EARL MICHAELS - PROGRESS STAFFING               1

#-PAT ID     $-PAT REVIEW
     MD: Okay. Earl Michaels. Okay, oh, you           3 -#-$
       staffed him last week. Okay --                 4 -#  |
                                                            |
#-PROBLEM
       Okay, he's got some musculoskeletal            6 -#  |
       problems. What are you doing in                7 -#  |
       physical therapy?                              8    -$

!-TREAT
     PT-1: Relaxation, muscle stretching --          10!

#-MOTIVE      #-EVAL        #-PAIN        #-PROGRESS     #-EVIDENCE
     PT-3: He's well motivated and he's ready       12 -#
       to get better.  I think he's tired of        13  |
       the life style that he's been living.        14  |
       He's shown -- (------) pain slips            15  |
       steadily decreasing (-----).                 16 -#

#-DIAGNOSIS
     MD: Are you all clear on what the final        18 -#
       physical diagnosis was for him. You          19  |
       know, we were questioning the spinal         20  |
       cord tumor. We were questioning              21  |
       multiple sclerosis.                          22 -#

#-HISTORY
       As you reconstruct the history, when         24 -#
       he fell -- this guy fell off the back        25  |
       of his truck. The first thing that           26  |
$-SIGNS
       happened he had -- he had weakness or        27  |-$
       paralysis and numbness in both his           28  | |
       legs. Couldn't move for almost an            29  | |
       hour. And it began to come back. And         30  | |
%-PAIN
       ever since that time he's had these --       31  | |-%
       these weird sensations and pain --           32  | | |
       pain has gone from his legs. Bladder         33  | |-%
       and bowel disturbance. Had a GU              34  |-$
$-DIAGNOSIS
       workup. They can't document that he          35  |-$
       has a (---------). I think he does.          36  | |
       Impotence. And I think he contused the       37  | |
       spinal cord is what he did.                  38 -#-$
```

The Ethnograph Figure 5. Printout of a fully coded data file. The codes applied in the two preceding figures are all visible. Note that the coding symbols are arbitrarily used, and recycled as needed. The same symbol can allude to different codes. The "brackets" showing code applications are intended to mimic the way you'd hand-draw brackets on hard copy; they're sometimes less than clear because they're broken at the code-name lines or where there is a paragraph space (see lines 4-6, 26-27, 30-31, 34-35 for examples). Note that, when multiple codes are applied to one segment (e.g., lines 12-16), only one bracket is drawn.

ments if you wish. "Quick code" also lets you apply an additional code word to the original segment.

The program keeps a record of codes applied to any given file, which you can ask for. However, more helpful is a master code list, which you create by telling the program all the relevant names of coded files. Then you can pop up the master list (it's alphabetical, in a small window) and select codes to be entered into either the "code sets"

```
       CODING DATA FILE: CASE42                            METHOD: Code Sets
START  STOP CODEWORD         STOP CODEWORD         STOP CODEWORD         STOP CODEWORD
  3-      4 #PAT ID             8 $PAT REVIEW

  6-      7 #PROBLEM

 10-     10 !TREAT

 12-     16 #MOTIVE            16 #EVAL              16 #PAIN              16 #PROGRESS
         16 #EVIDENCE

 18-     22 #DIAGNOSIS

 F1=Help  F2=Print  F3=Find  F4=Goto  F5=Memo  F6=View  F8=Code  F9(ESC)=Exit
```

The Ethnograph Figure 6. Display of code sets. For the data file CASE42, we see all the code applications, with start and stop lines. The user can shift back and forth between this display and coding, either with full text on screen or a blank screen while he or she is working from hard copy. The same options exist for this screen as in Figure 4.

or the "quick codes" dialog boxes, without having to type them in.

There is a modest search facility for use during coding: You can search for character strings, codes, or both, and you are popped to each hit, one at a time. You can also go to a specific line. That just helps you get around in the file; you still have to type in the code or use the repeated "quick code" method if you want to apply the same code to each hit.

As you add codes, you immediately see, at the top left of each coded segment, the code name and a symbol for the code, such as #, $, or %. The symbol, and bracketlike lines, appear at the right, showing the segment to which the code has been applied (see Figure 4).

This is a feature that most other code-and-retrieve programs lack, and it's helpful. (The price you pay is the limitation to 12 codes per segment and seven levels of nests/overlaps—that's all that can be fitted in.) *Caution*: the symbols are simply recycled as needed, so the same code does *not* always have the same symbol—a feature that bothers many users, especially new ones. A fully coded printout is illustrated in Figure 5.

You can also get a display of "code sets" (in this case, that means code applications) while you are coding (Figure 6) or choose the option "View Nothing," which you might want if you were working from hard copy (as in Version 3.0). Then the code entry window appears, and you just type in code names and start/stop lines.

Codes can be deleted, and the size of applicable segments changed, *but* with one specific limit: You can't push the start of a segment (to which you want to apply, say, CODE2) back if there's another preceding code start line (for, say, CODE1) in the way, nor similarly forward. What you have to do is delete CODE2, then reapply it in the larger range.

At any time, you can get a list of coded segments, speaker/section identifiers, or both (Figure 7).

Happily, your coding scheme can be globally modified (in effect, renaming all instances of a code, though you have the option to accept or reject each change), or all instances of a code can be deleted (again with the option to accept or reject each change). You also get a report of all changes made.

There's also a Codebook procedure—a very useful feature, especially for multi-researcher studies—that lets you enter a list of codes (or import a master list), identify them as first-level or "parent" codes, and type in definitions of up to 255 characters. According to the developer, parent codes can have parents, so there's no apparent limit to levels of codes. The list can be sorted by parent if you wish, and can be edited at any time. *However,* parent codes cannot be used in making searches. *And* the codebook and the

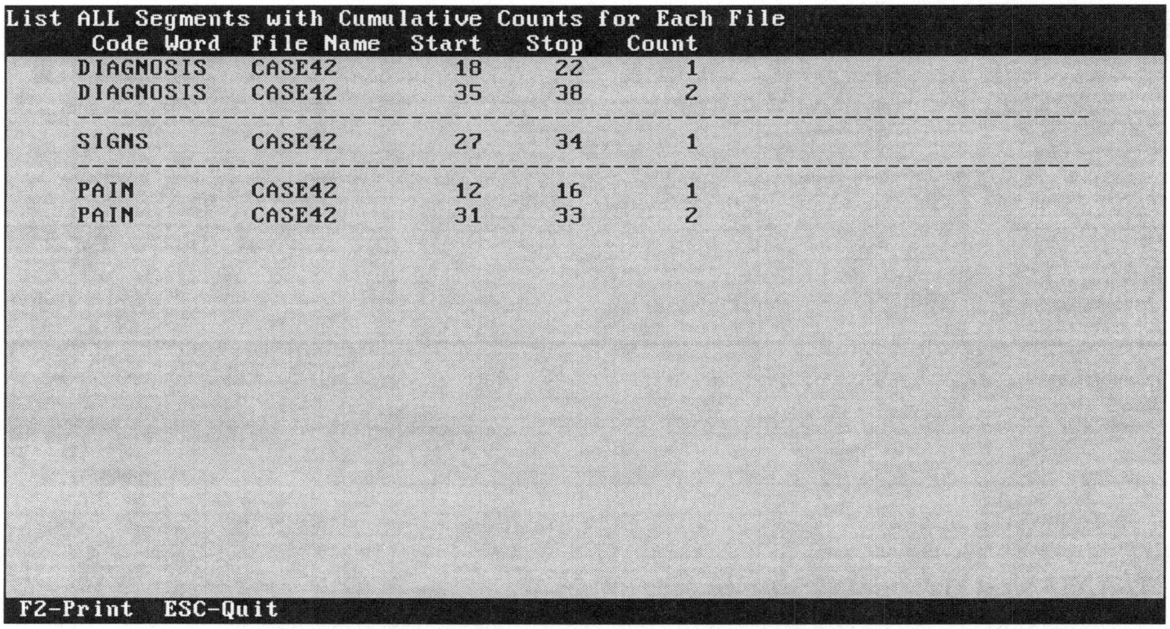

```
List ALL Segments with Cumulative Counts for Each File
     Code Word    File Name   Start    Stop    Count
     DIAGNOSIS    CASE42        18      22       1
     DIAGNOSIS    CASE42        35      38       2
     ---------------------------------------------------------------
     SIGNS        CASE42        27      34       1
     ---------------------------------------------------------------
     PAIN         CASE42        12      16       1
     PAIN         CASE42        31      33       2

 F2-Print  ESC-Quit
```

The Ethnograph Figure 7. A list of coded segments. Shown are the code names, the filename, the start and stop lines, and the cumulative counts. A similar list can be pulled up for speaker/section identifiers.

master list should be automatically integrated, but they do not know that the other is present. *You* have to be the link between them.

There is a good facility for specifying "face-sheet" variables (which apply to an entire file) and "speaker-sheet" variables (which apply to individuals, or sections, for whom you have identifiers within a file). Such information can be used in filtering/selecting files and in searching for segments. Thus you might want to identify a file by the research site, the date, the researcher involved, and whether it was a first, second, or third visit. For speakers within the file, you might want to indicate their age (numerical data are OK), ethnicity, gender, role, and so on.[3] You create a basic template (like the definition of fields in a database); up to 40 variables are possible. You save the template, then "activate" it by attaching it to relevant data files. Then, file by file and speaker by speaker, you enter the values of the variables (missing values are OK); values are editable at any time as you learn more about the file or speaker. (If you later want to revise the template itself, you can do so and apply it to a file that already has face-sheet and speaker-sheet variables, transferring old values that are still relevant, and transferring values between variables with different names.)

Finally, you can enter the memoing facility while you are coding. A box pops up with fields for the line numbers of the text you want to attach the memo to, your name, the time, the date, the topic, and up to three existing codes. Then you enter text in the window (up to 2K, though if you need to write more, up to 24 memos of that size can be attached to any given line) (see Figure 8). You can print memos separately or with the data they reference (page 1 has the memo, and page 2 has the data). In our second beta-test version, the printing worked, but the feature caused a computer crash.

Searching

The Ethnograph searches only for codes, and for speaker/section identifiers, looking for their line numbers. If you search by specific speaker/section identifiers, you'll get all the text down to the next identifier. (You can type in identifiers or choose them from your master identifier list.) Speaker/section identifiers can be used together with codes in searches. Your output can be viewed or printed with or without codes. There are two basic searching options: "single codes" and "multiple codes."

3. Although the documentation always calls these "speaker sheets," they can easily be used to specify variables for different *sections* of a file. For example, if the same file had interview data interspersed with sections labeled "Observation," you could specify the settings, times, and so on of the observation data in your basic template. That would let you search later for all observations in classroom 6A, or those made in morning hours, and so on.

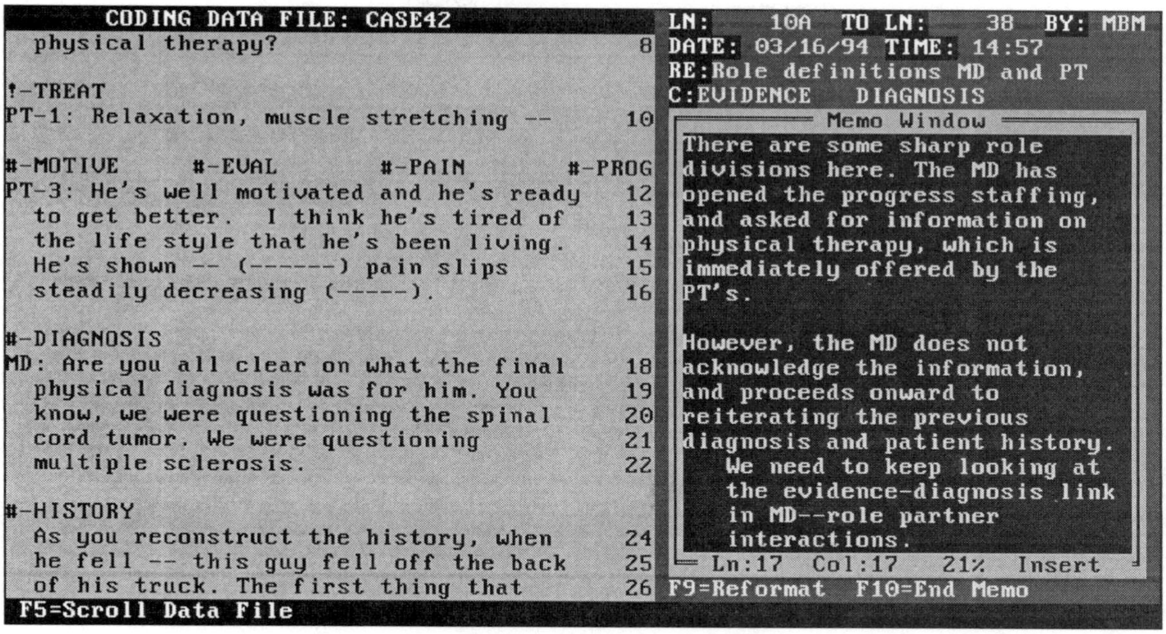

```
     CODING DATA FILE: CASE42                 LN:     10A  TO LN:     38  BY: MBM
  physical therapy?                        8  DATE: 03/16/94 TIME: 14:57
                                              RE:Role definitions MD and PT
!-TREAT                                       C:EVIDENCE    DIAGNOSIS
PT-1: Relaxation, muscle stretching --    10  ══════════ Memo Window ══════════
                                              There are some sharp role
#-MOTIVE     #-EVAL       #-PAIN     #-PROG   divisions here. The MD has
PT-3: He's well motivated and he's ready  12  opened the progress staffing,
  to get better.  I think he's tired of   13  and asked for information on
  the life style that he's been living.   14  physical therapy, which is
  He's shown -- (------) pain slips       15  immediately offered by the
  steadily decreasing (-----).            16  PT's.

#-DIAGNOSIS                                   However, the MD does not
MD: Are you all clear on what the final   18  acknowledge the information,
  physical diagnosis was for him. You     19  and proceeds onward to
  know, we were questioning the spinal    20  reiterating the previous
  cord tumor. We were questioning         21  diagnosis and patient history.
  multiple sclerosis.                     22     We need to keep looking at
                                                 the evidence-diagnosis link
#-HISTORY                                        in MD--role partner
  As you reconstruct the history, when    24     interactions.
  he fell -- this guy fell off the back   25  ═ Ln:17   Col:17    21%  Insert ═
  of his truck. The first thing that      26  F9=Reformat  F10=End Memo
 F5=Scroll Data File
```

The Ethnograph Figure 8. Writing a memo. The user has popped to the memo box from the display of coded text. At the right in this figure, the starting line (10) to which the memo will be attached has been typed in; the letter A signifies the first memo on this line. The memo applies to lines up to 38. The BY line has the author's initials. The date and time are entered automatically. The topic is typed in after RE:, and there is space for three established codes to be entered. In this case, EVIDENCE and DIAGNOSIS have been used. Then the text is typed in the memo window. At the bottom, we see how much (21%) of the available space has been used. The <F9> key will be used in a minute to reformat the memo to full flush left. To scroll the text, you have to "end" the memo with <F10>; it goes off screen. After scrolling <F5>, you can <Esc> back to the memo to write more if you want to. When the memo is complete, you "accept" the memo (another <F10>) and are popped to a list of memo titles in the current session, with starting line for each specified; a list of all memos can also be pulled up at any time, and you can see any memo immediately by choosing its title. There is no memo icon in the text.

Single-Code Searches

If you choose "single codes," you can specify a particular code, or a list of up to 100 single codes, either typing them in or picking them from your master code list. This is in effect an OR list; you'll get all the segments to which the single codes have been applied.

There's a wildcard option, which can help simulate two-level coding if you've organized your codes systematically. For this workaround, you might have a root code name used to produce several different codes—for example, TEACH-ENG, TEACH-MATH, TEACH-PHYS for teaching of various subjects. If you ask for TEACH-*, you'll get all the segments with these codes. Wildcards are also usable in multiple-code searches.

Multiple-Code Searches

The other option is "multiple codes" (confusingly named, because the list of "single codes" is in fact a multiple OR search). What the label means is codes that in *combination* apply to a segment. With this option, you can compose expressions with up to five codes linked by AND or NOT, in sequence. (You can list up to 20 such expressions at a time; the program retrieves all of them; the different expressions are treated as though they're connected by OR.) In a next step, you can look at the results involving just one search request if you wish.

Parenthetical expressions are not supported; if you ask for segments with requests like CODE1 and CODE2 but not CODE3 and CODE4, the program just looks for segments that include CODE1, CODE2, and CODE4, but not CODE3. With any multiple AND search expression, you get segments that have all the codes in the expression attached; the segments may be identical, overlapping, or nested (see below).

However, the presence of a list of search expressions lets you mix AND and OR to approximate some parenthetical expressions. You can specify an AND expression, say CODE1 AND CODE2, and follow it on the list with another AND expression, say, CODE3 AND CODE4; this would be the equivalent of (for example) (CODE1 AND

```
Code:     1 PROBLEM                                                    Marked:NO
File: CASE42            Display: All Segs      For: All Codes    For: All Files
CASE42    MD              + EARL MICHAELS - PROGRESS STAFFING

E: $-PAT REVIEW

SC: PROBLEM

#-PROBLEM
  Okay, he's got some musculoskeletal        6 -#  |
  problems. What are you doing in            7 -#  |

Ctrl-PgDn=Next  Ctrl-PgUp=Prev    F2=Print   F5=Display   F6=Mark    ESC=Quit
```

The Ethnograph Figure 9. Search results for a single code. The user has chosen to see all segments, for all codes in the list specified, for all files. This is the first (and as it turns out, the only) hit for the code PROBLEM. The "E:" shows that the code PAT REVIEW has a nested or overlapping relationship with code PROBLEM (see Figure 5). "SC" specifies the search request—in this case, PROBLEM as a single code, and the actual lines covered by the code, without additional context, are displayed. The functions at the bottom let the user scroll to other hits (if any), to print this hit, to change the display to show all segments, or only those for a specific code or file, or only those that have been marked. <F6> marks this hit (for later search, display, or printing); at the upper right, you see that this segment has not been marked. All the display options show hits one by one.

CODE2) OR (CODE3 AND CODE4). NOT operators can be folded in too.

You can also ask for multiple codes by sequence (CODE2 following CODE1), but the sequence search was not working in the beta-test copies. For a proximity search, you specify the number of lines between applicable segments, which can range from 0 to 9999—that is, the whole file.

As we've noted, The Ethnograph's face-sheet and speaker-sheet capabilities are good. They can be used as search filters (with logical operators EQUAL, OR, NOT), or numeric operators including =, < >, or a range of variable values to select a portion of your database, either alone or with codes. And up to six values for face-sheet data and six for speaker-sheet data can be listed with your output, thus enlarging your source-tag information. Note: Speaker-sheet information (which specifies a series of applicable variables) and speaker-*identifier* information (which is merely a label) cannot be used in the same filtering operation. That's not a serious limitation; it just means that you can't select a batch of speakers by identifiers and then refine the selection with speaker-sheet variables—or vice versa.

Display of Hits

However, what you get from a code search is unfortunately very limited (see Figure 9). For any single-code search, you get precisely the lines, with their numbers, to which the codes were attached, without added context. You can expand the context for any given hit for up to 10 lines by hitting <F3> and specifying the number of lines. But The Ethnograph does not remember this information for other hits you are looking at. Furthermore, when you try to print the expanded segment, it doesn't work—you only get the original contextless hit.

You do get source-tag information: the code you asked for, the filename, the current contextual comment, and the speaker/section identifier. The names of other codes that overlap, coincide, or nest with the requested code are shown. You can scroll from hit to hit, but you only see one hit at a time on screen, without context, unless you ask to expand it for that hit. Each one has a number showing you its sequence in the hits for that code, but you never know (until the end) how many hits there are. The developer says a count of hits is available, but it did not appear in the beta-test versions we saw. You can send everything to

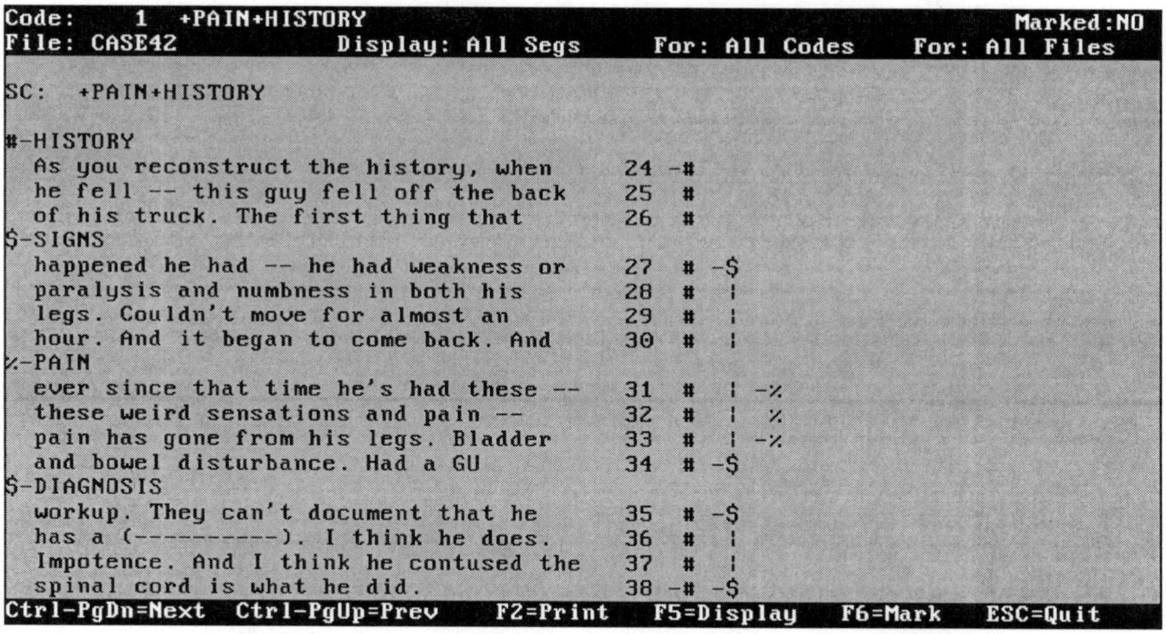

```
Code:     1  +PAIN+HISTORY                                              Marked:NO
File: CASE42              Display: All Segs      For: All Codes     For: All Files

SC:  +PAIN+HISTORY

#-HISTORY
  As you reconstruct the history, when       24 -#
  he fell -- this guy fell off the back      25  #
  of his truck. The first thing that         26  #
$-SIGNS
  happened he had -- he had weakness or      27  # -$
  paralysis and numbness in both his         28  #  |
  legs. Couldn't move for almost an          29  #  |
  hour. And it began to come back. And       30  #  |
%-PAIN
  ever since that time he's had these --     31  #  | -%
  these weird sensations and pain --         32  #  |  %
  pain has gone from his legs. Bladder       33  #  | -%
  and bowel disturbance. Had a GU            34  # -$
$-DIAGNOSIS
  workup. They can't document that he        35  # -$
  has a (----------). I think he does.       36  #  |
  Impotence. And I think he contused the     37  #  |
  spinal cord is what he did.                38 -# -$
Ctrl-PgDn=Next  Ctrl-PgUp=Prev    F2=Print   F5=Display   F6=Mark   ESC=Quit
```

The Ethnograph Figure 10. The "Big Picture" display for a multiple code search. Here the user has asked for all instances where the codes PAIN and HISTORY coincide on any lines. You see the full application of HISTORY (lines 24-38) and the nested application of PAIN (lines 31-33). The "Small Picture" display would show you only the actual intersection (lines 31-33).

printer or disk, or just the hit on screen. As you browse through the hits, you can also mark particular ones you want to be sent to printer or file.

For a multiple-code AND search, which will normally bring you overlapping and nested codes, or a proximity result, you can see a bit more. There are two options: the "Small Picture" and the "Big Picture." The Small Picture is indeed small—you only see the actual lines that include both codes, without further context, as usual. If you ask for the Big Picture (Figure 10), you will see the full segments that overlap or nest (still, however, without any larger context unless you request it).

The documentation points out that if you are doing code frequency counts and use the Big Picture when two coded segments (say they were both coded with CODE2) are nested within or overlap another coded segment, named CODE1, the program counts only the first example of CODE2.

The documentation has a helpful section making overlaps and nesting very clear, and describing how you may get "false positives" and "false negatives" when CODE1 ends on a line and CODE2 starts on the same line.

You can also ask for "summaries," which are simply the code applications: code name, start and stop lines, filename, and cumulative count (Figure 7). And you can get frequency counts and percentages, both within a file and/or across several files. Thus you can in effect get all the data you need for a crosstab, of which the rows might be files (e.g., TIME1, TIME2) and the columns might be codes (CODE1, CODE2, CODE3) appearing in those files. The program will show you frequencies and compute both column and row percentages, as in any contingency table. Note: The Ethnograph does *not,* however, export the data to statistical packages—you have to do that by hand. (See the "Update" section.)

During any particular searching session, as you ask for new single or combined codes, the program first shows you what the previous search request(s) were. You can either wipe them out, revise them, or add the new request(s) to the list. If you do the latter, you could use this as a workaround to produce a quasi-log—a record of all the search expressions used, up to a total of 20. *But*, because it's an OR list, the program will look for and find *all* the segments for *all* prior search expressions; to get your most recent one, you have to cycle through all the output until you come to the most recent request. (You can, of course, delete all the prior search expressions if you want to simplify life, but then you've lost your quasi-log.) *In any case,* there is *no* log saved when you exit the search module, unless you print the search list (there doesn't seem to be a way to save it to disk).

An annoying feature is that you specify the code names on one screen, then are jumped to the next screen to specify a sequence or proximity search. Then you can no longer see the names of the codes you are searching for. If your short-term memory is not so hot, or you get distracted, you may be in trouble as you try to remember which one was listed first and which second. You can, however, <Esc> back to the Multiple Code screen, then hit <F10> to return to the coding options—or print the search list. But all that is more time consuming than it should be.

Output

You can choose data output to screen, printer, or disk. You can print all or part of unnumbered, numbered, or coded data files, and send a "generic" (ASCII) file to disk. Remember that search outputs are printed without context—even if you've expanded the context while viewing a hit—and appear just as they initially do on screen.

Theory Building

Although the developer usefully characterizes qualitative analysis as including three basic activities ("noticing interesting things in your data, marking those things with code words, and retrieving those things for further analysis"), The Ethnograph is not at all strong in its support for *thinking* about coded and collected information. If the search facility for multilevel coding is added, that will be a plus.

Meanwhile, the only support for theory building is the memoing facility. It's helpful that you can show a list of memos, and sort it, but the memo file cannot be searched by code (except for "memo codes" that you assigned when you wrote the memo in the first place) or by string. Furthermore, there is no icon in the coded text to signal that a memo is attached at a particular point.

User Friendliness

Version 4.0 of The Ethnograph isn't hard to learn. The documentation (it is not yet a manual) is clear and straightforward; the explanation of line-level coding is one of the clearest we've seen. Though the program has 22 different file types, each is clearly described for you in the documentation, with suggestions about how to manage the database. You do have to remember filenames (i.e., what you called your master code list, the codebook, your catalogs, and so on), though the program does supply you with a pick list. The filename complexity could cause problems for you if you wanted to work on your data in the field or at home on another computer; it's not always easy to copy your database onto diskettes correctly.

The menus work well, by and large; it's usually easy to Esc back when you want to get out of something. However, there are very few help screens; we only found one that was working, and it only listed a series of commands.

For most operations (coding, searching), you specify actions, then are asked to "accept" them (by hitting F10); thus if you have made a mistake, you can always correct it first. You're always warned if your files are not set up right or if a disk has insufficient space left. Error messages are clear and are further explained in the documentation, with possible causes and solutions.

Technical support is supplied on the phone by the developer, who was quickly responsive to specific questions raised.

The quick tour is clearly laid out; it takes a Level 3 person only an hour or so. It goes through the basics of importing files, coding and searching, using a one-page data file—though it does not cover the important details of memoing, face sheets, or speaker sheets.

Part of user friendliness is ease of use once learned. Though the program is certainly not hard to use, the interface has a kind of awkwardness (e.g., the repeated need to specify files and output/display options, the need to shift between different modules) that uses more energy than it should.

Miscellaneous

There is a workable file manager, which lets you change or create directories, view lists of files, scroll in a file, and select, copy, rename, or delete files. You can also select certain categories of files (data files, coded files, face-sheet files, output files, and so on). It's accessible from the opening menu or from any filename entry screen (your first step when you are coding, searching, printing, or doing almost any other task). It can handle 2,700 files (more than this and you lose the Copy, Delete, and Rename functions), but note that each data file may have as many as 10 program-generated files associated with it (for codes, speaker identifiers, line numbering, and so on). Thus for practical purposes the upper limit for text files in any one directory is something like 270. (The Ethnograph can only work with 200 text files at a time, in any case.) The viewing window displays only 72 files, but you can see the remainder when you need to.

The documentation keeps saying that special files (e.g., the master code lists or templates for face-sheet data) are stored in a subdirectory called ethno4\stuff, but this did not happen. There are bugs (e.g., you can't escape from memoing except by "accepting" a blank memo; if you want to print several retrieved segments, you only get one at a time).

Instructions for conversion of codebooks, catalogs, and memo files prepared with Version 3.0 are included in the documentation; these and the occasional references to floppies as storage sites are naturally aimed at the upgrade audience of 3.0 users.

Update

In the past, the developer has supported a newsletter for registered users called *Cut and Paste*; this may resume when Version 4.0 is ready. A training video suitable for site licenses and classroom use is contemplated, though there will not be a demo version of The Ethnograph.

Version 4.0 was expected to be released after January 1995. Sequence searching is promised for it but is not yet working in either beta-test version we saw. A systematic procedure for backing up all levels of file (text, coded text, memos, catalogs, codebooks, and so on) is being implemented for 4.0—a definite plus for research team use as well as a protection for the single user. A Windows version is also being explored.

Comparative Remarks

Compared with other code-and-retrieve programs, Version 4.0 fares moderately well. It's better than almost any other program at showing your codes as they apply to text. It's better put together and easier to use than QUALPRO or AQUAD. Its coding capabilities are better than those of QUALPRO, though less flexible than HyperRESEARCH's. It has good face-sheet and speaker-sheet capability.

However, its setup for searching, though simpler than AQUAD's, is weaker than Kwalitan's. Kwalitan is stronger for those taking a reflective, grounded-theory approach, doesn't require preformatting or line-level coding, and has more data capacity, along with a hierarchical code outline. Its ease of use is similar. The Ethnograph completely lacks the data-linking capacity of HyperQual2 and HyperRESEARCH. In thinking about choosing The Ethnograph, you should also compare it with ATLAS/ti and NUD•IST, which keep you much closer to the meaning of your data, have strong theory-building features in addition to their basic code-and-retrieve functions, and are much more intuitive and user friendly.

Summary

Version 4.0 of The Ethnograph, when it appears in user-ready form, will be a fairly sturdy, straightforward program designed for doing line-level coding, showing you your coded text, and retrieving coded segments. Despite some residual stiffness from Version 3.0 and an awkward interface, it's relatively easy to learn. Its substantial improvements over Version 3.0—the on-screen coding, memoing, editing, and the code master list—will make it attractive to existing 3.0 users. Others may agree with our assessment: Despite the struggle to catch up with the features of other programs, The Ethnograph isn't wholly there yet. Still, Version 4.0, when it appears, looks like a sensible choice for researchers who are devoted to line-level coding, can accept the rather limited search-and-retrieval facilities, and do not mind the interface.

References

Miles, M. B., & Huberman, A. M. (1994). *Qualitative data analysis: An expanded sourcebook* (2nd ed.). Thousand Oaks, CA: Sage.

Seidel, J. V. (1991). Method and madness in the application of computer technology to qualitative data analysis. In N. G. Fielding & R. M. Lee (Eds.), *Using computers in qualitative research* (pp. 107-116). Newbury Park, CA: Sage.

Seidel, J. V., & Clark, J. A. (1984). The Ethnograph: A computer program for the analysis of qualitative data. *Qualitative Sociology, 7*(1-2), 110-125.

Seidel, J. V., Kjolseth, R., & Seymour, E. (1988). *The Ethnograph: A user's guide (version 3.0).* Amherst, MA: Qualis Research Associates.

Tesch, R. (1990). *Qualitative research: Analysis types and software tools.* New York: Falmer.

7

Code-Based Theory-Builders

In this chapter, we turn to programs that take a next step beyond those we've just looked at. They too (except for one program, QCA) can do code-and-retrieve operations effectively, but they have structures and functions that provide assistance in building and testing theory as well. They help you to develop categories and outlines, extending your coding scheme; to annotate your data, write memos, and link these to your codes; to formulate and test propositions or hypotheses; and sometimes to see graphical representations of the relationships among your concepts. They're often organized around a formal system of rules or logic.

Other programs that overlap significantly with this category, and the chapters they are reviewed in, include the following:

□ □ □

AQUAD 4.01

Available for DOS

Günter L. Huber[1]
University of Tübingen
Department of Pedagogical Psychology
Münzgasse 22-30
D-72070 Tübingen, Germany

Phone: 49-7071-292113
Fax: 49-7071-294954
E-mail: 100115.230@compuserve.com

Price: $195

Hardware Requirements:

- IBM PC: any
- DOS 2.0 or better
- Hard disk with 1.2MB free
- 640K RAM

Overview

AQUAD, named for "Analysis of Qualitative Data," is designed to supplement a basic code-and-retrieve facility with other modules that help you build theory: creating second-level codes, memoing, building of text matrices, testing of hypotheses about code co-occurrence in text, and doing cross-case configural analysis (like the QCA program) as a way of looking at causality. It also contains some content-analytic features: counts as well as retrieval of keywords in context.

It's written as a descendant of an earlier program, QUALOG (Shelly & Sibert, 1985). Though its menus are clear, and it's much less narrow and rigid than, say, QUALPRO or MECA, its interface with the user is sometimes awkward (e.g., difficulty in writing more than a very brief memo, clumsy shifting from screen to printer output). However, version 4.01 is much easier to use than the old 3.0. Its basic structure is that of a series of modules accessed through a shell; as you exit a module, your work is automatically saved to a file with a certain module-specific file extension. Mostly you can only work in one module at a time.

1. U.S. distribution and technical support is by Qualitative Research Management, 73425 Hilltop Road, Desert Hot Springs, CA 92240. Phone: (619) 329-7026.

If you specifically want its theory-building features, AQUAD may be useful to you, but don't expect the flexibility and ease of, say, ATLAS/ti, HyperRESEARCH, or NUD•IST. It claims to be usable both for inductive, grounded-theory and deductive, hypothesis-testing approaches, but its narrowness makes it difficult to do the former easily and intuitively. Its claims to test hypotheses rest largely on the co-occurrence of codes within a specified distance of each other, rather than on actual causal connections. AQUAD also works somewhat abstractly, at a distance from your text data (e.g., its searches bring you line numbers rather than actual text). Its search capabilities as such are limited. However, its implementation of configural analysis is more user friendly than that in QCA.

This review is based on the 3.0 manual, and the 4.01 version of the program, which has a number of new features not explained in the old manual but partially described in on-line help screens. Some features of version 4.03, just available as we revised this, are discussed as we go. An updated manual was expected in the fall of 1994.

The developer has also written a number of helpful articles about AQUAD. Huber and Marcelo Garcia (1991, 1993) provide an overview of the program and illustrate its use well with a study of student teachers; Huber (1992) describes the analytical assumptions AQUAD is built around (categorization, distance analysis, matrix display, configuration analysis), with illustrations from the same study.

Database Structure

AQUAD works with basic ASCII text files, a number of which you can organize in a "catalog"—a useful concept shared by several programs (Orbis, Kwalitan, WordCruncher, The Ethnograph, and so on); you can work with all the files for several persons, or for one or several research sites, or for specified time periods, and so on. The easiest way in AQUAD is to consider each file as a case—multiple files per case are more difficult to manage well. AQUAD works with the file as the basic unit, and codes and retrieves information on a line-by-line basis.

It's possible to specify temporary, partial, or new catalogs as you go—you just have to tell AQUAD exactly *which* catalog (with its extension, .NAM) you want to be working in. Once you start working in a catalog, AQUAD treats it as a default, to be returned to whenever you switch to a new module. Unless you skip to particular files within the catalog, AQUAD just assumes you want to work on all the files in the catalog, in order.

Your basic text files must each have the same five-character label, with a unique numbered extension (thus a file of interviews might be called INTER.001, INTER.002, and so on). (Note that those constraints limit your ability to give meaningful filenames, which often help you in keeping track of and sorting data.) From these text files, AQUAD's various modules produce the following six kinds of output files, each with its own unique file extension. (It's a good idea for you to know these when using AQUAD, because you are sometimes asked for the file extension.)

(.NUM) line-numbered data files
(.COD) lists of code applications (i.e., index)
(.COL) lists of code applications, sorted by line number
(.COA) lists of code applications, sorted alphabetically
(.MEM) memo files
(.TCO) line-numbered data files with codes attached

(In version 4.03, .TCO files exist only as "virtual" files, created "on-the-fly" when you need to code, view, or print line-numbered, coded files; they are never saved to disk. This move saves storage space; see below.)

Like many other programs, AQUAD indexes your files and then searches the index; your text files remain untouched. For 4.01 you need three to four times the space occupied by your original ASCII files. The developer says that use of the "virtual" .TCO files in 4.03 keeps space requirements to twice your original files (assuming that you store them somewhere else). The 4.03 program can handle 1,000 files of up to 500KB each in size.

There appears to be a facility for handling off-line data; in the coding module, you tell AQUAD you do *not* want to work with "transcriptions," and the program locks you out from accessing text files, a feature designed to keep the program from crashing if you asked it to code an off-line nontext file. However, the details of off-line work are not explained.

Data Entry

There's an initial "setup" module that lets you choose the length of codes (see below) and whether you want to be able to exit temporarily to DOS and return. You're also asked to say what the default output device will be (screen, printer, file). You can change your mind from this default as you work within each module, but if (for example) you see something on screen, you cannot then print it immediately but have to exit the module, change the default to printer or file, and then repeat the analysis—an annoying process. (There is also a bug when printing, which kicks you out of the program to the DOS prompt, even though printing does proceed.)

You produce text files with your word processor, convert them to pure ASCII, and give each one a main name and unique numbered extension. As noted above, you can only have five characters in the filename, because AQUAD adds other characters later. (For example, a basic file IN-

TER.001, when line-numbered, would be called INTER001.NUM, and so on.)

You also need to leave enough margin at the right so that you can type in codes and very brief comments (mini-annotations, in effect) in the margin later on. The suggestion is to have text lines no longer than 48 characters (this permits use of up to 10 three-character codes per line, or comments occupying a similar space).

You can edit your data within AQUAD (and indeed your data files after AQUAD has added line numbers and you have added codes); there's function-key support for simple word processing functions (string search and replace, copy, move, delete); you can also work in and/or copy from a second document. *However,* as with most line-numbered programs, once AQUAD has inserted line numbers and the codes are in place, any editing you do that changes line numbering will automatically mess things up, because the codes apply to the *line numbers,* not to specific text. Thus editing and revision of your basic text files should be completed at the front end, so that paragraph breaks, speaker identification, and so on are just as you want them.

After you've built text files, the setup module also lets you create one or more catalogs; you type in the filenames you want included in your named catalogs. (Later you can use it to choose among catalogs as well.)

Version 4.03 includes a subprogram for converting AQUAD version 3.0 files for current use.

Working on the Data

The default length of codes is three characters, presumably so you can get several codes on a line. But this is terribly limiting, forcing you toward abstract, thin code names rather than easily meaningful ones. You can set code length to any number of characters you like, but the length must be standard; if you use eight characters as your code length, all your codes must have eight characters—an annoying limitation. Say a code is CONFLICT, and you want to also have a code POWER. You will either have to call it POWER_, or POWERXXX, or POWER (followed by three spaces) to fill up the eight characters. Otherwise, you get an error message until it's fixed. (In 4.03, you can select a "longer codes" option, and AQUAD will fill up the empty spaces with a row of asterisks.) Note that the question of code length interacts with how much room you've left in the right margin (assuming that you want to avoid line wraps) and whether you expect to do a lot of multiple coding of segments.

AQUAD lets you work with one-step (on-screen) or two-step (with hard copy) coding. To do *one-step coding,* you tell AQUAD you want to work with "transcriptions" and ask AQUAD to number the lines of the files in the catalog you'll be coding. Then you ask for a numbered set of files. You'll be popped into the first file, where you can scroll around and apply codes by typing them in. (See Figure 1.) At the end of the line where you want a code application to begin, you type "[codename-," followed by up to four digits signifying the line number where you want the code application to end. Depending on your available space, you can add other code names.

For example, [CONFLICT- 22 [POWERXXX- 19 would apply code CONFLICT from the current line to line 22, and code POWERXXX from the current line to line 19. As with most line-by-line coding programs, code applications can thus overlap or be nested—but they can't apply to irregular blocks starting in the middle of lines. That limitation, the standard code length, and the space limitations make AQUAD's coding paradigm less than strong.

AQUAD deals with the problem of "header" information for a file by asking you to choose and assign certain codes, such as MALE, TEACHER, HISTORY (which would have to be rendered as something like MALE,TEAC,HIST if you'd specified four characters as the standard code length) only once to a file.

An interesting feature is that you can use numeric codes—for example, if you enter /a40, it can stand for age 40—however, there is no easy way to compute means or other statistics from these "numbers" within AQUAD; the developer says that he deliberately avoided including a computational module. With heavy technical help, the numerical codes can be converted to integers in the "linkage" module (see below under "Theory Building") and treated algebraically, but that's not really useful if you want to see a frequency distribution of ages. There's a feature called "semiautomatic" coding, but it isn't really anything more than a search for strings in the text; when you get there, you still have to type a code in the margin as usual.

You can add brief annotations to code applications, also as in Figure 1. However, the code(s), annotation, and ending line number(s) should for convenience fit within your margin limits; otherwise, they will wrap to the next line (the page numbering of your text is not altered). That has no serious consequences, other than throwing off the paging of your printing. The annotations will be displayed in file printout or search results, but cannot themselves be searched for.

You can exit from coding and return later to make additions or revisions without difficulty.

To do *2-step coding,* you tell AQUAD you want to use transcriptions (the default), after having marked up a hard copy of your line-numbered text with the usual brackets from starting to ending lines, and code names. Then you are asked to type in your starting and ending line numbers and the code name. Annotations can be added, and you can correct prior errors just by reentering the correct information.

The developer reports a nice feature: Coding done in either coding module (one step or working from hard copy)

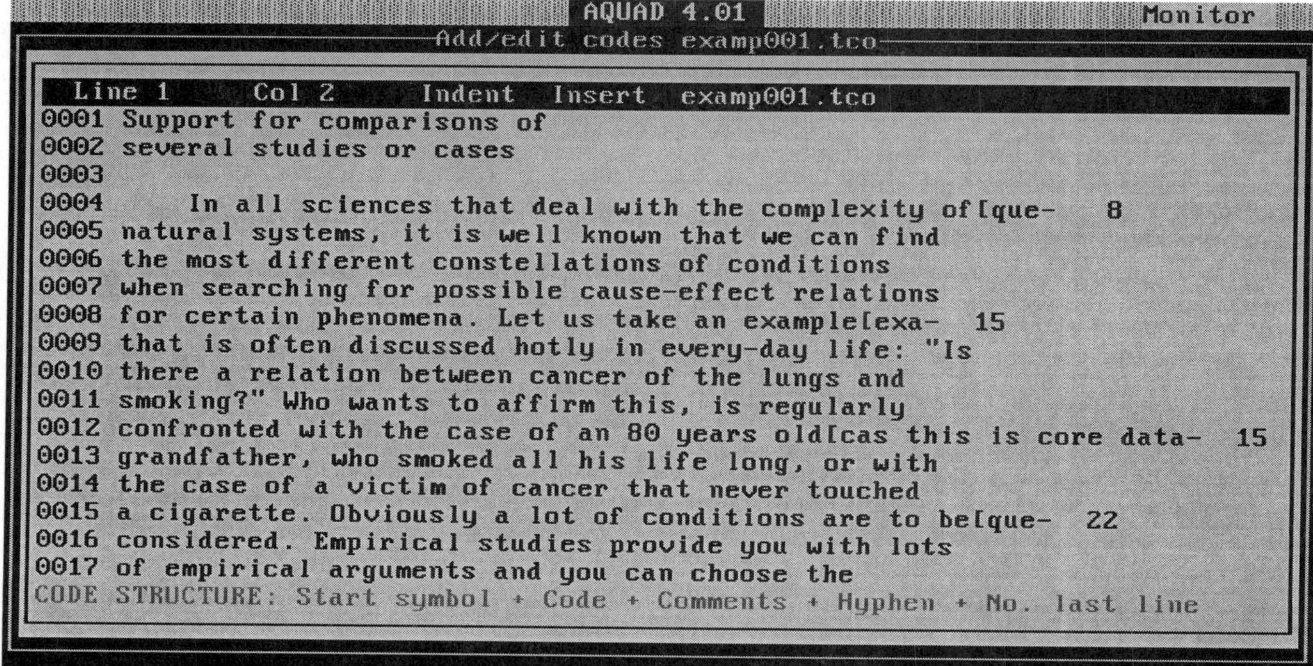

AQUAD Figure 1. Editing a text. On line 0008, the code "exa," followed by a -, is entered at the right, just after the left bracket ([). The number 15 that follows shows that the code is applied from the present line (0008) until line 0015. On line 0012, we see an example of an annotation, entered after the code "cas,"—"this is core data." If the annotation exceeds the right margin, it will wrap into the next line, but the line numbering will not be changed. The explanation of code structure at the bottom appears when editing begins but disappears thereafter. The function key list across the bottom shows the different editing functions you can perform. searching for strings, search and replace ("substitute"), copying text, moving it, deleting it, editing an external text, and copying external text into the present text.

automatically appears in the overall list of code applications (see below).

In a big improvement over version 3.0, AQUAD maintains a master code list for you; for some applications (e.g., in building matrices, or "retrieval catalogs" of codes you want to search for), it pops up in a separate window, and you can take codes from it. (It doesn't have any code definitions attached—a difficulty if you've kept the three-character default for code length.) Incidentally, in version 4.01, if you change your code length, say, from three to eight, the code list will include all the three-character codes along with the eight-character codes. This can make for some blips—for example, see the comment ("this is core data") following an old three-character code "cas" (see Figure 1, line 0012). When code length was shifted to eight characters, AQUAD just took the first five characters of the comment and added it on to the three, making a new code (called "cas this"). In 4.03, to avoid this sort of thing, you use the "longer codes" option, which in this example would fill up the five spaces with ***** and keep your comment separated from the code.

Note that when you ask AQUAD to "show codes," it gives you a list of all the code *applications*—sorted either alphabetically or by line number (Figure 2). If code POWER has been applied 12 times, you will see all 12 instances, in all files, with line numbers, along with all the other codes. You can also get a count of code and/or word occurrences.

Finally, AQUAD lets you build and edit second-level codes, called "meta-codes." To do this, working in the "coding" module, you first create a meta-code "script" by giving a name to the meta-code, then specifying how many subcodes there will be, then listing the subcode names. (In short, it's rather difficult to work upward from codes to a larger, more inclusive category, as you can in most other multilevel coding programs.) The meta-codes are not automatically linked to any particular catalog you're using, but are stored in another subdirectory. The developer says that when you want to use the meta-codes for retrieval, you copy your original codes to another subdirectory and copy the meta-codes to the usual code directory—then search and retrieve—an awkward procedure almost guaranteed to make the use of meta-codes infrequent.

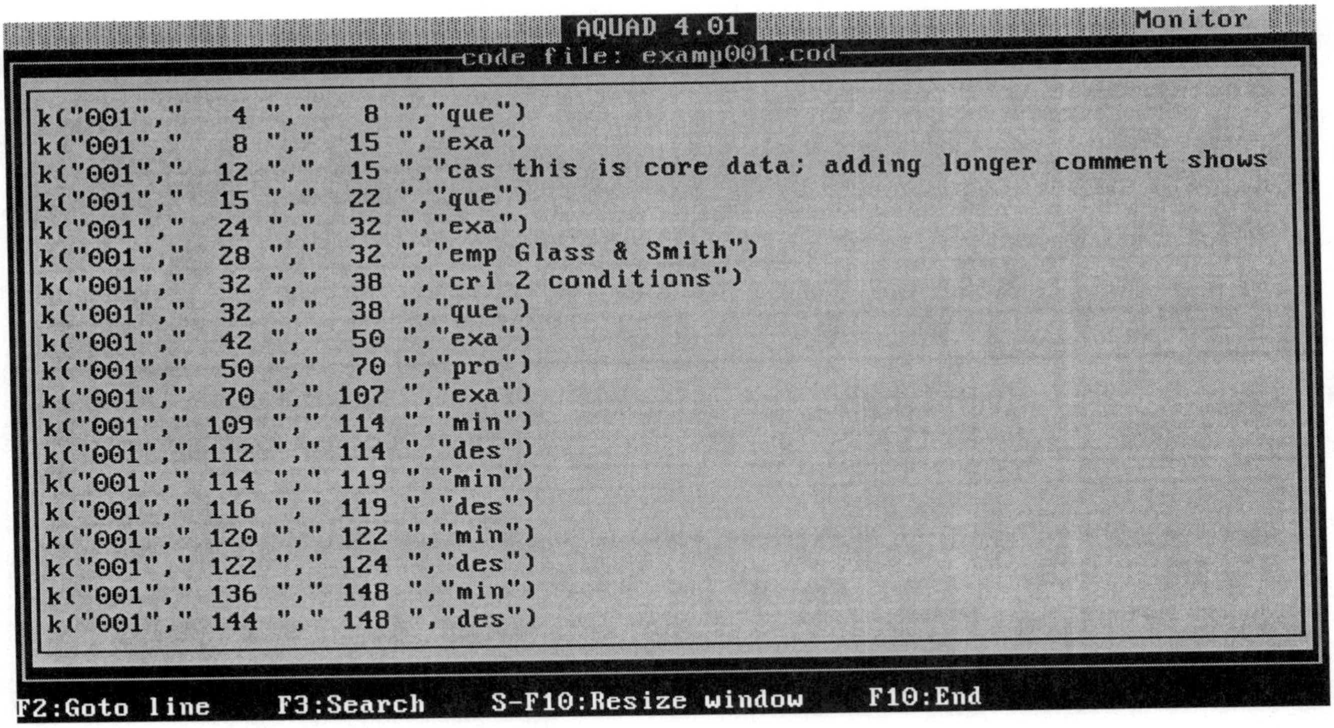

```
AQUAD 4.01                                                     Monitor
                     code file: examp001.cod
k("001","   4 ","   8 ","que")
k("001","   8 ","  15 ","exa")
k("001","  12 ","  15 ","cas this is core data; adding longer comment shows
k("001","  15 ","  22 ","que")
k("001","  24 ","  32 ","exa")
k("001","  28 ","  32 ","emp Glass & Smith")
k("001","  32 ","  38 ","cri 2 conditions")
k("001","  32 ","  38 ","que")
k("001","  42 ","  50 ","exa")
k("001","  50 ","  70 ","pro")
k("001","  70 "," 107 ","exa")
k("001"," 109 "," 114 ","min")
k("001"," 112 "," 114 ","des")
k("001"," 114 "," 119 ","min")
k("001"," 116 "," 119 ","des")
k("001"," 120 "," 122 ","min")
k("001"," 122 "," 124 ","des")
k("001"," 136 "," 148 ","min")
k("001"," 144 "," 148 ","des")

F2:Goto line    F3:Search    S-F10:Resize window    F10:End
```

AQUAD Figure 2. Code applications. The "show codes" command produces this list. K at the left means "code." "001" refers to the text file number. The next two numbers in the first row, 4 and 8, are starting and ending lines, and the last three-letter item, "que," is the code applied to those lines. An annotation in the third row ("this is core data; adding longer comment shows") is also appended but has run off the edge of the screen. (In the printed version, the remainder of the comment wraps to the next line.)

As in most search results screens in AQUAD, the bottom row shows commands that let you go to a specific line to search within the display for a particular word or number (<Shift-F3> repeats this command) and resize the window (smaller than the full size shown here).

(Going beyond second-level codes is possible, but difficult—you have to build "meta-meta" codes by writing a new meta-code script for the meta-codes—thus a meta-meta code.)

The size of code files is limited only by the boundary of 10 codes per segment. There is no maximum number of codes per file.

Searching

If you are interested in one or more codes, AQUAD will collect information on them for you. You can get all the instances of a single code (up to a total of five at one request). Figure 3 shows a request for two codes. You'll see the text segments (the lines to which codes were attached), the line numbers, the filename, and the total number of times the code appears in that file. *But* you do not see any context of retrieved segments. (You also have to accept the information on *all* files in the current catalog, unless you create a "partial" temporary catalog. That isn't made easy, because you have to decide this by filename rather than explicitly via header information.)

You can also search for a single meta-code, which will pull up all the segments with its subcodes—but this involves the awkward procedure mentioned earlier. Neither the old manual nor the very brief on-line help screen explains this for you.

Unfortunately, the program does not "know" the converse: that a specific subcode automatically belongs to its meta-code. (This is important if you want to retrieve the other subcodes belonging to the meta-code.) If you have forgotten which meta-code applies to your subcode, you can look at the meta-code script you created—but you shouldn't have to look it up. The program should do this automatically.

More-complex code searches, as always, are done in all files of the current catalog—unless you specify a partial or temporary one. The retrieval module provides a range of search options. You can get all the instances of nested or overlapping codes, or multiple codes assigned to the same

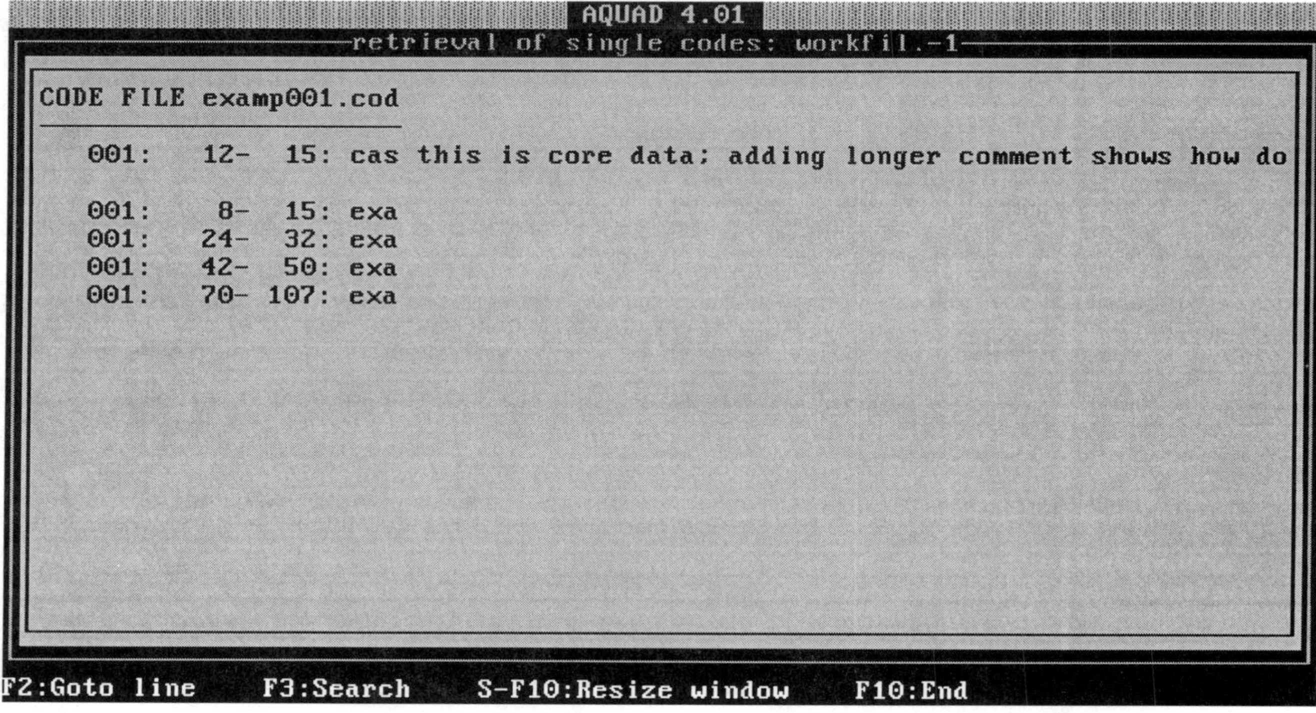

AQUAD Figure 3. A search result. The request was for instances of code "cas" or code "exa." Shown are the file ID, starting and ending lines, and the code name. An appended comment for lines 12-15 is also shown; it runs off the screen but will be shown wrapped when printed.

segments, as well as finding the actual line distances between codes. You can either work with "general" searches (e.g., all examples of all nested codes) or "specific" ones (e.g., all cases where code POWER is nested within code CONFLICT or within any other code). *Note*: You cannot do a simple AND search for two codes such as POWER and CONFLICT—you have to ask AQUAD whether they (a) overlap, (b) are nested, or (c) occupy the same segment as multiple codes. However, there's a nice feature: You can see which codes in your master list have not been used.

Note: These searches do *not* bring you the text of lines but simply the data file number, the starting/ending line numbers, and the code names (see Figure 3). You will have to look at hard copy or bring up the numbered, coded files involved to understand the substance. The feeling is thus rather abstract and distant from the meaning of the data. The developer says this is deliberate and claims that it aids conceptualizing by showing you the overall distribution of code applications, but most qualitative researchers would disagree; the meaning of qualitative data is primarily found in context rather than in disembodied counting. (The developer agrees with the latter statement—but limits his proposed solutions to the idea of warning the reader in the manual to look back at the text. Almost all other code-based programs will simply bring you the text of search hits, often in context, rather than requiring you to trudge back through hard copy; AQUAD should too.)

AQUAD will not count all words, but it will give you a count of whatever strings you set up in an "inventory." However, it's quite strict: It looks only for actual strings. If you ask for "term," as the 3.0 manual notes, you will get "terminology," "interminable," and so on. If you put a space before and after "term," you'll get the word—but miss it when it's at the end of a sentence, because there is no space before the period. The search is also case sensitive, so you wouldn't get "Term," and AQUAD won't find hyphenated strings.

You can also ask for an actual word, shown in the context for each of its occurrences (KWIC, or "keyword in context"). The normal context, however, is only the *line* the string appears in, and your output is all of the collected lines: fairly incoherent, as Figure 4 shows. The 3.0 manual says the software could be customized to change this to a larger context but doesn't explain how.

AQUAD was deliberately designed to permit the retrieval of text for insertion in matrices as an important

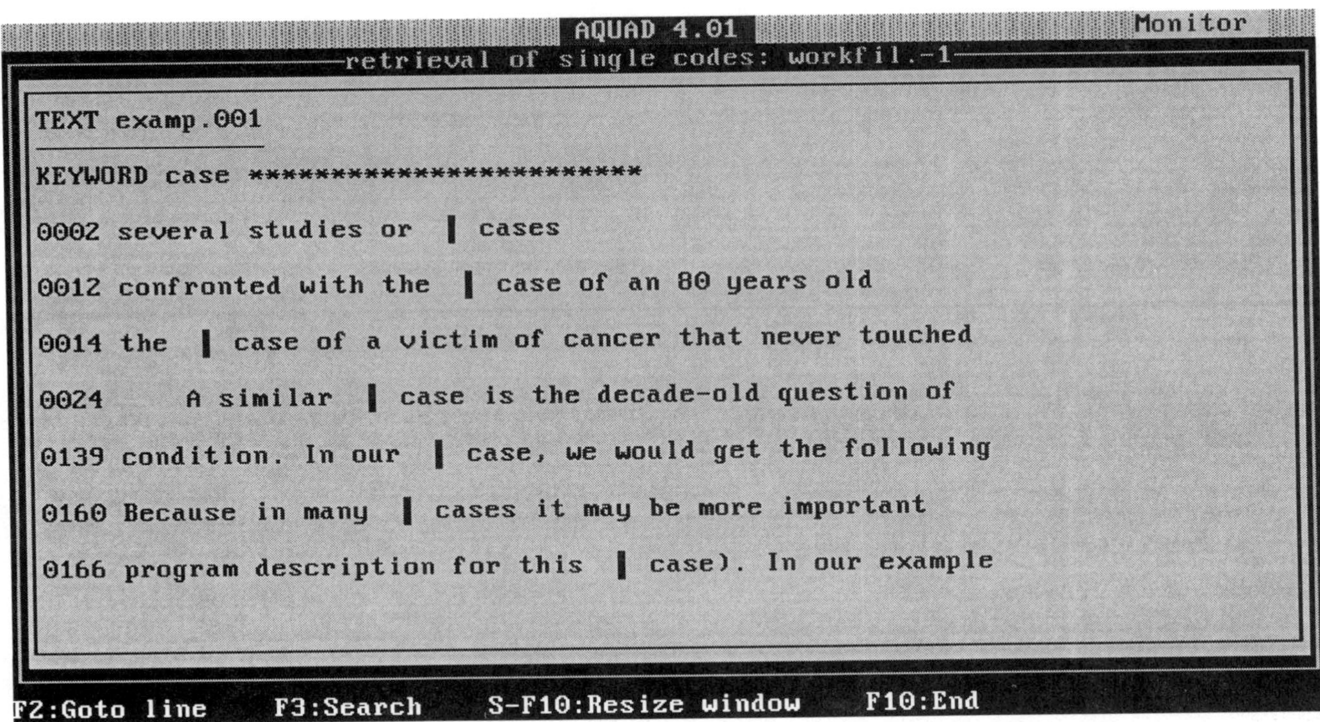

AQUAD Figure 4. A keyword in context (KWIC) search result. The word "case" has been asked for. Each line containing the keyword is displayed, with a vertical mark before the keyword. The file ID is above.

analytical strategy, and it calls this a "search." You enter the "table analysis" module and tell AQUAD the files you want to use. You then specify the codes that will define matrix columns (these must be "singular," headerlike codes that appear only once in a file). The columns are thus always *files*, and the column headers are defined as mutually exclusive (males, females, for example). Then you specify rows, using specific other codes that are applied repeatedly within files. (See Figure 5.) Rows thus bring you segments of coded text. AQUAD then works cell by cell, printing out or sending to file all the segments in all files. You see the file and line numbers (Figure 6).

To make the actual matrix, the cell printouts have to be assembled by hand on a wall or other surface—or converted to table form in your word processor. A good feature is that your matrix specifications are automatically saved and can be reused and/or edited.

It's a pleasure to see a matrix-building facility, but its limitations are serious. The displayed text chunks do not show the intersection of *codes,* but are only instances of the row codes that occur anywhere in the files you've chosen by headerlike information. Furthermore, you cannot specify rows (or columns) via combinations of codes—which you nearly always want to be able to do. So, within any given file, the facility only makes a list of different code occurrences for that file, as in Figure 6; you can't display their relationships at all, as you always want to do in within-case analysis (Miles & Huberman, 1994, chaps. 5, 6, 9).

For multiple files, you are always stuck with one column per type of file—say, males. That's also a serious limitation, because you may want to further divide males by age. Finally, when you see the text segments collected, they do *not* include codes or annotations.

Because segments are not editable, and all relevant segments from all files in the current file catalog are included, output can naturally get quite enormous. AQUAD also offers two types of reduced output. One gives you just the file numbers and the line numbers of segments. That may be useful if you've added annotations earlier (which are also displayed in this mode), but essentially it's just a sort of index rather than a real text-filled matrix. The other option is cell frequencies, which are helpful for an initial fast scan and for quantitative analysis, but this option ignores the text, which is the centerpiece of qualitative matrices. After looking at frequencies, you will still have to ask for code applications, and after that collect the text you want for your matrix.

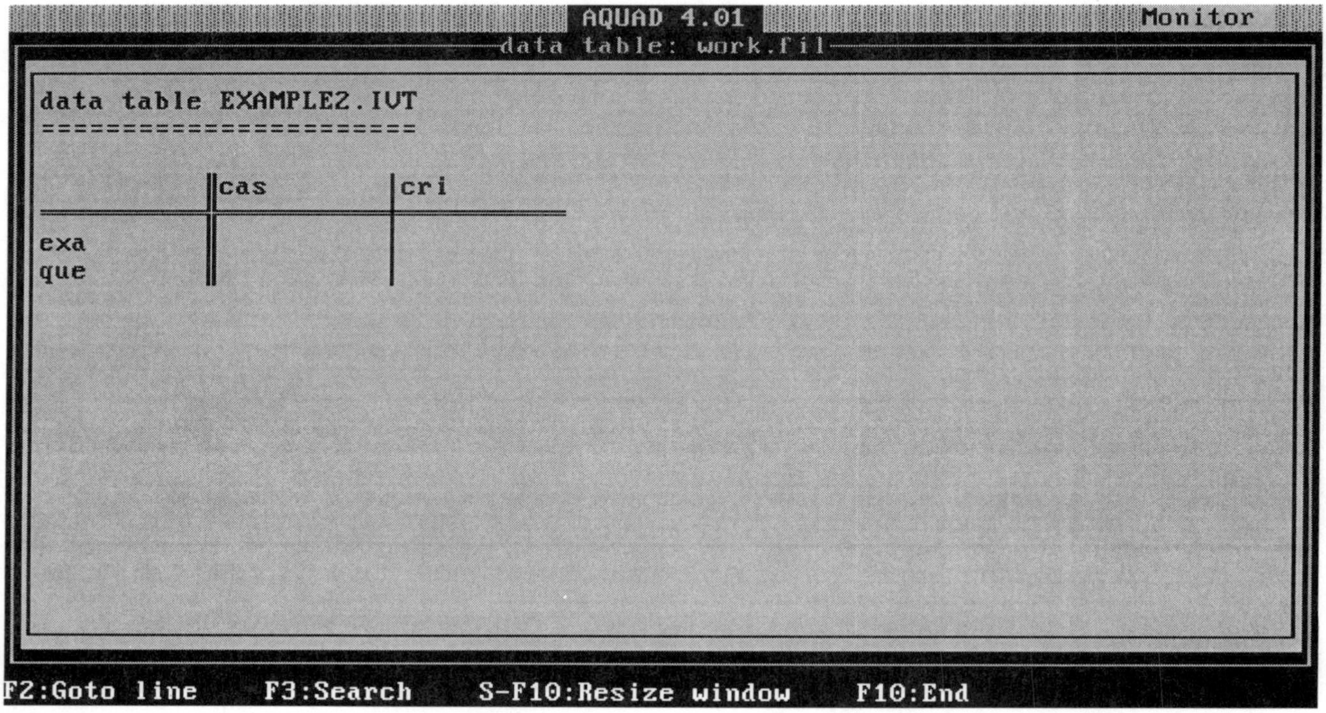

```
AQUAD 4.01                                    Monitor
                data table: work.fil
data table EXAMPLE2.IVT
=======================

              ||cas          |cri
exa           ||             |
que           ||             |

F2:Goto line    F3:Search    S-F10:Resize window    F10:End
```

AQUAD Figure 5. Specification of matrix columns and rows. The column variables are file identifiers. In this example, "cas" and "cri," which are considered header information, must have only one instance in any particular file. The file identifiers must be mutually exclusive; a given case can be "cri" or "cas," but not both. The row variables "exa" and "que" are specific codes. This table format is stored and can be reused. Figure 6 shows a section of sample output for this matrix.

Output

In the setup module, you specify a default output device, which for early work is usually the screen. When you finish coding or editing something, you always exit by hitting <F10>, which automatically saves the output to a properly named file. You can repeatedly view a piece of output (e.g., search results) if you want, but if you want to print it or send it to a particular file, you usually have to leave the analysis, reset to printer or file, then pull up the analysis again. In some cases when we did do this, the program kicked us back to the DOS prompt while printing was occurring. You get the printout, but AQUAD has to be reloaded.

Theory Building

AQUAD helps you build theory through its facilities for memoing (and brief annotation), for "hypothesis testing," and for cross-case configural analysis. (Its second-level coding and matrix-building features also contribute here.)

Annotations

This facility is limited because of the length constraint (whatever space you have left in a line after codes have been applied) and because annotations can't be searched for.

Memoing

The memoing setup is entered from the main menu. You identify the file number, the line you're writing the memo about, a relevant code, and an "index" word of your choice; you can write up to five 48-character lines (non-word-wrapped), a constraint that feels quite oppressive if you're accustomed to expansive memo writing (see Figure 7).

However, you can exceed the five-line limit by going to a new memo; AQUAD asks you for the identifier information again—you have to remember it, because the program doesn't help you. You type in the identifier information again, and write some more. The continuation of the memo through subsequent five-line portions will be displayed when you search for it. Why do things have to be this difficult?

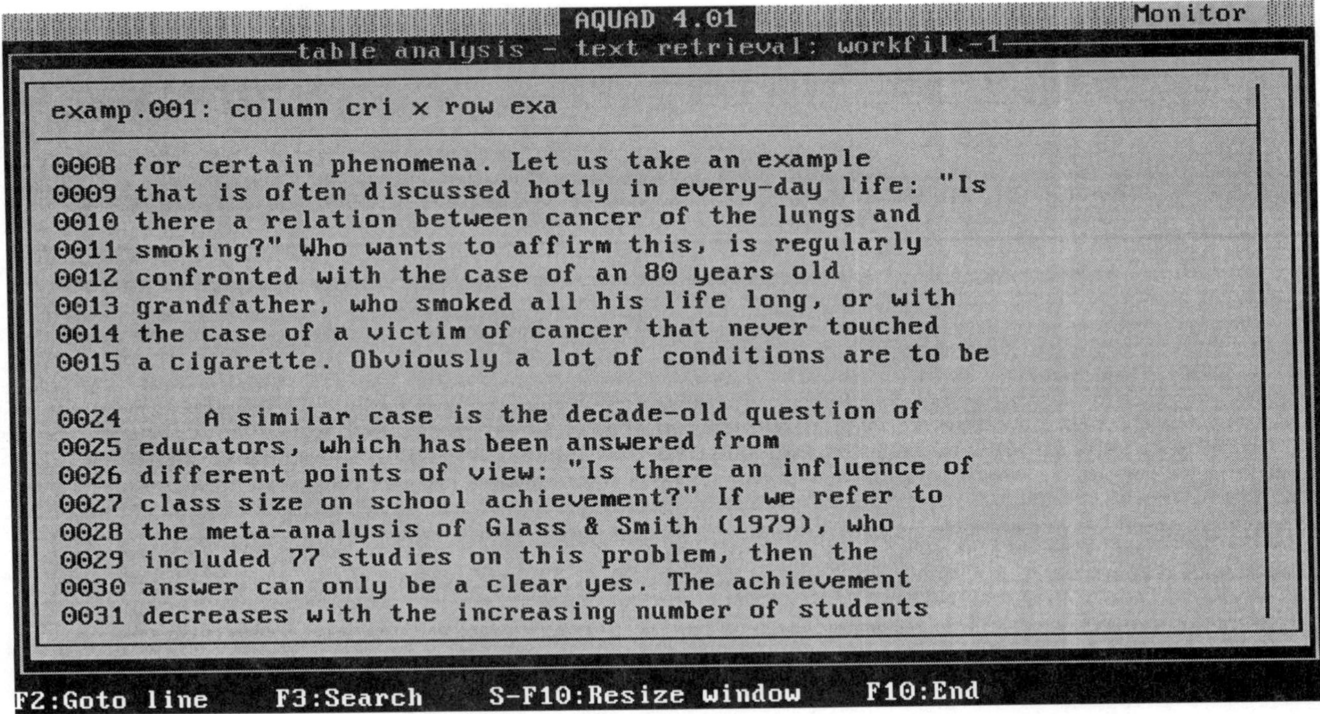

AQUAD Figure 6. Portion of output for matrix display. Shown are the first segments from file examp.001 that fall in the intersection of the column defined by the "cri" code (which is an identifier code appearing only once in the file) and the row defined by the "exa" code.

Memos are editable, either as you go or later. They are all stored for one catalog in a single file (.MEM), and they are searchable (AND, OR) via file, line number, code, or keyword. However, when you look at your coded text (.TCO) files, there is no marker showing you that a memo exists at any particular line. You'd have to do this yourself, perhaps by adding a letter M or other symbol in front of the codes for that line. A useful feature is being able to either write or retrieve memos during the two-step coding process. On balance, the memoing capabilities are adequate, but quite narrow, and not as flexible and accessible as in, say, ATLAS/ti, Kwalitan, or MetaDesign.

Hypothesis Testing

The "linkage" module is designed to let you "test hypotheses," which are essentially phrased in terms of co-occurrence of codes within text files—which, as we'll point out in a minute, is different than the co-occurrence of variables in the real world. The program includes 12 "hypotheses," as shown in Figure 8.

For example, H2 lets you ask for all instances where code 1 is followed within a specified distance (such as five lines) by code 2, plus all instances where this condition was not met. You see the results, file by file, expressed in terms of line numbers and attached codes. *Again,* for meaning beyond just counting the co-occurrences, you will have to go back to hard copy or the .TCO file to see what's happening.

Other "hypotheses" let you look at three rather than two codes, choose the sequence of codes, ask for an inclusive OR (all instances of the codes), look at nested codes (the developer says this shows a "hierarchical" structure, but a coded segment could easily be nested in another, conceptually irrelevant segment), and overlapping codes. You can also get all the codes that follow code X within a specified distance. H11 reports the number of instances of a quantitative code in the first versus the second half of the file (the example given is length of pauses in an interview). And H12 computes the "Tanimoto coefficient": the ratio of co-occurring codes A&B to the sum of A, B, and A&B—a rough coefficient of agreement that can be used in textual analyses (or in assessing coder reliability, by the way).

This list of hypotheses is based on some important assumptions: (a) that textual co-occurrence within a specified distance, or in a sequence, reflects association of the variables (codes) in the real world—an assumption open to doubt, as Richards and Richards (1994) have pointed out, and as we've said in our review of HyperRESEARCH,

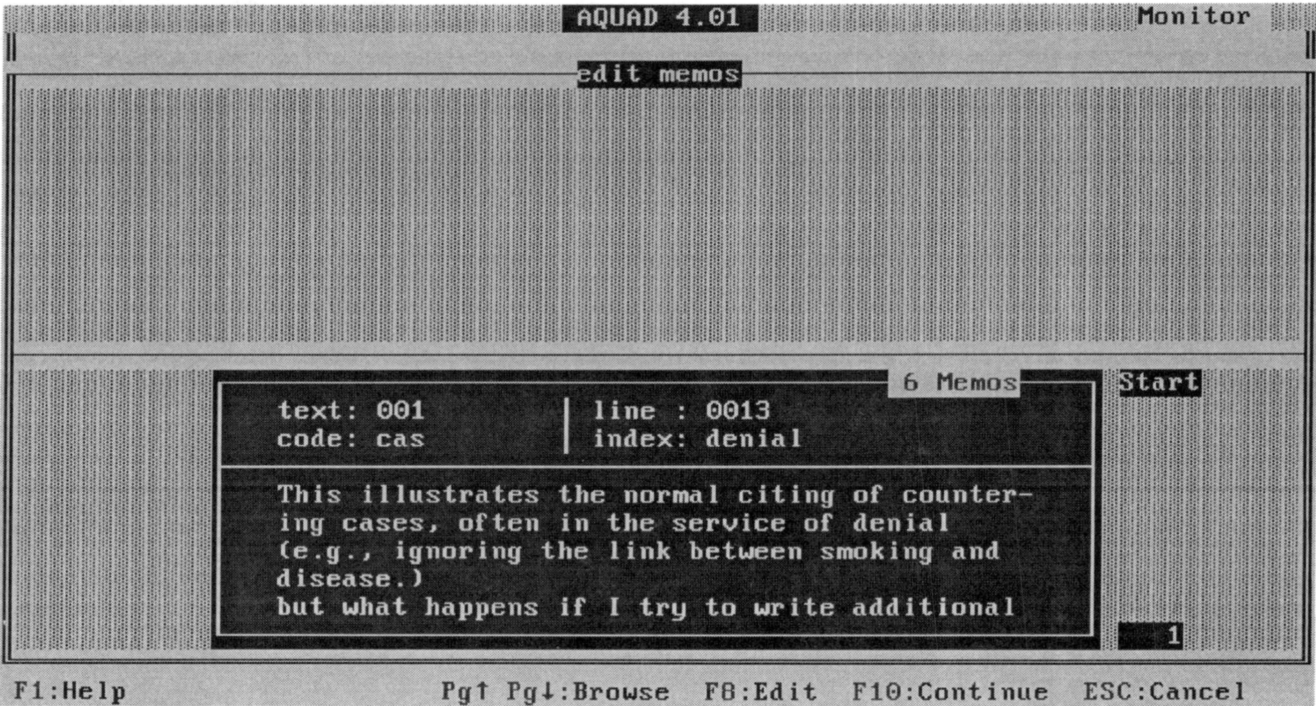

AQUAD Figure 7. Editing a memo. The researcher has typed in the ID of the text file (001), named a code to which the memo is linked and the line number involved, and optionally specified an "index"—a keyword describing the memo's content. Five lines of 48 characters have been filled. At this point, the display pops to a new blank memo form; you have to enter the same four items of information (which you must remember) to do a continuation of the memo. The total number of memos in the system is shown above.

and (b) that simple frequencies of code co-occurrence carry unambiguous meaning. If you share those assumptions, then AQUAD may be helpful, but if you don't, AQUAD does not make it easy for you to look at actual causal sequences or the meaning of your text.

Chapter X of the 3.0 manual, acknowledging that the 12 "hypotheses" are quite limited, explains how to use the programming language Turbo Prolog 1.1 or 2.0, or PDC Prolog (any of which you need to purchase separately), to design your own hypotheses, up to a working total of 20. Even a reasonable Level 3 computer user might quail at the directions for writing a source code to translate a hypothesis into instructions that AQUAD could read in its "linkages" module. (Huber & Marcelo Garcia, 1991, say that students needed 6-20 hours of training for this, although part of the time was formulating the hypotheses clearly in the first place.) Fortunately, registered users of AQUAD can get e-mail help in formulating linkage hypotheses; the developer, given your request, will send back a "linkage.exe" file for you to run, if you have the PDC Prolog programs "encode" and "decode."

Cross-Case Configural Analysis

AQUAD's final theory-building module is the "configurations" module, which, like the program QCA, lets you study how combinations of variables across a number of cases are associated with an outcome. Though it's accessed through the AQUAD shell, this module is conceptually freestanding and (in version 4.01) doesn't use output from the other modules; you have to key in the data for your cases. In 4.03 you can create data tables, importing code frequency counts produced in the "count" facility of the Retrieval module. The manual is clear but bare-bones in its description of the production of truth tables and their minimization. See also Huber (1992) for a helpful discussion of Boolean analysis as used for comparative analysis. Briefly stated, configurational analysis aims at finding patterns or configurations of variables within each of several cases and at showing how, across the cases, these patterns lead to an outcome. We won't repeat our discussion of configurational analysis here, but refer the reader to the QCA review for clarity on how configurational analysis works in detail.

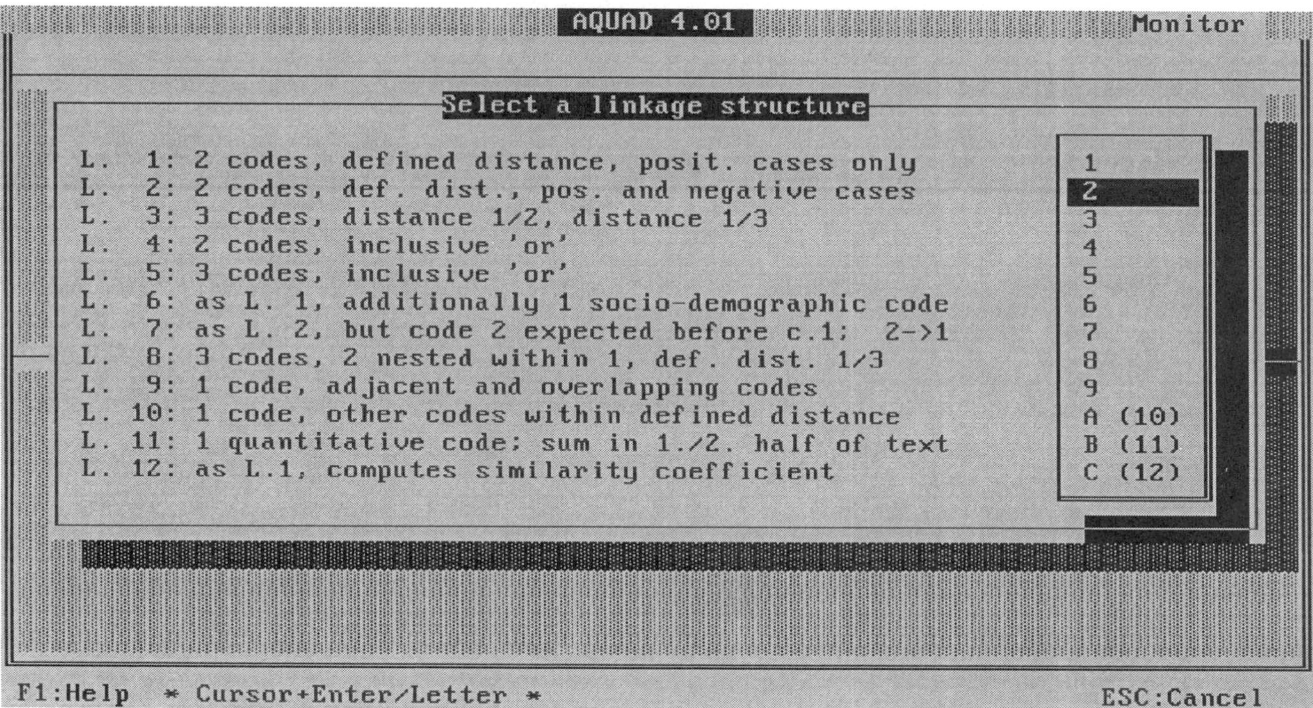

AQUAD Figure 8. Display showing a menu of standard search requests ("linkage structures"). The researcher is about to select option 2, which will produce all the segments that occur within a specified number of lines from code 1 to code 2.

Unlike QCA, which works with variable names of up to eight characters, AQUAD restricts you to single-letter variable names (A, B, C, D, and so on); these can be enlarged to four characters if you wish, but this restricted labeling remains thin—another example of AQUAD's abstractness and distance from a meaningful level of data. You can insert 9s and 1s to signify "true" and "false," or you can put in actual quantitative values for any of the variables; AQUAD will convert them later to "true" and "false" values (the standard cutoff is half a standard deviation below the standardized mean, treating roughly the lowest third of scores as "false," but you can set your own cutoffs). AQUAD, like QCA, can handle up to 12 variables, computes truth tables for your data, and minimizes them to help you find prime implicants—the patterns of variables associated with outcomes.

It's more flexible than QCA in that you can choose *any* variable in your list that you like as your dependent variable (outcome). AQUAD will also look for "secondary implicants," a set further reduced from the first prime implicant set. Like QCA, AQUAD will identify the cases involved in each prime implicant, so that you can begin to see clusters or families of cases. However, unlike QCA, it does *not* keep a log of the various steps in an analysis—you have to save the outputs to differently named files, keep track, and then call them up when you need them. This is a serious weakness (note that in QCA you can easily backtrack to any particular step, pull up the piece of analysis, and do new operations using it).

User Friendliness

The 3.0 manual is well organized and reasonably clear; it includes plenty of screen shots showing you how menus looked in that version. Working with 4.01 in the absence of an updated manual is sometimes puzzling, but it gives you a more user-friendly feeling than you have with 3.0. You can move about easily and escape out of what you are doing, and most error messages are succinct and clear. The flavor of the program is brisk and direct, and it isn't hard to learn. However, as we've noted at a number of points, it's often narrow and rigid, with frustrating use requirements (remember as one example the way you have to write longer memos).

Help screens are available only for the major modules (setup, coding, tabling, linkage, implicants, and so on); they are clear but quite general and brief. Actual run-time help (that you can use when you get stuck on something) is only available in the configuration module.

To get technical support, you phone Qualitative Research Management; minor questions are answered immediately. More-technical questions about the program are referred to the developer by QRM, and the developer calls you back.

Miscellaneous

The only substantial customization feature is the opportunity to write your own "hypotheses" using Prolog, a demanding task—but one you can get substantial technical help on, as noted. You can also change the standard number of characters in a code (though this feature seems to have a bug in 4.01) as well as the start character that signals when a code is coming (default is a "[").

Update

We've described the new features of version 4.03 along the way; the English manual for it was expected for the fall of 1994. The developer says that he expects to add a text editor to the next version to make it easy to return to text rather than just view code names and line numbers, as well as to write memos.

Comparative Remarks

We've already compared AQUAD's configurational analysis setup with that of QCA. Considering other code-based theory-builders, it's fair to say that both ATLAS/ti and NUD•IST keep you closer to your data, are more powerful in developing and applying multilevel coding schemes, and can more easily support your reflections through memoing. Both are more user friendly as well. HyperRESEARCH is also more user friendly and lets you develop and test hypotheses much more easily, though it's weaker on coding and retrieving. All three make logs of their work as they go, which AQUAD doesn't.

Summary

AQUAD was deliberately designed to go beyond code-and-retrieve to aid theory-building via annotation, memoing, testing of hypotheses about code co-occurrences, matrix building, and configural analysis. We'd consider it only moderately successful on these counts. Its limitations are mostly those of a mainframe, content-analytic heritage: the need to work in one module at a time, few multiple or linked windows, the assumption that frequency counts and distances between codes in the text are sufficient for understanding, the limited context of retrieved information, and the awkward movement between different output modes. The matrix option deserves *much* fuller, richer implementation.

Still, if you like to do line-by-line coding, want to see your coded text easily on screen with codes attached, like to think systematically and content-analytically about your data, don't worry too much about working at a more distant, abstract level, and want to do cross-case configuration analysis, it's a reasonable candidate.

References

Huber, G. L. (1992, October). *Analysis of linkages and configurations in qualitative data: Reconstruction and comparison of implicit theories.* Paper read to the International Conference on Qualitative Computing, Bremen, Germany.

Huber, G. L., & Marcelo Garcia, C. (1991). Computer assistance for testing hypotheses about qualitative data: The software package AQUAD 3.0. *Qualitative Sociology, 14*(4), 325-347.

Huber, G. L., & Marcelo Garcia, C. (1993). Voices of beginning teachers: Computer-assisted listening to their common experiences. In M. Schratz (Ed.), *Qualitative voices in educational research* (pp. 139-156). London: Falmer.

Miles, M. B., & Huberman, A. M. (1994). *Qualitative data analysis: An expanded sourcebook* (2nd ed.). Thousand Oaks, CA: Sage.

Richards, T., & Richards, L. (1994). Using computers in qualitative analysis. In N. Denzin & Y. Lincoln (Eds.), *Handbook of qualitative research* (chap. 28, pp. 445-462). Thousand Oaks, CA: Sage.

Shelly, A., & Sibert, E. (1985). *The QUALOG user's manual.* Syracuse, NY: Syracuse University School of Computer and Information Science.

Tesch, R., & Huber, G. L. (1992). *AQUAD user's manual.* Desert Hot Springs, CA: Qualitative Research Management; Tübingen, Germany: Department of Pedagogical Psychology, University of Tübingen.

ATLAS/ti, Release 1.1E

Available for DOS

Thomas Muhr[1]
Scientific Software Development
Trautenaustr. 12
D-10717 Berlin
Germany

Phone/Fax: 49-30-861-1415
E-mail: thomas.muhr@tu-berlin.de

Price: "Graded":
 Educational versus commercial
 Single user versus network
 Campus License available
Price Examples:
 Single User Commercial 650DM ($395)
 Single User Educational 440DM ($275)
 Single User Student 250DM ($165)

Hardware Requirements:

- IBM-compatible 80286 or better PC with system speed ≥ 20 MHz (386DX 40 MHz or better recommended)
- At least 4MB RAM (8MB recommended)
- VGA graphics adapter and monitor
- Hard disk with at least 2MB free space
- Mouse, Microsoft compatible
- DOS 3.0 or higher

Overview

ATLAS/ti is a powerful, well-designed, user-friendly program for coding and interpreting text. But more than that, it provides an unusually wide range of powerful tools for theory building, such as a network editor that allows you to graphically create, manipulate, and examine the logical relations (hierarchical or not) among your codes. You can also include text segments in your network views. ATLAS/ti also provides numerous options for memoing and commenting on text segments, source documents, codes, and relations. Memos can also be included in network views.

The screen display is particularly nice. ATLAS/ti calls your overall project a *Hermeneutic Unit* or *HU.* The HU editor shows you the text in the currently selected source file (*Primary Text,* or *PT*), a list of all the PTs, a list of references to all defined text segments (quotations), a list of codes, a list of memos, and the text of any memo associated with the currently selected quotation (see Figure 1, drawn from the demonstration files that come with the

1. Also available from Qualitative Research Management, 73425 Hilltop Road, Desert Hot Springs, CA 92240. Phone: (619) 329-7026.

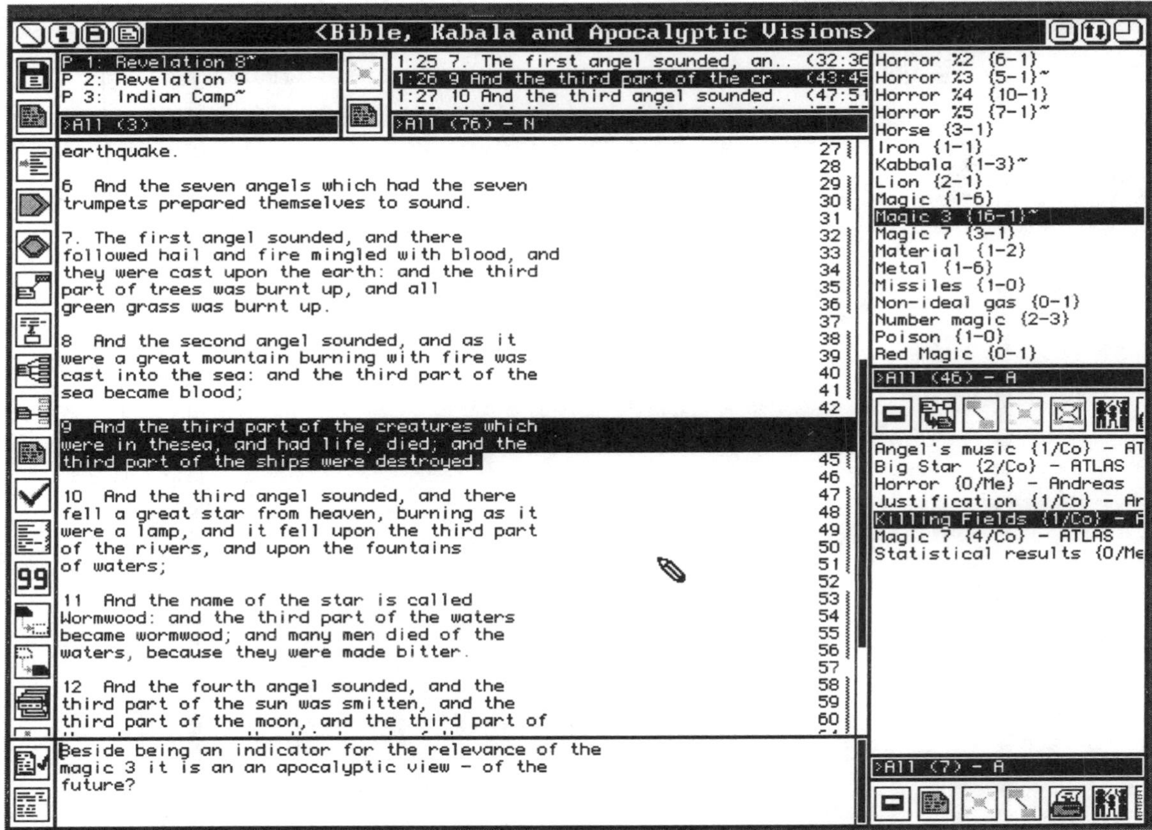

ATLAS/ti Figure 1. A sample hermeneutic unit. The major window panes are the list of primary texts, numbered P1 to P3 (top left); the list of quotations, or segments (top center), the highlighted entry (1:26) being for the twenty-sixth quotation from P1; the list of codes (top right); the list of memos (bottom right); text of the memo for the current quotation (bottom left); and the text of the current PT with the current quotation highlighted (center). Each of the list panes has the entry associated with the current quotation highlighted. Note the tildes (~) marking several of the codes and PTs, indicating the presence of comments.

program). Clicking with the mouse on a quotation reference, a code name, or a memo name highlights the associated objects, whether they are quotations, codes, or memos. ("Objects," in ATLAS/ti, refers to all the elements of the HU: PTs, quotations, codes, memos, comments, and so on.)

The display at first looks complex, but it really isn't. Commands are easily given. For most actions, there are "buttons," icons arranged in a strip, or toolbar, below or to the left of the appropriate window pane, which you click on with the mouse (see Figure 1). In addition, for all actions, there are menus associated with each pane, which you pop up by clicking with the right mouse button anywhere within the pane.

The program falls somewhat short in text retrieval and compatibility. The search routines will be adequate for many researchers and/or projects but will not be for others: Read on, then think it through. Compatibility issues include the need for Windows users to maintain separate configurations for their computers for ATLAS/ti and for everything else. This becomes a real hassle if you use a Windows word processor: To go back and forth between ATLAS/ti and your word processor, you have to reconfigure and reboot your computer each time. Note, though, that ATLAS/ti does come with utilities that let you automate the process.

Database Structure

Like HyperRESEARCH or NUD•IST, ATLAS/ti has no internal database. The data reside in separate ASCII files that you create with a word processor or text editor and that you must not delete. When you add one of these files to an HU, it is not physically imported, despite the fact that its text appears in the text window. Quotation locations are kept track of by an index of line and column numbers, so all codes and memos are referenced, not to the words in the text but to a position in the file. This means that you must be careful *not* to edit your data files: If you edit them, the same text is no longer in the same position in the file, and the wrong text is referenced.

How you distribute your data among different primary texts (PTs) is up to you. You can have as many primary texts associated with an HU as you want. PTs are only limited in *size* by the amount of RAM in your machine; the developer's recommendation is that, if you have 4MB of RAM, you should limit PTs to about 500KB each. (Just about all limits in ATLAS/ti work this way. Because it's designed to use all of your free RAM, it will let you make as big a PT as can be loaded into RAM after ATLAS/ti is already there, along with any other programs or device drivers you may have running. Only one PT is in RAM at a time, so you don't have to worry about what they add up to. The same is true of most things in ATLAS/ti, like network views, memos, comments, and so on. The reason such a low guideline is given—500KB if you have 4MB of RAM—is so you'll be less likely to get into trouble if you try to have a PT, a memo, a comment, and a network view all up on the screen at once. If you do run out of memory, you just close some things down.) The number of PTs—or other objects—you have is limited only by the space on your hard disk. Because you can filter (select which PTs are accessible to a particular process or analysis) and group PTs, you may want to organize them accordingly: such as a file for each person, interview, meeting, week, or town.

Data Entry

You create your text with a word processor or text editor that can save files in ASCII format. Because ATLAS/ti can recognize paragraphs as delimited by a blank line, you should single space your text, with a blank line between paragraphs, so you can take advantage of this feature. Also, to facilitate viewing the data in the HU editor, you should limit lines of text to about 50 characters. If you prefer to have longer lines, you can switch to a smaller font and/or change various aspects of the configuration of windows on the screen so that you can see up to 120 characters per line. ATLAS/ti will also let you scroll horizontally to see any text that does go beyond the window. You can enable editing of the text in the HU editor if you wish, but, as noted above, once you begin working (coding, annotating, memoing, linking, and so on) with your text in ATLAS/ti, you should not make any edits that change even the number of characters on a given line (for safety's sake, ATLAS/ti requires you to turn on text editing explicitly before you start editing). However, it's a simple matter to add text files as new PTs, even if a study is well under way. If you have to edit text, there are features that help you correct your quotations by hand, one at a time.

There's a facility for printing a line-numbered copy of the text file, and you can choose to see line numbers on screen with the data, although they are not actually inserted into the data file.

Working on the Data

This is where ATLAS/ti really excels. In addition to very flexible coding, you can do extensive memoing and commenting on the text *and on the codes.* You can then examine and define relationships in the graphical network views, but this crosses over into theory building; we'll discuss it further below.

Coding and Chunking

You can code either manually or automatically. For manual coding, having loaded the text file(s) as PTs, you begin to read through them in the large text pane of the HU editor (see Figure 1). When you come to a passage—of any length—you wish to code, you drag the mouse over it to select it. Or you can click with the mouse once to place the cursor, twice to select the current word, three times for the sentence, or four times for the paragraph (as delimited by a blank line).

With a segment of text highlighted, you have several options for assigning a code. (When you assign the code, if the segment hasn't already been made a quotation, it is defined as one.) You can click on (a) a button that lets you define one or more *new* codes (which can be virtually as long as you want) for this passage of text (open coding); (b) a button that lets you select a code or codes from the *existing* list (axial coding); or (c) a button that assigns the currently selected code to the selected text (quick axial coding). In addition, you can choose to have the highlighted text itself, if less than 40 characters, added as a code that applies to this segment (e.g., you might want the words "Joe got angry" coded as "Joe got angry").

Finally, you can autocode. You define a text search (see below), choose or create a code, and tell ATLAS/ti the size (word, sentence, or paragraph) of the quotations you want defined. Then, for every search hit, the specified range of text is marked as a quotation and coded with the chosen code. You have the choice of manually confirming each hit before it is coded.

In each of the above cases, the segment is automatically defined as a quotation and added to the quotation list. Quotations can overlap or be nested within one another without restriction and can have as many codes as you want. Both codes and quotations can also be easily created independently (without reference to any other object) and are referred to as "free" codes and quotations. This can be useful for building code structures independently of text or if you want to prepare your quotations and/or codes first and then start connecting them.

You can request listings of codes in various formats, with various accompanying information. These options are discussed under "Searching" and "Output," below.

Working with Codes

ATLAS/ti is a little light on code revision features; you can't do things like apply new codes based on old codes (e.g., any quotation coded "smiles" AND "laughs" should also be coded "happy"), though you can "merge codes" so that the two original codes disappear and a new code (with a new name) appears with all the quotation and other references of the originals. On the other hand, ATLAS/ti lets you do a lot of other powerful manipulations with codes, which are described under "Theory Building," below.

Families and Filters

There are a variety of options for "filtering" PTs, quotations, codes, and memos. A filter defines a set of objects that are active at a given time. When a filter is set, only the included objects show in the list panes, and almost every operation (like searching or printing) affects only those objects. For example, you can set the codes filter to those associated with the selected PT, "free" codes (not attached to any other objects), "abstract" codes (not attached to any quotations), codes created today (or not today), only codes created by me, only codes created by the defined coauthors, or only codes with (or without) comments. There are similar sets of options for filtering PTs, quotations, and memos.

You can also create "families" of PTs, codes, or memos: groupings that can be used as filters. For example, you could designate a PT family that consisted of all PTs on a particular person. Then, you could set the PT filter to that family and only those PTs would appear in the PT list and be available to whatever operations, such as searches, you carried out. A given code, PT, or memo can belong to multiple families or to none.

Families can function as a sort of limited broad coding scheme for selecting, say, based on demographic variables. For example, you could create a PT family that contained all interviews with male subjects and select just these for analysis.

Memos and Comments

Another really outstanding feature of ATLAS/ti is its extensive facility for adding memos and comments to various aspects of your HU. You can attach a single *comment* exclusively to any quotation, code, code family, PT, PT family, memo family, network view, code-to-code link, or quotation-to-quotation link in a network view, or to the HU itself. Like most things in ATLAS/ti, comments can be almost any length, limited only by RAM. Any item with an associated comment will be marked with a tilde (~) in its associated list pane (see the PT and code list panes in Figure 1).

Memos differ from comments; they can be attached to multiple objects at once, including quotations, codes, PTs, or other memos. Memos can also be "free": unattached to any other objects at all. In addition, you can define different types of memos: commentary, definition, method, and theory are provided (according to the manual—our copy of the program has commentary, critique, and method), and you can define your own types as well. Memo types can provide useful information to you and can be used as a basis for filtering.

Memoing and commenting are easy to do. For example, to attach a memo to a quotation, you select the quotation, then click on the memo button on the left side of the screen. You are asked to name the new memo, and the cursor then appears in the memo pane at the bottom of the HU editor (see Figure 1), ready for you to type your memo. The name of the new memo appears in the memo list on the right (see Figure 1). The memo editor has a variety of nice options for pasting in data such as a selected block in the PT, a quotation, or quotation reference information. To attach a comment, you select the item you want to attach it to, right-click with the mouse to pop up a menu, and choose "Comment." An editing window appears where you can type the comment.

Searching

ATLAS/ti departs from some other programs we have examined in choosing not to support much in the way of logical searches, while it has fairly good, and extremely user-friendly, facilities for exploring the text in other creative ways (we'll get more specific about all this in a moment). The developer, Thomas Muhr (1993b), has described the choice as intending ATLAS/ti to be "a tool which allows the researcher to go deeper into less material for which it makes sense to have it more directly available through the user interface, for instance, by 'direct manipulation' techniques: Click on a code and browse through the results."

For simple queries, there are many retrieval options. First, you can click on a code in the code list, and the associated quotation will immediately appear, in its full context, highlighted in the main text window. In curly brackets { } next to each code are two numbers, the first being the number of quotations associated with that code

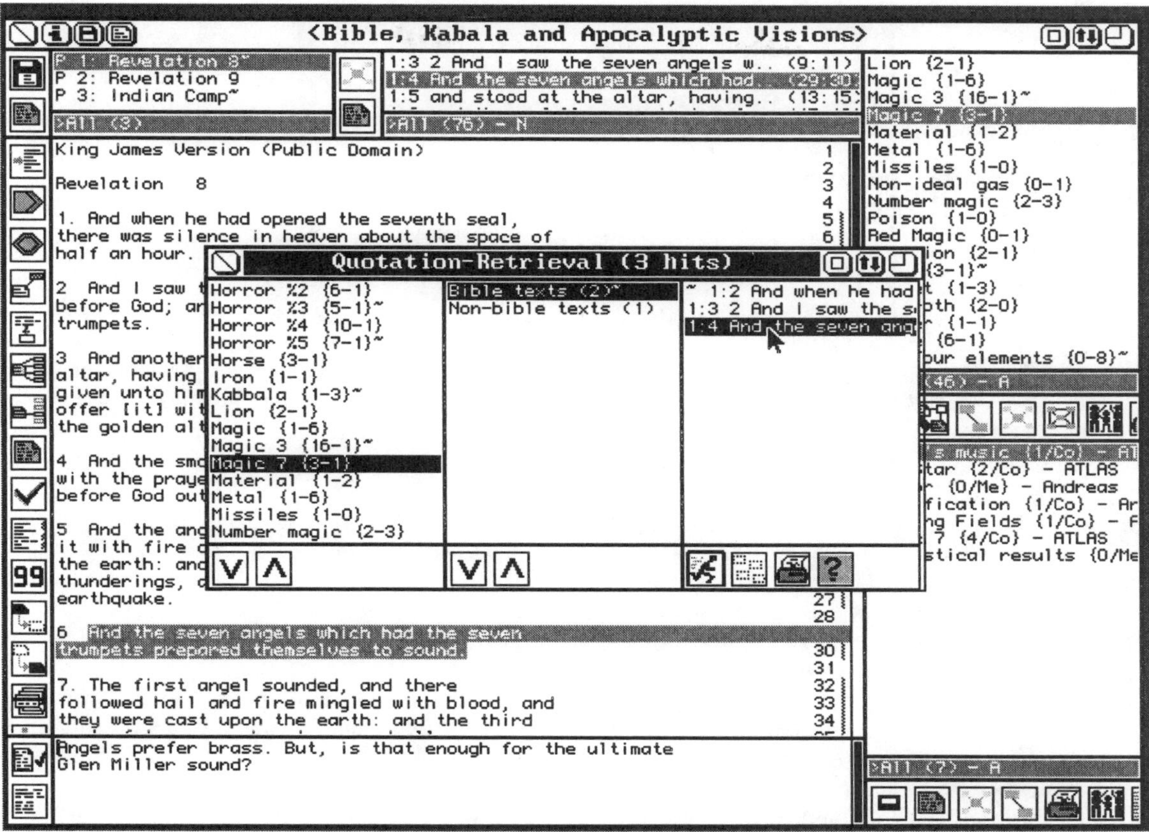

ATLAS/ti Figure 2. The Quotation-Retrieval window overlays the main HU editor window. A simple search has been executed for the code "Magic 7" (left-hand column) in the Bible texts PT family (center column). The resulting quotation references appear in the right-hand column. The quotation corresponding to the highlighted reference appears highlighted in the main text window.

and the second being the number of codes and memos associated with that code (see Figure 1). If there is more than one quotation associated with the code, you will be presented with a list of quotations in a pop-up list, each one identified with its quotation reference information (PT number, quotation number from that PT, line number range, and the first 30 characters of the quotation), and you can click on the one you want to see. (The problem is that you may not be able to tell from this information what the quotation is.) Once you've selected a code, you can browse sequentially through all the quotations coded with it by repeatedly clicking on a browse button. You can also browse through your data by selecting from the quotation, PT, and memo list panes, setting filters on any or several of these lists, and sorting them on such criteria as creation date (any list), order in the text (quotations), or alphabetical order (codes, memos).

More interestingly, you can search for quotations associated with all codes that are subordinately related to the current one (see the discussion of "relations" below), so you can retrieve according to a multilevel coding scheme. There are numerous other options for collecting and printing the information associated with a code. These are discussed under "Output," below.

For more complex searches, support for Boolean operators is limited. If you're searching for words in plain *text*, the only operator available is OR. These are referred to as *category* searches; you can string together a number of terms into a category so that any of its members will be found. Categories can be named and saved for reuse. You can define a set of, say, five words in a category. Furthermore, you can then include them all in a larger category simply by including the name of the first category. This strategy of having one category include another is called "recursive" searching in ATLAS/ti.

If you're searching for *quotations* with certain combinations of codes (via the *quotation retrieval* function; see Figure 2), you have a choice of AND and OR operators—but you can only use one at a time. So, you can do a conjunctive search (with AND) for quotations that have all the

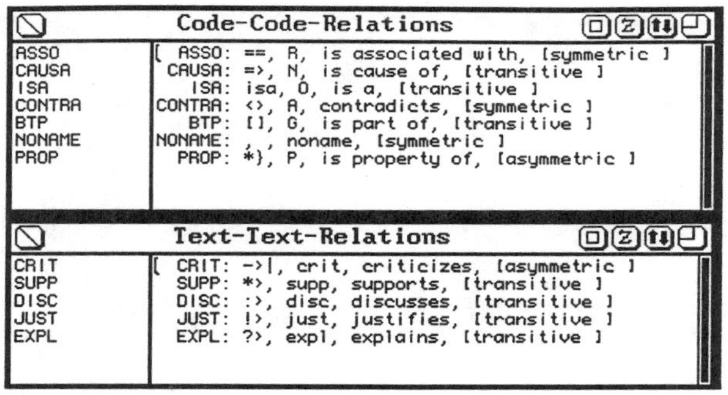

```
Code-Code-Relations
ASSO      [ ASSO: ==, R, is associated with, [symmetric ]
CAUSA      CAUSA: =>, N, is cause of, [transitive ]
ISA          ISA: isa, O, is a, [transitive ]
CONTRA    CONTRA: <>, A, contradicts, [symmetric ]
BTP          BTP: [], G, is part of, [transitive ]
NONAME    NONAME: , , noname, [symmetric ]
PROP        PROP: *}, P, is property of, [asymmetric ]

Text-Text-Relations
CRIT      [ CRIT: ->|, crit, criticizes, [asymmetric ]
SUPP        SUPP: *>, supp, supports, [transitive ]
DISC        DISC: :>, disc, discusses, [transitive ]
JUST        JUST: !>, just, justifies, [transitive ]
EXPL        EXPL: ?>, expl, explains, [transitive ]
```

ATLAS/ti Figure 3. The lists of predefined code-code and text-text relations. On the right are the name of the relation, the symbol optionally used to represent it in network views, the label that can be used instead of the symbol, the meaning of the relation, and its logical attribute.

codes you select, or a disjunctive search (with OR) for quotations that have any of the codes you select, but you cannot combine AND and OR logic in the same search or create any more complex Boolean queries. One logic refinement is that you can also create a conjunctive or disjunctive list of *PTs,* or *PT families,* to be included in the search. There is no way to implement NOT logic.

When you use the quotation retrieval feature to get quotations by conjunctive or disjunctive combinations of codes, a list of quotation references is provided (see Figure 2). You can then browse the quotations themselves; as you click on each quotation reference, the quotation appears highlighted in the text window. You can delete quotations (if you wish) from the retrieved list, and then output the final group to printer, file, or the built-in text editor (see "Output," below). Along with the full quotations, you get the quotation reference (the PT name, PT and quotation numbers, and line numbers), the author (the name of the user who originally defined the quotation), and the names of all codes and memos associated with the quotation.

A new, "prototype" feature in release 1.1E for collecting text for "code-matrices" allows one more sophisticated type of Boolean statement, but you lose the preview function of the quotation retrieval tool, and output goes straight to editor, printer, or disk. The code-matrix builder lets you define two different OR lists, connected by an AND, retrieving any segment with one or more elements from each list. For example, the statement "(boy OR girl) AND (athletic OR nurturing)" would get any segment with (boy AND athletic), OR (boy AND nurturing), OR (girl AND athletic), OR (girl AND nurturing). Because the output is sorted (all quotations with a given combination of codes are printed together), you could then easily arrange the resulting quotations in matrix form in your word processor, with the rows defined by "boy" and "girl" and the columns by "athletic" and "nurturing." (See Miles & Huberman, 1994, chaps. 5 and 9, for a detailed discussion of the use of such matrices.)

Theory Building

No program can honestly be said to build theory, nor would you want one to. But ATLAS/ti provides several extremely useful facilities to help you in theory-building efforts. You can create links among quotations, codes, and memos; give the links different logical properties; graphically view, manipulate, and print the resulting networks; and conduct searches based on the logical relations in the networks. You can also export an entire code network and import it into a new HU, allowing the application of your theoretical structure to a new data set—or allowing another researcher to try coding the same data with the same theoretical structure and comparing your results. Note too that if you set a code filter before you export, you can export a partial network structure.

Hypertext Linking

You can create links among objects in several ways. The links between quotations are called "hyperlinks," signifying their traditional hypertext functionality, although they function virtually identically to the other types of links. You can create links either in the HU editor, selecting objects in the list panes, or in the graphical network editor (see below), drawing the links among objects imported into the network view. Regardless of which method you choose, the links function the same way. When made among *quotations,* they can function as a kind of hypertext: You select one of the linked quotations, call up a graphical view of the network formed by this quotation and the objects linked to it (a focused network view, discussed below), and, as you click on the icon for each of the hyper-

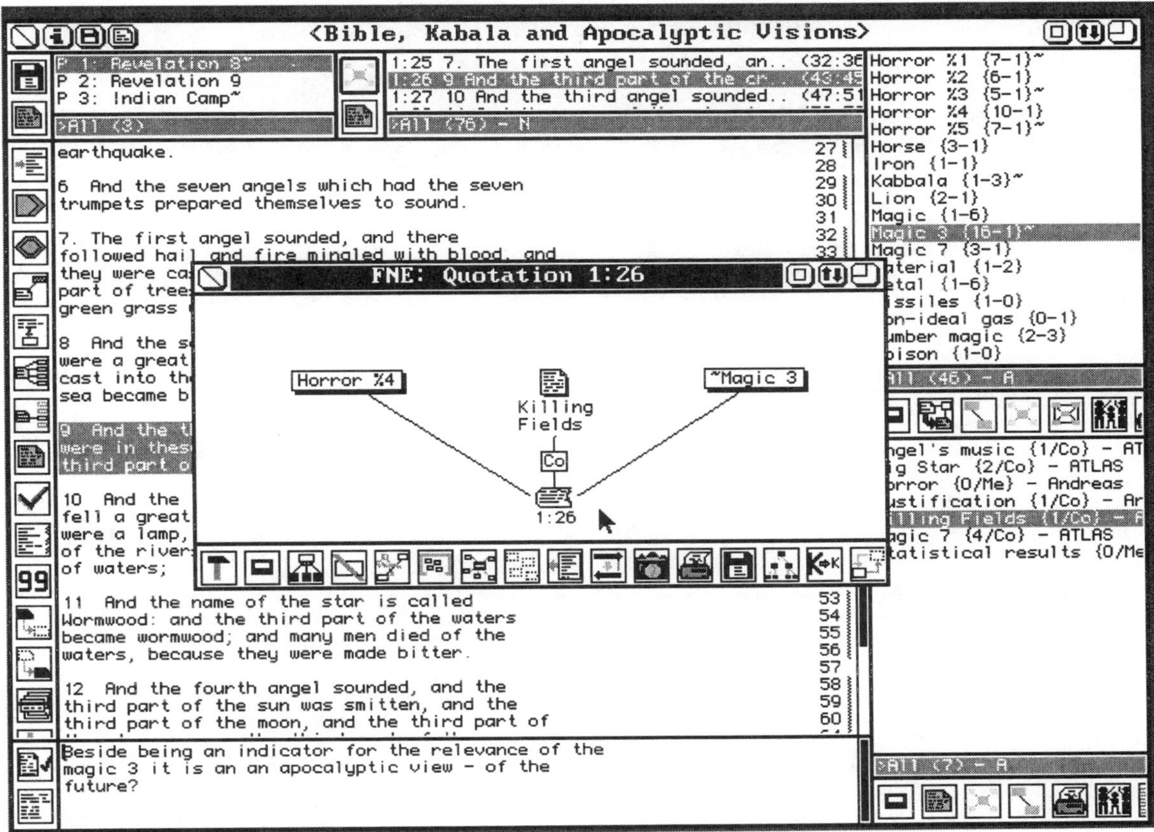

ATLAS/ti Figure 4. The network editor overlays the HU editor, showing a focused network for quotation 1:26, which includes an icon for the quotation as well as icons for the three objects—two codes, "Horror %4" and "~Magic 3," and a memo titled "Killing Fields"—it is directly linked to. The letters "Co" on the link to the memo indicate that the memo is of the type "commentary."

linked quotations, they are highlighted in the text window of the HU editor (see Figure 5).

You can also create links among codes, among memos, and between codes, memos, PTs, and quotations (when you "code" a quotation, you actually create a link between the quotation and the code). The links among codes, among quotations, and between memos and any type of object can have different properties, representing different types of relations.

Relations

The ability to define different relations for linking objects is another excellent theory-building aid in ATLAS/ti. There are seven different logical (or semantic) relations you can choose from for linking codes to codes, and five for linking quotations to quotations (see Figure 3). You can also define your own relations if you want and attach comments to each relation. Each of these relations has formal logical attributes, such as transitive, symmetric, or asymmetric. These affect representation in networks. Symmetric relations have no arrowheads because they run equally in both directions, while asymmetric relations have an arrowhead pointing toward the target.

Transitive relations can be used for retrieval by code. (Transitivity means that, if A > B and B > C, then it must be the case that A > C. A real transitive relation might be as follows: The school is in the district, the classroom is in the school, therefore the classroom is in the district. Note that it's not the case that, if John likes Mary, and Mary likes Joe, John must like Joe—this one is *not* transitive.)

You can retrieve not only all quotations associated with a given code but also all quotations associated with codes that are (subordinately) transitively linked to the code of interest (so, if you search for the district, you get the school and the classroom as well). Unfortunately, the relation does not "stick" in any other sense: When you examine a quotation, you'll only see a list of *directly* linked codes,

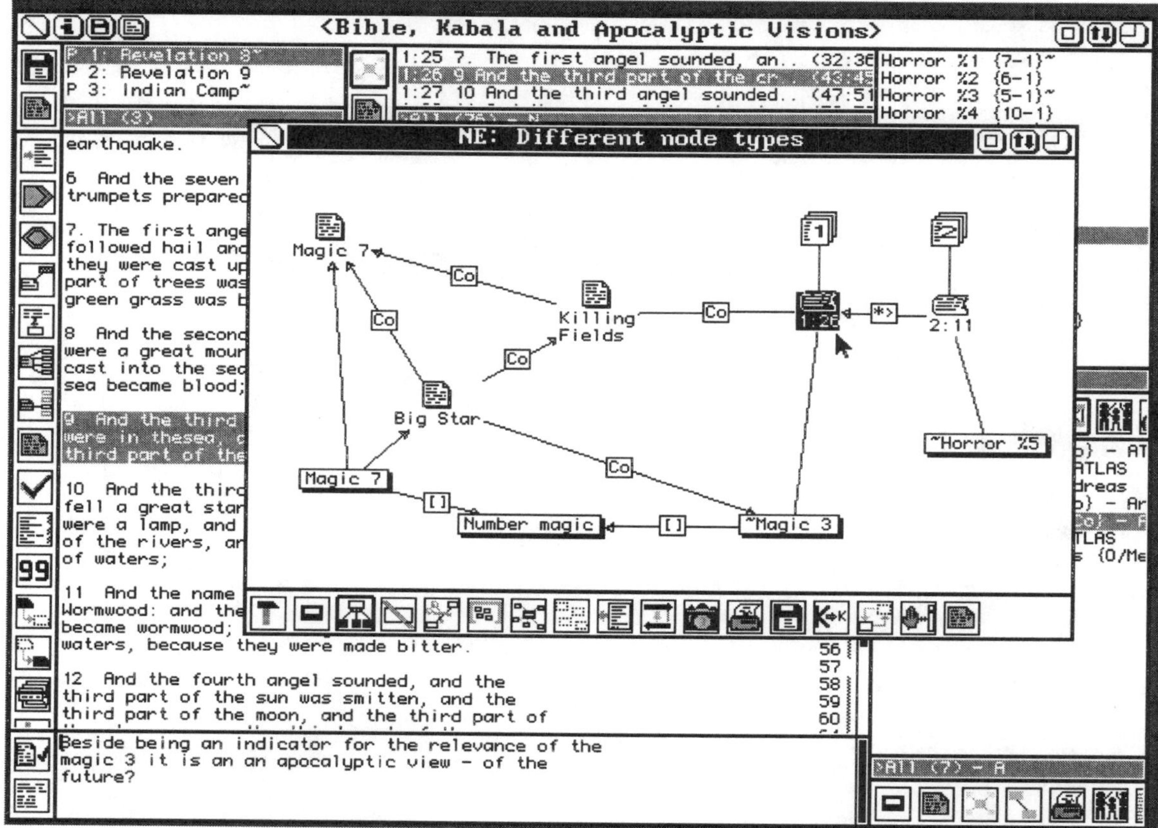

ATLAS/ti Figure 5. A more elaborate network view, named "Different node types." Note the different icons for quotations (e.g., 1:26), codes (e.g., Magic 7), memos (e.g., Big Star), and PTs (e.g., 1). Clicking on the icon for quotation 1:26 has caused the main window in the background to scroll to that quotation, which appears highlighted. This can be done with one quotation after another. Symbols on links indicate different types of relations (see Figure 3 for definitions).

unless you open a focused network view for the quotation and import the codes related to each of the codes attached to the quotation.

Networking

ATLAS/ti provides a graphical network editor that helps you explore and visualize the relationships among the different objects in your HU. The simplest way to use the network editor is to call up a "focused network view" for a quotation, code, or memo. When you click on the appropriate button, the network editor pops up (see Figure 4), displaying a network in which the current object (whether a quotation, code, or memo) is displayed along with all the objects that are directly related to it.

Alternatively, you can create and save your own network views (Figure 5 shows a more elaborate network view). There are different icons for each type of object, and you can choose different display modes for each, such as a text icon or the first few lines of text for a quotation. Any objects can be connected or disconnected while in the network editor—so you can build, revise, and extend the theory embodied in the relationships shown while working in a "right-brain" style.

All windows are synchronized, so that you can use a network view to explore an HU. For example, you can click on a quotation icon in the network view and see the quotation highlighted in the HU. You can pop up and edit *comments* for any object with a couple of mouse clicks. You can even create new codes and memos while you're in the network editor and connect them with other objects graphically; all these actions are reflected in the HU.

The network editor sports a wide assortment of tools. You can delete objects from the database entirely or just have them disappear from the network view. There is a tool for merging codes. There are tools for importing objects from lists and for importing all objects directly related to the currently selected objects(s). Tools are provided for

```
HU:  Bible, Kabala and Apocalyptic Visions
File:   [c:\textbank\bible]
Edited by: Super
Date/Time: 19 Nov 1993 - 17:37:25
____________________________________________

Codes hierarchy
Code filter: All
____________________________________________

Abaddon  <is>  Root

Animal  <is>  Root
  Horse  <is a>  Animal
  Lion  <is a>  Animal
  Scorpion  <is a>  Animal

Magic  <is>  Root
  Black Magic  <is a>  Magic
  Kabbala  <is associated with>  Magic
    Alchemie  <is associated with>  Kabbala
      Gold  <is part of>  Alchemie
        The four elements  <is cause of>  Gold
          Air  <is part of>  The four elements
          Earth  <is part of>  The four elements
          Fire  <is part of>  The four elements
          Water  <is part of>  The four elements
            Fire  <contradicts>  Water
      The four elements  <is part of>  Alchemie
        Air  <is part of>  The four elements
        Earth  <is part of>  The four elements
        Fire  <is part of>  The four elements
        Water  <is part of>  The four elements
          Fire  <contradicts>  Water
    Bible  <contradicts>  Kabbala
```

ATLAS/ti Figure 6. Excerpts of a printout of the code hierarchy for the sample textbase. Subordinate codes are indented outline style and listed in statements, with the relation that connects them to their immediate superordinate code given in angle brackets. The word "Root" indicates that a code, such as Abaddon, is the base of a "tree" of codes, that is, it is not related subordinately to anything.

inverting the relationship between two objects and for undoing the last repositioning of a code. Finally, there is a tool for automatically arranging an entire network hierarchically.

Graphics Editing

The network editor, while essentially an analytical tool, does provide decent tools for working with the graphical aspects of a network (though it's not in the same class as a dedicated diagrammer like MetaDesign or Inspiration—it's not intended to be). You can drag nodes (singly or in groups) around anywhere in your network, and all the links move and stretch with the nodes they're attached to. There is one auto-arrange feature. As mentioned above, this lets you arrange the network into a hierarchy. This can be very handy for bringing order out of chaos, especially if your nodes are related hierarchically, but can sometimes be confusing; a series of nodes may get lined up vertically, one right below the other, so that all the link lines get overlaid, and you can't tell what's connected to what. To fix this, you just drag one or more of the nodes out to the side so the link lines separate. There are no auto-align or auto-space features. Links can only be single, straight line segments.

You can choose between two different icons each for codes (either the code name or the first line of its comment) or quotations (either the quotation's reference number or its first 30 characters). Link labels can be switched between two different sets of symbols. You can also choose different thickness lines for different relations, and there are five different primitive fonts (most of them are represented in the figures).

Networks can be saved as .PCX files, the format used by the program Paintbrush, which comes with Microsoft Windows. If you want to do any drawing or writing on a network, beyond the sorts of things discussed above, you can do so in Paintbrush (if you have it) or in a more primitive drawing package included with ATLAS/ti as the "Mouse Training" program. (The latter, while not nearly as good as Paintbrush graphically, at least has the advantage of being usable during an ATLAS/ti session.)

Output

Again, the purpose of the network editor is to provide a powerful analytical tool and let you produce crude figures, but not high-quality publication graphics. When it comes to graphic output, what you see here is what you get. There

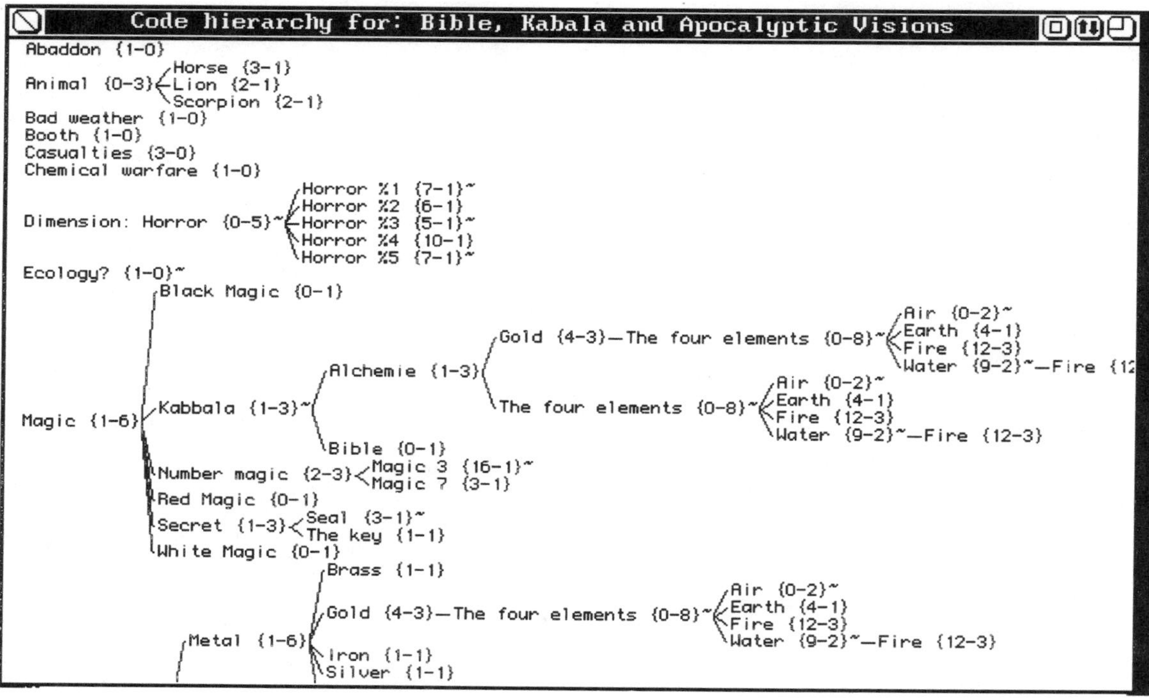

ATLAS/ti Figure 7. Partial code forest for the sample textbase. The forest is made up of code trees, each of which begins with a root, such as Abaddon or Dimension.

is no way to create higher quality pictures than those shown in Figures 4 and 5. You can either print directly or save the network as a .PCX file. If you do the latter (and have Windows and Paintbrush), then you can reconfigure and reboot your computer, start up Windows, and use Paintbrush to add to, or erase from the figure, but you won't be able to modify the existing objects. Then again, no other package does even this much.

The text output options are extremely rich, only lacking a bit in the extent of user control of the information that's included with a given printout; you may sometimes get more than you want. You also need to make note of what each printout is; most types, but not all, are clearly labeled.

There are different print options in the menus for each pane, offering different kinds of output (in virtually every case, the output can be sent to the editor, a file, or the printer). From the PT list you can get a list of PTs, a hierarchy of quotations, codes, and memos for a PT (with subordinate entities listed below and indented), the text of all quotations for a PT, or a line-numbered version of a PT.

From the quotation list, you can get the selected quotation with source info, codes, comments, and memos, or you can get all quotations with all the same accompanying information. You can also get a list of all quotation references with source info but without the actual quotation text.

From the memo list, you can get a list of memos or print the text of the current one, along with info about all the objects it is related to: PTs and line numbers for all quotations, names of all codes and memos, as well as the memo's type.

Where text output really gets interesting is at the codes list. From the CODES—Print menu, you can print all the quotations for the current code (with the names of all other codes and memos attached to each quotation) or just their references. You can get all quotations for the current code and all its subordinate codes (with the names of all other codes and memos attached to each quotation). You can print a code list, a complete code hierarchy (see Figure 6), or just a list of codes with their immediate neighbors (like Figure 6, but going down only one level, or up a level, or "sideways" to a symmetrically related neighbor). You can get a table of the frequencies of codes in each PT, with full marginal totals (for each code, PT, and grand total). Finally, you can get a list of all codes with their comments and quotation references.

Altogether, pretty amazing! Even more—from the CODES—Miscellaneous menu, you can get code "trees" and "forests," graphical representations of the hierarchical relationships among codes, though this option will not work if there are circular structures among your codes. A code tree shows the hierarchical structure of all codes subordinate to the current code, while a code forest shows the entire code structure (see Figure 7).

SPSS Output

ATLAS/ti can also output data for use in SPSS. If you choose this option, ATLAS/ti creates an SPSS program file that will define and read in a data set in which quotations are cases and codes are variables, with a "1" indicating the code is present for a case and a "0" indicating that it is not. You can also create numeric variables before you create the SPSS file. To do this, you create a series of codes with the same root name followed by a % and a number. In the example provided, these are as follows:

Horror %1
Horror %2
Horror %3
Horror %4
Horror %5

When you create the SPSS file, you get a single variable, Horror, with values from 1 to 5. Thus you could code your data quantitatively. This makes ATLAS/ti very useful as a program for analyzing structured interviews with numeric variables for which you intend to do both qualitative and quantitative analyses. There are also variables giving PT, starting and ending lines, and columns, which could be useful in selecting, grouping, and so on. There are compute statements that automatically create variables for PT families.

User Friendliness

As you can see, there are a tremendous number of features to assimilate in ATLAS/ti. But because of its interface, the program is easy to learn and use. There are no tutorials as such to get you going, but there are a number of well-developed sample HUs for you to explore. You can expect to be up and running in very little time—it took me only a couple of hours to get comfortable using the program—and you can also expect it to be quite some time before you learn everything the program can do.

The manual, completely redone for version 1.1E, is fair but much more professional than most of the programs from independent, academic sources. It's pretty clearly written, though the grammar and spelling still need some work (it's been translated from the original German). The biggest disadvantage of the manual is that its organization by conceptual sections (e.g., "Working with ATLAS/ti—The Textual Level" and "More Textual Level Functions" or "Advanced Techniques—The Conceptual Level")—which makes sense if you read it like a book—is not very helpful when you need to find out, for example, how to change symbols in the network view. Once you've spent a little time with it, though, you should be able to find what you need, and you almost certainly will be able to understand it.

Help screens are unusual, but very helpful. You can't pop into a big on-line manual system as you can in many commercial packages. What you can do is click on virtually anything on the screen with the right-hand mouse button, and a little help message, usually just a single, very helpful sentence, pops up in a little box. It is this feature more than any other that makes ATLAS/ti so easy to learn and use.

Technical support may eventually be available through a U.S. representative but for now you must rely on the developer, Thomas Muhr, in Germany. You can contact him by e-mail, phone, fax, or mail, and he is extremely responsive and helpful. E-mail is generally the cheapest, fastest method.

Miscellaneous

Four features to be dealt with are the text editing capabilities of ATLAS/ti, hardware and software compatibility, multiauthoring, and customization.

Text Editor

There's a text editor that pops up in a window on screen for a variety of functions. You can send any text output to an editor window, or you can load an ASCII file from your disk into the editor. There are slightly modified versions of the editor for editing PTs, memos, and comments. The editor has a clipboard so you can cut, copy, and paste text. You can perform category searches for words (see "Searching," above) within the edited document. Files can be appended to the current file, and you can print either the entire file in the editor or just a selected block of text.

Compatibility

Compatibility is a problem for some users, particularly those who use Microsoft Windows. If you don't and don't plan to, you can ignore this.

ATLAS/ti has a conflict with the way Windows manages memory and therefore cannot be run from within Windows. Furthermore, Windows's memory usage is normally supported by a program called SmartDrive. You must reconfigure and reboot your computer to remove SmartDrive from memory before you can run ATLAS/ti, and vice versa (the reconfiguration can be automated, however). One solution is to buy a third party disk-caching program to replace SmartDrive and use a memory-clearing utility that comes with ATLAS/ti. You'll still have to exit Windows to use ATLAS/ti, but you won't have to reboot. If you're used to Windows, then you're probably used to being able to run multiple programs at once. Even if you aren't, and you use a Windows word processor, you may get annoyed by having to exit your word processor, and Windows, and possibly reboot every time there's something else you want to check in your data.

Multiauthoring

A very nice aspect of ATLAS/ti is its support for multiple authors. All users must log in (identify themselves with a user name and a secret password) to use ATLAS/ti. (You can disable this if you work alone.) The system "administrator" (you) can define new users and their level of privilege; either they are administrators like you and can define and redefine other users, or they are "users" and can't. Either users or administrators can "author" HUs.

The "author" of an HU can change the degree of access to the project. You can declare the HU to be "public," so that any user can use and edit it, or "public—read only," so that anyone can look but they won't be able to save any changes. Finally, you can declare the HU to be private—meaning no one can even load it. If you do this, you can declare a list of coauthors who will be able to do anything with the HU except change the degree of access.

Every object created in ATLAS/ti is "stamped" with the time and date and the name of the person who created it. This allows you to filter things by "mine" and "not-mine." In addition, if there are coauthors defined, you can filter things by the name of any of the coauthors.

These features are excellent for managing large multicase, multistaff projects. But they can also be used for purposes of teaching qualitative analysis, improving coding reliability, and so on.

Customization

You can customize a number of aspects of the way ATLAS/ti works. For example, toolbars are customizable, there are a couple of different layouts available for the HU (with different functional advantages), and the colors in which most things are displayed can be selected (nice if you're partially or completely color-blind or work on a laptop or other monochrome display).

There are no macros as such. The closest things to macros are the search categories, which are like saved search macros. These are particularly nice in that they can be nested "recursively," as explained under "Searching," above.

Update

A Windows version of ATLAS/ti is now under development. This version is planned to run under Windows 3.1, Windows/NT (a 32-bit, "high performance" version of Windows), and the next version of Windows, which is currently being called Windows 95. The developer plans to have full compatibility with earlier versions; a better, less cluttered interface, including "floating" tool menus and memos (floating objects appear to be hovering above the window you're working in and can be moved around for convenience); more features for laying out network views, more sophisticated text search, and access to all Windows resources, including the clipboard and text attributes (fonts and so on). Beta-testing of the Windows version is currently projected to begin in fall 1994, so do not expect the actual release until sometime in 1995, at the earliest.

Comparative Remarks

ATLAS/ti is certainly one of the more versatile and, for most purposes, more powerful programs available for analyzing qualitative data in a text-coding paradigm. The interface is arguably the best of all the code-and-retrieve programs, allowing simultaneous viewing of all relevant information. In addition, it offers the unique and powerful network editor. The graphical output quality and graphical manipulation tools can't come close to those of a dedicated network mapper like MetaDesign or Inspiration, but ATLAS/ti has the significant advantage of tying your maps to your data in a fully dynamic linkage (changes in one place show up in the other).

ATLAS/ti is steadily improving in its support of searching by logical combinations of codes or words, but it still doesn't have the full-blown Boolean logic of search programs like The Text Collector or Metamorph, textbase managers like Folio VIEWS or Sonar Professional, or even other code-and-retrieve programs like HyperRESEARCH or NUD•IST. Nor does it deal with special co-occurrences like overlaps, nesting, following, and so on. ATLAS/ti is one day intended to support such complex search logic. Right now, this is about the only area in which it doesn't lead the pack.

Summary

It should be obvious by now that ATLAS/ti is an extraordinary program. If you can live with its shortcomings in Windows compatibility and search logic, you will get a host of features and advantages that simply can't be had elsewhere. We generally find ourselves comparing other code-and-retrieve, and code-based theory-building, packages with ATLAS/ti, and ATLAS/ti keeps coming out on top. The only program in this category it's not a clear winner over is NUD•IST, and the choice between the two is not clear cut: You'll have to weigh the strengths and weaknesses and match them against your needs.

References

Miles, M. B., & Huberman, A. M. (1994). *Qualitative data analysis: An expanded sourcebook* (2nd ed.). Thousand Oaks, CA: Sage.

Muhr, T. (1993a). *ATLAS/ti: Computer aided text interpretation & theory building: User's manual.* Berlin: Author.

Muhr, T. (1993b, January 21). [E-mail message; sender: thomas.muhr@tu-berlin.de].

•

HyperRESEARCH 1.55

Available for Macintosh and Windows[1]

ResearchWare, Inc.
P.O. Box 1258
Randolph, MA 02368-1258

Phone: (617) 961-3909
E-mail: paul@bcvms.bc.edu

Price: $225 + shipping
Quantity discounts for three or more
Lab pack licenses available

Hardware Requirements:
For Macintosh
- Apple Macintosh computer
- 2MB RAM (4MB or more for System 7)
- Hard disk
- System version 6.0.7 or later (System 7 recommended)
- HyperCard 1.2.5 or later (HyperCard 2.1 or HyperCard 2.1 Player recommended)

For Windows
- 286 or better processor (486 recommended)
- 4MB RAM (6MB recommended)
- 1.44MB (3.5 in.) diskette drive
- DOS 5.0 or later
- Windows 3.1 or later
- Mouse or other pointing device

Overview

HyperRESEARCH is a code-and-retrieve program with a powerful and unique theory-building module hooked on. It is especially intended, and especially good, for a cross-case analytic approach. For example, when you search for a Boolean combination of codes, the program selects out the *cases* with that combination of codes. Then you can generate a report for those cases, in which you can include chunks as identified by a single code (but not by combinations of codes). HyperRESEARCH could be, if certain serious limitations were overcome, one of the better programs available for qualitative data analysis. As it is, it is quite capable and could be helpful for many researchers; consider the limitations and the unique strengths, and decide for yourself.

HyperRESEARCH is now available in virtually identical versions for the Macintosh and for Windows[2] on IBM compatible computers. It is designed for the coding, re-

1. At the time this manuscript was being prepared, ResearchWare had been forced to suspend shipping of the Windows version of HyperRESEARCH due to a problem with Toolbook 3.0, a HyperCard-like program it is built on. At this point, HyperRESEARCH for Windows has reportedly been fixed, using a prerelease version of the new release of Toolbook 3.0. However, ResearchWare is not allowed to sell it until Toolbook is officially released.

2. See footnote 1.

trieval, and analysis of text. Perhaps its most outstanding feature is that it allows for the computerized testing of hypotheses about qualitative data through the evaluation of IF . . . THEN rules created by the researcher.

Database Structure

When you're using HyperRESEARCH, the data for a project actually remain in their original source files. These must be standard ASCII text files, which you create with any word processor or optical character recognition (OCR) software and scanner.

Your files can be organized in any way you like. For example, you can have a file for each interview, a file for each day's notes, and a file for each questionnaire. Or you can lump your notes together, your interviews together, and so on—however you like to work. You can use as many source files, and as large source files, as will fit on your hard disk.

One of the more interesting features of HyperRESEARCH is the unique structure it employs for its database. Your entire project is called a "study." Within the study, you can define multiple cases (up to 900). A case might, for example, be a person in your study, or a village, a classroom, a day—whatever unit of analysis makes sense for your study. You can name cases, either with meaningful names or simply as Case 01, Case 02, and so on.

You have complete freedom in associating chunks of text from source files with different cases. You can associate chunks of different files with the same case (you might have an interview with Jim Nelson, your own observations of Jim, and an informant's comments about Jim). You can also associate chunks from a single file with multiple cases (an interview with one person might have information relevant to several different cases). You see a case as an index card on the screen (see Figure 1), and each case holds the references to the locations of the chunks you define and the names of the codes you apply to them. Each of these references acts as a hypertext link, identified by a code name, from the case to the source text, as described below under "Data Linking."

This organization of data from multiple sources by case is a unique and outstanding feature of HyperRESEARCH. For some cross-case analytic approaches, this program is clearly the one to choose.

There is also fairly good freedom in chunking. Chunks can range in size from a single word to a whole "page." (A "page" in HyperRESEARCH *can* be up to 16,000 characters long, though you may want to keep these pages to the same length as the *real* pages of your printed data. This is explained under "Data Entry," below.) Chunks can overlap and a single chunk can have as many codes, applying to as many cases, as you want.

The first problems with the program appear here. First, the limitation of the size of chunks to a "page" (no matter how defined) will be a serious constraint for some projects. A chunk cannot run across page boundaries even if the chunk is only a couple of lines in length.

The second problem is more complex. HyperRESEARCH confuses the concepts of *code* and *chunk.* Each entry on a case, which consists of a reference to a *chunk* and the *code* that applies to it, is called a "code." So, the entire first entry in Figure 1, "char 1 to 319 of page 1 of INV01.TXT, non trad field," is referred to not as a *chunk* and its *code* but as a "code." The label "non trad field," in the abstract, is referred to as a Master Code. (For simplicity's sake, we'll use quotation marks around "code" whenever we're referring to HyperRESEARCH usage.) The program treats each of these "codes" completely independently, with the result that the program never knows if there is more than one code (in the usual sense) on a given chunk. Instead, it treats two codes on the same chunk as two entirely independent entries on the case, as though there were two unrelated chunks (the significance of this limitation will be discussed below). You could even code exactly the same range of text onto the same case with the same code twice and the program would never know.

Data Entry

You don't "enter" data directly in HyperRESEARCH. You either type up text files in your favorite word processor or scan text in. Then you start up HyperRESEARCH and code the externally created materials. This means you can't edit from within the program. Furthermore, because the program tracks chunks by an index of line and column positions, if you edit a source file, you're likely to wind up with the wrong text referenced. The folks at ResearchWare correctly suggest that you lock your source files (make them read-only) so they *can't* be edited. Implication: The program is best suited for data that won't be altered after you start working on it, though you can always easily add new source files to your study with additional information.

When you prepare your text in your word processor, you must insert a tilde (~) on a line by itself to indicate every page break. Your "pages" can be up to 16,000 characters long (remember, there are about 3,000 characters on a single-spaced page). Because your coded chunks can't cross page boundaries, the placement of the ~'s becomes very important. Although your HyperRESEARCH pages *can* be 16,000 characters long, the manual points out that, if you want to be able to easily find text you're interested in on hard copy, you may want to keep your HyperRESEARCH pages the same length as your printout pages. On the other hand, this may prove to be too restrictive in terms of cod-

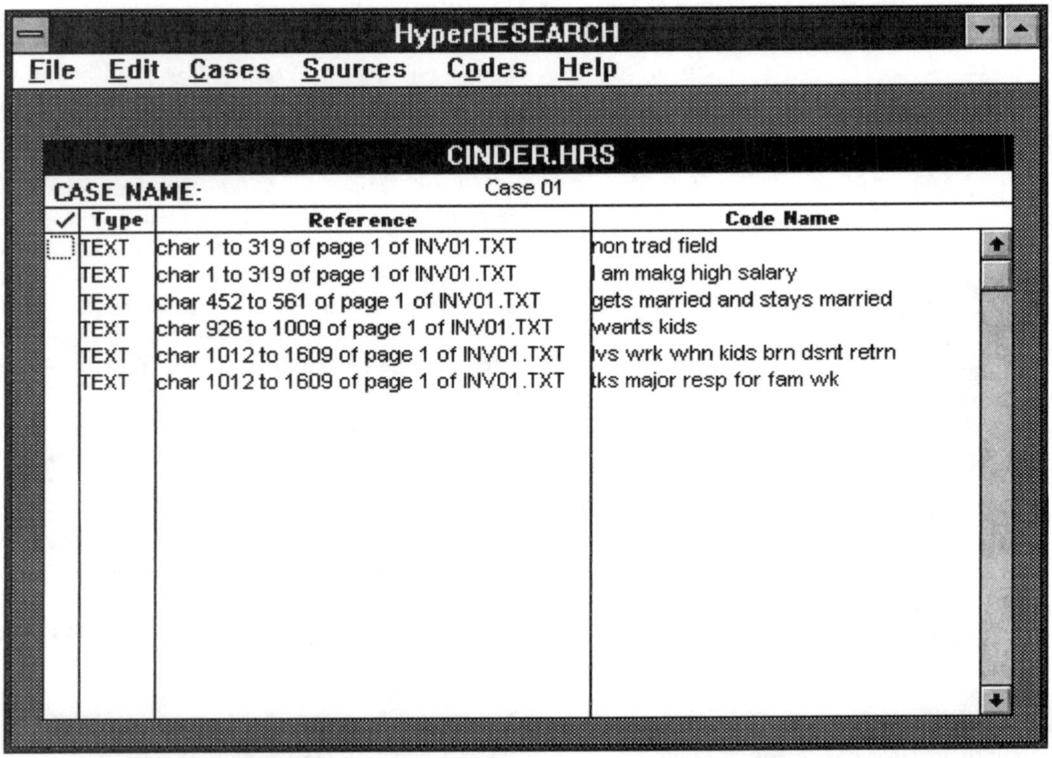

HyperRESEARCH

File Edit Cases Sources Codes Help

CINDER.HRS

CASE NAME: Case 01

✓	Type	Reference	Code Name
	TEXT	char 1 to 319 of page 1 of INV01.TXT	non trad field
	TEXT	char 1 to 319 of page 1 of INV01.TXT	I am makg high salary
	TEXT	char 452 to 561 of page 1 of INV01.TXT	gets married and stays married
	TEXT	char 926 to 1009 of page 1 of INV01.TXT	wants kids
	TEXT	char 1012 to 1609 of page 1 of INV01.TXT	lvs wrk whn kids brn dsnt retrn
	TEXT	char 1012 to 1609 of page 1 of INV01.TXT	tks major resp for fam wk

HyperRESEARCH Figure 1. A sample case with several entries. Note that, although all the entries in this instance come from the same file, INV01.TXT (interview 1), they don't have to.

ing. Also note that determining where your 16,000 characters runs out can be difficult, at best.

Working on the Data

Most of this work you do from the "Generate Codes" screen, where you see the index card representations of your cases and can pop up your source files. You can sort the entries on the case by code name or by chunk reference. The latter option is helpful for finding out when the same chunk is coded with more than one code.

Coding and Chunking

With a case (such as Jim Nelson or Case 01) displayed on the screen, you pop up a source file in a window. As you read through the file, you use the mouse to select a segment of text that you want to code. A dialogue box pops up, giving you the option of applying any existing code or adding a new code, which will then be available for all future chunks. The code and the reference to the chunk you have just defined are then added to the index card for the current case. Codes can be up to 32 characters in length. Punctuation in codes is not permitted.

Alternatively, you can choose to Autocode. With this procedure, you have the program search for a text string and apply a code *to that string*. Unfortunately, the program does not allow the use of Boolean logic in Autocode, so you cannot ask it, for example, to code all paragraphs containing two specified strings, or one string OR another, or one string but NOT another. Autocode also does not supply an interactive mode, which would allow you to review found text before it is coded: a real drawback.

As mentioned above, you can code chunks from a source file onto as many cases as you want, and you can code as many source files as you want onto a case.

Working with Codes

At the case screen, you can click on any "code" entry and you will be given the choice of displaying, renaming, copying, or deleting that coded chunk. If you choose "display," HyperRESEARCH brings up the source file in a window and highlights the chunk referenced by the "code" entry you've asked for. If you choose rename, you can change the code for that chunk. Copy lets you create a new entry for the same chunk, with another code. Delete removes the code entry on the case without affecting the original source material.

Copy, rename, and delete functions can also be run for an *entire case* or on a global basis for *every case* in the study. It would be nice if you could limit these operations to a subset of cases or source files—but that isn't possible. By using either the global or the local copy commands, it is easy to add higher-order codes. The program doesn't know they're higher order, though, so you should come up with a naming scheme that tells you. For example, if you have a code "rain" and want a higher-order code "precipitation," you might name it "2precipitation." Next you could have "3weather." This scheme, though, doesn't tell you what lower level codes are associated with "3weather." If you want a program that's really built for handling code hierarchies, go with one like NUD•IST or ATLAS/ti.

It's also easy to get a code list at any time, for the whole study or for a subset of cases. Unfortunately, because all coded chunks are recorded independently (even if they refer to the same source text), global copy, rename, and delete operations cannot be carried out according to logical expressions. So you can't, for example, recode all passages with a given combination of codes or text strings.

There are some other "copy" operations as well. You can copy a "code" (chunk reference and code) or group of "codes" from one case to another, even if the destination case is in another study! You can also copy an entire case from one study to another.

Aside from these shortcomings, the coding facilities in HyperRESEARCH are very flexible and very easy to use. If the shortcomings mentioned here don't bother you (or, better yet, if ResearchWare fixes them!), you will find it easier and more flexible for coding than most available programs.

Memoing

It has become increasingly clear to us that any good code-and-retrieve or code-based theory-building program should include a memoing facility of some sort. Unfortunately, HyperRESEARCH provides no way to annotate or write memos about your work.

Searching

You can retrieve text based on codes. (You cannot search for character strings in the text.) This is done by making "reports" through the Analyze Codes window (see Figure 2). You can choose any case, all cases, or a subset of cases, either by criteria using the Build Expression box or by name using the Select Cases box. The criteria are logical expressions made up of codes, using the Boolean operators AND, OR, and NOT. Parentheses are allowed. Expressions can be up to 32,000 characters in length (in other words, much longer than you'd ever need). All cases that match your criteria are eligible for inclusion in the report.

Next, you specify a list of codes in the Codes to Include box (there is a dialog box with a list of all codes from which you can choose). All chunks in the selected cases having the specified codes are then included in the report. Again, because the program treats two code references to the same chunk as independent entries, it doesn't know if a chunk has more than one code. As a result, you can't specify a logical expression for selecting chunks. This is a serious problem, and one that is not present in most competing programs.

Output

Reports from "Analyze Codes"

Reports can be viewed on screen, exported to a text file, or printed out. You can get a source tag (see below) with each chunk showing its origin, but you cannot view it in context. If you need context, you'll have to go back to the individual cases and ask to display the chunk for each relevant "code" entry.

This is another of the weaknesses of the program. Ideally, you would have the option of viewing each identified chunk in its context as the search progressed. Alternatively, because the program is HyperCard based on the Mac, and Toolbook based on the PC, it could be rewritten to maintain links to the source files so that you could, say, click on the chunk in the report to view it in context.

There are numerous options for customizing your reports. You can generate a list of the cases included by your selection criteria and a list of the codes in your report (you can use this option to get a list of all the codes in your study). These lists can be generated on their own or at the beginning of a longer report. You can also ask for the selection criteria to be printed out.

The retrieved chunks can be labeled with source tags showing case name, code name, frequency of the code within the case, source type (text, picture, video, or audio), and source reference (character range, page number, and filename). The output can be sorted either by case or by code.

Finally, you can save all of the settings for a report, so that the whole thing can be retrieved and rerun, for example, with some modifications, or after you have modified the data. If you don't care about seeing context (a big "if"), this is a very nice, complete, customizable report.

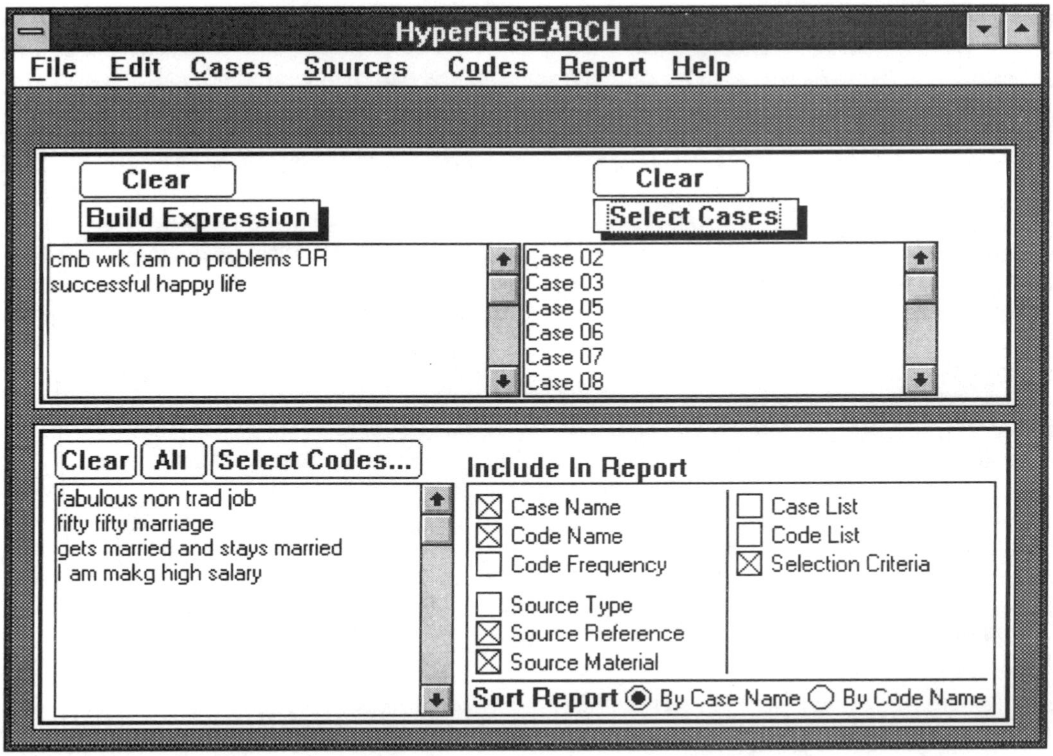

HyperRESEARCH Figure 2. The Analyze Codes window consists of four work areas: the Build Expression box, for building expressions to select cases by; the Select Cases box, where you can choose to select either by the expression or by case name; the Codes to Include box, where you select the codes to retrieve text by; and the Include in Report checkboxes, to specify the type of material you want in your report.

Theory Building

The hypothesis tester is what makes HyperRESEARCH such a unique and important program. ResearchWare's assertion is that this capability finally brings replicability to qualitative data analysis. It's a reasonable claim, even if, like some researchers, you have doubts about the importance of replication in qualitative research.

The hypothesis tester allows you to build a series of IF . . . THEN rules. The IF statement is a logical expression built of codes with AND, OR, and NOT statements. The THEN action can be either adding or deleting a code from the case (although only for the duration of the hypothesis-testing run—they never *really* get added to or deleted from the case card). Typically, you will be saying IF some combination of codes exists for this case, THEN add a new code representing my assertion about this combination of codes. Subsequent rules can refer to these added codes. (The ability to delete codes as well gives you more flexibility in building your set of rules. Conceivably, you might want a step in your series of rules to remove a code under certain conditions.) You could also specify multiple actions in the THEN statement. This all sounds pretty abstract. Let's turn to the example in the manual and tutorial, which is a good illustration (though it only uses rules that add codes and none that delete them).

The tutorial study is called the Cinderella Study and consists of eight interviews with college-age women about their expectations for their lives at age 40. The hypothesis to be tested is that these women have unrealistically high expectations about having both highly successful career and family lives and experiencing no conflict between the two goals. The hypothesis is operationalized using the following codes:

fabulous non traditional job

I am making high salary

gets married and stays married

wants kids

cmb wrk fam no problems

successful happy life

Figure 3 shows the tutorial hypothesis being constructed. The first rule says IF (I am making a high salary

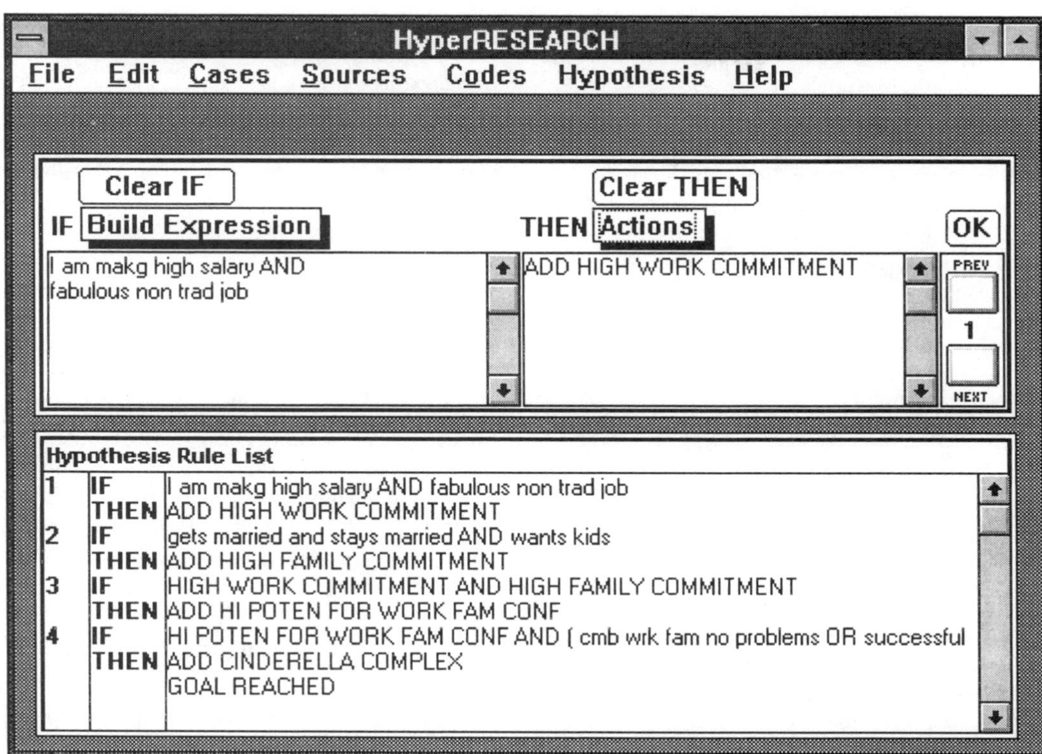

HyperRESEARCH Figure 3. The hypothesis tester window. In the top two windows, Rule 1 is being worked on; the IF portion on the left and the THEN portion on the right. In the bottom window, the entire rule list appears.

AND have a fabulous non traditional job), THEN (ADD high work commitment). This represents the researcher's conclusion that, if the respondent received both codes in the IF statement, THEN she is highly committed to a successful career. The second rule says IF (gets married and stays married AND wants kids), THEN (ADD high family commitment). The third rule uses the codes added by the first two. It states, IF (high work commitment AND high family commitment), THEN (ADD hi poten for wrk fam conf). This says that, if the respondent has proved true on the first two rules, then (in the researcher's opinion) she is headed for some conflict between the two goals. The fourth rule uses the results of the third. It states, IF (hi poten for work fam conf AND [cmb wrk fam no problems OR successful happy life]), THEN (ADD Cinderella complex). This states that, IF the respondent has the two conflicting (in the researcher's opinion) goals, AND has one of two codes indicating that she expects no problems in balancing the two, THEN she fulfills the original hypothesis. To indicate that this rule fulfills the hypothesis, you also add to the THEN statement a GOAL. If the final rule proves true, and thus the GOAL is reached, HyperRESEARCH reports that the hypothesis has been supported by the current case.

(A more conservative way to look at this is that the pattern you've specified and constructed has been found to exist in this case. True hypothesis testing takes place at the next step when you, for example, look at the proportion of cases for which the pattern holds or does not. Another approach is to compare your conclusions with an objective measure. If you find that a case has a pattern of codes that you think will predict, say, poverty, you should then have an objective measure of poverty to check your findings against. The implication is that you have to be careful that your outcome variable can be legitimately inferred from the data. Richards and Richards, 1994, provide a thorough discussion of this issue.)

The program makes numerous passes through the case, executing each rule in turn, until there are no more rules whose IF statements are true. The reporting for each case shows which rules applied and the final conclusion. After running an analysis, the researcher can revise the original rules, adding new codes or changing logical expressions (though if you want to delete anything from a rule, you'll have to clear that part of it—IF or THEN—and start over). For example, you might want to use more of the codes about career expectations to identify high work commitment cases. Finally, you will have a set of cases for which the hypothesis was "true" and a set for which it was false. Such results could easily be subjected to statistical analysis. In addition, new hypotheses could be tested on the set for which the first hypothesis proved true and the set for which it proved false. (Note, though, that you'll have to do this by adding more rules to the original hypothesis because HyperRESEARCH *doesn't retain* the codes it applies during hypothesis testing.)

There's yet another layer of possibilities here. The hypothesis tester determines whether the hypothesis is true or not for a case by whether or not the rule, usually the final one, which has a GOAL in the THEN statement, is true. But you can designate GOALS in multiple rules of a hypothesis, providing for several ways for a hypothesis to be "true."

Data Linking

HyperRESEARCH provides one type of hypertext linking: one-way links from the case cards to the coded chunks in context. As shown in Figure 1, the case card lists references to coded chunks, which include the location (filename and position) and the name of the code applied to the chunk. When you select one of these references with the mouse, you are given the option to "display" the chunk, which pops up the entire source file in a window. The chunk is highlighted, and you can scroll around in the text. You can make new coded entries on the case for the current chunk or select and code new chunks if you wish. It would be nice to be able to print source text from this window, but you can't; you have to go to Analyze Codes to print the coded chunks or open up the source file with an editor or word processor to print more extensive, or different, chunks. (As a workaround, you could apply a new code, "PRINT," to free-form segments you want to print, and then go to Analyze Codes to print them.)

This is it for hypertexting in HyperRESEARCH. The links are one way, so you can't scroll through source text and pop from there to the cases, and there's no way to create links between text files, between cases, or between codes.

User Friendliness

This is another high point of the program, especially as compared with some of the DOS programs. Even though the manual was not finished at the time we first reviewed HyperRESEARCH, the program was extremely easy to learn and get working on. The help system actually helps a lot. You turn on help mode, then click on any menu item, and, instead of the command being executed, an explanation appears in the help window. Inexperienced researchers may be a bit confused at first by the organization of the data into study and cases, and the independence of the source files from these, but beyond this they should find the program extremely user friendly.

Technical Support

During the first exploration of the program, two calls were made for technical support. The first time, we got some help from the person who answered the phone, and then got a call back a couple of hours later for answers to some more technical questions. The second call (on a Saturday) was answered by an answering machine, and it took about a week for a call back. Both times, the people on the phone were friendly, patient, and helpful.

Comparative Remarks

What HyperRESEARCH has that other programs don't are organization by cases, onto which you can code from multiple source files, and the hypothesis tester—both strong features that make it worth serious consideration. It doesn't have the sophistication in coding that other code-based theory-builders like NUD•IST and ATLAS/ti or even code-and-retrieve programs like The Ethnograph have. The inability to retrieve based on the combination of codes on a *chunk* is a real problem, and a unique one among these sorts of programs. It also lacks memoing, a surprising omission for a program in this group, and has only one, albeit powerful, type of data linking.

Summary

HyperRESEARCH is, in several respects, an important, innovative program. Its ease of coding and unique database structure are important strengths. But its outstanding features are the hypothesis "tester" and the organization of data into cases.

On the other hand, there are important limitations, discussed throughout this review, such as the size of chunks, the inability to recognize multiple codes on the same chunk and apply logical expressions to chunks, the absence of any facilities for memoing or data linking, the lack of Boolean logic for Autocode and copying and renaming codes, and the inability to see search/report results in context.

All in all, the program is worth serious consideration, and you can get a fully working demo version (it just won't save your work) for free from a BBS or on a disk from the company for $10. This would be an easy way to check out how well the program meets your needs. If ResearchWare addresses the problems discussed here, HyperRESEARCH will be one of the better programs available and well worthwhile.

References

Dupuis, A., & Tornabene, E. (1993). *HyperRESEARCH(TM) from ResearchWare: A content analysis tool for the qualitative researcher.* Randolph, MA: ResearchWare, Inc.

Richards, T., & Richards, L. (1994). Using computers in qualitative analysis. In N. Denzin & Y. Lincoln (Eds.), *Handbook of qualitative research* (chap. 28, pp. 445-462). Thousand Oaks, CA: Sage.

NUD•IST 3.0

Available for Macintosh and Windows

Qualitative Solutions & Research Pty. Ltd.[1]
Box 171
La Trobe University Post Office
Melbourne, Victoria 3083, Australia

Phone: 61 (3) 459-1699
Fax: 61 (3) 479-1441

Prices:

Power Version $555 (Educ. Price $333)
Entry Version $333 (Educ. Price $200)
Various multiple licenses and network deals available

Hardware Requirements:
For Macintosh
- Macintosh with System 6.0.4 or later, or System 7.0.1 or later
- 2.5MB of free RAM (3MB strongly recommended)
- Hard disk with at least 4MB free space

For Windows
- 386 or better—the faster the better
- Windows NT or 3.1
- 5MB of free RAM[2]
- Hard disk with at least 3MB free space
- VGA or better monitor

Overview

NUD•IST (for Non-numerical, Unstructured Data Indexing, Searching and Theorizing) is a program designed for the storage, coding, retrieval, and analysis of text. Conceptually, it is one of the best-thought-out programs around: The developers have gone to great pains to figure out the types of actions and features required for various methods of text analysis and to provide for them. With the release of version 3.0, the program has a graphical user interface (GUI) that does justice to its capabilities and a set of features improvements that make the program one of the best for plain code-and-retrieve or code-based theory-building work. The structuring of your database according to a hierarchically organized "index system" of codes, together with a collection of code search operators unmatched in terms of power, variety, or relevance, are what give this program its particular appeal.

During regular use, when you start the program up, you're looking at a hierarchical tree diagram of your coding scheme (see Figure 1), and you can navigate and ex-

1. Distributor for the United States and Canada: Learning Profiles, Inc., Attn. Dr. Jim Adams-Berger, 2329 West Main St. #330, Littleton, CO 80120-1951. Phone: (303) 797-2633, ext. 17. Fax: (303) 797-2660. E-mail: jimab@omni.org.

2. The manual says you need 3MB free RAM but, in practice, NUD•IST will try to take about 5MB. The manual says that if you have only 4MB total RAM, or have 8MB and want to be able to run other applications at the same time as NUD•IST, you'll need a permanent Windows swap-file of 5-10MB. We ran into severe low memory problems with 8MB of total RAM and a 3MB swap-file.

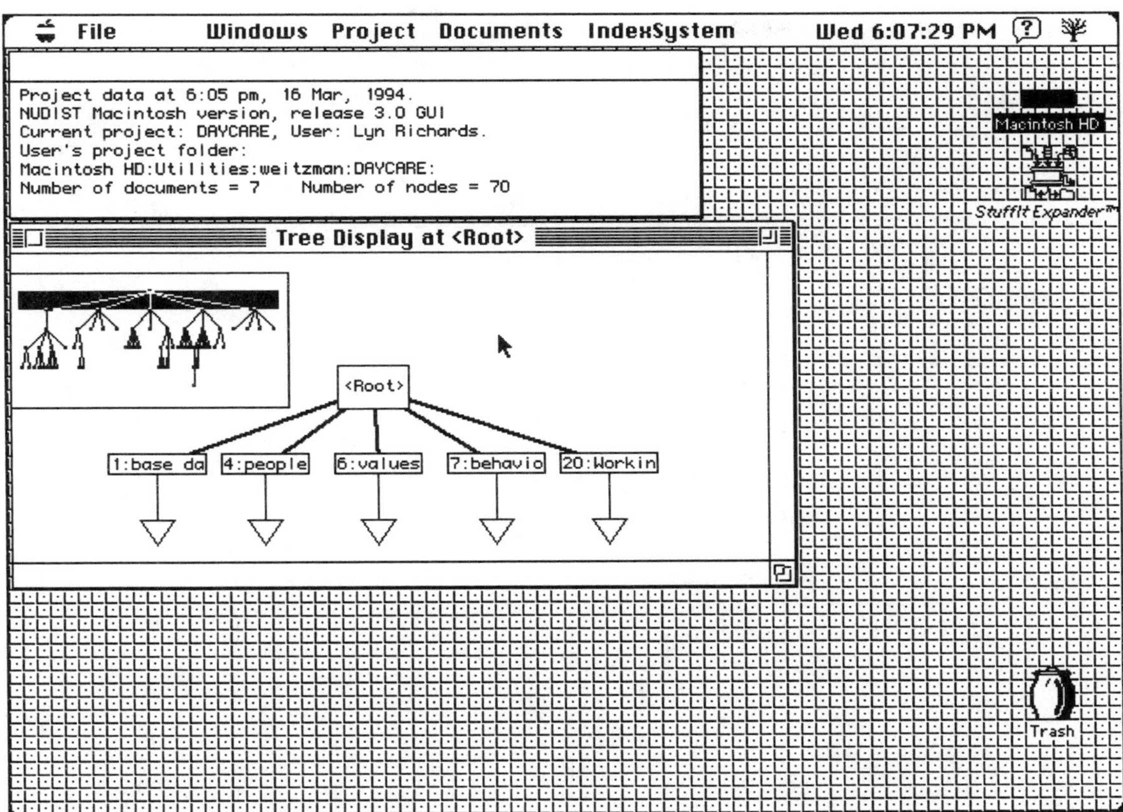

NUD•IST Figure 1. This is the basic view in NUD•IST. At the top is an information window with basic information about the project (in this case, the tutorial that comes with the program). The lower window contains both "current" and "summary" (small inset) views of your coding scheme (index system), but you just work with the current view, which shows the current code and its immediate children (in this case, the current code is <ROOT>, a meaningless code that is simply the starting point of the tree). You can scroll around the current view by clicking on arrows, which indicate that there's more to be seen in a given direction. By clicking on a node (the boxes that represent codes), you get a menu with options to perform various operations on nodes, such as to make reports on them and the text they apply to, or to rearrange or merge them.

plore your codes and the referenced text either graphically or with commands from pull-down menus. In addition to this hierarchical index (code) system, which can be easily "pruned" and rearranged, the program also maintains a document system. You can explore your data from either one, the latter organizing your investigations on the basis of documents first, codes second, while the former works on a codes first, documents second basis. This is explained further, below. Codes are conceived of hierarchically in NUD•IST, though you can avoid hierarchy if you only establish first-level codes. Each first-level code is the root of an unlimited tree of subcodes. Because of this tree conception, codes are referred to as "nodes."

The developers' approach to designing NUD•IST is particularly sound, conceptually. Tom and Lyn Richards are a husband and wife team; he's a computer scientist and she's a qualitative researcher. They've pooled their respective expertise and done quite a bit of writing and thinking about the issues involved (see, e.g., Richards & Richards, 1994).

Because the program is conceptually rich, it will take some discussion here to explain it. As a result, this review may make the program seem complicated, but it's actually quite user friendly.

Database Structure

All of the data for a given project are organized in, logically enough, a "project." Your data for each project are organized and referenced by two separate but parallel databases, or "systems"—the "document system" and the "index system." The document system keeps track of all of your documents (text files), as the name implies, while the

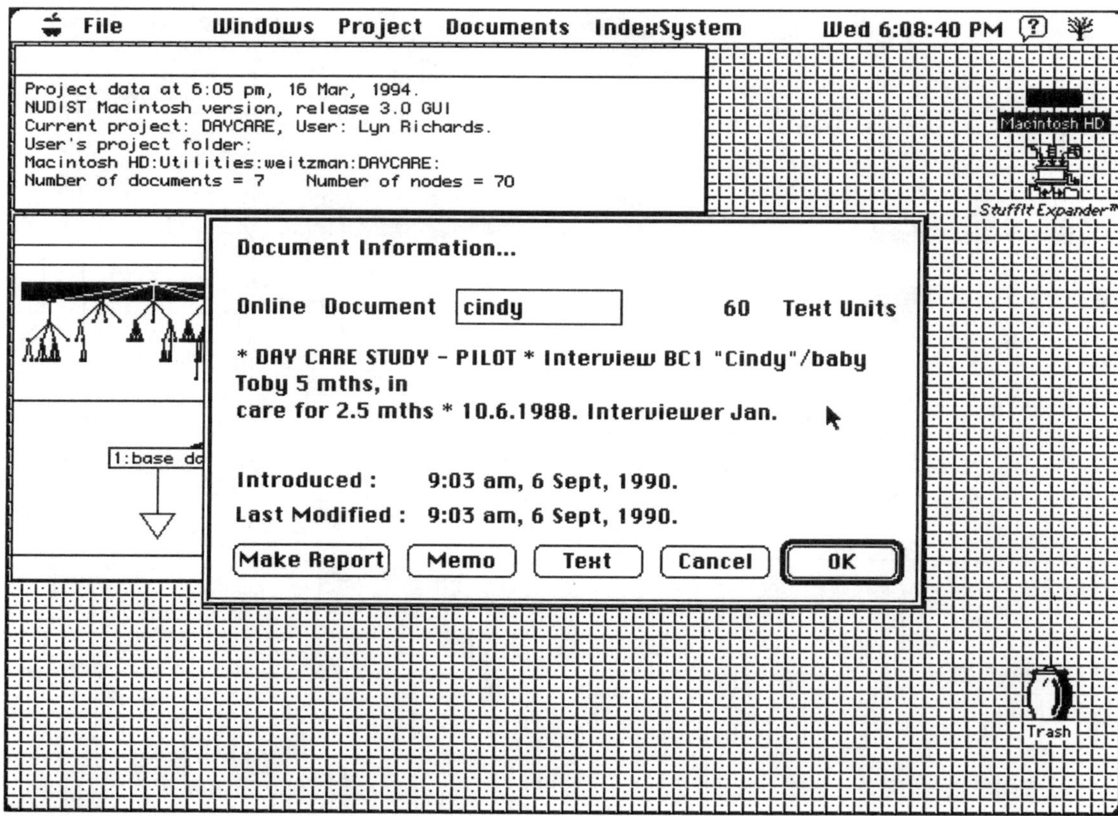

NUD•IST Figure 2. The Document Information dialog box shows you the name of the document, the number of text units it has, its header (the cursor arrow is pointing to it), and the dates on which it was introduced and last modified. There are options to make a report on this document, to view or edit its memo, or to view, edit, or index (code) its text.

index system organizes your codes and keeps track of the way in which they "index" your text.

The Document System

There are numerous options for investigating documents, allowing you to ask questions about the coding that has been applied to a particular document—applying codes, editing data files, writing and reading memos about documents, and so on. These are described further along. The various types of information about a document are accessed through the Document Information dialog box (see Figure 2). You can have as many documents as will fit on your hard disk. The size of documents is limited by disk space and RAM. The "rule of thumb" provided in the documentation is that you will need (in addition to the 2MB of disk space taken up by the program itself) .5KB of disk space for each node and document in the project, plus the space taken up by the actual document files themselves. This means that 2,000 nodes and/or documents will require an additional 1MB of disk space. Similarly, you will need (in addition to the 2.5MB of RAM needed by the program itself) .5KB of RAM for each node and document in the project (but you don't need RAM to hold the text of each document file). Again, 2,000 nodes and/or documents will require 1MB of RAM.

Text units. NUD•IST does not support completely free-form coding, which allows you to simply select the exact range of text, from one character position to another, to which you want a code to apply (programs like HyperRESEARCH and ATLAS/ti let you do this by simply dragging across the text of interest with a mouse). Rather, you must specify a range of "text units" to which you want the code to apply. Text units are always delimited by hard carriage returns, which would typically get you paragraphs. If you want a unit other than paragraphs, you have to prepare the raw text with, say, a return after each line, sentence, or word. The latter two options may make your text hard to read, because each sentence or word, respectively, will start on a new line. In the case of words, this seems an untenable approach; even folks who do word-oriented analyses generally want to see the word of interest in a line or sentence, not all by itself.

To apply a code to a segment of text larger than a text unit, as mentioned above, you apply it to a *range of text units* so that what you may want to think about as your coded chunk (as you can in many other programs) is actually a range of chunks. A serious problem, beyond lack of flexibility, arises from this approach in the way text is displayed with codes. If you want to see the codes that apply to some text (the nodes at which the text is indexed), the codes are printed after *each* text unit. This means that, if your text units are lines, and you've applied codes to a range of lines, like an entire paragraph, the text in your printout will be interrupted after every line with a list of the codes, even though they are virtually the same for every line, as shown in Figure 3, which is drawn from the tutorial. This can get particularly annoying if you've applied some codes to the entire file, such as **/base data/interviewees/gender/female** in Figure 3. But this is worse than an annoyance; look again at Figure 3, and see how long it takes you to figure out where the various codes begin and end. (Imagine what this would look like with the list of codes appearing after every *word*!) Compare this with The Ethnograph's depiction of code applications with brackets in the margin. At the very least, this situation could be improved by moving those codes that apply to the whole document (e.g., demographic information) to the top of the listing for that document, so that the number of codes listed after each line could be reduced.

Headers and subheaders. You can place one "header" at the beginning of each file. You simply begin the first text unit of the file with an * and type whatever information you would like to have in the header. This information will appear with any text you subsequently retrieve from the document. So, you might enter information concerning the names of the interviewer and interviewee, the date, time, and place of the interview, and any other identifying or contextual information you wanted.

Subheaders are used to divide the document into sections. Any text unit, after the header, that begins with an * will be treated as a subheader and will appear with a retrieval of any text between it and the next subheader. You might use subheaders as speaker identifiers or to provide context for a part of the file. For example, in the interviews in the tutorial, subheaders are used to provide contextual information like "*INTERRUPTION: BABY CRYING. MOTHER NOT CONCENTRATING." This information would appear with any text retrieved from between that subheader and the next, which reads "*BABY SETTLED, ASLEEP FOR REMAINDER OF THE INTERVIEW."

One limitation here is that you have only two levels: headers, which apply to the whole file, and subheaders, which divide the file into contiguous sections. You cannot use subheaders as hierarchical outline levels.

On-line versus off-line documents. The document system provides explicit support, not only for the text documents you actually have on the hard disk ("on-line" data) but for "off-line" documents that you don't have in computer form at all, such as books or archival data, which are impractical or impossible to scan or transcribe. For off-line documents, NUD•IST keeps a place in the document system, and you can call up the Document Information dialog box (Figure 2) just as though the text were on line. You can attach memos to them and edit their header information. You specify the number of text units in the document when you "introduce" it to NUD•IST, so you can even index (code) "text units" of an off-line document. Because the data are off line, you're not subject to NUD•IST's hard carriage return restriction on text units and can make them anything you like. Note that NUD•IST won't be able to retrieve the text itself in response to a search, but it will give you text unit numbers, and you can then look up the text in your off-line documents.

This basic strategy could, in essence, be used with any code-and-retrieve or code-based theory-building program by setting up dummy text files—with no actual text, just references to, say, book chapters or individuals at a site—and then coding these references. NUD•IST's explicit support for off-line documents, however, is clean, clear, and user friendly. It encourages you to think about and explore possible applications of this technique.

The Index System

The "index system" is the real heart of the program. Coding is conceived of in NUD•IST as a process of indexing your text, so that your coding scheme can be used as an index for retrieving text. Accordingly, the sense one gets is that, rather than codes being applied to text (the way we usually think about it), each code has a list of references to the text it indexes. Because the coding scheme is conceived of as a hierarchical tree structure, the codes, being the branch points in the tree, are referred to as "nodes." Coding, then, is referred to as a process of *indexing text at a node.*

Nodes. Nodes are identified by an address and title, which include the addresses and titles of any superordinate nodes. For example, in the tutorial project, the fourth subnode of the first subnode of the sixth first-level node is node 6 1 4, whose title, **/values/child's needs/development**, gives the titles of all three nodes involved. *However,* and this is important, text with this code is essentially coded just with this one node, "development." If you want the parent nodes "values" or "child's needs" to apply as well, you'll have to apply them explicitly (there are features to automate this,

```
NUD•IST Macintosh Version 3.0 GUI.
Licensee: eben weitzman.

PROJECT: DAYCARE, User Lyn Richards, 6:13 pm, 16 Mar, 1994.

*******************************************************************************
(20 5)                  /Working nodes/IndSysSrch2
*** Definition:
Search for (OVERLAP (7 1 1) (7 2 2 4))
+++++++++++++++++++++++++++++++++++++++
+++ ON-LINE DOCUMENT: cindy
+++ Retrieval for this document: 32 units out of 60, = 53%
++ Text units 4-28:
4     CINDY:    Yeah, I hated it.  Even when he was here with me.  I hated it.
(1 1 1 2)               /base data/interviewees/gender/female
(1 1 2 2)               /base data/interviewees/age-group/30s
(1 1 3 4)               /base data/interviewees/religion/no religion
(6 1)                   /values/child's needs
(6 1 1)                 /values/child's needs/love
(6 3 2 2)               /values/childcare/physical/cleanliness
(6 3 2 3)               /values/childcare/physical/safety
(7 2 2 4)               /behaviour/mothers'/adapting/settling in
(7 2 8)                 /behaviour/mothers'/accepting
(20 5)                  /Working nodes/IndSysSrch2
5     I really did.  Because well you know you look at the floor, there's sand
(1 1 1 2)               /base data/interviewees/gender/female
(1 1 2 2)               /base data/interviewees/age-group/30s
(1 1 3 4)               /base data/interviewees/religion/no religion
(6 3 2 2)               /values/childcare/physical/cleanliness
(6 3 2 3)               /values/childcare/physical/safety
(7 2 2 4)               /behaviour/mothers'/adapting/settling in
(7 2 8)                 /behaviour/mothers'/accepting
(20 5)                  /Working nodes/IndSysSrch2
6     in the carpet and you vacuum it till your fingers are worn out but its
(1 1 1 2)               /base data/interviewees/gender/female
(1 1 2 2)               /base data/interviewees/age-group/30s
(1 1 3 4)               /base data/interviewees/religion/no religion
(6 3 2 2)               /values/childcare/physical/cleanliness
(6 3 2 3)               /values/childcare/physical/safety
(7 2 2 4)               /behaviour/mothers'/adapting/settling in
(7 2 8)                 /behaviour/mothers'/accepting
(20 5)                  /Working nodes/IndSysSrch2
```

NUD•IST Figure 3. Printout showing where codes apply to text. In this case, text units have been defined as lines, and the entire list of codes that apply to each line is listed after it, no matter how redundant this is. At left are the node (code) addresses (defined under "The Index System," below) and at right are actual code names. This listing was produced by searching for the overlap of two codes, with addresses (7 1 1) and (7 2 2 4).

described below). Nodes can have longer definitions for reference that include comments automatically generated about the creation of the node as well as any additional comments you type in. Each node can also have its own memo. Finally, nodes have references to text units (or *ranges* of text units).

The developers have written at length (e.g., Richards & Richards, 1994) about the flexibility of this system. For example, they argue that nodes can represent anything you want, whether coding categories, concepts, individuals, and so on. You can thus use the index system not only to index (code) text but also to represent the relationships among concepts you are working with (though you can't explicitly name these relationships). You could also use it to set up a casewise organization of your data for cross-case analysis. You would accomplish this by indexing all the text for a case at a "case node," which might be identified by a subject's or site's name or ID number. This setup would allow you to have the data for a case scattered around multiple documents, for example, an interview with the subject of that case, field notes from your observations of the subject, and interviews with other informants who might have mentioned the subject.

Manipulating the index system. When you create a node, you choose its place in the index system's hierarchy. If you're not clear about hierarchy yet, you can start by making all your codes first-level codes and then move them down to subordinate levels later if you want.

So you might start with a set of codes including "supportive," "student involvement," "competition," "trainer style," and "teacher/trainer interaction." After working with these a while, you might decide that the first four codes were all about (were subcodes of) the "social environment," while the last two were about (were subcodes of) the "training implementation." You would then create the new parent codes, "social environment" and "training implementation," as first-level nodes, and then shift the original nodes down to the second level, under their new parents. This could get somewhat disconcerting, as your data-level codes could wind up changing their positions and levels in the coding scheme quite a bit, and you could wind up with data-level nodes at different levels in the hierarchy, depending on how many levels of abstraction were above them.

Note that this is the reverse of the way we usually talk about code hierarchies. We usually talk about our base-level codes as first level and then call higher-order codes second level, third, and so on. In NUD•IST, you work in the opposite direction: The top of the tree (most general) is the first level, and subordinate levels are second, third, and so on. You can shift nodes (of any level), and their subtrees, from place to place in the coding scheme. You can also copy the contents of a node (comments, references, and so on) to another node, or merge the contents of two nodes.

The implication of this top-down structure is that it's a little harder (or at least a little more awkward) to take an inductive, grounded-theory approach. It also invites you to name parent codes early—though you don't have to accept the invitation, of course.

Another interesting aspect of NUD•IST is that the results of most searches are stored as a new node, which you can name, write memos to, and to which you can add or delete text references. Thus, if you search for text with both the codes "motives" and "critical incidents," you will wind up with a new node for this combination of codes. A node can wind up representing very complex sets of codes or other facts about the text. (See further discussion of this below under "System Closure.")

Data Entry

On-line documents are text only, although if you buy a separate program, you can use video too (more about video below). Typically, you would create your text files with your word processor and then save them as text only, or ASCII, files. NUD•IST has its own text editor, which is not bad and could certainly be used for writing up text files, but if your files are even moderately lengthy, you'll probably be better off with a full-fledged word processor.

Several formatting requirements must be met. First and foremost, you must make sure that your text units are separated by hard carriage returns. If you want, for example, sentences as text units, you'll have to insert hard returns after each sentence. If you'll be using lines as text units, most word processors will, upon request, end each line with a hard return when saving the file as an ASCII file. The manual warns that, if you're using lines, you should make sure there are no more than 72 characters per line, or the text will be forced to wrap after NUD•IST adds line numbers to the file. You are also cautioned not to use tabs or indents in your text files as they "may disrupt the format" of the text.

Headers and subheaders are typed directly into the text. Headers begin on the first line of the file, with an * in the first column. If there is more than one text unit of header (as defined by carriage returns), as long as there is nothing in between, you can just begin each one with an *. Subheaders are typed in wherever you want, also beginning with an *.

After your data are prepared, you place all of the documents for a project in a single folder (directory). From within NUD•IST, you then "introduce" documents into a project. You tell NUD•IST whether your document is on line or off. In the former case, you select the name of the file, and then give it a title, or document name, for NUD•IST to use in the project. This can be a longer, more intuitive, or more informative name than the filename. (If you're introducing an off-line document, you then specify the number of text units you want it to have.)

Video

NUD•IST 3.0 for the Macintosh, with the help of another program, can use videotape as data. This is accom-

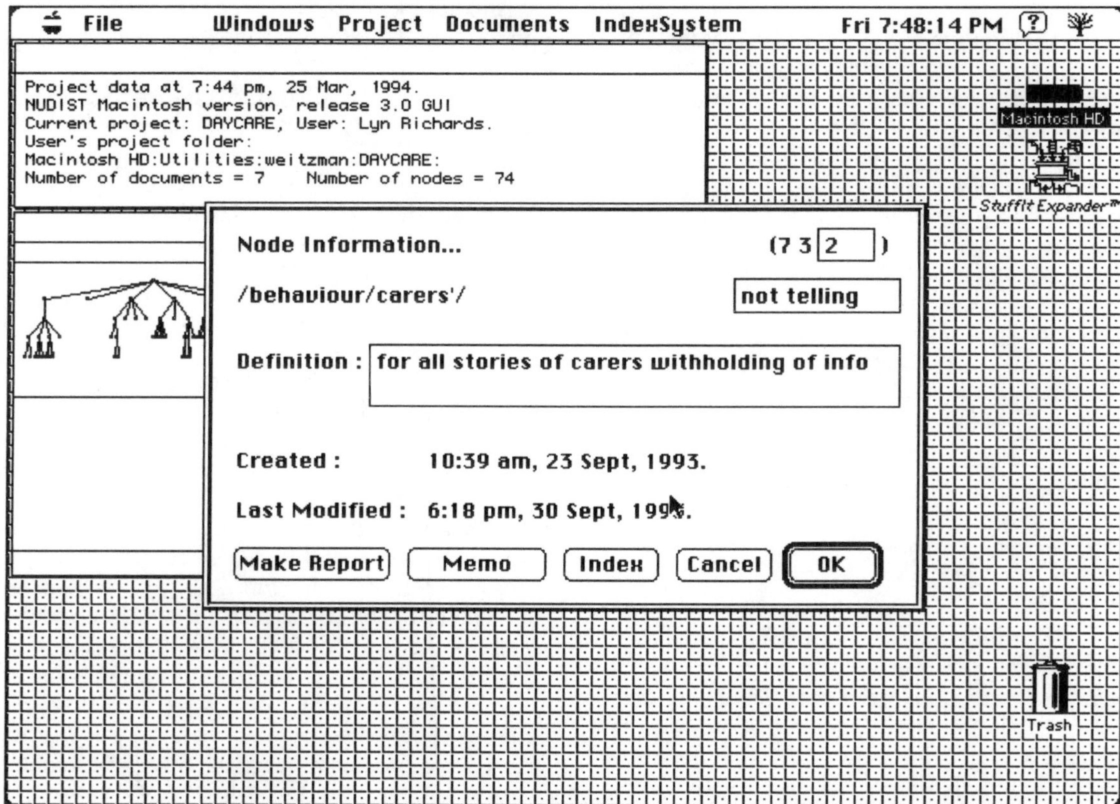

NUD•IST Figure 4. The Node Information dialog box. At the top right is the node's address (7 3 2); the address of the node's parent is (7 3), and the current node's numbering under this, (2), appears in a box where you can edit it. The title of the parent is **/behavior/carer's/** and the current node's own title is in the box at right, **not telling**. The full title of this node is then **/behavior/carer's/not telling**. There are options to make a report on the node, view or edit its memo, or add or delete indexing with this node (apply it to text or remove its applications from text).

plished via a program called CVideo.[3] CVideo runs with a videotape deck connected to your Macintosh with a cable. It allows you to control your tape deck, and it will record tape count numbers to locate scenes you want to mark for later retrieval. These numbers are recorded in a text file, which you can edit, adding annotations or memos about the video scenes. You can then export the text file to NUD•IST as a document. The tape count numbers will be formatted as subheaders, so that they will show up with any of the following text that you later retrieve. Thus you could write extensive notes or descriptions of the video scenes, and code and search them in NUD•IST, and any text you retrieved would come with the tape count number of the appropriate video segment. Apparently (we weren't able to check this out), if you have both NUD•IST and CVideo running at the same time,[4] you can select the tape count in the subheader in the NUD•IST output and have CVideo find and play the indexed portion of video.

Working on the Data

There are several ways to work on your data in NUD•IST. First you can index, or code it. You can attach memos to both nodes and documents. And you can edit your text. You can also work extensively on your index system, or coding scheme (see above, under "Manipulating the Index System," in the "The Index System" subsection of the "Database Structure" section).

Nodes are created and their various aspects accessed through the Node Information dialog box (see Figure 4).

3. Produced by Dr. Jeremy Roschelle, Knowledge Revolution, 15 Brush Place, San Francisco, CA 94103. Phone: (415) 553-8153. Fax: (415) 553-8012. Price for version 1.5: $150.

4. This means you must have System 7 and adequate RAM.

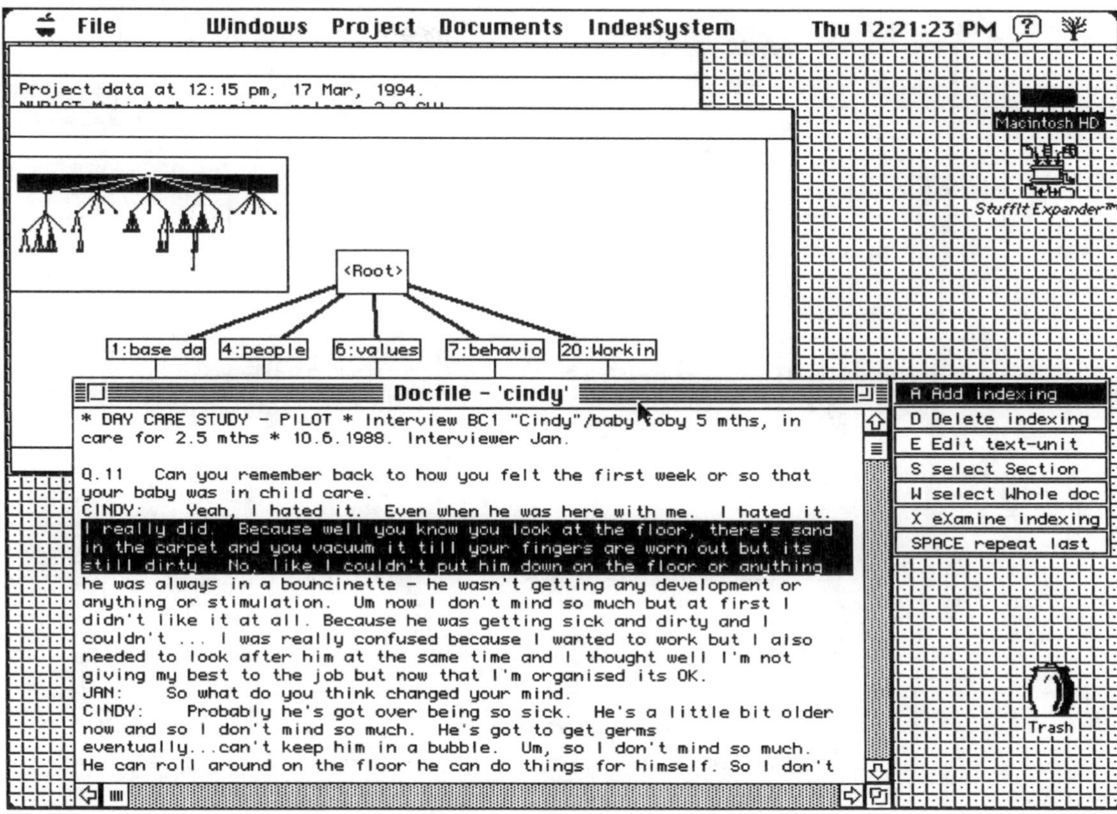

NUD•IST Figure 5. Working on a document. This window is accessed with the Text button in the Document Information dialog box (see Figure 2). After selecting some text (shown in reverse colors) with the mouse, you can press the letter "A" or click on the Add Indexing button on the right, and then type in or choose the code (node) you want to apply to this range of text units. Note that you do not see text unit numbers in this view, nor can you tell whether text units are lines, paragraphs, or something larger.

From here you can do things like edit a node's name, definition, or memo or apply it to text.

Indexing (Coding)

You can approach coding in two different ways. Beginning with version 3, you can do on-screen, one-step, mouse-drag coding, though you're still limited to coding by text unit. Or you can do two-step coding from a dialog box, where you type in or select node address, document name, and text units. The manual suggests that two-step coding may be preferable when a document is off line, when you've done your coding on hard copy first, or when you want to specify references to many documents at once for the same node. You also might find this a useful approach when applying codes, such as for demographic information, to entire documents at once.

One-step coding. This is an important addition to the program. From the Document Information dialog box (see Figure 2), if you select the Text button, the document will pop up in an editing window (Figure 5). To the right of the text are buttons that allow you to add or delete indexing for the currently selected text units. If you choose to add indexing, you're given a box into which you can type node addresses. If you don't know the address of the node you want to apply, you can pop up the Select Nodes dialog box, which lets you navigate down through the hierarchy of nodes to the one you want to apply (see Figure 6). There are also options to select a whole section (as defined by subheaders) or the entire document, after which you can add or delete indexing for these larger selections. You can also ask to "examine" the indexing for a selected text unit, which pops up a dialog box showing a listing of codes that index that text unit. You can delete from, but not add to, this list.

Two-step coding. If you prefer a two-step coding approach, you can use the Add/Delete Indexing dialog box, shown in Figure 7, which is reached from the Node Information dialog

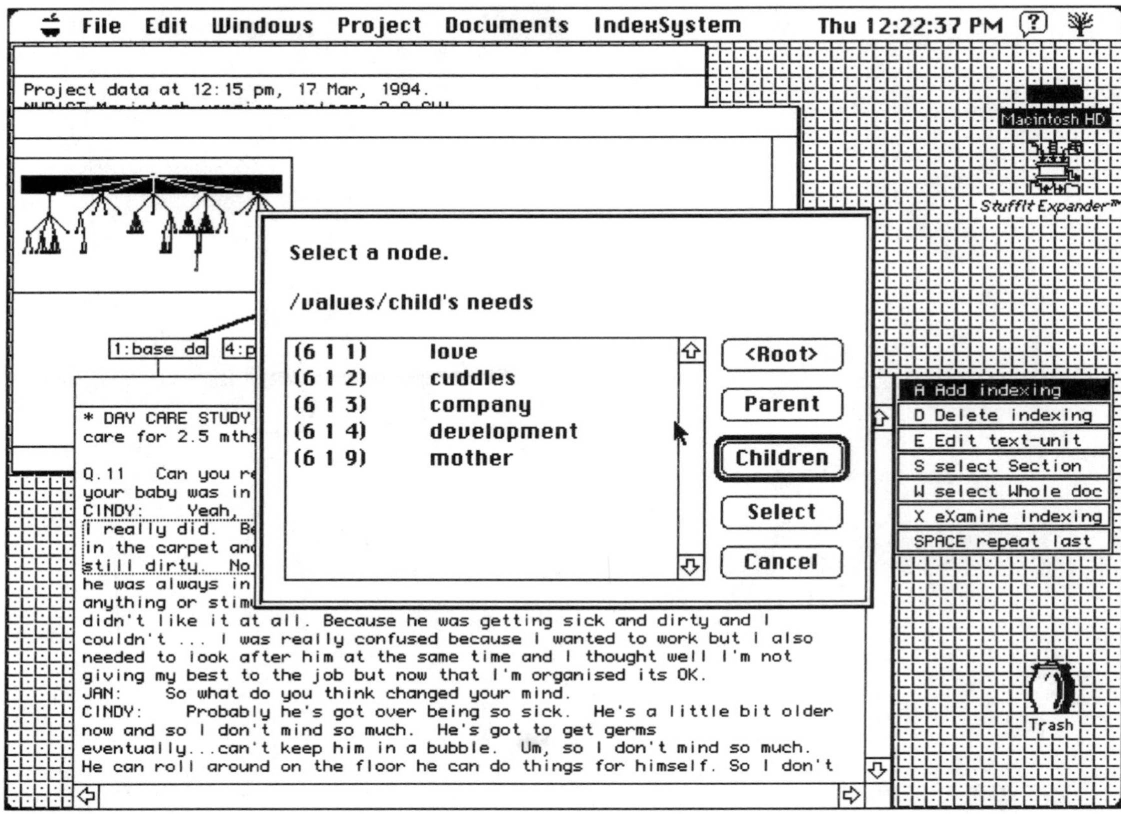

NUD•IST Figure 6. The Select a node dialog box can be popped up if you don't know the address of the node you want. It is available not only when coding but any time you are asked to specify a node address. Shown is a list of the children nodes of node (6 1), **/values/child's needs**. You can click on any of these and ask to see its children, go back up one level to the parent of **/values/child's needs** (you would see *all* the children of **/values**, including **/values/child's needs**), or all the way back up to the <ROOT>. You can also click on any one of these and then choose Select, which will choose that code for the operation you are doing (in this case, coding text).

box. This can be reached by clicking on the node you want to use in the tree display or through the IndexSystem menu. In the Add/Delete Indexing box, you choose a document name and a node address (you can get the Select Nodes box here too—see Figure 6) and specify either a range of text units or the entire document.

This is generally an older, slower method of coding than one-step coding, but as mentioned above, it can be a useful option in certain circumstances. For example, if you're applying demographic codes to whole files, it would probably be most efficient just to name one document after another in this dialog, repeatedly applying, say, the node **/base data/interviewees/gender/female**.

Automated Coding

The results of any search, whether for text or combinations of codes (nodes), can be saved as a new node. For example, you could do a search for a particular character string (say, a word or phrase) and have every text unit with that string indexed at the new node (more about NUD•IST's powerful facilities for text search under "Searching," below). You can have the program stop and show you each find, so you can decide whether or not to include it. When the search is done, you can have the indexing "spread" so that the references at the new node are not just to each found text unit but to a given number of text units, the section, or the document it was found in. Note that when you specify the distance to "spread" the indexing, this same distance is applied to all the hits in the current search; you can't do it on a hit-by-hit basis.

As indicated above, you can also use searches for combinations of codes to create new codes. Because the results of a search for a combination of codes are stored at a new node, the name of this new node becomes, essentially, a new code applying to all text that satisfied the search criteria. The power of this feature becomes more clear when you consider the range of types of code combina-

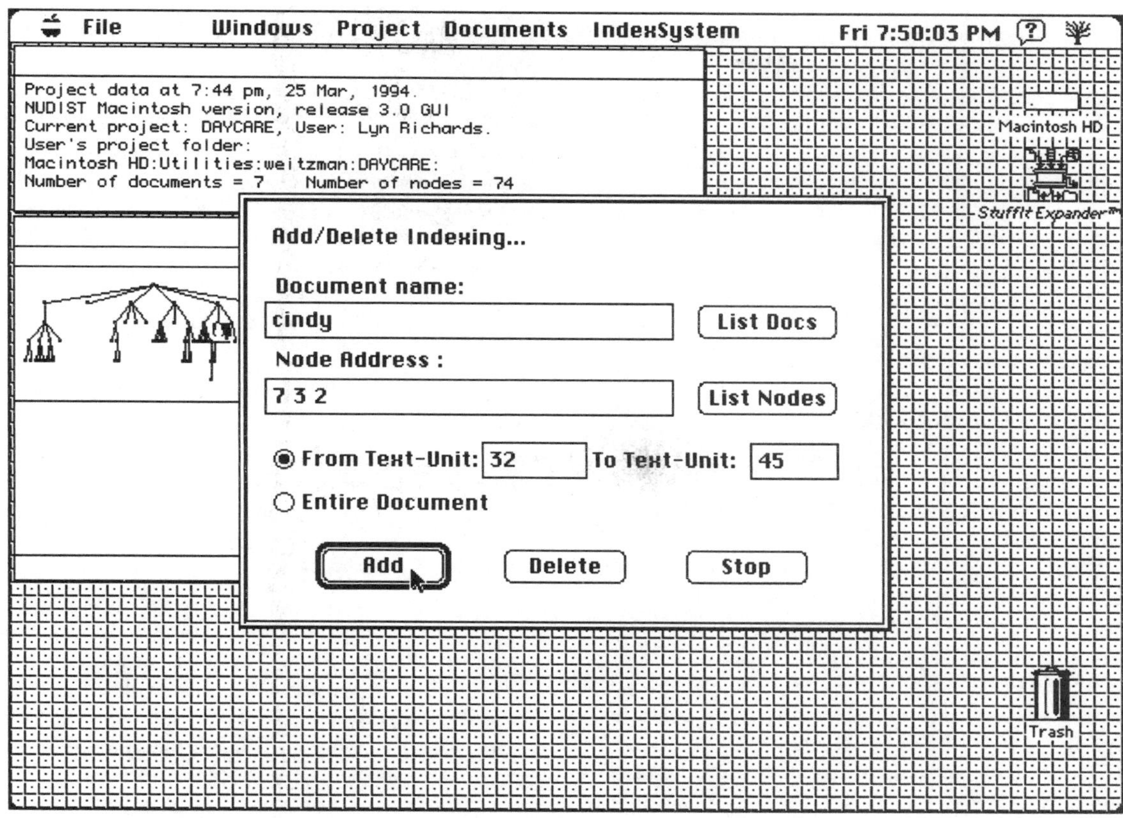

NUD•IST Figure 7. The Add/Delete Indexing box allows you to do two-step coding. You type in document name, node address (the List Nodes button will pop up the Select a node dialog box shown in Figure 6), and specify either a range of text units or the entire document. You can either add or delete indexing.

tions you can specify when searching, which are discussed below.

Editing Text

Also beginning with version 3, you can do some limited editing of your text files, as long as you don't add or delete text units (if you do, your nodes will now index the wrong text, because they work by text unit number). When you pop up the text in an editing window from within NUD•IST (see Figure 5), as when applying codes via the one-step method, there is a button at the right to edit the current text unit. If you choose this option, the text unit is opened up in a separate editing window. (In the Windows version, you can only edit text units from within NUD•IST if the text units are under 32K. This limit should not often be a problem, unless you are using entire documents as your text units.) As long as you don't add any carriage returns, your indexing will not be affected. However, you may wind up with inconsistent text units. For example, if you've been using lines as text units, and you add enough text to make your text unit wrap to another line, you'll wind up with one two-line text unit while the others are all one line. But your text unit numbering will still be OK, and therefore so will your indexing. Also, if you delete all the text in a text unit, the program will still remember the text unit, so that the numbering of all the other ones (and their indexing) is not affected.

Memos

The memoing facilities in NUD•IST are in some ways excellent but in other ways very limited. First, the good news: You can attach memos to nodes (codes) as such—as well as to documents—an important ability sadly lacking in many of the other programs. They are easily accessed from either the Nodes Information or the Documents Information dialog boxes. Memos can be quite long: about 150K (varying with available RAM), which is about 50 pages of single-spaced text, in the Mac version. In the Windows version, you can only edit memos in NUD•IST that are under 32K. This means that your memos are essentially limited to 32K (or about 10 pages of single-spaced text) because you write them with the internal editor.

If you want memos to be indexed or searched, you can easily save them as new documents, adding your own reflections to the database. This provides a certain amount of "system closure" because the results of your analyses can become part of the data.

Now for some rather disappointing news: First, you only get one memo per node or document. (This problem is somewhat offset by the fact that you can always go back and add to a memo so you could make multiple sections of the same memo, and treat them like multiple memos.) You don't have the important flexibility to add memos or annotations at various points in your text files. You also can't search memos as long as they're attached to your documents or nodes; you have to save them out to text files and introduce them as new documents. Further, while you can get memos along with data in some retrieval operations, you can't get them in others. For example, if you do a node-based search, you can get *node* memos with your output, but not the memos attached to the *documents* whose text is retrieved in the course of the search. If you "make a report" on a given node (see "Output," below), you can include the node's memo, *but only* if you're *not* including the text referenced by the node in the report. If you make a listing of all nodes, you can't get their memos with them either (though you can get their definitions). The only way to get document memos is when you make a report on a given document (again, see "Output," below).

Searching

NUD•IST has by far the most extensive and powerful set of code-based retrieval operators around. It provides 18 functions—Boolean and beyond, including references to all sorts of sequencing, overlapping, and nesting of coded ranges of text—for specifying logical combinations of nodes to retrieve, study, or save as new nodes for later study. You can also search for text strings or patterns in the raw text and have the option of saving those results to a new node, which can be used, as we've noted, for automated coding.

The simplest way to search is to retrieve all the text indexed at a certain node (coded with a certain code). This is done from the Node Information dialog box, where you select the Make Report option. One kind of report you can make includes the text references for the node (all the text units indexed at the node). If you want to see what other nodes apply to the retrieved text, you ask for cross-references, which can be just node addresses or can include node names. (Remember, though, that they'll all appear after each text unit, no matter how redundant this gets. See Figure 3.)

Whatever kind of search you do, the retrieved text will be only the coded (indexed) text units. You will not get the surrounding context. You can later do separate operations, which we'll talk about below, to expand the indexing so that you retrieve larger chunks. But you will never be shown search results in their full surrounding context. (Yes, we know we said that twice.)

Searching the Index System

This is where NUD•IST has all the others beat, hands down. There are 18 different operators for specifying relationships (co-occurrence, proximity, and so on) among codes that you want to use in retrieving text. The results of an index system search are saved to a new node. This means that a new node is created, on the "node clipboard," that indexes all the text found by the search, and that you can then add to your index system (code hierarchy) either by attaching it as a subnode to an existing node, or by merging it with an existing node. This is an important aspect of NUD•IST's system closure capabilities; any search you do can become a permanent part of your data. The new node can be given its own name, definition, and memo and has references to all the text units that matched the search request. (If you want, you have the option, while the node is still on the clipboard, to "spread" the indexing from the orginally-indexed text unit[s] to an entire section or document or by a specified number of text units.) Then you can look at the text with the new code. If you merge it with an existing node, the new text references get added to the existing node, so what you're really doing is saying, "I want all text found by the search request coded with this existing code." Another way to look at it is as applying an existing code to the newly found text.

We mentioned parenthetically, in the paragraph above, that you can spread the indexing of the text units on the node clipboard. This is where NUD•IST gives you some control of the context you see your hits in. But you have to make a global decision, for everything retrieved by the current search, about how much you want to spread by, and the result is that you change the size of your output chunks rather than seeing the original chunk in its context. Put another way, you can't just look at each hit in the full context of its source file, unless you spread all your hits over their full files and make whole files your output for the entire search.

So what are these 18 operators we keep referring to? The manual breaks them down into five categories, which help conceptually.

Collation. These are the operators that are most like those in other packages, and they allow you to specify various types of co-occurrence of codes on a segment of text (one or more units). For any of these, you can specify as many nodes as you like. *Intersect* is like an AND list; it finds text units indexed by all of the nodes specified. *Union* is like an OR list; it finds text units indexed by any of the nodes specified. *Less* lets you find text units that are indexed by the first node in a list but by none of the others. *Just-One* is like an exclusive OR, or XOR, search; it finds text units indexed by any one of the nodes you list but none of the others. (The difference between Less and Just-One is that in the former case the first node must be found, whereas in the latter it could be any one node in the list you provide.) *Overlap* finds an Intersection of at least two of the nodes you list, but then shows you all of each of the overlapping text unit ranges, including parts that fall outside the Intersection. This is akin to the "Big Picture" in The Ethnograph. For example, if text units 10-20 are coded "discipline" and text units 15-25 are coded "disruption," the Intersection is text units 15-20, but Overlap will get you text units 10-25.

Contextual. This category overlaps a bit with the last. The operators here are intended to find text coded with a given code, based on its contextual relation to text coded with another code. *At-least* might be better categorized as a collation operator. You specify the number of codes, out of those you list, that must be present for a text unit to be retrieved. So you might ask for text with At-least three of four listed codes. The Overlap operator described above is like an At-least two request. At-least is essentially a set logic operator that lets you say how many intersections among the items you specify must be found; see the review of Metamorph for a fuller description of set logic.

If inside finds ranges of text units that are coded with a given code, if they are completely nested inside a range of text coded with another code. *If outside* is the opposite; it finds ranges of text with a given code that completely surround ranges with another code.

Near is a proximity operator; it allows you to specify the distance within which you want two codes to co-occur. You can specify number of text units, same section, or same document. You can retrieve the first, second, or both of the text unit ranges coded by the two codes. *Followed-by* works just like Near but also lets you specify the order in which the two codes must appear in the text for the search request to be satisfied.

Spread is not really a search operator at all; it lets you extend the indexing for a particular node from the originally-indexed text unit(s) to an entire section or document, or by a specified number of text units in either direction.

Negation. There is only one negation operator, *Not-in,* which is just a NOT operator; it finds text units NOT indexed with a given node. (Actually, in logical terms, *Less* is a negation operator also, but it's grouped with the collation operators.)

Restriction. These operators allow you to filter or restrict the scope of the search and are typically used in conjunction with other operators. *Including-docs-from* lets you restrict your search to those documents that have references to a particular node. *Excluding-docs-from* does the opposite; it restricts your search to documents that do NOT have references to a particular node. You might, for example, use these operators to filter, or subset, your database on demographic variables so that a search might only include data from female subjects. Or you might want to exclude documents indexed as researcher reflections. Unfortunately, you can't restrict by document name.

Tree structured. There are two subgroups of this category, with two search operators each. The first two allow you to get text indexed at nodes higher or lower in the hierarchy than the node of interest. This is important because the program doesn't automatically understand the relationships among parent and child nodes; if you have some text coded **/climate/solitary behavior**, it will only show up in a search for "solitary behavior" and *not* in a search for "climate."

Inherit lets you get all the text referenced by a given node's ancestor nodes, going all the way up the tree. To use the manual's example, if you have a code **/mammals/carnivores/felines/cats**, Inherit will let you create a new node that has references to all text coded cats, felines, carnivores, or mammals so that you can get the more general information that applies to cats, *assuming* that everything you've coded "mammals" is general enough to apply to cats. *Collect* works in the opposite direction, collecting all the references from the given node and its children. For example, you might want a search for the code mammals to turn up all text coded with any of mammals' children, including not only carnivores, felines, and cats but herbivores, omnivores, and all their subcategories as well. As always, you can save the results as a new node, or merge them into the "mammals" node, so that it now indexes everything indexed by any of its children.

The second subgroup of tree-structured operators helps you build matrices defined by two sets of codes. (Actually, matrices can be *more* than two dimensional! But hang on a minute.) *Matrix* lets you specify a set of codes to define the rows of a matrix, and a set to define the columns, and then find the text that satisfies the combination of the pair of codes that define each cell of the matrix. But wait, there's more: This is not just an AND combination of each pair of row and column codes; you can use any of the other operators that apply to two codes (e.g., Intersect, Union, If-inside, and so on). The output is not actually in matrix form (a challenge no software has conquered yet), but the data for each cell are listed together and are clearly marked as to which cell they are for and what nodes defined the current row and column.

NUD•IST expects you to want to use the children of one node as the rows and the children of another as the columns. When you specify the search, you just give it one parent node to define the rows and another to define the columns. This may often be just what you want. It is also a restriction, but it can be overcome; if the matrix *you* want to make doesn't satisfy these criteria, just create a new node (call it "ROWS") and attach all the nodes you want to use for rows as children, then do the same for columns. Then you do a matrix operation for ROWS and COLUMNS.

As mentioned above, matrices can be more than two dimensional. Because a matrix is stored as a special node (all the cells are like invisible children), you can use it as a node in building a new matrix. By Matrixing a matrix node with a new node, the new node's children define the third dimension of the matrix. For example, say you've created a matrix of educational level by professional achievement. If you then matrix this node against age group, you'll get an education × achievement × age-group matrix. This can go on as long as you like, creating *n*-dimensional matrices!

The last operator is *Vector,* which makes a one-row matrix. The first node you specify is *itself* cross-tabulated (by whatever operator you choose) with the children of the second node.

Text Searches

NUD•IST also provides good text search capability. You can search for specific strings of characters in the text—typically words, phrases, or numbers—or you can search for *patterns* of characters. For example, a social security number can be described as a pattern of three digits, a hyphen, two digits, a hyphen, and four more digits. In NUD•IST, you would specify this as

```
[0-9][0-9][0-9] - [0-9][0-9] - [0-9][0-9][0-9][0-9]
```

Each set of brackets in this example refers to an OR specification of any of the digits from 0 to 9. Implied in this example: You can also use pattern searches to execute an OR search. An example given in the manual is the pattern search

```
^John:.*I [wish|want|need|feel]
```

This finds all text units beginning with "John:" (presumably those in which John's speech is recorded) and containing any one of the phrases: "I wish," "I want," "I need," or "I feel." NUD•IST's pattern matching syntax is fairly comprehensive, though not quite as extensive as Metamorph's REX syntax (which might make NUD•IST a little easier to learn, if less powerful).

As mentioned earlier, the results of text searches (whether for a character string or pattern) are saved as a new node, which you can place or merge wherever you want. In other words, all text units containing the text you've searched for are coded with this new code, so that text searches by default accomplish automated coding. Because the new node can also be merged with an existing node, you can use this technique to apply existing codes to text found with a text search.

Output

Output is a slightly mixed bag for NUD•IST. The options are fairly rich, and the material you can retrieve is extensive, but there are problems with how the output is organized.

Node Reports

When you execute a search, you don't get shown the results right away. The index references just get recorded in a new node. This happens very quickly. Then, if you want to actually see the results, you go to that new node and make a "report" (see Figure 8). There are two different types of node reports—with and without the actual text—and several options for each. If you do *not* include text, you can include memos; if you do include text, you can find out what other nodes index (cross-reference) the retrieved text. Reports are presented on screen, and you can print them out or save them to files on your hard disk for later printing or editing with your word processor.

The biggest problem has to do with the way codes are printed with text, though this is only a problem *if* you want to see the codes that apply to the retrieved segment. Because NUD•IST works with rigidly defined text units, even when you're coding ranges of them, you must get all the codes that apply to each text unit after that text unit. As we showed in Figure 3, this can be a real problem, especially if you use lines as text units to allow relatively fine coding.

Source tags are pretty thorough. You get information on the node the report is about, including its name and address (which tell you what its ancestors—parent, grandparent, and so on—are), its definition (which tells you what search operation created the node, if appropriate), its creation and last modification dates, its siblings, and its children. You also get information on each document from which text is retrieved: the document name, the subheader (if any) that applies to each range of retrieved text units, the count and

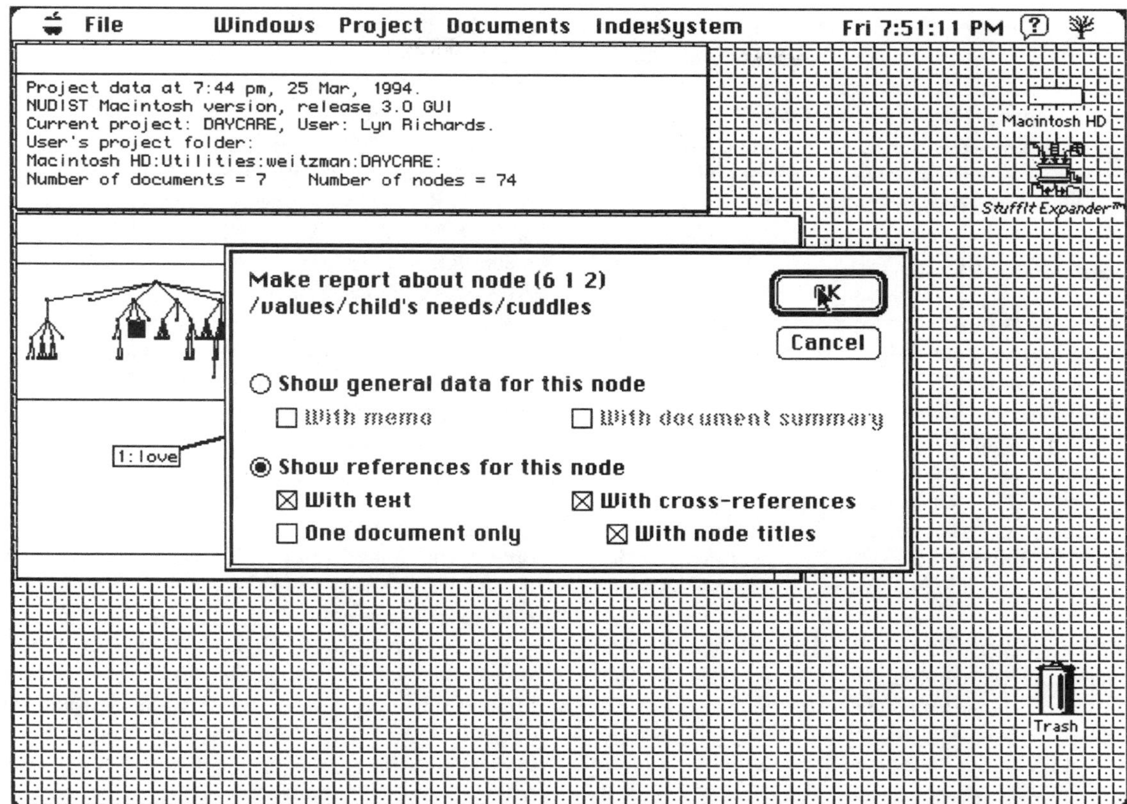

NUD•IST Figure 8. The dialog box for making a report on a node, whether it simply represents a code, or the output of a search. Choose "Show general data . . ." if you don't want to see actual text or text references. Choose "Show references . . ." if you do.

percentage of text units retrieved, and the numbers of all text units retrieved.

Matrix output, as noted before, is not really in matrix form. However, data are organized by the cell they come from and have tags that tell you the cell number (e.g., Cell (2 3) is in the second row, third column) and the codes that defined the row and column. This information is a big help whether you're actually cutting and pasting the data into the cells of a table in your word processor or reading through, cell by cell, to write summaries for your table (see Miles & Huberman, 1994, for a thorough discussion of strategies for making qualitative matrices).

You can also get a few summary statistics on your searches. For each document that had hits in the search, you get the number of text units retrieved, the total number of text units, and the percentage of the total text units retrieved. At the end of the report, you get the total number of text units retrieved; the total number of documents in the project and the number and percentage of them from which text was retrieved; the total number of text units in the documents with retrievals, and the percentage of them retrieved; and the total number of text units in all documents, and the percentage of them retrieved.

Document Reports

You can also make reports on documents. You have options to display no indexing (codes), summary of indexing only, or all node addresses. If you're *not* printing out the text itself, you can get node titles as well (they're listed with the text unit numbers they apply to). This is not too friendly, but the developer says this limitation is a bug that has been fixed. You can also get document headers, memos, and text.

Node Lists

Finally, you can get a list of some or all of the nodes (codes) in your project. You can restrict the listing to a tree or part of a tree. Nodes can be listed by address or title. You can get the node definitions, but not memos, with the list. There is some information about the documents indexed by each node available too: You can get the titles of the documents, their headers, the percentage of each document's text units that are indexed by the node, and the numbers of the specific text units. You can also restrict this to documents either indexed or not indexed at another specified node (see the Including-docs-from and Excluding-docs-from operator under "Searching").

Tree Diagrams

You can also print out the tree diagrams that represent your coding hierarchy (or index system), but you cannot save these diagrams to a file or paste them into, say, a word processor document. There are limits to what you can do here, but the diagrams can be helpful. If you look back at Figure 1, you'll see that there are two versions of the tree. One view shows you one node and its immediate children, with node numbers and at least part of the titles. The other view, in a smaller window, shows an overview of the whole tree, with no labels. You can print either of these two views: one node with immediate children (Figure 9) or a complete overview (Figure 10). The first option gives you the same labels that you see on screen. The second option will give you a little more information *if* there's room on the page; you'll get local node numbers (i.e., node (6 2) will just be marked with a 2—you can tell that it's a child of 6 by looking above) as long as the tree will still fit on a single page. If the tree starts getting too big, some of the node numbers start getting left off the level(s) that are too wide. Depending on your printer, the Macintosh print setup dialog box or the Windows page setup dialog box will let you print the tree in landscape mode (sideways) to get a wider diagram and/or reduce the size of the diagram, so that more fits on the page.

Theory Building

There are three main ways in which NUD•IST supports theory building: memoing, elucidating structure through building and modifying the index system (code tree), and system closure (allowing you to treat the products of your work as more data). NUD•IST lacks any hypertexting functions. Memoing was discussed above, so we'll focus primarily on the other two issues here.

Elucidating Structure

Working with a hierarchically structured tree of codes (or nodes) *forces* you to think about the relationship among your codes and strongly encourages you to do it in hierarchical terms. This may or may not be a good thing—it depends on your personal style, your methodological approach, your data, and the theory (or theoretical ideas) you're working with. If you don't want, for any reason, to arrange your codes in a hierarchical tree, you can simply make them all first-level nodes.

There's an unusual twist, and theoretical implication, to the tree structure of NUD•IST's index system; it works from the top down. In most research paradigms, you begin at the level of the data, applying codes representing the meaning(s) of particular chunks of text. These are your "first-level" codes. You may start with a theoretical structure that organizes these codes, or you may simply begin to see relationships among, or superordinate categories that subsume, the first-level codes. These are often called "higher-order" or "second-level" codes. So you build your way up from the data to first-level codes, second-level codes, and so on.

In NUD•IST, on the other hand, your highest-order codes are the first level. You work your way *down* through progressively finer categories, until you get to the bottom-level codes (or node tips). Typically, it is these nodes with which you index your text, although you *can* index with any node (remember, though, that you can start indexing with first-level codes and then move them lower in the hierarchy as you start to realize what their superordinate categories are). This results in the nodes that actually index the text often being at different levels in the hierarchy (subtrees will often be of different depths). This is quite different conceptually than the normal situation in which all your codes are at the same level, with varying levels of abstraction above them.

There are advantages to NUD•IST's coding system, which may be appropriate for your project. The manual provides good guidelines for designing and creating index systems. For example, it suggests that you begin by deciding on some general categories to organize your coding scheme; create a subtree for factual, or demographic, data; use each node's "definition" box, and write memos, to keep track of how each node was made, what it represents, and what ideas you have about it; watch out for redundant categories in the system; and, finally, "keep the index system simple, elegant, and efficient. Use cut, shift, copy and merge facilities to prune, rearrange and tighten the index system" (Replee, 1993, p. 7-6). (*Cut, shift, copy,* and *merge* are the commands used to carry out the earlier mentioned operations for deleting, moving, replicating, and joining nodes.) Another good suggestion is to create a subtree for working nodes you've created with searches and so on and haven't decided where to put yet.

System Closure

NUD•IST also makes a priority of supporting *system closure.* The developers argue for a process in which one's

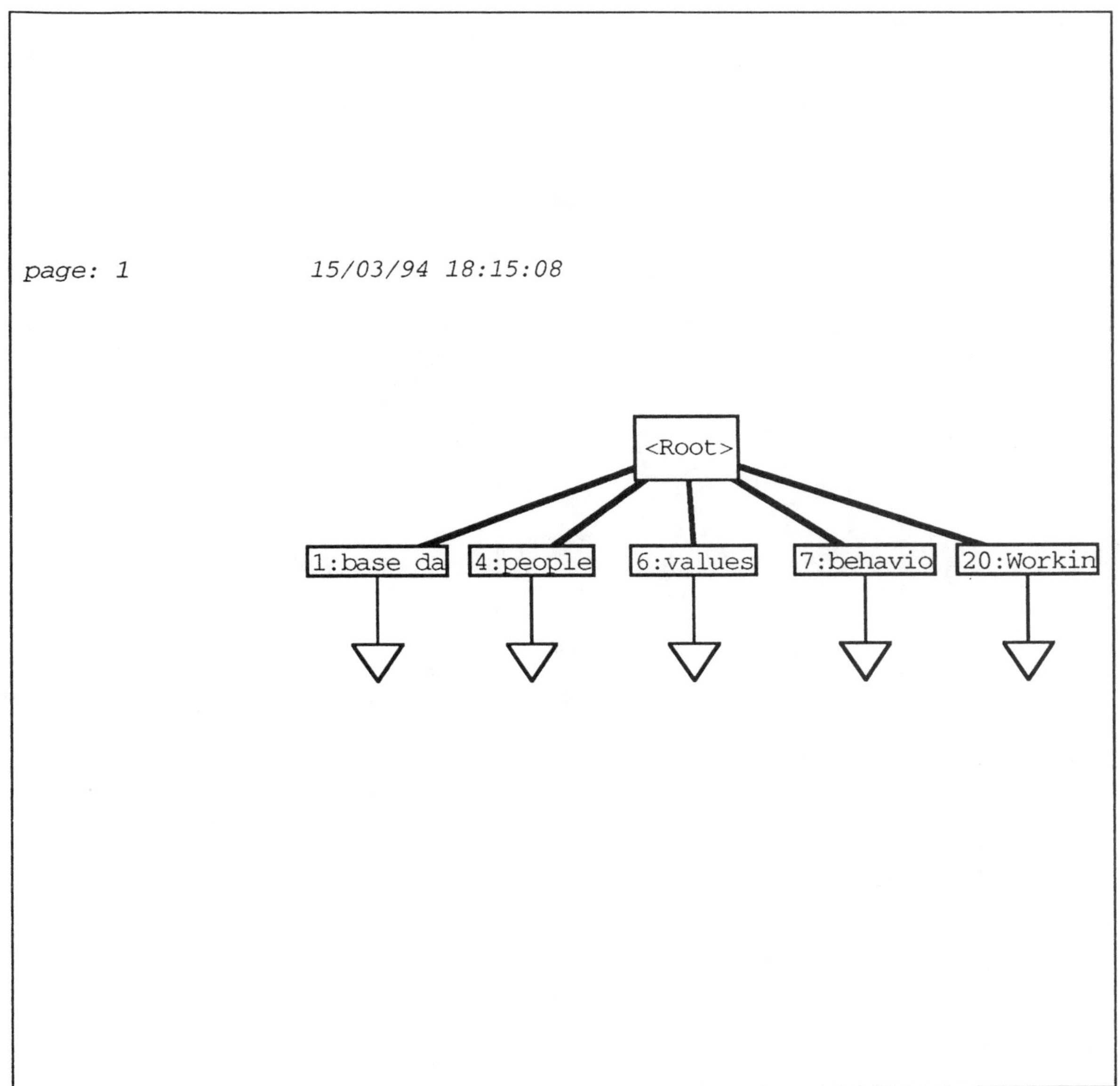

NUD•IST Figure 9. A printout of the current view of the index, which includes just the current node (in this case the <ROOT>) and its immediate children. Note that node titles are truncated to fit in the boxes.

"growing nets or hierarchies of concepts, evidence links, groupings of ideas, and so on" can be kept with the original data and, in fact, become part of it (Richards & Richards, 1994, p. 449). NUD•IST supports this approach by saving all of your searches, so that every question you ask of the data, whether it's a phrase you've searched for in the text or a particular combination of codes, becomes a permanent part of the code structure (unless you don't want it to). These new nodes are just like any others and can be used in new searches, building text matrices, and so on. Further, as mentioned earlier, your memos, whether on nodes or documents, can be saved to freestanding text files at any time and then introduced as new documents to be memoed, indexed, and searched. You might even set up a separate subtree devoted to coding and categorizing information in your memos.

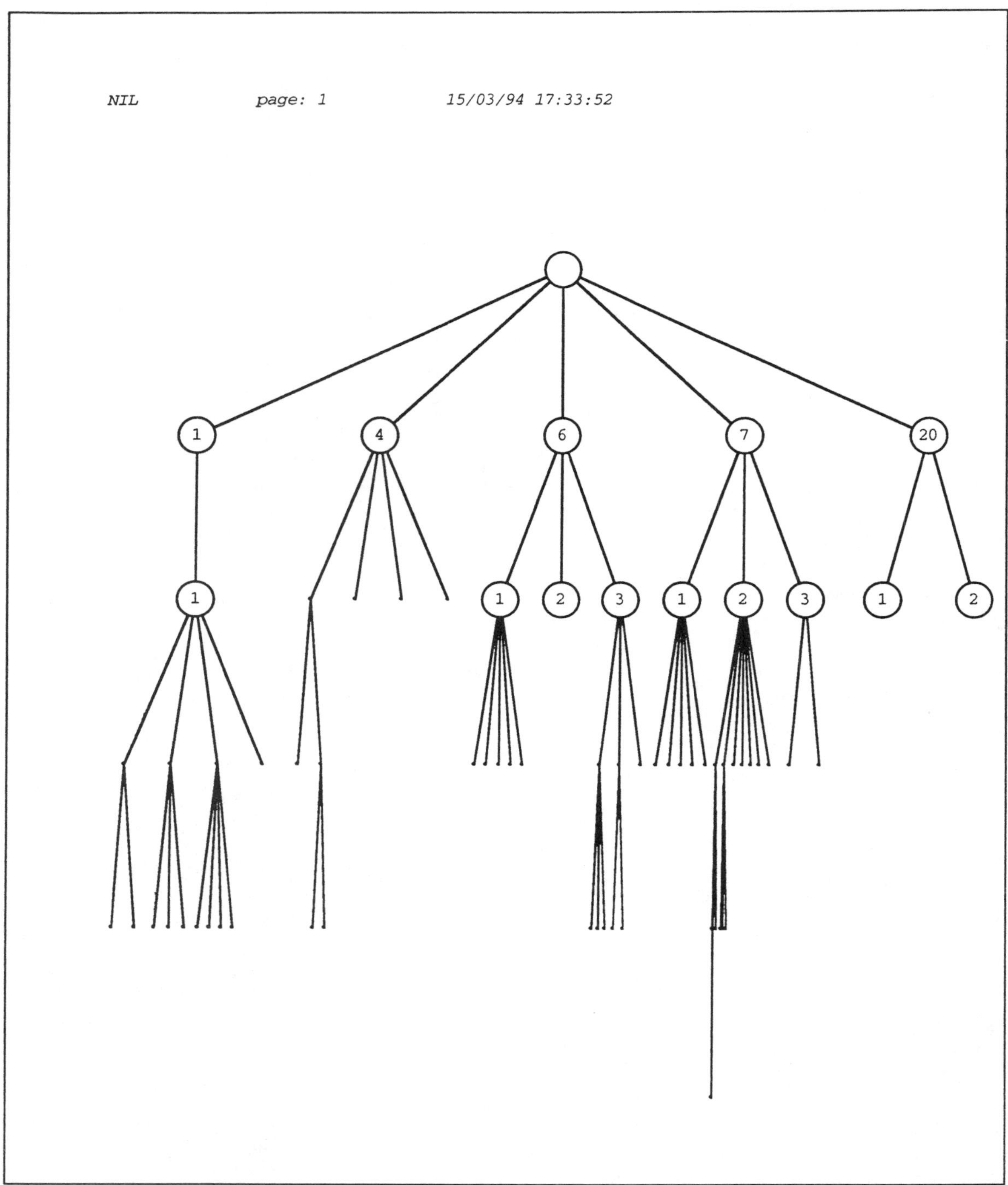

NUD•IST Figure 10. A printout of the summary view of the index system. Nodes are numbered, but not labeled. The root node does not get a number. As you go down the tree to levels with more nodes, fewer nodes are displayed so that the tree fits on a page.

Graphics Editing

Although NUD•IST supports some basic graphic output, described above, you can't edit or manipulate it at all. The most you can do is specify portrait (normal) or landscape (sideways) printing and scale the image to make more or fewer of the node numbers appear on the tree. (See Figures 9 and 10.)

User Friendliness

NUD•IST 3.0 is much easier to learn and use than its predecessors. The old versions all relied on an old-fashioned, mainframe style, scroll-mode interface, which made it extremely tedious and confusing. Version 3.0, however, takes full advantage of the Macintosh's and Windows's graphical user interfaces (GUIs), which let you give commands and do things by pointing to things on the screen (graphically) rather than typing commands. The ability to browse around the index system by clicking on nodes and arrows in the index tree, do on-screen coding by selecting text with the mouse, and the use of dialog boxes for setting up all sorts of procedures makes this program very pleasant to learn and use.

The one real drawback here is that NUD•IST tends to distance you from your data. You develop a very intimate feel for your index system, and can retrieve from it easily, but you don't see your hits in context. The only time you work from a view of your text is when you code, though you can keep text windows and document report windows open on the screen and go back and forth to explore things.

The manual is well written and clear. If you can find the information you want, you'll almost certainly be able to understand it easily. There are very helpful discussions on designing and creating an index system and document system. And there's a chapter on research design aimed at making the best use of the program's unique capabilities.

But the manual suffers from a couple of organizational problems. There's a tutorial with the program, and the sample project used for the manual is included, which helps when you want to play around with different functions to see how they work. Chapter 5 also has a section, titled "Menus," which is described as a "guided tour of the software." But the fifth chapter is an odd place to find such a thing; it's hard to find out that it's there, and it's really just a summary of all the menu items rather than a tutorial (which is what a "guided tour" usually is). But for what it is, it's helpful, and there is a tutorial as well.

Other things are in odd places too. For example, to find out about hardware and software requirements, you have to look in the appendix on trouble-shooting. We were recently told by the developer that this information is also in the installation guide, an add-in at the front of the manual, but this section is not tabbed like the others, isn't in the table of contents, and there's no entry in the index that we could find.

The other major problem with the manual is that it's a bit sparse. There are quite a few issues not addressed at all. The 4-page index in the October 1993 manual we started out with rarely had the term we were looking for, but, as of May 1994, it had been expanded to 12 pages and seemed much more complete.

Technical support is good. Until recently, you had to phone, fax, or send e-mail to the developers in Australia, and either Tom Richards or Boyd Sharrock, the programmers, would get right back to you with clear, helpful answers. Now there's a distributor/support organization in the United States: Jim Adams-Berger of Omni Research & Training, Inc., in Colorado (though you can still always contact the folks in Australia). Dr. Adams-Berger is friendly, patient, and helpful. At the time of this writing, he had just started supporting NUD•IST and so didn't yet know the answers to some questions. However, he checked with the developers and had answers the next day.

Miscellaneous

The main things we haven't discussed yet are automation and cross-platform portability.

Command Files

Automation is accomplished through "command files." The command file language has commands for virtually every NUD•IST function. You can set up complex processes to run in a batch simply by executing the command file. This is particularly useful for complex processes that you have to run repeatedly. Command files are even easier to create in version 3.0 because you can use the friendly Search Index System dialog boxes to set up your complex searches and then have them pasted into a command file you're building. This saves you the headache of figuring out some pretty tricky command syntax.

Command files can be used to store search requests that you'll want to use repeatedly. This is important because, while the results of a search, say, for the intersection of codes A & B, can be saved as a new node, that node will not automatically know about text that is *later* coded both A & B; you'll have to run the search again to update it.

Cross-Platform Portability

NUD•IST "projects" can be transferred back and forth between the Macintosh and a PC running Windows (assuming both machines have the appropriate versions of NUD•IST). You accomplish the transfer via a program that comes with the Macintosh called Apple File Exchange, using DOS-formatted disks.

Network Use

NUD•IST, as shipped, will run on a network; you don't need a special network version. Before installing on a network, you simply pay for the number of workstations you intend to run it on.

Comparative Remarks

NUD•IST ranks as one of the top two or three programs available for coding-oriented qualitative data analysis, along with ATLAS/ti and Folio VIEWS (which doesn't really have theory-building features). It has unparalleled power when it comes to code-based searching and has and will continue to command a faithful following for this reason. It's the only one of the three available for the Macintosh, though Folio VIEWS is now available in a read-only version for the Mac and a full Mac version is reportedly on the way.

The operators provided for index system searching in NUD•IST are more sophisticated than anything else available for searching by codes. If this is your priority, the choice is probably easy. On the other hand, Folio VIEWS has a lot of powerful search operators too, though fewer, but it can also apply them to text strings, field variables, and memos and annotations.

In most other respects, the program also compares well with the competition. The index system has a lot of strong features (e.g., system closure, collect and inherit, matrices, and indexing off-line documents), and the only other program that supports working with the relationships among codes so thoroughly is ATLAS/ti. NUD•IST's firm but flexible hierarchical structure, along with the ability to reorganize and "collect" and "inherit," are superb; but ATLAS/ti allows nonhierarchical as well as hierarchical nets, has multiple link types with different logical properties, does searches according to logical link properties, and lets you graphically edit your network views both for thinking and for presentation. Which approach is better depends on you and your project.

NUD•IST probably facilitates getting to know your coding scheme better than most programs. On the other hand, it keeps you more distant from your data than ATLAS/ti or Folio VIEWS, both of which keep the data in front of you at all times.

The necessity to code by fixed text units introduces rigidity not found in HyperRESEARCH, ATLAS/ti, or Folio VIEWS. As a result of this structure, printing codes with text is particularly frustrating, but no program has as good a solution to this problem as The Ethnograph.

Memoing is not as flexible (one per node or document) as in ATLAS/ti, The Ethnograph, or Folio VIEWS. On the other hand, NUD•IST lets you attach a memo to a code, which neither The Ethnograph nor Folio VIEWS does, but ATLAS/ti lets you attach as many as you want (HyperRESEARCH doesn't support memoing at all). The explicit facility for turning memos into documents to be indexed, searched, and memoed themselves, while it could probably be mimicked with a workaround in most programs, is very nice.

Summary

The operators for index system searching in NUD•IST are the program's forte. In our informal conversations about types of searches, we have discovered that we don't have an adequate vocabulary for them and so wind up talking about Boolean operators, set logic operators, and NUD•IST operators. The comparative remarks above may look like a mixed bag, but when you add them all up, NUD•IST comes out as an excellent package in many respects, with a few drawbacks—distance from the data, context-less search hits, cumbersome output for line-level data, and hierarchical-only coding.

A lot of folks get drawn to the program because of the tree-structured index system and the powerful search capabilities. For many researchers it will be the best choice. Keep the limitations in mind, compare the relative merits of ATLAS/ti and Folio VIEWS, and make a customized choice for yourself based on your individual needs.

References

Miles, M. B., & Huberman, A. M. (1994). *Qualitative data analysis: An expanded sourcebook* (2nd ed.). Thousand Oaks, CA: Sage.

Replee Pty Ltd. (1993). *NUD•IST user guide: Version 3.0 for Macintosh.* Victoria, Australia: Author.

Replee Pty Ltd. (1994). *Q.S.R. NUD•IST version 3.0: User guide.* Victoria, Australia: Author.

Richards, T., & Richards, L. (1994). Using computers in qualitative analysis. In N. Denzin & Y. Lincoln (Eds.), *Handbook of qualitative research* (chap. 28; pp. 445-462). Thousand Oaks, CA: Sage.

QCA (Qualitative Comparative Analysis) 3.0

Available for DOS

Kriss A. Drass and Charles C. Ragin
Center for Urban Affairs and Policy Research
Northwestern University,
2040 Sheridan Rd., Evanston, IL 60208-4100
(orders: Audrey Chambers)

Phone: (708) 491-8712
E-mail: kadrass@nevada.edu
cragin@nwu.edu

Price: $25

Hardware Requirements
- IBM PC: any
- DOS 3.0 or better
- 640K free RAM

Overview

QCA is a special-purpose program designed to analyze quantified data from multiple cases. It's a theory-building, data processing program, *not* a code-store-retrieve program as such, so it's a deviant case in this section. It's built around Ragin's (1987, 1993b) ideas on comparative analysis, using Boolean logic. The aim is to find patterns or configurations of variables *within* each case, and to show how, across a number of cases, these patterns lead to an outcome. The same outcome may in fact be achieved through different causal combinations, so "families" of cases can be sorted out.

Unlike regular statistical programs, which take a solely variable-oriented approach (e.g., looking at SES, parental expectations, and peer support and seeing how these relate to the outcome of going to college), this program aims to *preserve configurations* within particular cases (e.g., the pattern of mid-SES, high parental expectations, and moderate peer support for a particular individual) and see how such a pattern of variables accounts for an outcome (see also Ragin & Becker, 1989).

Qualitative comparative analysis is actually a combination of case-oriented and variable-oriented analysis. It's important to get this distinction clear. Imagine a data matrix showing persons in the rows and variables in the columns. A variable-oriented analysis looks through the matrix vertically, variable by variable: How do parental expectations relate to college going? The answers are "smoothed" across a whole population of cases, so that we never really understand how a particular case works.

A case-oriented analysis, on the other hand, would look across rows at particular cases—*persons,* in this instance—and how their idiosyncratic pattern or configuration of variables looked. The results are not "smoothed," but very case-specific—even though it may turn out that certain cases fall into clusters or "families," helping us form generalizations beyond single cases but well grounded in their local configurations. (For more on this important distinction, see Ragin, 1987, 1993b, and Miles & Huberman, 1994. We also discuss it further in Chapter 10 of this book.)

Database Structure

You create raw data in the form of an ASCII matrix (cases by predictor variables and a single outcome). The cell entry is either 1 or zero, signifying high/low or present/absent. There's also an ASCII file with the names of your variables. These are inputs for QCA. (QCA can also read other data files as input, with integer, real, and label

Case-Ordered Predictor-Outcome Matrix: Additional Factors Related to Early Implementation

	ROUGHNESS Ease of early use, by cases	PRESS Users (1st generation) volunteered or pressured	BADFIT Actual classroom/ organizational fit	CHANGE Actual degree of practice change	LOWLAT Latitude for making changes	SIZE Actual size/scope of innovation +
	Smooth early use [a]					
0	Astoria (E)	constrained 1	good$_F$ 0	minor$_F$ 0	high$_F$ 0	small 0
0	Burton (E)	pressured$_F$ 1	good$_F$ 0	minor$_F$ 0	high$_F$ 0	small$_F$ 0
	Mostly smooth					
0	Lido (E)	pressured$_F$ 1	moderate$_B$ 1	moderate$_B$ 1	high$_F$ 0	small/moderate 0
	Mixed [b]					
0	Calston (E)	pressured 1	poor$_B$ 1	moderate$_B$ 1	mod./high$_B$ 0	small 0
0	Perry-Parkdale (E)	volunteered 0	moderate –	moderate$_B$ 1	high$_F$ 0	moderate 1
	Rough					
1	Banestown (E)	pressured 1	moderate –	major$_B$ 1	high 0	small/moderate 0
1	Masepa (E)	volunteered 0	good 0	major$_B$ 1	low$_B$ 1	large 1
1	Carson (L)	volunteered$_F$ 0	moderate –	major$_B$ 1	high/mod.$_F$ 0	large$_B$ 1
1	Dun Hollow (L)	volunteered 0	poor$_B$ 1	minor$_F$ 0	moderate –	small$_F$ 0
1	Plummet (L)	volunteered$_F$ 0	poor$_B$ 1	mod-major$_B$ 1	high$_F$ 0	large$_B$ 1
1	Proville (L)	pressured$_B$ 1	moderate –	minor 0	high 0	moderate$_B$ 1
1	Tindale (L)	pressured$_B$ 1	moderate$_B$ 1	major$_B$ 1	low$_B$ 1	moderate/large 1

(E) externally-developed innovation
(L) locally-developed innovation
[a] field researcher judgment from users' responses and/or from observation of practice in use
[b] smooth for some users, rough for others
underline signifies researcher estimate that factor was decisive in affecting ease of early use
F = factor facilitated early use
B = factor was a barrier to successful early use
* substantial role changes, but for limited populations
+ as contrasted with pre-implementation size/scope

QCA Figure 1. An original data display, used as a worksheet for data entry. This text-filled matrix is drawn from Miles and Huberman (1994). It orders 12 named cases (Astoria, Burton, and so on, which are school districts) according to a main dependent variable (ease of early use of innovations) and shows data on five predictor variables thought to be associated with that outcome. To make interpretation easier, the dependent variable has been renamed "ROUGHNESS," and brief names have been written for the predictors (PRESS, BADFIT, CHANGE, LOWLAT, and SIZE). For all six variables, the researcher has written in a 1 to show presence or a 0 to show absence and a "–" when it wasn't possible to decide.

data; the formats include Gauss, Lotus, Stata, SPSSX Export, and Systat.)

QCA's structure includes several other "objects," including "truth tables," "minimized truth tables," hypotheses, and tests of the hypotheses. They are hooked together in an "object hierarchy"—from your results, you can get quickly back to the hypotheses, the minimized table, the truth table, and the original data matrix. Your work is recorded in a Log that keeps track of what you've done and lets you cycle back to relook at results, make new truth tables, and test new hypotheses. (These different "objects" are explained below.)

All of the objects can be edited as you go along (exception—you cannot change the names of variables in a data matrix).

QCA will accept up to 255 variables in a data matrix. However, when you move to any particular truth table, you must select at least 3 and not more than 12 variables (be-

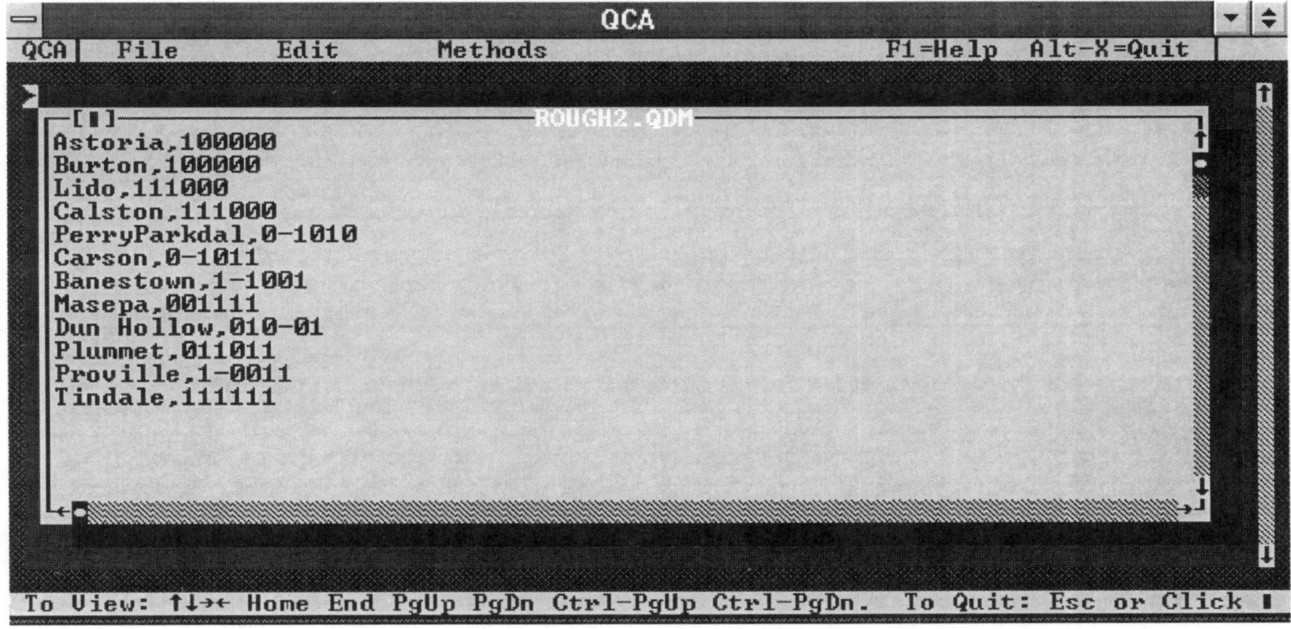

QCA Figure 2. A data file. The file, in ASCII, lists the IDs of each case (Astoria, Burton, and so on), followed by a comma and the data for each variable.

cause the permutations of configurations mount so rapidly). The number of cases is unlimited.

Data Entry

You can input data directly, which we did using data from a study of school innovation (see Figure 1, drawn from Miles & Huberman, 1994, p. 216).[1] For each predictor variable, such as "users volunteered or pressured," you decide whether the value should be 1 (for "present") or 0 ("absent"); you do the same for the outcome variable, which in this case is "roughness of implementation."

The step before inputting data was to mark up the 1s and 0s on the original data display, as you see. Note that you need to decide whether a description such as "moderate" should be classified as 1 or 0, based on what you know about the case. QCA does provide an option of "don't care" as well, which you can use to indicate that the variable for practical purposes could be either 0 or 1. Later computations will use this information rather than treating the cell as having missing data. The matrix entry for "don't care" is "–" (you can also use "2," but that looks a bit confusing).

1. These data were also used in the review of Tabletop; the comparison shows the programs' different ways of handling cross-case analysis.

You create a series of case IDs (up to 12 characters) and key in your data. The data matrix file looks like Figure 2. If you've already produced a data matrix with some other statistical package, you can import it. As noted above, QCA has a menu that lets you read in data from several other matrix programs.

The program, happily, will accept "contradictory" data—when the same pattern of predictors leads to different outcomes. (Real life is not always logical.)

You also need to assign names to your variables (up to eight characters) by creating an ASCII file. The variables used (five predictors and one outcome variable) are shown in Figure 3.

If needed, you can edit the original raw matrix, though there's no recode function—you just enter new data, cancel or revise old data, and so on.

Working on the Data

You start by building a truth table with selected variables from your raw data matrix. You must include your dependent variable, and can include up to 11 other (predictor) variables. The total number of variables must be at least 3. Figure 4 shows how you make these requests.

From the 1s and 0s that it takes from your data matrix file, QCA uses Boolean logic to compute "truth tables."

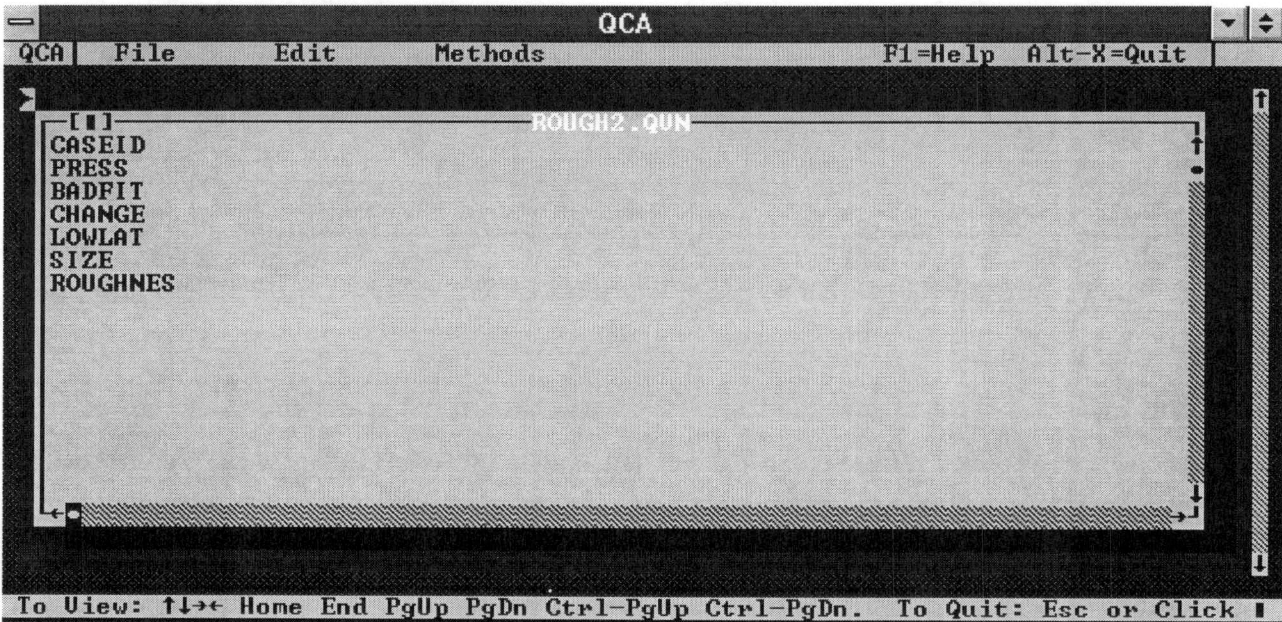

QCA Figure 3. A file with variable names. After the case identification label, the name of each variable is listed using ASCII characters.

Each row of the truth table shows a different pattern of variables, such as 10001, or 11001, enabling you to see which patterns of variables (out of all possible ones) are actually present in your data, and for how many cases.

A nice feature is that you can select cases from your total case file based on values in your total variable file (not just the 3-12 variables in the truth table you are building). So you could take only schools in District 13, or those recently adopting an innovation, or urban ones. Multiple choices can be made; the program treats them as connected by logical ORs. The operators are "equal to," "not equal to," "greater than," "lesser than," "greater than or equal to," and "lesser than or equal to." (If you ask for cases where District = 13, or School = Elem, or CASEID > 36, *every* case will be included that meets *any one* of these conditions.)

Figure 5 shows how a summary of the truth table looks. For example, it shows you that, of 32 possible configurations among the five variables (2 to the 5th power), there are only 9 actually existing within our 12 cases. You can see which patterns are associated with the presence or absence of the outcome, and you can ask for the IDs of cases with a particular pattern, such as the one highlighted in Figure 5.

At first glance, Figure 5 looks pretty puzzling. The configurations are quite diverse and don't make much sense on the face of it. The next step is to ask QCA to "minimize" the table, finding prime implicants (the simplest configurations of within-case variables that are associated with the outcome).

Let's clarify what "prime implicants" are. Suppose that you were studying three independent variables, A, B, C, and a dependent variable, D. We'll use the convention that QCA does: Uppercase "A" means that the variable is "true" or present, and lowercase "a" means it is "false" or absent.

You might get a truth table that looked, in part, like this:[2]

Configuration		Frequency
1. A B C	D	2
2. A B c	D	9
3. A b C	D	5
4. a B c	D	4

Let's look, as QCA does, at the configurations pair by pair. Comparing configurations 1 and 2, we note that variable C/c can be eliminated; only A and B are associated with D. Comparing configuration 1 and 3, we can eliminate B/b, leaving A and C as predictors. Comparing configurations 2 and 4, we can eliminate A/a, leaving Bc. Thus the dependent variable D will be present whenever a configuration contains AB, or AC, or Bc. In Boolean notation: D = AB + AC + Bc (the + signifies an OR).

However, note that configuration 1 can be explained either by AC or by AB, so AB is not necessary (configu-

2. We've adapted this example from the manual for AQUAD, another program that does qualitative comparative analysis.

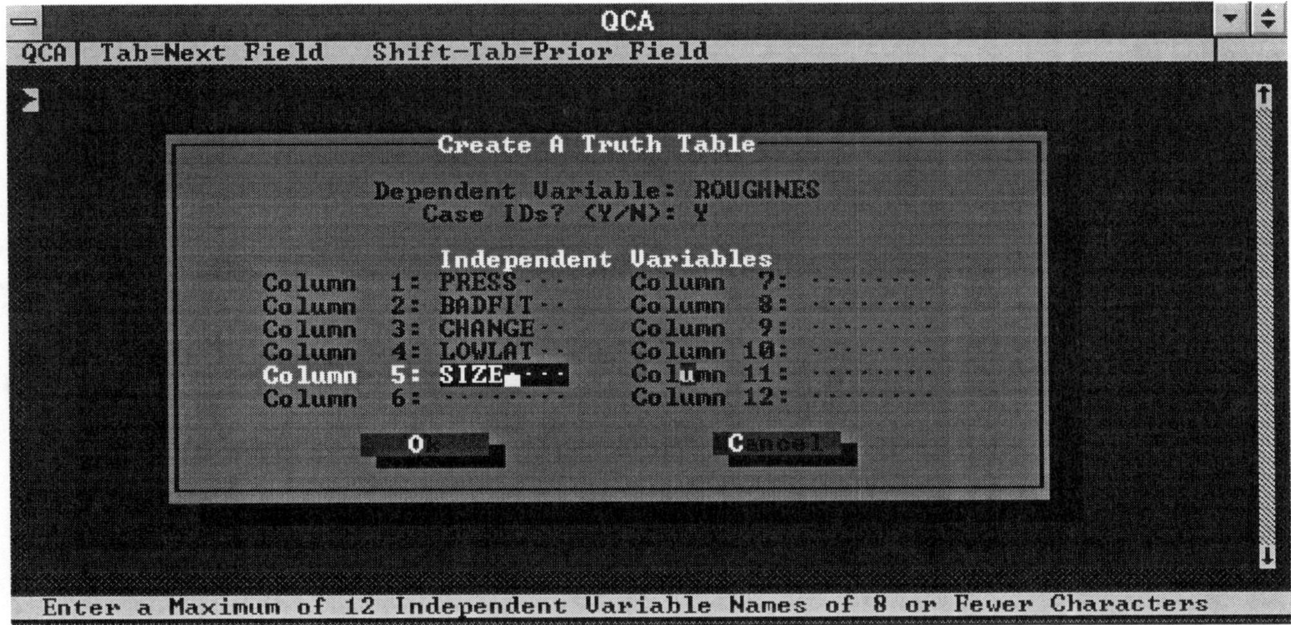

QCA Figure 4. Creating a truth table. The names of the dependent variable and the predictor variables have been typed in. In this case, all the variables in the data file have been used; usually, there will be a selection.

ration 2 is explained by Bc). So our finally reduced set of prime implicants—those really essential for D—is D = AC + Bc.

Another truth table can give us the prime implicants for "d," the absence or falsity of the dependent variable.

To get a minimized truth table, you indicate whether you want to include configurations where the dependent variable is present, or absent. You can also include or exclude "contradictory" configurations, and include or exclude the instances of "don't care" values.

QCA works stepwise, letting you look at each step. You can go back or ahead as well (actually, the program does all the steps, then you look at them). If it cannot find a good solution, there is a provision for you to fiddle and work out a "good enough" solution; you can mark the particular prime implicants you want included. QCA will tell you, as you go, how many configurations you've covered; the aim is to cover all the configurations with the least number of implicants.

Figure 6 shows two minimized solutions. Truth Table 2 was just for configurations associated with roughness of implementation; 3 was configurations associated with the absence of roughness. We can begin to see a possible hypothesis: that SIZE of the innovation, when combined with the CHANGE it requires, leads to ROUGHNESS, but this pattern only occurs for three implicants. A check back with the truth table summary (Figure 5) shows us that we've covered only five of the seven ROUGH cases. We would have to reduce the implicants more by hand.

But for our low-roughness cases, small size (shown in lowercase letters) and small "lowlat" accompanied by PRESS, mean less roughness for all configurations and all cases. In other words, we have an emerging hypothesis: If an innovation is small, and its users have latitude in its use, implementation will be smooth, not rough, even if there was pressure to use the innovation. (Note, however, that the picture for rough cases is *not* a mirror image; either LOWLAT or lowlat may be occurring.)

Theory Building

Now we have two hypotheses, drawn from looking at the prime implicants. The program lets you test your hypotheses' "intersection" with the relevant truth tables; this process, iterated, helps you build theory about what is happening in your cases. An "intersection" just pulls out the prime implicants that your "hypothesis" fits, in effect (see Figure 7).

This is all logged as you go. To return to a particular piece, such as a truth table or an associated hypothesis (QCA numbers them as you go), you cursor to that part of the log and click (practically all commands can be done by your choice of keyboard or mouse). Because the variable names in any particular configuration are shown in upper-

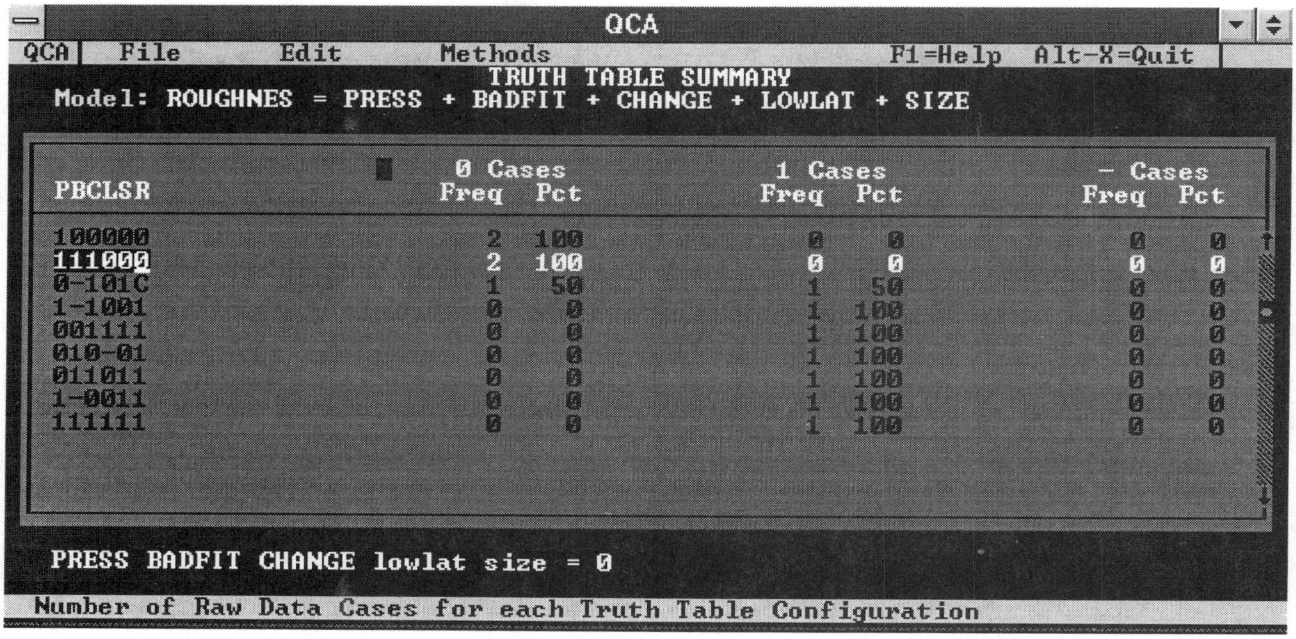

QCA

QCA | File | Edit | Methods | F1=Help | Alt-X=Quit

TRUTH TABLE SUMMARY

Model: ROUGHNES = PRESS + BADFIT + CHANGE + LOWLAT + SIZE

PBCLSR	0 Cases		1 Cases		– Cases	
	Freq	Pct	Freq	Pct	Freq	Pct
100000	2	100	0	0	0	0
111000	2	100	0	0	0	0
0-101C	1	50	1	50	0	0
1-1001	0	0	1	100	0	0
001111	0	0	1	100	0	0
010-01	0	0	1	100	0	0
011011	0	0	1	100	0	0
1-0011	0	0	1	100	0	0
111111	0	0	1	100	0	0

PRESS BADFIT CHANGE lowlat size = 0

Number of Raw Data Cases for each Truth Table Configuration

QCA Figure 5. A truth table summary. The model being tested is shown at the top. The initials PBCLSR refer to the variables PRESS, BADFIT, CHANGE, LOWLAT, and SIZE and the dependent variable ROUGHNESS. The highlighted configuration 111000 appears in two actual cases, which have the value "0" (absent, false) of the dependent variable (see the column headed "0 cases"). The column "1 cases" shows the configurations associated with presence of the dependent variable. The "–" column shows contradictory cases—where the same configuration appears for outcomes of both 0 and 1. At the bottom, you see variable names for the highlighted configuration. the variables PRESS, BADFIT, and CHANGE are all present, and the variables lowlat and size are absent, as shown by uppercase and lowercase letters, respectively.

case and lowercase letters, you retain a commonsense idea of what you are getting. (QCA's use of complete variable names is better than AQUAD's, which gives you only variable initials expandable to four characters.)

As you see the log's successive steps, you can annotate it with notes about what you think it means, what some good next steps might be, and so on. (This feature is confusingly called "label function" and is not explained in the documentation.) You can also build new truth tables with different variables drawn from the same original raw data matrix, thus following up hunches—a feature lacking in AQUAD.

The prime implicants do help in theory building—for example, they underlined something in the data that had been ignored during the eyeballing of the original matrix: that cases with low outcomes (smooth implementation) actually had high pressure, along with high latitude and small size.

You can also pull up the "complement" of a minimized truth table function (implicant) or a hypothesis—the minimized function of all configurations *not* implied by the original function or hypothesis. It wasn't wholly clear to us what that does for you; perhaps it helps you exclude unworkable hypotheses.

Searching

This is really a data-processing program, not a code-and-retrieve program or even a database program. However, you can ask for cases that fit a certain configuration, thus enabling you to see families or clusters.

Output

Typical outputs are a matrix of cases by variables, the "truth table" (also a matrix), and the names of key variables in a pattern that predicts the outcome. These all go to screen and can be printed or sent to a disk file as you wish. The log, which you work with on screen, can be sent either as a screen or as a total file to a printer or disk. In the latter case, it can be appended to an existing file if you wish, so your results cumulate in one place. It appears, however, that you can't call up and use an old log directly; you create a new log each time—though you could, of course, start with ideas from a printed-out old log.

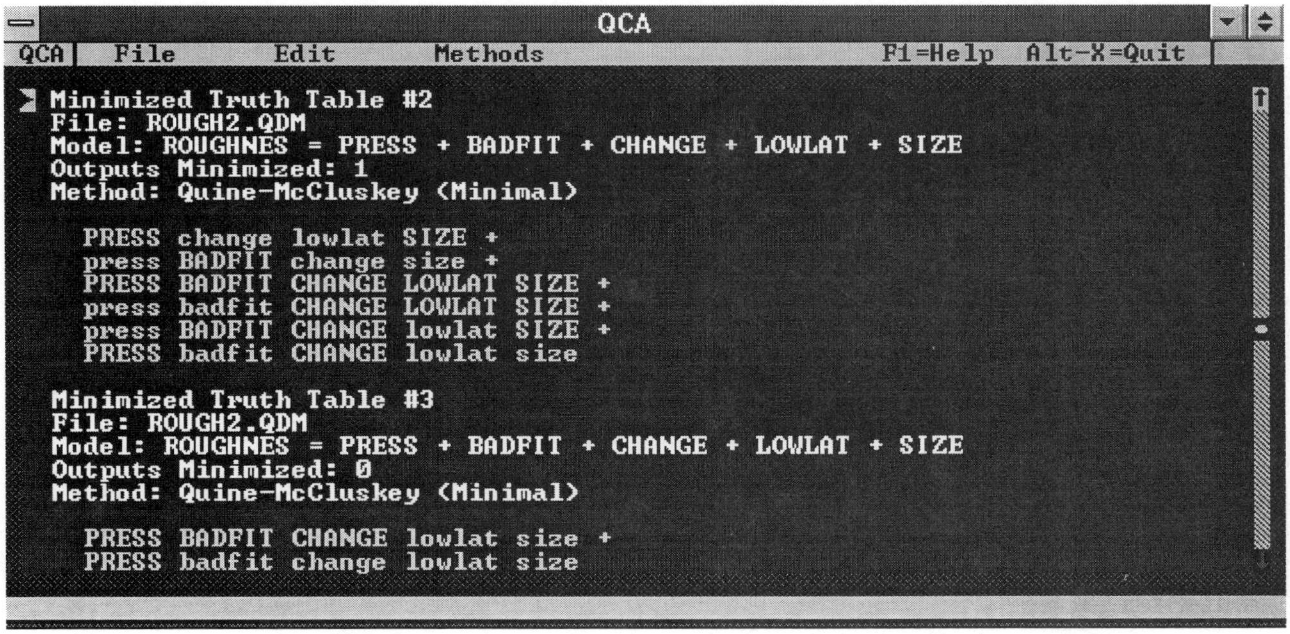

```
QCA
QCA  File  Edit  Methods                    F1=Help  Alt-X=Quit

Minimized Truth Table #2
File: ROUGH2.QDM
Model: ROUGHNES = PRESS + BADFIT + CHANGE + LOWLAT + SIZE
Outputs Minimized: 1
Method: Quine-McCluskey (Minimal)

  PRESS change lowlat SIZE +
  press BADFIT change size +
  PRESS BADFIT CHANGE LOWLAT SIZE +
  press badfit CHANGE LOWLAT SIZE +
  press BADFIT CHANGE lowlat SIZE +
  PRESS badfit CHANGE lowlat size

Minimized Truth Table #3
File: ROUGH2.QDM
Model: ROUGHNES = PRESS + BADFIT + CHANGE + LOWLAT + SIZE
Outputs Minimized: 0
Method: Quine-McCluskey (Minimal)

  PRESS BADFIT CHANGE lowlat size +
  PRESS badfit change lowlat size
```

QCA Figure 6. Portion of the log, showing two minimized truth tables. Table 2 shows that there are six prime implicants (reduced configurations leading to ROUGHNESS), and Table 3 shows that there are two prime implicants leading to absence of roughness.

User Friendliness

Even though the menus are clear, most commands are reasonably easy, and mouse capability helps, QCA is not as friendly as it should be.

Basically, you have to have a good grasp of how this brand of Boolean work is set up (which you can get from the very thoughtful discussion in Ragin, 1987, or 1993b—the documentation doesn't help much on this). A Level 2 user with a reasonable sense of the concepts of "truth table" and "prime implicants" didn't get to a sense of fluent use of the concepts after a day's work with the program.

The beta-version documentation (Drass, 1992) is totally bare-bones; it mostly copies the help screens, without giving you any real-world examples, like those in this review. (Ragin, 1993a, helpfully describes a study of pension systems in 18 capitalist societies, and Ragin, 1987, is useful in showing you how to make sense of prime implicants.)

The documentation doesn't have any examples of the way screens look. There aren't explanations of hypothesis testing, or of what "assumptions" mean when they're displayed, or of what a "complement" can be useful for. So the net feeling is a bit forbidding; it's not really a user's manual. You have the sense that you're not quite getting it. The developer says that the manual is "simply a guide for using the software" and that Ragin (1987) should be used in parallel with the program as an introduction to QCA and Boolean analysis. (See the "Update" section.)

There is no tutorial, though a file of data from Bill Gamson is included, presumably for practice. However, it has only initials for variable names, so it's hard to get much meaning from it.

The developer does not offer any formal technical support but will respond to e-mail queries about specific problems.

So, in general, QCA was developed by researchers for researchers knowledgeable about this brand of comparative analysis, without much attention to learning support. Of course, it may be expecting too much to ask this of a noncommercial $25 program.

Miscellaneous

QCA has a series of editors, which you can use to create or revise different "objects": raw data matrix, specific "functions" (the 0s, 1s, and –'s in a particular configuration of variables), the truth tables, and the hypotheses.

However, you can't change variable names, which makes for some conceptual rigidity. For example, one of the original variables in the implementation study was "latitude for making changes." This was turned around to

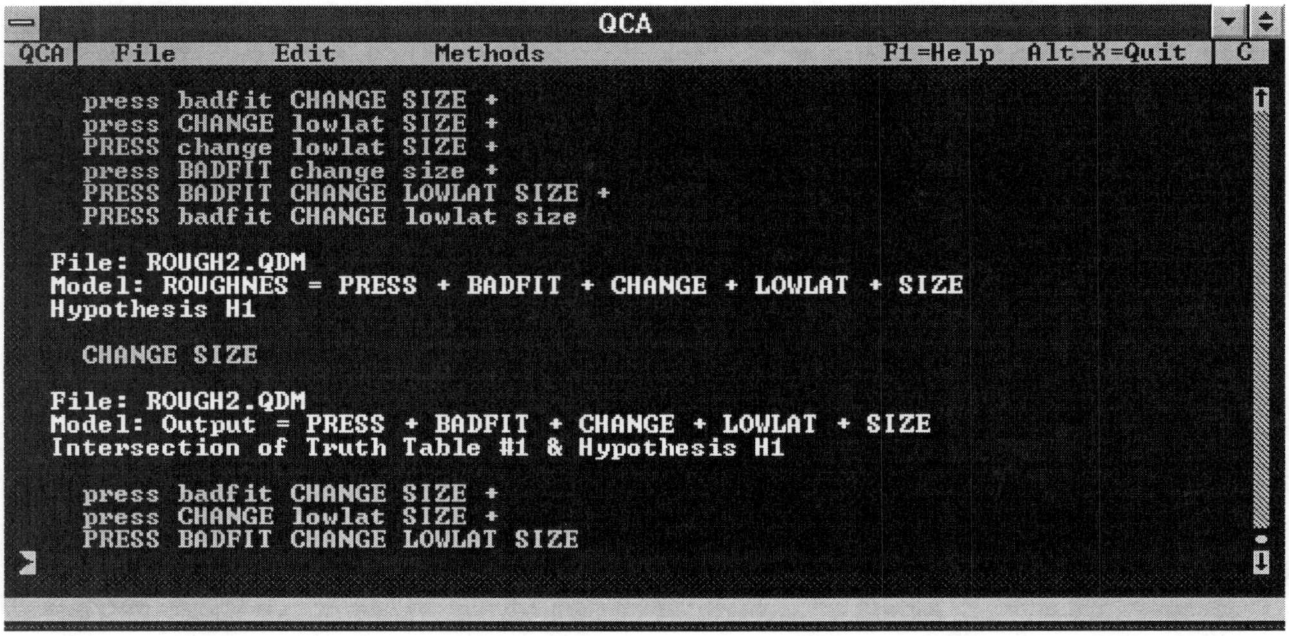

```
QCA
QCA   File        Edit        Methods                  F1=Help   Alt-X=Quit   C

    press badfit CHANGE SIZE +
    press CHANGE lowlat SIZE +
    PRESS change lowlat SIZE +
    press BADFIT change size +
    PRESS BADFIT CHANGE LOWLAT SIZE +
    PRESS badfit CHANGE lowlat size

  File: ROUGH2.QDM
  Model: ROUGHNES = PRESS + BADFIT + CHANGE + LOWLAT + SIZE
  Hypothesis H1

    CHANGE SIZE

  File: ROUGH2.QDM
  Model: Output = PRESS + BADFIT + CHANGE + LOWLAT + SIZE
  Intersection of Truth Table #1 & Hypothesis H1

    press badfit CHANGE SIZE +
    press CHANGE lowlat SIZE +
    PRESS BADFIT CHANGE LOWLAT SIZE
```

QCA Figure 7. Testing a hypothesis. At the top is shown the list of prime implicants for the presence of ROUGHNESS, from Truth Table 1 (label not shown). Hypothesis H1 has been proposed (that the two variables of CHANGE and SIZE, taken together, account for ROUGHNESS). At the bottom, the hypothesis has been "tested," by showing the intersection between Truth Table 1 and H1. We can see that the intersection shows us that, for the three implicants where CHANGE and SIZE occur, the variables PRESS, BADFIT, and LOWLAT are not consistently present or absent. Thus we've reduced the implicants. ROUGHNESS = CHANGE SIZE. We still need to reduce the other three implicants, however.

LOWLAT, because it seemed to make more sense that way as a predictor. But it was confusing, because "lowlat" (absence of the variable) would thus mean high latitude. But in QCA you can't change LOWLAT to a clearer name, such as RESTRICT. You would have to make a whole new data matrix; the way to transfer the data from the old matrix to a newly named one isn't clear. Perhaps there's a way.

The Log doesn't go purely sequentially but puts the results of hypothesis tests next to the relevant truth table, so you have to page up and down a bit to find things. When you're working on various parts of your database—truth tables, the raw data, hypotheses, and so on—it's sometimes confusing in terms of how to get out of what you're doing. At times it's <Esc>; at other times you have to go to the command line and exit the editor you're in.

The necessary Boolean restriction of "1," "0," and "don't care" can make for a bit of forcing (as Figure 1 shows). You could probably get around this by defining variables not just as PRESSURE (1 or 0) but by adding a variable, say, MODPRESS, 1, or 0, to allow for intermediate levels. (See also Ragin, 1993a, for a way he developed to use cluster analysis of causal and outcome variables to make mathematically precise assignments of 1 and 0.)

Update

Work on updating QCA was scheduled for the fall of 1994. The aim is to make it available for multiple platforms, with a simpler, more user-friendly interface. The documentation will be rewritten as an actual manual. Version 4.0 was expected in mid-1995.

Comparative Remarks

QCA is specialized, only doing configurational analysis across cases. AQUAD also does configurational analysis (in a somewhat more user-friendly way, with better documentation) and also can do coding, search, and retrieval of text. However, it does not keep a log of your work, which is one of QCA's strengths. Tabletop is more friendly as well, and helps you sort your cases on multiple variables (but can only manage three, in effect); it may be more helpful for exploratory work.

Summary

This inexpensive program's real strength is in helping you think clearly about a few key variables and their configural relationships within cases—but seen across as large a number of cases as you have. In qualitative research, it is no longer rare to have multiple cases, sometimes ranging up to 20, 30, or more. But your mind usually goes blooey when it's faced with the patterns within more than a dozen or so cases.

QCA successfully combines "case-oriented" and "variable-oriented" views of your data, enabling a coherent understanding; you can both build and test theory. It achieves this power at some cost, of course: forcing the values of your case-level variables into a "present/absent" mode or, at best, a "high-medium-low" mode. Still, you can learn a lot that way.

References

Drass, K. A. (1992, October 15). *QCA 3.0: Qualitative comparative analysis* (Beta release). Evanston, IL: Northwestern University, Center for Urban Affairs and Policy Research.

Miles, M. B., & Huberman, A. M. (1994). *Qualitative data analysis: An expanded sourcebook* (2nd ed.). Thousand Oaks, CA: Sage.

Ragin, C. C. (1987). *The comparative method: Moving beyond qualitative and quantitative strategies.* Berkeley: University of California Press.

Ragin, C. C. (1993a). A qualitative comparative analysis of pension systems. In T. Janoski & A. Hicks (Eds.), *The comparative political economy of the welfare state* (pp. 320-345). New York: Cambridge University Press.

Ragin, C. C. (1993b). Introduction to qualitative comparative analysis. In T. Janoski & A. Hicks (Eds.), *The comparative political economy of the welfare state* (pp. 299-319). New York: Cambridge University Press.

Ragin, C. C., & Becker, H. S. (1989). How the microcomputer is changing our analytic habits. In G. Blank et al. (Eds.), *New technology in sociology: Practical applications in research and work* (pp. 47-55). New Brunswick, NJ: Transaction.

8

Conceptual Network-Builders

The software in this chapter also helps you build and test theory, using semantically meaningful networks. The networks contain "nodes" (representing your key variables) and "links" (representing the relationships among the variables). These are not just programs for drawing or diagramming. They base their graphic displays on your concepts, your thinking about your data, and your higher level propositions—and facilitate your ongoing conceptual work.

Other programs that overlap significantly with this category, and the chapters they are reviewed in, include the following:

Inspiration 4.0

Available for Macintosh and Windows

Inspiration Software, Inc.
2920 S.W. Dolph Court, Suite 3
Portland, OR 97219

Phone: (503) 245-9011
(800) ~~775-4292~~ 877-4292
Fax: (503) 246-4292

Price: $175 Mac, $135 Windows
$95 Educational
$625 Network/Site 10-pack

Hardware Requirements:
For Macintosh

- MacPlus or better
- System 6.0.4 or 7
- At least 1MB RAM
- Either: two 800K drives *or* one Superdrive or hard disk

For Windows

- 386SX or better
- Windows 3.1
- 4MB RAM
- VGA or better monitor
- Math coprocessor used if present but not required
- Mouse or other Windows-compatible pointing device

Overview

Inspiration gives you lots of powerful, easy-to-use tools for making stunningly beautiful network-type diagrams (hierarchical or not), but what really sets it apart from other network diagrammers is that it can translate these diagrams into text outlines, it gives you powerful, easy-to-use tools for manipulating and editing your outlines, and it can also translate your outlines into diagrams. It treats your outline and your diagram as two different "views" of the same document. A third view, called "text" view, is a good enough word processor that you can turn your outlines into finished documents (though for really long ones you may want to export to your word processor).

This combination of features makes the program a fine "thinking tool," and the promotional literature makes a lot of the ability the program gives you to toggle between "right-brain" (creative/artistic/spatial-relational) and "left-brain" (critical/analytical/linear) thinking. Other features that make it a good thinking tool include multiple shortcuts for creating new nodes quickly and easily. One method, "Rapid Fire," lets you simply type, striking the Enter key between ideas, and each idea is automatically put in a separate node, with a link to the node you began to Rapid Fire in.

You can attach a pop-up Notes window to a symbol (node), in which you type more extensive text, although you can have about five single-spaced pages of text in a

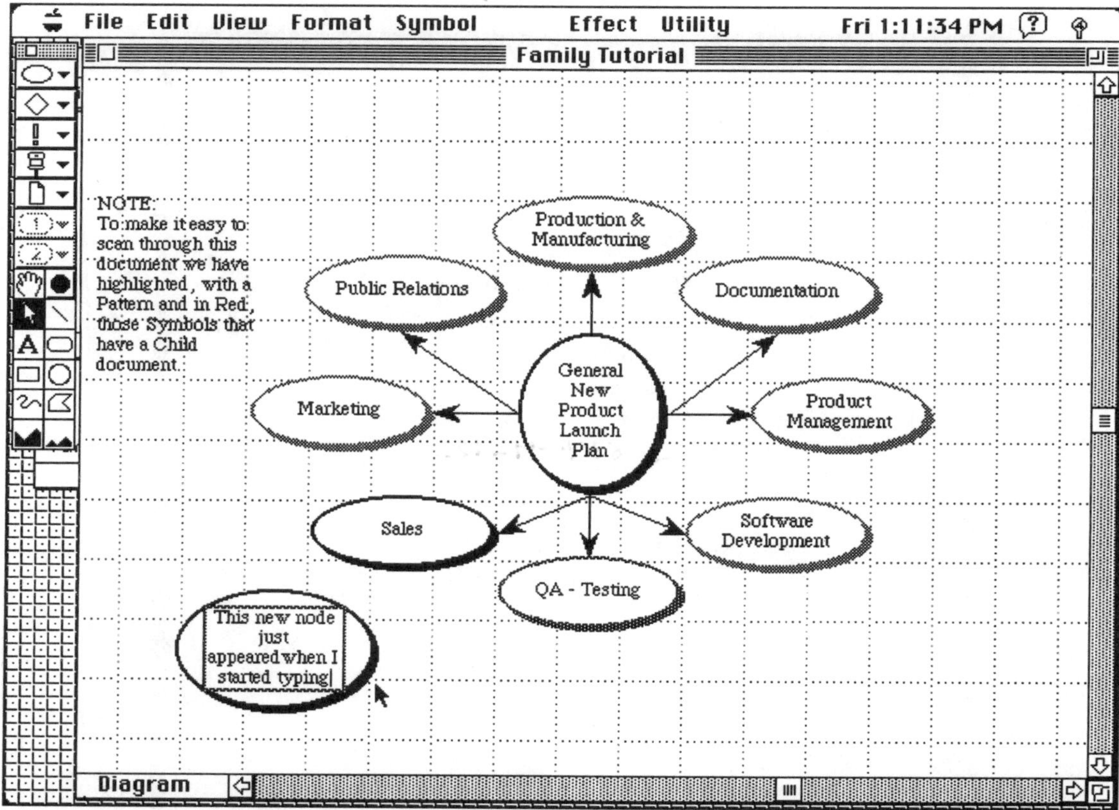

Inspiration Figure 1. The node at lower left has just been created by simply clicking on a square in the grid and starting to type. The "toolbar" at left gives quick access to a number of basic features.

symbol if you want. Graphics can be pasted in and either used simply as embellishments or actually treated as nodes. You can also create "child" documents associated with a node. These are separate drawings that are linked to the "parent" node, enabling you to travel from document to document by clicking on nodes: essentially a hypertext arrangement.

Originally a Macintosh program, Inspiration has just been released in a virtually identical Windows version. Most of the work for this review was done on the Macintosh version, before the Windows version was released. The few subtle differences are discussed in the "Update" section, below. For qualitative researchers, examples of good uses are building a framework for a study, drawing causal or conceptual maps, or writing reports.

Database Structure

Inspiration lets you create a network of nodes and links. You can divide each file into as many hierarchically interrelated subdocuments as you want, creating "child" documents attached to each node (one child to a node). Children can have children, and so on, so that you can have multiple, nested levels of documents. Each child, or subdocument, is a complete diagram/outline, hyperlinked to the node it's a child of. The entire "family" of subdocuments is stored in the same file with the top-level document, so that the whole thing is retrieved together when you open the document. Each diagram (document or subdocument) can be *huge,* covering up to 638 pages when printed out.

Each node can hold up to 15,000 characters, or about five single-spaced pages, of text. In addition, its pop-up Note can hold another 15K of text. You can create any pattern of interconnections among your nodes.

Nodes correspond to Topic Headers in the outline view. When you convert a diagram into an outline, an arrow from one node to another tells Inspiration that the second node is a subtopic of (is subordinate to) the first, and thus it creates the outline. Notes text is treated as body text under the Topic Header/node it was attached to in the diagram. If you have circular relationships among nodes, or a node

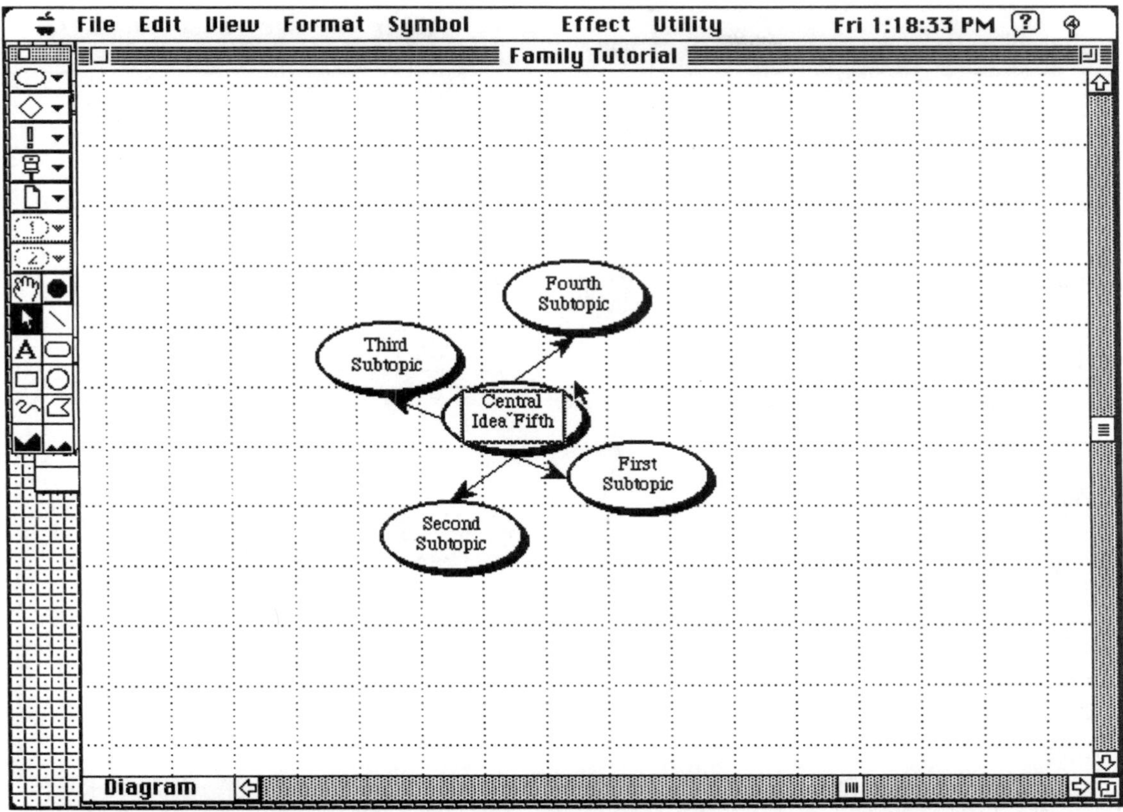

Inspiration Figure 2. Generating new subnodes using the Rapid Fire mode. All the typing is being done in the "Central Idea" node (the "Fifth Subtopic" node is just in the midst of being defined), and striking <Enter> after typing the text for each node causes it to be "spat out" into a new node. The new subtopic nodes are arranged around the original one and can be rearranged later—the purpose here is to get them down as fast as you think of them, and it works!

is subordinate to more than one other node, Inspiration will look at the connection that was created first to determine where the subtopic goes in the outline. If you don't like this, you can easily rearrange the outline.

When you create a new document, there's one node on the screen, called the "Main Idea." You can change this to whatever *your* main idea is and have all your other nodes branching off it. Or, you just as easily can have nodes that are completely unconnected to it. You can even just delete the text from the Main Idea and have its node hidden, or change which node is the Main Idea. In your outline view, the Main Idea will appear at the top, like a title. All the nodes directly connected to it will be treated as first-level topics in the outline, as will nodes that you haven't attached to it and that have no other superordinate node.

Data Entry

Entering data in the diagram view is fast, easy, and flexible, and it's designed to be that way so you can spew out ideas at brainstorm speed. There are lots of ways to go here. You can just click on a box in the grid on screen to select it, and then start typing (see Figure 1). Inspiration will create a node around the text you type. If you hold down the command key (⌘) while you click on a box (⌘-click), the new node you create will be automatically attached with a link from the previously selected node. Or, with a node selected, you can click one of eight directional arrows (up, down, left, right, and all four diagonals), and a new node, with a link from the previously selected node, will appear in the direction corresponding to the arrow. Finally, the "Rapid Fire" option lets you quickly jot down all the subtopics for a node and have them automatically arranged around the first node (see Figure 2). To use Rapid Fire, you just start typing in a node, and when you're finished with the text for that node, rather than starting a new node, you hit <Enter> on the Mac (Return won't do) or <F9> on a PC, and then type the text for the first subordinate node. When that text is all in, you hit <Enter> again, and, bingo, it gets moved to a new subordinate node. Keep typing, hit

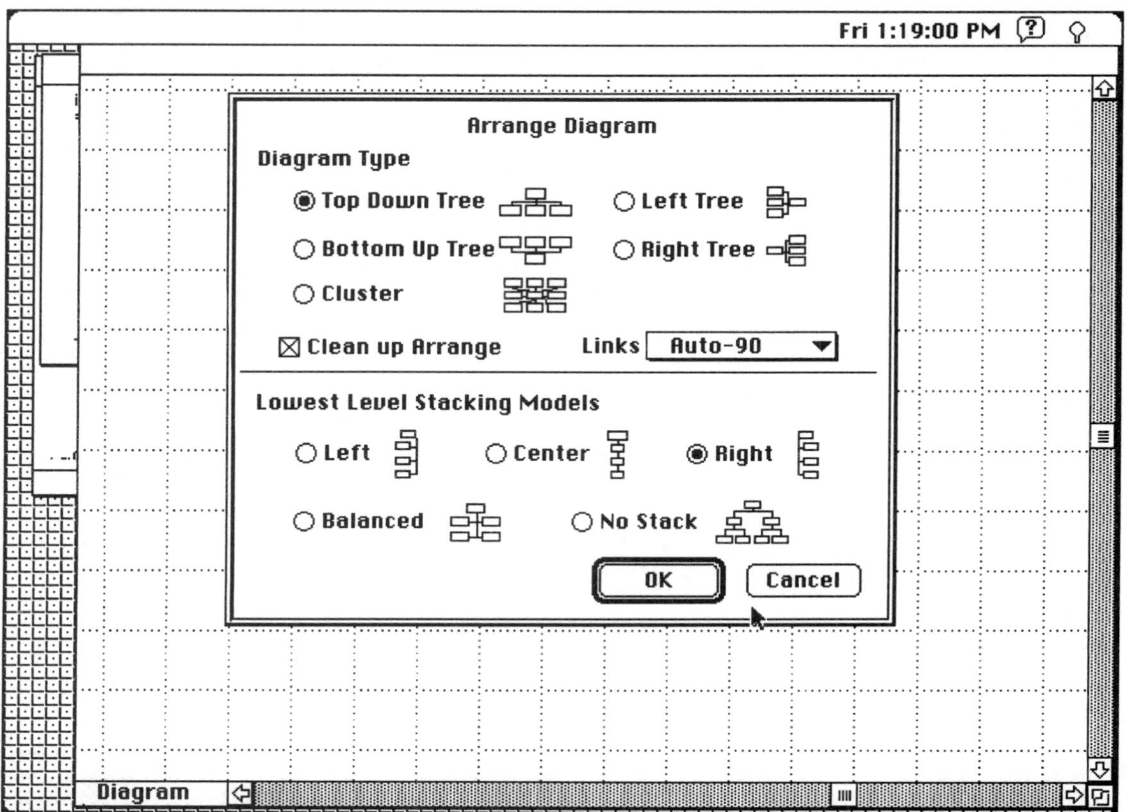

Inspiration Figure 3. The "Arrange Diagram" dialog box. The top half gives options for various types of automatic layouts, both hierarchical and cluster style. The Clean Up Arrange checkbox prevents Inspiration from making any major changes, which is nice for "cleaning up." Links lets you specify whether you want straight, direct links or you want them to stick to the horizontal and vertical, bending at 90° angles. The lower half of the dialog box lets you specify how the lowest level of nodes should be arranged in a hierarchical layout.

<Enter> again, and you get another subordinate of the original node. The subordinates are arranged either in a circle around the superordinate node or in a variety of hierarchical formats (discussed under "Working on the Data," below) depending on what you choose. To start making subnodes of one of the other nodes, you just click to select it, place the cursor at the end of the text, hit <Enter>, and start typing.

The outline mode gives you all the power of a dedicated outliner. If you prefer to work from this mode, you can simply start typing topic headers. There are a variety of ⌘-key combinations and menu choices for creating subtopics, topics at the current level, topics at higher levels, or inserting new topics of different levels in the middle of an outline. You can hit <Tab> to move a topic to a lower level or <Shift-Tab> to move it to a higher one. There are also ⌘-key combinations to move topics around in the outline, commands to make topics switch places, and so on. You can also use the mouse to drag topics and their attached Notes text around in the outline. Whenever you do any of these operations, all the topics are automatically and instantly renumbered.

You can also import text files into the outline view. If you do this, the first sentence of each paragraph will be the first-level topic header and the rest of the paragraph will be Notes text for that outline. When you convert to diagram view, the topic headers become nodes and the Notes text is available in the pop-up Notes text windows.

Working on the Data

You can work with your document in outline, diagram, or text views. In text view, topics are simply listed, one under the other, without the usual indented outline format. You can also create elaborate "families" of subdocuments and navigate through them.

Text View

Here you can work on your text as you would in a word processor, creating a text document to suit your needs. You

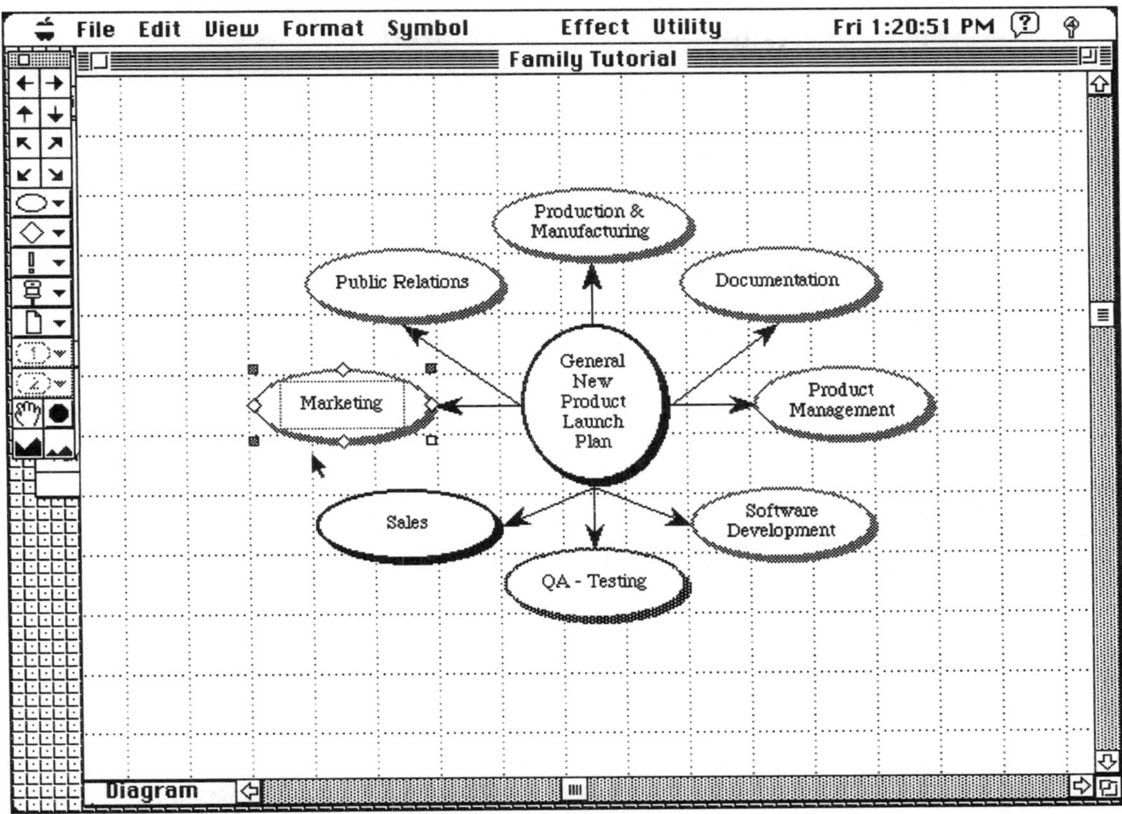

Inspiration Figure 4. The "Marketing" node is selected. Three of the four corner handles around it are gray, indicating (and giving access to) various things. upper right is for a child document, upper left is for Notes text, and lower left is for hidden subtopic nodes. The lower right handle is for resizing the node. The diamond-shaped handles can be used for creating new links—just drag from the diamond handle to a new node.

could format headers of different levels to meet APA style guidelines, for example, or you could do things you found more aesthetically pleasing, using a full complement of character and paragraph formatting attributes (fonts, including TrueType, bold, italic, underline, and color for the former; and indents, justification, line spacing, and so on for the latter). "Styles" can be defined, so that text of a particular type will all be formatted in the same way. You can define styles for each topic level, for Notes text, and for page headers and footers. You can also have topic headers hidden and just work with the Notes text. Graphics can be pasted in to appear with text views when printed. Text view functions as quite a decent word processor, and you can produce very good-looking documents with it.

Working with Diagrams

You can drag nodes around in diagrams, resize them, change the symbols they show as, and edit their text and their Notes text. There are, in fact, a wide variety of functions for manipulating and graphically embellishing your diagrams (including drawing on them or pasting in graphics) that are more properly discussed under "Graphics Editing" below, including various automatic alignment and spacing options.

One particular feature that warrants discussion here is the excellent Arrange feature. This pops up a dialog box that gives you access to a host of different automatic arrangement options (see Figure 3). You select a diagram whose subtopics you want to arrange and then pop up this dialog box. You can choose from among top-down, bottom-up, left-to-right, and right-to-left hierarchical trees. There's an option to choose whether links can go at a diagonal or must zigzag at right angles, keeping to horizontals and verticals. You can also choose "Cluster," and the subtopics will be arranged in a circular array around the selected topic. For hierarchical arrangements, there are also a variety of options for specifying how the lowest level of topics will be stacked (see Figure 3).

When you select a node, a dotted rectangular outline appears around it, with four little boxes, called "handles," at the corners (see Figure 4). These handles have different functions. The upper-left corner handle will be shaded in gray if there is a Note text attached to the node. Double-clicking on this handle will cause the Note to pop up so you can write, read, or edit it. The upper-right corner will be gray if the node has a child document attached to it (see "Families," below). Double-clicking here will jump you to the subpage. The lower-right handle is used for resizing the node by dragging with the mouse. The lower-left handle will be gray if there are hidden subtopics attached (see "Hiding Things," below). Double-clicking here will hide or show the attached subtopics.

Working with Outlines

Outline topics can be edited, as can their attached Notes text. They can be moved and rearranged in various ways, some of which were described under "Data Entry," above. One of the most powerful and useful tools in the outliner is new to version 4. You can select multiple "discontinuous" topics—from different places in the outline—with the mouse, and then choose Collect & Move from a menu. The first topic you selected in the group stays where it is, while all the other selected topics get moved, becoming subtopics of the first.

Families

Each node in a diagram (or topic in an outline) can have a "child" document attached to it, and each child can be stored in text, outline, or diagram view, independent of which view the parent is in. Every node in a child document can have its own child as well, allowing for an infinite hierarchy of subdocuments in a file (assuming, of course, that you have infinite RAM and disk space, as we do). Typically, the child document of a given node contains detailed information about that node. If you decide that all the subnodes of a given node are cluttering up your diagram, you could cut them to the clipboard, create a child document for the node, and paste the subnodes into the child document, in essence removing detail from the main document to the child. This has the added benefit of saving RAM, because only diagrams that are open on the screen need to be loaded into RAM. Or as the manual puts it: "Children do not use memory until they are opened" (Helfgott & Schmidt, 1992b, p. 93).

Children can be "disowned," deleted, or saved to separate files, and all their families (a subdocument's family consists of all its progeny), if they have them, will go too. Readers who love children need not despair, however, because you can also "adopt," bringing in other Inspiration files as children of the selected node.

Lists of children are available in two places. You can select the Open Any Child option from the File menu, and you'll get a list of all the children in the document. Children are listed directly beneath their parents, and their names are prefaced with a •. Grandchildren are listed directly below *their* parents and are prefaced with a •• and so on. The effect is of an outline of the entire family. The other option is to pull down the Utility menu, at the bottom of which is a similar list, the only difference being that it only lists children that are open at the time.

Hiding Things

In any view, you have the option of hiding nodes/topics or hiding just their Notes text (in diagram view, the Notes are hidden anyway until you open them up). This is controlled by hiding or showing all the subtopics of a particular node/topic, either from the menu or by double-clicking on the appropriate node handle, as described above.

You can also control hiding and showing globally. Remember that topics have levels, "first" being the highest, or broadest, topics in the outline, and subtopics having progressively higher level numbers (lower levels). Because outline and diagram are inherently linked, nodes have levels too. There's a setting that lets you determine how high a level (again, first is the highest) a topic/node must be to show on screen or print.

This capability can have a broad range of important applications. For example, you can *easily* create overview diagrams with varying levels of detail, with the level set either globally or specifically throughout the diagram. You can also simplify the diagram to the major topics to make rearranging easier and clearer, and then redisplay the subtopics. A very nice suggestion in the manual is that you can use the hide and show feature for on-line presentations, starting with only the major nodes showing and then progressively revealing subtopics as the presentation progresses.

Searching

Searching is very simple but can be indispensable. Inspiration has basic word processor Find (which finds a simple text string) and Find and Replace (which finds one simple text string and replaces it with another) features. Note, though, that you can do such a search through an entire diagram (or outline), which can be particularly helpful when you're working with a diagram that extends way beyond the borders of your screen. There are also options to match case (upper or lower) and to find whole words only (so if you type "see" you won't get "seeking"). Best of all, there's an option to extend the search throughout the entire family, including all the children and grandchildren and so on, enabling you to find a node or some text even if you don't know which diagram or outline it's in.

Output

Output from Inspiration, particularly on a laser printer, is spectacular. The assortment of built-in node symbols are both very functional, providing lots of information, easy differentiation, and plenty of customization options, and also very aesthetically pleasing.

Diagrams that are too big to fit on a single page of paper will be printed on multiple sheets, which you can then assemble in a rectangle. Remember that this rectangle can be composed of up to 638 sheets of paper. You can choose whether you want it to print the matrix of pages left to right or top to bottom. You can also choose whether the individual sheets are printed in landscape or portrait orientation. There are a variety of different ways you can have your output constrained, forcing it to be scaled to particular numbers of pages.

One of the program's few weaknesses shows up here. Because most printers (including laser and ink jet printers) don't print all the way to the edge of the paper, you're going to have to trim the margins off (with scissors or paper cutter) to get the links and symbols on one page to match up with those on the next. Other programs, such as MetaDesign, have options for printing with overlap so that this is easier to accomplish.

In general, though, Inspiration takes full advantage of the Mac's (and now Windows's) graphic capabilities. It handles pasted-in graphics beautifully, uses TrueType fonts (if you're on a Mac, you'll need System 7), and produces crisp, clean output.

Theory Building

Inspiration is an excellent tool for recording, representing, and manipulating the theorizing you're doing. Ray Padilla (personal communication, April 1994), developer of HyperQual2, for example, uses Inspiration in conjunction with his program to represent the emerging patterns he finds in his data. We've used it in brainstorming and then developing, elaborating, and representing a model of the "Ideal Program" for qualitative analysis. We know people who use it for designing lectures and workshops and who find working from a network diagram, either alone or side-by-side with an outline, to be a great new way to work—but this is getting somewhat far afield of theory building. The point is that you can use Inspiration in many different ways to pull ideas together, work with them, and represent them. An "Idea Book" that comes with the program suggests a wealth of possibilities, from storyboarding to Total Quality Management work to flowcharting to creating cognitive maps (see Figures 7, 8, and 9 for examples).

Graphics Editing

Inspiration's graphics-editing capabilities are outstanding, and this is significant whether you care about aesthetics or just want more power and flexibility in laying out your network to better represent your ideas. It's only possible to give a general overview of the program's features here. So, we'll cover three broad areas: tools and features for rearranging diagrams, the variety of predefined symbols for nodes and the things you can do to create your own, and other general aesthetic refinement-type features.

Rearranging Diagrams

A couple of the major features here have already been described, including the Arrange dialog box and the use of hide and show to facilitate rearranging things. A few others warrant mention here.

As in any decent network diagrammer, links are "intelligent"; that is, when you drag nodes around on the screen, their links move with them, keeping them connected. By default, nodes automatically "snap to grid," meaning they align precisely on the grid showing in the background. You can change the spacing of the grid, and you can turn off snap to grid so that you can position nodes more freely.

Also, as in any good network diagrammer or graphics editor, there are a wide variety of options for automatically aligning a selected group of nodes horizontally (lining up the nodes' tops, bottoms, or horizontal center lines) or vertically (lining up the nodes' left sides, right sides, or vertical center lines). You can also evenly space a selected group of nodes either horizontally or vertically, whether these nodes are aligned or not.

You can "group" a number of nodes so that you can operate on them all at once and make sure that they stay in the same spatial relationship to one another. A group can be dragged around the screen all at once. A group can also be changed all at once (e.g., you can change all nodes in a group to a new symbol or a new symbol size).

There are a variety of commands for selecting specific or multiple objects at once. You can Select Main Idea, Select All, Select All Symbols, Select All Links, Select Subtopics, Select This Level (e.g., to change all nodes of a particular level to one symbol), or Select All Draw Objects (you can add freehand drawing objects and pasted-in

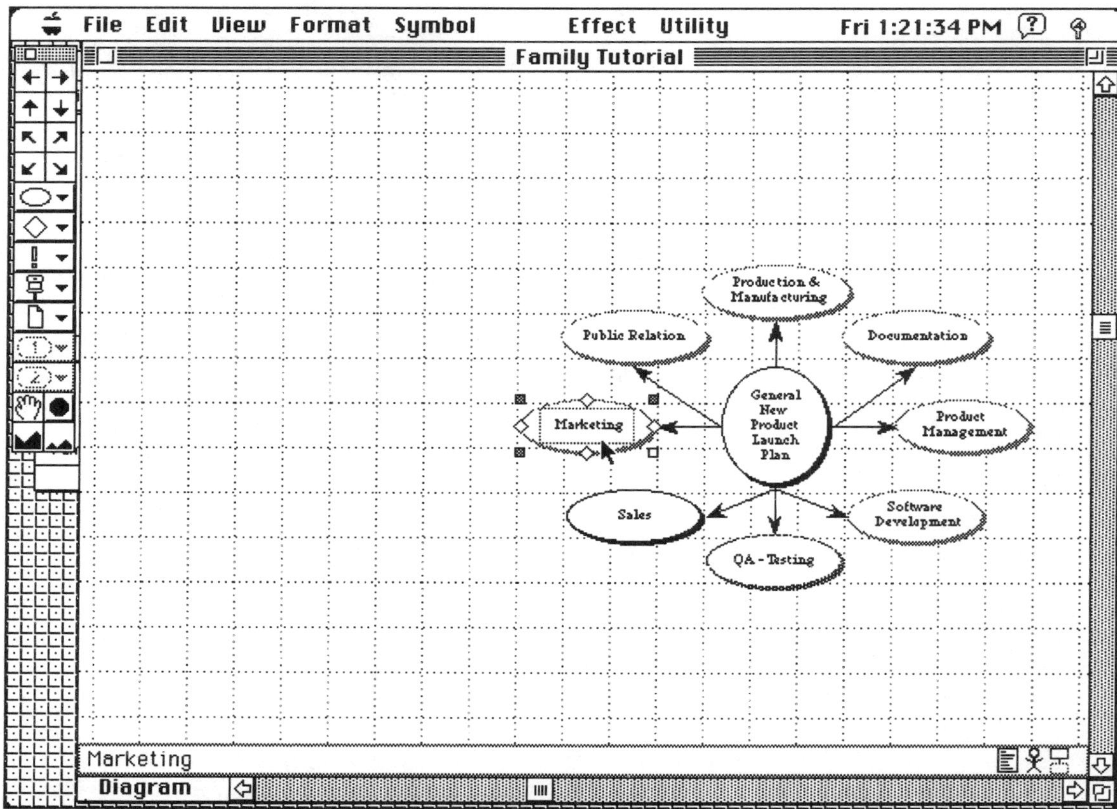

Inspiration Figure 5. The same view that was shown in Figure 4, except that we have used the "zoom" feature to reduce size and see a larger area of the diagram. The Magnify Text box appears near the bottom of the screen and shows the text of the node (Marketing) the mouse is pointing to (clicking is unnecessary), and icons (far right) to show that there is Notes text, a child, and hidden subnodes, respectively.

graphics, as discussed in "Other Aesthetic Enhancements," below).

You can zoom out and in, focusing on greater detail or larger areas. A new feature in version 4 called Magnify Text helps you work with reduced images. When you zoom out, and text gets small and hard to read, you can just move the mouse cursor to a node, and the node's text shows in a box at the bottom (or top) of the screen (see Figure 5). The Magnify Text box also displays icons to show you if the node has children, Notes text, or hidden subtopics—all information you'd normally get by looking at whether the node's handles were gray.

Symbols for Nodes

Inspiration provides a startling array of predefined symbols for nodes, far beyond what MetaDesign offers. All node types can be set to "autogrow," expanding as necessary to accommodate the text you type in. If you don't let them autogrow, then text that doesn't fit simply won't show on screen. If you place the cursor in the text, however, and use the arrow keys to move it up and down, the rest of the text will scroll through the visible text window in the node.

There are menus of 10 basic shapes, 14 ANSI-standard flowchart symbols, 15 business symbols, 11 "designer" symbols, and 12 "image" symbols. The business and designer symbols are what are called "strip symbols," as shown in Figure 6, with an icon in a strip down the left side of a text rectangle. You can also create your own custom strip symbols by pasting in a graphic for the strip, typing text to appear in the strip, or editing a graphic for the strip. In addition, any graphic you paste in using the clipboard (any graphic that can be placed on the clipboard can be pasted in) will be treated as a node. If you want to use a graphic regularly as a node symbol, you can add it to one of two "user symbols" menus, which hold 50 symbols each.

It may be overkill to say it here, but *all* of the symbols provided with Inspiration look good. They are easy to dis-

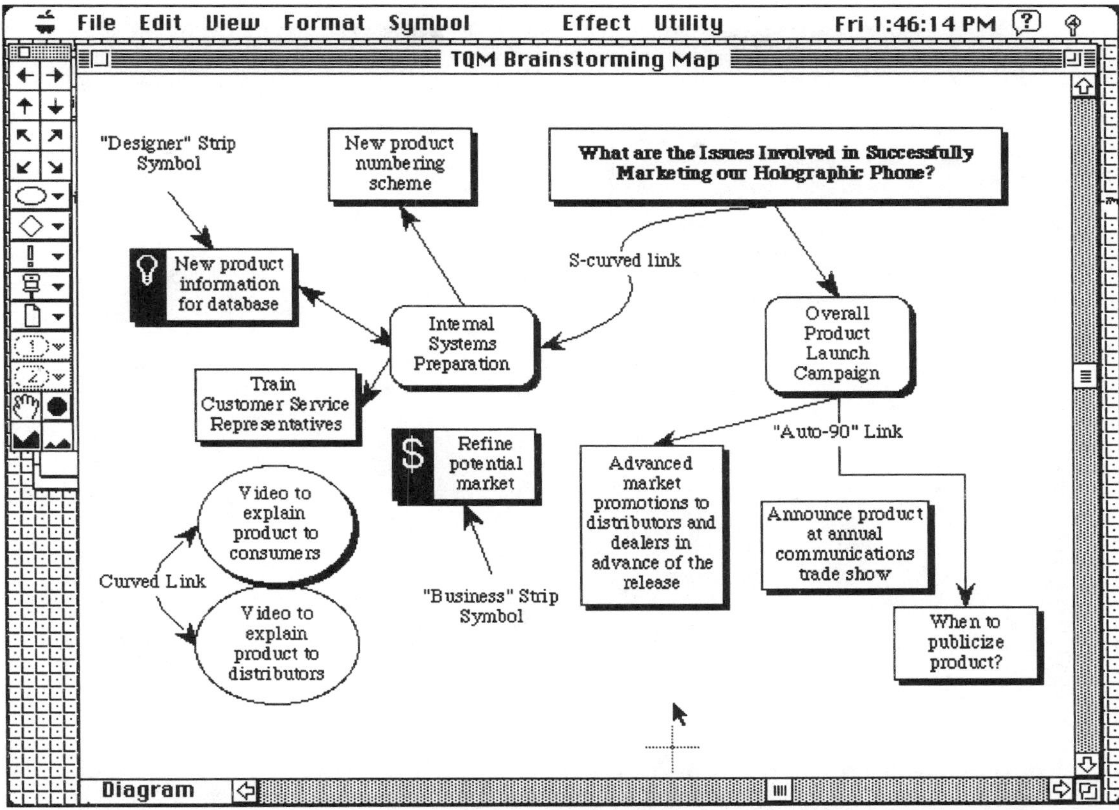

Inspiration Figure 6. A sample diagram, showing a variety of different node symbols, in different styles, with different types of links.

tinguish, aesthetically pleasing, and well designed for communicating information.

Other Aesthetic Enhancements

Links can be straight, curved (a simple curve or an "S" curve), or segmented (consisting of straight segments connected at "elbows"). Curving and segmenting can be done manually or automatically. Links can connect to any of 32 points around the perimeter of a node, and multiple links can connect to the same point, offering you lots of different looks to give your diagram. You can attach text to a link and place the text box anywhere along the link. Inspiration creates a little break in the link line so that the text shows clearly and is easy to read. Links can have different line thicknesses, different styles of arrowheads, even different colors and different shadings and crosshatchings for the arrowheads.

Nodes can be shadowed, for a three-dimensional look, or not (see Figure 6). They can be colored and shaded using an editable color palette and selecting from among 24 fill patterns.

There's a simple selection of Draw tools for drawing straight lines (with or without arrowheads), plain or rounded rectangles, ovals, polygons, or freeform lines. You can use these tools to enhance your diagrams any way you want, without being forced to try to use symbols and links to represent everything.

User Friendliness

To top it all off, Inspiration is great fun to use, and it is surprisingly easy to learn thoroughly. We spent a little over 3 hours on the excellent tutorials for version 3 and learned the program very thoroughly. The tutorials for version 4 look more comprehensive and, if anything, like more fun. The manuals are well written and laid out, though at times the explanations, in trying to be simple and clear, are somewhat incomplete, and you have to experiment to see what will happen. The indexes are fairly thorough, but not spectacular. The "idea book" gives a wide range of examples of the kinds of things you can do with Inspiration and can be very helpful in seeing unexpected applications of the

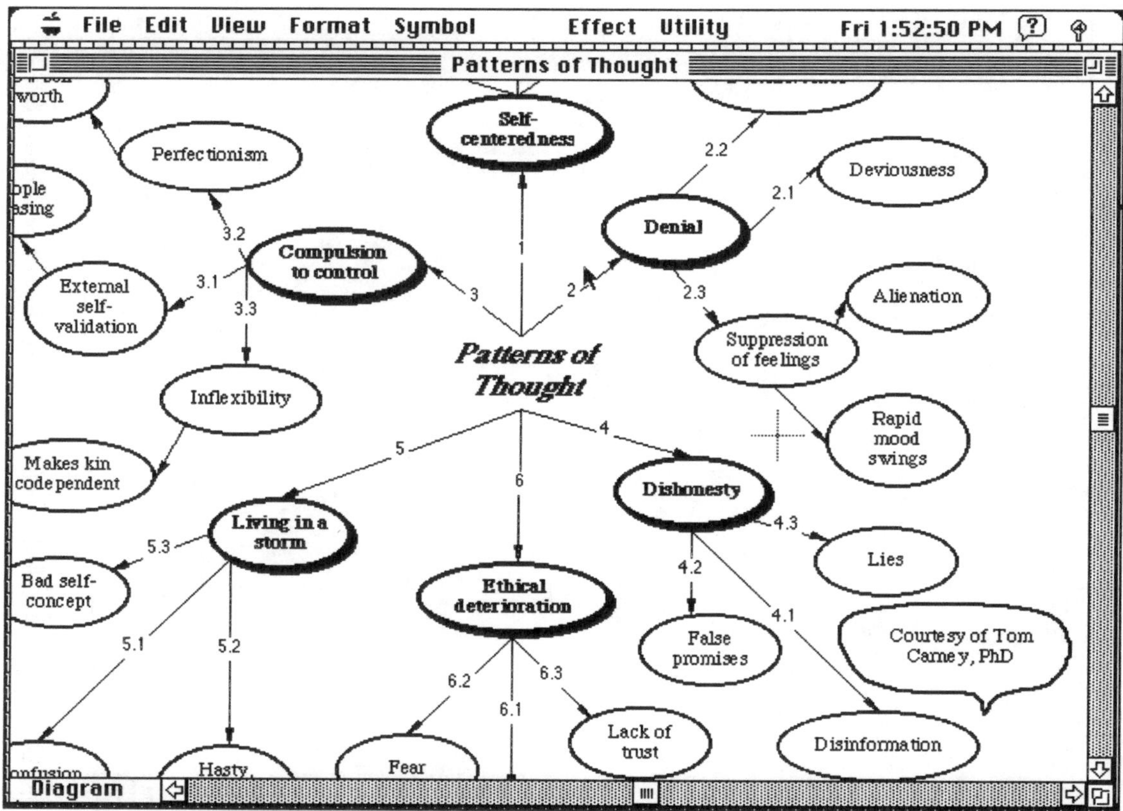

Inspiration Figure 7. A sample diagram that comes with the program, showing a model of "Patterns of Thought." Note that outline position numbering is used as link labels.

program (see Figures 7, 8, and 9 for a few examples). Most of these are available as Inspiration documents that come on the program disks.

On-screen help is provided in the Macintosh version, if you have System 7, through the most thorough implementation of help balloons of any of the Mac programs reviewed in this book. Every menu and dialog box item we checked had a help balloon, and the information provided was usually very helpful. In the Windows version, on-screen help is provided through a standard Windows help setup, a particularly nicely done one.

Technical support is available from 8 to 5 Pacific time. The only phone number in the materials that came with our evaluation copy was a long-distance, toll number. However, a call to 800 directory information turned up the toll-free number provided in the information box at the beginning of this review. The 800 number gives you access to sales, technical support, and some information about frequently asked questions. The tech support people we dealt with ranged from quite competent to excellent and were always friendly and patient.

Miscellaneous

Inspiration will run on a network. For specific information about things like simultaneous users, contact the developer.

Update

With the Windows version, Inspiration Software introduced a number of new or enhanced features, all of which they are working to implement in the Macintosh version as well. The set of ready-to-go symbols is expanded from 63 to 525. The extra symbols are provided in 12 "libraries," which you can load into the custom symbol spots on the toolbar. Many of the new symbols are whimsical; quite a few are useful. Finally, they have replaced their old spell-checker, which had 70,000 words, with one from Houghton-Mifflin, which has 200,000. Transfer of documents back and forth between the two platforms was expected for the summer of 1994. As we've pointed out in other

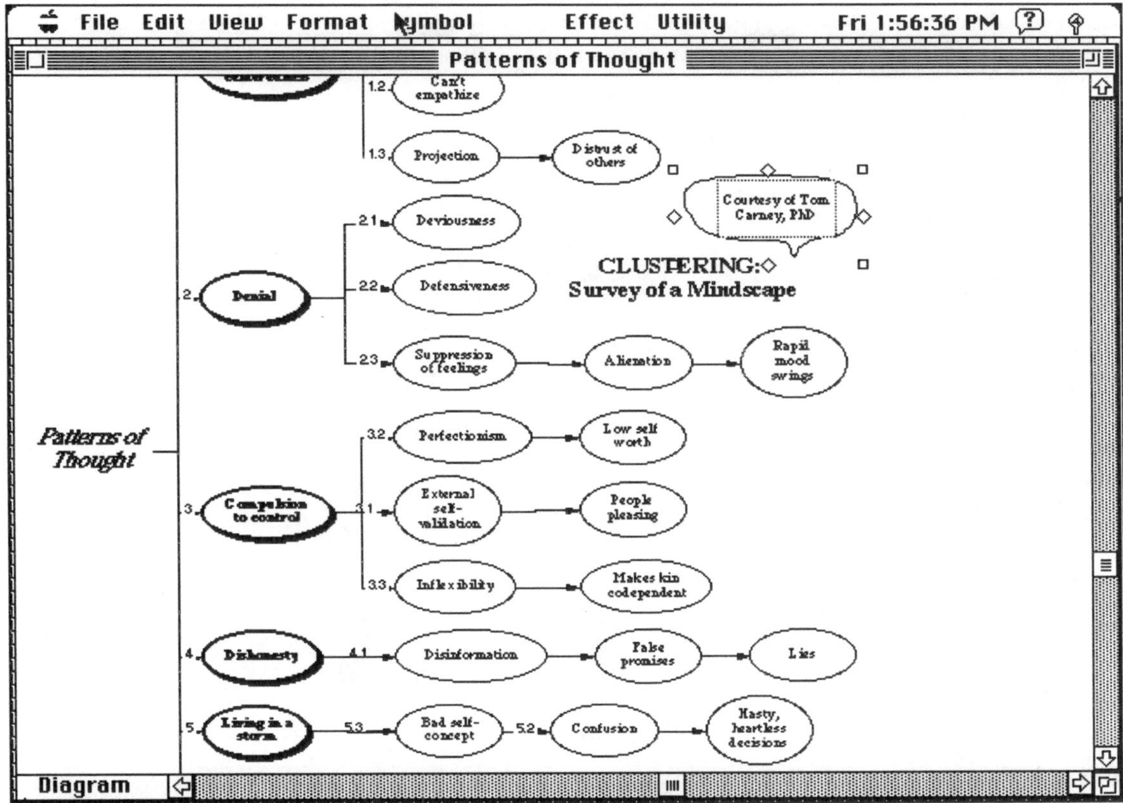

Inspiration Figure 8. The diagram from Figure 7 has been rearranged in one step using the Arrange Diagram dialog box, so that it now appears as a left to right hierarchical tree.

reviews, such predictions are virtually always optimistic; wait and see.

Comparative Remarks

Inspiration, being a dedicated graphic-mapper, is *much* better in terms of graphics than programs like ATLAS/ti, NUD•IST, MECA, or even SemNet, which are not intended to compete in this area. It would be great if programs like those had an export feature that allowed you to send their networks, retaining connected, movable nodes and links, to programs like Inspiration, but as of now they don't.

The only program reviewed here that is directly comparable with Inspiration is MetaDesign, and the comparison is tricky because MetaDesign Version 4.0 is only available for Windows, while Mac users must settle for Version 3.0. When Inspiration was a Mac-only program, this made the choice simple: If you used a PC running Windows, we'd say use MetaDesign, and if you used a Mac, we'd say choose Inspiration. But now Inspiration is available for both platforms. So here's a summary of some key differences:

Inspiration Can, MetaDesign Can't

1. Outline Outline Outline
2. Make larger visuals
3. Create diagrams more quickly and easily, with more options for new node generation
4. Let nodes automatically grow to fit text (MetaDesign makes you issue a command to do it)
5. Use strip symbols—rectangles with a customizable icon in a vertical strip on the left side
6. Break an imported text document down into outline form: first sentence of each paragraph becomes a Topic Heading, with rest of paragraph as Notes text (topic Heading level is determined by indentation in text document)
7. Produce higher quality graphics more easily

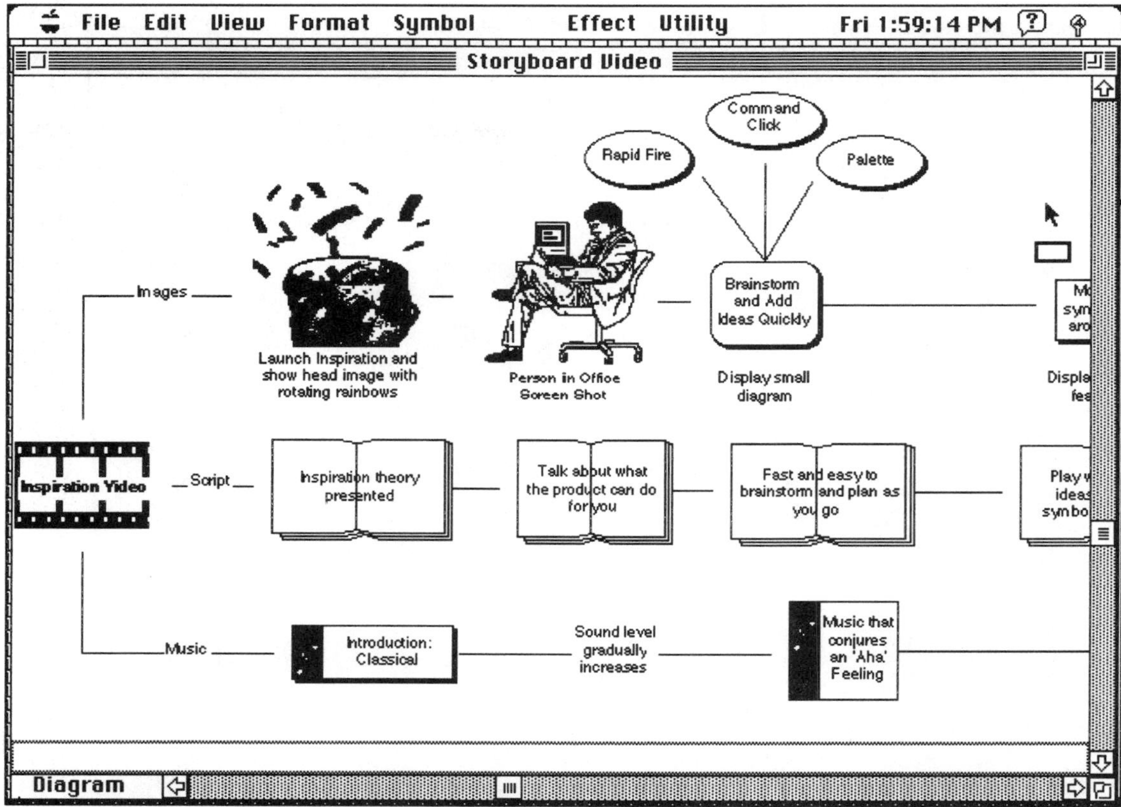

Inspiration Figure 9. Another sample from the tutorial diagrams. This one incorporates pasted-in graphics as node symbols.

MetaDesign Can, Inspiration Can't

1. Provide "page structure" view for navigating among relatives (Inspiration provides only an outline of the family structure)
2. Load external text into a node with a single command (with Inspiration, you have to load the text into a word processor, copy it to the clipboard, and paste the text from the clipboard into the diagram; on the Mac, if you don't have System 7, or MultiFinder, this means you'll have to exit Inspiration to get to your word processor, then exit the word processor to get back to Inspiration)
3. Parse text by delimiters (see MetaDesign review for details)
4. Provide scroll bars for viewing text that extends beyond the boundaries of a node
5. Provide hypertext linking between specific nodes and more flexibility in creating hierarchical relationships among various objects in a document

Summary

If it's not clear by now, we loved this program. Even though it's not a dedicated analysis tool, its range of possible applications in qualitative research, and in intellectual work in general, is wide. The biggest problem with Inspiration was always that it was only available for the Mac, but, happily, that's no longer true. It's a powerful thinking tool, allowing you to develop and represent your ideas and conceptual frameworks in *both* graphic and outline (or free-text) forms *simultaneously.* And it creates gorgeous, high-quality graphics suitable for any publication or presentation purpose.

References

Helfgott, M., & Nakell, C. (1992). *Inspiration idea book.* Portland, OR: Inspiration Software, Inc.

Helfgott, M., & Schmidt, R. (1992a). *Inspiration getting started manual.* Portland, OR: Inspiration Software, Inc.

Helfgott, M., & Schmidt, R. (1992b). *Inspiration user's manual.* Portland, OR: Inspiration Software, Inc.

MECA, Version 1

Available for DOS, Unix, and Macintosh

Kathleen Carley
Department of Social and Decision Sciences
Carnegie Mellon University
Pittsburgh, PA 15568

Phone: (412) 268-3225
E-mail: kathleen.carley@centro.soar.cs.cmu.edu

Price: $60 individuals
$200 for classes (four copies)
Unix: price negotiated

Hardware Requirements:
For DOS
- IBM PC XT or better; DOS 2.0 or higher
- 640K RAM
- Hard disk with 1-2MB free (depending on data file size)

For Macintosh
- Mac II or better; system 6 or higher
- 604K RAM

For Unix
- Sun or Dec workstations
- Berkeley Unix
- 1MB RAM

Overview

MECA, Version 1, is a specialized research collection with 15 programs—routines for constructing and working analytically with the structure of conceptual networks (i.e., mental models) and doing numerical content analysis of the data. It includes only a minimal program for graphic network display. It can be used for either exploratory or confirmatory analysis.

MECA is built around four key ideas: (a) *concepts* (such as Bill or Jane); (b) *relationships* (such as "loves," "hates"); (c) *statements* (such as "Bill hates Jane"); and (d) a *map*, which is a collection of statements.[1]

1. In MECA's language, a "map" is just that. a collection of statements that express the relationships among a set of concepts. Only one MECA program shows you a graphic map (a circle of concepts with lines showing relationships). You don't see a usual "network" as in other programs such as MetaDesign, Inspiration, ATLAS/ti, or NUD•IST.

MECA will give you data about conceptual maps primarily in quantitative form (matrices, content-analytic information, or simple statistical summaries). Its graphic display is limited: only a circle of concepts with relationships lines drawn between them. (To produce this, if you are working in the DOS version, data must be transferred to a Macintosh and printed with MacDraw.)

In its present version, MECA is a bare-bones collection of programs, which are not linked together in a package. You enter each program as needed, run it, and then have an output file that you can use as you enter another program in the collection.

MECA has a clear *conceptual* rationale and is supported by several articles supplied as documentation. On-line help is minimal. MECA can be used both to study the conceptual maps of your respondents and (with less

TEXT

Interviewer:	Step by step... What's the first thing that you do?
[1] Student:	Get a topic.
Interviewer:	What do you mean by a "topic"?
[2] Student:	What you are going to write on.
Interviewer:	Okay, then what would you do after that?
[3] Student:	Go to the library and find out something about **it**
Interviewer:	How would you find out...
[4] Student:	**Magazines,** books, encyclopedias...
Interviewer:	Anything else.
[5] Student:	Nothing offhand,
[6]	I mean there's things,
[7]	if you had resources you would know something offhand.
Interviewer:	Okay, you have the books and magazines. What would you do next?
[8] Student:	Read **them** (laughs).
Interviewer:	Okay, after you have read them?
[9] Student:	**Decide specifically what** you are going to write down,
[10]	**which side of** the issue or something,
[11]	trying to get down ideas,
[12]	make a general outline,
[13]	just a few ideas of what you are going to write about.
Interviewer:	So you would move from a topic to an issue that you would write about? What would the issue be?
[14] Student:	Like **for or against** whatever the topic was.

EXTRACTED CONCEPTS	GENERALIZED CONCEPTS
book	books
decide specifically what	topic
encyclopedia	encyclopedia
facts	fact
find	find
for or against	sides
ideas	idea
issue	issue
it	topic
library	library
magazine	books
outline	outline
read them	research
research writing	writing
resources	books
topic	topic
which side of	sides
write	writing

MECA Figure 1. Annotated text segment. The analyst has underlined concepts and also converted them to more generalized form in many instances. The generalized concepts can now be entered in a setup file via STARTUP (see Figure 2) or a text editor.
SOURCE: Drawn from Carley and Palmquist (1992).

ease) to clarify your own evolving theory.[2] But don't expect a fully developed program like most of the others we're reviewing (QCA is the only other program that has a similar technical-researcher flavor). We include it here as an instance of a specialized, researcher-developed program that may work for you if you have interests in the domain of mental models and their analysis. The flavor of the program is mainframe; you get prompts and work in line mode, without the possibility to scroll back up.

This preliminary review used the DOS version and is based on 11 of the 15 programs, along with three items—two articles and a set of overheads—included as documentation, and the experience of running some of the programs with the brief sample text files provided. It was also important to understand the conceptual basis of the research the program is designed to support. In one article, Carley (1993) does a very clear job of making the basic case for distinguishing map analysis (essentially, constructing networks) from traditional content analysis (essentially, counting frequencies); see also Carley (1991, 1994). An appendix to the 1993 article reviews MECA's various programs. Another article (Carley & Palmquist, 1992) places the "mental models" or cognitive mapping approach in the literature of cognitive science, linguistics, and content analysis, and then runs you through the first two basic steps of using MECA. A set of overheads used in presentations (Carley, 1990) are very useful in providing an overview of the concepts and programs of MECA. Other useful articles are cited as we go.

2. The developer points out that MECA is explicitly designed to represent the content of text, and says, "To the extent the researcher has a theory, that theory is embedded in the coding scheme (e.g., types of concepts and relations chosen), and the researcher's theory can be tested using the output" (Carley, personal communication).

WELCOME TO STARTUP V4

Copyright (c) 1990 Carley

This program is used to enter the set-up information used by the following MECA programs -- CLIST, CMATRIX, CODEMAP, COMPRA, CUBE, SCOMPRA, SKI, SMATRIX

This program is entirely interactive. A series of questions will be asked. After answering the question simply type a carriage return.

The output file is an asci file.

What would you like to call the file containing the set-up information?
??? mysetup.dat ← *this can be any name that you would like for the template file*
You can classify concepts into a maximum of 9 categories
How many concept categories are there?
??? 1 ← *because Palmquist did not distinguish categories*

Name of concept category 1? book2 ← *must be one word*
Are statements:
1) Some uni- and some bi-directional
2) All uni-directional
3) All bi-directional
??? 3 ← *because Palmquist did not want to distinguish directionality*
Are you using strength:
1) To denote existence
2) To denote existence and sign
3) A range of strengths
4) Number of occurrences of this fact
??? 1 ← *because Palmquist only wanted to denote that there was a relationship*
You can classify relationships (links) into a maximum of 9 types
How many types of links are there?
??? 0 ← *because Palmquist did not distinguish any special types of relationships*

How many concepts in category book2 do you currently have? 0 ← *because Palmquist took an exploratory approach to concept definition*

THANK YOU FOR USING STARTUP

Your data is being stored in the file mysetup.dat.
It can be edited with a standard text editor.

MECA Figure 2. Creating a setup file. This material is not a screen shot but an annotated version. The program's prompts are in bold, the user's choices in normal type, and explanatory remarks added by Carley and Palmquist are in italics. The figure should be read through in sequence to get a feel for how STARTUP works.
SOURCE: Excerpted from Carley and Palmquist (1992).

Database Structure

If you are working in an exploratory mode, you begin work by looking at a text (spoken or written—it could be an interview, a soliloquy, a written essay, story, document, and so on). As one option, this can be done with hard copy. You identify generic concepts in the text, most easily by highlighting, circling, or listing them in the margin. Concepts can be at almost any level you like (e.g., "friend," "Red Riding Hood," "writing," "library," "walked to Grandmother's house," "hunger").

Figure 1, drawn from Carley and Palmquist (1992), shows an example of how you might go about the extraction of concepts using hard copy.

It's also possible to create text files (ASCII) in a text editor, using no more than 500 characters per line and separating paragraphs with $$ markers. If you do this, there are programs for simplifying your list of concepts, either through concept deletion or through creating a synonym list. The program DELCON takes concepts out of your text that you don't want, in one or several text files (they could be a sort of "omit list" of nuisance words). The program TRANSLATE will convert concepts in one or several text files, using a synonym list that you create with a text editor (the key concept is marked with a $, followed by synonyms on subsequent lines). In effect, it too deletes surplus concepts; whenever it finds a synonym, it replaces it with the key concept. Such simplified text files, when printed out, may

```
WELCOME TO CODEMAP V4
Copyright (c) 1990 Carley

What is the name of the set-up file? mysetup.dat ← the template file
What is your name? coder ← full name, initials, or any id
What is the date? 3/90
What is the name of the text? (one word) student ← must be one word
Output will be put into the file student.map. ← .map is automatically
        appended
Directions? (y/n) n
Concept? (<concept name>, #, <cr>, ?, or -quit) ? ← a "?" always causes
        CODEMAP to print help if it exists
For each sentence you may have 1 or more Concepts. First check to see if
the Concept is already in the list of Concepts If it is, then all you need to
type is the first word or unique characters If it is not, then type the entire
phrase. A '#' will print out a list of the available Concepts in category
book2. A -quit returns you to the question -
CONTINUE? A carriage return <cr> acts like a quit. ← CODEMAP is
        automatically modified by the template file. Note the use of
        "book2" for concept category.

Concept? (<concept name>, #, <cr>, ?, or -quit) wri ← you need not type in
        the complete concept only the first few unique characters
Do you want the Concept: writer? (y/n) n
Do you want the Concept: writing? (y/n) y
Concept? (<concept name>, #, <cr>, ?, or -quit) topic ← can be multiple
        words topic is not listed as a Concept of type concept
Do you want to add topic to the Concept list? (y/n) y
----------------------------------------------------------------
The Concepts are:
        (1) topic
        (2) writing
Current Information:
        strength No Relation
        directionality bi-directional - directionality can not be altered
Do you wish to change any of this information? (y/n) y ← since the only
        choice is to change the strength, no-relation will
        automatically be changed to presence of relation
```

MECA Figure 3. Coding the statements. As in Figure 1, bold type shows program prompts; normal type, the user's input; and italics, annotated remarks inserted by the authors. This excerpt shows the user (a) making initial entry to the program; (b) asking for concepts beginning with "wri" and choosing "writing"; (c) adding a new concept, "topic"; and (d) creating a statement linking the concepts "topic" and "writing." The user continues by (e) creating a statement linking "issue" and "sides," then (f) creating a statement linking the concepts of "topic"—which has now been added to the setup file as a result of step c—and "issue." CODEMAP concludes (g) with a report of the output map file's contents.
SOURCE: From Carley and Palmquist (1992).

be easier to use in setting up your basic data files, which we'll turn to in a moment.

Back to the hard copy: You also think through the types of relationships you are interested in—the links or ties between concepts. They can be equally varied: "loves," "does," "leads to," "is less likely than," "is a kind of." Relationships (links) have four formal properties: *directionality* (one- or two-way); *strength* (which can be defined as intensity, certainty, emphasis, frequency, and so on); *sign* (positive or negative); and *meaning* (the content, such as "is friends with," "works with"). (Carley suggests that in most cases link types do not need to be differentiated, so it's possible to specify relationships in a completely minimal way if you wish: Two-way directionality, no strength, no sign, and no different meaning of the link would simply link concepts as being "connected.")

Look in the text at hand for statements showing how concept 1 is linked to concept 2 ("papers have abstracts," "cooling causes condensation," "Bill is a tutor"). As Carley and Palmquist point out, you are functioning as a sort of (exploratory) literary scholar, inferring from the text what the relationships are between the concepts. These statements, taken together, will describe a network. The list of statements is called a map. (Remember that in MECA a "map" is just that—a list—not necessarily the graphic network that can be drawn from it.)

The approach in a confirmatory or hypothesis-testing mode is similar, except that concepts, relationships, and statements are drawn from the prior literature, instruments, and existing theory. You are functioning more as a "subject matter expert" in defining statements.

MECA's capacity per any given map is limited to 500 concepts (which can be sorted into up to nine categories),[3]

3. It isn't wholly clear how having categories of concepts can be useful when you're using MECA. Two possibilities are (a) creating submaps, each restricted to one of your categories, or (b) arranging graphic output (see below under DRAWMAP) so that concepts in a category adjoin each other.

```
CONTINUE? (y/n) y
Concept? (<concept name>, #, <cr>, ?, or -quit) issue
Do you want the Concept: issue? (y/n) y
Concept? (<concept name>, #, <cr>, ?, or -quit) sides
Do you want the Concept: sides? (y/n) y
-------------------------------------------------------------
The Concepts are:
        (1) issue
        (2) sides
Current Information:
        strength No Relation
        directionality bi-directional - directionality can not be altered
Do you wish to change any of this information? (y/n) y
CONTINUE? (y/n) y
Concept? (<concept name>, #, <cr>, ?, or -quit) topic
Do you want the Concept: topic? (y/n) y ← the template file has now been
                changed and includes the concept topic
Concept? (<concept name>, #, <cr>, ?, or -quit) issue
Do you want the Concept: issue? (y/n) y
-------------------------------------------------------------
The Concepts are:
        (1) topic
        (2) issue
Current Information:
        strength No Relation
        directionality bi-directional - directionality can not be altered
Do you wish to change any of this information? (y/n) y
CONTINUE? (y/n) n
Thank you for coding this text.
The output will be in the file student.map.
Do you wish to code another text? (y/n) n
                        THANK YOU FOR USING CODEMAP

The contents of the output-file student.map are:
        created by coder 3/90:
        1$book2$issue$book2$sides$2
        1$book2$issue$book2$topic$2
        1$book2$sides$book2$issue$2
        1$book2$topic$book2$issue$2
        1$book2$topic$book2$writing$2
        1$book2$writing$book2$topic$2
```

MECA Figure 3. Continued.

nine types of relations (which you specify), and 8,000 statements. (The program helps you by offering the idea of "key concepts," with the same limit of 500, but each one may have up to 500 synonyms.) Practically speaking, most studies take 200, sometimes up to 400 concepts, according to Carley. The number of statements is usually far less than the theoretical maximum (e.g., for 200 concepts, there can be 19,900 bidirectional links); the impression in several studies cited by Carley is that the number of statements is only a small multiple of the number of concepts.

Data Entry

You use STARTUP, a program that creates a template, called a "setup file," for coding your text and performing later analytical operations. This basic startup data set is used in many of the other programs. STARTUP (see Figure 2) asks you for your list of concepts, one by one (usually up to about 200 for a particular situation or task); concept names must be under 40 characters. They can be sorted into up to nine different categories if you wish, with labels supplied by you. (Later, after you have created a map, a program called CLIST shows you the list of concepts you have used in it.)

Considering the relationships you will be examining, you also indicate the *directionality* (one-way, two-way, or mixed); the *strength* and *sign* (simple existence of a link, existence plus sign—positive, negative, or a mix), a range of strengths (say, –3 to +3), or the number of occurrences of the relationship; and the *meaning* (advice is to limit the numbers of different meanings—the maximum is nine types—so as not to balloon the number of statements). All this is done interactively—the program asks you for your decisions, item by item. You can't scroll back, but you can exit and correct the setup file you've created with a text editor.

Figure 2, excerpted from Carley and Palmquist (1992), shows how this works in a very simple instance, using concepts and relationships from the text in Figure 1. STARTUP automatically creates a "template" or setup file when you finish providing the information.

Working on the Data

The next step is to "code" your data. Note carefully: In MECA, "coding" does not mean attaching keywords to text for use in later search and retrieval. Rather, you are creating a series of "statements," each one linking two concepts. The program CODEMAP does this by asking you

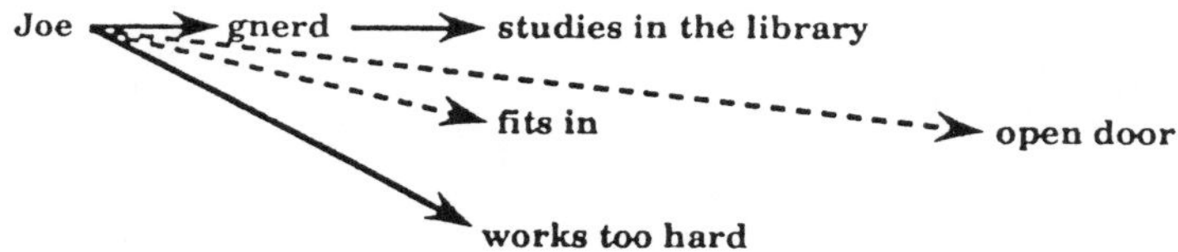

MECA Figure 4. Graphic representation of a concept map. This map, hand-drawn from the analytical "map" statements, shows how the text above can be formally depicted. Solid lines show a positive relationship; dotted ones, negative.
SOURCE: Drawn from Carley (1993).

for two concepts at a time, then asking you to specify the statement that involves them. This is also done interactively. Note that this can get to be a very long job if you have lots of concepts, more than one type of relationship, and so on. It's slow work, but probably no slower than the process of assigning codes on a line-by-line basis.

Figure 3, also from Carley and Palmquist (1992), shows how CODEMAP works. You enter concepts first (CODEMAP will bring them to you from your setup file, one at a time, if you ask for the initial letter or first few letters). When you have a pair of concepts, you specify the relationship between them. Again, you cannot scroll back. CODEMAP does, however, ask you to confirm whether you do or don't want a particular concept you've entered, and it allows you to change a relationship you've specified or delete the whole statement. Once you've entered a full statement, however, it's on to the next. If you want to make changes later, it will have to be done in a text editor working on CODEMAP's output file, which is in ASCII. It looks like this, for a simple one:

```
1$book2$issue$book2$sides$2
```

In this example, the initial "1" shows that the "strength" of the relationship is indicated as "exists" (rather than having a sign, a range, or a frequency); "book2" names the general category of the concept "issue," which is linked to the concept "sides," also in the category "book2." The concluding "2" indicates that the relation is bidirectional (rather than unidirectional). The $ signs are separators; the next statement will appear on the next line. A "map" is a complete set of such statements. The output can be edited by reentering CODEMAP or by using your word processor or a text editor such as Epsilon or emacs.

The reader interested in networks may say "Ugh! How can a map made from such statements tell me anything?" Remember: These "maps" are used as basic input to programs that will provide you with numerical summaries and one type of actual graphic display.

MECA includes an interesting-sounding program called SKI, which helps you make implicit "expert" knowledge about the domain covered in a coded map explicit. Using CODEMAP first, you create a map of "definitives," which embody well-defined social knowledge. To illustrate this, Figure 4 shows a "hand-drawn" map (via MacDraw) of statements entered using CODEMAP from the following text, drawn from Carley's (1985) study of college resident tutors and reported in Carley (1993):

> Joe's a gnerd [*sic*] who always studies in the library and doesn't fit in. His door is never open, he works too hard.

Carley suggests a whole series of implicit social knowledge items that lie "behind the text" here. For example, most people would know:

> If someone studies in the library, then he/she is not accessible.
>
> If someone is a gnerd, he/she is not friendly.
>
> If someone has an open door, he/she interacts with students.
>
> If he/she is accessible, then the door is open.

To use SKI, in addition to such "definitives" (if concept 1 is used, everyone in the social group involved would agree that concept 2 is always implied), you also input a map of knowledge labeled "logicals" (concept 1 always has the same implied *logical link* to concept 2) and a map of "simples" (concept 1 is always linked in the *same way* to concept 2—even though it may not be "logical"). You also input the basic map you want to recode. SKI, working in batch mode, redoes the map in light of the definitives, logicals, and simples—in effect making it more complex. SKI could thus be used to correct and extend the "coding" done by less expert people (e.g., new research assistants). SKI can also be used to compare explicit and implicit knowledge. See Kaufer and Carley (1993) for additional ideas on coding text.

MECA also includes an "automatic" coding procedure. Once you have a setup file produced by STARTUP, a program called GENMAP can be used to generate statements

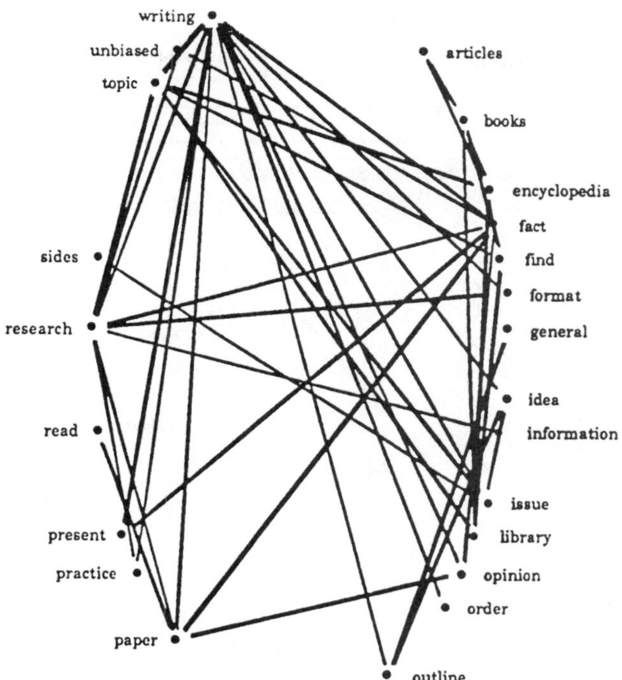

MECA Figure 5. Example of DRAWMAP output as printed by MacDraw. The 23 concepts have been arranged (an option) around the circle (here, more of an ellipse) alphabetically. In this instance, the lines depicting statements are bidirectional (have no arrowheads) and have no strength differences (differing line weights) or positive-negative sign (solid versus dotted lines).
SOURCE: From Carley and Palmquist (1992).

"automatically" from a text file. You set a "window" of the number of words to be searched through to make a statement; all concepts within the window and before the end of the paragraph are linked automatically to make statements. This program was not included on the available disk, so it wasn't clear how this works (it probably uses only a simple, "exists"-type link and relies on the assumption that proximity of two concepts in text implies a relationship).

Output

MECA will use the "maps" (lists of statements) you've produced to get you output in matrix, statistical, or one type of network form.

Once you've created your database of "setup files" via STARTUP and coded it with CODEMAP, another program, CMATRIX, will count the presence/absence (or frequencies) of each of a specific list of concepts in one or more maps, also creating an ASCII output matrix readable by standard statistical packages such as SYSTAT and SAS. (The program CMATRIX2 will do the same with raw text files—it will treat every word as a concept.)

The SMATRIX program will look at the statements in a number of map files, telling you the names of the files they appear in and/or showing you the "union" of *all* statements in the maps, or only the statements *shared* by a set of maps (the "intersection"). It ignores strength as well as types of links and concepts.

When you run any program, such as CMATRIX, MECA does *not* show you the results on screen or print them, but outputs them to a new file, automatically naming it simply CMATRIX.DAT. If you already have a file with this name, it renames the old file OLDCMATR.DAT, telling you so. Thus (a) you have to open the file in a text editor or word processor to see what it looks like; (b) you'd better rename CMATRIX.DAT and OLDCMATR.DAT right away, or the next time you run CMATRIX you'll lose OLDCMATR.DAT—not to mention that the name MECA assigned gives you no clue as to *which* CMATRIX.DAT this one was. The same procedure applies to other output files: the program SMATRIX will produce SMATRIX.DAT, CMATRIX2 gives you CMATRIX2.DAT, and so on. You also have no choice of where MECA will create the file; it just goes to the current directory. All this illustrates the bare-bones character of MECA.

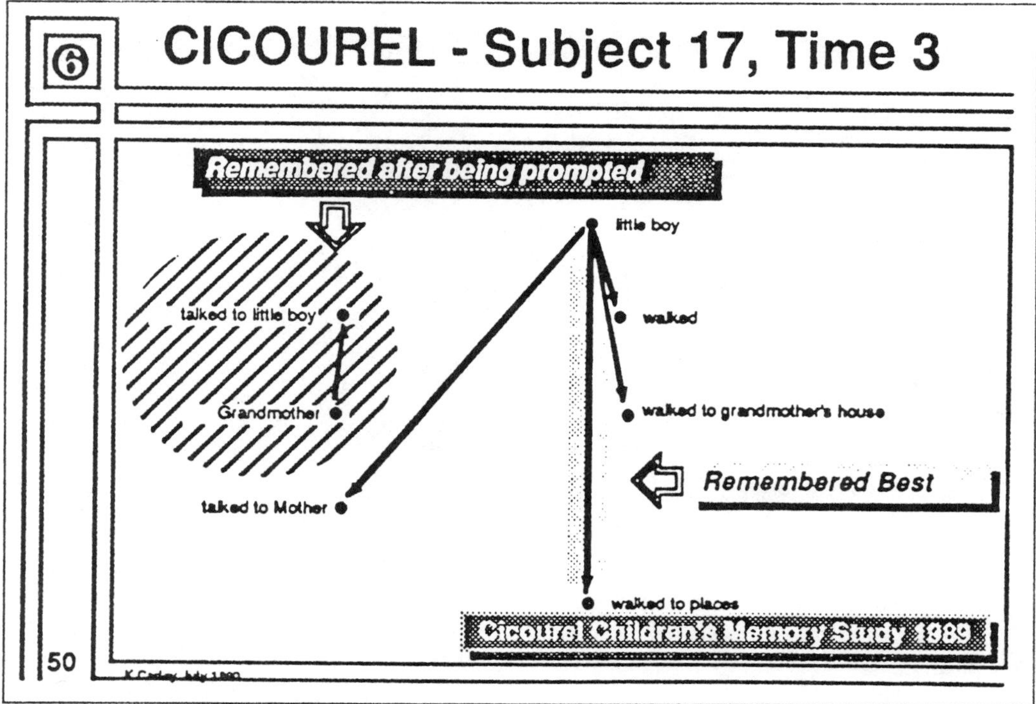

MECA Figure 6. Graphic output showing map differences. The graphic at the right shows the statements developed from an interview with a child about what was "remembered best" in a story; the crosshatched graphic at the left shows only those statements that were based on what the child remembered after being prompted. The display was edited using MacDraw, with annotations added, from a "difference" request made in the program COMPRA, comparing the "best remembered" map with the "prompted" map.
SOURCE: From Carley (1990).

A program called DRAWMAP displays your concepts in a circle (you can do some pre-editing to arrange the sequence if you wish, and specify abbreviations for the concept names to make readability easier) and draws the connections among them, illustrating the statements. Figure 5 shows an example of how this looks. DRAWMAP is restricted to handling 100 concepts, but the display is naturally much easier to read when limited to about 40. It can show strength of relationships (via heavier lines or labels), positive or negative sign (dotted lines or labels), and directionality (via arrowheads)—but *not* the type of concepts or relationships (that is, meanings).

The output of DRAWMAP is a file that needs to be printed via MacDraw; if you are working in DOS or Unix, you will have to transfer it to a Mac machine, then use Binhex to upload it for MacDraw use. If you are using the Mac version of MECA, your document will already be a MacDraw 1.9 document and can be printed directly (it may often be usefully edited for readability, clarity, and so on).

A program called EXTRACT will apparently (it had a help screen, but was not on the available disk) pull out the submap that is built around a particular concept (that is, all the statements that include it).

There are also programs for comparing maps: COMPRA, which compares two maps on total number of concepts, number of links, and computes the "union" (*all* statements in map1 and map2) and "intersection" (shared statements —those that appear in *both* map1 AND map2) as well as the "difference"—statements that occur *only* in each map (map1 but not map2; map2 but not map1). It also does measures of association (tau-beta and Somers d, chi-square, phi, Q [gamma]). Map comparison can be very useful—time 1 versus time 2, expert versus novice, teacher versus student, treatment A versus treatment B, and so on. COMPRA-produced data, as well as those from SMATRIX, can be output to DRAWMAP, so that maps of the unions, intersections, or differences can be shown graphically. Figure 6 illustrates this.

Another program, SCOMPRA, will do analyses on a larger set of maps (paired comparisons of map files in list 1 with those in list 2), ignoring concept and link types and ignoring strength.

CUBE (another program described on a help screen but not included on the disk) makes a data matrix that includes three variables called density, transitivity, and consensus. These variables are explained in Carley and Kaufer (1993). In brief, *density* is the number of other concepts to which a particular concept is connected; *transitivity* (conductivity) involves the directional paths to and from a particular concept, measured by multiplying in-links times out-links for a concept; and *consensus* is the number or percentage of people in some social population who agree that two concepts are linked—shared social knowledge is implied. The "level" of transitivity and consensus is defined as the number of links that meet or exceed some preset threshold. For CUBE, this is the average. The RECUBE program (also not on this disk) allows you to set new threshold ("cutoff") values and recategorizes the data accordingly.

Searching

There isn't searching capability as we've usually defined it—remember that "coding" in MECA is simply constructing statements, not attaching keywords to text. However, as we've seen, MECA will find the frequencies of concepts and statements in the intersection, union, or differences across pairs of map files; these correspond roughly to the Boolean ideas of AND, OR, and NOT.

It's also hard to talk about data linking in our usual terms—the whole program centers on links among concepts.

Theory Building

The program is not set up for doing theory building in the way most other programs we review do it (through coding and retrieval, outlining, memoing and annotation, proposition testing, conceptual network display, and so on), but it is actually a way of specifying and depicting a network of statements (i.e., propositions) and can be used, as Carley notes, either in a confirmatory or an exploratory, theory-building mode. We suspect that working with the complex sort of propositions involved in most qualitative studies (with multiple levels of concepts and different types of links, for example) might prove difficult, because some of the programs ignore concept and link categories. (See also the "Comparative Remarks" section, below.)

User Friendliness

MECA is really a technically-oriented set of research programs, not a linked package. You use each program one at a time; there are no menus to get you from one to another. Carley and some colleagues have used MECA in several different studies, from some of which she shows illustrative findings in the photocopied overhead set (Carley, 1990). Carley and Palmquist (1992), the article used as partial documentation, is quite clear on the basic programs of STARTUP and CODEMAP, but the others are not described. The appendix to Carley (1993) sketches them only briefly.

If you turn to the help screens to find out about the other programs, the text is extremely sparse, usually giving only a bare outline of what the program does, what its typical input and output files are, and how you format commands. You have to go to the photocopied set of presentation overheads supplied with the documentation (Carley, 1990) to see how things work; they are much clearer, with annotated advice to the user. (The figures in this review are not actual screen shots, but are drawn from these overheads, because they were more informative than what you actually see on screen.)

It also helps to print out all the help screens, so you have a hard copy to refer to. (This is laborious: You have to ask for help on a program and then do <Print Screen> for each one.)

The determined user at what we've called Level 2 or 3 could probably set up files and process them without too much difficulty. The diskettes have a few minimal example files that you can run and see what happens.

The developer, Kathleen Carley, says that the software is provided "as is." She will answer technical questions, most easily by e-mail.

Basically, you need to be at least a Level 2 computer user and should expect to do a lot of the figuring out of MECA on your own, with the aid of the "documentation." You also need a clear idea of what this kind of map analysis is about and what it involves.

If MECA sounds interesting and promising for your needs, you could begin by reading Carley (1993) for a very clear conceptual overview of map analysis, as well as Carley and Palmquist (1992). If you decide to purchase MECA, the best introduction is the overheads. They, with reference to the help screens, should be enough to get you started trying some of the sample files to see how the programs work.

Miscellaneous

How much disk space you need really depends on how many maps, how many concepts, and how many statements you are working with. Carley gave as an example that 15 maps, using a general "vocabulary" of 200 concepts, with 200 statements in each map, might occupy about a megabyte (this includes everything—the setup file, the maps, the modified maps, unions, intersections, and statistics).

Except for STARTUP and CODEMAP, most of the programs can be run in batch mode (see the Glossary) as well as interactively. SKI works only in batch mode.

Though MECA as a whole is called Version 1, and hasn't changed much since 1991, a number of the specific programs are denoted Version 4, suggesting developmental effort.

The class version (four copies, with one copy of documentation) can be run on a network, though there aren't guarantees; some networks have routines that may interfere with printing and windowing.

Comparative Remarks

MECA is probably better set up to study the details of respondents' mental maps than to clarify your *own* evolving theory drawn from analysis of text—though see footnote 2. Programs such as ATLAS/ti, Inspiration, or MetaDesign are more flexible and user friendly in helping you clarify your ideas and showing them to you instantly in full-blown network form.

But if your main interest is in clarifying someone *else's* implicit conceptual network, and taking a mostly numerical, summarizing approach, then MECA looks as if it will work reasonably well. You should compare it with SemNet, another mapping program that retains rich semantic meaning, also creates data matrices for statistical packages, has a well-developed user interface, and is graphically powerful.

Summary

MECA is a technical collection of programs—not linked together—for creating and analyzing mental maps—collections of "statements," defined as the linkages between pairs of concepts. It's all about conceptual networks, but it approaches them analytically and numerically; its actual network display capacity is very limited. Supplementing MECA with a good drawing program, such as MacDraw—or, even better, one with good conceptual support, such as SemNet, MetaDesign, or Inspiration—will be helpful.[4] MECA's dollar costs are low, but learning to use it fluently may take you a while.

References

Items included with purchase as documentation:

Carley, K. (1990, August). *Computer analysis of qualitative data: Copy of overheads for didactic seminar.* Paper presented at the annual meeting of the American Sociological Association, Washington, DC.

Carley, K. (1993). Coding choices for textual analysis: A comparison of content analysis and map analysis. In P. Marsden (Ed.), *Sociological methodology* (Vol. 23, pp. 75-126). Oxford: Blackwell.

Carley, K. (in press). Extracting culture through textual analysis. *Poetics.*

Carley, K., & Palmquist, M. (1992). Extracting, representing and analyzing mental models. *Social Forces, 70*(3), 601-636.

Other items:

Carley, K. (1985). An approach for relating social structure to cognitive structure. *Journal of Mathematical Sociology, 12*(2), 137-189.

Carley, K. (1988). Formalizing the social expert's knowledge. *Sociological Methods and Research, 17*, 165-232.

Carley, K. (1991). *Textual analysis using maps.* Pittsburgh, PA: Carnegie-Mellon University, Department of Social and Decision Sciences.

Carley, K. (1994). Content analysis. In R. E. Asher et al. (Eds.), *The encyclopedia of language and linguistics* (Vol. 2, pp. 725-730). Edinburgh, U.K.: Pergamon.

Carley, K., & Kaufer, D. (1993). Semantic connectivity: An approach for analyzing semantic networks. *Communication Theory, 3*, 183-213.

Kaufer, D., & Carley, K. (1993). *Communication at a distance: The influence of print on sociocultural organization and change.* Hillsdale, NJ: Lawrence Erlbaum. (See chapter on coding text.)

Krackhardt, D., Lundberg, M., & O'Rourke, L. (1993). KrackPlot: A picture's worth a thousand words. *Connections, 16*(1-2), 37-47.

4. It also occurs to us that the output of CODEMAP might be usable in one or another of the programs that have long been available for the analysis of sociometric data; they produce meaningfully clustered graphic networks. One such program is KrackPlot (Krackhardt, Lundberg, & O'Rourke, 1993).

MetaDesign, Version 4.0/3.0[1]

Available for Windows and Macintosh

Meta Software Corporation
125 CambridgePark Drive
Cambridge, MA 02140

Phone: (617) 576-6920
Fax: (617) 661-2008

Price: $199

Hardware Requirements:
For Macintosh
- 1MB RAM
- System 6.0 or 7.0
  System 7.0 allows virtual memory and TrueType fonts

For Windows
- 286 or better CPU (386 or better recommended)
- 3MB RAM
- Windows 3.1
- Hard drive with at least 1MB free space
- Mouse
- EGA, VGA, Hercules Monochrome, or other Windows-compatible graphics adapter and display
- Windows-compatible printer

Overview

This program lets you draw complex networks of nodes and links (MetaDesign calls them "connectors") with text in/on both, make hypertext connections, and insert graphics (pictures) while establishing complex hierarchies within and between pages. The program is thus valuable for much more than drawing; it is a powerful tool for organizing and clarifying *ideas,* whether you use it for brainstorming (it's that easy to use), developing elaborate propositions and theories, or as a sort of visually organized text database. The "workspace" for a given "page" (see below) covers multiple sheets of paper; it can extend seven 8½ × 11 inch sheets in width by five sheets in length. The entire workspace can be printed at once; the program can be asked to reduce it to one page or print it on multiple "tiled" pages for you to assemble.

The program itself is very easy to learn and use. Some of the things you can do with it are complicated and a little hard to understand at first, but even these are easy to learn *how* to do—hardly a criticism.

MetaDesign for Windows is now up to Version 4.0, but the Macintosh version is stuck at 3.0 until they get enough user requests for an upgrade. (This is disappointing, because part of the beauty of 3.0 was that the two versions were nearly identical and you could transfer files back and forth.) For this review, we'll concentrate on Version 4.0 for Windows, and in a section below we'll talk about its differences from the Mac and Windows Versions 3.0.

1. The Windows version of the program has recently been upgraded to 4.0, but there are no current plans to upgrade the Macintosh version.

Database Structure

A given file can be divided into a series of "pages," which can be organized and linked hierarchically if you want (more on this under "Theory Building," below). Text can be typed or pasted into nodes, which can be arranged and linked any way you want. MetaDesign allows you to put 30,000 characters of text in a node—figuring about 3,000 characters on a single-spaced page with one-inch margins, that's over 10 pages of solid text. Meta Software's recommendation is that you limit a given file to 32,000 objects (such as nodes and connectors) for "optimum performance." That's a lot of data.

Any real "structure" to the database is provided by you. You can do this by the way you arrange your nodes and connectors and through various hierarchical organizing and hypertexting capabilities discussed below.

Creating a Diagram

Because this is largely a diagramming program, we have created this additional section for this review. We cover here the issues normally covered under "Data Entry," "Working on the Data," and "Graphics Editing."

Nodes

You draw nodes on the screen and type text into them if you want to. Text options, node resizing, and automatic alignment and even spacing of nodes are all good. Next, you draw connections among nodes. Connectors (links) can be labeled and have different styles, and can be straight, curved, or angled. Connectors are "intelligent": when you move a node, its connectors are automatically moved. You can choose to see a grid of dots on the screen, which is helpful for lining things up, and you can also choose a "snap to grid" option, which forces all objects to line up precisely with the nearest gridlines.

For creating nodes, you can choose among tools to create boxes (rectangles), rounded boxes, ellipses, polygons, regular polygons, diamonds, and wedges (see Figure 1 for samples). The program also comes with several "palettes" of fancier shapes and pictures you can use for nodes, and you can create your own custom palettes as well. The Windows version comes with "Booch" (unexplained in the documentation), Flowchart, Network, DataFlow, OrgChart, and Project Management palettes, while the Mac version comes with Flowchart, Network, Logic, DataFlow, and Arrows palettes. Finally, any graphic object that the Mac System or Windows will paste between applications can be pasted into MetaDesign as a node. Both colors and text in a Paintbrush graphic that was pasted in were retained.

Nodes can be easily repositioned by dragging with the mouse. There are 14 different options for automatically aligning groups of nodes, and you can have them evenly spaced. You can choose among 8 line thicknesses, 5 line types, 36 fill patterns (patterns of crosshatch to fill an object), and 16 colors each for outlines and fill patterns.

Connectors (Links)

Connectors between nodes can have arrowheads at either end, both ends, or neither. They can go directly from node to node (in either a straight or curved line) or have multiple bends (such lines are called "segmented"), which can be sharp or curved. You can lock any bends in your connectors to 90° angles. Connectors can attach anywhere along the perimeter of a node, or they can be linked so that they always point to the center of the node, their point of contact changing as the two nodes are moved relative to each other. You can set line styles, fill patterns for arrowheads, and colors for both with all the same options as for nodes. As mentioned above, when you move nodes, the connectors attached to them move also—a fine feature. Each connector can have text attached to it. This would usually be just a label, but it could be up to 30,000 characters if you wanted.

There are an array of 22 different types of arrowheads and other markers to use for both origin and destination ends of connectors. These are designed for an advanced form of charting known as Entity-Relationship charting (E-R). This allows you to use different-looking connectors to represent different types of relationships among nodes.

Text

To add text to a node, you click on the node and enter the text mode by clicking on a button, making a menu choice, or just beginning to type. (The latter is obviously preferable if you're typing new or added text—you only have to do one of the other operations if you want to make changes to existing text.) A node can hold more text than will show in the box that represents it. You will see only the lines of text that fit in the node, and scroll bars appear so you can view text that doesn't fit. You can also paste in text from the clipboard. You can resize a node to show more or less of its text if you want, and there is an option to fit the node to the text. Unfortunately, there's no way to have the node just stretch as you add text, as you can in Inspiration.

You can choose options like bold, underlined, and italic text; left, center, or right justification; and whatever fonts and point sizes your Macintosh System or Microsoft Windows has. However, you can't mix text attributes within a

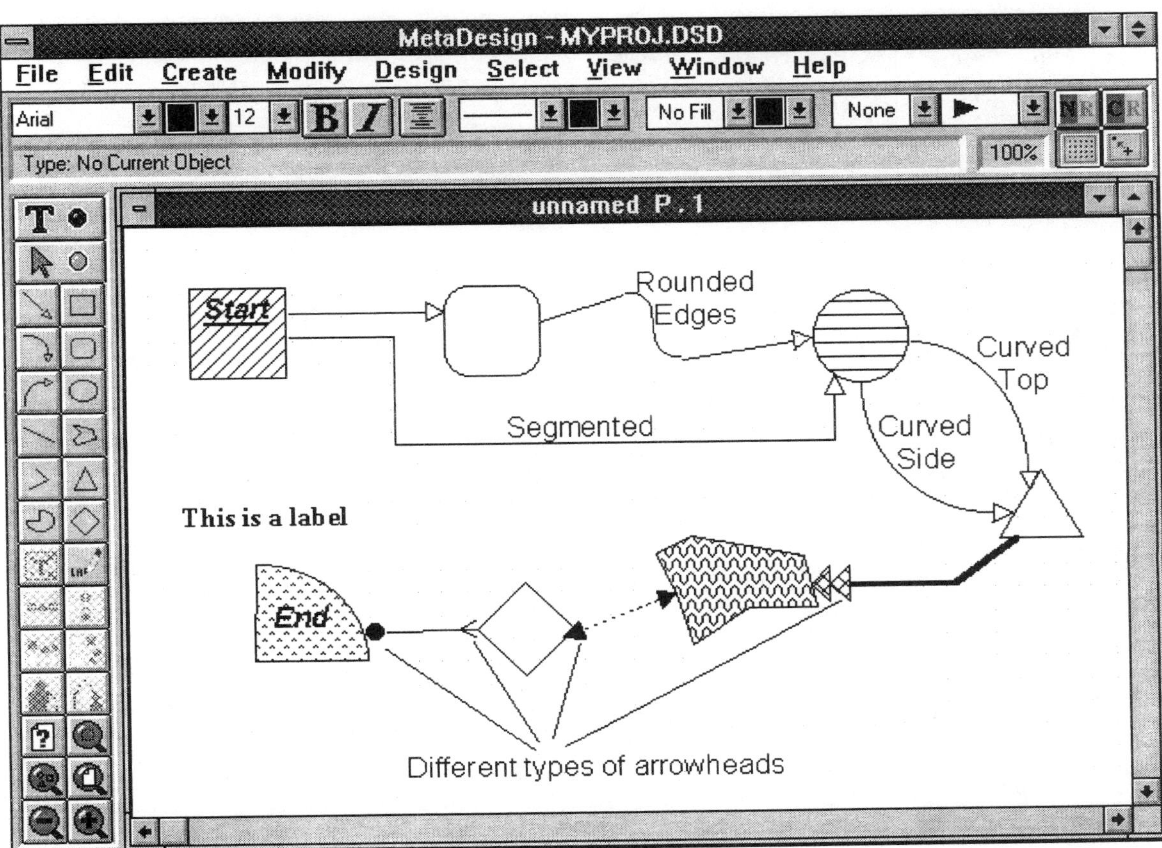

MetaDesign Figure 1. A simple drawing, using the default node types and connectors. Specialized graphics can be pasted in as nodes from the palettes. The icon bar on the left side of the screen provides quick and easy access to most major functions.

node—a real drag if you want, for example, to underline or italicize certain words.

You can also create "labels," which are special text nodes with invisible boundaries. You would use labels for text, such as titles or annotations that you do not want to appear as nodes or, as an optional way to create connector text.

Importing text. In addition to simply pasting text into nodes, there are elaborate routines for importing and parsing (chunking) text, some of them designed for computer programmers. Each chunk is placed in a separate node. For simple text, you can have the file broken into chunks of a size you specify, up to the limit of 30,000 characters per node. You can also specify characters such as { } to delimit blocks of text if you don't want to do it by size. If you nest blocks within one another, a nested block will be placed in a separate node, with a hypertext link to the node for the block it was nested in.

Theory Building

Theories often involve a hierarchy of concepts. MetaDesign allows you to create hierarchical relationships among pages, nodes, and text. Before we describe how this works, let's get a little terminology down; then the discussion should be fairly easy to follow. For simplicity's sake, we'll talk about nodes, although these concepts apply to any object. A node that is hierarchically *above* another is called, variously, *superordinate, coarse, higher order,* or a *parent.* The node below that one is *subordinate, finer, lower order,* or its *child.* Most of these terms are also used in verb forms, as in *to subordinate* (move down the hierarchy) or *coarsen* (move up the hierarchy).

Suppose that you have too much complexity on a page. You might want to take some of the detail out and move it to a subordinate page. You choose a node and instruct the program to "coarsen" it. That node is now a coarse node, connected to its own subpage (or child) on which you create

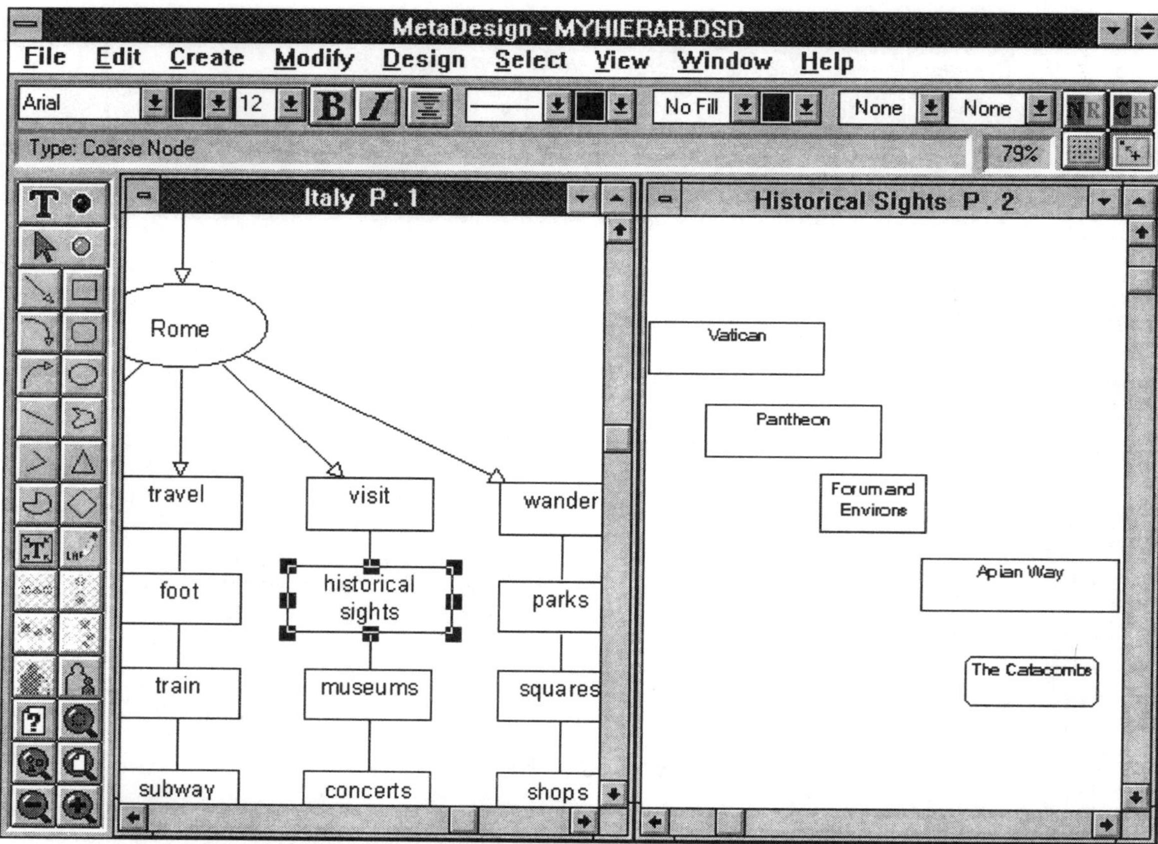

MetaDesign Figure 2. This drawing was created following the tutorial from Version 3.0. The window on the left is the top-level page, Page 1, and contains a breakdown of a trip to Italy. The "historical sights" node is selected (the eight sizing "handles" around the edges, which can be dragged to change the size and shape of the node, also indicate that the node is selected), and the status bar indicates this is a coarse node. The subpage, or "child," shown on the right (Page 2) is a map of the historic sights the traveler plans to visit.

the detail. Double-click on the coarse node, and you instantly flip to the associated subpage (see Figure 2). A page can have multiple subpages, and subpages can have their own subpages. There can also be multiple pages at the first (top) level. The Page Structure command gives you a view, either a tree diagram or an outline, of the overall structure of pages in your diagram. (See Figure 3.) Click on the name of any page and, bingo, you're there.

If you select multiple objects at once, you can have one of them coarsened and the rest "subordinated": sent to the subpage. This presents a little problem: What happens to links between the subordinated nodes and other nodes on the page? Any connectors between a subordinated node and other nodes on the page are redrawn connecting the other nodes to the coarse node. Then, on the subpage, the subordinated node has a connector going to a black dot, called a "port node," at the boundary of the subpage. The port node represents the connected node back on the original page. This is a reasonable solution, but a little buggy: The new connectors may get drawn in the wrong direction.

You can also create "regions" of nodes—essentially child objects but, rather than being on a subpage, they can be on the current page. One advantage of this is that when you move the parent object around, the child moves with it. Another advantage of this is that if you select any object (node, text, or picture) you can ask to travel to its parent or child. You can thus create dynamic, on-line diagrams.

Finally, you can "attach" nodes to other pages, without implying a hierarchical relationship. Thus you can set up a node, which, when double-clicked, will move you to another page, regardless of the relationship of the two pages in the hierarchy.

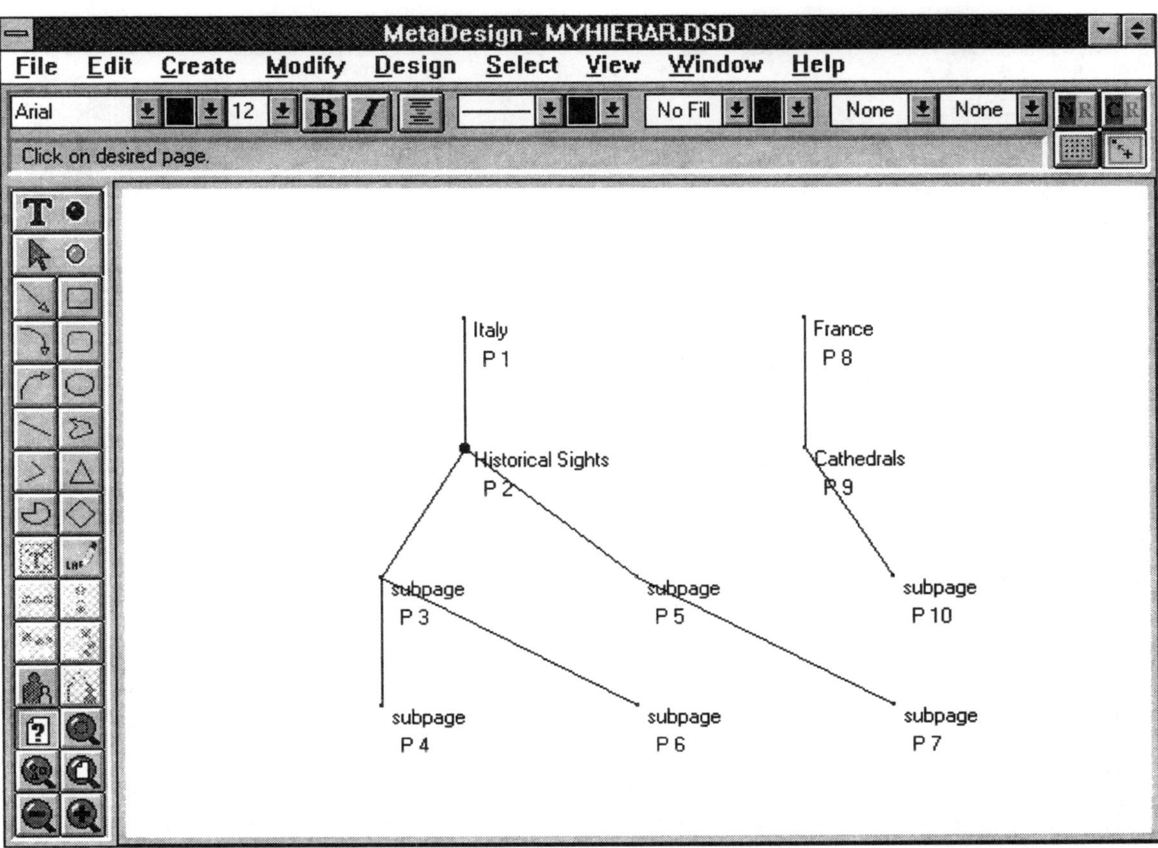

MetaDesign Figure 3. A page structure tree diagram for a complex diagram. Each branch point represents a page or subpage and is labeled with a page number. If the page has been named, the name appears; otherwise, it is simply named "page" or "subpage." The large dot on Historical Sights indicates that this is the current page.

Hypertext

As mentioned above, you can type extensive text (30,000 characters) in nodes. You can hypertext by "coarsening" text. The terminology here is confusing, because you're actually having some selected text moved to a *child* node—what's coarsened is the original node. To do this, you enter text mode, select the text that you want moved, and give the command to coarsen. Rather than placing the detail on a new page, as is the case when you coarsen a node, the text in the original node is replaced with a (parent) reference symbol (a number in international quotation marks: « ») and the text is moved to a new (child) node. (See Figure 4.) If you double-click on the reference, you pop to the child text. The child text node can then be moved to another page, if you so desire. Note that coarsening implies a hierarchical, "parent-child" relationship. You can also "attach" text, creating a hypertext link between text that's already in different nodes. A reference symbol is inserted into the parent node.

Searching

MetaDesign provides text searching features that, while they don't hold a candle to a serious text search program, are better than those in many word processors. For a program like this, they strike us as quite good. You can search the text in an object (node, connector, picture, and so on), in the entire document, in a page (see the "Theory Building" section, above), in an object and its substructure (meaning its regions and subregions, *not* its subpages—see "Theory Building," above), or along the path of hypertext tracers from the current object down through its children.

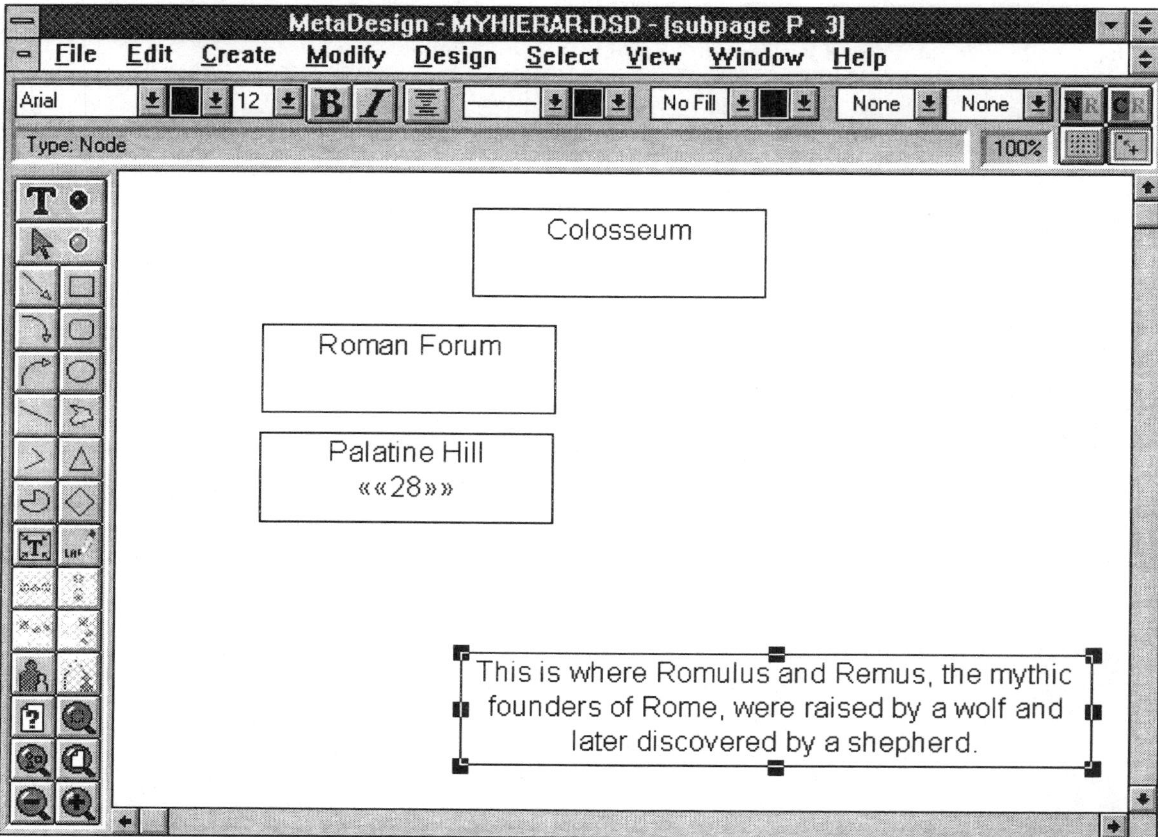

MetaDesign Figure 4. This page is a child of Page 2, shown in the right half of Figure 2, and is linked to the "Forum and Environs" node. The selected node (marked with sizing handles) is a child of the "Palatine Hill" node on this page. Double-clicking on the reference mark («28») in the "Palatine Hill" node moved me to the child node. Note that the parent and child do not both have to be visible within the same screen; this makes jumping back and forth even more interesting.

Output

Once you have created and dressed up your diagram, you have several ways to print it. You can print the page structure diagram. You can print a given page in a couple of ways. First, you can print "normally": the central 8½ × 11 inches of a page's total workspace. Or you can scale the entire workspace to fit on one piece of paper. As mentioned in the overview, you can also have the entire workspace of a page "tiled": printed on multiple sheets of paper, which you can then tape or paste together. Printing on a laser printer left about a quarter of an inch at the edge of the paper, so it was necessary to do a little trimming. There's a second tiling option that overlaps each row and column by one quarter of an inch, which seemed to make it easier to line up the pages. The total workspace printout was seven pages across and five pages down: *What a wall chart!* And remember: That's just one page! You can have thousands of pages in a document. Such wall charts can be especially useful for large cross-case analyses. Remember that MetaDesign will just print the text that actually shows in a node, but a node can be larger than one screen.

Graphics Editing

Graphics editing is such a large part of what you do when you work in MetaDesign that we've covered these issues above in the section "Creating a Diagram."

User Friendliness

As noted above, the program, in both versions, is extremely easy to learn and use. The three lessons of the tutorial for Version 3.0 for the Macintosh—"The Basics,"

"Managing Complexity," and "Polishing and Printing"—took a Level 3 person 30 minutes, 45 minutes, and 15 minutes, respectively, to master. In an hour and a half, we were really ready to use the thing! In fact, you learn most of the program in that hour and a half and will probably have only occasional need to go into the rest of the manual.

The tutorial for Version 4.0 for Windows is different. The manual tells you to budget 40, 30, 15, and 20 minutes, respectively, for the four lessons for a total of an hour and three quarters, but it didn't take that long. This tutorial is very entertaining, although we had a little trouble getting one feature to work correctly (text was overflowing one of the nodes). Unfortunately, it doesn't go into hypertexting at all and spends much less time on hierarchy in general than the Version 3.0 tutorial did. The Windows version, however, also has the advantage of Windows-style on-line help.[2]

The manuals are more professional than a lot of the ones you'll find reviewed here, but they could use a little work. The indexes are a little sparse, and some features aren't explained too clearly. But as mentioned earlier, you won't need to go to the manuals all that much unless you're really trying to do some fancy stuff.

The tech support folks are only available Monday through Friday, 9-5 eastern time. The manual lists a toll-call number, but they do have a toll-free number also: (800) 227-4106, found in *PC Magazine*'s review (Miller, 1993). Our experiences with them have been mixed—about two thirds of the time they've been extremely knowledgeable and helpful. Unfortunately, we did run into one guy who wasn't all that competent; he seemed to have to check with other people to answer any question and wasn't good about returning phone calls. Usually, however, they are extremely friendly, patient, and helpful. When you call, you're likely to get one of the people identified in the manual as developers: They ought to know what they're doing, and they do!

Differences Between Versions

There are two issues here: Windows versus Macintosh and, if you're going the Windows route, Versions 3.0 versus 4.0. Version 4.0 is clearly superior, and the only reason you'd want to choose Version 3.0 for Windows (which is still available) would be if you want to be able to transfer diagrams *from* a PC *to* a Mac (Version 4.0 will read Version 3.0 files, but not vice versa).

2. Windows-style help gives you an on-screen index of help topics. You click on the topic you want and get popped to the explanation. Most help screens have "related topics" listed at the bottom, which you can also select. Depending on your version of Windows, there are a variety of "buttons" on the screen for traveling through the help info.

Version 3.0 Versus Version 4.0

There are a number of differences between Versions 3.0 and 4.0, not least among them are 4.0's icon bar on the left side of the screen and the control ribbon across the top. (See Figures 1-4.) The icon bar lets you quickly toggle text mode on or off; start creation of the various shapes of nodes (the diamond is new), both straight and curved connectors, straight and segmented lines, and labels; fit a node to its text; align or space objects; jump to a parent or child object; go to the page structure view; or zoom to any of several standard views. The control ribbon gives you quick access to control of such text attributes as font, size, bold, italic, and justification; line styles and colors; fill patterns and colors; source and target arrowheads; and toggling of the "snap to grid" options. The menus have also been rearranged and are now more logical and convenient.

The snap to grid options, standard in the better drawing packages, are a new addition for Version 4.0. Also, you can now adjust the size of the invisible, rectangular text box in a node. This is an important addition because in Version 3.0 the corners of the text boxes stuck out past the boundaries of elliptical nodes so that you had to do a lot of fiddling to get the text all inside the node. Text mode in 4.0 can be activated simply by selecting a node and starting to type. In Version 3.0, you had to make a menu selection or hit a function key.

There's a bit more control of options in Version 4.0. You can have various settings, like default line and node attributes, zoom settings, and so on retained from one session to another. Some of the options, though, are not too user friendly. For example, you can change grid dot and page break options but you have to put commands like

```
[Grid]
GridDotColor=0x00808080
```

into the "DESIGN.INI" configuration file (the numbers describe the color). If you want to use the program in a video mode other than VGA (i.e., Super VGA, EGA, or Monochrome), you will also have to edit the "DESIGN.INI" file to get the icon bar and control ribbon to display properly.

One advantage in Version 3.0: When we made the biggest page possible in the Windows version and printed it out, it came to nine sheets of paper across by seven down, as compared with seven by five sheets in 4.0. Note that you've still got a chart covering 35 sheets of paper.

Version 3.0: Mac Versus Windows

The manuals for the Windows and Macintosh 3.0 versions are virtually word-for-word identical, that's how close the two versions are: menus, dialog boxes, the whole darn

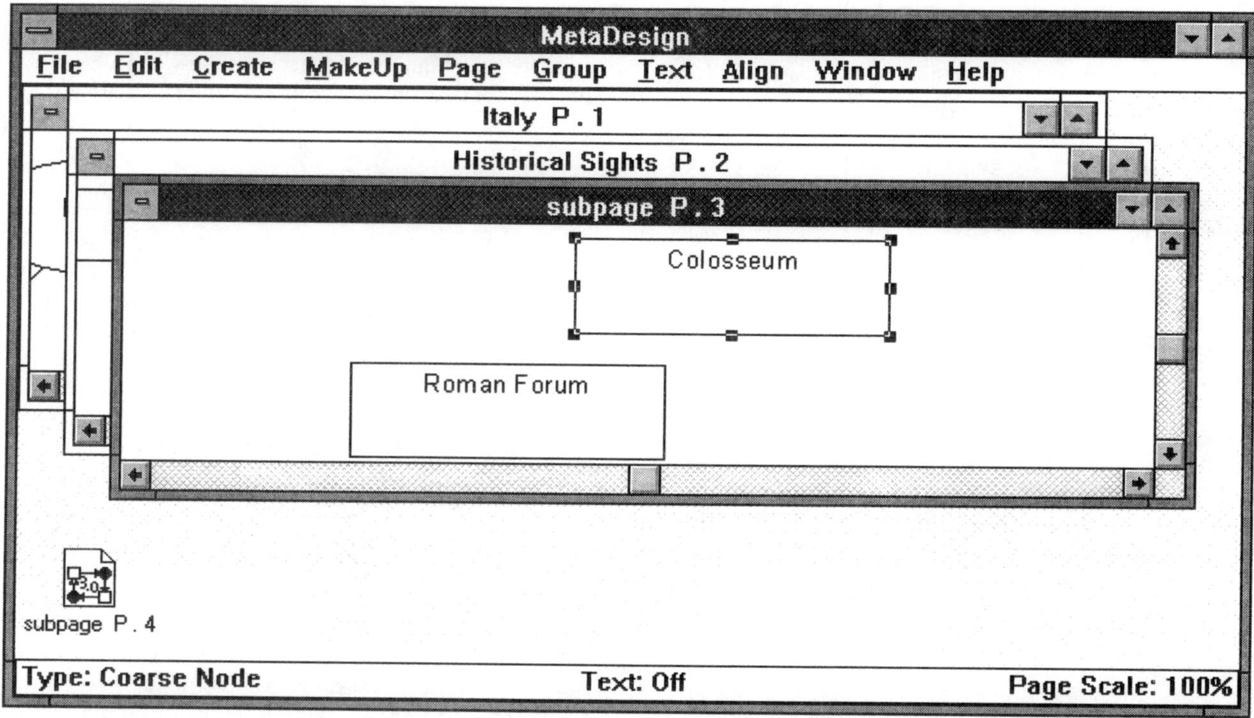

MetaDesign Figure 5. Cascaded windows in Version 3.0 for Windows. At the bottom of the larger MetaDesign window is an icon for Page 4, which is a child of the Colosseum node. Note the absence of the very useful icon bar on the left and control ribbon on top in the previous figures, from Version 4.0.

thing seems virtually identical—and you can easily transfer diagrams, with all their complexity, back and forth.

The Mac version has two available "add-on" features. The first of these add-ons is called "Arrows." This gives you a subset of 11 of the "Entity-Relationship" (E-R) arrowheads, which are now standard in Version 4.0 (but not available in 3.0 for Windows). These are used for an advanced form of charting (E-R).

The second add-on is a simulator, based on "the token game" in Petri net methodology. (What?) This simulator will walk through the steps of a Petri net—places (or states) connected by transitions (or events)—either one step at a time or continuously. If you don't know what Petri nets are, the manual helps.

The Windows version takes advantage of a couple of Windows conventions not available on the Mac. For example, you can minimize a page's document window, dropping it down to an icon at the bottom of the MetaDesign window, so if you're working with several pages at once, you can keep the desktop a little neater (see Figure 5). You also get the standard Window menu, which allows you to tile your windows (arrange them side by side; see Figure 2) or cascade them (arrange in a neat overlapping cascade, as in Figure 5), or select which one you want active. As Windows users know, and Mac users can imagine, the Window menu is nice to have. Finally, the Windows version's zoom control (which lets you adjust magnification) is a bit more flexible, including a Zoom dialog box that the Mac version doesn't have. This lets you choose 3 automatic scaling options or type in anything from 10% to 400% view and choose to have your choices applied to the current page, all existing pages, or future pages. The Mac version simply gives you Enlarge and Reduce options that step you through several zoom levels.

Miscellaneous

Both the Macintosh and the Windows versions of MetaDesign will run on a network. However, they are not designed to let multiple users work on the same document simultaneously, so doing so could have unpredictable results.

Comparative Remarks

For its graphics editing and production capabilities, MetaDesign is clearly in a different league than a program like ATLAS/ti, NUD•IST, or SemNet. Then again, it doesn't have the data-analytic functions of those programs.

The other program reviewed here that has similar capabilities is Inspiration. We've run down the comparison between the two programs in greater detail in the Inspiration review. Here's a brief summary. Inspiration *adds* the ability to jump back and forth between viewing your document as a text outline and a diagram; has a "rapid fire" feature that lets you just type text into a node, hitting the <Enter> key every time you want to start a new, linked node; can make diagrams up to 660 by 660 pieces of paper; can hold even more text per node; has special pop-up notes for each node; has nodes that can automatically grow to fit text; and has a more interesting variety of symbols for nodes.

Inspiration *lacks* MetaDesign's ability to create hypertext links (though you can have child pages linked to nodes), doesn't have an equivalent to the page structure view, can't load external text into a document (you have to copy to the clipboard from another application, then paste it in), can't parse (chunk) text by delimiters, and doesn't have scroll bars to read text that extends beyond the boundaries of a node.

Summary

This is an excellent program. It is extremely powerful and easy to learn and use: a dream combination. It should be clearer by now what we meant in the "Overview" when we said that this was much more than a drawing program. The ease of the program makes it very attractive even for first-cut brainstorming, alone or with colleagues: Several of you could huddle around the monitor while one of you effortlessly throws the group's ideas into nodes; rearranging and reorganizing the drawing would be fast, easy, and flexible. MetaDesign diagrams could be extremely helpful in clarifying coding schemes or developing them using the constant comparative method. You could also use the program as a sort of visual database, which could include complex hierarchy if you wanted, elaborate hypertext links if you wanted, or graphic symbols, drawings, and text indicating relationships among nodes. MetaDesign could productively be used for developing and exploring propositions, or networks of propositions. The Mac version could be used for testing hypotheses that are appropriate for Petri net methodology. As mentioned above, large wall charts can be vital in huge cross-case analyses.

References

Laverty, M., & Albright, R. (1993). *MetaDesign user's guide: Version 4.0 for Microsoft® Windows.* Cambridge, MA: Meta Software Corporation.

Miller, R. (1993). Designing your thoughts. *PC Magazine, 12*(22), 161-174.

SemNet 1.1β6[1]

Available for Macintosh

SemNet Research Group
1043 University Avenue Suite 215
San Diego, CA 92103-3392

Phone: (619) 232-9334
E-mail: jfaletti@sciences.sdsu.edu
or kfisher@sciences.sdsu.edu

Price: Undetermined[2]

Hardware Requirements:

- System 5.0 minimum, 6.0.5 or later recommended
- 512K RAM for small nets, > 1MB sufficient for large ones

Overview

SemNet is a Mac program designed for both graphically mapping and analyzing semantic networks (nets). It is currently used most by researchers in knowledge acquisition, elicitation and engineering, and expert systems work. You define the concepts for a map, the different kinds of relations between them, which concepts are related to each other, and in what way each pair, or "instance," is related. All of this information is entered into user-friendly, intelligently designed dialog boxes that do a lot of the work for you and offer helpful shortcuts.

In SemNet's graphic mode, you see any *one* concept as the central node surrounded by all the concepts directly related to it (see Figure 1). You can attach pop-up notes, pictures, and lists of synonyms to each concept, which you open up with mouse clicks. To see the rest of the map, you navigate around in various ways, making different concepts the central node at different times. The different options provide a lot of nifty ways of finding your way around a net, which we'll discuss under "Searching," below. You can get overview graphic displays, which show you more, or all, of the concepts in a net. But they're difficult, if not impossible, to read, let alone interpret. There's an add-on program called MapMaker (available from Wally Axmann at Kansas State University) that facilitates the creation of larger scale maps from SemNet files.

You can also view your data (the contents of your net) in a variety of lists. You can see lists of concepts, relations, or instances, each in different sort orders and with different optional information. For example, you can see the number of instances in which a concept occurs—but more on this as we go. You can print your data in any of the formats you view them in.

The manual is very helpful in suggesting a number of different types of uses for the program. For example, in addition to various uses for research purposes, the developers also suggest the use of SemNet as a learning tool: for teachers to prepare nets for students (there's an Intro Bio Starter Net included), for students to use in representing what they're learning, and for a variety of testing techniques.

1. This will be released as version 1.1. Current plans are to have one version available as shareware through the Internet, meaning you can get and try it for free, and then, if you like it, you are expected to contact the developer and volunteer to pay something like $40 for individual use or $100 for group use. There will also probably be "Academic" and "Professional" versions, which will have different prices. The versions will differ in their capabilities.

2. See footnote 1.

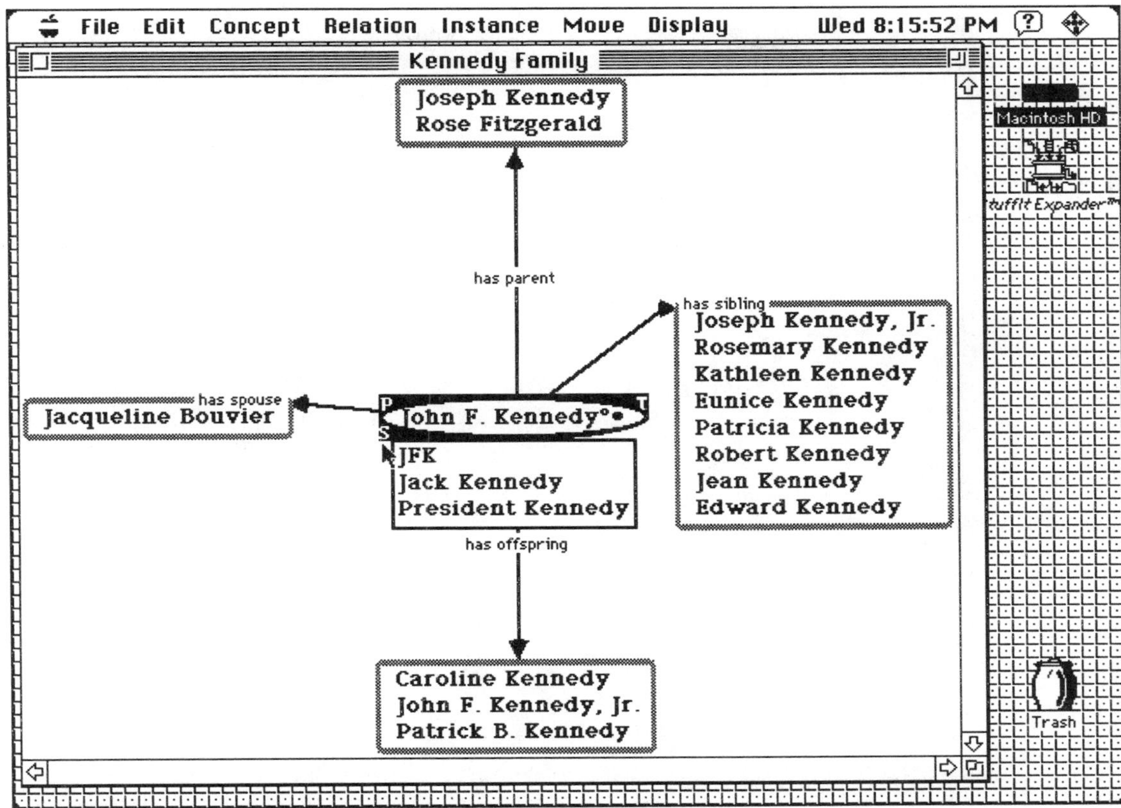

SemNet Figure 1. The basic view in SemNet: looking at a concept (in this particular case, I have made John F. Kennedy the central concept) and those it is directly connected to. The relations that connect it to other concepts are represented by labeled arrows. All concepts in the same relation to the central concept (e.g., all offspring) are listed together in a box. Double-clicking on any concept will make it the central concept and display it with its directly related concepts. Clicking and holding with the mouse on the "S" in the corner of the central concept has caused the list of synonyms to drop down. Clicking on the " T " would pop up a text note, and clicking on the " P " would pop up a picture.

Database Structure

There are three basic elements to your database: concepts, relations, and instances. Concepts and relations can have additional "elaborations," such as text notes and pictures, attached to them.

Concepts

Concepts are the items you're mapping the relationships among. They can be things, people, ideas—whatever you want. You can type a label up to 31 characters long for each concept. (A special version of the program, which accepts labels 90 characters long, is available from the developers.) You can put up to 32,767 concepts in a net. Each concept can have a note attached to it with up to 255 characters of text, a picture in Macintosh PICT file format that you paste in from the clipboard (you can apparently also use QuickTime movies, but we weren't able to test this), and a list of as many synonyms for the concept as you want. A synonym can be substituted anywhere you specify a concept name (e.g., when jumping to a concept). For example, in one of the tutorial nets—a family tree for the Kennedy family—synonyms for John F. Kennedy include Jack, Jack Kennedy, JFK, and so on. The only limitation here is that each synonym counts toward the total limit of 32,767 concepts per net. Text, pictures, and synonym lists can all be easily displayed by clicking with the mouse on marked regions of the concept's node (the box or oval that represents a concept in a network is called a node) and can also be printed with concept lists.

Relations

You can define up to 32,767 relations for a net (note that a single relation can be used to connect many different

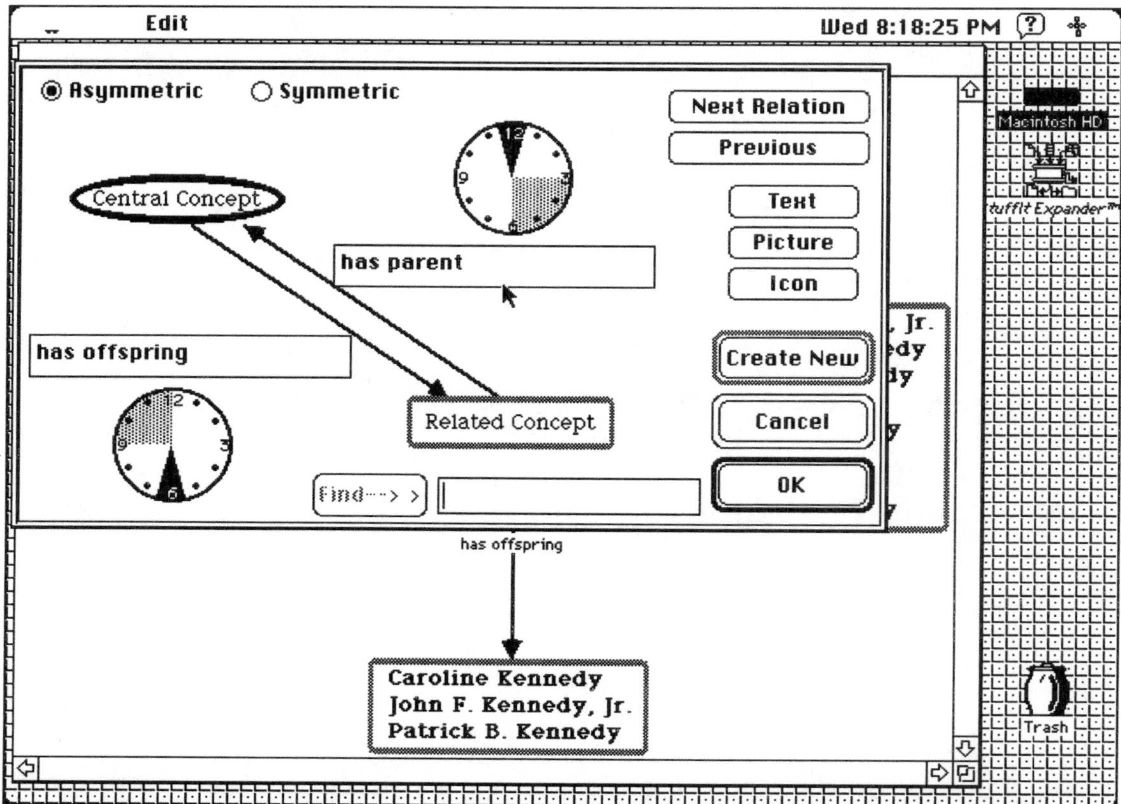

SemNet Figure 2. The Create Relation dialog box. There are boxes for defining the two rays of the concept (in a symmetrical relation, these would be identical). The clock faces are for choosing where on the screen concepts related by each ray will appear. The black area is the selected orientation; the gray area is being recommended *not* to be used for this relation by SemNet (how this is chosen is not explained). Note. Multiple relations can have the same orientation. If there are two, they will be displayed just slightly to either side of the orientation chosen; if three, the third will be moved 1 hour "later"; and so on.

pairs of concepts). Each direction of a relation is called a "ray." Relations can be symmetric (e.g., a sibling relationship is a sibling relationship on both rays: has sibling/has sibling[3]) or asymmetric (the relationship between a parent and child is different depending on which ray you're looking at: has parent/has child). You can only use a ray name *in one relation* in a net (though relations can be used repeatedly). So if you want, for example, to make gender-specific sibling relations, you can't have has brother/has sister, and has brother/has brother, and has sister/has sister. You could get around this limitation by using abbreviations, or alternate designations, like using has bro' for the brother ray in one of the relations or not using the word "has" in one of the relations.

When you define a relation, you specify the spatial orientation of each ray on a clock face (see Figure 2). For example, you might specify that "has parent" should appear at 12 o'clock. All parents of the current central concept will then be listed in a box directly above. If you define "has child" as appearing at 6 o'clock, children will appear directly below. (But you don't have to. You could, for example, put them at 3 o'clock.) The advantage to lining up the rays of an asymmetric relation (e.g., has parent/has child) opposite each other (say, at 12 and 6 o'clock) is that later on, as you choose to move up through parent after parent, the parent moves down to center and the former central concept moves down to the child box at the bottom, creating a scrolling effect. Relations can also have text and pictures associated with them. In addition, you can paste in a PICT graphic to act as an icon, appearing on the relation arrow in diagrams, in place of the relation's name.

Instances

The third major element of the database is the "instance." Each pair of concepts, with the relation that connects them,

3. This notation represents the two rays that make up a relation. Read as ray-in-one-direction/ray-in-the-other-direction.

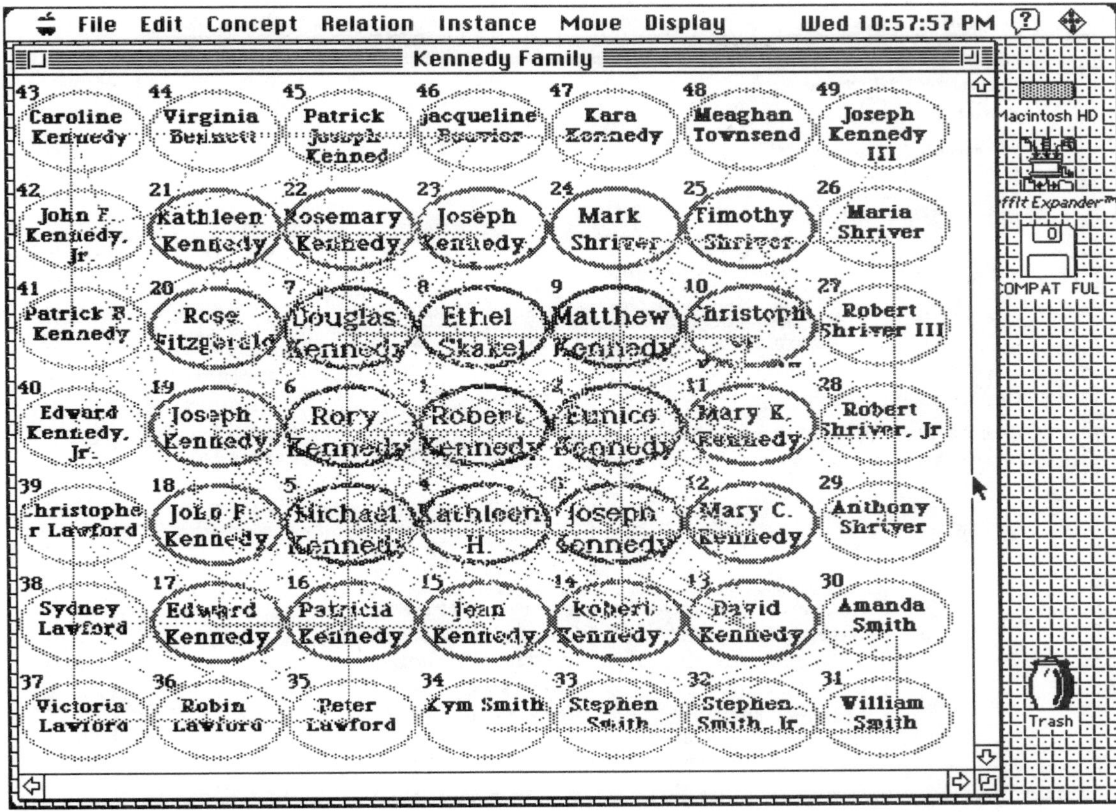

SemNet Figure 3. The "knowledge core" for the Kennedy family net. The more "embedded" concepts have darker borders. The spiderweb-like lines representing relations among concepts make the display very hard to read.

is called an "instance." (MECA calls them "statements.") You can have up to 32,767 instances in a net, and a given concept or relation can be involved in as many instances as you want. The number of instances a concept is involved in can be reported and/or used for sorting the list of concepts.

"Embeddedness" is a different kind of measure of the degree of connectedness, or centrality, of a given concept with the rest of the net. It is calculated by taking the number of unique paths from a concept to another concept two steps away and summing across all concepts two steps away. Lists of concepts can include and be sorted by concepts' embeddedness. Embeddedness is also used to determine the "knowledge core" of the net. You can get a display of the 49 most embedded concepts in the net, arranged in a rectangular matrix, with the most embedded concepts at the center and the rest spiraling outward (see Figure 3). The concepts are numbered by embeddedness, and there are unlabeled lines connecting all related pairs of concepts (that is, instances). As you can see in Figure 3, this display can be very hard to read. (But see the "Update" section of this review: This feature has been substantially enhanced in the most recent version we have seen.)

Data Entry

Your "data" are concepts (which can, again, be things, people, facts, ideas, variables, and so on), the relations that can connect them, and the related pairs of concepts, called "instances." You can start your data entry at any point: creating concepts, relations, or instances. Creating instances can often be the most efficient way to go (see Figure 4), as the concept names and relations you use to create the instances are automatically learned by the program. (On the other hand, the manual urges taking the time to carefully create your set of *relations* first and then building your instances. Which is best probably depends on your project.) To define an instance, you fill in the name of the central concept (for this instance), the relation, and the related concept. Note two things here. First, in the relation box, you're actually filling in the name of the ray that goes from the central concept to the related concept. The other ray of the relation is automatically implied. Second, remember that any concept can be the central concept when you want it to be, so we could specify an instance as "Eben — has child → Ned" or we could specify the same

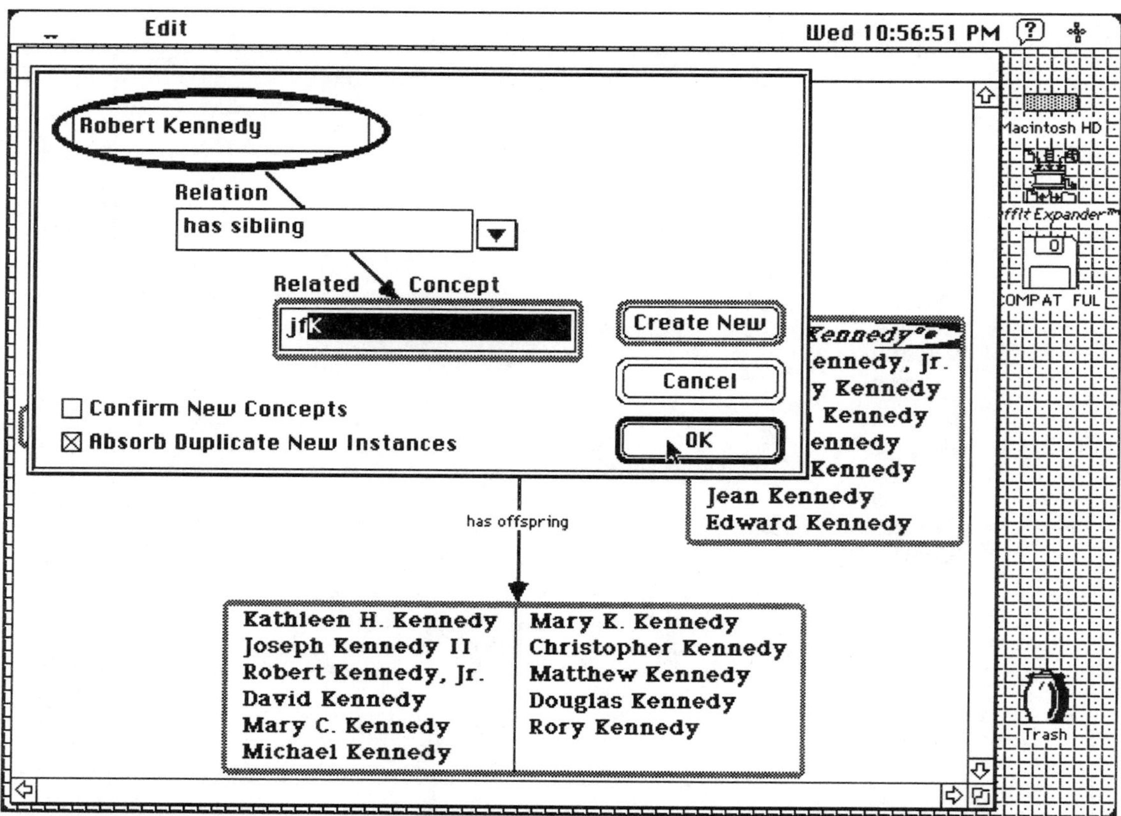

SemNet Figure 4. The Create Instance dialog box. "jfk," a synonym for John F. Kennedy, is being defined as a sibling of Robert Kennedy (in this case, the central concept). "jf" has been typed, and SemNet has completed the name with a "k." Note the checkbox options at the bottom of the box, which let you get a prompt to confirm that you have typed a new concept name (in case you made an error), and automatically "absorb," or ignore, instances you create if they duplicate what's already there (e.g., this one would duplicate the already existing instance, which has JFK as the central concept related as a sibling to RFK).

instance as "Ned — has parent → Eben." Either of these implies the other.

SemNet has an excellent "word completion," or intelligent search, feature: As you type in, say, a concept name, SemNet tries to complete it by matching the typed letters to the concepts it knows (this also works with relations and rays). This makes data entry fast and easy, because you often have to type only a couple of letters to specify a concept name. You can have SemNet warn you if you've typed a new concept name, in case you meant to use an existing one but made a typo. After you define a concept name while creating a given instance, it will remain in the "central concept" box for the next instance, and the same relation will stay in the relation box, so that you could very quickly enter, say, all your uncles one after the other. If you need to define a new relation while working in the Create Instance dialog box, just type the name of the new relation and the Edit Relations dialog box will automatically appear.

Another nice data entry feature is that, when you define one ray of a new relation, SemNet will try to guess the name of the other ray for you. For example, if you type "has child" as the name of the first ray, SemNet will suggest "child of" for the other. If this isn't what you want, there's nothing lost—you just go ahead and type in the name you want.

SemNet will not make any assumptions about instances you might consider implicit. For example, just because you create an instance representing that both Aram and Lara are your siblings, SemNet won't know that that means they are each other's siblings until you create *that* instance as well.

SemNet's combination of word completion, and its ability to learn concepts and relations in multiple places, make it a very easy and powerful way to enter the data for a net. Sally Gordon (personal communication, July 1993), a psychologist at the University of Idaho who uses SemNet for representing knowledge structures, uses it just because it's so easy to enter the data, even though there are other programs that could give her a more flexible graphic representation.

Importing

There are also a couple of ways you can import data to SemNet from text-only files. The most simple thing you can do is import a list of concepts, one to a line. You can then use these concepts in a net. You can also import a list of concepts *with* attached texts (notes). You just put a <tab> between the concept and its text and make each concept-with-text a separate paragraph. This might be useful, for example, for importing a glossary; all your glossary items would be set up as concepts, and their definitions would be available in pop-up text boxes and in list-type output. The third import option is to import *pairs* of concepts. You set them up one pair to a line, separated with a <tab>. All pairs you import at a given time get set up as instances using the same relation (which you specify). The example in the manual is importing from an address list. One column could be names, the other could be phone numbers, and you could specify the relation "has phone number." If you have a text file with more than two columns of data—for example, one exported from a database program—you can tell SemNet which two columns of data to take on a particular import operation. This is nice because it can save you from having to make a separate text file for each pair of variables.

Working on the Data

There are a couple of ways you might work on a net after it's been created: writing notes or memos, masking concepts, and editing the net itself.

Notes

As you explore the net (which we'll discuss under "Searching," below) and learn more about it and its implications, you can write or edit the text (notes) attached to your concepts and relations. Although each text is limited to 255 characters, and they are intended as "elaborations" of your concepts and relations, they could also be thought of as short memos about the parts of the net.

Masking

SemNet has a feature for masking concepts and relations. A masked concept's or relation's *name* does not show in the net, but you still see the box or arrow that represents it. The manual suggests several uses of this feature. For example, you could have the central concept always masked, and as you move around the net (you can jump randomly), see if you've included enough information to be able to tell what the central concept is from its displayed instances. As another example, students could test their knowledge by masking all related concepts in a view and seeing how many they can remember.

Editing Instances, Relations, and Concepts

All three basic elements of the net can be edited at any time. You may want to redefine a concept, change one or both rays of a relation (or the "clock" orientation at which the ray is displayed), or change particular instances of relations between two concepts. All three types of elements can be edited with their respective editing dialog boxes at any time, and the change will be represented throughout the net.

Most interesting is the Edit Instance dialog box (Figure 5). This dialog has a Cycle button, which brings up one instance after another for review and editing. You can control the manner in which Cycle works by "anchoring" the relation, the central concept, or both. If you anchor the relation, you'll cycle through all the instances using that relation. If you anchor the central concept, you'll cycle through all of its relations. If you anchor both, you'll cycle through all of the instances of that central concept and that relation, so that you could, for example, cycle through all of the instances of a person and her or his children.

The Edit Instance dialog box also has a Flip button, which lets you reverse the direction of the relation between two concepts. In terms of what you see in the dialog box, this is not actually done by changing the ray that shows in the dialog box (e.g., from "has parent" to "has child"). Rather, it is done by switching the central and related concepts, so that what was the related concept is now central, and vice versa. Because the ray stays the same, the relation has been reversed. This does not affect the relationships of either of these concepts with other concepts. There's also a button to Make Central the related concept. Like Flip, this switches the two relations showing, but unlike Flip, it also switches to the other ray of the relation, so that the concept that was, say, the child, remains the child (to return to an earlier example, we replace "Eben — has child → Ned" with "Ned — has parent → Eben"—two different ways of stating the same instance).

As shown in Figure 1, all of the concepts related to a particular central concept with the same relation show in a list in a box at the specified orientation. You can move each related concept up and down in this list.

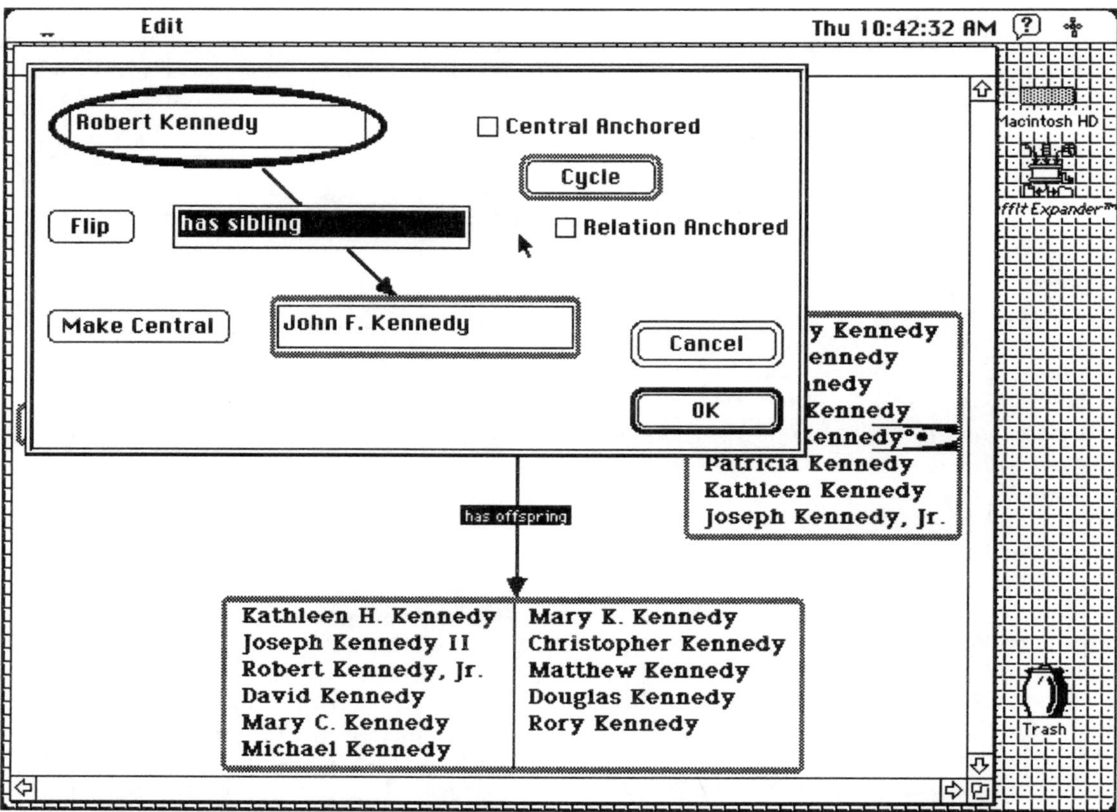

SemNet Figure 5. The Edit Instance dialog box lets you review and edit each instance. The Cycle button, in conjunction with the "Anchored" checkboxes, will let you cycle, one at a time, through all instances in the net, all instances with the current relation, all instances for the current central concept, or all instances with both this concept and this relation. The Flip and Make Central buttons are described in the text.

Searching

SemNet does not search for text, as we normally think of it. For example, it won't search through the text of your notes. However, it does have a couple of different, very useful ways of navigating through, or "searching," your net. The simplest thing you can do is double-click on a related concept name. That concept instantly becomes the central concept, shifting the entire display. You can continue to browse the entire net in this way.

The most significant method of navigation has already been referred to: name completion. If you give the Jump command, a dialog box pops up, asking for the name of the concept you want to jump to. You begin typing the name of the concept you want to jump to and SemNet fills in the rest of the name as soon as you've given it enough letters. Here's where synonyms come in handy: If you type a synonym instead of the actual concept name, SemNet matches that too and still jumps you to the right concept. So if you don't remember whether you named the concept "John F. Kennedy" or "JFK," it doesn't matter—either one will get you there.

Another thing you can do is a random jump. This is exactly what it sounds like. When you give this command, SemNet jumps you to a concept chosen at random. This might be useful if you were quizzing yourself or if you wanted to break out of standard patterns you were following in browsing the net.

Finally, you can "traverse" the net. This allows you to select criteria and, in effect, search the net according to them. You set a number of options for selecting concepts, such as selecting all concepts, those with a certain number or range of numbers of instances, or only those with text or pictures (see Figure 6). You can also designate concepts as start and end points for traversing, or else SemNet will simply show you all concepts matching your criteria. When you begin to traverse, SemNet takes you, one at a time, through the concepts selected by your criteria, and

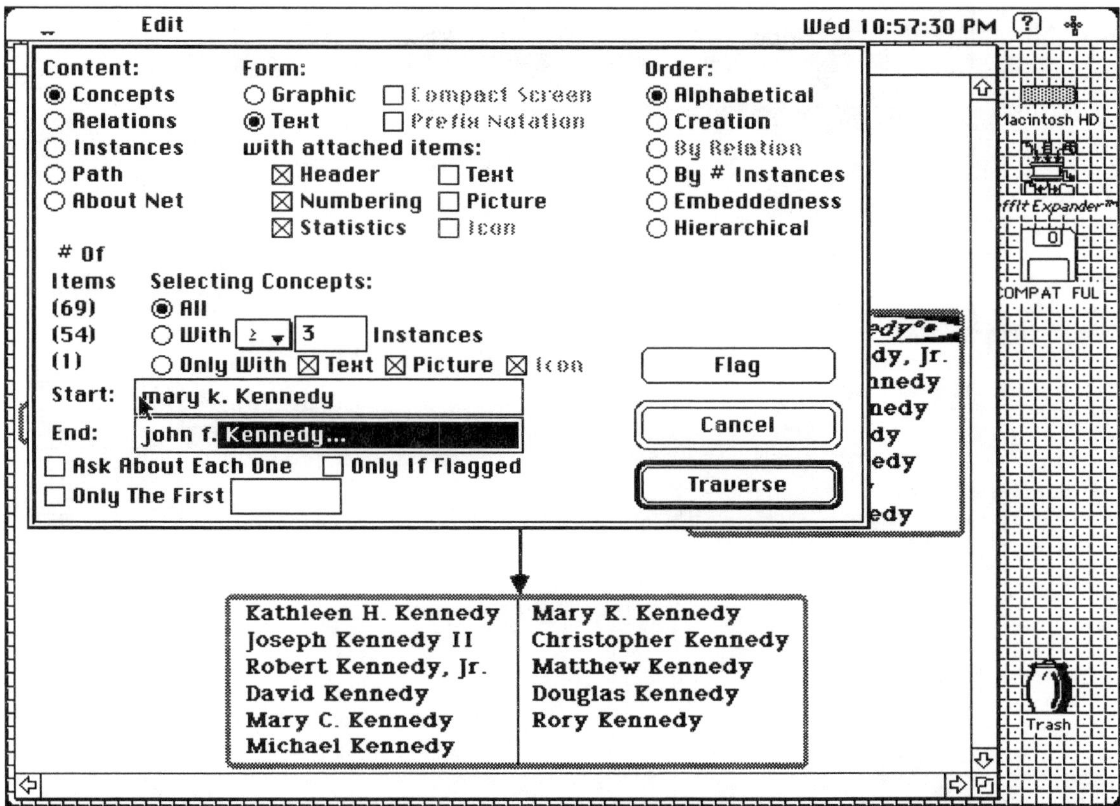

SemNet Figure 6. The traverse dialog box, which is essentially similar to the print dialog box. You choose whether you are interested in printing concepts, relations, instances, the path (audit trail), or the About Net statistics. Graphic output is only available for concepts. You can specify what additional information (attached items) you want, the order you want output sorted in, and the items to be selected.

you can go back and forth through this set as you please. There's an option to have the traverse function automatically flag all of the concepts found by your criteria. Flagged concepts can later be traversed again or printed as a batch (though this wasn't working properly in our beta copy).

As you move around the net, SemNet keeps an audit trail of where you've been. It calls this the "path." You can replay the path, to review everywhere you've been, or use the path with additional criteria to direct a new traverse operation or for printing. You can also see or print it in list or graphic form. The list form shows you the names of the relations you followed, as well as the concept names, but the graphic form just shows unlabeled lines (it looks a lot like the knowledge core display in Figure 3). You can select a concept in either display to make it the current concept and then go back to the normal display, as in Figure 1.

Finally, you can specify two concepts and ask SemNet to display the shortest path between them. The path is displayed graphically, from left to right, as a series of bubbles with concept names. Relations are shown simply as unlabeled lines connecting bubbles; their names are not displayed.

Output

There are three issues we'll discuss here: printing, the different types of displays you can get on the screen, and exporting data, including numerical matrices suitable for cluster analysis and multidimensional scaling.

Printing

You can print information either graphically or in list form. Both types of printouts come out looking pretty much the way their corresponding displays do on screen. Graphic output is fairly poor on an ImageWriter but is quite acceptable, for either overheads or publication, on a laser printer. The simplest print option is to graphically print the

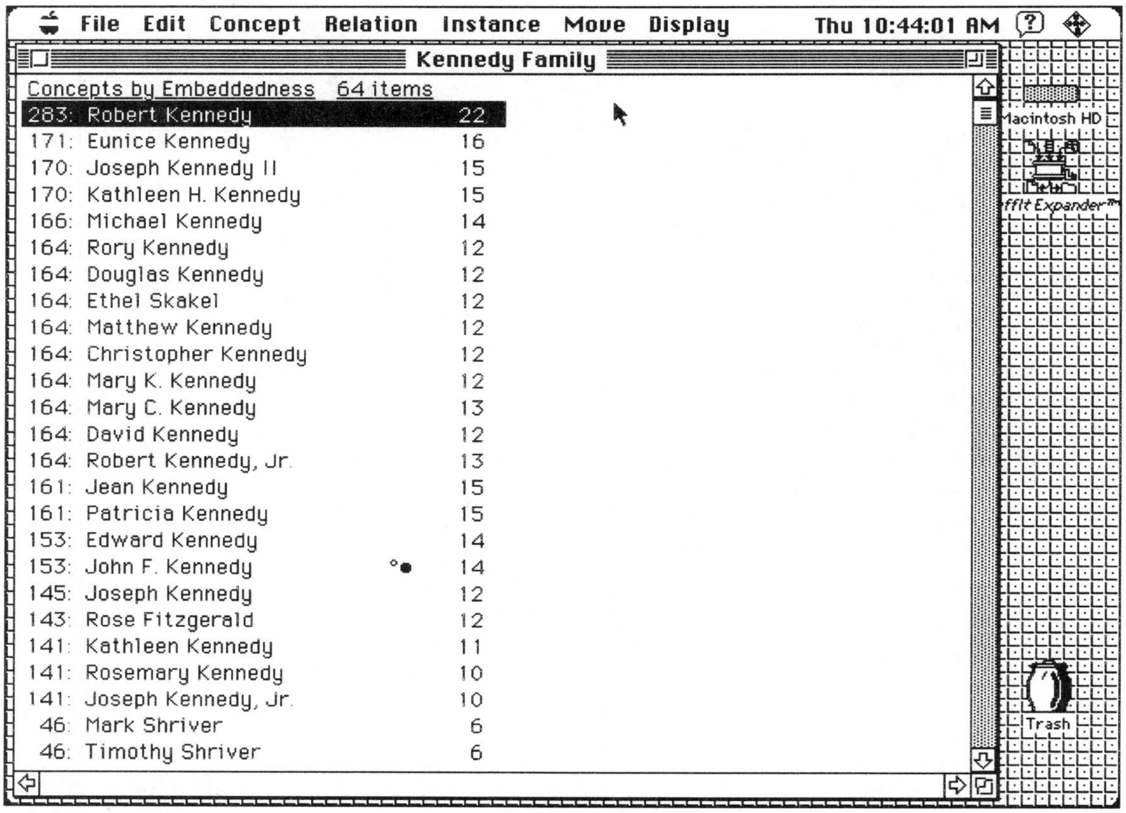

File Edit Concept Relation Instance Move Display Thu 10:44:01 AM

Kennedy Family

Concepts by Embeddedness 64 items

283:	Robert Kennedy	22
171:	Eunice Kennedy	16
170:	Joseph Kennedy II	15
170:	Kathleen H. Kennedy	15
166:	Michael Kennedy	14
164:	Rory Kennedy	12
164:	Douglas Kennedy	12
164:	Ethel Skakel	12
164:	Matthew Kennedy	12
164:	Christopher Kennedy	12
164:	Mary K. Kennedy	12
164:	Mary C. Kennedy	13
164:	David Kennedy	12
164:	Robert Kennedy, Jr.	13
161:	Jean Kennedy	15
161:	Patricia Kennedy	15
153:	Edward Kennedy	14
153:	John F. Kennedy °•	14
145:	Joseph Kennedy	12
143:	Rose Fitzgerald	12
141:	Kathleen Kennedy	11
141:	Rosemary Kennedy	10
141:	Joseph Kennedy, Jr.	10
46:	Mark Shriver	6
46:	Timothy Shriver	6

Macintosh HD

Trash

SemNet Figure 7. Display of concepts, sorted by embeddedness. Embeddedness is shown at left, and number of instances at right. The symbols ° and • indicate that this concept has a picture and a text note, respectively.

current concept, which gives you a paper copy of the basic view of a concept with its instances, as shown in Figure 1. Or you can use the Copy Window command to paste it into a word processor or paint program.

You can also print using a dialog box that is virtually identical to the Traverse dialog box, shown in Figure 6, with only a couple of minor differences. This selects the concepts to be printed in the same way as for traversing, and you can choose how many concepts' views (as in Figure 1)—1, 2, 3, 4, 6, or 8—to print on a page (the more you squeeze on a page, the smaller they'll each be). Remember that you'll get a separate diagram for each selected concept! (There are about 64 in the Kennedy family tree.) To print other graphic displays, you use the Copy Window command to copy the current display as a PICT file, which you can paste into a word processor or paint program. We'll discuss the different types of displays under "Displays," below.

You can also choose to have the concepts printed in list form, and if you do this you can have associated text, pictures, and statistics (numbers of instances and embeddedness) printed too. You can also print lists of relations, the path (audit trail), or an "About Net" listing. The last will give you the number of elements, synonyms, texts (notes), pictures, and names for each of the concepts, relations, and instances; counts and percentages of concepts having 0, 1-2, 3 or more, 6 or more, 10 or more, or 20 or more instances; the "most developed concept" (the concept with the most instances) with its number of instances; the most embedded concept with embeddedness (the total number of indirect paths to all concepts two steps away); and the most used relation with number of instances. The information you can print in lists of concepts and relations corresponds to the information in the different types of displays discussed next.

Displays

In addition to the standard graphic display (Figure 1), and the knowledge core (Figure 3), you can see (and then copy and paste) the graphic display of the path you've followed. You can also see (and copy and paste) a graphic display of the entire net. This works basically like the knowledge core, except concepts are ordered left to right,

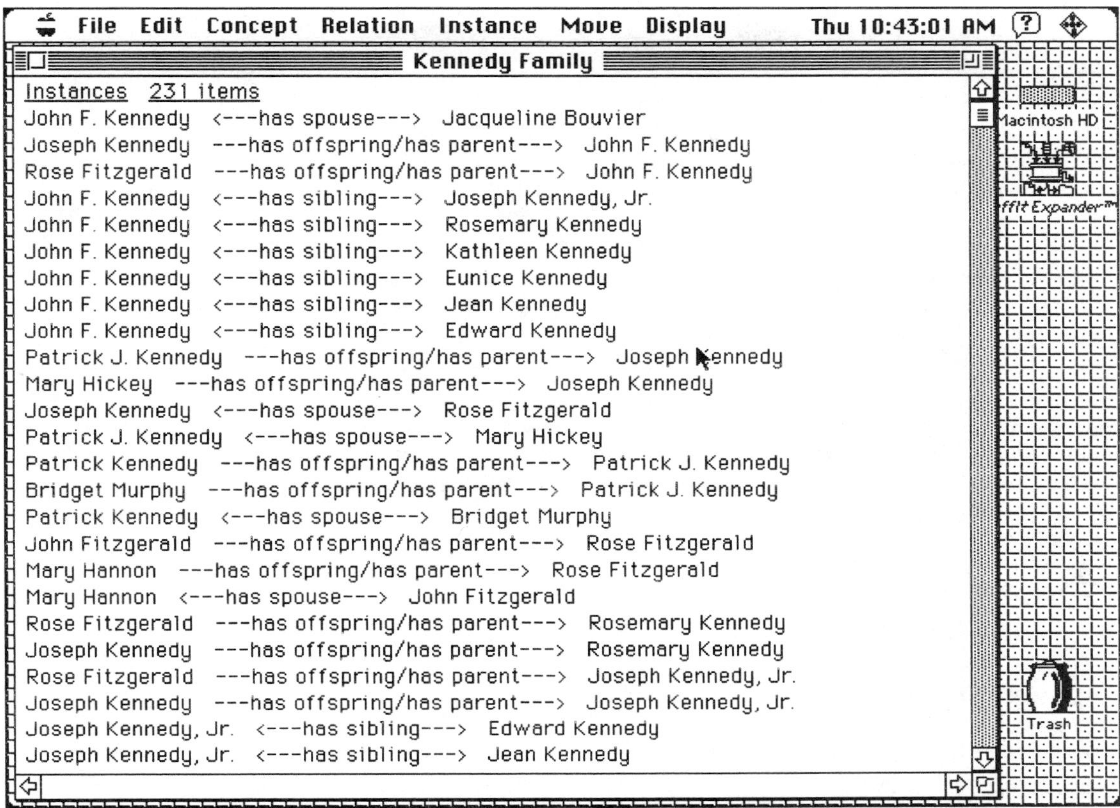

SemNet Figure 8. Display of instances, sorted by creation order. The first and last columns show the two concepts in an instance, and the center shows the relation that connects them. Notice that symmetric relations are shown as a single name, with arrows in both directions, whereas asymmetric relations are shown with the names of both rays, separated with a /, and a single arrow.

top to bottom, and they're *all* there, instead of just the most embedded 49, so the display is even worse.

You can see concepts by number of instances (with embeddedness also listed), by embeddedness, as shown in Figure 7 (with number of instances also listed), alphabetically, or in creation order (with both number of instances and embeddedness). Relations can be listed in alphabetical or creation order with orientation and number of instances. Instances can also be listed in creation order, as shown in Figure 8. ("Creation order" can work in one of two ways; it can be fixed, or it can work so that, if a relation is deleted, the next one you add goes in its slot.)

Exporting

You can export a portion of the net to a new net: you choose whether to have all or none of each of concepts, relations, instances, texts, and pictures. You don't have complete freedom here. For example, to save instances, you have to save concepts and relations.

Of more interest, you can export tables of data to text files. You use a dialog box like the print and traverse dialog boxes to select concepts, relations, or instances. Each column of text is separated from its neighbors by <tab>s (this is known as "tab delimited"). This makes it easy to create neatly formatted tables in a word processor or to tell a spreadsheet or statistical program where the columns of data should be separated.

By now you are surely wondering what types of data are exported. First, you can export lists like those described above, the tabs creating neat columns of—for an instances list, say—the first concept, the relation, and the second concept.

You can also create numerical matrices showing three different measures of association among concepts: adjacency, similarity, and distance. The concepts selected via the print dialog box define the rows and columns of the matrix, so that each cell represents the intersection of two concepts. Adjacency shows a 1 in a cell for two concepts that are directly connected in an instance and a zero for two concepts that are not so related. Similarity shows the number of concepts to which *both* the row and the column concept for that cell are directly related. Distance shows the number of steps in the shortest path between the row and column concepts (if there is no path, the total N of concepts is printed instead). These matrices are suitable for either cluster analysis or multidimensional scaling or for conventional sociometric analysis.

Theory Building

A major way of thinking of a theory is that it's a network of variables connected through various kinds of relationships. What SemNet does is help you represent a map of these related variables and give you some statistics about their interconnectedness. Theory building is, essentially, what SemNet is all about, and it assumes that you take an approach that is supported through the specification and exploration of such networks of concepts.

Graphics Editing

The program is surprisingly weak here. In fact, aside from specifying the orientation of your relations, and supplying pop-up pictures and also icons for relations, you have no control of the graphic appearance of your nets. You type in data, and you navigate graphically, but you do not edit or refine the graphics in any way. A good idea suggested in the manual is to use Copy Window on selected concept views and paste them into another graphics program, where you could add lines and other embellishments to represent relationships among these different views.

There's an add-on program called MapMaker that's been floating around in a prerelease version for over a year now (implication—there's still no release version), which imports SemNet nets, lets you "cut" your concepts into groups based on how embedded they are, and then paste them, one at a time, from these groups onto a map (implication—it's still a lot of work). When you place a concept on the map, MapMaker draws connections between it and all the other concepts it was related to in SemNet. Links are intelligent—meaning you can drag a concept around on the screen and it will remain connected to its related concepts. There are very few graphic refinements available, but one thing you can do is have concept nodes automatically sized according to embeddedness.

User Friendliness

SemNet is both user friendly and fun to use. The tutorial took the better part of a day (5 or 6 hours) but we suspect this was because we were having fun and got carried away. The tutorial is quite comprehensive, giving you a very good introduction to the program. The manual is a marvel for a "small unfunded team of five people all holding full-time jobs doing research and teaching, much of it not directly related to SemNet." (A number of the developers of software reviewed in this book resemble this description.) Though neither slick nor professional looking, it is clear, complete, and easy to find stuff in (with a great index) and has lots of helpful suggestions.

Drawbacks? No on-screen help. While tech support is available by phone if you make the toll call to California, 9-5 Pacific time, you're cautioned that the phone will be answered by office staff who aren't full-fledged tech-support types. You're advised to send detailed information on your problem via e-mail, which will be answered by one of the developers. Include your phone number and they'll call you back if that seems to them to make most sense in your situation. An e-mail message with a couple of questions received a clear, complete response via e-mail in less than 24 hours. If you don't have access to e-mail, they will *presumably* find a way to get you on the phone with one of the developers.

Miscellaneous

SemNet cannot be run on a network. You must install a copy on each computer you want to run it on.

Update

Just as we were finishing our edits to this book, we received a newer beta version, designated as β14, which contained several enhancements.

You can now attach pictures to instances as well as to concepts and relations.

The display of knowledge cores and overall views of nets have been substantially enhanced, and our complaints earlier in this review no longer altogether apply. In these views, concepts' nodes are now represented by rectangles, as opposed to ellipses, as in Figure 3. Rather than seeing an illegible spiderweb of all relations, you now click on a concept and see just the lines for the relations directly connecting that concept to others (if you want, you can set the number of steps away you want displayed). The names of these relations are displayed in small type in a corner of each of the concept nodes.

You can also have the embeddedness, number of instances, and symbols for attachments displayed in each node. You can click on different concepts, displaying their relations one at a time. (If you want, you can still see all relations at once.) The overall effect is of a very readable, and very useful, interactive display.

There's a feature that let's you list a "hierarchy" for a given concept and relation. So, you could ask for a hierarchy of John F. Kennedy, using the relation has parent/has offspring. You would get a listing in outline form, in which JFK appears somewhere in the middle, offspring (children, grandchildren, and so on) appear indented below, and parents, grandparents, and so on appear above. For each generation removed from JFK that a concept (or, in this case, a relative) is, it is indented once. Note that there are typically many interconnected hierarchies in any net.

The developers also intend to allow you to create links from concepts, relations, or instances to documents external to SemNet. These documents could be, for example, word processor files or graphics. The developers also intend to allow such links to work with videodisks and CD-ROM. They say they have these features working but haven't decided exactly how the interface will look yet. As with any promised, but not yet incorporated, feature, don't buy SemNet for these features unless you first verify that they wound up in the final release.

It's also now possible to merge nets together. Thus you can create a series of smaller nets, say, one per interview, and then merge them together and explore the resulting new patterns.

Comparative Remarks

SemNet is mostly in a category unto itself, although it overlaps a bit in different ways with different programs. MECA is its closest relative, but MECA is oriented to a quantitative approach, whereas SemNet is largely graphically oriented, although it can also create matrices for multidimensional scaling and cluster analysis.

Another possible comparison is with ATLAS/ti, which also allows you to specify different types of relations among different types of concepts. Further, ATLAS/ti takes as its network nodes (concepts in SemNet) codes you've applied to your data, selected chunks of text, and your research memos and maintains the connection between the node icons and the data they represent, so that you can make hypertextlike jumps from the network view to the data, and vice versa. It also gives you much more flexibility in creating and arranging custom views of your nets. SemNet, on the other hand, is dedicated to semantic network creation, provides a variety of powerful options for creating and navigating nets and for analyzing the connections within them, and provides better support for specifying and using greater numbers of relations. Its graphic output—at least of views of a concept and its instances—on a laser printer is of higher quality.

Graphically, SemNet cannot compete with dedicated graphic-mappers such as Inspiration and MetaDesign. For more information on these programs, which are dedicated to drawing and refining networks from a graphic standpoint, see their reviews.

Summary

SemNet is a unique program. Its special features for creating, exploring, and analyzing semantic networks can make it a powerful theory-building tool if it fits your needs. It also generates association data for use in cluster analysis and multidimensional analysis. Its one serious drawback is its inability to usefully display more than a view of one central concept and its instances at a given time. If you can live with this, or are happy using MapMaker or pasting different concept views into a graphic program (Inspiration or MetaDesign could work nicely for this) and elaborating and integrating them there, you could have a lot of fun and do a lot of good work with SemNet.

Reference

Miller, B., Faletti, J., & Fisher, K. (1991). *SemNet user's guide version 1.0.* San Diego, CA: SemNet Research Group.

9

Program Features

A GUIDE TO THE RATINGS

The matrix appearing at the end of this chapter is designed to display program features in a specific, comparative way. It, used with the reviews in Chapters 4 through 8, gives you detailed information so you can narrow down your choices and take next steps (e.g., asking colleagues or friends who have used the program about their reactions; calling the developer for specific information, a program brochure, or demo version; or making a purchase).

The programs, which are shown in the columns, are roughly bunched according to general type, or "family" (text retrievers, textbase managers, code-and-retrieve, code-based theory-builders, and conceptual network-builders), and are alphabetized within family. Remember, though, that you will often want to make comparisons across families. Specific features are shown in the rows, clustered into areas, such as *Data Entry/Structure.* Each area has a general rating with our assessment (strong, OK, weak, absent). Then there are subaspects of the area. Here's a brief explanation of the rows of the matrix, with a section for each area; the rows are discussed in the exact sequence appearing in the matrix. See also the legend for the meaning of specific entries. These explanations may be clearer if you occasionally refer to the matrix as we go.

If a particular term used here isn't clear to you, check the Glossary.

Matrix Categories

Data Entry/Structure

How do you get data into the program? Once they're there, how are they stored?

The items here show whether a text editor or word processor is included, and how strong it is, whether data must be specifically preformatted in some way, and whether you can input data directly (or must use other software to do so). The names of word processors that are compatible with the program are shown. Programs may be able to accept graphics, numbers, audio or video data as well as text. Another feature is whether the program can show links to "off-line" data, which are not actually in your database (e.g., it will show you that there's an audiotape recording in the files for interview number 4 with person G.W.).

Some programs number lines of text automatically, which is very helpful when you are doing close-up, detailed analysis of words, phrases, meanings.

The revisability of your basic data documents is often important; can you easily edit, update, revise, and extend data files, or must they be kept inviolate? (It's almost always *possible* to revise your data, but sometimes the consequences are severe.)

Programs vary in their database structure; some have formal fields and records, and some are unstructured. Some use internal files (imported or created), and others set up a separate index[1] paralleling your text files, whose elements stay separate as external files. Indexing has the virtue of leaving your original text untouched but the liability that, if you edit your text, the references in the index file become meaningless. Depending on the type of index, you may be able to give a command to reindex or you may have to redo some or all of your coding, annotation, and so on.

Most programs have a facility for "unitizing" or chunking data—that is, making the "pieces" you will attach codes to. Some programs do this in a uniform way (always lines, or sentences, or paragraphs, and so on). Some let you choose among several standard sizes, and some can accept varying sizes from you. Some programs allow what we have called "free-form" chunking, so you can simply select whatever range of text you want, from one particular character to another. Some programs do chunking automatically, and some let you do it flexibly in the program. Others require you to insert specific chunk "delimiters," such as an "@" sign after each chunk in your original text.

Standard chunk sizes can vary from single characters to words, sentences, paragraphs, pages, sections, or whole files. Codes themselves may be limited to a single word or abbreviation or be limited to a phrase.

The program's capacity is shown in terms of the number and/or size of files it can accommodate. (The text of reviews sometimes specifies other limits, such as the number of chunks and/or codes.)

1. Note that there are two basic types of indexes here, which we don't distinguish between. To speed up text search, some programs set up "inverted" files, which list all the words in a file along with pointers to all the places in the file each word occurs. This is what programmers typically mean by "indexed." The other setup we're calling "indexed" is where the program keeps track of all your coding, annotating, linking, and so on in a file separate from the actual text, with pointers to the places in the text these items refer to.

Coding

Many researchers want to attach codes or keywords to various pieces of their data so they can retrieve them easily for analysis. As with data entry, we provide an overall rating of the strength of coding capabilities.

On-screen or "one-step" coding permits you to assign codes directly to text as you view it; when this is absent, you usually work by jotting down codes on a hard copy printout of your data, then key in codes in a second step.

Some programs permit you to assign multiple codes to the same chunk, usually with some upper limit (no more than eight codes, for example). If we don't specify a number, then there's no limit. Or you can "overlap" or "nest" codes across chunks (example: code CONFLICT is applied to lines 6-19, code RACIAL is *nested* within CONFLICT for lines 10-13, and code POWER, on lines 17-26, *overlaps* CONFLICT). Codes can also be organized hierarchically, and given at a first level, at a second, more abstract level, or at successively higher levels.

Programs vary in how easy it is to revise and update your coding categories as you go; for some, it's a big production, and for others, it's very simple. For example, you might want to give a higher-level code of CHANGE to all first-level codes of INNOVATION, CRISIS, REFORM, and RESTRUCTURING or reallocate INNOVATION and a new code INCREMENTALISM to a new higher level code called SMALLCHANGE. Can this be done with a few keystrokes, or must it be done laboriously, item by item? Some programs also provide for automated code assignment (e.g., applying code CONFLICT whenever the words "argument," "fight," "disagreement" are found in the text). Programs also vary in how easy it is to revise code *applications*: Can you correct, revise, and update your coding of specific chunks?

When you want to see your whole code list, some programs can't do it at all, and others offer you a list. Some give you an outline, or a network display, showing levels of codes.

A final issue here is whether the program can store and use facts that are not in your text. For example, there might be a long interview with someone, but nowhere in the interview text is there anything to indicate that the person (a) is a principal, (b) is female, (c) is new on the job, (d) is a close friend of the guidance counselor, (e) attended a recent training workshop. This is sometimes called "face-sheet" or "source" information, but the issue is broader than that: Can the program incorporate such facts, whether or not they are mentioned in your text? Without them you are limited to what's in the text.

Memoing/Annotation

Researchers need to reflect on their data, figure out what it means, make sense of it. Programs can vary a good deal in how much they support your reflective activity, and we provide a general rating.

It's important to know whether the program allows you to edit/revise your database as you go or requires you to keep it inviolate. Some programs permit you to add marks to the text, such as redlining, underlining, or highlighting certain words or phrases. Others let you annotate it by writing inserted or marginal remarks. With others, you can write extended memos reflecting on what you are seeing in the text. While annotations are typically not more than a few sentences, memos are typically longer, sometimes running many pages in length. Annotations are also typically attached to one particular point in the text, whereas memos may apply to whole files, discontinuous chunks of text, codes, or cases. Such additional material may be in a separate file, or appear in an adjacent or alternate window when you want to see it.

It's important to know whether your memos are just sitting in another file and have to be called up by file name when you want them—or are clearly linked to some part of the original text, or to particular codes, or to specific annotations. For example, you might see a marker in the text showing that at that point the researcher wrote a memo; clicking on the marker will pull up the memo immediately.

Some programs permit you to code the memos and/or annotations as well as the original text, so they too can be retrieved via codes.

Data Linking

As analysis proceeds, you typically see more and more connections among different parts of the database. Some programs offer very little support for incorporating these observations, and others are quite thorough and ingenious. For example, when you suddenly see a connection between, say, codes for PROBLEM, COPING STYLE, and ACTIVE/PASSIVE, you can actually link them, as well as linking a memo on, say, "proactiveness," to all three of these codes. That way, the next time you or a colleague want to think some more about "proactiveness," you don't just read the memo but can see what things have been linked to it and instantly pull up the relevant coded chunks without having to search for them one by one.

The entries here, after a general rating, show what kinds of links can be made. First, links can be made *within* classes of objects such as your basic text, codes, annotations, memos, and "off-line" material such as videos, documents, or other material not actually in your text database. So you could have text-to-text links, code-to-code links, and so on. Second, links can be made across parts (e.g., linking codes to memos, or annotations to text). Programs with strong linking functions, perhaps in a "hypertext" mode, let you "browse" or "navigate" easily through your growing database.

It's important to note that links made among chunks of text and memos are essentially hypertext links. To assess a program's hypertext functions in the matrix, look both here and under "Conceptual/Theory Development," below.

Search and Retrieval

How good is a program in looking for, finding, and showing you particular information you're looking for? The rating gives a general idea.

In more detail, we show the relative speed of search and retrieval compared with other programs. Note that these are rough impressions, not the result of strict quantitative measurements.

Next we look at how search requests are formulated. That can be done in several ways:[2]

Boolean: Combinations of AND, OR, NOT, and so on using algebraic parentheses to formulate very precise requests

Set logic: Similar but with possibilities like "inside" (nested), "overlaps," "at least 3 of these 5," and so on[3]

Relational: Items that are linked in some specified way (usually, searching for text coded with all subcodes of a given code)

Fuzzy: Items spelled approximately like your request

Sequence: Items occurring before or after another

Proximity: Items co-occurring within a specified distance (e.g., within 5 words, or two paragraphs, or 10 lines)

Wildcard: Request includes symbols like * or ? that can stand for any characters (thus a search using "decisi*" will get you "decisive," "decision," "decision-making," and so on)

Phonetic: Words that sound like your request

Synonyms: Items of equivalent meaning to your request

For each applicable type, we give a "strength" rating.

When you're searching for more than one code, as in Boolean, set logic, sequence, or proximity requests, you should know just where the co-occurrence will be looked for: within standard chunks, such as a line, sentence, or paragraph; within free-form chunks you've defined; within a specified distance (as in a proximity search); or within a file (document) as a whole.

2. Each of the following is described in more detail in the Glossary.

3. Technically, set logic and Boolean algebra are both part of Set Theory and, to heavy mathematical types, are functionally equivalent, using different language to accomplish the same things. The differences in language, however, often lead to real differences in program implementation, as reflected in the distinction we make here.

Programs can search for codes or "keywords" (traditionally, keywords are marked words in your text, while codes are labels you apply to your text, but this distinction often breaks down) and/or for any naturally occurring words (or strings that can be parts of words or whole phrases) in your text. Some can search for cases as a whole. Some can select sections, subgroups, or segments of your data and work just within those (e.g., only female respondents, or only in second-grade classrooms, or in combinations of these—second-grade classrooms taught by women). When the program finds a requested chunk (a "hit"), it may highlight the whole hit (if the hit is shown in context), or just the string or code you were looking for, or not highlight anything. It's also important to know whether you see the hit by itself or in the context of preceding and following text. We also provide a rating of the adequacy of "source tags" attached; they let you see which person, which observation, which interview, which line, which file, and so on the hit came from. You may also want to be able to find just where in the file the hit is (line number, page number, and so on).

A few programs also make an automatic record or log of your various searches and retrievals. That's important, because you may want to return to an earlier search to check something or to refine your search question. You're building up a database that includes your useful searches (many will have been dead ends), the results, and your memos and annotations.

A final, important issue is whether your hits can be revised or processed. Perhaps you can only see them (as in a library search program). Or perhaps you can actually edit them (sometimes in a window or clipboard), summarize, abstract, or select from them as you go, before you send them to an output file or printer.

Conceptual/Theory Development

Here the issue is how good a program is in helping you think and conceptualize about your data. That's what analysis is for. Good coding and retrieval features, and memoing/annotation features, can be a big help in your efforts to make good conceptual sense of your data and to build and test overarching theories. But some programs go farther, providing features specifically designed to support, expand, and record your theory-building work. We provide a general rating here. Note, though, that just what kinds of conceptual/theory building help are useful to you will depend on your own analytical style; see the discussion in Chapter 10 for more help with this issue.

As a minimal feature, some programs have an "outlining" facility that sets up a structure for what you're writing and shows it in various levels of detail.

The theory-development aspects of the program usually have an underlying system. These come in several types. One type is built on a *code-and-retrieve* metaphor (attach codes to chunks, retrieve chunks, build higher level codes). Another type is *rule-based* (if certain combinations of codes are found, assign a specific higher level code). Or the system may be *logic-based* (testing propositions or hypotheses in IF . . . THEN form). Another type is *network-based* (developing a conceptual structure of named "nodes" and "links" between them, either in a tree—hierarchical—or more general network form). For further discussion of these types, see Richards and Richards (1994).

Programs using networks may have links of a single, unnamed type (which just says, "These things are connected."). Or there may be multiple types (such as "is a kind of," "causes," "requires," "follows"). You may be able to define your own link types, either in a standard or an idiosyncratic way. Links may also have logical properties, such as "symmetric," "asymmetric," "transitive."

Links can also be hypertext links. Look at the ratings both here and under "Data Linking," above.

Some programs permit direct testing of hypotheses or propositions in your data, such as "Administrative pressure and technical support lead to effective program implementation; program implementation leads to high student impact." Note that you can often achieve the same results with sophisticated, complex code-based search requests such as those available in NUD•IST, but we reserve this rating for programs that have specific, built-in features or routines set up specifically for this purpose.

Others enable cross-case analysis of the complex configurations or patterns of predictors associated with outcomes within each of a number of cases. For example, Huberman and Miles (1984) studied schools that had high student impact. They found two different "families" of high-impact schools: One had high administrative pressure along with tech support. The other had a different configuration: tech support without pressure and high-quality staff who had mastered the new program and were strongly committed to it. (There were also "low-impact" families.)

A final, important feature is "system closure." In some programs, the results of theory-building efforts are recorded and fed back into the database. They can be coded, retrieved, and used in the next step of conceptualization.

Graphics Editing

A program may or may not have graphics capability. If it does, an important issue is how well it manages the production and revision of graphics. This rating is followed by two others. First, the program's output may be of high quality (clear, wide ranging, flexible) or may be less good (muddy, narrow, restricted). Second, some programs have many aesthetic refinements (shading, different fonts, styles) and others few.

Most programs with graphics capability focus on network presentation (as contrasted with matrix or table presentation). It's important to look at a number of network editing features.

For example, if you move a network node, are its links "intelligent," stretching and moving as the node moves? Are there other automatic features, such as automatic network arrangement, either in hierarchical form or to permit maximum readability? Some programs will align nodes automatically, and some will make automatic spacing among nodes.

Programs may also provide a range of node styles (circles, ellipses, boxes, triangles) to which you can assign special meanings. Nodes may also be resizable or not.

Links can also have a range of styles (light or heavy, dotted or solid, and so on), and links may be segmented or not (i.e., just go in a straight line or be bent around corners).

A final, very important feature is whether each node can only have a label (such as "administrative pressure") attached to it or can include extended text (say, a long memo on administrative pressure, which will pop up from the graphic when you ask for it).

Data Output/Display

A crunch question is how programs give you information. Some programs do a marvelous job on this count, and others are limited and frustrating. The rating gives a general judgment on this.

Most will send output to the screen, to a printer, or to a file. Some work with extra windows on screen, or with split screens, or alternate screens.

A few programs will produce output that can be displayed in matrix (table) form; the cell entries may be numbers, codes, or text. Others, as we've noted, will show you results in a network of nodes and links.

Some programs will do frequency counts (of codes, words, strings, hits, and so on), and some will export quantitative data to statistical software such as SPSS, BMDP, and the like.

Other Features

Some programs have deliberate provision for "customizing" the software for your particular needs and tastes. Others do this only partially or not at all.

You can also look for whether certain routines can be set up to run automatically, often via "macros" (essentially, miniprograms, or recorded sequences of keystrokes to accomplish specific tasks). Some programs have additional capability: You can write new subprograms that revise what the software does for you.

Some programs will run only on one "platform" (DOS or Macintosh, for example). Some have multiple versions, each usable on a different platform (Windows, Unix, mainframe, DOS, Macintosh). Most flexible are those that let you transport your data across platforms (the laptop Mac you use for field notes and the DOS machine in the office).

User Friendliness

Qualitative data analysis is hard enough without having to struggle with difficult, unfriendly software. The issue of user friendliness is quite crucial in the choice of a program because it relates to investments of time and energy. Will your investments be justified in terms of what you're getting?

Here we provide a general judgment of overall user friendliness and the amount of learning effort the program requires. We also rate the quality of tutorials, on-screen help, and available documentation (manuals, articles, and so on).

The matrix does not include ratings of the subjective "feel" of the program, but look in the reviews for comments about this. For example, some programs are quite flexible; you can "work around" their features, doing what you want without too much hassle. Others are rather unforgiving and will do only what they were built for.

There is probably no program that can be wholly trouble-free; you'll always encounter problems and glitches that you need help with. Thus the quality of tech support is important and is rated using criteria like these: Can you get it from the developer or distributor easily and quickly, preferably over the phone, or by fax or e-mail? Is it concrete and helpful? Does it cost you anything? Some programs also have user groups who exchange information and mutual help; some have newsletters. Our tech-support ratings are conservative. Very few developers got a rating of "strong," and quite a few developers who provide very good support got ratings of only OK. Nobody's perfect, and almost every tech support system had some frustrations involved. For example, a developer might be extremely friendly, responsive, patient, detail oriented, and helpful but not have a toll-free line—or work primarily via e-mail so that there could be a full day's delay before getting a question answered, often with a request for more information, adding another day. If you live on the other side of the globe from the developer, these problems can be exacerbated by time differences.

We saved the "strong" ratings for developers who had truly extraordinary tech support, like the company that produces Metamorph, who, if they can't solve your problem over the phone, will send you a modem and special software so that they can take over your machine by remote control and set things up properly for you.

One developer, who provides excellent tech support, said that "the best support is, when it is not needed." We agree with this statement but did feel it necessary to tease the issue of tech support apart from the issues of program reliability and general user friendliness—factors that affect the need for tech support. You should go to the "User Friendliness" sections of the reviews and get a richer description of tech support rather than relying exclusively on the ratings.

There's also a rating of how easy the program is to use once you've learned it. (Complex programs that take a while to learn can turn out to be really easy to use, and some quickly learned programs are actually awkward to use.)

Price

Prices were given as of Summer 1994, in U.S. dollars. If multiple packages are offered (single user, professional, student, network, demo, Mac, DOS, and so on), a range is shown, and the full information appears in the title boxes of the reviews in Chapters 4 through 8.

Operating System

This lists the availability of the program for DOS (and Windows), Mac, Unix, mainframe, and so on, indicating the minimal version needed.

Hardware Requirements

Normally, this includes what the developer says is needed for minimal and/or optimal use: CPU, such as IBM 286, 386, 486, and system level for Mac; amount of free RAM needed; space needed on hard disk; math coprocessor; video (CGA, VGA, SVGA, and so on); mouse. This information is given in more detail in the title box at the beginning of each program review.

Using the Matrix

Because the columns of the matrix are bunched according to program type, if you know what general style of program you're looking for, you can concentrate on that region of the matrix. But you'll notice quickly that there isn't a precisely standard set of features for, say, "code-and-retrieve" programs. Furthermore, each program has a distinctive configuration of features. So, within a region, you need to look carefully, comparing the configurations and going back to the specific reviews when the matrix raises a question in your mind about Program X.

Scanning across the rows in areas that are important to you (e.g., coding or theory building) can be very helpful in pointing you toward specific program reviews that will tell you more. It may also aid you in a strategy that can be very useful: defining a list of "must" features, such as "must have memoing capability," "must have on-screen coding," "must not cost over $300," "must not have high learning effort." Such a list, perhaps supplemented by a list of "desirable" features that would be nice to have (e.g., "wildcard search if possible," "prefer highlighted hits") is a good way to locate candidate programs rapidly and winnow them down.

You also need to refer back to, and keep updating, the notes you made in your worksheet copy of Figure 2.1. Your matrix scanning should be grounded in your answers to basic questions about you, your data, and your expected analyses.

To winnow, if you have several programs in mind as candidates, it's easy to compare their features rapidly, column to column. Then you need to cycle back to the detailed reviews for fuller information about a feature or general rating and to be sure your "must" and "desirable" features work as you'd like them to. That process may also help you frame specific questions you want to ask the developer or program distributor about particular features.

The matrix can also be helpful in surfacing and clarifying trade-offs, which are normally inevitable. For example, to get a sophisticated textbase manager for the complicated study you're planning, you may have to accept a steeper learning curve or pay more than you'd hoped. Or you may discover that a nominally simpler, cheaper program has some rigid, unpleasant features. The issue is finding trade-offs you can live with, given what your "musts" are like.

TEXT RETRIEVERS

FEATURES	Metamorph	Orbis	Sonar Professional	The Text Collector	WordCruncher
DATA ENTRY/STRUCTURE	◎	●	◎	◎	○
editor/word processor	D: ◎	●	—	—	○
data preformatting	not req'd	helpful	helpful	not req'd	req'd
direct data input	—	✔	—	—	—
compatible with word processors	ASCII, WordPerfect (With others lose formatting)	XyWrite, Nota Bene (which can import from others)	Many - see review	All or Many	WordPerfect ASCII
data types accepted	D: T / W: T, OLE	T	T/Q/G/V	T	T
handling of off-line data	—	—	●	—	—
line numbering	—	—	—	✔	✔
data files easily revisable	D: ✔ / W: ✔	✔	—	✔	—
database structure	unstructured external-files	unstructured internal-files indexed	records-fields unstructured external-files indexed	unstructured external-files	semi-structured external-files indexed
chunking/unitizing	flex/auto	uniform	uniform/flex	flex	flex
standard chunk sizes	character/line/ sentence/para/page/ file/User-defined delimiters	line/para/page/file	word/para/file	word/line/sentence/para/ parentheses/ quotes/ records/User-defined delimiters	line/sentence/para/ page/file
database capacity	No limits	1,000,000 files, 16,000MB per file	∞ files K per file limited by RAM	No limits	1,000 files ∞ K per file
CODING	D: ○	○	—	—	—
code length	phrase	keyword/phrase	N/A	N/A	N/A
on-screen (one-step)	—	✔	N/A	N/A	N/A
code applications	D: MU	MU	N/A	N/A	N/A
multi-levels	D: more than 2	none	N/A	N/A	N/A
automated coding	D: ◎	—	N/A	N/A	N/A
code revision easy	D: ★★	★★	N/A	N/A	N/A
codes display	D: with text	none	N/A	N/A	N/A
store facts not in text	—	—	✔	—	—
MEMOING/ANNOTATION	◎	○	●	—	—
text editable	✔	✔	✔	—	N/A
text markable	—	redlining/under-lining/highlighting	redlining/under-lining/highlighting	—	—
text annotation	✔	✔	—	—	—
accepts memos	✔	—	✔	—	—
memos attached to:	text	—	text	—	—
memos/annotations codable	—	p	—	—	—
DATA-LINKING	●	—	◎	—	○
links made within:	T	—	T	—	T
links made among:	T-0	—	T-M	—	T-Graphics
SEARCH AND RETRIEVAL	●	◎	●	●	◎
speed	high	high	med	high	high
search request types	● set logic ● fuzzy ● proximity ● wildcard ● synonyms	● Boolean ● wildcard ◎ synonyms	● Boolean ● sequence ● proximity ○ wildcard ● phonetic ◎ synonyms ◎ relational	● Boolean ● wildcard ◎ phonetic	◎ Boolean ◎ sequence ◎ proximity ◎ wildcard ○ synonyms
co-occurrence by:	chunk/proximity document	chunk	chunk/proximity document	chunk/document	chunk/proximity
search for:	text strings	codes/text strings	text strings/cases	text strings/cases	text strings
select subgroups of data	✔	✔	✔	✔	✔
hits highlighted	string/chunk	string/code	string	string/chunk	string
show hits in context	full	full	full	full	full
source tags attached	●	○	●	◎	◎
searches logged, recorded	✔	✔ (weak)	✔	✔	—
hits editable, processable	✔	✔	✔	—	✔

TEXT RETRIEVERS

FEATURES	Metamorph	Orbis	Sonar Professional	The Text Collector	WordCruncher
CONCEPTUAL/THEORY DEVELOPMENT	—	—	○	—	—
outlining	—	✔	—	—	—
system type	—	code-retrieve	logic-based	N/A	logic-based
hierarchical/tree structure	—	—	—	—	—
other network structure	—	—	—	—	—
link types	specifiable	—	single	—	single
logical link properties	none	none	none	none	none
hypothesis-testing	—	—	—	—	—
multi-case configural comparison	—	—	—	—	—
system closure	—	—	✔	—	—
GRAPHICS EDITING	—	—	—	—	—
output quality	—	—	—	—	—
aesthetic refinements	—	—	—	—	—
intelligent links	N/A	N/A	N/A	N/A	N/A
auto arrange	N/A	N/A	N/A	N/A	N/A
auto align	N/A	N/A	N/A	N/A	N/A
auto space	N/A	N/A	N/A	N/A	N/A
different node styles	N/A	N/A	N/A	N/A	N/A
resizeable nodes	N/A	N/A	N/A	N/A	N/A
different link styles	N/A	N/A	N/A	N/A	N/A
segmented links	N/A	N/A	N/A	N/A	N/A
node text	N/A	N/A	N/A	N/A	N/A
DATA OUTPUT/DISPLAY	◉	◉	●	◉	◉
output goes to:	screen/file	screen/printer/file	screen/printer/file	screen/printer/file	screen/printer/file
split or alternate screens	✔	✔	✔	✔	✔
matrix output	—	text	—	—	—
network output	—	—	—	—	—
frequency counts	—	✔	✔	—	✔
numerical data export to:	—	—	—	—	—
OTHER FEATURES					
customization	D: ● / W: ◉	◉	◉	●	◉
automation	D: macros D: batch jobs D: replayable searches	macros (XPL Programming Language)	macros	batch jobs	none
cross-platform portability	—	—	✔ (Win ↔ Mac)	—	—
USER FRIENDLINESS	D: ◉ / W: ●	◉	●	●	○
learning effort required	moderate	high XyWrite, low Orbis	moderate	low	high
tutorials	◉	◉	—	●	◉
on-screen help	D: ● / W: ◉	◉	◉	●	◉
documentation	D: ○ / W: ◉	●	●	●	○
tech support	●	◉	◉	◉	◉
easy to use once learned	D: ★★ / W: ★★★	★★	★★★	★★★	★
PRICE $	1644 400 (Faculty)	149 + 495 (XyWrite)	795 295 (non-Professional)	69	395
OPERATING SYSTEM	DOS, MAC, UNIX, Windows [3.1], MVS, and will customize for others	DOS [3.3]	Windows [3.1] MAC [System 7]	DOS [2.0]	DOS [2.1, Preferably 3.2]
HARDWARE REQUIREMENTS	286 Hard Disk (≥ 4MB free) 450K free DOS RAM, LPT1 parallel port	IBM PC/PS 2 286 or better, 384K RAM Hard Disk (≥ 2-7MB free) EGA or better monitor	**Windows:** 386 or better 4MB RAM (8MB recommended for Windows)	128K RAM	IBM PC AT or better 512-640K RAM Hard Disk (≥ 1.2MB free)

● strong
◉ OK
○ weak
— absent

N/A Not Applicable

✔ yes
p partially
— no

★★★ definitely
★★ mostly
★ is awkward

D: Dos
W: Windows
(if unspecified, same for both)

Data Types
T text
Q quantitative
G graphic
AU audio
V video

Code Applications
MU multiple
OV overlapping
N nesting

Data Linking
T text
C codes
A annotations
M memos
O off-line

	TEXT RETRIEVERS	TEXTBASE MANAGERS			
FEATURES	ZyINDEX	askSam	Folio VIEWS	MAX	Tabletop
DATA ENTRY/STRUCTURE	○	●	●	**○**	**○**
editor/word processor	—	W: ● D: **○**	●	○	—
data preformatting	not req'd	not req'd	not req'd	req'd	req'd
direct data input	—	✔	✔	✔	✔
compatible with word processors	ASCII, WordPerfect, MS-Word, MS-Write, Ami Pro, Word for Windows, dBASE III and IV, VolksWriter/ Total Word, WordStar, Display Write, XyWrite, Multimate	ASCII WordPerfect 5.x, RTF, dBase III+ and IV	ASCII, WordPerfect 5.1/5.2/6.0 (DOS and Windows), Word for Windows 2.0, MS-Word 5.5, LEXIS/NEXIS	ASCII	ASCII
data types accepted	T/Q/G	T/Q/G/AU/V W: OLE	T/Q/G/AU/V/ OLE 1.0	T/Q	T/Q
handling of off-line data	—	—	●	—	—
line numbering	—	—	—	✔	N/A
data files easily revisable	—	✔	✔	p	✔
database structure	unstructured/ external-files/indexed	records-fields/ unstructured/ internal-files	records-fields/ unstructured/ internal-files/indexed	records-fields/ unstructured/ internal-files/indexed	records-fields/ internal files
chunking/unitizing	flex	flex	flex/free-form	flex	N/A
standard chunk sizes	line/sentence/para/ page/file	word/line/sentence/ para/file	para	line/para/page/file	N/A
database capacity	50 million files, 20 Gigabytes per index, search 8 indexes at once	∞ K per file 16,000 lines (300 pages) per record	16,000,000MB per file	999 files, 5.9MB per file	200 records 50 fields
CODING	—	—	●	○	N/A
code length	N/A	N/A	phrase	keyword	N/A
on-screen (one-step)	N/A	N/A	✔	✔	N/A
code applications	N/A	N/A	MU/OV/N	MU/OV/N	N/A
multi-levels	N/A	N/A	none	none	N/A
automated coding	N/A	N/A	**○**	—	N/A
code revision easy	N/A	N/A	★	★★	N/A
codes display	N/A	N/A	list	list	N/A
store facts not in text	—	✔	✔	✔	N/A
MEMOING/ANNOTATION	**○**	**○**	●	○	**○**
text editable	—	✔	✔	—	✔
text markable	—	redlining/underlining/ highlighting	redlining/underlining/ highlighting	—	—
text annotation	✔	✔	✔	—	—
accepts memos	✔	✔	✔	—	✔
memos attached to:	text	text	text	—	databases, analyses, fields
memos/annotations codable	—	—	—	—	—
DATA-LINKING	**○**	**○**	●	—	—
links made within:	T	T/M	T	—	—
links made among:	T-M, T-A	T-M	T-A, T-M, T-O	—	—
SEARCH AND RETRIEVAL	●	●	●	○	**○**
speed	high	high	high	med	low
search request types	● Boolean ● set-logic ● sequence ● proximity **○** wildcard **○** synonyms	**○** Boolean ● sequence **○** proximity ○ wildcard	● Boolean **○** sequence ● proximity **○** wildcard **○** synonyms	**○** Boolean	○ Boolean ○ set-logic
co-occurrence by:	chunk/proximity/ document	chunk/proximity/ document	chunk/proximity/ document/field/section	chunk/document	R[1]
search for:	text strings/cases	text strings/cases	codes/text strings/cases	codes/text strings/cases	cases
select subgroups of data	✔	✔	✔	✔	✔
hits highlighted	string	string	string/chunk	string (arrows, not highlight)	N/A
show hits in context	full	full	full	no	N/A
source tags attached	○	**○**	●	○	●
searches logged, recorded	✔	✔	✔	—	✔
hits editable, processable	✔	—	✔	—	—

	TEXT RETRIEVERS	TEXTBASE MANAGERS			
FEATURES	ZyINDEX	askSam	Folio VIEWS	MAX	Tabletop
CONCEPTUAL/THEORY DEVELOPMENT	—	—	◉	—	◉
outlining	—	—	✔	—	—
system type	—	—	code-retrieve	code-retrieve	logic-based
hierarchical/tree structure	—	—	✔	—	—
other network structure	—	—	—	—	—
link types	single	single	multiple	—	—
logical link properties	none	none	none	none	—
hypothesis-testing	—	—	—	—	—
multi-case configural comparison	—	—	—	—	✔
system closure	—	✔	✔	—	✔
GRAPHICS EDITING	—	—	—	—	○
output quality	—	◉	●	—	○
aesthetic refinements	—	○	—	—	○
intelligent links	N/A	N/A	N/A	N/A	N/A
auto arrange	N/A	N/A	N/A	N/A	by criteria
auto align	N/A	N/A	N/A	N/A	✔
auto space	N/A	N/A	N/A	N/A	✔
different node styles	N/A	N/A	N/A	N/A	preset[2]/specifiable[2]
resizeable nodes	N/A	N/A	N/A	N/A	✔[2]
different link styles	N/A	N/A	N/A	N/A	N/A
segmented links	N/A	N/A	N/A	N/A	N/A
node text	N/A	N/A	N/A	N/A	label[2]
DATA OUTPUT/DISPLAY	◉	◉	●	○	◉
output goes to:	screen/printer/file	screen/printer/file	screen/printer/file	screen/file	screen/printer/file
split or alternate screens	✔	✔	✔	—	✔
matrix output	—	—	—	quant	quant/text
network output	—	—	—	—	—
frequency counts	—	✔	—	✔	✔
numerical data export to:	—	—	ASCII	SPSS/SYSTAT/ dBASE	ASCII
OTHER FEATURES					
customization	◉	●	●	—	○
automation	macros search macros	macros/reports D: Programming	macros / various utility program	none	none
cross-platform portability	—	✔ (DOS ↔ Win)	✔ (Win ↔ DOS) (Win or DOS → Mac)	—	✔(Win ↔ Mac)
USER FRIENDLINESS	○	W: ● / D: ◉	●	◉	●
learning effort required	moderate	moderate	low (High to learn everything)	low	low
tutorials	—	W: ●	●	◉	◉
on-screen help	○	●	●	○	○
documentation	○	◉	◉	◉	◉
tech support	◉	◉	●	◉	◉
easy to use once learned	★★	W: ★★★ / D: ★★	★★	★★	★★★
PRICE $	395	395 99.95 (Educational)	495 150 (Educational)	220	100
OPERATING SYSTEM	DOS [3.1] Windows [3.0]	DOS [2.0] Windows [3.1]	DOS [3.0] Windows [3.0] Mac [System 7]	DOS [2.0]	Windows [3.1] Mac [System 6]
HARDWARE REQUIREMENTS	High density diskette drive, Hard Disk or Network drive	**DOS**: PC, 384K RAM Mono, CGA, EGA, VGA **Windows**: 386 PC 4MB RAM Hard Disk (≥ 5MB free) Windows compatible graphics	**Windows/DOS**: 286 or better 2MB RAM (4MB recommended) One high density floppy drive (3.5" or 5.25") Hard Disk (≥ 17MB free for full installation) **Mac**: 68030 Mac or better 2MB RAM (4MB recommended)	286 or better 540-640K RAM Hard Disk	**Windows**: 386 or better 4MB RAM Hard Disk (≥ 1.5MB free) **Mac**: Mac II or better 2.5MB free RAM Hard Disk (≥ 3MB free)

● strong
◉ OK
○ weak
— absent

N/A Not Applicable

✔ yes
p partially
— no

★★★ definitely
★★ mostly
★ is awkward

D: Dos
W: Windows
(if unspecified, same for both)

Data Types
T text
Q quantitative
G graphic
AU audio
V video

Code Applications
MU multiple
OV overlapping
N nesting

Data Linking
T text
C codes
A annotations
M memos
O off-line

[1] Record
[2] nodes=icons for records

CODE-AND-RETRIEVE PROGRAMS

FEATURES	HyperQual2	Kwalitan	Martin	QUALPRO	The Ethnograph
DATA ENTRY/STRUCTURE	○	◎	◎	◎	◎
editor/word processor	○	○	◎	○	◎
data preformatting	not req'd	req'd	helpful	req'd	req'd
direct data input	✔	✔	—	✔	✔
compatible with word processors	ASCII	ASCII	ASCII	ASCII	MS-Word, WordPerfect, AmiPro
data types accepted	T/G	T	T	T	T
handling of off-line data	◎	—	—	—	—
line numbering	—	— (sentence #'s)	—	✔	✔
data files easily revisable	✔	✔	—	—	—
database structure	records/fields internal-files	unstructured internal-files	unstructured internal-files	unstructured external-files indexed	unstructured internal-files
chunking/unitizing	free-form	flex	free-form	flex	flex
standard chunk sizes	—	sentence/para/page/file	—	line/para/file	line
database capacity	∞ K per file 512MB per stack, 30K per field 16,777,216 cards per stack	65,000 files, ∞ K per file	∞ files 50K per file	1,000 files ∞ K per file	200 files 300K per file
CODING	◎	●	◎	○	◎
code length	keyword	phrase	phrase	keyword	keyword
on-screen (one-step)	✔	✔	✔	—	✔
code applications	MU/OV/N	MU(25)/OV	MU/OV/N	MU(1,000)/OV/N	MU(12)/OV/N
multi-levels	none	more than 2	none	none	more than 2
automated coding	○	◎	—	—	—
code revision easy	★★★	★★★	★★★	★★	★★
codes display	list	list/outline	list	list	list
store facts not in text	✔	✔	—	✔	✔
MEMOING/ANNOTATION	◎	●	◎	○	◎
text editable	✔	✔	✔	✔	✔
text markable	—	—	—	—	—
text annotation	✔	✔	✔	—	—
accepts memos	✔	✔	✔	✔	✔
memos attached to:	text (stack version only)	text/codes	text[3]	—	text
memos/annotations codable	p	p	—	✔	✔
DATA-LINKING	◎ (stack v. only)	◎	○	—	—
links made within:	T (stack v. only)	C	—	—	—
links made among:	T-M (stack v. only)	A-T, M-C	M-T	—	—
SEARCH AND RETRIEVAL	○	◎	○	○	◎
speed	med	med	med	low	med
search request types	○ Boolean	◎ Boolean ◎ wildcard	● Boolean ◎ wildcard	◎ Boolean	○ Boolean ◎ proximity ◎ wildcard
co-occurrence by:	chunk	chunk	chunk	chunk	chunk/proximity document
search for:	codes/text strings	codes/text strings/cases	codes/text strings	codes/cases	codes
select subgroups of data	✔	✔	✔	✔	✔
hits highlighted	string	no	string	no	no
show hits in context	full	limited	full[4] / no[5]	no	no
source tags attached	◎	◎	○	○	◎
searches logged, recorded	—	—	—	—	—
hits editable, processable	—	—	—	—	—

CODE-AND-RETRIEVE PROGRAMS

FEATURES	HyperQual2	Kwalitan	Martin	QUALPRO	The Ethnograph
CONCEPTUAL/THEORY DEVELOPMENT	○	⭘	⭘	—	—
outlining	—	—	—	—	—
system type	code-retrieve	code-retrieve	code-retrieve	code-retrieve	code-retrieve
hierarchical/tree structure	—	✔	✔[6]	—	—
other network structure	—	—	—	—	—
link types	single	single	single	—	—
logical link properties	none	single	none	none	none
hypothesis-testing	—	—	—	—	—
multi-case configural comparison	—	—	—	—	—
system closure	✔	—	✔	—	—
GRAPHICS EDITING	⭘	—	—	—	—
output quality	⭘	—	—	—	—
aesthetic refinements	⭘	—	—	—	—
intelligent links	—	N/A	N/A	N/A	N/A
auto arrange	none	N/A	N/A	N/A	N/A
auto align	—	N/A	N/A	N/A	N/A
auto space	—	N/A	N/A	N/A	N/A
different node styles	preset	N/A	N/A	N/A	N/A
resizeable nodes	—	N/A	N/A	N/A	N/A
different link styles	✔	N/A	N/A	N/A	N/A
segmented links	✔	N/A	N/A	N/A	N/A
node text	extended text	N/A	N/A	N/A	N/A
DATA OUTPUT/DISPLAY	⭘	⭘	⭘	⭘	⭘
output goes to:	file	screen/printer/file	screen/file	screen/printer/file	screen/printer/file
split or alternate screens	✔	—	✔	—	—
matrix output	—	quant	—	quant/codes/text	—
network output	—	—	—	—	—
frequency counts	—	✔	—	✔	✔
numerical data export to:	—	SPSS	—	—	—
OTHER FEATURES					
customization	⭘ (stack v. only)	○	○	○	—
automation	none	none	none	none	none
cross-platform portability	—	—	—	—	—
USER FRIENDLINESS	⭘	●	●	⭘	⭘
learning effort required	low	low	low	low	low
tutorials	⭘	⭘	○	●	⭘
on-screen help	—	⭘	●	⭘	○
documentation	⭘	⭘	●	●	●
tech support	⭘	⭘	⭘	⭘	⭘
easy to use once learned	★★	★★	★★★	★★	★★
PRICE $	180, stack v. 360	250	250	88, Student 44	200
OPERATING SYSTEM	Mac [System: any] HyperCard [2.0 for stack version]	DOS [3.0]	Windows [3.0]	DOS [2.0]	DOS [any]
HARDWARE REQUIREMENTS	1MB RAM 4MB w/System 7 Hard Disk	IBM PC, XT, AT, PS/2 350K RAM Hard Disk recommended, 2 floppies OK	386 or better 4MB RAM Hard Disk VGA monitor, Mouse	IBM PC-any 128K RAM Hard Disk recommended, 2 floppies OK	IBM PC-any 450K RAM Hard Disk (≥ 2MB free)

● strong
⭘ OK
○ weak
— absent

N/A Not Applicable

✔ yes
p partially
— no

★★★ definitely
★★ mostly
★ is awkward

D: Dos
W: Windows
(if unspecified, same for both)

Data Types
T text
Q quantitative
G graphic
AU audio
V video

Code Applications
MU multiple
OV overlapping
N nesting

Data Linking
T text
C codes
A annotations
M memos
O off-line

3 to cards
4 for text string search
5 for code search
6 cards/folders/groups

CODE-BASED THEORY-BUILDERS

FEATURES	AQUAD	ATLAS/ti	HyperRESEARCH	NUD•IST	QCA
DATA ENTRY/STRUCTURE	◯	●	—	◯	◯
editor/word processor	◯	◯	—	◯	◯
data preformatting	req'd	helpful	req'd	req'd	req'd
direct data input	—	✔	—	✔	✔
compatible with word processors	ASCII	ASCII	ASCII	ASCII	ASCII
data types accepted	T	T	T	T/V[8]	Q
handling of off-line data	—	—	—	●	—
line numbering	✔	✔	—	✔	—
data files easily revisable	—	—	—	✔	✔
database structure	unstructured external-files indexed	unstructured external-files indexed	unstructured external-files indexed	unstructured external-files indexed	records-fields internal-files
chunking/unitizing	flex	free-form/auto	free-form	flex	N/A
standard chunk sizes	line	word/sentence/para	word	line/para	N/A
database capacity	1000 files 500K per file	K per file limited by RAM/∞ K total	900 files, ∞ K per file 900 cases	∞ files ∞ K per file	255 vars, ∞ cases
CODING	◯	●	◯	●	N/A
code length	keyword	phrase	phrase	phrase	N/A
on-screen (one-step)	✔	✔	✔	✔	N/A
code applications	MU(10)/OV/N	MU/OV/N	MU/OV/N	MU/OV/N	N/A
multi-levels	2	more than 2	—[7]	more than 2	N/A
automated coding	—	◯	○	●	N/A
code revision easy	★★	★★	★★★	★★★	N/A
codes display	list	list/network	list	list/network	N/A
store facts not in text	✔	✔	—	✔	N/A
MEMOING/ANNOTATION	◯	●	—	◯	◯
text editable	✔	✔ (inadvisable)	—	✔	N/A
text markable	—	—	—	—	N/A
text annotation	✔	✔	—	—	—
accepts memos	✔	✔	—	✔	✔
memos attached to:	text/codes	text/codes/memos/networks/links/ relations/families/projects	—	codes/documents	analyses
memos/annotations codable	✔	✔	—	p	—
DATA-LINKING	○	●	—	○	○
links made within:	—	T/C/M	—	C	—
links made among:	T-M, C-M	T-M, C-M	—	C-O	M-analyses
SEARCH AND RETRIEVAL	○	◯	◯	●	○
speed	med	high	med	med	high
search request types	○ Boolean ○ set logic ◯ sequence ◯ proximity ◯ wildcard	○ Boolean ◯ wildcard ● synonyms ● relational	◯ Boolean	● Boolean ● set logic ● sequence ● proximity ● wildcard ◯ relational	◯ Boolean
co-occurrence by:	chunk/proximity document	chunk	case	chunk/proximity document	case
search for:	codes/text strings	codes/text strings	codes/cases	codes/text strings/cases	cases
select subgroups of data	✔ (limited)	✔	✔	✔	✔
hits highlighted	no	string/code/chunk	no	string	chunk (cases, configurations)
show hits in context	no	full	no	limited	N/A
source tags attached	○	●	●	●	◯
searches logged, recorded	—	—	✔	✔	✔
hits editable, processable	—	✔	✔	✔	✔

CODE-BASED THEORY-BUILDERS

FEATURES	AQUAD	ATLAS/ti	HyperRESEARCH	NUD•IST	QCA
CONCEPTUAL/THEORY DEVELOPMENT	◉	●	◉	●	◉
outlining	—	—	—	—	—
system type	code-retrieve logic-based	code-retrieve logic-based, network-based	code-retrieve rule-based	code-retrieve logic-based, network-based	logic-based
hierarchical/tree structure	—	✔	—	✔	—
other network structure	—	✔	—	—	—
link types	—	specifiable	—	single	—
logical link properties	none	multiple	none	none	none
hypothesis-testing	—	—	✔	—	✔
multi-case configural comparison	✔	—	✔	—	✔
system closure	—	✔	✔	✔	✔
GRAPHICS EDITING	—	◉	—	—	—
output quality	—	○	—	◉	—
aesthetic refinements	—	◉	—	—	—
intelligent links	N/A	✔	N/A	N/A	N/A
auto arrange	N/A	hierarchical	N/A	N/A	N/A
auto align	N/A	—	N/A	N/A	N/A
auto space	N/A	—	N/A	N/A	N/A
different node styles	N/A	preset-w/choices	N/A	N/A	N/A
resizeable nodes	N/A	—	N/A	N/A	N/A
different link styles	N/A	✔	N/A	N/A	N/A
segmented links	N/A	—	N/A	N/A	N/A
node text	N/A	label	N/A	label	N/A
DATA OUTPUT/DISPLAY	○	◉	◉	◉	◉
output goes to:	screen/printer/file	screen/printer/file	screen/printer/file	screen/printer/file	screen/printer/file
split or alternate screens	—	✔	✔	✔	✔
matrix output	quant/codes/text	quant/text	—	text	quant
network output	—	✔	—	✔	—
frequency counts	✔	✔	✔	✔	✔
numerical data export to:	—	SPSS/ASCII	—	—	ASCII
OTHER FEATURES					
customization	○	●	—	—	—
automation	none	none	Replayable searches	command files	none
cross-platform portability	—	—	p	✔ (Win ↔ Mac)	—
USER FRIENDLINESS	◉	●	●	●	○
learning effort required	moderate	moderate	low	moderate	moderate
tutorials	—[9]	—[9]	●	○	—
on-screen help	◉	●	●	—	○
documentation	◉	◉	◉	◉	○
tech support	◉	◉	◉	◉	○
easy to use once learned	★	★★★	★★★	★★★	★★
PRICE $	195	Commercial 395 Educational 275 Student 165	225	Power version 555 (Educ., 333) Entry version 333 (Educ., 200)	25
OPERATING SYSTEM	DOS [2.0]	DOS [3.0]	DOS [5] Windows [3.1], Mac [System 6.0.7] HyperCard [1.2.5]	Mac [System 6.04 or 7.01] Windows [NT or 3.1]	DOS [3.0]
HARDWARE REQUIREMENTS	IBM PC-any 640K RAM Hard Disk (≥ 2MB free)	**Min:** 286 ≥ 20 MHZ 4MB RAM Hard Disk (≥ 2MB free) VGA, Mouse **Recommended:** 386DX 40 MHZ or 486DX with 8MB RAM	**Windows:** 286 or better 4MB RAM 1.44MB floppy drive Mouse **Mac:** 2MB RAM (4MB for System 7) Hard Disk	**Mac:** 2.5-3MB free RAM Hard Disk (≥ 4MB free) **Windows:** 386 or better 5MB free RAM Hard Disk (≥ 4MB free) VGA monitor	IBM PC-any 640K RAM

● strong
◉ OK
○ weak
— absent
N/A Not Applicable

✔ yes
p partially
— no

★★★ definitely
★★ mostly
★ is awkward

D: Dos
W: Windows
(if unspecified, same for both)

Data Types
T text
Q quantitative
G graphic
AU audio
V video

Code Applications
MU multiple
OV overlapping
N nesting

Data Linking
T text
C codes
A annotations
M memos
O off-line

[7] more than 2 during hypothesis-testing only
[8] with add-on
[9] example materials included

CONCEPTUAL NETWORK-BUILDERS

FEATURES	Inspiration	MECA	MetaDesign	SemNet
DATA ENTRY/STRUCTURE	●	○	●	●
editor/word processor	●	—	○	○
data preformatting	not req'd	req'd	not req'd	req'd
direct data input	✔	✔	✔	✔
compatible with word processors	ASCII, MORE III	ASCII	ASCII	ASCII
data types accepted	T/G	T	T/G	T/G
handling of off-line data	—	—	—	—
line numbering	—	—	—	N/A
data files easily revisable	✔	—	✔	✔
database structure	internal-files	external-files	unstructured internal-files	internal-files
chunking/unitizing	N/A	N/A	flex	N/A
standard chunk sizes	N/A	N/A	User-defined delimiters	N/A
database capacity	15K / node ∞ nodes	∞ K per file 500 concepts, 8,000 statements per file	30K text per node, 32,000 nodes total	32,767 concepts, 32,767 relations, 32,767 instances
CODING	N/A	○	—	N/A
code length	N/A	phrase	N/A	N/A
on-screen (one-step)	N/A	—	N/A	N/A
code applications	N/A	—	N/A	N/A
multi-levels	N/A	2	N/A	N/A
automated coding	N/A	○	N/A	N/A
code revision easy	N/A	★	N/A	N/A
codes display	N/A	list/network	N/A	N/A
store facts not in text	N/A	✔	N/A	✔
MEMOING/ANNOTATION	●	—	●	◉
text editable	✔	N/A	✔	✔
text markable	underlining highlighting	—	underlining	—
text annotation	✔	—	✔	✔
accepts memos	✔	—	✔	—
memos attached to:	text/nodes	—	text	concepts, relations
memos/annotations codable	—	—	—	—
DATA-LINKING	●	◉	●	●
links made within:	T/A/M	C	T/M	concepts
links made among:	T-M, T-A	—	T-M, T-A, A-M	—
SEARCH AND RETRIEVAL	◉	○	○	◉
speed	med	med	high	high
search request types	◉ relational	○ set logic	—	—
co-occurrence by:	—	document	—	—
search for:	text strings	—	text strings	concepts
select subgroups of data	✔	✔	✔	✔
hits highlighted	string	N/A	string	N/A
show hits in context	full	N/A	full	limited
source tags attached	N/A	N/A	N/A	N/A
searches logged, recorded	—	—	—	✔
hits editable, processable	✔	—	✔	—

CONCEPTUAL NETWORK-BUILDERS

FEATURES	Inspiration	MECA	MetaDesign	SemNet
CONCEPTUAL/THEORY DEVELOPMENT	◎	○	◎	◎
outlining	✔	—	✔ (among pages)	—
system type	network-based	network-based	network-based	network-based
hierarchical/tree structure	✔	—	✔ (among pages)	✔
other network structure	✔	✔	✔	✔
link types	multiple/specifiable	multiple/specifiable	single	specifiable
logical link properties	none	none	none	multiple
hypothesis-testing	—	—	—	—
multi-case configural comparison	—	—	—	—
system closure	✔	—	—	✔
GRAPHICS EDITING	●	○	●	○
output quality	●	○	●	◎
aesthetic refinements	●	—	●	—
intelligent links	✔	—	✔	—
auto arrange	hierarchical/readability/cluster	readability	hierarchical (among pages)	readability
auto align	✔	—	✔	✔
auto space	✔	✔	✔	✔
different node styles	specifiable	none	specifiable	preset
resizeable nodes	✔	—	✔	—
different link styles	✔	✔	✔	—
segmented links	✔	—	✔	—
node text	label/extended text	label	extended text	label
DATA OUTPUT/DISPLAY	●	○	●	◎
output goes to:	screen/printer/file	file	screen/printer/file	screen/printer/file
split or alternate screens	✔	—	✔	✔
matrix output	—	quant/codes	—	quant
network output	✔	✔	✔	✔
frequency counts	—	✔	—	✔
numerical data export to:	—	ASCII /SYSTAT/SAS	—	ASCII
OTHER FEATURES				
customization	●	—	◎	○
automation	none	none	none	none
cross-platform portability	—	✔	p (DOS→MAC)	—
USER FRIENDLINESS	●	○	●	●
learning effort required	low	moderate	moderate	moderate
tutorials	●	—[10]	●	●
on-screen help	●	○	●	—
documentation	●	◎	◎	●
tech support	◎	◎	◎	◎
easy to use once learned	★★★	★	★★★	★★★
PRICE $	135 Windows, 175 Mac 95 (Educational) 625 (Network/site 10-pack)	60-200	199	to be determined-- see review
OPERATING SYSTEM	Mac [System 6.04 or 7] Windows [3.1]	DOS [2.0] Mac [System 6] Unix [Berkeley]	Windows [3.1] Mac [System 6 or 7]	Mac [System 5.0 minimum, 6.0.5 recommended]
HARDWARE REQUIREMENTS	**Mac:** Mac Plus or better 1MB RAM, 2 800K drives or 1 super drive or Hard Disk **Windows:** 386SX or better, 4MB RAM VGA or better monitor, Math coprocessor used if present; *not required* Mouse	IBM PC XT or better MAC II or better 640K RAM for DOS and MAC 1MB RAM for Unix Hard Disk (≥ 1-2MB free)	**Windows:** 386, 486, Pentium (286 works, but *slowly*) 3MB RAM Hard Disk (≥ 1MB free) Mouse **Mac:** 1MB RAM	512K for small nets 1MB for large ones

● strong
◎ OK
○ weak
— absent

✔ yes
p partially
— no

★★★ definitely
★★ mostly
★ is awkward

D: Dos
W: Windows
(if unspecified, same for both)

Data Types
T text
Q quantitative
G graphic
AU audio
V video

Code Applications
MU multiple
OV overlapping
N nesting

Data Linking
T text
C codes
A annotations
M memos
O off-line

[10] example materials included

N/A Not Applicable

PART III

Reflections and Resources

Part III begins with Chapter 10, "Reflections and Hopes," where we reflect on the current state of software for qualitative data analysis, and talk about the needs we see for future developments and the trends that are, or are not, visible in those directions. We then provide a series of resources for users of the book.

The Appendix contains contact information for all the programs' developers.

The Glossary contains definitions of terms, from both computing and research worlds, that might be new or confusing to readers. We started it by defining all the terms we thought might be difficult, and then built it further by incorporating every suggestion we received from each of 15 reviewers of the manuscript—who ranged in computer use level from 1.5 to 4, and in qualitative data analysis experience from novice to expert—plus quite a few of the developers.

We have also provided a list of Annotated References on computer-aided qualitative data analysis.

Next comes the full list of References for the book, including repeats of the references listed at the end of each review. Following that is the Index.

10

Reflections and Hopes

In this chapter, we first make some reflective generalizations about the state of software for qualitative data analysis, based on the journey we've taken through 24 programs. We'll include what we see as promising signs, and identify some concerns. Then we turn to a discussion of needs and hopes for development, a sort of wish list: What might software look like that closely addresses researchers' special and general needs?

Reflections

Promising Signs

On the upbeat side, if we compare what's available now with what researchers could draw on, say, 5 years ago, there are some real advances. Generally speaking, it's fair to say that user interfaces are much more graphic, friendly, direct, easy, and intuitive than they were before. Mainframelike programs with strict sequences of prompts and limited scrolling and no mouse capability are the exception rather than the rule. That's an important shift, making a large difference in programs' usability.

Back of that change is a historical trend. At first, qualitative researchers mostly had to make do with business-oriented, commercial programs not developed with their needs in mind. Luckily, because commercial developers are well staffed with sophisticated programmers, their programs (e.g., Folio VIEWS, MetaDesign, or Metamorph) are often easy to use. Even so, they often have to be "worked around" to accomplish a particular qualitative analysis task.

The early programs developed by qualitative researchers had researchers' real needs in mind, but were often awkward and hard to use because their developers were not really professional programmers. That picture is changing, as we can see from programs like ATLAS/ti and NUD•IST, where the user interface shows clear signs of thoughtful attention by a developer who combines research interests with strong programming skills.

There's also encouraging evidence that more than a few developers are user-driven, recasting and improving their programs on the basis of actual researcher experience with programs rather than on abstract ideas about the management and analysis of text. Changes of this sort have occurred, for example, in Kwalitan, QUALPRO, The Ethnograph, ATLAS/ti, and NUD•IST.

A specific example of a feature that meets user needs well is casewise data organization, seen best in HyperRESEARCH. In much qualitative work, information relevant to specific cases, such as individuals, is widely scattered through interviews with other people, observations, documents, and the like. Neither a narrow "records-and-fields" approach nor an open "free-form" approach to assembling such data really works well. The HyperRESEARCH ability to build a case file using diverse data from many sources is very useful and deserves wider imitation.

Today's code-and-retrieve capabilities are more flexible and sophisticated, with easier on-screen coding and simpler, richer searching. They more and more include theory-building features, such as memoing, annotation, and multilevel code lists.

More generally, it seems clear that theory building and theory testing are increasingly seen as central features of good programs, and they are being implemented in a more systematic, user-friendly way. Programs that make easy linkages among text, codes, annotations, and memos, or test hypotheses, or display concepts and their linkages in network form, are more frequently found. Software will never "do" theory building for you (see Dreyfus, 1992), but it can explicitly support your intellectual efforts, making it easier for you to think coherently about the meaning of your data. The inductive, grounded-theory approach to understanding qualitative data is now fairly well served, both by simple, straightforward programs like Martin and Kwalitan and by more elegant programs like ATLAS/ti and NUD•IST. Hypothesis-testing features appear in HyperRESEARCH and QCA.

Finally, we'll reemphasize that there are some outstanding—even amazing—programs not designed for qualitative research as such, but quite applicable to the needs of researchers—for example, programs like Folio VIEWS, Metamorph, Inspiration, and MetaDesign.

Some Concerns

The reviewing function. We believe that qualitative data analysis programs, like restaurants, appliances, and cars, will improve in direct relation to the presence of informed user choice and user demand. A book of critical reviews like this one can support user choice and may stimulate demand. But it's no substitute for a regular, *continuing reviewing function* to help link user needs with developer invention and development. As ambitious as this book has been, there are probably at least a dozen other reasonable candidate programs that aren't included. Furthermore, programs are constantly changing and developing. Journal reviews and program descriptions, such as those that have appeared from time to time in *Qualitative Studies in Education, Qualitative Sociology,* or the *CAM Newsletter,* have been sporadic, not a regular feature. Qualitative researchers have nothing like the frequent, regular reviews of software that appear in *PC Magazine, PC Computing, Windows Magazine, Macworld,* or *MacUser.* They deserve something comparable.

User awareness. Beyond the question of informed choice, writing about software should keep emphasizing user awareness of how programs are interacting with the users' analytical work. We like Pfaffenberger's (1988) comment:

> A technology is like a colonial power—it tells you that it is working in your best interests and, all the while it is functioning insidiously to dim your critical perception of the world around you. You will remain its victim so long as you fail to conceptualize adequately what it's up to. (p. 20)

Fielding and Lee (in press), however, caution against an overpessimistic view: "[The fear of] facile analyses, analyses steered in a particular direction by program conventions and features, or the loss of craft skills, does not seem realistic on the basis of experience with programs at their present level of sophistication" (p. 9).

Still, the issue of awareness during use is important. As with the history of quantitative data packages like SPSS, there's the risk of naive, unthinking use of a technology, especially by novices. As Pfaffenberger (1988) points out, it's equally naive to believe that a program is (a) a neutral technical tool or (b) an overdetermining monster. The issue is understanding a program's properties and presuppositions, and how they can support or constrain your thinking to produce unanticipated effects. For example, using a line-level code-and-retrieve program may well lead you in the direction of too-fine analyses and get you bogged down in coding, as Lee and Fielding (in press) found in their study of users. Or using a strong textbase manager may encourage you to collect far more data than you really need because it's so easy to retrieve. Or a program that retrieves chunks without showing you their context may lead you to quite faulty conclusions and interpretations.

We are pleased that empirical studies of this issue are beginning to appear. For example, Weaver and Atkinson (in press) compared the analytical experience of using The Ethnograph 3.0 as a classic code-and-retrieve program with that of a generic hypertext program, GUIDE, using the same database. They found that The Ethnograph, with a cut-and-paste metaphor, tended to encourage "thin," partially predetermined coding schemes that remained static after the first coding pass, and was poor at representing intercode relationships, though it was good at searching. By contrast, GUIDE permitted the creation of multiple, inductive links among data, codes, and memos throughout analysis, and easy movement across analysis levels, avoiding fragmentation; its metaphor is an evolving network of "associative trails." However, there were difficulties in using GUIDE: Getting lost in the network was a risk; GUIDE had to be "authored" and customized as the analysis proceeded; the "cognitive load" was heavier; and production of final analytical text was not easy.

Similarly, Horney and Healey (1991) compared the hypertext program Entryway with a relational database program, Foxbase/Mac; the latter was good at theme finding, content analysis, and concordance making; the hypertext program was better at mapping and browsing among larger information chunks and their linkages. Walker (1993) compared The Ethnograph, GATOR, and Martin on the same database, concluding that The Ethnograph and GATOR were useful in labeling, pattern finding, and synthesis into categories, while Martin in addition helped with developing "thick descriptions."

We believe it's important to do more such comparisons so the connections among program structure, specific features, and possible types of analysis can be made clearer.

User influence on developers. It seems that there are few good channels from users to developers. It's hard for developers to find their users, and users mostly don't know who's trying to create new and better software. Most developers distribute their own products, and qualitative analysis programs don't make it into shareware networks. There has been until recently only one American distributor of programs, Qualitative Research Management, performing a useful function, but it handles only 6 of the 24 programs we review here, and now provides only limited technical support. Other distributors are beginning to appear, but most handle only one or two programs for qualitative analysis.

A few developers (e.g., Kwalitan, NUD•IST, The Ethnograph) have created user networks that provide mutual advice and support as well as feedback on needed features. There is an electronic listserv bulletin board (QUALRSL @UGA.BITNET) that focuses on qualitative research and features frequent discussions about software. Another, QUALNET@CHIMERA.SPH.UMN.EDU, emphasizes qualitative organization studies. In the United Kingdom, there are several university centers (Stirling, Cardiff, Surrey) that provide user advice. The series of International Conferences on Computers and Qualitative Methodology held in 1989 (Surrey), 1991 (Breckenridge), and 1992 (Bremen) has been helpful in building a community of developers, disseminators, and users (though the latter have been underrepresented).

Furthermore, developers of general-purpose programs such as text retrievers or textbase managers don't really know what the real demands of qualitative research are. Even developers who are themselves qualitative researchers may have a narrow view, not understanding what a particular variety of user—say, a grounded theorist, a narrative-oriented, ethnographic, hermeneutic, critical theorist, or action researcher—really needs and wants. We'll discuss these special concerns below.

The basic issue is how to make the market drive constructive development, rather than encouraging developers to make only incremental improvements in a program that doesn't work too well to begin with—or to add complicated bells and whistles just because their competitors are doing so. The focus needs to be on *accessible, useful* features that meet real needs.

Researcher Needs and Hopes for Development

In what follows here, we'll try to play a surrogate role, speaking as best we can to developers on behalf of users. Any wishes and hopes we express here need to be based on real needs. What might they be?

Needs and Hopes Based on the Logic of Qualitative Analysis

First, the needs of qualitative researchers depend on a basic issue: the logic of qualitative analysis they are following—an issue that is not as visible as it should be in the thinking of developers—and, indeed, users. We adapt here ideas from Miles and Huberman (1994), Maxwell (1992), Ragin (1987), and others.

Two basic approaches to analysis. We can distinguish two types of analysis: variable-oriented analysis and case-oriented analysis. A *variable-oriented* approach (Ragin, 1987) is "paradigmatic," dealing with the relations among well-defined concepts. For example, you might study adolescents' decisions to attend college by examining the relationships among variables such as socioeconomic class, parental expectations, school grades, and peer support.

A *case-oriented* approach considers the case as a whole entity, looking at configurations, associations, temporal sequences, causes, and effects within the case—and only then turns to comparative analysis of a limited number of cases. A case-oriented approach is "syntagmatic," or process-oriented, following the events in a specified case context over time (Abbott, 1992; Maxwell, 1992; Mohr, 1982). For example, you might study a particular adolescent, Kim Taylor, over a period of several months to follow the events in her life (such as a poignant discussion with her mother on why she had never worked outside the home, or her friend Jane's experience in dissecting a frog) that were related to her decision to go to veterinary school.

Each approach has pluses and minuses. Variable-oriented analysis works well in finding probabilistic relationships among variables in a large population, but it's poor at handling the usual tangle of local causality (where multiple causes affect each other as well as the final multiple "effects"); it's also weak at handling multiple subsamples, and its findings are often rather general and vague. Case-oriented or process-oriented analysis is good at finding specific, concrete historically-grounded patterns common to small sets of cases, but its findings often remain particularistic and not generalizable.

Howard (1991) has also pointed out that this distinction is not just a researcher preference: We retrieve information from memory in different forms—the paradigmatic and the narrative. We represent much of what we think or remember either through propositions or through stories.

The issue is combining and synthesizing the approaches, as nearly all of the authors just cited emphasize. Good explanations usually involve cycling back and forth between (or synthesizing) strategies aimed at understanding case dynamics *and* at seeing the effect of key variables. As Miles and Huberman (1994) note: "Stories without variables do not tell us enough about the meaning and larger import of what we are seeing. Variables without stories are ultimately abstract and unconvincing" (p. 302).

Two major display types. The variable/process distinction also appears when we consider data displays. There we can see two main categories: matrices and networks. Matrices involve the crossing of two or more main dimensions or variables (often with subvariables) to see how they interact. The cells of a qualitative data matrix typically contain text, not just numbers. Matrices lend themselves well to a variable-oriented analysis style, and they can be expanded to a more holistic case-oriented style (for examples, see Miles & Huberman, 1994).

Networks, on the other hand, are not dimensional in the way matrices are. They involve a series of nodes connected by links. They lend themselves well to a case-oriented, "syntagmatic" approach that re-creates the "plot" of events over time, as well as showing the complex interaction of variables. They give us the kinds of narratives that tend to get chopped up analytically in matrices. They give us process dynamics more easily than matrices do (see also Miles & Huberman, 1994, for examples). But they are less strong than matrices in letting us see systematically how *classes* of variables affect each other.

Related needs and hopes. What do these distinctions imply about needed software features? First, we'd like to see features that permit easy movement from a variable-oriented to a case-oriented view, and vice versa. Most coding schemes are essentially variable-oriented, and it's not always easy to see the text of coded chunks arranged coherently for a *single case, across a number of codes.*

We'd also hope that, within programs, there could be a simple connection between matrix and network display modes. Users should be able to pop from one to another easily.

In many respects, network displays have advanced faster than matrices. Programs such as ATLAS/ti and NUD•IST, for example, offer the user facilities for making network views of codes and their relationships; ATLAS/ti also lets you do the same for relations among chunks, memos, and text files, and you can use many different types of network links (and do memos and annotations for them). Conceptual network-builders such as SemNet, Inspiration, and MetaDesign are quite strong. (We'll have some added suggestions in a minute.)

Matrix displays in existing software are presently quite weak. Researchers need the ability to fill matrices with rich text, not just code references or numbers. A few programs (e.g., NUD•IST, AQUAD, ATLAS/ti) will use codes to retrieve text for each of the cells of a matrix, which you can then insert using your word processor. But usually you don't want all the text; programs need to include much better and easier ways of selecting and reducing text, such as using split or alternate screens to write a shorter, summary version, as in the Orbis/XyWrite combination. Furthermore, no current program actually *produces* text-filled matrix displays; what's needed is automatic tabling and automatic insertion of edited text by cell. The capacity of matrix display programs is also important; in multicase studies, which may involve a dozen or more cases, each with multiple variables, displays can get very big.

Generally speaking, we hope for much easier, richer displays that retain the look and feel of networks and matrices on paper. Good displays are a major support for qualitative data analysis, and users deserve better.

The configurational methods used by the programs QCA and AQUAD are a powerful way to combine a variable-oriented and a case-oriented approach across a number of cases. But at present they're not very user friendly, and they involve a very heavy data reduction. We need better combined methods that can go well beyond 1s and 0s. One possibility is creating routines that would let the user move back and forth easily between a set of case-specific "causal networks" with an associated multicase causal "antecedents matrix," which displays the immediate and remote causes of variables and lets you see the *absence* of causal links too (for detail, see Miles & Huberman, 1994, pp. 233-234).

Needs and Hopes Based on Specific Approaches

It's important to keep in mind that there are many varieties of qualitative researchers, each with differing approaches to drawing conclusions from qualitative data and thus different needs for software features. We can't be exhaustive here[1] but would like to propose some possible needs and related hopes present in six different approaches to qualitative research, as we understand them. We hope these suggestions will encourage researcher-developer dialogue at a far more specific level, getting wish lists clearer and programs built closer to researchers' hopes.

Grounded theory. Researchers in this tradition tend to proceed inductively, examining their text, selecting chunks of it, and applying first-level codes, often in the language of respondents ("in vivo" codes). As they proceed, they begin to generate second-level "pattern" codes or themes with more theoretical power; this work is supported and extended by conceptual memos written to apply across different data chunks, persons, research sites, and so on (see, for example, Chesler, 1987, as reported in Miles & Huberman, 1994, pp. 87-88; Glaser, 1978, 1992; Glaser & Strauss, 1967; Lonkila, in press; Strauss & Corbin, 1990).

Software has served grounded-theory work fairly well with a range of provisions for coding, annotation, and memoing.[2] However, it seems important, heeding Glaser's (1992) warnings about too-easy "forcing" of concepts, to have program features that keep grounded theory really grounded in the data. These might include *text underlining* for "in vivo" codes and use of *wide margins* for restating them more generally; provisions for *chunk sorting and clustering* (as in Martin, HyperQual2, and so on); much easier and more powerful *code revision;* easy, fluid use of *multilevel coding;* and aid, perhaps with *thesaurus or synonym searching*, in finding chunks that can be coded abstractly as "strategies," "causes," or "consequences" (Strauss, 1987). A good program for grounded-theory building also needs to maintain an automatically updated code list in either *hierarchical outline or network* form, so the theory's progress is clearly seen, and the analyst can see when the data set is "saturated" (no new codes emerge from the data).

Narrative studies. Some researchers, as noted above, have a strong interest in narrative, sequence, and chronology. They aim to discover, reproduce, and create basic "stories" and to see if "generic narratives" can be discovered across cases (see, for example, Abbott, 1992; Connelly & Clandinin, 1990; Josselson & Lieblich, 1993; Vitz, 1990).

What are some hopes here? For one, it would be nice to be able to retrieve chunks by actual *chronological sequence* rather than only by their sequence in the text. We have also been musing about the idea of a set of *story templates* that could be called up and used to aid with annotation and/or with narrative production. It may also be that *hypertext* writing programs like Storyspace (Eastgate Systems, 1993) could be thoughtfully adapted for narrative analysis. Finally, it would be good to have a facility where *causal networks* and *the specific analytical narratives* that accompany them could easily be worked on in a split-screen mode; Miles and Huberman (1994) have stressed the importance of their parallel development. ATLAS/ti is helpful on this; you can easily pop up text (notes, memos) that applies to the overall structure, or to specific nodes or links of a network. Or you can place your specific narrative in the background and refer to it at any point as needed.

Ethnography. Social anthropologists and others often aim to produce a comprehensive, wide-ranging description of the patterns and behavioral regularities—the culture—of a social setting, using multiple data sources over a long period of time, with links to general theory (see, for example, Agar, 1986; Wolcott, 1980).

We suggest that ethnographers could benefit in particular from much-expanded *off-line facilities* permitting retrieval and analysis of photos, audiotape, videotape, and extended documents. In addition, flexible, powerful *multilevel coding schemes* should be more available than they are. At present there are only a few programs (e.g., ATLAS/ti, NUD•IST, Kwalitan) that do a reasonable job of linking text, codes at several levels, annotations, and memos. To understand a culture well through a rich range of data and analyses really requires software that will let you navigate easily among different parts of your data set, your codes, your memos, and your evolving conceptual representations—preferably at the click of a mouse—without getting lost or confused. We'd hope for strengthening of current programs with hypertext features to accomplish this.

Interpretivist/hermeneutic analysis. Some researchers emphasize the in-depth analysis of multiple levels of meaning in a text, subject to personal and diverse interpretations, on the part of both researchers and respondents. Coding is used less, and researchers rely more on reading, annotating, and rewriting field notes, rereading this text, and distilling deeper and deeper core meanings (see, e.g., Denzin, 1989; Fischer & Wertz, 1975; Noblit, 1988; Pearsol, 1985; Polkinghorne, 1988).

For researchers working in this style, it seems that *easy annotation* needs to be a central feature, along with *redlining* for elimination of dross, and *highlighting* or *underlining*. One should also easily be able to see the basic *text and annotation in parallel* rather than in a pop-up window. Even more important, one would hope for *multilevel annotation* (which would permit successively higher orders—

1. For reviews of the full range of qualitative research approaches, see Wolcott (1992), Tesch (1990), Jacob (1987), Crabtree and Miller (1992), Denzin and Lincoln (1994, Pt. III), and Miles and Huberman (1994).

2. Lonkila (in press) argues that grounded theory has strongly influenced both the general discussion around qualitative data analysis and the development of certain theory-building programs, notably ATLAS/ti and NUD•IST.

first thoughts, later ones, distilled judgments, and so on). All annotations and memos need to be easily *searchable*.

Critical theorists. Researchers in this tradition aim to clarify and make explicit the "taken-for-granted" aspects of social life—especially oppressive, often invisible power relations in institutions. The aim is to be "emancipatory" and empowering for corrective action (see, for example, Carspecken & Apple, 1992; Popkewitz, 1990). The analytical style is often to move from descriptive data to more interpretive levels, often via dialogue with study respondents, to get at normative meanings and effects of the larger social system.

Here too we might hope for *multilevel annotation*, perhaps in matrix form, where the text could be at the left, and several different columns used at the right to display different levels of analysis, such as objective, normative, or system-level. We might also think of adapting the *"story template"* idea above, perhaps with versions at several levels.

Collaborative or action research. This style of qualitative research involves collective action aimed not just at studying but at improving a social setting. The distance between researchers and "respondents" is reduced as they attack jointly-defined problems and work on their resolution (see, for example, Oja & Smulyan, 1989; Watkins, 1991).

Here we'd hope for features permitting easy comparison/juxtaposition of analyses by different partners. There are usually multiple researchers and multiple field partners, so some kind of common *networked database* is needed with authorship of different contributions identified (as currently implemented in ATLAS/ti, Orbis/XyWrite, and Folio VIEWS). It would be helpful to have more routines for *interresearcher coding reliability*, as in QUALPRO. Showing analyses in *parallel annotation* or *matrix* form would also be very helpful.

Some Cut-Across Needs and Hopes

Regardless of the specific approach being taken to qualitative analysis, we can distinguish some cut-across needs and hopes, which we've labeled as follows: multitasking; closeness to the data; improved coding and chunking; search and retrieval; logging and system closure; information beyond the text; co-occurrence, sequence, and causality; research team use; automation; and a standard "floor."

Multitasking. We don't mean to be implying that every software program should have all the desirable features we've mentioned built in. Wholly comprehensive programs are not only a superhuman task for developers but are unwise—they too easily get complex and cumbersome. The issue is more one of taking a thoughtful approach to *multitasking*, with a user-friendly interface. For example, programs with Windows or Mac System 7 versions can be easily popped out of to your word processor or a statistical analysis program. Or, while you're writing something in your word processor, your search-retrieval software could be doing a long job. With easy multitasking, it's more likely that report writing will be closely linked to analytical work.

For straight DOS users, it might be nice to see more development (with user advice) of *connected* programs, which work as well-linked adjuncts to specific word processors (like Orbis with XyWrite or Nota Bene). Many researchers who already rely heavily on their word processors could get a boost with the use of add-on packages (e.g., for textbase management and conceptual networking). This will naturally require thoughtful collaboration between developers of word processors and of qualitative analysis packages.[3]

Many programs currently encourage use in parallel with word processors (MAX, QUALPRO, and The Text Collector, for example), but they haven't really provided the easy links from their specialized packages to your word processor that exist, for example, in the Orbis/Nota Bene/XyWrite setup.

Another, parallel, hope is for much more sophisticated and friendly programs for linking and managing *qualitative and quantitative* data from the same cases. The qualitative/quantitative distinction is *not* the same as "variable-oriented versus process-oriented." Either general analytical approach can be used with either kind of data. Historically, variable-oriented researchers have often used quantitative data, and case- or process-oriented researchers, qualitative data—but there are many, many examples of the converse in each case.

Furthermore, there is growing agreement in the qualitative research community that linking qualitative and quantitative data in study designs and analyses can enhance validity, develop richer analyses, and lead to deeper theoretical insight (e.g., Brannen, 1992; Greene, Caracelli, & Graham, 1989; Howe, 1985, 1988; Miles & Huberman, 1994; Rossman & Wilson, 1984).

Our hopes here are for much more than the usual exporting of data to SPSS or similar programs. Rather, we'd like to see extensions of programs like MAX that maintain comparable qualitative and quantitative data on a set of cases *and* that would include easily accessible routines for simple, illuminating analyses such as crosstabs, cluster analysis, chi-squares, scatterplots, box-and-whisker displays, and other exploratory data analysis methods (Hartwig & Dearing, 1979).

3. R. Lee and N. Fielding (personal communication) report the existence of WPIndex, a WordPerfect add-on, and a program being built around DataPerfect.

There are many programs available—none reviewed in this book—that can perform key project management functions in qualitative studies: coordination of staff time, data collection, and so on; timelining; and physical document storage and management. Here again we hope for easy linking to such programs, through Windows or other means.[4]

Closeness to the data. Judging from the electronic mail we've seen, many users place high value on "staying close to my data." But this is a complicated issue. Some feel that so-called one-step (on-screen) coding is "further away" from data than coding on hard copy, for example. Some programs (e.g., AQUAD) work at a more abstract, quasi-numerical level than those that stay with fully reported data chunks (e.g., Martin, Kwalitan). Some programs' awkwardness of use (e.g., QUALPRO, The Ethnograph) may have a similar distancing effect: You can't get to your data easily and quickly within the program—you have to use hard copy.

These different meanings of "closeness" point to several hopes. We believe that fears of "losing touch" when using on-screen coding have stemmed primarily from the awkwardness and tedium involved in early versions of programs such as The Ethnograph. It's important for users to see their text and its codes clearly and easily on screen, and not get lost or disoriented as to where they are in their text as they work.

To us, it's clear that flexible, simple, on-screen coding (mouse-dragging to define chunks, unrestricted overlapping and nesting, ability to scroll up and down and recode easily, and so on) actually keeps you in much *closer* contact with your data. ATLAS/ti is the best exemplar here, though it has some limitations (e.g., it only highlights one coded chunk at a time, so doesn't show you overlaps clearly). The hope here is for easy, on-screen, free-form coding that will let you keep your nose right in the data as you read and code, and reread and recode.

Another hope is obvious but apparently hard to implement. Researchers using code-and-retrieve programs ought to be able to see their original text displayed with *code names* attached just where they have been applied—as you might see them on hard copy. We may need some new display ideas: different ways of using margins, interlinear presentation, highlighting with different colors. Some programs (e.g., ATLAS/ti) show you the code names that apply to a segment in a pop-up box, or list them in a box beside the chunk (e.g., Kwalitan, HyperQual2), but none has achieved the most natural display: text with codes alongside. Both TEXTBASE ALPHA, reviewed by Tesch (1990), and The Ethnograph come close; you see the code name on the line before the chunk, with brackets delimiting the chunk. AQUAD has you type in several codes at the end of the first line of the chunk to which they apply, but you're restricted to very brief code names because of space limits, and the end of the chunk is only reported as a line number.

To put it another way, researchers ought to have "pencil-level richness" in their displays, with margins or interlinear spaces usable for codes and annotations. Software designed for use on bigger monitors will help.

A more general hope is for displays that will easily show you not only text and codes, but annotations and memos as well. ATLAS/ti shows you memo windows below the text window. Folio VIEWS is ingenious in showing you icons, or visual attributes marking text such as underlining, boldface, and colors; clicking on the icon or the attribute brings you the note or memo involved. More along these lines would be helpful. Color in particular seems underused to clarify meaning in displays.[5]

These hopes for richer displays may very well mean that software will need to support printers and word processor formats more fully than at present; ASCII, even though it's universally readable, may no longer be adequate.

A third important hope: As we'll emphasize later, retrieved hits always ought to appear in a *controllable context.* That is, a highlighted hit should always appear in its textual surroundings, which you can scroll up and down in to see antecedent and consequent data. And the size of the context boundaries for output should be changeable on-the-fly (from several sentences to a paragraph, section, or the document as a whole).

Improved coding and chunking. To expand a bit on the suggestion above, we hope for simpler *and* more automated chunking and coding features. Chunking via mouse-dragging (as in ATLAS/ti, NUD•IST, Folio VIEWS, HyperRESEARCH, and HyperQual2) should be more widespread. It should also be easier than it is in most programs to do chunking automatically according to sentences, paragraphs, or interview questions. Changing chunk boundaries after initial chunking should be easier. More programs should be designed to work with both strings and codes. It would be nice to see software using some of the features of IZE, a now-discontinued program, including automatic coding of strings that appear on a code list, grouping of chunks for coding, and automatic coding of the immediate context of a string. ATLAS/ti and NUD•IST both do the

4. It's also important to remember that some qualitative analysis software programs can be easily adapted to such uses, as Legewie (1994) has pointed out; he has used ATLAS/ti to keep a personal journal, track staff meetings, maintain a project calendar, and maintain bibliographies.

5. A literal scissors-and-paste method using different colors of paper for different respondents' data has been developed (Radnofsky, 1994); a program for it could probably be developed.

latter. NUD•IST will also automatically create new codes based on the combination of several old codes.

We noted earlier that theory-building features have advanced, including provisions for *multilevel coding*. Programs like ATLAS/ti and NUD•IST can easily find all the lower-level code applications associated with a higher-level one. However, as far as we know, no current program understands that a lower-level code, such as "rain," *automatically* implies the presence of the higher-level code, such as "weather," and assigns the higher-level code. (There's a feature in NUD•IST that lets you do this one code at a time, but it's not automatic.)

Search and retrieval. Some hopes in this domain include wider availability of complex Boolean requests (using parentheses); more flexibility in specifying the scope, range, or context of a search (e.g., within a sentence, paragraph, page, section, or a complete document); wider availability of synonym searches (as in Metamorph); and increased use of set logic search requests (as in Metamorph, ZyINDEX, NUD•IST, and AQUAD). Quantitative programs such as SPSS have excellent dialog boxes to let you choose variables and operators for complex search requests quickly and easily. For qualitative analysis, the need is for dialog boxes that will let you see and choose from codes, strings, search operators, and choices to select subsets of your data.

We also believe that straightforward "bundling" of hits into a collection for output, while useful, needs to be supplemented by more flexible output. You need to be able to look at each hit, scroll around in it, expand or contract the size of the surrounding context, edit or select parts of the hit or even discard it, and *then* export it to another display, such as a matrix or list. Orbis/XyWrite does all this easily, and more programs should.

We'll also reemphasize that annotations and memos need to be easily searchable—not just coded chunks and strings in the text.

Logging and system closure. We also hope for much more widespread availability of features that maintain a detailed *log* of analysis operations as you go. That not only helps analysts steer their strategies as they go, but leaves an "audit trail" that can be used for later write-up and/or verification by another analyst. The best of such features truly entail *system closure*: The results of analysis are not just recorded but can be used to execute later analyses; you can click on an earlier analysis and bring it up instantly for redoing, reworking, or combining with a new one.

Information beyond the text. A number of programs now include a "header"/"face-sheet"/"speaker ID" function that records *factual information* about cases, whether or not that information appears in the text being analyzed. These headers are often used to sort cases for selective analysis. We believe such functions need to be considerably expanded, both to enrich the range of real-world information included, and to make it available in a relational database format so that it's possible to link across multiple data tables.

Co-occurrence, sequence, and causality. As Richards and Richards (1994) point out, even though codes co-occur in a chunk or even larger region of text, that does not necessarily tell us anything about their actual causal or temporal relation in the world the text refers to. To find that a chunk coded BETRAYAL is followed shortly by one coded ANGER in a particular interview does not tell us anything very illuminating. The actual events may have been, for example, as follows:

1. *Person A betrayed a confidence offered by Person B; Person B was furious.* That's the conclusion we might have leapt to. *But* the events may have been otherwise. For example:
2. *Person A was angry at Person B and decided to reveal the confidence.* The causality is reversed, and the anger belongs to a different person. *Or*:
3. *Person A betrayed a confidence offered by someone, but it had nothing to do with Person B, who was angry about something else.* No causal connection at all.

We've discussed this issue in our reviews of HyperRESEARCH and AQUAD. We definitely need programs to give us co-occurrences and find the sequence of coded chunks and strings. But this is not enough; the basic need for software is to include *connected social "facts"*—within or across our cases, and organized temporally—that can be used in conjunction with the text chunks we code and retrieve to understand causal sequences. Some annotation facilities could be used for making "cause notes," for example.

Research team use. Qualitative research is more and more frequently carried out by research teams (often multidisciplinary and multilevel) rather than by individuals (Miles & Huberman, 1994). Even solo researchers often involve colleagues as advisers or "critical friends." Lee and Fielding (in press) have documented the problems of research teams in reconciling diverse perspectives during coding and other analytical operations, in spotting and correcting errors, and in using software effectively on a shared basis.

About half of the programs described here are set up for network use, so that team members can each work on a common database. However, simple "network use" is not sufficient for supporting team use well. Normally, effective network use requires specifying levels of access to the data (with some basic files editable only by team leaders, for example, but "multiauthoring" possible on others) along with other special facilities. Such facilities appear in ATLAS/ti, ZyINDEX, Orbis/XyWrite, and Folio VIEWS. In ATLAS/ti, any coded chunks have a tag showing which member of the research team did them, and all chunks by specific coders can be filtered out for analysis. The "redlining" feature of Orbis/XyWrite permits different members to edit or update text, and then dates and tags their contributions. ZyINDEX has levels of access (full and read-only) and can distinguish between "public" and private notes and hyperlinks. We'd like to see more use of "shadow files," copies of texts that can be customized, annotated, edited, and coded differently by different team members, as in Folio VIEWS.

Coder reliability checks are a useful feature, but only QUALPRO includes this explicitly; AQUAD has a coefficient of agreement that can be adapted for this purpose.

Some programs let you export your complete coding scheme for use by another researcher or in a new data set (Martin, Kwalitan, ATLAS/ti, NUD•IST). Very few programs (Martin and ATLAS/ti) provide facilities that help you transfer a complete data set—text, codes, annotations, and memos—easily to another computer without having to copy everything laboriously, file by file. That facility is essential for research teams.[6]

Automation. On balance, it's probably desirable for developers to include features that will run more or less automatically and reduce labor-intensive input by users. For example, programs using standard chunking should provide a facility for doing this (always overridable, of course); more programs should include automatic attachment of codes to found strings, automatic second-level coding, and so on. We have encountered instances where developers deliberately refused to include such features (e.g., HyperQual2, The Ethnograph) on the grounds of "loss of contact with the data." Similarly, the AQUAD program was deliberately designed *not* to bring you full search hits automatically, only their line numbers—which is supposed to make you think more "abstractly." Such restrictions seem inappropriate to us; developers should not prejudge how their products will be used, and should not put "governors" on programs to reduce their speed and power. Developers should give users the tools to be rigorous and not try to "enforce" rigor by truncating their designs.

6. The question of data set transfer to other *programs* is also important. At present, this is only partially approached through ASCII files. It may be that the next step is developer agreement on languages such as SGML (Standard General Markup Language) that will permit it.

It can be argued that too much automation will make for superficial, mindless analysis; it can also be argued that automation will promote more rigor through easier replication, cross-checking, and testing of assumptions and conclusions. But these arguments need to be resolved empirically, not asserted a priori.

A standard "floor." In the world of word processors, certain things are now taken for granted; you should be able to center text, justify it, control margins, cut and paste blocks of text, have a spell-checker, and so on. We think there is a parallel case to be made for qualitative analysis software.

At the minimum, we'd suggest, a good program should include the following:

- some facility for managing files in the database
- simple, natural on-screen (one-step) coding
- easy, rich searching for both codes and strings (including Boolean, proximity, and sequence operators)
- search hits displayed in full, controllable context
- provision for annotating and memoing, with such products searchable and linked to each other
- some form of logging
- some method of display of conceptual schemes (outlines, networks)

Note that we are *not* suggesting the creation of an "ideal" program; there is no such workable thing, given the diversity of analytical approaches and databases. Nor are we suggesting uniformity; continued innovation is essential. Rather, our hope is for more or less accepted minima that a good program should incorporate in some form.

Concluding Comments

Software for aiding qualitative analysis has burgeoned in the last decade. The analyst looking for help in setting up databases, doing coding, searching and retrieving relevant data segments, thinking about the meaning of data, and developing and testing theories to explain findings now has an amazing range of choices. But as we've noted, the fit between what qualitative researchers need and what they're getting is not as close as it should be. We hope our reflections and critical comments will support steady, sustained dialogue between users and developers and keep bringing us richer, more powerful tools for qualitative work.

Appendix

PROGRAM DEVELOPERS AND DISTRIBUTORS

AQUAD: Günter L. Huber, University of Tübingen, Department of Pedagogical Psychology, Münzgasse 22-30, D-72070 Tübingen, Germany. Phone: 49-7071-292113. Fax: 49-7071-294954. E-mail: 100115.230@compuserve.com*

askSam: askSam Systems, P.O. Box 1428, Perry, FL 32347. Phone: (800) 800-1997; (904) 584-6590 (support). Fax: (904) 584-7481.

ATLAS/ti: Thomas Muhr, Scientific Software Development, Trautenaustr. 12, D-10717 Berlin, Germany. Phone and fax: 49-30-861-1415. E-mail: thomas.muhr@tu-berlin.de*

Folio VIEWS: Folio Corporation, 5072 North 300 West, Provo, UT 84604. Phone: (801) 229-6700; (800) 543-6546 (sales); (801) 229-6650 (support). Fax: (801) 229-6790.

HyperQual2: Raymond V. Padilla, 3327 N. Dakota, Chandler, AZ 85224. Phone: (602) 892-9173.*

HyperRESEARCH: ResearchWare, Inc., P.O. Box 1258, Randolph, MA 02368-1258. Phone: (617) 961-3909. E-mail: paul@bcvms.bc.edu

Inspiration: Inspiration Software, Inc., 2920 S.W. Dolph Court, Suite 3, Portland, OR 97219. Phone: (503) 245-9011; (800) 775-4292. Fax: (503) 246-4292.

Kwalitan: Vincent Peters, Postbus 9104, 6500 HE Nijmegen, The Netherlands. Phone: 31-80-612038/615568. Fax: 31-80-612351. E-Mail: U211384@vm.uci.kun.nl

Martin: Simonds Center for Instruction and Research in Nursing, School of Nursing, University of Wisconsin—Madison, 600 Highland Ave., Madison, WI 53792-2455. Phone: (608) 263-5336. Fax: (608) 263-5332. E-mail: pwipperf@vms2.macc.wisc.edu

MAX: Udo Kuckartz, Free University of Berlin, Institute for Social and Adult Education, Arnimallee 12, D-

14195 Berlin, Germany. Phone: 49-30-838 5539; 49-30-813 7201 (distributor and Thursday hotline). Fax: 49-30-838 5889.*

MECA: Kathleen Carley, Department of Social and Decision Sciences, Carnegie Mellon University, Pittsburgh, PA 15568. Phone: (412) 268-3225. E-mail:kathleen.carley@centro.soar.cs.cmu.edu

MetaDesign: Meta Software Corporation, 125 Cambridge-Park Drive, Cambridge, MA 02140. Phone: (617) 576-6920. Fax: (617) 661-2008.

Metamorph: Thunderstone, Expansion Programs International, Inc., 11115 Edgewater Drive, Cleveland, OH 44102. Phone: (216) 631-8544. Fax: (216) 281-0828.

NUD•IST: Qualitative Solutions and Research Pty. Ltd, Box 171, La Trobe University Post Office, Melbourne, Vic. 3083, Australia. Phone: 61-3-459-1699. Fax: 61-3-479-1441. E-mail: tom@qsr.latrobe.edu.au U.S. and Canada distributor: Learning Profiles, Inc., Attn. Jim Adams-Berger, 2329 West Main St. #330, Littleton, CO 80120-1951. Phone: (303) 797-2633, x-17. Fax: (303) 797-2660. E-mail: jimab@omni.org

Orbis: The Technology Group, 36 South Charles Street, Suite 2200, Baltimore, MD 21201. Phone: (410) 576-2040. Fax: (410) 576-1968.

QCA: Kriss A. Drass and Charles C. Ragin, Center for Urban Affairs and Policy Research, Northwestern University, 2040 Sheridan Rd., Evanston, IL 60208-4100. Orders: Audrey Chambers. Phone: (708) 491-8712. E-mail: kadrass@nevada.edu; cragin@nwu.edu

QUALPRO: *Impulse* Development Co., 3491-11 Thomasville Rd., Suite 202, Tallahassee, FL 32308, or Dr. Bernard Blackman, 2504 Debden Court, Tallahassee, FL 32308-3035. Phone: (904) 668-9865. Fax: (904) 668-9866.*

SemNet: SemNet Research Group, 1043 University Avenue, Suite 215, San Diego, CA 92103-3392. Phone: (619) 232-9334. E-mail: jfaletti@sciences.sdsu.edu, or kfisher@sciences.sdsu.edu

Sonar Professional: Virginia Systems Software Services, Inc., 5509 West Bay Court, Midlothian, VA 23112. Phone: (804) 739-3200. Fax: (804) 739-8376.

Tabletop: TERC (Technical Education Research Centers), 2067 Massachusetts Ave., Cambridge, MA 02140. Phone: (617) 547-0430. Distributor: Broderbund Software, P.O. Box 6125, Novato, CA 94948-6125. Phone: (800) 521-6263.

The Ethnograph: Qualis Research Associates, P.O. Box 2070, Amherst, MA 01004. Phone: (413) 256-8835. Fax: (413) 256-8472. E-mail: qualis@mcimail.com*

The Text Collector: O'Neill Software, P.O. Box 26111, San Francisco, CA 94126. Phone: (415) 398-2255.

WordCruncher: Johnston & Co., P.O. Box 6627, Bloomington, IN 47407. Phone: (812) 339-9996. Fax: (812) 339-9997.

ZyINDEX: ZyLAB Division, ZyCO International, Inc., 19650 Club House Road, Suite 106, Gaithersburg, MD 20879. Phone: (301) 590-2760; (800) 544-6339. Fax: (301) 590-0903.

* These programs are also distributed and in some cases supported by Qualitative Research Management, 73425 Hilltop Road, Desert Hot Springs, CA 92240. Phone: (619) 329-7026.

Glossary

We've formatted this Glossary with extra room in the margins for your note taking, scribbles, and other annotations.

Annotation: A brief remark, comment, abstract or summary that's directly linked to one or several lines of text. Memos, by contrast, are typically longer and may be linked to a variety of things in addition to a single spot in the text. See also **Memo**.

ASCII: (pronounced "askie") "Pure" text (including numbers) that doesn't have special formatting commands like those inserted by word processors or other programs (e.g., underlining, boldface, centering). From American Standard Code for Information Interchange. "Pure" text files on the Macintosh are often referred to as "plain text" files.

Audit trail: A record of work that has been done. Can be used to check the steps in an analysis, or to attempt to reproduce results. In some programs, an audit trail can be "replayed" so that the program automatically repeats the recorded actions.

Autocoding: See **Automated coding**.

Automated coding: The computer does *not* read your text and decide how it should be coded! Rather, it may do things like apply a code wherever a search string you specify occurs, or apply a new code (or alter existing coding) wherever a specified combination of codes has already been applied.

Automation: Some software allows you to automate various procedures through "macros" and "programs." There are two types of macros.

In one, called "keystroke macros," the software has the ability to remember a series of keystrokes, including those you use to navigate menus and give commands. So, if you have a repetitive task, you can do it once, record it, and then "play it back," so that the computer does the whole task by itself.

Another type of macro has a "macro language," which allows you to write out the set of steps you want the software to carry out, including commands to issue and text to insert.

"Programs" are usually more intelligent than macros, allowing complex IF . . . THEN statements and various error-catching devices.

Batch program/file: A file that contains several commands in sequence; typing the name of the batch file will execute all the commands.

Beta-test version: A near-final, prerelease version of a program that's undergoing evaluation by expert users. Usually will have some bugs and/or missing features.

Boolean logic: Logical operations such as AND, OR, XOR (either A or B but not both), and NOT, based on Boolean algebra; often used in formulating search requests (see **Search**). See also Ragin (1987, pp. 86-102) for an overview of Boolean algebra; see also **Set logic**.

Braces: The characters { and }.

Brackets: The characters [and].

Browse: The activity of looking through one or several files, not necessarily with a precise search objective in mind. As a search option, usually lets you see search results right in the original files (in full context) rather than just seeing the extracted found text (hits).

Bug: An error in a program. May have minor consequences such as displaying information incorrectly (e.g., in the wrong position) or major consequences such as crashing the computer and losing your data. See **Crash**.

Button: In Windows and Mac displays, a place (usually marked with an icon) where you can click with a mouse to perform some command (e.g., save, search, browse, print). In hypertext programs, an icon you can click on that lets you make a link between two places in text that you consider related. Subsequent clicking on the "button" will jump you immediately to the linked place.

Case: The unit of analysis for a given study. Examples of cases: James Robertson, a third-grade student; Brenda Keeler as she works in her third-grade classroom; the social studies department at Washington School; Washington School in its district context; the ABC reading program as implemented in all of the district's schools; the school district in its community and state context. A qualitative case usually includes a key social unit as the focus of attention, embedded in its surrounding context. (Quantitative cases, whether of individuals or larger units, usually strip away the context.)

Character: A digit, letter or symbol, usually occupying one space on the computer screen.

Chunk: A segment of text, which can be as short as a single character, word, or sentence, or as long as a paragraph, a page, or an entire document.

Code-and-retrieve program: Program that helps you divide text into chunks, attach codes to chunks, and retrieve chunks with one or a combination of codes.

Code-based theory-builder: Program that extends code-and-retrieve capabilities to include theory-building features such as higher-order classifications, code networks, or making and testing of propositions.

Codes: Words or phrases attached to a chunk of text that indicate its meaning, or what category it falls into. These may be all at one conceptual level (e.g., "rain," "hail," "snow," "sunny," "cloudy") or include higher-level codes (e.g., "weather reports") that subsume other codes. Codes can thus be hierarchically organized.

Conceptual network-builder: Program that helps you clarify concepts and theory via systematically built, semantically meaningful graphic networks.

Concordance: A collection of search **Hits**, usually showing each hit embedded in the midst of the line of text it occurs in, along with a page or line reference. Concordances may also include only the hit and the page reference, and thus can be used for making a conventional index of your text.

Configural analysis (or configurational analysis): See **Cross-case configural analysis**.

CPU: The central processing unit of a computer. For personal computers, the main chip—identified in IBM and compatibles as 286, 386, 486, Pentium, and so on, and in Mac as 68030, 68040, and so on. The term has also sometimes been used to refer to the main box of the computer that holds all the hard and floppy drives and into which you plug your monitor, keyboard, printer, and other peripherals, though this use is somewhat outdated.

Crash: When a program, or in the worst cases the entire computer, stops responding to your commands or keystrokes, or shuts down entirely. In some cases, the machine may simply reboot (momentarily turn off and then restart). In almost any case, any data you have not saved before the crash is irretrievably lost, though the program can often be used again. A *hard disk* **crash** is very serious; the hard disk completely stops functioning, cannot be restarted, and *all data on it are lost,* though, if you're lucky, a specialist may be able to retrieve some of it.

Cross-case configural analysis (CCA): A type of analysis conducted across several cases to find case-specific patterns of predictors associated with an outcome, as described by Ragin (1993a, 1993b). Working with true/false variables (such as presence or absence of a code), you specify the outcome variable you're interested in, and the program goes through the cases in your database, generating a list of all the combinations of predictors associated with this outcome, removing redundancies. It then uses **Boolean logic** to reduce these patterns, finding the common necessary elements of the patterns.

Customization: Program capacity that permits you to change features such as screen color, screen layout, menus, hot-keys, keyboard options, formatting of output, and other aspects of program operation.

Database: A more or less systematically-organized set of data. Databases may include both text and numerical information.

"Flat-file" databases consist of a single table of data. The records (see **Records and fields**) are arranged sequentially, and each has a certain fixed collection of data, organized by fields (see **Records and fields**).

"Free-form" databases don't require every record to have the same field structure.

"Relational" databases (Codd, 1990; Kalman, 1991) have several connected tables of data. For example, one table might have a record with information on each doctor at a clinic. Another table might have information on each patient, including his or her doctor's name. When you ask for the information on a given patient, the patient's information from the second table and the doctor's information from the first table can all be presented together, as one record.

Nonrelational databases access records sequentially, so that the user navigates through them one at a time or makes simple searches.[1] Relational databases access records at a logical level; the user defines a request, naming or giving examples of the information wanted, and the software decides on the best way to organize and present the results.

Database management system (DBMS): A program for managing databases. Often called a "database program." Examples are dBASE, FoxPro, Access, and Paradox.

Data linking: Feature that lets you make direct, structural connections among or between chunks of text, codes, annotations, memos, or files. "Direct" means that if you are, for example, looking at an annotation, the linked chunk of text will be automatically visible or retrievable for you. See also **Hypertext**.

DBMS: See **Database management system**.

Default: The value of a program option that will occur normally (by default) unless you choose to change it. For example, the default time for automatic saving might be every 30 minutes, or the default line spacing might be single space.

Delimiter: One or more characters, such as a period, paragraph marker, or symbol like @, $, or #, used to signal the beginning and end of a chunk. Other naturally occurring examples include **parentheses** ( ), **brackets** [ ], and **braces** { }.

Dialog box: A window on the screen that lets you specify several options, commands, or parts of a command at once. May contain boxes into which you type information, lists to select from, and check boxes to click on and off.

1. There are also sophisticated database structures, such as object-oriented databases (which we don't deal with here), that provide nonsequential access, but are also not relational. We're oversimplifying a bit by contrasting databases that are relational with those that aren't.

Directory: A division of your hard or floppy disk. You can create multiple directories to store different groups of files (see **File**), and you can create subdirectories within directories. This makes it possible to organize your files and find them more easily. On a Macintosh, directories are called folders.

Driver: A routine in a program, often contained in a separate file, that the program uses to run the printer, the video display, the keyboard, or other features.

Fields and records: See **Records and fields**.

File: The basic unit of organization for the information in your computer. For example, each document (letter, interview text, article, and so on) you create with your word processor gets stored in its own file. In addition to basic text, files can include graphics, programs, specialized files produced by programs, system or device drivers, or commands assembled into a batch.

Folder: See **Directory**.

Free-form text: Text without any particular formatting constraints, or substantive structure, arranged on the page or screen in whatever way you like. Often used in contrast to a strict **records and fields** approach, or structured text, such as that in interview questions and answers.

Fuzzy search: See **Search**.

Graphical user interface (GUI): Lets you interact with the computer using a graphical display. Gives you information graphically and lets you issue commands by pointing to what you want with a device such as a mouse. GUIs typically rely a lot, for example, on **dialog boxes**. The most common examples are the Macintosh System, Microsoft Windows, OS/2, and XWindows for Unix.

Graphic-mapper: Program that provides a graphical representation of concepts, usually shown as **nodes**, and their relationships, usually shown as **links**. Links may be named (e.g., "implies," "requires," "is part of") or only understood generally as "connected to." See also **Conceptual network-builder**.

GUI: pronounced "gooey." See **Graphical user interface**.

Header: Information attached to a file indicating its characteristics (e.g., the individual, situation, or time it's about, or background or demographic information). See also **Source tag**. In printed output, "running headers" appear at the top of each page, showing section or chapter, page number, or the like. "Headers" may also mean the titles of sections in a text.

Hit: A retrieved chunk, found in response to a search request.

Hot-key: A key (such as <F10>) or key combination (such as <Alt-X>) that has been set up to issue a complex command; instead of typing out the command, you just hit the hot-key—don't even have to press <Return>.

Hyperlink: See **Hypertext**.

Hypertext: A nonlinear approach to connecting various noncontiguous pieces or sources of information, and permitting rapid movement among them. On the one hand, hypertext can be implemented with explicit, fixed, or "hard" links. Another approach to hypertext is referred to variously as implicit, dynamic, or intelligent hypertext (McAleese, 1993)

With *explicit* hypertext, you have text or other material that includes links and associations among chunks of text (or other "objects," such as graphics, memos, or whole files); by hitting a key or clicking on a "button" or icon, you "jump" instantly to the linked item. Hypertext-creating programs are designed to create such links, and may also keep a record of your "navigation" from item to item along a trail of links.

Implicit hypertext is accomplished by having the computer carry out various actions, such as a search for other places where the same word or phrase as you are reading occurs, so that you jump around among the places in the text where the same topic is discussed. For a more extended discussion of hypertext, see Chapter 3, under "Data Linking/Hypertext."

Icon: A graphical symbol that indicates the meaning of a program, file, command, and so on. Usually can be used to issue a command by clicking on it with a mouse.

Import: To bring data into a program (typically data created by a different program) and store it in that program's **proprietary format.** Normally, the original data file is untouched, and the information in it is simply *copied* into a new file created by the program.

Indexing (of database): Approach used in textbase managers and text retrievers to aid fast searching. The program creates an "index" separate from the actual data files, then searches the index rather than the files themselves to find wanted material.

Keyword in context (KWIC): A listing of all occurrences of a word (or phrase), with a set amount of each occurrence's surrounding context (typically you get the entire line on which the word occurs).

Keywords: In this book, largely synonymous with **codes,** though formally a keyword actually exists in the text, while a code is a label applied to the text, but need not actually appear in the text. May also mean a character string, as in **keyword in context** searches, where a word or phrase you're searching for is retrieved and displayed within a line or two of surrounding text. In information retrieval systems such as "Psychlit," "ERIC," or library reference retrieval systems, "keyword" means a tag, placed in or ahead of the text, that summarizes some aspect of the material in a particular article, book, and so on.

KWIC: See **Keyword in context**.

LAN: See **Network (2)**.

Link: Formally, a connection between two nodes in a network. See also **Relation**. In a program, a direct connection between various "objects" (see **Object**), such as chunks, codes, annotations, memos, analyses, files, or off-line material.

Local area network (LAN): See **Network (2)**.

Macro: See **Automation**.

Matrix: A crossing of two lists, appearing as the rows and columns of a grid. Rows and columns can be defined as persons, roles, cases, concepts, times, or other variables. Each row-column intersection is a "cell." The entries in cells can be numbers or text. Numerical matrices can be processed by spreadsheet and statistical programs. For analysis of text matrices, see Miles and Huberman (1994, chap. 9).

Memo: Material written by you, reflecting, commenting on, abstracting, or summarizing themes or issues in text, codes, project methods, or other general topics: essentially, recording your thinking about your project. Longer than an **annotation**, it may be linked directly to codes, discontinuous chunks of text, files, or other memos, while annotations are typically just linked to a single spot in the text.

Memoing: Program feature that lets you write memos and directly link them to codes, to text, to one or several files, or to other memos.

Menu: A list of choices, usually appearing in a "pull-down" or "pop-up" mode, that lets you execute specific commands, either by mouse clicks or by a keystroke.

Navigation: Moving around in a file or group of files. In hypertext programs, the activity of moving along an associative trail of links from one place to another in text. You should be provided with information that helps you know where you are, so you don't get bewildered and lost. See **Hypertext**.

Network (1): A collection of **nodes** or points, connected by lines (**links**). Nodes usually have specific names or labels, and can represent people, events, chunks of text, variables, concepts, and so on. Links may be a simple connection, or may have specified meanings, such as "causes," "is a kind of," or "includes." Links may vary in strength, and be unidirectional or bidirectional. Networks can also show chronology and causation. A hierarchy or "tree" is a special form of network.

Network (2): A connected group of computers that can to varying degrees interact and share programs and data. Also called a local area network or LAN. May have a central computer called a file server, which holds programs and data files for use by the other computers, or "workstations," on the network.

NEXIS: A commercial on-line information service providing access to a wide range of publications and transcripts, primarily from the news media.

Node: A point in a **network**, often represented by a rectangle, ellipse, or other symbol. May hold extensive text or just a label, depending on the program.

Numerical operators: Indicators of quantitative relationships. For example:

= equals
< less than
> greater than
≤ less than or equal to
≥ greater than or equal to
<> not equal

Object: A generic name for any piece of information: may be a chunk of text, a drawing, a memo, a network node, a chart, or the like. See also **Object linking and embedding**.

Object linking and embedding (OLE): The name used by Windows for a process that lets you take an object created by one program and place it in a document in another program, while still keeping it connected to its original application. For example, you can "embed" a piece of a spreadsheet in a word processing document, such as a report, and have it appear and print as part of the report. If you want to edit the spreadsheet table from within your word processor, you can double-click on it, and the spreadsheet program will appear temporarily so you can make your changes. If you "link" the object as well as embedding it, any time you change the original document (e.g., the spreadsheet), the changes will automatically be made to the object embedded in the new document. On a Macintosh, this process is called Publish and Subscribe.

Off-line: Information (such as audio, video, or text) that is usually not loaded into the computer. Programs that can handle off-line data may be able to keep track of a reference to the information (the videotape is in drawer 22 of the cabinet) or actually access it when it is needed (the videotape in the recorder will jump to minute 1.63 to display a specific coded chunk you are searching for).

OLE: (pronounced olay) See **Object linking and embedding**.

On-the-fly: In the midst of a process. For example, reviewing and editing search hits **on-the-fly** means you get to read each search hit, and edit it, *as the search progresses*. Changing program options **on-the-fly** means you can alter the way a command is executed *while it's happening*.

One-step coding: Applying codes to text on screen, in a single step. By contrast, two-step coding requires you to mark up your codes on a line-numbered printout of your text (step one) and then, one at a time, type in codes and the line numbers of the text segments they are to be attached to (step two). See Chapter 3 for a fuller discussion.

Operating system: The basic program that gets your computer running, accepts your commands, and controls your computer's operations as you load programs and issue commands. For personal computers, the most common operating systems are MS-DOS and the Macintosh System; Windows is an enhancement of DOS. Unix is a workstation and mainframe operating system.

Output: Information resulting from program operations, such as retrieved chunks, summary statistics, code networks; may appear on screen, be saved to a file, or printed.

Parentheses: The characters (and).

Phonetic search: See **Search**.

Platform: Broadly, the operating system and associated hardware. A program that's "portable" across platforms lets you move your data from one to another, say, from your IBM laptop to the Mac in your office.

Proprietary format: A file format that only the program that created the file can read. Most programs, including word processors, database managers, spreadsheets, and graphics programs, store data in proprietary format. This allows them to store information about things like formatting and footnotes, keep track of records and fields, and record graphics information. By contrast, **ASCII** files have nothing but plain characters (letters, numbers, and symbols like !@#$%^&*[]{}) in them (see **ASCII**).

Proximity search: See **Search**.

RAM: Random access memory, the memory the computer uses to temporarily hold your program and data while you are using them. In contrast to a hard or floppy disk, information in RAM is temporary, and will be lost when the computer is turned off if it is not saved to a file on a disk. Programs require differing amounts of RAM in order to run: Check to make sure you have enough for the program you want to use!!! If not, depending on the capacity of your computer, you may be able to buy and install additional RAM in the form of chips or cards.

Records and fields: A flat-file database, the simplest example, is arranged into records and fields. Think of records as the rows in a table, and fields as the columns. Generally, you have a row, or record, for each observation or unit of analysis. For example, if your database has information on a group of teachers, you might have one record for each teacher (Brenda Keeler, Michael Logan, and so on).

Each record is divided into fields, which correspond to the variables on which you have information. To continue the example, you might have a field for the teacher's last name, one for first name, one for ID number, one for gender, one for attitude toward school, one for experience as a teacher, one for comments about the principal, and so on.

Note that records can be set up not only for individuals but for groups (the social studies, art, and English departments) or organizations (Washington School, P.S. 122, and so on).

Relational databases (see **Database**) also have records and fields. Free-form databases are very flexible; they permit having a common field structure but do not require it.

Relation: A named link in a network. Examples of relation are "is a kind of," "leads to," "includes," "loves," "requires."

Relational database: See **Database**.

Relational DBMS: A DBMS that works with relational databases (see **Database**).

Relational search: Searching through a database based on the relations among items. Typically, this means searching for all codes, or nodes, in a network that are linked, or *related,* to a starting code or node, and retrieving the text found there.

Scrolling: Moving the text up, down, or sideways as it appears on screen. "Scrolling up" gives you the feeling of moving the cursor back up (the text is actually moving down). In Mac or Windows displays, scrolling is often managed by a "scrollbar" at right or left that lets you move up and down easily via mouse.

Search: How the program finds text you are looking for.

Boolean searches let you combine different search terms with Boolean operators such as AND, OR, XOR, and NOT. AND lets you ask for all chunks that include the words "principal" AND "conflict." OR lets you find all chunks that include "principal" OR "conflict" or both. Because chunks with both will be included, this is called an "inclusive OR." XOR is an "exclusive OR." It lets you find chunks with either "principal" XOR "conflict" but not both. NOT lets you find chunks that do NOT contain "conflict." You can also use NOT to get a *complement* (see **Set logic**) such as all chunks with "principal" but NOT "conflict."

A program with good support for Boolean operators uses all four of these and also allows the use of parentheses to define complex searches. So you can ask for ("principal" OR "teacher") AND "conflict." This will find all chunks that have either the word "principal" or the word "teacher" in combination with the word "conflict."

Relational searches let you search for information according to relationships in the data, most often as represented by **network** links. See also **Relational search**.

Wildcard searches let you substitute a "**wildcard**" character for a letter or letters in your search string. Searching for "electr*" will find all words beginning with "electr" such as "electricity," "electrical," "electron," "electrode."

Fuzzy searches find words spelled approximately like the one you enter.

Phonetic searches find words that sound like the one you enter.

Synonym searches find words with similar meanings to the one you enter.

Proximity searches find strings that are within a specified distance of each other (e.g., 10 words, same paragraph), or that follow or precede each other.

Search engine: Usually, the part of a program devoted to searching. Occasionally, a freestanding program devoted exclusively to searching. In both cases, implies powerful search capabilities.

Segment: See **Chunk**.

Set logic: Approach to search and retrieval that involves comparing collections of entities (sets), as in this Venn diagram.

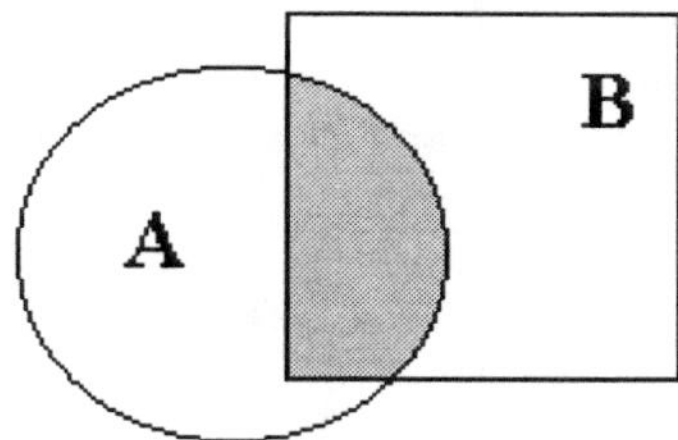

The "intersection" is the items that are included in both sets A and B (shaded area). This is equivalent to a **Boolean** AND. The "union" is all the items that occur in A, or in B, or in both. This is equivalent to a **Boolean** OR. The "complement" of A is all the items in the "union" that are not in A (unshaded area in B). A set may also be contained in another set (think of a circle within a circle). Some programs (e.g., Metamorph or NUD•IST) use set logic to allow you to create complex searches, but the way they implement it varies widely. See the individual program reviews.

Shell: A program that helps you choose among and manage the use of several other programs, usually with a screen display that shows you a number of choices, enhancing or simplifying the use of your operating system (e.g., MS-DOS or the Macintosh System). Common examples are Norton Commander, PCTools, and MS-DOS Shell. Microsoft Windows shares similarities with shells, but is much more than that.

The word "shell" is also used as a verb, to describe the action of temporarily suspending a program so that you can use the operating system to do things like look for or manage files. So you might "shell to DOS," copy some files, and then return to your program.

Source tag: Information attached to a retrieved chunk that tells you where it came from (case, file, page, line, and so on). May include "header," "face-sheet," or demographic information on the file, individual, or case at hand. See **Header**.

Stack: In the HyperCard program, a file consisting of a set of "cards," each with related information. This is essentially a **database**, where each card is a **record**, though the stack is presented on screen visually as a stack of cards.

Stand-alone: A program or module that can run by itself, without the aid of another program. For example, Windows programs are *not* considered stand-alone because they require Windows to run. HyperCard-based programs (for Macintosh) are typically not stand-alone unless the developer builds in essential parts of HyperCard so that the program can run alone.

String: A sequence of characters, such as "principal," "P.S. 122," "school impr," "facili-," or "X5067??." A program searches for, retrieves, and/or connects strings; it doesn't know the meaning of words or phrases.

Structured data: See **Database**.

Synonym search: See **Search**.

Syntax: The various parts of a command and the way you must type them. Includes the order in which the parts must appear, any symbols or abbreviations for different options, and so on. For example, to get a listing of certain files in a DOS directory, the syntax is:

dir [drive]:\[directory]\[filename]

When you type in the appropriate information for the brackets, say, to get a listing of all files whose names end in ".doc" in the docs directory on the C: drive, the final command might look, for example, like this:

dir c:\docs*.doc

System closure: Program feature that allows you to store the results of analyses within the program as you go, thus steadily extending and enriching the database.

Textbase manager: A database manager specifically designed for handling text. It organizes, sorts, and makes subsets of your text files, as well as doing search and retrieval. It may also allow the embedding of nontext objects (e.g., graphics).

Text editor: A program, often available with your operating system, that performs limited editing and word processing capabilities on ASCII files. In DOS, examples are MS-DOS Editor, or Edlin. A text editor generally has much more limited functions than a word processor.

Text retriever: Program that finds all the instances of words, phrases, and combinations of these you are interested in locating, in one or several files. Some have content-analytic (counting, displaying words in their context, creating word lists) capabilities as well.

Toolbar: Part of a **Graphical user interface** (e.g., Mac or Windows) display that lets you issue a range of commands, usually by clicking on an icon.

Two-step coding: See explanation under **one-step coding**, and fuller discussion in Chapter 3.

Unstructured data: See **Database**.

Video: Type of screen display, with such labels as EGA, CGA, VGA, SVGA, referring to monochrome, degrees of gray, or color, and fineness of screen detail. May also refer to moving images, as on videotape.

Wildcard: A symbol (or character) that can stand for any other character (or characters)—most commonly an asterisk (*)—in a search expression or command. More elaborate wildcard schemes may have different symbols that stand for "any uppercase letter(s)," "any lowercase letter(s)," "any number," and so on.

Wildcard search: See **Search** and **Wildcard**.

Word processor: Program designed for producing, revising, and formatting text. Also used, originally, to mean a special type of computer that only does word processing, like the old WANG machines.

Workaround: A way of getting a program to accomplish something it wasn't originally designed to do. Example: If a program can only handle one level of codes, you could decide to denote first-level codes by lowercase letters, and second-level codes by CAPITALS.

WYSIWYG: (pronounced "Wissie-wig) What You See Is What You Get. Text as viewed on screen is formatted exactly as it will be printed (paragraphing, margins, and so on).

Annotated References

These references largely deal with general issues in computer-aided qualitative research. References specific to particular programs appear with the reviews in Chapters 4 through 8. For a complete list of all citations, see the following References section.

Bernard, R. (1991). About text management and computers. *Cultural Anthropology Methods Newsletter, 3*(1), 1-4, 7, 12.

A practical, straightforward summary for researchers: covers fieldnote production, databases, content analysis.

Conrad, P., & Reinharz, S. (Eds.). (1984). Computers and qualitative data [Special issue]. *Qualitative Sociology, 7*(1-2).

One of the first collections of articles (11) on the topic. Includes an annotated bibliography of prior work (1966 onward). The conceptual pieces are still helpful, though the comments on specific software are no longer relevant. Includes a good overview of computer-aided content analysis.

Drass, K. A. (1989). Text analysis and text-analysis software: A comparison of assumptions. In G. Blank et al. (Eds.), *New technology in sociology: Practical applications in research and work* (pp. 155-162). New Brunswick, NJ: Transaction.

Discusses limitations of "notecard" approaches to software, and proposes desirable characteristics of good text analysis programs.

Fielding, N. G., & Lee, R. M. (Eds.). (1991). *Using computers in qualitative research.* London: Sage.

Eleven thoughtful articles: overviews by the editors, by Tesch, and by Richards and Richards; descriptions of analysis in specific projects (Davies, Fischer, & Finkelstein; Cordingley); review of event structure analysis (Heise); data confidentiality (Akeroyd); and two reflective pieces on computer use (Seidel, Agar).

McAleese, R. (Ed.). (1993). *Hypertext: Theory into practice.* Oxford: Intellect.
A state-of-the-art collection of 12 articles. Concrete and helpful; many screen shots to illustrate issues of navigation, browsing, and searching and learning in hypertext, as well as creating it.

Miles, M. B., & Huberman, A. M. (1994). *Qualitative data analysis: An expanded sourcebook* (2nd ed.). Thousand Oaks, CA: Sage.
Comprehensive collection of analytical strategies and techniques, distinguishing data reduction, data display (emphasizing matrices and networks), and conclusion drawing as aspects of analysis. Includes section on computer use in qualitative projects and an appendix on software (a microversion of the present book).

Pfaffenberger, B. (1988). *Microcomputer applications in qualitative research.* Newbury Park, CA: Sage.
Thoughtful introduction to strategies of qualitative data analysis and how they can be aided and mediated (and hindered) by various types of programs: word processors, textbase managers, concordance makers, frequency counters, thesauruses/dictionaries, outliners/idea processors, hypertexters, and artificial intelligence programs.

Ragin, C. C., & Becker, H. S. (1989). How the microcomputer is changing our analytic habits. In G. Blank et al. (Eds.), *New technology in sociology: Practical applications in research and work* (pp. 47-55). New Brunswick, NJ: Transaction.
Comments on strategies of data reduction: variable-oriented (explaining variation) versus case-oriented (comprehending local diversity); discusses impact of microcomputing in integration of conceptualization, data collection, and analysis, going beyond "handicraft production."

Reid, A. O., Jr. (1992). Computer management strategies for text data. In B. F. Crabtree & W. L. Miller (Eds.), *Doing qualitative research* (pp. 125-148). Newbury Park, CA: Sage.
A practical summary, emphasizing use of word processors, including macros, for data preparation, identification (chunking), and manipulation (searching).

Richards, T., & Richards, L. (1994). Using computers in qualitative analysis. In N. Denzin & Y. Lincoln (Eds.), *Handbook of qualitative research* (chap. 28, pp. 445-462). Thousand Oaks, CA: Sage.
The best available current overview of the topic. Discusses relation of data to theory and analytical styles; reviews general types of software, emphasizing their "architecture" and purposes, and illustrates with brief descriptions of nine programs.

Tesch, R. (1989). Computer software and qualitative analysis: A reassessment. In G. Blank et al. (Eds.), *New technology in sociology: Practical applications in research and work* (pp. 141-154). New Brunswick, NJ: Transaction.
Speculates on slow diffusion rates of software among researchers, discusses requirements for good programs, benefits, outlook for future.

Tesch, R. (1990). *Qualitative research: Analysis types and software tools.* New York: Falmer.
A thoughtful review and classification of approaches to qualitative analysis; discussion of the mechanics of qualitative analysis and software types and functions. Detailed, systematic descriptions of six programs (ETHNO, TAP, QUALPRO, The Ethnograph, TEXTBASE ALPHA, and HyperQual) in their 1990 versions.

Tesch, R. (Ed.). (1991). Computers and qualitative data II. [Special issue, Pts. 1, 2]. *Qualitative Sociology, 14*(3, 4).
Includes useful introductory overview (Tesch) distinguishing descriptive-interpretive, theory-building, and content-analytic programs. Articles on concept modeling (Padilla) and user practice (Tallerico), plus articles on specific programs (HyperRESEARCH, NUD•IST, AQUAD, ATLAS/ti, and SAGE).

Tesch, R. (1993). Personal computers in qualitative research. In M. D. LeCompte & J. Preissle, *Ethnography and qualitative design in educational research* (2nd ed., chap. 8, pp. 279-314). San Diego, CA: Academic Press.
A clear discussion of analytical tasks computers can aid with, sorted into categories: data preparation and storage; segmenting, coding, and collating; establishing linkages; and transferal and display. Illustrative examples from specific programs, including The Ethnograph, HyperQual, QUALPRO, TEXTBASE ALPHA, AQUAD, HyperSoft, HyperRESEARCH, NUD•IST, ATLAS/ti, and ETHNO.

References

Abbott, A. (1992). What do cases do? Some notes on activity in sociological analysis. In C. Ragin & H. Becker (Eds.), *What is a case? Exploring the foundations of social inquiry* (pp. 53-82). New York: Cambridge University Press.

Agar, M. H. (1986). *Speaking of ethnography* (Qualitative Research Methods Series, Vol. 2). Newbury Park, CA: Sage.

Bernard, R. (1991). About text management and computers. *Cultural Anthropology Methods Newsletter, 3*(1), 1-4, 7, 12.

Blackman, B. I. (1993). *QUALPRO text database and productivity tools: User's manual, version 4 for IBM and PC compatibles.* Tallahassee, FL: *Impulse* Development Co.

Bogdan, R. C., & Biklen, S. K. (1982). *Qualitative research in education: An introduction to theory and methods.* Boston: Allyn & Bacon.

Brannen, J. (Ed.). (1992). *Mixing methods: Qualitative and quantitative research.* Aldershot, U.K.: Avebury.

Brigham Young University. (1993a, October 9). *System documentation, WordCruncher for Windows (evaluation copy): WCView for Windows.* Provo, UT: Author.

Brigham Young University. (1993b, August 19). *System documentation for WordCruncher for Windows: WCIndex for Windows.* Provo, UT: Author.

Carley, K. (1985). An approach for relating social structure to cognitive structure. *Journal of Mathematical Sociology, 12*(2), 137-189.

Carley, K. (1988). Formalizing the social expert's knowledge. *Sociological Methods and Research, 17,* 165-232.

Carley, K. (1990, August). *Computer analysis of qualitative data: Copy of overheads for didactic seminar.* Paper presented at the annual meeting of the American Sociological Association, Washington, DC.

Carley, K. (1991). *Textual analysis using maps.* Pittsburgh, PA: Carnegie-Mellon University, Department of Social and Decision Sciences.

Carley, K. (1993). Coding choices for textual analysis: A comparison of content analysis and map analysis. In P. Marsden (Ed.), *Sociological methodology* (Vol. 23, pp. 75-126). Oxford: Blackwell.

Carley, K. (1994). Content analysis. In R. E. Asher et al. (Eds.), *The encyclopedia of language and linguistics* (Vol. 2, pp. 725-730). Edinburgh, U.K.: Pergamon.

Carley, K. (in press). Extracting culture through textual analysis. *Poetics.*

Carley, K., & Kaufer, D. (1993). Semantic connectivity: An approach for analyzing semantic networks. *Communication Theory, 3,* 183-213.

Carley, K., & Palmquist, M. (1992). Extracting, representing and analyzing mental models. *Social Forces, 70*(3), 601-636.

Carspecken, P. F., & Apple, M. (1992). Critical qualitative research: Theory, methodology and practice. In M. LeCompte, W. Millroy, & J. Preissle (Eds.), *The handbook of qualitative research in education* (pp. 507-554). San Diego, CA: Academic Press.

Codd, E. F. (1990). *The relational model for database management: Version 2.* Reading, MA: Addison-Wesley.

Connelly, F. M., & Clandinin, D. J. (1990). Stories of experience and narrative inquiry. *Educational Researcher, 19*(4), 2-14.

Conrad, P., & Reinharz, S. (Eds.). (1984). Computers and qualitative data [Special issue]. *Qualitative Sociology, 7*(1-2).

Crabtree, B. F., & Miller, W. L. (1992). *Doing qualitative research.* Newbury Park, CA: Sage.

Denzin, N. K. (1989). *Interpretive interactionism* (Applied Social Research Methods Series, Vol. 16). Newbury Park, CA: Sage.

Denzin, N., & Lincoln, Y. (1994). *Handbook of qualitative research.* Thousand Oaks, CA: Sage.

Diekelmann, N. L., Lam, S., & Schuster, R. M. (1991). *Martin, v. 2.0 user manual.* Madison: University of Wisconsin—Madison, School of Nursing.

Drass, K. A. (1980). The analysis of qualitative data: A computer program. *Urban Life, 9,* 322-353.

Drass, K. A. (1989). Text analysis and text-analysis software: A comparison of assumptions. In G. Blank et al. (Eds.), *New technology in sociology: Practical applications in research and work* (pp. 155-162). New Brunswick, NJ: Transaction.

Drass, K. A. (1992, October 15). *QCA 3.0, Qualitative comparative analysis* (beta release). Evanston, IL: Northwestern University, Center for Urban Affairs and Policy Research.

Dreyfus, H. L. (1992). *What computers still can't do: A critique of artificial reason.* Cambridge: MIT Press.

Dupuis, A., & Tornabene, E. (1993). *HyperRESEARCH*(TM) *from ResearchWare: A content analysis tool for the qualitative researcher.* Randolph, MA: ResearchWare, Inc.

Eastgate Systems. (1993). *Storyspace*(TM). Watertown, MA: Author.

Electronic Text Corporation. (1987). *The Constitution papers* (WordCruncher Bookshelf Series, Bicentennial Edition 1787-1987, 10 disks). Provo, UT: Author.

Electronic Text Corporation. (1989a). *WordCruncher: WCIndex retrieval software (version 4.30).* Provo, UT: Author.

Electronic Text Corporation. (1989b). *WordCruncher: WCView text retrieval software (version 4.30).* Provo, UT: Author.

Fielding, N. G., & Lee, R. M. (1991). *Using computers in qualitative research.* London: Sage.

Fielding, N. G., & Lee, R. M. (in press). Confronting CAQDAS: Choice and contingency. In R. G. Burgess (Ed.), *Studies in qualitative methodology.* Greenwich, CT: JAI.

Fischer, C., & Wertz, F. (1975). Empirical phenomenological analyses of being criminally victimized. In A. Giorgi (Ed.), *Phenomenology and psychological research* (pp. 135-158). Pittsburgh, PA: Duquesne University Press.

Folio Corporation. (1993). *Folio VIEWS personal electronic publishing software: User's guide, Version 3.0, for the Windows graphical environment.* Provo, UT: Author.

Glaser, B. G. (1978). *Theoretical sensitivity: Advances in the methodology of grounded theory.* Mill Valley, CA: Sociology Press.

Glaser, B. G. (1992). *Emergence vs. forcing: Basics of grounded theory analysis.* Mill Valley, CA: Sociology Press.

Glaser, B., & Strauss, A. L. (1967). *The discovery of grounded theory: Strategies for qualitative research.* Chicago: Aldine.

Goetz, J. P., & LeCompte, M. D. (1984). *Ethnography and qualitative design in educational research.* Orlando, FL: Academic Press.

Goldman-Segall, R. (1990). A multimedia research tool for ethnographic investigation. In I. Harel & S. Papert (Eds.), *Constructionism* (pp. 467-496). Norwood, NJ: Ablex.

Goldman-Segall, R. (1993). Interpreting video data: Introducing a "significance measure" to layer description. *Journal of Educational Multimedia and Hypermedia, 2*(3), 261-281.

Greene, J. C., Caracelli, V. J., & Graham, W. F. (1989). Toward a conceptual framework for mixed-method evaluation designs. *Educational Evaluation and Policy Analysis, 11*(2), 255-274.

Hancock, C., & Kaput, J. J. (1990, July). *Computerized tools and the process of data modeling.* Paper read at the 14th International Conference on the Psychology of Mathematics Education, Mexico.

Hancock, C., Kaput, J. J., & Goldsmith, L. (1992). Authentic inquiry with data: Critical barriers to classroom implementation. *Educational Psychologist, 27*(3), 337-364.

Hartwig, F., & Dearing, B. E. (1979). *Exploratory data analysis.* Beverly Hills, CA: Sage.

Hecht, J. B., Roberts, N., & Schoon, P. (1994, April). *VTLOGANL: A computer program for coding and analyzing data gathered on videotape.* Presentation at the annual meeting of the American Educational Research Association, New Orleans.

Helfgott, M., & Nakell, C. (1992). *Inspiration idea book.* Portland, OR: Inspiration Software, Inc.

Helfgott, M., & Schmidt, R. (1992a). *Inspiration getting started manual.* Portland, OR: Inspiration Software, Inc.

Helfgott, M., & Schmidt, R. (1992b). *Inspiration user's manual.* Portland, OR: Inspiration Software, Inc.

Horney, M. A. (1994, March 2). [E-mail message; sender: mhorney@oregon.uoregon.edu].

Horney, M. A., & Healey, D. (1991, April). *Hypertext and database tools for qualitative research.* Paper read at the annual meeting of the American Educational Research Association, Chicago.

Howard, G. S. (1991). Culture tales: A narrative approach to thinking, cross-cultural psychology, and psychotherapy. *American Psychologist, 46*(3), 187-197.

Howe, K. R. (1985). Two dogmas of educational research. *Educational Researcher, 14*(8), 10-18.

Howe, K. R. (1988). Against the quantitative-qualitative incompatibility thesis or dogmas die hard. *Educational Researcher, 17*(8), 10-16.

Huber, G. L. (1992, October). *Analysis of linkages and configurations in qualitative data: Reconstruction and comparison of implicit theories.* Paper presented at the International Conference on Qualitative Computing, Bremen, Germany.

Huber, G. L., & Marcelo Garcia, C. (1991). Computer assistance for testing hypotheses about qualitative data: The software package AQUAD 3.0. *Qualitative Sociology, 14*(4), 325-347.

Huber, G. L., & Marcelo Garcia, C. (1993). Voices of beginning teachers: Computer-assisted listening to their common experiences. In M. Schratz (Ed.), *Qualitative voices in educational research* (pp. 139-156). London: Falmer.

Huberman, A. M., & Miles, M. B. (1984). *Innovation up close: How school improvement works.* New York: Plenum.

Jacob, E. (1987). Qualitative research traditions: A review. *Review of Educational Research, 57*(1), 1-50.

Johnston & Co. (1991-1992). *WordCruncher 4.5: Upgrade summary and reference guide.* American Fork, UT: Author.

Johnston & Co. (1993). *WordCruncher: Getting started.* American Fork, UT: Author.

Josselson, R., & Lieblich, A. (Eds.). (1993). *The narrative study of lives* (Vol. 1). Newbury Park, CA: Sage.

Kalman, D. (1991, May 28). 15 relational databases: Easy access, programming power. *PC Magazine,* pp. 101-108.

Kaufer, D., & Carley, K. (1993). *Communication at a distance: The influence of print on sociocultural organization and change.* Hillsdale, NJ: Lawrence Erlbaum.

Kibby, M. R., & Mayes, T. (1993). Towards intelligent hypertext. In R. McAleese (Ed.), *Hypertext: Theory into practice* (pp. 138-144). Oxford: Intellect.

Krackhardt, D., Lundberg, M., & O'Rourke, L. (1993). KrackPlot: A picture's worth a thousand words. *Connections, 16*(1-2), 37-47.

Krauss, R. M., Morrel-Samuels, P., & Hochberg, J. (1988). Videologger: A computerized multichannel event recorder for analyzing videotapes. *Behavior Research Methods, Instruments, & Computers, 20*(1), 37-40.

Kuckartz, U. (1993). *MAX user's manual.* German version—Berlin: Free University of Berlin, Author. English version—introduction, translation and design by R. Tesch; Desert Hot Springs, CA: Qualitative Research Management.

Laverty, M., & Albright, R. (1993). *MetaDesign user's guide: Version 4.0 for Microsoft Windows.* Cambridge, MA: Meta Software Corporation.

Lee, R. M., & Fielding, N. G. (in press). Users' experiences of qualitative analysis software. In U. Kelle (Ed.), *Computers and qualitative methodology.* Thousand Oaks, CA: Sage.

Legewie, H. (1994, March 17). [E-mail message on list ATLAS-TI%DBOTUI11; sender: atla0230@zrz.mailszrz.tu-berlin.de].

Lofland, J., & Lofland, L. H. (1984). *Analyzing social settings: A guide to qualitative observation and analysis* (2nd ed.). Belmont, CA: Wadsworth.

Lonkila, M. (in press). Grounded theory and computer assisted qualitative data analysis. In U. Kelle (Ed.), *Computers and qualitative methodology.* London: Sage.

Maxwell, J. A. (1992). *The logic of qualitative research* (Working paper). Cambridge, MA: Harvard Graduate School of Education. [Submitted to *Cultural Anthropology Methods Newsletter*].

McAleese, R. (Ed.). (1993). *Hypertext: Theory into practice.* Oxford: Intellect.

Miles, M. B., & Huberman, A. M. (1984). *Qualitative data analysis: A sourcebook of new methods* (1st ed.). Beverly Hills, CA: Sage.

Miles, M. B., & Huberman, A. M. (1994). *Qualitative data analysis: An expanded sourcebook* (2nd ed.). Thousand Oaks, CA: Sage.

Miles, M. B., & Weitzman, E. A. (1994). Appendix: Choosing computer programs for qualitative data analysis. In M. B. Miles & A. M. Huberman, *Qualitative data analysis: An expanded sourcebook* (pp. 311-317). Thousand Oaks, CA: Sage.

Miller, B., Faletti, J., & Fisher, K. (1991). *SemNet user's guide version 1.0.* San Diego: SemNet Research Group.

Miller, R. (1993). Designing your thoughts. *PC Magazine, 12*(22), 161-174.

Mohr, L. B. (1982). *Explaining organizational behavior.* San Francisco: Jossey-Bass.

Morales, A. (1993). Computer software review: QUALPRO v4.0. *NOTAS, 2*(1), 8.

Morse, J. (1991). Analyzing unstructured interactive interviews using the Macintosh computer. *Qualitative Health Research, 1*(1), 117-122.

Muhr, T. (1993a). *ATLAS/ti: Computer aided text interpretation & theory building. User's manual.* Berlin: Author.

Muhr, T. (1993b, January 21). [E-mail message; sender: muhr@cs.tu-berlin.de].

Noblit, G. W. (1988, February). *A sense of interpretation.* Paper presented at the Ethnography in Education Research Forum, Philadelphia (University of North Carolina, Chapel Hill).

Oja, S., & Smulyan, L. (1989). *Collaborative action research: A developmental approach* (Social Research and Educational Studies Series, 7). London: Falmer.

O'Neill Software. (1987). *The Text Collector: User's manual.* San Francisco: Author.

Padilla, R. V. (1993). *HyperQual2 for qualitative analysis and theory development.* Chandler, AZ: Author.

Pearsol, J. A. (1985, April). *Controlling qualitative data: Understanding teachers' value perspectives on a sex equity education project.* Paper presented at the annual conference of the American Educational Research Association, Chicago (Columbus: College of Medicine, Ohio State University).

Peters, V., & Wester, F. (1989). *Kwalitan as a tool for qualitative data analysis.* Nijmegen, the Netherlands: University of Nijmegen, Social Science Faculty, Department of Research Methodology.

Peters, V., & Wester, F. (1990). *Qualitative analysis in practice: Including user's guide, Kwalitan version 2.* Nijmegen, the Netherlands: University of Nijmegen, Social Science Faculty, Department of Research Methodology.

Peters, V., & Wester, F. (1993). *Qualitative analysis in practice. Supplement: A short help to learn version 3.1.* Nijmegen, the Netherlands: University of Nijmegen, Social Science Faculty, Department of Research Methodology.

Pfaffenberger, B. (1988). *Microcomputer applications in qualitative research.* Newbury Park, CA: Sage.

Polkinghorne, D. E. (1988). *Narrative knowing and the human sciences.* Albany: State University of New York Press.

Popkewitz, T. S. (1990). Whose future? Whose past? Notes on critical theory and methodology. In E. G. Guba (Ed.), *The paradigm dialog* (pp. 46-66). Newbury Park, CA: Sage.

Radnofsky, M. (1994, April). *Minimizing chaos in qualitative analyses of multiple transcriptions the* Chromacode® *way.* Paper read at the annual meeting of the American Educational Research Association, New Orleans (Garden City, NY: School of Education, Adelphi University).

Ragin, C. C. (1987). *The comparative method: Moving beyond qualitative and quantitative strategies.* Berkeley: University of California Press.

Ragin, C. C. (1993a). A qualitative comparative analysis of pension systems. In T. Janoski & A. Hicks (Eds.), *The comparative political economy of the welfare state* (pp. 320-345). New York: Cambridge University Press.

Ragin, C. C. (1993b). Introduction to qualitative comparative analysis. In T. Janoski & A. Hicks (Eds.), *The comparative political economy of the welfare state* (pp. 299-319). New York: Cambridge University Press.

Ragin, C. C., & Becker, H. S. (1989). How the microcomputer is changing our analytic habits. In G. Blank et al. (Eds.), *New technology in sociology: Practical applications in research and work* (pp. 47-55). New Brunswick, NJ: Transaction.

Reid, A. O., Jr. (1992). Computer management strategies for text data. In B. F. Crabtree & W. L. Miller (Eds.), *Doing qualitative research* (pp. 125-148). Newbury Park, CA: Sage.

Replee Pty Ltd. (1993). *NUD•IST user guide: Version 3.0 for Macintosh.* Victoria, Australia: Author.

Replee Pty Ltd. (1994). *Q.S.R. NUD•IST version 3.0: User guide.* Victoria, Australia: Author.

Richards, T., & Richards, L. (1994). Using computers in qualitative analysis. In N. Denzin & Y. Lincoln (Eds.), *Handbook of qualitative research* (chap. 28, pp. 445-462). Thousand Oaks, CA: Sage.

Roschelle, J., & Goldman, S. (1991). VideoNoter: A productivity tool for video data analysis. *Behavior Research Methods, Instruments, & Computers, 23*(2), 219-224.

Rossman, G. B., & Wilson, B. L. (1984, April). Numbers and words: Combining quantitative and qualitative methods in a single large-scale evaluation study. *Evaluation Review, 9*(5), 627-643.

Seaside Software, Inc. (1991a). *askSam reference.* Perry, FL: Author.

Seaside Software, Inc. (1991b). *askSam user's guide.* Perry, FL: Author.

Seaside Software, Inc. (1991c). *Getting started with askSam.* Perry, FL: Author.

Seidel, J. V. (1991). Method and madness in the application of computer technology to qualitative data analysis. In N. G. Fielding & R. M.

Lee, *Using computers in qualitative research* (pp. 107-116). Newbury Park, CA: Sage.

Seidel, J. V., & Clark, J. A. (1984). The Ethnograph: A computer program for the analysis of qualitative data. *Qualitative Sociology, 7*(1-2), 110-125.

Seidel, J. V., Kjolseth, R., & Seymour, E. (1988). *The Ethnograph: A user's guide (version 3.0).* Amherst, MA: Qualis Research Associates.

Shelly, A., & Sibert, E. (1985). *The Qualog user's manual.* Syracuse, NY: Syracuse University, School of Computer and Information Science.

Silverman, D. (1993). *Interpreting qualitative data: Methods for analyzing talk, text and interaction.* London: Sage.

Strauss, A. L. (1987). *Qualitative analysis for social scientists.* Cambridge: Cambridge University Press.

Strauss, A. L., & Corbin, J. L. (1990). *Basics of qualitative research: Grounded theory procedures and techniques.* Newbury Park, CA: Sage.

The Technology Group. (1993a). *Orbis for XyWrite.* Baltimore, MD: Author.

The Technology Group. (1993b). *XyWrite 4.0: Command reference guide.* Baltimore, MD: Author.

The Technology Group. (1993c). *XyWrite 4.0: Customization guide.* Baltimore, MD: Author.

TERC (Technical Education Research Centers). (1989). *Use numbers.* Menlo Park, CA: Dale Seymour.

TERC (Technical Education Research Centers). (1994). *The Tabletop (Senior) user guide: The condensed quickie version.* Cambridge, MA: TERC.

Tesch, R. (1989). Computer software and qualitative analysis: A reassessment. In G. Blank et al. (Eds.), *New technology in sociology: Practical applications in research and work* (pp. 141-154). New Brunswick, NJ: Transaction.

Tesch, R. (1990). *Qualitative research: Analysis types and software tools.* New York: Falmer.

Tesch, R. (Ed.). (1991). Computers and qualitative data II [Special issue, Pts. 1, 2]. *Qualitative Sociology, 14*(3, 4).

Tesch, R. (1993). Personal computers in qualitative research. In M. D. LeCompte & J. Preissle, *Ethnography and qualitative design in educational research* (2nd ed., chap. 8, pp. 279-314). San Diego, CA: Academic Press.

Tesch, R., & Huber, G. L. (1992). *AQUAD user's manual.* Desert Hot Springs, CA: Qualitative Research Management; Tübingen, Germany: University of Tübingen, Department of Pedagogical Psychology.

Thunderstone Software. (1991). *Metamorph version 3.4 for DOS & Unix: Operations manual.* Cleveland, OH: Author.

Tyk, S., & Mohler, K. D. (1993a). *askSam for Windows getting started guide.* Perry, FL: Seaside Software, Inc.

Tyk, S., & Mohler, K. D. (1993b). *askSam for Windows user's guide.* Perry, FL: Seaside Software, Inc.

Virginia Systems Software Services, Inc. (1994). *Sonar: Macintosh combined user's guide, Sonar and Sonar Professional, version 8.5.* Midlothian, VA: Author.

Vitz, P. C. (1990). The use of stories in moral development: New psychological reasons for an old education method. *American Psychologist, 45*(6), 709-720.

Walker, B. L. (1993). Computer analysis of qualitative data: A comparison of three packages. *Qualitative Health Research, 3*(1), 91-111.

Watkins, K. E. (1991, April). *Validity in action research.* Paper presented at the annual meeting of AERA, Chicago.

Weaver, A., & Atkinson, P. (in press). From coding to hypertext: Strategies for microcomputing and qualitative data analysis. In R. G. Burgess (Ed.), *Studies in qualitative methodology.* Greenwich, CT: JAI.

Weitzman, E. A., & Miles, M. B. (1991). *Computer-aided qualitative data analysis: A review of selected software.* New York: Center for Policy Research.

Wester, F., & Peters, V. (1989). *Qualitative analysis.* Nijmegen, the Netherlands: University of Nijmegen, Social Science Faculty, Department of Research Methodology.

Wolcott, H. (1980). How to look like an anthropologist without being one. *Practicing Anthropology, 3*(1), 6-7, 56-59.

Wolcott, H. F. (1992). Posturing in qualitative inquiry. In M. D. LeCompte, J. Preissle, & W. L. Millroy (Eds.), *The handbook of qualitative research in education* (pp. 3-52). San Diego, CA: Academic Press.

Wolcott, H. F. (1994). *Transforming qualitative data: Description, analysis, and interpretation.* Thousand Oaks, CA: Sage.

ZyLAB Division, Information Dimensions, Inc. (1993). *ZyINDEX for Windows user's guide.* Buffalo Grove, IL: Author.

Index

EDITORS' NOTE: Bold face page numbers indicate Glossary entry.

About the Authors

Eben A. Weitzman received his Ph.D. in social and organizational psychology from Columbia University. He is currently Visiting Assistant Professor of Psychology in the New York University Department of Psychology's Industrial/Organizational Psychology program; Research Associate at the Center for Policy Research, New York; and Research Associate at the International Center for Cooperation and Conflict Resolution at Teachers College, Columbia University. His interests are in conflict resolution, intergroup relations, and the determinants and effects of cooperation and competition. He has worked as a database programmer and conducted extensive training in computer use. His current research is in cultural differences in attitudes toward conflict, in-group/out-group formation in response to social diversity, alienation and commitment in organizations, effects of constructive conflict resolution training, and effects of cooperation and competition on small group processes.

Matthew B. Miles, a social psychologist, has been Senior Research Associate at the Center for Policy Research, New York, since 1970. Before that he was Professor of Psychology and Education at Teachers College, where he worked from 1953 onward. He has had long-term interest in planned change in education, leading studies of leadership and intensive group training, school organizational renewal, educational innovation, program implementation, design of new schools, and the work of "change agents." Recent books he has coauthored include *Lasting School Improvement* (Acco, 1987), *Assisting Change in Education* (ASCD, 1990), *Improving the Urban High School: What Works and Why* (Teachers College Press, 1990), and *Qualitative Data Analysis* (Sage, 1994). His current research focuses on cognitive mapping of school restructuring, educational reform in developing countries, and advances in qualitative data analysis.